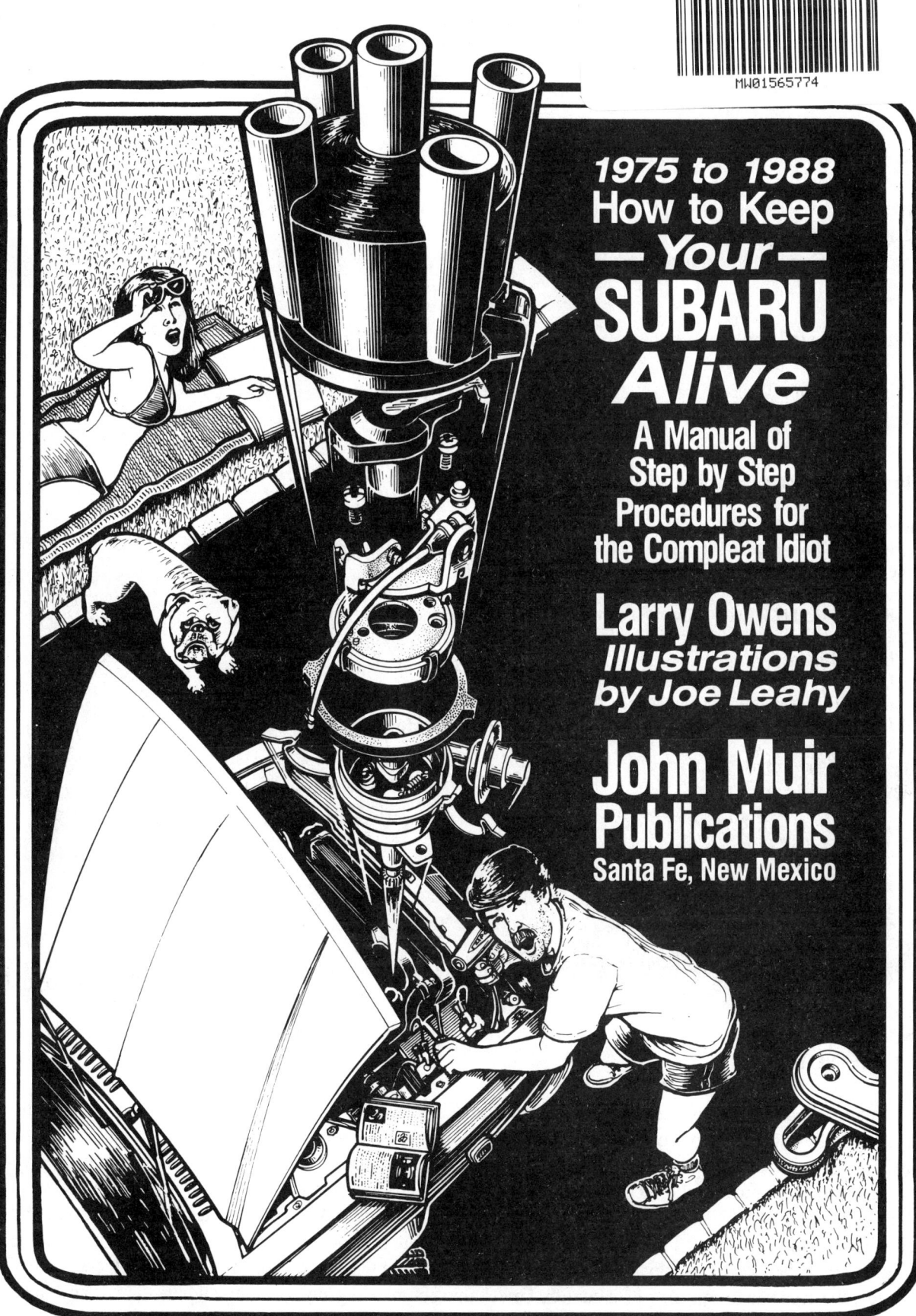

1975 to 1988 How to Keep *Your* SUBARU *Alive*

A Manual of Step by Step Procedures for the Compleat Idiot

Larry Owens
Illustrations by Joe Leahy

John Muir Publications
Santa Fe, New Mexico

John Muir Publications, P.O. Box 613, Santa Fe, NM 87504

© 1986, 1989 by John Muir Publications
All rights reserved. Published 1986
Printed in the United States of America
Second edition. Second printing, January 1995

Typeface: Text: Times Roman; Illustrations: Bookman Demi Italic, Venture Script and Helvetica Italic
Designer: Jim Wood
Typesetter: Copygraphics, Inc. Santa Fe, NM

Distributed to the book trade by:

Publishers Group West
Emeryville, California

Library of Congress Cataloging-in-Publication Data

Owens, Larry, 1942-
    1975 to 1988—how to keep your Subaru alive: a manual of step by step procedures for the compleat idiot/Larry Owens; illustrations by Joe Leahy.—2nd ed.
    p. cm.
    Rev. ed. of: 1972-1984—how to keep your Subaru alive. 1st ed.
©1986.
    Includes index.
    ISBN 0-945465-11-4
    1. Subaru automobile—Maintenance and repair. I. Owens, Larry, 1942-
1972-1984—how to keep your Subaru alive. II. Title. III. Title: How to keep your Subaru alive.
TL215.S84097   1989
629.28'722—dc20   89-9457
                                                                                                              CIP

PLEASE NOTE:

    The repair and maintenance procedures in this book are based on the training, personal experiences and research of the author, and on recommendations of responsible automotive professionals. If you follow all the directions specifically, you should be able to complete the procedures in this book successfully and safely.

    Please understand that the recommendations and warnings herein cannot cover all conceivable ways in which service procedures may be done, or every possible hazard and risk involved. The author, illustrator and publisher are not responsible for any adverse consequences that may occur in connection with the procedures explained in this book. Please do not use the book unless you are willing to assume the risk of adverse consequences. We urge you to consult with a qualified mechanic before using any procedure where there is any question as to its completeness or appropriateness.

    We especially advise you to heed all WARNINGS and CAUTIONS, to use all recommended safety precautions called for throughout the book—and to use common sense. Thanks.

ACKNOWLEDGMENTS

Finally I get to publicly thank all the people who have helped me put this book together. From the tips and technical material of the pros, to the people who greased their hands and noses to check out the procedures, you have all been great.

My heartfelt thanks to all the people at John Muir Publications and to Joe Leahy for the wonderful illustrations. I hope we all work together again in the near future.

Thanks to Dan Youngberg, Fred Heyler, and Steve Davis at Subaru of America, Inc., Pennsauken, New Jersey, Ryoji Katow at the Subaru Technical Center, Garden Grove, California, Frank Barrow, Al Giles, and Javier Limon at Tom Williams Subaru, Santa Barbara, California, and to Frank Morales at Vreeland Subaru, Ventura, California, for the valuable technical assistance.

Special thanks to Pam, Dennis P. Lewis (24 years in the business), Ken Antognini, Scott Taylor, and my main man Mike Mahneke of Mahneke Motors, Goleta, California. You kept me going when the going got tough.

Thanks also to Dave Rees and Ralph at Import Auto Parts in Santa Barbara for letting me pester you so much.

More special thanks to the people who "idiot tested" the book: Jeff Rosedale, Mark Schaenzer, Randy Aslin, Paul Reid, Peter Porinsh, and Paul Chesnut.

Others who helped in the project are my wife Camille (Mimi), my son Oscar (Oz), Billy J. Trucker, Greg Drust, Peter and Liz Porinsh, and Crystal LaVenture. And of course the good people at Santa Fe Auto Machine in Santa Fe, New Mexico: Elmer Townsley, Mary Nichols, Mike Rodriquez, and Cris Deubel. Thanks to all of you.

Thanks to John Muir for starting the whole thing. John, we miss you. I hope you're proud of this book.

Wilbur Kleenex—where are you?

This book is dedicated to Elmer Townsley, a wonderfully patient, understanding man who has helped countless "idiots" like myself make sense out of mechanical and personal dilemmas.

CONTENTS

INTRODUCTION 7

CHAPTER 1   HOW TO USE THIS BOOK 9

CHAPTER 2   UNDER-HOOD ORIENTATION...AND A LITTLE HISTORY 13

CHAPTER 3   SAFETY 21

CHAPTER 4   HOW A SUBARU WORKS 31

CHAPTER 5   TOOLS, PARTS, AND BOOKS 45

CHAPTER 6   HOW TO BUY A SUBARU 55

CHAPTER 7   MAINTENANCE, LUBRICATION, AND TUNE-UP 65

CHAPTER 8   DRIVING FOR ECONOMY AND LONGEVITY 147

CHAPTER 9   TROUBLESHOOTING 151

CHAPTER 10   THE ELECTRICAL SYSTEM 165

CHAPTER 11   FUEL SYSTEMS 205

CHAPTER 12   EXHAUST AND EMISSION CONTROL SYSTEMS 243

CHAPTER 13   BRAKES 267

CHAPTER 14   SUSPENSION AND STEERING 317

CHAPTER 15   CLUTCH, TRANSMISSION, AND DRIVESHAFTS 349

CHAPTER 16   COOLING SYSTEM 377

CHAPTER 17   ENGINE REMOVAL AND REPAIR 401

CHAPTER 18   MECHANIC'S TIPS, SECRETS, ODDS 'N ENDS 453

INDEX 465

INTRODUCTION

Whether you're thumbing through this book in a store or you've already bought it, in the back of your mind you might be wondering if you can really do the maintenance and repair procedures in the following chapters. Believe me, if you can read, you can do it. Here's why.

In the 60s and early 70s, Wilbur Kleenex, Billy J. Trucker, and I owned and operated an independent Volkswagen garage in Santa Fe called the Grease Pit (some people thought it was a restaurant). In 1969 John Muir started hanging around the garage saying he was writing a VW repair manual for people with no mechanical experience. We wondered how anyone could work on their own car without having first read all the hot rod and custom car books in the Fifties! Anyway, we shared knowledge and experiences with John and sure enough he wrote *How to Keep Your Volkswagen Alive: A Manual of Step-by-Step Procedures for the Compleat Idiot*.

We soon had a steady stream of transient flower children (and a few lawyers, housewives, musicians, outlaws, etc.) wanting to do their own VW repair work in the Grease Pit parking lot. At first we were quite skeptical whether John Muir's "idiots" (especially the spaced-out hippies) could actually do repair work like rebuilding an engine or repairing the brakes without us ending up doing most of the work for them (for free, of course!). But in the spirit of those times, we wanted to help our fellow man, so we gave them a spot in the lot and let 'em go for it. It didn't take long to convince us that given a John Muir book and a little space, any man, woman, or adolescent who could read *could* rebuild an engine, *could* do a brake job, and *could* do almost everything necessary to keep their cars in safe, dependable working order. Some of the parking lot people enjoyed working on their cars so much they ended up working with us at the Grease Pit. Through John's "Idiot" book we made a lot of good friends, had a lot of fun, and were usually rewarded with a couple of dollars for the use of the parking lot and an occasional tool. In all that time we were never ripped off! John's book soon became the standard of the industry for Volkswagen repair manuals and sold in the millions.

The times they have changed, but people haven't. There are still friendly people in garages who will help if you get stuck with a broken bolt or crossed wire. In fact, most mechanics and automotive machinists are impressed by mechanically inexperienced people who have the ambition and guts to work on their own cars. When you find a friendly, helpful mechanic or machinist, reward him with an occasional bag of donuts, a cold six-pack, or whatever, so he'll stay helpful, knowing he's really appreciated.

Like the Volkswagen book, *How to Keep Your Subaru Alive* is written for people with little or no mechanical experience. I've tried to write it so you'll feel as if my friendly hand is on your shoulder as you go through the procedures. Working as a team, you and I can keep your Sooby Doo in tip-top condition.

This book covers the maintenance, diagnosis, and repair of all Subarus imported to the United States from 1975 through 1988, except Justys. Due to special tools, safety factors, and/or complexity, instructions for the diagnosis and repair of air conditioning, power steering, and cruise control systems are not included in this manual. Also, diagnosis and repair of the fuel injection and turbocharger systems that are on some 1983-88 models is not covered. However, other than the fuel injection, turbocharger, and a few related parts on the engine, these models are the same as non-fuel-injected models, so all other maintenance, diagnosis, and repair work for those cars is included.

Subarus are good, tough cars that are easy to work on. They are also rather forgiving and can stand an occasional flub by an amateur mechanic. Their engines are built on essentially the same pattern as the old air-cooled VW engines. But, since Subaru engines are water cooled, they don't have the tendency to commit suicide by breaking exhaust valves or throwing rods like the old hot-running Volksies did. Subarus tend to live long, useful lives, aging gracefully with plenty of warning signs that resurrection time is approaching. Maintenance is the key to keeping your Soob safe and reliable year after year.

Contrary to popular belief, modern cars are not too complicated for the average owner to maintain—often at a savings of $100-$1000 per year! In fact, in most cases, it's easier now to do the maintenance than it ever was because more and more things are computer-controlled and never require maintenance.

True, the computers and a few other high-tech gadgets on the newer cars are beyond the home mechanic's means to deal with; but these systems rarely need to be messed with. All those hoses, wires, and mysterious looking gizmos under the hood just make things look a lot more complicated than they really are. Basically simple things like replacing the oil and oil filter, checking and changing the air and fuel filters and spark plugs, keeping the tires properly inflated and rotated, and so on, are the same as they have always been—well within the ability of the average car owner.

Due to the engine design of your Subaru, a few of the repair procedures require engine removal, and at least partial disassembly of the engine, to get to the broken or worn out parts. Don't panic at the thought of disconnecting all those wires and hoses in the engine compartment, then trying to find where they all go when the engine is back in the car. Take it one step at a time, with adequate attention to detail, and you'll find it's really quite easy. Same with tune-ups, brake jobs, and other repairs—take it one step at a time, pay attention to what you're doing, and you'll reincarnate the old Soob so it runs like new again.

If you're still unsure of yourself after this pep talk, read Chapter 1: *How to Use this Book*, then do the Vital (yet simple) Chapters and Procedures listed at the end of that chapter, to slowly wade into the book. As you build up confidence, gradually go deeper and deeper into Chapter 7. Soon you'll be changing the oil and filter, massaging away your Soob's aches and pains, and eventually you'll be doing thorough, competent tune-ups and repairs that you would have to pay most garages a wad of money to do. Also, you'll have the satisfying security of replacing worn parts before they fail completely, which might have left you on the side of the road with a roast in the oven, the kids stranded at school, a hungry date waiting to be picked up, ad infinitum. Write to me at John Muir Publications to let me know how it goes. I'm always open to suggestions for easier or better ways to do things, interesting stories, compliments and complaints.

Just remember, *IF YOU CAN READ, YOU CAN DO IT!*

ASA NISI MASA

Larry Owens

LARRY OWENS

CHAPTER 1
HOW TO USE THIS BOOK

To get your money's worth from this book, you gotta read it. Skipping paragraphs or sentences, sometimes even skipping a word, can defeat hours of otherwise meticulous attention to instructions. When helping Volkswagen owners who got stuck using the *How to Keep Your Volkswagen Alive* book, and when testing this book on inexperienced mechanics, I found the most common problem was that people were skipping part of the instructions. The information was there; they just weren't using it.

To make this book really work for you, please read the *Orientation* and *Safety* chapters before diving into your Soob. *Orientation* will define some very important terms so you can correctly follow the instructions. "Right side" and "left side" sound simple and concrete, but they are actually relative to where you're standing when reading the instructions.

The Safety chapter will tell you how to do things Safely. I wrote this book for two reasons: to make some money and to help you save some money by doing your own car repairs. A trip to the emergency room could quickly wipe out the money you saved. I want you to come through the procedures with nary a scratch, let alone major damage.

Nobody knows it all! The people at the Subaru dealer will help you when they have time. I'll warn you about procedures that require special tools, skills, and/or experience that are beyond the home mechanic's means. That's when it's time to seek professional help. I also urge you to seek advice at a friendly, well-equipped independent garage that specializes in Subarus.

Almost every car has idiosyncrasies that give it character and personality. For example, you may hear horrible scraping sounds when you step on the brake pedal, or the glove box door might fly open every time you hit a bump. You can live with an open glove box door but the brake thing should be checked out right away. The idea is to keep a sense of priorities. Get what's important fixed right away, then mess with the true idiosyncrasies as you choose.

There are three types of procedures in this book: *Maintenance, Diagnostic,* and *Repair.*

Maintenance Procedures: If you regularly perform the maintenance procedures, which include checking the condition of almost everything on the car, the likelihood of having to use the diagnostic and repair procedures will be reduced considerably. You'll know when some of the parts, like brakes, are nearing the end of the trail and should be replaced. Waiting for something to break before replacing it won't save you money by squeezing a few extra miles out of the part. When it breaks, other parts could be damaged that were otherwise in good condition. It's a lot easier on the nerves as well as the bank account to replace certain parts during your maintenance procedures rather than at the side of the road—or after having a tow truck haul your Soob back home. The AAA estimates that 80 percent of road emergencies are caused by neglecting maintenance.

When you buy a used Subaru, assume the maintenance *hasn't* been done even if the seller swears on his mother's grave that it was faithfully performed daily. Go through the 12,000-mile and 30,000-mile maintenance procedures (Chapter 7, Procedures 5 through 15) to replace all the vital fluids and to check the condition of the various systems—brakes, steering, suspension, etc. This will acquaint you intimately with your "pre-owned" Soob.

Diagnostic Procedures: When there's a clue that something is amiss, from fresh spots of oil on the driveway to an engine that won't start or dies suddenly in rush hour traffic, use the diagnostic procedures in Chapter 9 to identify the problem. Chapter 9 describes the symptoms of various maladies, then either tells you how to fix the problem or directs you to the appropriate chapter. Incidentally, at the beginning of each procedure in this book, a **Conditions** paragraph describes the *existing conditions of the car* under which the procedure should be performed. Oftentimes, diagnosing a problem is much more difficult than fixing it. But Chapter 9 and the Conditions paragraphs will help you.

Repair Procedures: Eventually some parts, like the water pump and brake pads, will give up the ghost due to normal wear, no matter how well the car is maintained. When the telltale symptoms appear, use the diagnostic procedures in Chapter 9 to identify the problem, then turn to the appropriate repair procedure. Fix it as soon as possible so you don't end up stranded in rush hour traffic or the middle of the desert.

PROCEDURE LAYOUT

The chapters are divided into **Procedures** which are broken down into **Steps**. At the beginning of each procedure the **Conditions** are described under which the procedure should be performed. Occasionally, I'll have a few words to say about the system in question at the start of a procedure.

Next comes the **Tools and Materials** paragraph, which will tell you what tools, parts, and supplies (such as brake fluid, gasket sealer, etc.) are needed to do the procedure. The word Friend is capitalized because there are times when two people are required to perform the procedures. Don't macho out and try to do everything yourself—you might get hurt or become so frustrated you give up. Having a Friend around to help and give you support and encouragement will make the procedures go faster and they'll probably be more fun.

The **Remarks** section gives you special instructions for the procedure, reminds you about things that should be done before starting the procedure, etc.

Especially important are the **Cautions!** and **Warnings!** that alert you to possible dangers you might encounter in the procedure. Do not pass Go until you read and heed them.

Read the entire procedure through before you begin, then read each step and be sure you understand it before you do it.

YEAR AND MODEL VARIATIONS

As with any instruction manual, it is of utmost importance that you follow the directions that apply to your particular model. Below I've defined the various years and models; be sure you understand exactly which model you have before attempting any of the procedures.

Mechanically speaking, there are two similar, yet different, types of Subarus. Here's how I've defined the two types in the manual:

OHV models: All 1975-1984 models, all Hatchbacks, and all Brats have overhead valve engines and will be referred to as **OHV** models.

OHC models: 1985 and newer Sedans, Station Wagons, XTs and Three-Door models have overhead camshaft engines so they will be referred to as **OHC** models.

In addition to the different engines in the two types, there are other mechanical differences throughout the car. So even if the procedure you are following has nothing to do with the engine, if you have an OHV model, as listed above, be sure to follow directions for OHV models. Likewise for OHC models.

Within the procedures, different tools, parts, or techniques are required for working on the various years and models covered in this book. When there are differences, I'll indicate in boldface type which years and models the instructions are for. If the years are followed by the word **models** (for example **'75-'79 models**), it means **ALL** models (Sedans, Station Wagons, Brats, etc., made from 1975 through 1979). If the years are followed by **cars**, it means all models *except* Brats. Special instructions for Brats are always indicated by **Brats** after the applicable years. Likewise, special instructions for XT models will be indicated by **XTs**. If the years are followed by **OHC** or **OHV**, it means the instructions are only for whichever type is indicated.

Here's how I've designated other variations:

Instructions that apply to four wheel drive models are indicated by **4WD**, and instructions for non-four wheel drive models are labeled **non-4WD**.

Subarus designed to California specifications are called **California cars** and all others are called **non-California** or **49 State** cars.

Until 1983 all Subaru engines had carburetors. Now there are also two different types of fuel injection systems, plus a turbocharger on some fuel injected models. Here's how the various fuel systems will be referred to throughout the book: Models with carburetors will be called **carb models**, models with Single Point Fuel Injection will be called **SPFI**, and models with Multi Point Fuel Injection will be called **MPFI**. Instructions that are specifically for models with turbochargers will be referred to as **Turbos**.

Here's how to tell which type of fuel system you have. (See Chapter 2 if you aren't sure where some of the parts mentioned are located.)

Carb models: You have a large, flat, light blue, or black air cleaner sitting on the top center of the engine.

SPFI and MPFI models: The black, box-like air cleaner is located in the right front corner of the engine compartment.

MPFI (OHV models): This setup is only on '83-'84 models. Locate the spark plugs on top of the cylinder heads. The fuel injectors are mounted in the heads right below the spark plugs.

MPFI (OHC models): Look at the outer ends of the intake manifold. There are two spark plug-size things sticking out of the end of the manifold. Those are the fuel injectors. The rubber hoses attached to the ends of the injectors supply the fuel.

SPFI models: You **don't** have fuel injectors mounted in the cylinder heads or intake manifold like the MPFI models have. The throttle body mounted on the top center of the engine contains the single fuel injector.

Whew! All of this isn't really as complicated as it seems right now. You'll get the hang of it quickly, and it's actually quite simple once you start doing the procedures.

When you come to a section that applies to your particular Soob, follow the instructions to the end of the Step, or until you come to a section in the Step that doesn't apply to your car. Skip down through the section that doesn't apply until you either come to another section that applies to your year and model or to one that begins with the word **EVERYONE**. Obviously, everyone should do the EVERYONE section.

As you do the preliminary read-through, using a yellow marking pen to highlight the sections appropriate to your year and model will save you time and possible confusion later while you're actually doing the procedure.

12   Chapter 1

STEP-BY-STEP

Read each procedure all the way through before starting to work. Often something that doesn't make sense in the first part of the procedure will become obvious a little farther along. I've seen people become very perplexed and spend a lot of time trying to figure something out, whereas if they had only read the entire procedure before starting, they wouldn't have gotten hung up.

If possible, have someone read the steps to you as you perform the work so you don't have to stop and find your place in the book so often. Also, there's nothing worse than trying to turn pages with greasy hands or trying to read while lying under the car with dirt falling in your eyes. Have a pencil and paper handy so you, or your reader, can jot down notes as you go along—about parts needed, or the disassembly sequence, or if there's a discrepancy between what you have and what the book says you should have.

Take your time! Do the job once and do it right. DON'T IMPROVISE! Just do it the way it says. When you strip a thread, twist off a stud, break a bolt and disasters like that, don't slit your wrists—turn to Chapter 18. It was written for just these contingencies. Smile!

Keep everything clean as you go along. Clean parts so they shine, or get your Friend to do it. The job will go easier with fewer frustrations. When you're through working on your Soob, clean your tools and put them away before you take your funky clothes off. Then clean yourself and change your clothes before you drive the car, or at least cover the seat with something so you don't get the inside greasy. Old sheets, large towels, or blankets work well.

NOW WHAT?

Now that you know how to use this book, and before you jump into some of the full-scale repair procedures, I suggest you read and perform the simple, yet vital, chapters and/or procedures listed below to familiarize yourself with your Soob and the actual doing of procedures. The only tools required are the lugwrench, jack and jack handle that came with the car, a rag, and safety glasses. If any of these tools are missing, get them as soon as possible. Knowing how to change a flat tire and check the vital fluid levels in the engine compartment will give you confidence that you can perform the more complicated procedures when necessary.

VITAL (YET SIMPLE) CHAPTERS AND PROCEDURES

Chapter 2: Orientation. Learn the names and locations of some of the important parts in the engine compartment. While you're at it, copy the vital numbers for your Soob in the "My Specs" chart in Chapter 7. (If you want to know **how** your Subaru does what it does, read Chapter 4: *How a Subaru Works*.)

Chapter 3: Safety. Read the safety rap, then pretend you have a flat tire and follow the instructions in Procedure 2 to practice changing a tire. Having leisurely done this in your garage or driveway, you'll be assured the necessary tools are in the car, you'll know how to use the tools, and you'll have the confidence that you are prepared to do the job, if and when the dreaded event actually happens. Even if you belong to an auto club that will change the tire for you for free, think of the time you'll save and the sense of pride you'll experience by confidently handling the situation yourself!

Chapter 7: Maintenance, Lubrication, and Tune-up. Read the introduction to the chapter, then do Procedures 1 and 2 to check the vital fluid levels and condition of the drive belts in the engine compartment. Doing these two procedures (and Procedure 2 in Chapter 16) regularly will probably eliminate 80 percent of the causes of roadside breakdowns!

Chapter 16: Cooling. Procedure 2 tells you how to check and replace the rubber cooling system hoses. If any hoses look suspect (I tell you what to look for), replace them as soon as possible. It's a great way to get hands-on experience taking things apart and putting them back together, and it's almost as easy as eating homemade apple pie.

CHAPTER 2

UNDER-HOOD ORIENTATION... AND A LITTLE HISTORY

We'll get to the "under-hood orientation" in a few minutes, but first here's my personal, unofficial version of the coming to be of the Subaru. A little history, professor, if you please. There won't be a pop quiz at the end.

Subarus are what classical music composers would call a variation on a theme. They are related in many ways to their Japanese cousins, offering similar dimensions and body styles. The engine, however, is a rather unique variation on a very familiar German theme. The original theme was developed before World War II by Dr. Ferdinand Porsche (remember him?) for Adolf Hitler (remember him?). Hitler hired Porsche to design a simple, efficient, inexpensive (and built to stay that way!) car for the masses. The theory was that the German folks (*volks* in German) would give the Third Reich some of their money every year and the Third Reich in return would put the volks on wheels (*wagens*). Guess what car Porsche designed? Right, the Volkswagen.

As you know, old Adolf used the money and some of Dr. Porsche's designs for less honorable endeavors. Anyway, Porsche did what he was hired to do and developed a simple, efficient, horizontally opposed, air-cooled, four-cylinder engine, which bolted to a combined transmission and differential (called a *transaxle*), to be fitted in the rear of a small car. It eventually became one of the most popular automotive designs in the world.

The original Volkswagen, as well as some variations on the original theme (like 356, 911 and 912 Porsche sports cars), have become automotive legends. Other variations, like Chevy Corvairs, became less than legendary.

In the 1960s some clever fellows at Fuji Heavy Industries (a Japanese airplane and heavy equipment manufacturer) "borrowed" Dr. Porsche's engine/transaxle design, put it in the front (thus front wheel drive—yea!), used water to cool it (good idea!), made a few more improvements on the already good design (typically

Japanese, right?), put it in a modern body, and called it a Subaru. Why didn't I think of this? Clever people, those Japanese.

So in your Subaru you have a modern variation of an automotive legend living on and on. And doing quite nicely, I would add.

Subaru, by the way, is the Japanese word for the star constellation we call the Pleiades, or the Seven Sisters. Some starry winter night when the coyotes are howling at the moon, see if you can find a cluster of tiny stars in the sky, above and to the right of Orion, that looks like your grille ornament.

Since the Subaru is named for a star constellation, I can't resist calling it *Starship Subaru* and having Captain Quirk, Mr. Schpock, Snotty, and Dr. McJoy make occasional appearances in the following chapters.

OK, 'nuf of this. Now let's get on with the orientation.

WHICH WAY IS UP?

As a great philosopher once said, "Before we speak, let us first define terms." That's exactly what we need to do before jumping into the maintenance and repair procedures. It's important to eliminate directions that may be ambiguous because they're relative to things that change. For instance, you know which is your right hand and which is your left hand, but that won't necessarily help you when the directions say something like, "The widget is on the right side of the gizmo." Sounds simple, but right is *relative* to which side of the gizmo you're standing on.

To keep things straight, throughout the book **right** will mean the **passenger's side** of the car; **left** will be the **driver's side**. If you're standing in front of the car looking at the engine, the right side will be to your left because right is always the passenger's side. Got it?

The front of the car is the end with the headlights, and the rear end of the car has the taillights. So **front** always means toward the front of the car, **rear** means toward the back of the car. Assuming your Soob is standing on its wheels, the **top** is the shiny side and the **bottom** is the mysterious underneath side you seldom see. And that goes for every part on the vehicle. In other words, all directions (front, back, top, bottom) relate to the car itself.

Here are two more: **Inboard** means toward the center of the car; **outboard** means away from the center of the car.

When the instructions say, "Turn the key to ON," it means turn the key until the dash lights blaze, but don't start the engine. "Turn the engine ON" or "Start the engine" means just that, so turn the key all the way and start it.

Although it's technically inaccurate, for convenience I'll refer to nut and bolt sizes throughout the book by whatever size wrench it takes to fit the nut or head of the bolt (technically, the size is determined by the size of the threaded portion, not the wrench size). If you have to replace a bolt or nut, take the old one, or one just like it, to the parts store with you.

All bolts and nuts on your Soob have *right-hand threads* (at least all which you'll be removing or installing). Right-hand threads mean you screw the nut or bolt *clockwise* to tighten it and *counterclockwise* to remove it. That means *clockwise* or *counterclockwise* as viewed from the end of the bolt or nut you're turning. It gets a little confusing when you're on your back under the car and removing a nut screwed on from the top. You need to imagine an out-of-body experience so you can view the nut from above—the end you are turning. *Clockwise* and *counterclockwise* are sometimes italicized just to get your attention.

THINGS IN THE ENGINE COMPARTMENT

Knowing the names of some under-hood parts common to all Subarus will help you locate lesser known parts. For example, telling you the automatic choke housing is on the right side of the carburetor won't help much if you don't know where the carburetor is. Please learn the names of the major parts in this section (indicated in boldface) and where they are located in the engine compartment.

This section is only to familiarize you with the **names** and **locations** of common parts. What the parts do and how they do it is explained in Chapter 4: *How a Subaru Works*, or sometimes in the rap at the beginning of the chapter that covers maintenance and repair of the part.

To open the hood of your Starship, find the small black knob underneath the dashboard on the left, near your left knee when sitting in the driver's seat. Pull on the knob until you see the front of the hood jump slightly. Go to the front of the car and grope about in the center between the hood and the top of the grille for a little flat lever that releases the safety latch. Pull up on the lever and the hood will rise before you. Look for a long thin *prop rod* across the top of the grille, held in place by a rubber or plastic *clip*. Lift up on the free end of the rod and it will pivot in a rubber grommet on the other end. The free end of the rod fits into a *bracket* on the underside of the hood on early models, or hooks into a *hole* punched into the hood bracing on later models. (On '80 and newer models there's an arrow pointing to the correct hole.)

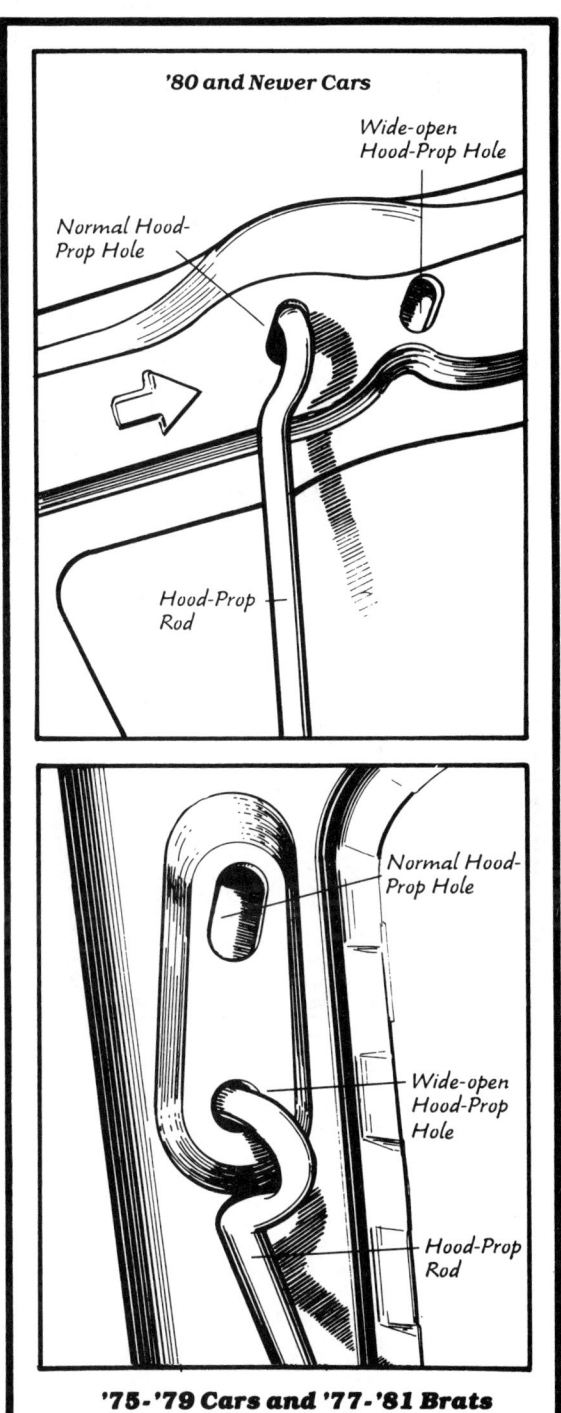

Subaru hoods can also be propped in a *wide open position* by wiggling the end of the prop rod out of the grommet and inserting it in a hole (or hole in a bracket) on one of the **strut towers**. The strut towers are those metal lumps that stick out into the middle of each side of the engine compartment. There's a round black rubber thing sticking up out of the center of each strut tower which you don't mess with. On models without a prop rod bracket on the hood, the hole for the prop rod when the hood is in the wide open position is either below or a couple of inches to the side of the regular hole (check the illustration).

On most Subarus the first thing you may notice and wonder about when you open the hood is that the **spare tire** is in the engine compartment. Actually, storing the spare in the engine compartment makes very good sense: more luggage space is available in the trunk on sedans, coupes, and hardtops, and more hauling space is available for hatchbacks, station wagons, and Brats. It's always accessible (you don't have to unload all the vacation luggage to get to it). Also, it offers a little more protection in case of an altercation with something, like a tree that grew where it shouldn't have or a kamikaze cab driver. I use the top of the spare tire to stash spare parts I may need on the road, such as drive belts, a clutch cable, and an accelerator cable.

Some people have actually told me that when they were shopping for a new car they didn't buy a Subaru because the spare tire in the engine compartment looked weird. That's a weird reason!

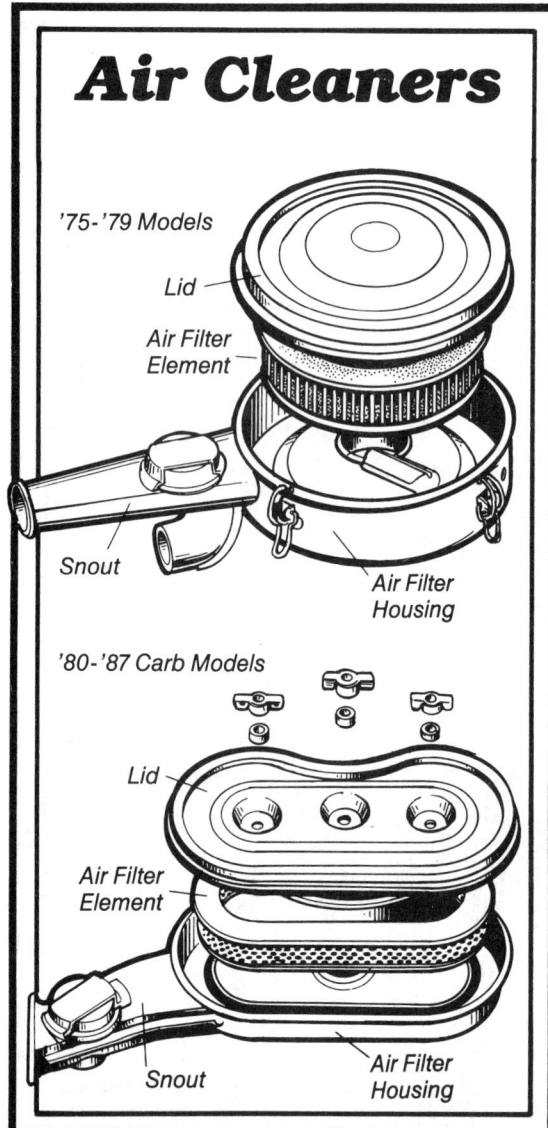

Air Cleaners

'75-'79 Models
- Lid
- Air Filter Element
- Snout
- Air Filter Housing

'80-'87 Carb Models
- Lid
- Air Filter Element
- Snout
- Air Filter Housing

If the spare tire isn't in the engine compartment, look under the rubber floor mat and piece of stiff cardboard in the trunk of sedans and coupes, or under the rear of the car on early station wagons. It's mounted in the trunk on XT models. Still no spare? It's gone AWOL and should be replaced as soon as possible. Look for a Subaru wheel and tire at a junkyard and save yourself some money.

Let's move right along with our engine compartment tour. Things are slightly different on carb models and fuel injected models.

Carb models: The next thing you'll probably notice is the light blue or black, round or oval-shaped **air cleaner**, smack dab in front of you. Inside the air cleaner is the engine **air filter element** that filters out the dust, bugs, and gravel before the air enters the engine. There's an air intake **"snout"** on the right (passenger's) side of the housing with a large, **hot air intake hose** attached to the bottom. On OHC models the end of the snout connects to a rubber hose. The **carburetor** is directly below the air cleaner housing, in among some pipes and wires, bolted to the top of the engine's **intake manifold**.

SPFI and MPFI engines: The large rubber **air intake boot** (hose) on the right (passenger's side) of the engine compartment connects to the **air cleaner housing**, located on the inside of the right fender. On non-Turbo models, the other end of the hose connects to the **throttle body assembly**, which is bolted to the top center of the engine's **intake manifold**. The fuel injection type (SPFI or MPFI) is probably stamped on the rubber boot. **Turbo models:** Large rubber ducts (air intake boots) connect the **turbocharger** to the air cleaner housing and to the **throttle body assembly**, which is bolted to the top center of the engine's **intake manifold**. The turbocharger itself is on the right rear corner of the engine, hidden beneath sheet metal heat shields so you can't see it.

OHV models: To the right rear of the engine, near the spare tire, you'll see the wire-loop handle of the **engine oil dipstick**. To the left rear of the engine and also near the spare tire is the metal **oil filler tube** and its cap. This is where you put fresh oil into the crankcase.

OHC models: The **engine oil dipstick** is conveniently located near the front center of the engine.

Under-Hood Orientation

The **oil filler tube** sticks up from the right front corner of the engine.

Automatic transmission models: You have a second wire-loop-handle dipstick. You'll find it to the left rear of the engine compartment, near the brake reservoir. It's called the automatic transmission **fluid level dipstick**.

The **distributor** is a fist-sized thing mounted near the top front of the engine slightly to the right of center on OHV models and on the top left rear corner of the engine on OHC models. (To see it on *some* OHV carb models you might have to peek around a black plastic shield clipped to the front of the air cleaner housing.) The distributor has large **high tension wires** plugged into the top of its plastic **distributor cap**. The wires around the top edge of the distributor cap are **spark plug wires**. They carry electricity to the **spark plugs** located on top of the two **cylinder heads** (just follow the wires to find the cylinder heads). The wire plugged into the center of the distributor cap is the **coil wire**. The other end of the coil wire is connected to the **ignition coil**, a cylindrical thing about the size of a soup can.

KEY
1. Hood Prop Rod
2. Wide Open Hood Prop Bracket (might be a hole next to the strut tower)
3. Strut Towers
4. Carburetor
5. Intake Manifold
6. Battery
7. Battery Cables
8. Terminal Posts
9. Battery Hold Down Bracket
10. Engine Oil Dipstick
11. Engine Oil Filler Tube
12. Automatic Transmission Fluid Dipstick
13. Distributor
14. Distributor Cap
15. Spark Plug Wires
16. Spark Plugs
17. Cylinder Heads
18. Coil Wire
19. Coil
20. Voltage Regulator
21. Valve Covers
22. Crankcase
23. Crankshaft Pulley
24. Drive Belt
25. Oil Pump
26. Oil Filter
27. Water Pump
28. Alternator
29. Master Cylinder
30. Brake Fluid Reservoirs
31. Master Vac
32. Windshield Wiper Motor
33. Windshield Washer Fluid Reservoir (might be on the other side)
34. Radiator
35. Radiator Cap
36. Radiator Hoses
37. Flywheel Housing
38. Double Offset Joint (DOJ)

The **battery** is the big, plastic rectangular box in one of the front corners of the engine compartment. Two **battery cables** attach by clamps to **terminal posts** on opposite ends of the battery. The battery is held in place by a **hold-down bracket**.

On 1975-1981 models, just to the rear of the battery is a black or bronze-colored metal box with a few wires running from it. That's the **voltage regulator**. It's usually larger than the other boxes you may find near it.

The **spark plugs** are screwed into the **cylinder heads**. There's one head on each side of the engine. The rounded things bolted to the outboard surface of each cylinder head, just below the spark plugs, are the **valve covers**. Lurking inside the valve covers are such mysterious things as *rocker arms, valves, and valve springs*.

A hollow aluminum **intake manifold** connects the carburetor (*throttle body* on fuel injected models) to the two cylinder heads. It bolts onto the heads right between the two spark plugs.

The large hunk of aluminum below the intake manifold and between the cylinder heads is the engine **crankcase** or block. The crankcase consists of a right and left half, bolted together in the middle. Within the crankcase are the *cylinders, pistons, crankshaft, connecting rods*, and on OHV models, the *camshaft*. How all these internal parts relate is explained in Chapter 4: *How a Subaru Works*.

On the front of the engine you will see some round pulleys. The pulley on the bottom front center of the engine is attached to the end of the crankshaft and is appropriately called the **crankshaft pulley**. It turns whenever the engine is running. Licorice-looking **drive belts** around the crankshaft pulley turn pulleys on other things (described later).

Straight below the crankshaft pulley on the front of the engine is the **oil pump**. You won't be able to see much of the oil pump unless you crawl beneath the front of the car. The round canlike **oil filter** sticks out of the left side of the oil pump on OHV models, and out of the right side of the pump on OHC models. On OHC models, you won't be able to see the oil pump because of the large plastic camshaft belt covers that enclose most of the front of the engine.

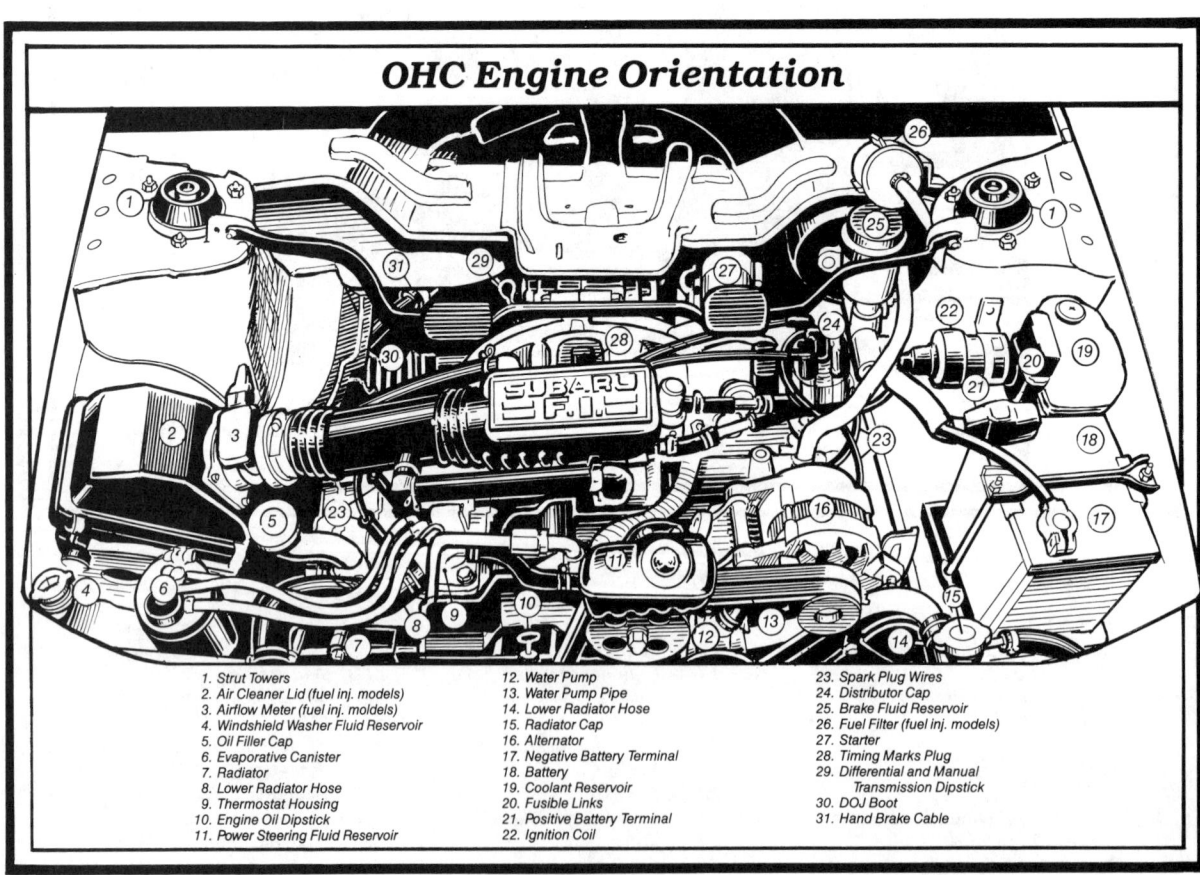

OHC Engine Orientation

1. Strut Towers
2. Air Cleaner Lid (fuel inj. models)
3. Airflow Meter (fuel inj. moldels)
4. Windshield Washer Fluid Reservoir
5. Oil Filler Cap
6. Evaporative Canister
7. Radiator
8. Lower Radiator Hose
9. Thermostat Housing
10. Engine Oil Dipstick
11. Power Steering Fluid Reservoir
12. Water Pump
13. Water Pump Pipe
14. Lower Radiator Hose
15. Radiator Cap
16. Alternator
17. Negative Battery Terminal
18. Battery
19. Coolant Reservoir
20. Fusible Links
21. Positive Battery Terminal
22. Ignition Coil
23. Spark Plug Wires
24. Distributor Cap
25. Brake Fluid Reservoir
26. Fuel Filter (fuel inj. models)
27. Starter
28. Timing Marks Plug
29. Differential and Manual Transmission Dipstick
30. DOJ Boot
31. Hand Brake Cable

The **water pump** is bolted to the left front of the engine. A pulley on the front of the water pump is driven by a drive belt from the nearby crankshaft pulley.

The **alternator** is mounted by brackets to the top left corner of the engine, on four-cylinder engines. On six-cylinder engines it's mounted on the top center of the engine. The alternator is about the size of a short fat coffee can sitting on edge. It has slots on the front and wires connected to the back. It has a metal fan-bladed thing with a pulley on the front that's turned by the drive belt from the crankshaft pulley.

If you have air conditioning, the large, clunky looking **air conditioner compressor** will be to the left of the alternator or between the alternator and carburetor or throttle body. A second drive belt from the crankshaft pulley goes around the pulley on the front of the compressor. Two hoses are attached to the compressor to carry freon gas under high pressure back to the passenger compartment. *Don't mess with these two hoses.*

If you have power steering on an OHV carb model, you'll have a third drive belt that turns a **hydraulic power steering pump**, located on the top front of the engine on the passenger's side.

Let's move away from the engine now and explore other delights under your hood.

The aluminum brake **master cylinder**, with one or two **brake fluid reservoirs** mounted on top, sticks straight out of the **firewall** (the wall between the engine and passenger compartments). It's near the left rear corner of the engine compartment. See the plastic filler cap(s) on top of it? A large, round, black **Master Vac** (vacuum assist unit) is between the master cylinder and firewall.

The **fuel filter** for '80-'81 models and all fuel injected engines is mounted near the brake master cylinder.

The soup can-sized thing in the top, left, rear corner of the engine compartment (above the master cylinder) is the **windshield wiper motor**.

There's a large, white plastic **windshield washer fluid reservoir** somewhere in the engine compartment. It's in the left rear corner on '75-'79 cars and '77-'81 Brats, and on the right side near the rear on '80-'84 cars, '82-'87 Brats and all hatchbacks. It has a cap on top. On OHC models, the reservoir is hiding near the right front corner of the engine compartment. You have to peek through a vertical oblong hole just beneath the filler cap.

The **radiator** is that large, flat black thing with a corrugated surface attached vertically to the body between the engine and grille. An **electric cooling fan** is mounted to its right rear side. Late models with air conditioning will have a second fan mounted on the left rear side of the radiator. The **radiator cap** is on the upper left corner of the radiator.

On OHC models, there's a white translucent coolant reservoir tank mounted on the left front side of the engine compartment. That's where you check the coolant level.

Two large, black rubber **radiator hoses** attach to the back of the radiator. One hose goes from the lower left corner of the radiator to the water pump; the other hose goes from the upper right corner of the radiator to a fitting on the intake manifold.

Now peer down beneath the spare tire (if it's in the engine compartment). Bolted to the back of the engine crankcase is the round **flywheel housing** and to the back of that, the transaxle.

The engine and transaxle are held in place by bolts and rubber **engine mounts** to the **front crossmember**, a long, black metal piece that runs from left to right, below and to the rear of the engine crankcase.

On either side of the transaxle you'll see the **axle shafts** sticking out, one going to each front wheel. The axle shafts have accordion-type rubber boots on each end.

We have now covered the main parts visible underneath the hood of your Subaru. Yes, there are sundry other pipes, hoses, and wires. Many of them deal with emissions, and I'll get to them in Chapter 12: *Exhaust and Emission Control Systems.*

NUMBERS

This little section tells you how to locate the engine and body serial numbers, the production date (when the car was made), and the engine type. I urge you to find the numbers now, then copy them down in the "My Specs" chart in Chapter 7. Always take these numbers with you when buying parts. Changes in parts are sometimes made during a model year run, so you may need more than just the year model of your Soob.

Production Date and Vehicle Identification Number (VIN): Open the driver's door and look for a metal plate on the rear edge of the door or on the pillar the door closes against. You'll see numbers like 10/73, 12/82, and so forth, that indicate the month and year the car was manufactured. That's the **production date**.

Near the bottom of the plate there will be a long **Vehicle Identification Number (VIN)**. The VIN is also stamped into the firewall in the engine compartment near the spare tire. On late models, the VIN is also on the top of the dash and you can read it by looking through the lower left corner of the windshield.

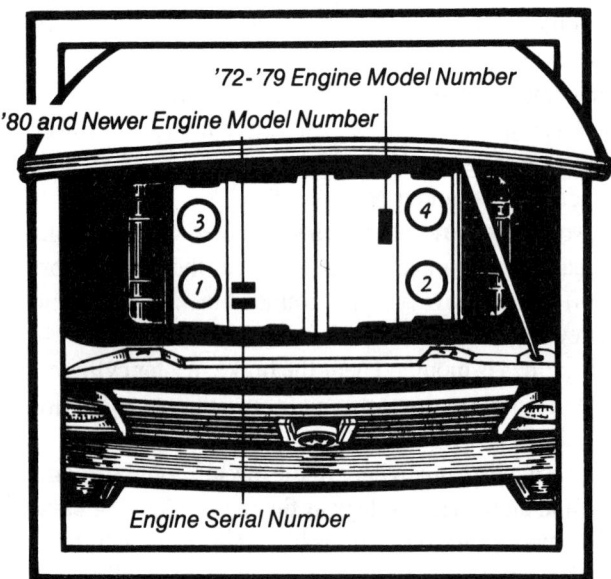

Engine Serial Number: Look on the top front of the engine, just to the right of center. You'll see a flat place with numbers stamped on it. That's the **engine serial number**.

Engine Model Number: A set of numbers cast (raised numbers) into the engine block identifies the size of the engine:

'75-'79 models: The engine model number is cast on the top left rear corner of the engine crankcase (it's just above the rearmost spark plug).

'80 and newer models: The engine model number is cast in place right above the engine serial number, on the top right front of the engine crankcase.

EVERYONE: The engine model numbers indicate the size of the engine in cubic centimeters (cc): EA71 = 1600cc; EA81 = 1800cc OHV; EA82 = 1800cc OHC; ER27 = 2700cc six-cylinder OHC.

UNDERHOOD STICKERS

Most models have a white **Emission Control Information** sticker on the underside of the hood which contains valuable information about your particular Subaru. If your sticker is missing, try to get a new one from the Subaru dealer. Be sure to take your vehicle identification number, engine model, and serial number with you to ensure getting the correct sticker.

Here's the pertinent information the sticker can tell you: If your model has an **exhaust catalyst**, or if it's a **non-catalyst** model (if the sticker doesn't mention a catalyst, you don't have one); the **tune-up specifications** for your engine (timing, valve clearance, idle speed, etc.); and the **model year**. If the car was built to **California specifications**, the sticker will say something like, "This model complies with State of California regulations applicable to 19?? model year new passenger cars when sold in the state of California." If California *isn't* mentioned on the sticker you have a **non-California (49 State)** car.

You might also have a handy **vacuum hose connections** sticker. You can use the sticker to identify some of the emission control gizmos and to see that all the vacuum hoses are connected to them correctly.

Models equipped with the skinny "T" type spare tire will have a caution sticker for using the tire. Read the sticker and follow the directions when using the tire.

Some models will have a sticker showing how to orient the jack if it fits under the spare tire.

There's probably a sticker on the brace across the top front of the radiator that identifies the paint color number for your Soob. Write the paint number in this book or in the owner's manual so you'll have it even if the sticker fades or falls off. Ok, that's it for Starship lore and orientation. To close the hood, hold it up with one hand while you lower the prop and stick it in its clip on the right side above the grille with the other hand. Then lower the hood about halfway, clear your fingers, and let it drop. Pull up on it to check that the safety catch has grabbed hold and will keep it snugly down.

Snotty, beam us to Chapter 3, a most important mission.

CHAPTER 3

SAFETY!

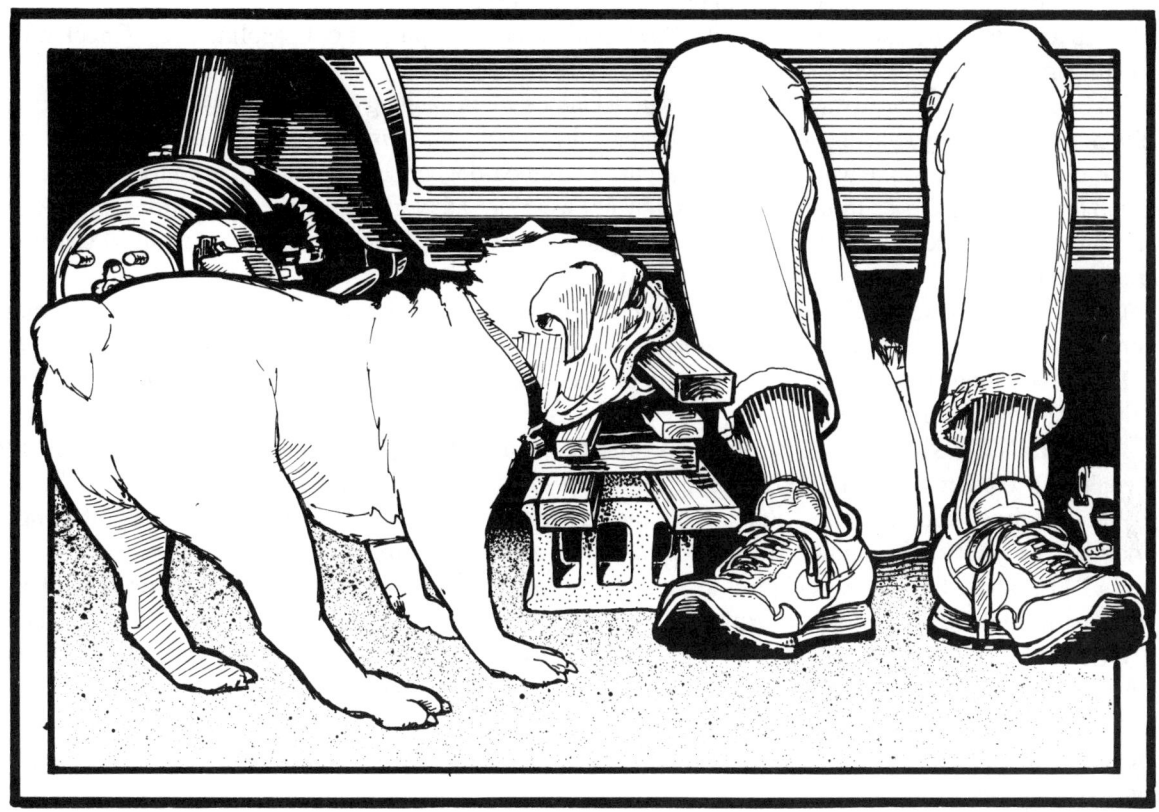

    Read this chapter all the way through, but don't let it scare you. It shouldn't intimidate you out of working on your Soob; it is intended to make you aware of a few simple safety precautions that will prevent common accidents. A trip to Dr. McJoy's sick bay could quickly cost more than you'll save by doing your own car work. Read on.
    Besides being a fine piece of automotive engineering, your Subaru, dealt with thoughtlessly, can also be dangerous and deadly. When working on your Soob, *concentrate* on what you are doing. If something is distracting you, STOP, deal with the interference, then go back to work with all your attention focused on the task at hand. It's hard to keep track of what you've done and what you are to do next when being constantly interrupted. No matter how tired, cold, miserable, or pissed off you get, don't make borderline decisions *for* convenience but *against* safety.
    Work at your own pace. Don't rush a job. And do EVERYTHING it says to do in the procedures. It's wise to allow at least twice the time you think you'll need. Remember, cleanup is part of the procedure, and that takes time, too. It's especially important to be patient near the end of a job. That's when you may be a little tired and tempted to take shortcuts or rush things. Don't. It's often toward the *end* of the job that mistakes and accidents happen.
    I can't possibly come up with every bizarre situation you might run into, but I'll list the most common causes of accidents, and how to avoid them:
    EXHAUST GAS: Carbon monoxide first makes you drowsy and careless, then kills you. So *never* run the engine in a garage with the large garage door closed. It's best to roll the car out of the garage far enough so the exhaust pipe is outside. I stick a ten-foot piece of rain gutter downpipe on the end of the exhaust pipe to get the fumes as far away from me as possible.

FIRE DANGERS: The combination of a spark and a puddle of gasoline can turn your Soob into a nasty black carcass in about ten minutes. Have you ever seen a car destroyed by fire? It's sickening. To prevent this from happening to you, wipe up all drips, spills, and puddles of gasoline right when they happen.

Don't smoke *anything* while working on your car. If you smoke, take a break away from the car (you can read the procedure or step you're about to perform while you light up).

Keep a modern fire extinguisher handy. Be sure it's capable of putting out gasoline fires. Check it regularly. Inform helpers of its whereabouts.

SAFETY GLASSES: Always wear clean safety glasses when banging on something with a hammer, when you're messing with any kind of spring, when checking the battery, when using a spray can of carb cleaner (brake cleaner, etc.), or when you're working under the car or dashboard where crud could fall in your eyes. Your sight is much too precious to even think about risking by not wearing safety glasses in these situations. I know there aren't any designer safety goggles around and most people look pretty foolish in them, but swallow your vanity and wear 'em.

CLOTHING: Take off all jewelry, including rings (finger, nose, or ear). Also remove scarves, neckties, or any loose clothing, and tuck long hair into a stocking cap when working on a car. Wear comfortable clothing. If you have long sleeves, either roll them up or button them properly (loose cuffs are notorious for finding their way into moving parts).

RUNNING ENGINE: When the engine is running, some of the pulleys, fans, and drive belts spin so fast you can't even tell they're moving. When doing a tune-up, BE AWARE and keep fingers, tools, rags, hair, clothing, and the wires from the timing light and/or the tach/dwell meter well away from the front of the engine. Remember also that some engine parts get *very hot* soon after the engine is started.

BATTERY ACID: Battery acid loves to eat clothing, and it should be kept away from your eyes at all costs. The vapor around the battery caps is explosive, so never check the battery fluid level with a match or lighter.

DUST MASK OR RESPIRATOR: Wear at least a dust mask (a painter's respirator is better) when working on the brakes or clutch. They contain asbestos, which can cause cancer if inhaled too often.

AIR CONDITIONING: If you have air conditioning (A/C), be very careful around the hoses attached to the A/C compressor. They contain gases under high pressure. If any A/C stuff has to be taken apart, have Subaru or a garage do it.

LIGHTING: You'll frequently need some kind of light to see what you're doing. Groping around in dim light is dangerous as well as frustrating. Use either a **flashlight** or a **drop light** (the kind with the bulb surrounded by a steel safety cage). Use "rough service" light bulbs. Never use a household type standing lamp. If it's knocked over, the bulb can shatter, exposing the metal filament. If any combustible fuels contact the filament, hope that your insurance is up to date. My recommendations for good work lights are in Chapter 5: *Tools*.

OILY RAGS: Don't keep a pile of oily rags in the corner of your garage. They have this weird ability to build up heat and ignite themselves. Put them in a metal trash can outside. There are companies that supply rags in bundles which you can buy or rent.

WASTE MATERIALS: Drain oil, coolant, and other fluids into a catch pan, then transfer them into a sealed metal or plastic container marked POISON. Dispose of waste materials properly—not down the drain. Recycling centers can tell you who accepts used oil if they don't.

BATTLE SCARS: Anyone who has worked on a car has experienced the skinned knuckle syndrome. To protect your pinkies, think about where your hand will end up if the wrench slips or the stubborn bolt suddenly breaks loose. If possible, position the wrench so you're pulling it toward you rather than pushing on it.

CLEANLINESS: Keep your work area clean and well organized as you go along. It's easier to find dropped screws, bolts, and washers on a clean floor rather than having to dig through dirt clods, grease blobs, and squished cigarette butts to find them. Stash the parts you remove from the car someplace where you won't be tripping over them, causing damage to the parts or yourself.

Safety! 23

GETTING UNDER THE CAR

Knowing the right way to jack up your Soob safely is very important, because it can be very dangerous if you don't do it right. Improper jacking is the most common cause of injury when working on a car.

When you need to support the car to work under it, support it well on *level* ground. Always put the gearshift in 1st (manual transmission) or PARK (automatic transmission), set the handbrake, and "chock" the wheels on the opposite end from the end you're raising—use blocks of wood so the car can't roll. Stuff the chocks under there snugly on both front and back of the tire. Use good quality **jackstands** to support the weight of the car once it's jacked up. Jacks are notorious for slipping or falling over, so don't get under the car when it's only supported by a jack.

Keep kids and spectators away from the car while it's jacked up. Have them take a walk or fix snacks.

If you're going to be working on the brakes, suspension, steering, axles, or other things that require the car to be raised, I recommend buying, borrowing, or renting an inexpensive hydraulic **floor jack** (they cost less than $50 now) and two *good* jackstands (about $10 each) to safely raise and support the car. The jack that came with the car is meant for raising one corner so a tire can be changed. It works fine for that but is not designed to raise the car high enough to make repair work convenient or safe. Besides, the place where you jack up the car with the Subaru jack is where the jackstand should be placed after the car is raised. A peculiar Catch 22. But it will motivate you to get that floor jack.

Here are a few *NEVERS* to keep in mind before getting under the car.

NEVER use a bumper jack to raise your Soob. The shock absorbers in the bumpers and probably the bumpers themselves will be bent and ruined.

NEVER use cinder (cement) blocks to support the weight of your car. They look strong and feel heavy, but they are very brittle. Without warning, they can crumble into a pile of dust. I would never get under a car supported by cinder blocks and you shouldn't either.

NEVER use a stack of lumber to support the car if you're going to be working under it. Unless you're using heavy beams at least 12 inches wide and several inches thick, the stack would be so wobbly by the time the car is high enough to crawl under that it would be unsafe.

OK, with all the warnings taken care of, here's how to properly *Chock, Jack,* and *Block* your Soob. Procedure 1 tells you how to use a floor jack and jackstands to get both front or both rear wheels off the ground. You'll be referred to this procedure through-

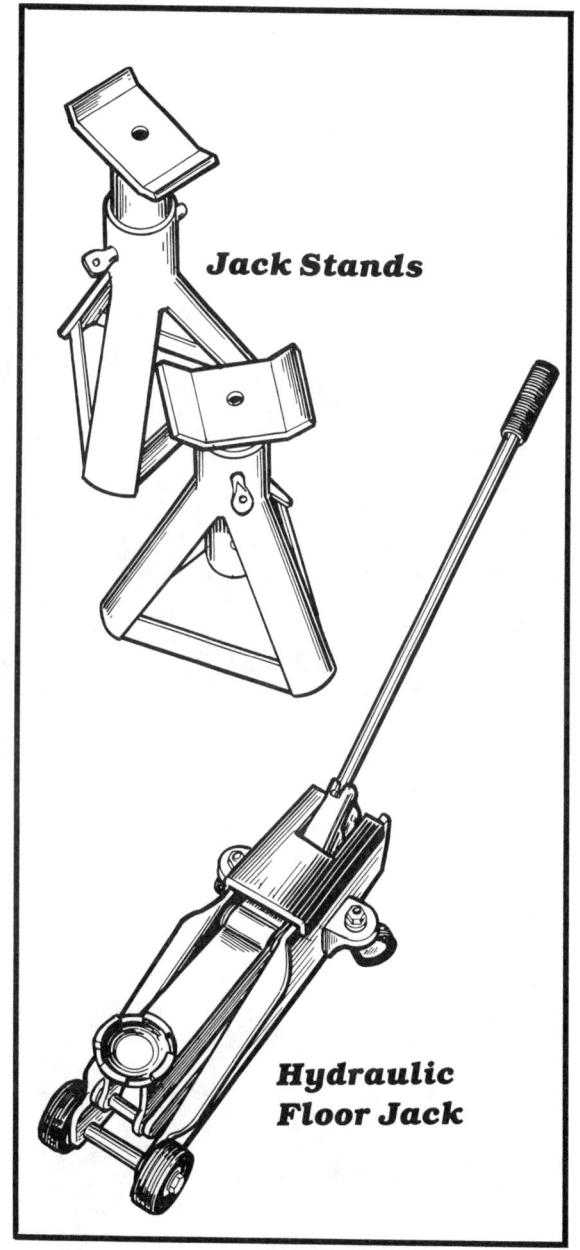

out the book, so be sure you have the equipment and know-how to do it correctly. Procedure 2 tells you how to use the Subaru jack to change a flat tire or rotate the tires so they'll wear evenly. Procedure 3 tells you how to tow a distressed car safely. Remember, read each procedure all the way through before you start the work.

PROCEDURE 1: CHOCK, JACK, AND BLOCK (using a floor jack and jackstands)

Condition: The car needs to be raised so the wheels can be removed; OR you need to get under the car to work on it.

Tools and Materials: A hydraulic floor jack, two jackstands, at least two chocks to keep the car from rolling. The chocks can be large blocks of wood (4x4 blocks about 12" long work well), wedge-shaped blocks of wood, or store-bought metal wheel chocks.

If you're removing wheels, you'll need a **lug wrench** or socket and ratchet. Depending on the kind of wheels you have (regular, spokers, or mags), the lug nuts are either 19mm or 21mm.

If you need to remove the axle nuts (those big nuts on the ends of the front axles on all models, and the center of the rear axles on 4WD models), you'll need a 36mm socket and ratchet.

Remark: If you need to remove a wheel, or a brake drum or disc, loosen the lug nuts and/or axle nuts a little *before* raising the car.

Wheel Chocks

Front Jacking Point
Use the black crossmember behind the Oil Pan - NOT the Oil Pan

Step 1. Park the Car.

Park on a level, hard, smooth surface. Pull the handbrake on, then put the car in 1st (manual transmission), or PARK (automatics). Jacking a car up on even a slight incline greatly increases the chance of an accident. If the ground is soft or muddy, you'll need to round up a large, thick, flat piece of wood to set the jack on or you'll end up lowering the jack into the ground instead of raising the car. Shoo people and pets out of the car before raising it.

Step 2. Chock the Wheels.

Place blocks of wood (called **chocks**) in front of and behind at least one of the wheels on the opposite end of the car from the end you're raising. It's especially important to block the rear wheels before raising the front of the car.

Step 3. Position the Jack.

Follow the directions that came with your floor jack for properly positioning, raising, and lowering it.

FRONT: Look under the front of the car. You'll see a black bulbous **oil pan** covering the bottom of the engine. 4WD models will have a steel **skid plate** below the oil pan to protect it from rocks and boulders. A little farther back than the oil pan or skid plate, you'll see a nearly flat, black, steel plate called the **front crossmember**. That's where you position the floor jack to raise the front of the car (not under the skid plate or oil pan).

REAR: Depending on the year and model, there are three different places to jack up the rear of the car:

'75-'79 non-4WD models: Look for two **U-shaped clamps** located on the bottom center of the car slightly forward from the rear wheels. The clamps attach two steel *torsion bars* to the bottom of the body. Center the jack on the two U-shaped clamps to raise the rear.

'80 and newer non-4WD models: Locate a **black steel tube** that runs across the bottom of the car about one foot in front of the rear wheels. Position the jack as close to the center of the tube as possible. The exhaust pipe or muffler might prevent you from getting the jack exactly in the center.

All 4WD models: Center the jack on the bottom of the **rear differential** (that aluminum box directly between the two rear wheels).

Step 4. Raise the Car.

If you're removing a wheel, brake drum, or disc, remember to slightly loosen the nuts before raising the car. Otherwise, a turn on the lug nut or axle nut will simply make the wheel turn around.

Place a small block of wood on the round, business end (lifting plate) of the jack, then pump it up so the block is directly under the proper jack point identified in Step 3. Slowly jack the car up until it's a little higher than it needs to be. To jack the car up higher, use a 4x4 block of wood on the lifting plate.

Step 5. Position Jackstands.

Do this every time the car is going to be up for more than just a quick wheel change. Never stick any part of your body under there without the jackstands in place.

Look for the *reinforced areas* along the bottom of the car body just behind the front wheel well and just in front of the rear wheel well (the places where you raise the car with the Subaru jack). Place a jackstand under the reinforced area on each side of the car—the forward points if you're lifting the front, the aft ones if you're jacking the back. If your jackstands are adjustable, adjust them so the top is as close to the car as possible. Be sure the *adjusting pin* or *lever* on the jackstand is locked securely in place. Now slowly lower the jack so the jackstands support the weight of the car. If the floor jack won't be in your

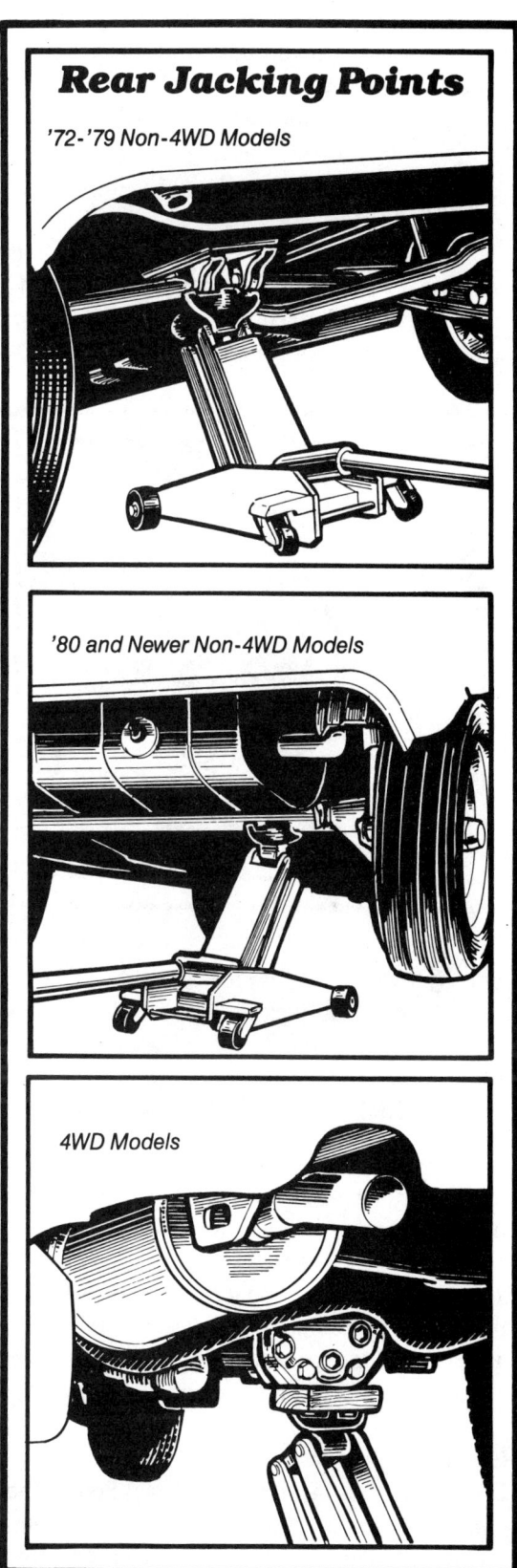

Rear Jacking Points

'72-'79 Non-4WD Models

'80 and Newer Non-4WD Models

4WD Models

way, leave it in position for added safety. (If the jack handle is removable, remove it. If it isn't removable, be aware the handle's there, and try not to trip over it.) Check the bottoms of the jackstands to be sure they're squarely on the floor, not tilted.

Now you can remove or work on the wheels, brakes, suspension parts, or whatever, without worrying about the car falling on you.

Step 6. Lower the Car.

When you've finished the repair work, fit the tires onto the lug studs, then install and snug down the lug nuts with a wrench. The final tightening has to be done after the car is lowered.

Be sure the wheel chocks are still in place, then use the floor jack to raise the car high enough so the jackstands can be removed. Now lower the jack until the car is back on all fours.

Step 7. Torque Lug Nuts.

If you removed any wheels, the lug nuts should be evenly torqued to 58-72 ft. lbs. with a torque wrench. The reason for using a torque wrench is to be sure each lug nut is tight enough so it can't loosen and fall off but not so tight it strips the threads on the bolt or will be a hassle to remove the next time. Unevenly tightened lug nuts can warp the discs (on cars with disc brakes) or drums (on cars with drum brakes), reducing the braking efficiency and causing premature wear on the brake parts.

When tightening the lug nuts, first tighten them in a crisscross pattern—tighten one, then the one directly across from it, then the other two. Then do a final check going around in a circle to be sure none were missed. If you don't have a torque wrench, tighten them as evenly as possible with the lug wrench. It would be wise for you to then take the car to a garage and have the lug nuts torqued.

Stash the jack, jackstands, and wheel chocks and you're finished.

PROCEDURE 2: CHANGING A TIRE

Condition: You're rotating the tires; OR you have a flat tire or a busted wheel; OR you don't have a floor jack and it's necessary to raise the car for repair.

Tools and Materials: Subaru jack, chocks for the wheels, lug wrench, jackstand(s) if you're doing repair work, an inflated tire mounted on a wheel that fits your car. The spare tire is stashed either in the engine compartment, in the trunk under a mat and piece of heavy cardboard, or under the rear of the car (on early station wagons). On some models you might need a 14mm wrench to remove the hub cap(s).

Remark: When rotating radial tires, all you do is put the front tires on the rear and the rear tires on the front. (Don't crisscross the tires on the car.) Follow the directions in this procedure and substitute the spare for each front tire while you move it to the rear, then mount the rear tire on the front. I keep the spare tire only as a spare, so I only have to buy four tires instead of five when the old ones wear out.

If you have a skinny "T-type" spare tire (also known as a space-saver spare), it should only be used to drive short distances at slow speed (less than 50 mph).

Step 1. Safety First.

If a tire goes flat while you're driving, don't slam on the brakes. Just carefully pull over to the side of the road and switch on the **emergency flashers** (the switch is on the right side of the steering column). *Don't* change a tire in the middle of the road, no matter how deserted it may seem. As soon as you get the car jacked up, sure enough someone will come blasting by in a semi-truck.

Ask your passengers to get out of the car and keep well away from the road. Safety! The shoulder on a busy highway is one of the most dangerous places on earth. Have someone hold onto small children, and keep pets in the car so they can't run around and cause havoc.

Step 2. Chock....

Put the car in 1st or reverse gear (manual) or PARK (automatics) and set the handbrake. Get your lug wrench. It's in the Subaru tool kit which is usually in the trunk, under a seat, or in the cubby hole on the left rear corner of '80 and newer station wagons. Maybe it's in the glove box. Or did you or a previous owner take it out of the car thinking you'd never need it?

Anyway, find some big rocks, bricks, or chunks of wood to *chock* the tire on the *opposite* corner from the one you're going to be changing. If you're changing a front tire, chock the rear wheel on the opposite side of the car. If you're changing a rear tire, chock the front tire on the opposite side. Force the chocks into the gap where the tire meets the road.

If there's a bolt visible at the center of the hub cap (even the small hub cap in the center of some "spoker" wheels), remove it with a 14mm (9/16″) wrench or crescent wrench. A 14mm wrench should be in the Subaru tool kit.

If the spare tire is mounted in the engine compartment, unscrew the large **wingnut-type bolt** (*counterclockwise* as viewed from the top). Remove the bolt and flat plate. If the jack isn't mounted on top of the spare tire, you can now remove the spare tire.

If the jack is mounted on top of the spare tire, the jack handle is mounted below the spare. To remove the jack, find the end that has a flat tab with a hole in it. Turn the tab *counterclockwise* (as viewed from the tab end of the jack) until the jack is loose in its holder. Remove the jack, then the spare tire, then the jack handle from its clips.

OHV models: The jack is stashed near the front left corner of the engine compartment. The jack handle is that long crooked metal rod with a hook on one end, mounted in clips near the jack. To remove the jack, twist the end that has a flat tab with a hole in it *counterclockwise* (as viewed from the tab end of the jack). That will loosen the jack from its holder so you can remove it. If it won't budge, use a screwdriver, pliers, or the jack handle (if it isn't secured by the jack) to turn the tab. Remove the jack handle from the clips on the side of the engine compartment.

OHC models: The jack is stashed either in the engine compartment or in a little cubby hole in the left rear corner of the vehicle. Your owner's manual will tell you where to find the elusive critter.

EVERYONE: Put the lug wrench squarely on one of the wheel lug nuts and loosen it by turning it *counterclockwise* (as viewed from the end of the nut). It won't move? The lug nuts were probably put on by a sadistic gorilla with an air impact wrench. You'll have to really throw your weight into it. Try this: put the lug wrench on the nut so the handle is on the left side and is as horizontal as possible. Be sure the wrench is fully and firmly engaged on the lug nut because if it slips you could end up with an ugly black and blue bruise on your shin. Put one foot on the handle, and press down with all your weight. Put your hands on the car for balance. Now bounce (carefully) on the handle, lightly at first.

Get all four nuts loose—just a half turn or so—we'll take them off later.

28 Chapter 3 Procedure 2, Step 3

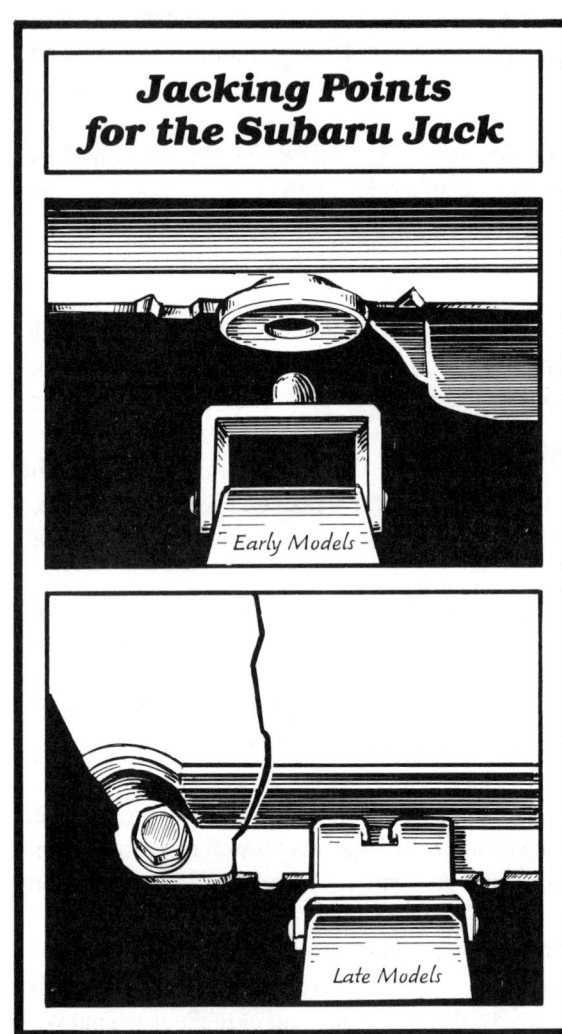

Jacking Points for the Subaru Jack
- Early Models -
Late Models

Step 3. Jack....

The Subaru jack is designed to fit into special reinforced areas of the car body. These are a couple of inches to the rear of each front wheel well and a couple of inches in front of the rear wheel wells. The top of your jack will have either a *round pin* sticking out of the top or a groove across the top. The bottom of the jack is flat. If your jack has a pin, find a hole in the reinforced area, then turn the tab on the end of the jack *clockwise* to raise it so the pin fits into the hole. No pin? Then the long slot in the top of the jack should be positioned between two small bumps hanging down from the flange along the bottom edge of body. Turn the tab on the jack *clockwise* until the groove of the jack fits itself onto the flange between the two tabs (see illustration).

Be sure the jack is sitting squarely on the ground, then hook the end of the jack handle into the hole on the tab. Hold the long part of the handle with one hand while cranking clockwise the short end of the handle with the other hand.

If the ground is soft or muddy, you'll have to round up a flat piece of wood to put under the jack to keep it from sinking. It's also probably getting dark and starting to rain. Anyway, keep turning the handle to jack the car up until the bottom of the flat tire clears the ground by at least an inch or so.

Step 4...and Block.

Block the car to prevent disaster in case the jack slips or fails. It happens more often than you might think, so please do this whenever you're doing more than just changing a tire. If you don't have a jackstand, large wood block, or large rock, put the *spare wheel* under the car right next to the jack. If the jack lets loose, the block (or wheel) will prevent the car from falling all the way to the ground—or onto your hand or foot. If the jack falls while the tire's off and you don't have a block under the car, you'll have a hell of a time getting it back up: there's no room to put the jack underneath again.

When it's safely jacked and blocked, rock the car gently to see if it is reasonably stable and safe. Too wobbly? Check the block, jack, and chock Steps again. And make sure the handbrake is on and the car is in gear or in PARK.

Step 5. Exchange Wheels.

Now remove all four lug nuts. Put them in the hub cap, your pocket, or someplace where they won't get lost. Gently remove the tire, using both hands and balancing your weight. Now roll your spare tire over to where you're working. If you used it for a safety block, drag it out from under the car and put the tire you removed in its place. Rotate the wheel until the holes in the wheel line up with the threaded **lug studs**. Lift the spare into position on the **wheel hub** and screw on a lug nut by hand. Now screw on the other three. Spin them down with the lug wrench until they are just firm. If you try to tighten them completely before the car has been lowered to the ground, the wheel itself will spin, or you might force the car off the jack and onto your foot. Remove the block or flat tire from under the car and lower the jack by turning its handle *counterclockwise*.

If you are rotating the tires, install the tire you just removed onto the other end of the car, then install that tire where you just installed the spare.

Once the tire(s) are mounted, use the lug wrench (or your torque wrench if it's with you) to tighten all four lug nuts. Tighten one, then the one directly across from it, then the other two. Now go around again to be sure you got them all. If you aren't very strong or have a bad back, try using a foot and part of the weight of your body on the lug wrench handle. Careful here: don't put all your weight on the lug wrench. One bounce on each lug nut should do it. Put the hubcap on (and tighten the 14mm bolt if yours has one). Torque the lug nuts when you get home, or have a garage torque them for you. The correct torque is 58-72 ft. lbs.

If you had a flat, head for the nearest service station or tire store because paranoia will lurk in your mind in the shape of a flat tire. So get it fixed right away.

If the jack is stashed in the engine compartment, set it in its holder inside the left front fender, then turn the cranking tab clockwise until the top of the jack is snug against the bracket on the body.

If your car has a T-type spare tire (the skinny low-rider kind), head straight for a garage or tire store to have the flat tire repaired or replaced. T-type tires are for *temporary* use only. On the way, don't drive over 50 miles per hour, avoid bumps and potholes like the plague, don't put the car in 4WD, don't pick your nose, and keep your elbows off the table.

PROCEDURE 3: TOWING

Condition: Your Starship is broken down at the side of the road; OR you're being a good Samaritan and helping a fellow motorist.
Tools and Materials: Friend, tow car, and *good* quality tow rope, chain, or cable (See Chapter 5: *Tools*).

Remarks: You're broken down on the side of the highway without the necessary tools or parts to get you mobile again. It's 110° in the shade, you're tired and hungry, the first mate is complaining, the kids are all crying, and all you can think about is getting the car towed to a safe harbor.

When help arrives, attach the towing chain or rope to one of the towing hooks below the bumper (some models have only one towing hook on the front). It's very important that you don't tie the rope or chain around either the front or rear bumper. A jerky tow driver may drag your bumper off to another galaxy and leave you and the rest of the Soob on the highway. Don't wrap it around any of the suspension parts under the car, either—could be costly and dangerous.

Before towing, be sure the parking brake is released and the transmission is in NEUTRAL. Turn the ignition key out of the lock position so the steering wheel can turn. If your Soob has an automatic transmission, keep the towing speed under 20 miles per hour and don't tow it more than six miles. Here's why: the automatic transmission has an oil pump that

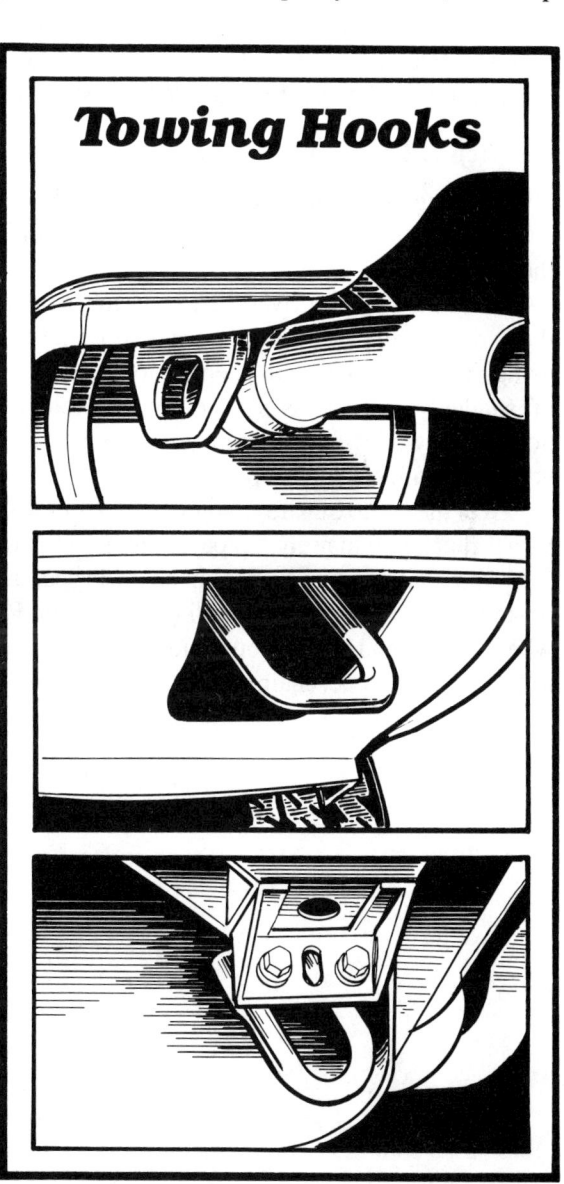

pumps only when the engine is working. So, if the engine isn't turning over while the car is moving, the transmission isn't being lubricated. The six mile, 20 mph towing limit is *absolutely crucial*. The dollars you try to save by towing the car a few extra miles will soon be in the hands of the transmission shop owner. If it's more than six miles to the nearest garage, and Snotty isn't around to beam you up, a tow truck will be needed to lift the front wheels off the ground.

Towing a Soob with a manual transmission should be held to a 30 mph limit for safety reasons, but you can tow it almost any distance. You should stop at least every fifty miles, however, to give everything a chance to cool down.

Step 1. Prepare to Tow.

If you have some paper or cardboard and a magic marker handy, make a sign reading "Car in Tow" and stick it in the rear window. Turn the **emergency flashers** for both vehicles ON.

Attach the tow rope, chain, cable, or strap through the **towing hooks** on the bottom of the car, and attach the other end securely to the vehicle doing the towing. Whatever rope, cable, or chain you use, the length between the two vehicles should be no longer than 15 feet or shorter than 8 feet. If it's longer, other drivers, not realizing you're being towed, may try to cut in between the tower and towee, with quite spectacular and alarming results! If you have a rag handy, tie it in the middle of the tow rope as a marker. If the rope's too short, you won't have much margin for error if Friend slows or stops abruptly, and you may have trouble going around turns.

Step 2. Tow Away.

Once again, be sure the handbrake is OFF, the ignition key is ON, and the transmission is in NEUTRAL.

Since you have vacuum-assisted brakes, you'll have to press on the brake pedal harder than usual to slow the car.

Have the tow car driver wave his arm when approaching a stop sign, or whenever he needs to slow down, then you should do the braking for both vehicles. If possible, the person being towed should be the only one using the brakes. This will keep the tow line tight at all times. If the tow line goes slack and the tow car takes off suddenly, extra stress is placed on both vehicles, the tow line (it might even break), and you. If the tow line does break while you're moving, don't slam on the brakes (someone might be close behind). Just coast until you find a safe place to stop.

Tow the car to Subaru if you're still under warranty. If you attempt to repair a part or system still covered by warranty, you may end up paying to have them complete the job.

Above all, keep your eyes on the towing car and the traffic ahead. If you doze off and the tower has to slow or stop, your grille will end up eating his bumper. Remember: you're a team, and it's your job to get on the brakes when your Friend signals you to slow or stop. If you're on a downhill grade, keep your foot lightly on the brake to keep the tow rope/chain/cable taut. Slack (in the chain or in your brain) is your enemy.

CHAPTER 4
HOW A SUBARU WORKS

    This chapter won't make you an automotive engineer, but it will help you understand the mechanical mysteries going on in your car as you glide down the road. Although thorough understanding of how your internal combustion engine works is not mandatory to carry out most of the procedures in this book, a general idea of how the parts work and their relationship to each other will make the maintenance, diagnostic, and repair procedures much more meaningful.

    Relative to most cars made in the last ten years, Subarus are very simple and easy to work on. If you ever had a VW bug or bus that you maintained yourself, you'll feel right at home working on a Subaru. The basic simplicity and efficiency of the old VWs are also cardinal virtues of the Subaru. A few high-tech smog control systems have crept in, but the people at Subaru seem to have tried to keep things as simple as possible.

    In this chapter, technical names for the different parts are followed by slang words or more common names for the part. After reading this chapter you'll be able to **talk** (*rap, chew the fat*) with any **mechanic** (*gear head, grease monkey*) in your favorite **cocktail lounge** (*honky-tonk, dive, watering hole*) about the **transmission** (*tranny, gearbox*) that you just **bought** (*scored*) for your **Subaru** (*Soob, Sooby Doo*) from the local **auto dismantler** (*junkyard*).

THE LAYOUT

    All Subarus (since 1970) are equipped with front wheel or four wheel drive, front mounted, horizontally opposed, four cylinder, four-stroke, internal combustion, water-cooled, gasoline engines. Whew! No diesels—yet.

Chapter 4

A few other cars of note which have horizontally opposed (flat) engines are Volkswagens until the advent of the Rabbit series; 356, 911, and 912 Porsches; and last but not least, old Chevy Corvairs. The major difference, and improvement in my opinion, between Subarus and these other famous cars is that the engine is water cooled and is in the front with front wheel drive.

Built into the body of your Subaru is the **frame** (*chassis*). The frame is like the skeleton of the car; it provides the strength and rigidity necessary to hold the various systems that make the car go and whoa. The engine, transmission, differential, steering gear, brake, and suspension systems are all bolted to this skeleton. Here's the basic layout:

The **engine** sits in the front of the car with a combined **transmission** and **differential** (called a **transaxle**) bolted on as a single unit behind it. An **axle shaft** sticks out of each side of the differential to carry the power from the engine to the front wheels. Four wheel drive (4WD) models have a **driveshaft** (*pilot shaft*) that transfers power from the transmission to a **rear differential** located between the rear tires. Two more axles carry the power from the rear differential to the rear wheels when the four wheel drive is engaged.

Let's go through these systems one at a time and see how they work and how they relate. But first, a little history.

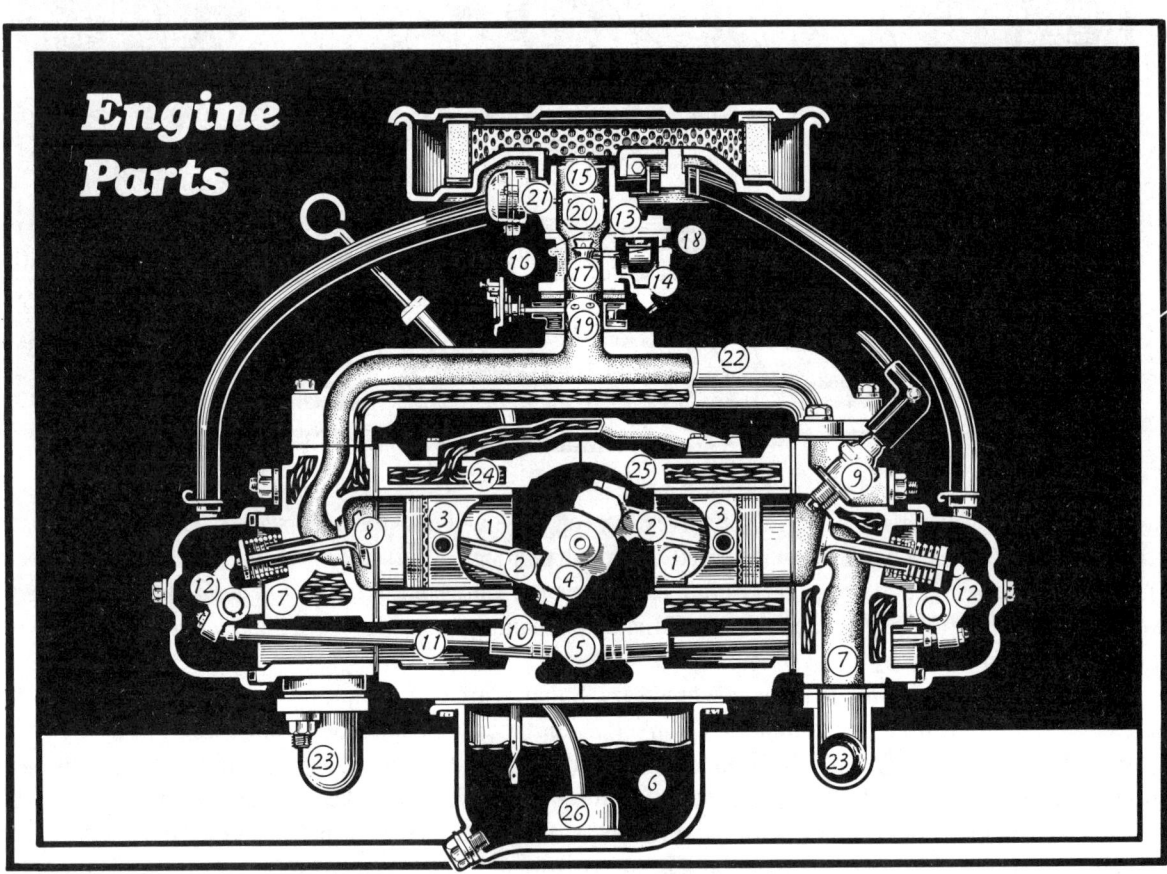

KEY
1. Cylinders
2. Connecting Rods
3. Pistons
4. Crankshaft
5. Camshaft
6. Oil Pan
7. Cylinder Heads
8. Valves
9. Spark Plugs
10. Cam Followers
11. Push Rods
12. Rocker Arms
13. Carburetor
14. Float Bowl
15. Barrels
16. Venturi
17. Fuel Nozzle
18. Fuel Nozzle Tube
19. Throttle Valve
20. Choke Plate
21. Automatic Choke
22. Intake Manifold
23. Exhaust Manifold
24. Water Jackets
25. Crankcase
26. Oil Pickup

A LITTLE HISTORY

Almost all of today's internal combustion engines are basically the same in design as they were over a hundred years ago. In 1862, a Frenchman, Jean Etienne Lenoir, built the first practical gasoline engine. Lenoir also became the first automotive commuter because he used his "mobile engine" to drive six miles to work and back. It only took about three hours each way. Sounds like rush hour in L.A.

Next, a German, Dr. Nikolaus Otto, studied Lenoir's design and improved on it by developing the "Otto Cycle," or **four-stroke system** that today's engines use. The four strokes (not a rock band) that made Dr. Otto almost as famous as the Beatles (a rock band), refer to four strokes of a **piston** within a **cylinder**, the basic components of the engine. A **stroke** occurs when the piston travels from one end of the cylinder to the other. Sounds simple, but it's the movement of the piston that is the heart of your internal combustion engine. We'll get back to the four strokes and how they work after a quick tour of the major mechanical parts of the engine and two systems (*fuel* and *electrical*) necessary to make the engine run.

ENGINE PARTS

The main engine parts are inside where you can't see them. Joe's pictures give you some x-ray vision to these basic components.

The engine description below is for a four cylinder engine. Subaru introduced a six cylinder engine in 1988, which is the same as the four cylinder OHC models described below, except that it has two extra cylinders.

Your Subaru engine has four **cylinders**, big holes bored into a strong, lightweight, two-piece aluminum alloy box called a **crankcase** (*case, block*). Steel **cylinder liners** (*sleeves*) are mounted in the crankcase cylinder bores. Each half (right and left) of the crankcase contains two of the cylinders; the two pairs lie flat and face away from each other. The center of the crankcase has front-to-rear holes bored through it—a large one for the **crankshaft** and, on OHV engines, a smaller one for the **camshaft**. Bolted to the bottom of the crankcase is an **oil pan** to collect, store, and help cool the engine oil that lubricates the moving parts inside the crankcase.

A flat-topped cylindrical-shaped **piston** fits snugly inside each cylinder. Three special **piston rings** made of spring steel fit into grooves on the pistons and press outward against the inside of the cylinder liner forming an airtight seal. (The top two rings prevent exploding gases in the cylinders from escaping past the piston, while the bottom ring prevents oil from the crankcase from entering the cylinder.)

The **crankshaft** (*crank*) is a heavy steel crooked-looking shaft. It has three **main bearing journals** and four **connecting rod journals** (*throws*), or attaching places, designed into it. Each of the pistons is connected to a journal on the crankshaft by a **connecting rod** (*rod*). A steel **piston pin** (*wrist pin*) attaches the piston to the small end of the connecting rod; the other (big) end of the rod fits around a connecting rod journal on the crankshaft. The big end is held in place on the crank with a **rod cap** and two **rod bolts**. The connecting rod journals are offset from the center line of the crankshaft, and change the back and forth movement of the pistons into the round and round motion of the crankshaft. Confused? It works just like pedaling a bicycle—your legs (connecting rods and pistons) push down on the pedals (crank throws), which rotate the sprocket (crankshaft).

The end of the cylinder that's opposite from the crankshaft is capped by a **cylinder head** (*head*). There are two heads, one for the pair of cylinders on the right, one for the pair on the left.

Each of the heads contains an **intake valve**, an **exhaust valve**, and a **spark plug** for each of the two cylinders it caps. The valves act like gates to control passage of fuel and air and exhaust into and out of the cylinder. Each cylinder has a pair of valves. A valve looks like a steel pencil stuck to the center of a disc about the size of a half dollar. The pencil part, called the **valve stem**, sticks through a brass **valve guide** in the cylinder head to the outside where it is held in place by **valve springs** and **valve keepers**. The coin-shaped end of the valve, called the **valve head**, fits tightly against a **valve seat** that surrounds a **port** (hole) on the inside of the cylinder head.

Chapter 4

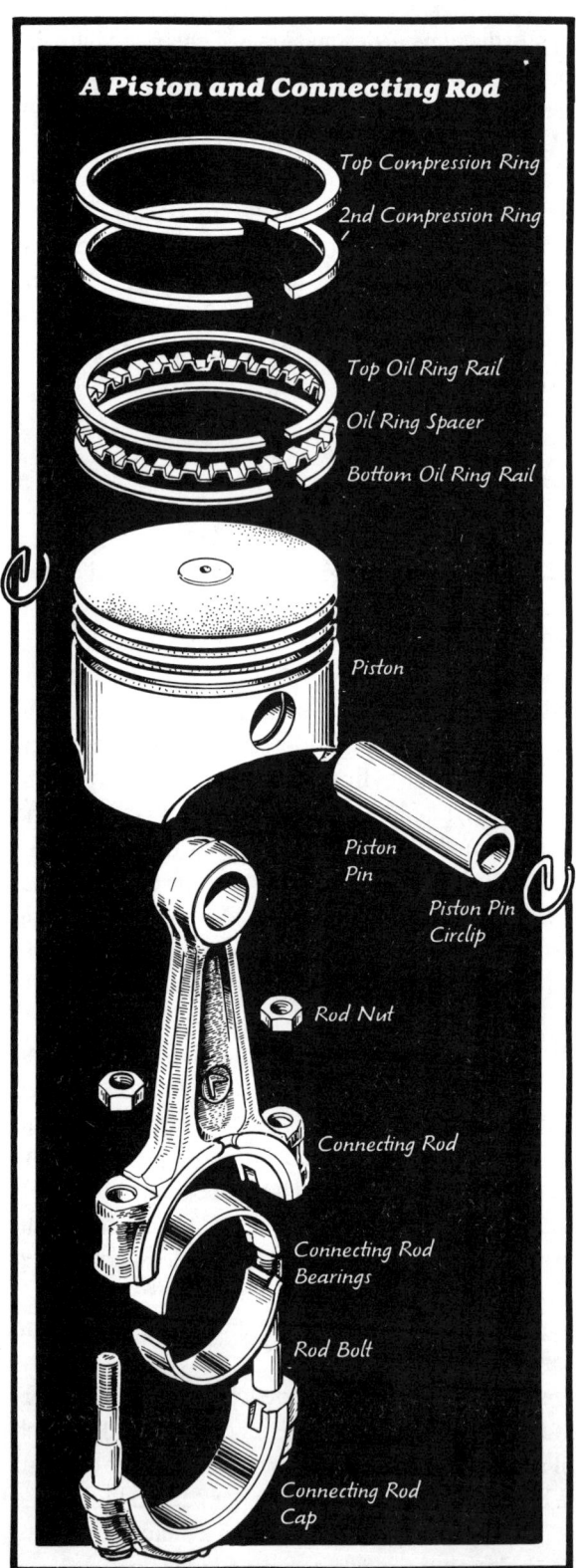

A Piston and Connecting Rod: Top Compression Ring, 2nd Compression Ring, Top Oil Ring Rail, Oil Ring Spacer, Bottom Oil Ring Rail, Piston, Piston Pin, Piston Pin Circlip, Rod Nut, Connecting Rod, Connecting Rod Bearings, Rod Bolt, Connecting Rod Cap

All of the valves are opened by the action of **camshaft(s)** (*cam(s)*). On OHV engines, the camshaft is mounted in the center of the crankcase, below the crankshaft. On OHC engines, there are two camshafts, one mounted on the outboard side of each cylinder head. A camshaft resembles a short piece of broom handle with the mumps. Here's how the camshafts work on the two types of Subaru engines:

OHV engines: A large gear on the rear end of the camshaft meshes with a gear on the crank. As the crankshaft turns the cam, the cam **lobes** (lopsided bumps on the cam) push against little tubular things about the size of your thumb called **cam followers** (*valve lifters, tappets*) that fit in small bores inside the crankcase. The valve lifters in turn push hollow, pencillike rods, appropriately called **push rods**, against one end of a seesaw-like mechanism called a **rocker arm** (*rocker*). The other end of the rocker arm presses against the end of a valve stem and causes a valve to open. When a lobe on the camshaft rotates past a cam follower, the corresponding push rod and rocker arm relaxes and a **valve spring** pulls the valve back to its closed position. The next time the lobe comes around the whole process happens again. Some late model OHV engines have hydraulic valve lifters that eliminate the need to periodically adjust the valve clearance.

OHC engines: Two long rubber camshaft drive belts connect the camshafts to a toothed pulley on the front end of the crankshaft. The toothed pulley turns the belts, and the belts turn the camshafts. As the camshafts turn, the **lobes** (bumps on the cam) press against short **rocker arms**, which press on the ends of the valve stems, causing the valves to open. As the cam lobe rotates past the rocker arm, the valve springs pull the valve closed. In addition to making the engine look a lot more awesome, the overhead camshaft arrangement eliminates the push rods, thus making the engine quieter and more efficient. Hydraulic valve lifters on OHC engines eliminate the need for periodic valve clearance adjustments.

EVERYONE: The camshaft must be correctly "timed" to the crankshaft so the valves open at the right time. In a four-stroke (*four-cycle*) engine, the crankshaft rotates *two times* per cycle and the camshaft only *once* per cycle. This is accomplished by connecting the crank to the cam with different size gears. The gear on the end of the crankshaft is smaller and has half the number of teeth of the larger camshaft gear, and thus the crank will make two revolutions for each revolution of the camshaft.

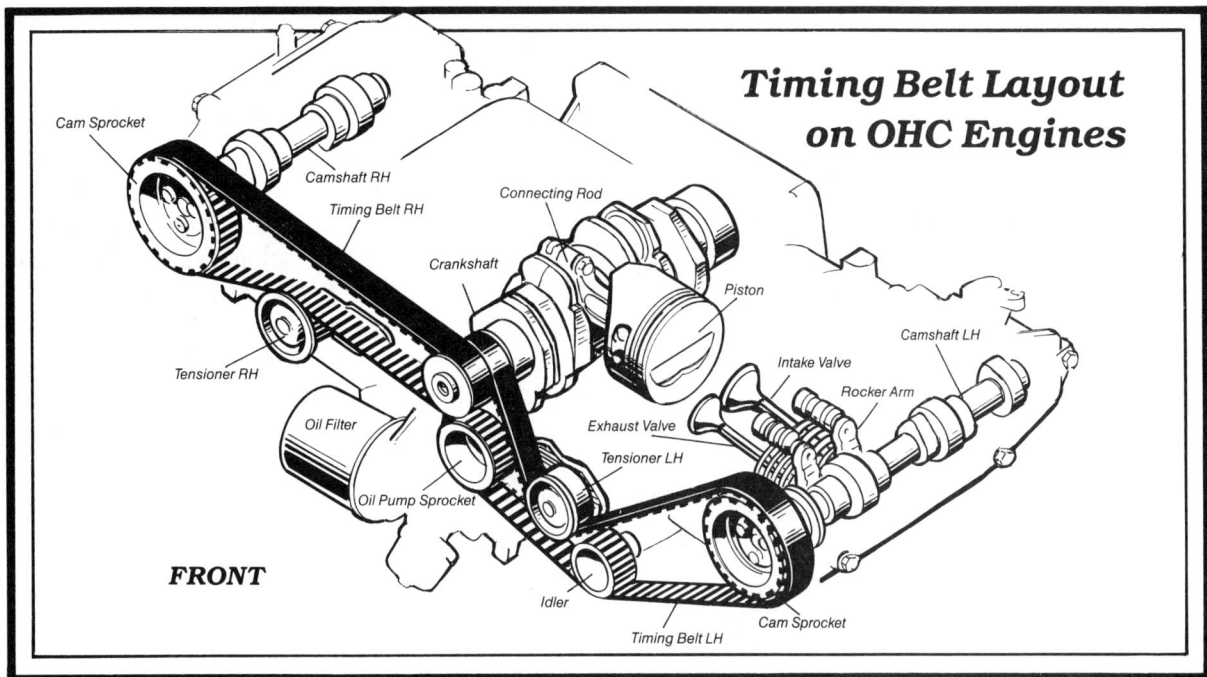

Thin metal shells called **bearings** are placed in vital locations where parts turn and rub against each other. These bearings minimize friction where there's a lot of it and also take the burden of wear in order to save the more expensive parts such as the crank and case. **Main bearings** fit at the places (journals) where the crankshaft and crankcase meet. **Rod bearings** fit where each of the connecting rods wraps around the crankshaft.

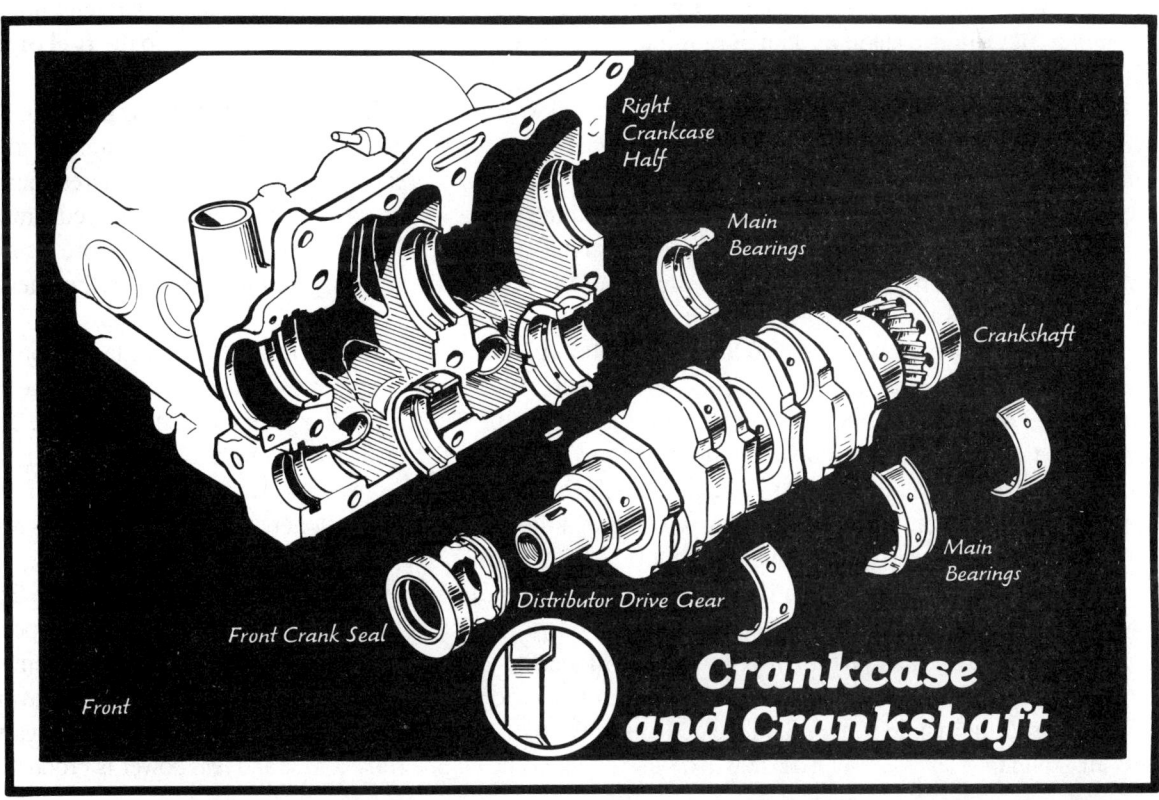

The crankshaft main bearings, connecting rod bearings, camshaft, cam followers, and rocker arms are all pressure lubricated with oil. Delivery and pressure of the oil is done by the **oil pump**.

The oil pump fits into the lower front of the crankcase, just below the **crank pulley**. On OHV models, the oil pump is driven by a short shaft that fits into a slot on the end of the camshaft. On OHC models, the oil pump is turned by one of the cam belts. When the oil pump is turned, oil is forced through the **oil filter** and then into small tunnels called **oil galleys** in the crankcase which deliver the oil to the vital locations. As the crank spins, it splashes oil on the cylinder walls, which lubricates the cylinders, pistons, and rings. One way or another, oil gets sprayed, squirted, splashed, or dripped on all those inside parts needing lubrication. Without this steady supply of the slippery stuff, the engine would quickly get super hot and come to a screeching halt.

Bolted to the front end of the crankshaft is the **crank pulley**, which drives a **drive belt** (*V-belt*, *fan belt*). The drive belt turns the **water pump**, which pumps coolant through the engine, the **alternator**, which makes electricity and charges the battery, and a **fan** on some 4WD and/or air-conditioned models. Other belts driven by the crank pulley turn the **air conditioner compressor** and/or **power steering pump**, if your Soob has these accessories.

OK, that covers the major moving parts of the engine. Now we need a *fuel system* to get an explosive mixture of fuel and air into the engine and an *ignition system* to supply a means of igniting the fuel mixture.

FUEL SYSTEM

Liquid gasoline will burn quickly when ignited, but in that state it won't make your engine run. The gasoline must be mixed with air in a certain ratio so it becomes an explosive *vapor*. The proper ratio for starting a cold engine, warmup, and acceleration is a "rich" mixture of about nine parts air to one part gasoline. For normal driving conditions, the ratio is "leaner"—about fifteen parts air to one part gasoline. If the mixture is too rich, the engine will "flood" and not start or run until some of the gasoline evaporates. If the mixture is too lean, it won't burn because there is not enough energy present in the form of vaporized gasoline. Here's how your Soob converts liquid gasoline into an explosive vapor: An electric **fuel pump** draws gasoline from the gas tank, forces it through a **fuel filter** to clean it, then pumps it to the **carburetor** (*carb*) on carb models or to the **fuel injector(s)** on fuel injected models.

Carburetor models: Here's how the gasoline is mixed with air inside the carburetor to become the explosive vapor needed by the cylinders: The first stop for the fuel is a reservoir called a **float bowl**. The fuel-air mixing takes place in two short vertical tubes called **barrels**. The front barrel is slightly smaller than the rear barrel and operates when the engine is idling or running at medium speed. When you press the accelerator pedal more than halfway to the floor, the larger rear barrel comes into action. With both barrels operating, more air and gas can be sucked into the engine to provide the power for accelerating quickly, climbing hills, pulling heavy loads, and racing Porsches.

The carburetor's barrels are shaped like a pair of hourglasses—slightly narrower in the middle than on the ends. The narrow area is called a **venturi**, and its shape creates a partial vacuum as air is drawn through the **air horn** on top of the carburetor and into the barrel. Located in the venturi is one end of a **fuel nozzle tube**. The other end of the fuel nozzle is attached to the float bowl. When the engine is running, vacuum created in the venturi sucks gasoline out of the float bowl and into the barrel(s) where it mixes with the downrushing air and becomes a volatile vapor. A **jet**, a brass plug with a tiny hole in it, is set in the float bowl. The jet regulates how much gas can be drawn out of the bowl and sent through the fuel nozzle into the barrel.

At the bottom of each barrel is a flat round **throttle valve** (*butterfly valve*) about the size of a quarter. The throttle valve is activated by your foot on the gas pedal. As you push down on the pedal, the throttle valve opens, allowing more air to be sucked into the engine. The increased airflow creates a greater vacuum in the venturi and more gas is sucked out of the float bowl. The more gas and air sucked in, the more volatile vapor is available so the faster the engine runs. When the pedal is released, a **throttle return spring** closes the throttle valve so less air—and thus less gas—can be drawn into the engine. The engine runs slower and less power is produced.

Another butterfly valve, called the **choke plate**, is in the round air horn opening at the top of the carb. Its function is to restrict only the airflow and not the gas flow. The choke plate enables the carb to make a gas-rich mixture when the engine is cold. All carb models have an electrically operated **automatic choke**.

Once the gas and air is mixed in the carburetor, it flows through the hollow **intake manifold** to the right and left cylinder heads, where it can be sucked into the cylinders when the intake valves are open. The volatile gas-air vapor is now ready to go to work, but it needs the ignition system to make it explode.

Fuel injection systems: Here's how the gas and air are mixed in a fuel injection system:

Single Port Fuel Injection (SPFI): This system utilizes a single **fuel injector** mounted inside a **throttle chamber**, which is bolted to the top center of the intake manifold, just like a carburetor. In fact, it looks a lot like a carburetor. The volume and density of air being drawn into the engine is measured by a **Hot-and-Cold wire system** located in the **airflow meter**, which is mounted on the engine side of the air cleaner housing. The cold wire measures the temperature of air flowing into the engine, then sends this information to the hot wire. The hot wire, also located in the airflow meter, measures the amount of air flowing through the meter by utilizing the heat transfer phenomenon between the incoming air and the hot wire (heating resistor). In other words, the more air flowing in, the more it cools the wire. The hot wire sends an electronic signal to the computer to let it know how cool it is and thus how much air is being drawn into the engine. The computer also receives electronic signals from other sensors which tell it such things as throttle position, coolant temperature, exhaust oxygen content, crankshaft angle, engine rpm, if the starter is in operation, if the air conditioner is on, and if the transmission is in gear. As the signals are received, the computer calculates the optimum amount of fuel needed by the engine, then sends a signal to the fuel injector, telling it how much gas to squirt into the engine. A nozzle on the end of the fuel injector sprays the gasoline in the form of a fine mist into the incoming air stream.

Multi Point Fuel Injection (MPFI): This system has four fuel injectors mounted in the cylinder heads near the intake valves (six injectors on six cylinder engines). A hot-wire system, similar to the hot-and-cold wire system used on SPFI models (described above), measures the volume of air passing through the airflow meter, then sends the information in the form of an electrical signal to the computer. The computer incorporates the airflow data with information from other sensors such as throttle position, coolant temperature, crankshaft position, engine rpm, and exhaust oxygen content, then sends signals to the fuel injectors to let them know how much gas to spray into each cylinder.

SPFI and MPFI: The computer for the fuel injection systems can "learn" the driving habits of the owner and react to them as well as automatically compensate for wear of various components within the system. Although these high-tech systems sound complicated, in terms of efficiency, reliability, and exhaust emission control, fuel injection is a great improvement over a carburetor.

Turbocharger: Turbochargers (turbos) are available on certain models that also have MPFI. Basically, what a turbo does is force the fuel and air mixture into the cylinders ("packs" it), rather than relying on atmospheric pressure and vacuum created by the pistons to fill the cylinders. Here's how the turbo works: On its way to the exhaust pipe, the exhaust gas passes through a **turbine housing** causing a windmill-like **turbine wheel** to spin. The turbine wheel is attached via a shaft to a **compressor impeller** located in a separate **compressor housing**. The compressor impeller sucks air through the air cleaner and forces it through the throttle body and into the cylinders. As engine speed increases, more exhaust gas is created, so the turbine automatically turns faster to meet the engine's demands. The turbine wheel/compressor impeller speed varies between approximately 20,000 and 130,000 revolutions per minute! Servicing the turbo unit should be left to the professionals because a misadjusted turbo can quickly ruin the engine.

The nifty thing about turbochargers is that what would otherwise be wasted energy (the exhaust gas) is used to make the engine more efficient.

38 Chapter 4

IGNITION SYSTEM

Each of the cylinders has a **spark plug**. In order for the fuel vapor in a cylinder to explode, a powerful electric spark must jump across the gap between two **electrodes** on the ends of the spark plug at just the right moment. The distributor is the gizmo responsible for getting a spark to each cylinder at the right time. And here's how it's done:

OHV engines: Inside the crankcase just behind the crank pulley, a funny sideways **worm gear** mounted on the crankshaft turns a gear (**distributor drive gear**) attached to the bottom end of the distributor driveshaft.

OHC engines: A **worm gear** mounted on the rear end of the left camshaft turns a gear on the bottom of the distributor driveshaft, which turns the shaft.

EVERYONE: A **rotor** mounted on the top end of the rotating distributor shaft points sequentially to four small **metal posts** inside the stationary **distributor cap**. Think of the cap and rotor as a clock: the rotor is like a hand and the cap is similar to a clock face with four numbers (the posts) on it. The metal posts are connected to the four large **spark plug wires** on the outside of the distributor cap, which carry electricity to the four spark plugs.

The basic function of the distributor is to act as a **switch** (like a light switch) to turn electricity in the ignition system on and off. Following is an explanation for why a switch is required:

Electricity is stored in your Soob's **battery**. When the ignition key is turned on, 12 volts of juice flow from the **positive (+) battery terminal** through a wire to the **ignition coil** (coil). A mere 12 volts isn't powerful enough to ignite the fuel/air mixture in the cylinders, so the coil boosts the original 12 volts up to about 30,000 volts. How? The coil has two electrical circuits: a **primary circuit** and a **secondary circuit**. Electricity is invisible and mysterious, so I'll try to make it as simple as I can. The 12 volts from the battery go through the primary

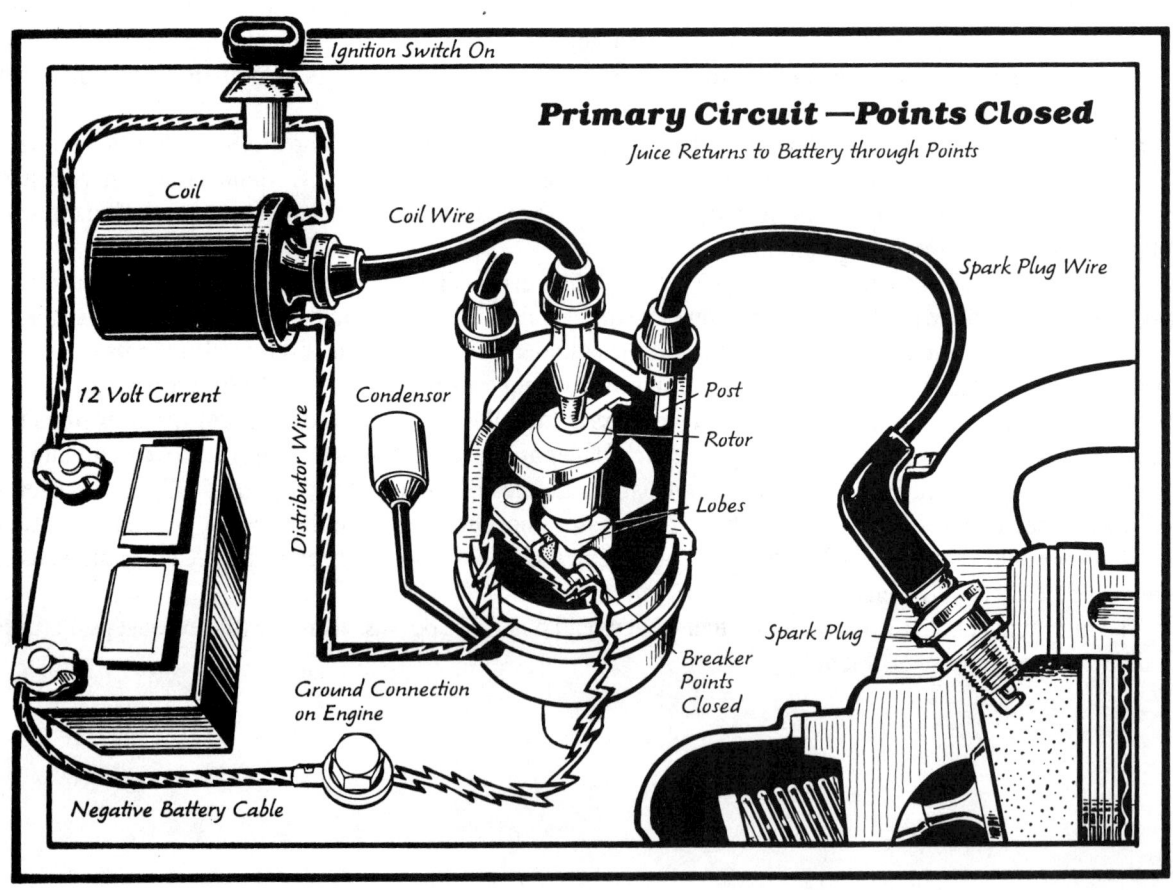

circuit **winding** (a wrapping of wires) inside the coil, then through a wire to the closed switch in the distributor, then to the distributor body, then back to the **negative (-) battery terminal** through the body of the car. As the juice passes through the primary winding of the coil, a concentrated electromagnetic field is created. High school science, remember?

The secondary circuit leaps into action when the distributor shaft is turned by the crankshaft. The switch in the distributor turns off the juice for just a moment, thus interrupting the flow of electricity through the primary circuit.

When the juice is off, the interruption of the primary circuit causes the magnetic field in the coil to "collapse," which generates a momentary but very powerful current in the **winding** of the secondary circuit, also inside the coil. It is in the secondary winding that the original 12 volts is boosted up to around 30,000 volts. At highway speed, this happens about 7,000 times a minute!

After the voltage has been boosted, it travels through the thick **high tension coil wire** that comes out of the end of the coil and goes to the top center of the distributor cap. From there the high-potency juice goes to an electrical contact on top of the rotor. As the rotor turns and points to one of the four metal posts inside the distributor cap, the juice jumps to the post. The 30,000 volt jolt then travels through the spark plug wire connecting that post to a spark plug. The current has to jump from the **insulated electrode** in the center of the spark plug to the **outer electrode** to complete its circuit. When it does, it creates a hot spark at just the right time to ignite the fuel/air mixture in the cylinder.

There have been three different types of distributor "switch" systems used on Subarus: breaker point; electronic breakerless; and light emitting diode (LED). Here's how the three systems work.

Breaker point ignition system: This system is on all pre-1977 California models and on all pre-1979 non-California models. On the distributor shaft, just below the rotor, there is a cam with four corners called **lobes**. The distributor lobes open and close **breaker points** (*points*, *points set*), which act as a switch to send electricity to the rotor each time it's pointed toward one of the metal posts.

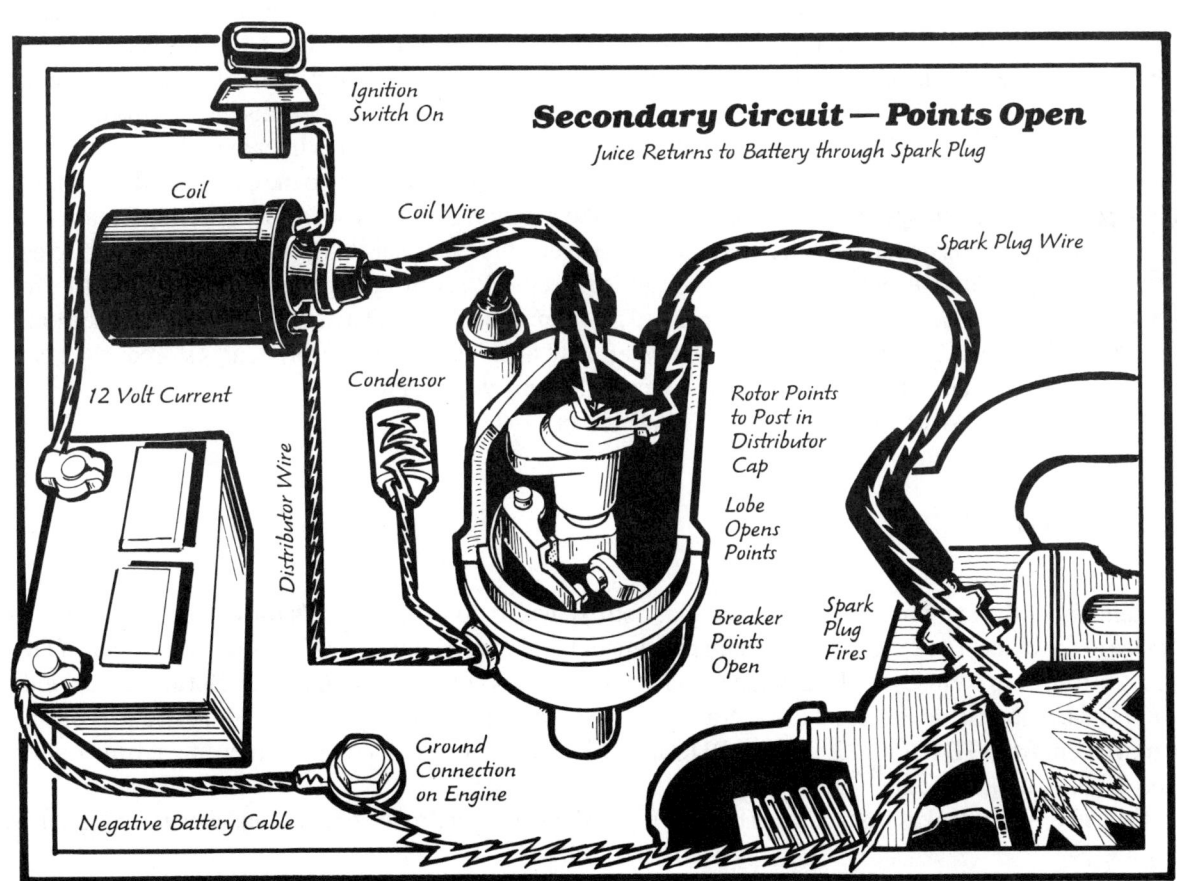

Electricity, like water, will follow the path of least resistance, so if one path is closed, it will follow another. A small cylinder, called the condenser, located on the outside of the distributor, is part of the path while the points are open (not touching). The condenser stops the 12 volt current and keeps it from jumping the point gap to get to the distributor body. This stopping of the current also prevents the points from burning and pitting too rapidly.

Breakerless (electronic) ignition system: Starting in 1977 on California cars and 1979 for all Subaru models, a new electronic ignition system was introduced which eliminated the use of breaker points. The advantage of the breakerless ignition system is the absence of the mechanical breaker points, which are prone to wear and thus require regular adjustment and replacement. Instead of four rounded lobes on the distributor shaft, there is a thick round chunk of metal with four raised tabs, called a **reluctor**. The reluctor on these distributors serves the same function as the breaker points, only it switches the electricity on and off electronically rather than mechanically.

The main *operational* difference between the breaker type and breakerless type is in the primary circuit. In the breakerless system, juice from the primary circuit of the coil travels through a wire to an **ignition control unit**, then back to the battery. The control unit is actually a very reliable high-tech switch. When one of the four tabs of the reluctor passes by a **pickup coil** mounted in the distributor, an electrical signal is sent to the ignition control unit which breaks (switches off) the primary circuit. This brief interruption activates the high voltage secondary circuit inside the coil, creating the 30,000 volt jolt—the same as opening the breaker points did in the breaker-type circuit. The difference in switching systems (points vs. control unit) may seem like a small one, but it makes a big difference in reliability.

Light emitting diode (LED) distributor: It was a great improvement in the late 1970s when electronic, breakerless distributors replaced the old, trouble-prone breaker point-type distributors. The new LED system even eliminates checking the air gap (easy as it is to do) on breakerless-type distributors. LED distributors are on all models with SPFI and 1987 and newer models with MPFI. Here's how the system works:

A flat, horizontal, rotating disc in the distributor has 360 slots around the outer edge, plus four slots near the center. Each of the 360 slots represents 1 degree of distributor rotation (since the distributor turns at half of the crankshaft speed, each slot represents 2 degrees of crankshaft rotation). The four slots near the center of the disc represent the location of Top Dead Center (TDC) of each of the four pistons. The LED is mounted directly above the rotating disc, and a photodiode light sensor is mounted below the disc. Light from the LED shines through the slots to the light sensor. As the disc rotates, the light beam is interrupted between the end of one slot and the start of the next slot. This interruption causes a signal to be sent to the computer. The computer combines this information with input from sensors on the position of the gas pedal and the temperature of the engine, then tells the secondary circuit in the coil when to send the electrical charge (via the distributor) to each of the spark plugs. Thus, the ignition timing is controlled electronically by the logic of the computer, rather than with mechanical and vacuum advance and/or retard mechanisms. The LED distributor can be checked out by connecting the test mode connectors for the computer. Any fault occurring in the system is stored in the computer's memory—even if the fault occurs only once. Pretty nifty stuff, eh?

We've covered a lot of territory, and here's the climax:

ALL TOGETHER NOW

Remember the four strokes? I explained that a stroke has to do with a piston's travel from one end of the cylinder to the other. The outer limit of piston movement within the cylinder is called **top dead center** (TDC). At TDC, the piston is closest to the cylinder head and farthest away from the crankshaft. **Bottom dead center** (BDC) is when the piston is closest to the crankshaft and farthest from the cylinder head. A stroke is one piston movement from TDC to BDC, or from BDC to TDC; in other words, a complete movement from one end of the cylinder to the other.

Each of the four strokes has a name and a function, which is related to the opening and closing of the valves. They are:

The Four Strokes

INTAKE STROKE:

The camshaft opens the intake valve and an explosive fuel/air mixture is drawn into the cylinder as the piston moves from TDC to BDC. The intake valve closes at BDC.

COMPRESSION STROKE:

The piston moves from BDC to TDC, compressing the mixture into the combustion chamber.

POWER STROKE:

The spark plug ignites the mixture which forces the piston from TDC to BDC.

EXHAUST STROKE:

The camshaft opens the exhaust valve and the burned mixture is forced out of the cylinder and into the exhaust system as the piston moves from BDC to TDC.

1. **Intake stroke:** The intake valve opens as the piston moves from TDC to BDC and the fuel-air vaporous mixture is sucked into the increasing space inside the cylinder (like sucking fluid into a syringe). When the piston reaches BDC, the intake valve closes.

2. **Compression stroke:** Both valves are closed as the piston moves from BDC to TDC, squeezing the fuel-air mixture in the cylinder into the small area between the top of the piston and the cylinder head. This space is called the **combustion chamber**.

3. **Combustion (power) stroke:** As the piston nears TDC, a spark from the ignition system jumps across the spark plug electrodes igniting the compressed fuel-air mixture in the combustion chamber. The resulting explosion forces the piston to BDC and causes the connecting rod to turn the crankshaft. It's the power stroke that does the work and turns the crankshaft as well as moving the pistons through the other three strokes. The power strokes of all four pistons help each other. I'll have more about that in a moment.

4. **Exhaust stroke:** The exhaust valve opens as the piston moves again from BDC to TDC. The piston forces the burned gas past the exhaust valve and into the **exhaust system**. At TDC the exhaust valve closes and the intake valve opens, starting the cycle again.

We have just gone through one complete *cycle* of one cylinder in your Soob's engine: The piston made four direction changes, giving us four strokes. The crankshaft was forced to make two complete revolutions, the camshaft one revolution, and each valve opened and closed one time during the cycle. At highway cruising speed, this cycle is repeated about 1,500 times every minute in each cylinder!

A multiple-cylinder engine runs smoother than a single-cylinder engine because the power strokes are distributed throughout a single rotation of the crankshaft. With a four cylinder engine, the locations of the connecting rod journals (connections) are staggered around the crankshaft so there are four power strokes for every two revolutions of the crankshaft—or, you guessed it, two power strokes for one crankshaft revolution.

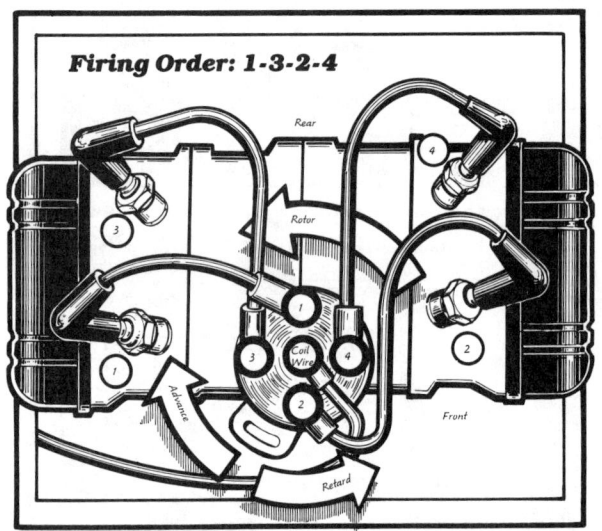

The combustion (power) strokes on a Subaru follow the same sequence over and over and over. The pistons are all linked to the crankshaft in a very specific pecking order. First, cylinder number one "fires"; then number three, number two, and finally number four. This is called the **firing order** and is shown as 1-3-2-4. The result is that as piston number one reaches BDC on its power stroke, number three fires, which helps force number one back to TDC. As number three reaches BDC on its power stroke, number two fires, forcing number three back up. Number four in turn helps number two get back to TDC. As long as the proper fuel/air mixture and a spark are supplied at the right time, the engine will continue to run.

All of these explosions are smoothed out and augmented by a heavy steel disc called the **flywheel**, which is bolted to the rear end of the crankshaft. The flywheel helps keep the engine rotating between power strokes by means of *inertia*. Inertia is the tendency for a rotating wheel to resist any change of speed. The flywheel absorbs some of the energy from each power stroke, then gives it back by keeping the crankshaft turning at an even speed through the other three strokes.

ON TO THE WHEELS

Now that the engine is running, let's see how the power gets to the wheels. We'll go first to the clutch and transmission (manual shift Soobs).

How a Subaru Works **43**

The engine is connected to the **transmission main shaft** via a **friction disc** in the **clutch assembly**, which is bolted to the rear of the flywheel. The clutch assembly allows you to disconnect the engine from the transmission when you want to change gears or stop the car without turning the engine off. The working of clutch is explained in Chapter 15.

Manual transmissions consist of different size gears that change the ratio between engine revolutions and wheel revolutions. More engine rpms are needed to take off from a standing start or to climb a steep grade than are necessary to cruise along a level highway or coast down a hill. The gears in the transmission allow you to select the proper ratio between engine speed and wheel speed.

Automatic transmissions work by hydraulics—the use of a fluid to move and turn parts. The fluid in this case is, of course, your automatic transmission fluid. Bolted to the flywheel (called a **torque plate** on automatics) is a large donut-shaped **torque converter**. Inside, a set of windmill-like vanes attached to the torque plate rotate and slosh fluid in a circular motion, which drives another windmill set of vanes attached to the transmission shaft. A complicated set of **planetary gears** behind the torque converter is driven by the transmission shaft. The gears are shifted automatically as you drive, through the magic of hydraulics. Automatic transmissions aren't covered in this book. They are complicated devils, and when something goes wrong they belong in the hands of a specialist.

From the transmission main shaft, the rotating power from the engine goes through the gears to another shaft called the **drive pinion shaft**, which connects the transmission to the **differential**. A clever device, the differential divides the power for equal delivery to the two front wheels. A **worm gear** on the end of the drive pinion shaft meshes with a large **ring gear** inside the differential. The ring gear in turn meshes with gears connected to the two **axleshafts**, which run out to the left and right front wheels which pull the car. The differential's magic is in how it delegates rotating speed to the two driving wheels:

As a car goes around a corner, the outside wheel has to travel farther than the inside wheel, right? If the axle was one piece with no differential, the inside wheel would drag slightly and wear out the tire very quickly. But the ring and pinion gears work in conjunction with small **spider gears** so the two drive wheels can rotate at different speeds while maintaining about equal driving power. Amazing, eh? I think the differential is one of the all-time niftiest mechanical inventions.

Located at the differential (inboard) ends of the axle shafts are **double offset joints** (DOJs). At the wheel end of the axles, **constant velocity joints** (CVJs) connect the axle shafts to short axles that pass through the **wheel bearing housings**. Splines on the ends of these axles mesh with splines in the **brake drums** or **rotors** (depending on the year and model) which are attached to the axles with large nuts. The DOJs and CVJs are similar to **universal joints** (*U-joints*)—they act as joints to allow the rotating axles to move up and down as the car goes over bumps or pot holes. The CVJs allow the front wheels to turn so you can steer the car.

The turning power from the crankshaft in your engine has now reached the driving wheels. You're on your way. Other vital parts and systems help out; for instance, to smooth out the bumps and holes in the road, **MacPherson struts** on the front and **torsion bars** or **coil springs** and **shock absorbers** on the rear fit between the body and the wheels.

EVERYTHING ELSE

Everything else, like brakes, steering, exhaust, smog control systems, lights, hiccups, as well as more thorough details on the systems just described, is covered in the appropriate chapters. If you want to know more about how the transmission works, see Chapter 15; if you'd like to understand your MacPherson struts, see Chapter 14, and so forth.

Chapter 4

CHAPTER 5

TOOLS, PARTS, AND BOOKS

Some professional mechanics have been known to spend more for tools each week than for food. Others can do quality work with a handful of tools they have collected in pawn shops, surplus stores, and at swap meets. My tools have somehow found their way from the far ends of the earth into my tool box. Each one has a specific purpose, so I'm not lugging around extra weight.

Tool selection is easiest if you're going to be working on the same car or the same make of car all the time. Subarus use metric sizes, fortunately, so you'll want to have metric tools. Keep a basic set in the car at all times so that if you're stuck on the road and a Mack truck driver stops to help, you'll have the right tools (and this book of course) to get you on the road again. Most of his truck tools won't fit.

There are two ways you can approach buying tools. If you have the money, just go out and buy what's on the list. If you can't afford to buy them all at once, read through the procedure you are getting ready to do and buy only the tools you need for that procedure. Gradually you will build up a full-fledged tool set. Dropping hints around Christmas time and birthdays sometimes works for me.

Ultimately, how much you need to invest in tools comes down to how independent of garages and dealerships you want to become. At the current hourly shop rates for garages, your tools will pay for themselves just by doing a couple of tune-ups or simple repairs yourself. Bashing around off-road in your four wheel drive Soob will be more fun knowing you have the tools, this book, and a few spare parts to get you back to civilization.

If you have a stash of tools for American cars, don't throw them away, because some of them can be used on your Soob. Here's a list of direct conversions:

14mm = $9/16''$ 19mm = $3/4''$ 22mm = $7/8''$ 17mm = $11/16''$ 21mm = $13/16''$

Tool prices vary radically from brand to brand. The most expensive and generally considered the best are **Snap-on** and **Mac Tools**. They look good, feel like silver jewelry in your hand, come with a lifetime guarantee, and cost about a third more than good medium-priced tools. If your last name is Rockefeller, go ahead and buy all Snap-on or Mac tools. They're sold mainly to shops and garages out of the large company vans you've probably seen around town. Even if you don't buy any tools, it's fun to look through the van. **Stahlwille** tools are my favorites, but they're not always easy to find. Sears' **Craftsman** tools are also good, guaranteed for life, and rather expensive. They also sell a cheaper line, just labeled "Sears." The most commonly used tools on Subarus are the 10mm, 12mm, and 14mm wrenches and sockets. If you want to splurge, get the expensive wrenches in those sizes.

You can buy good medium-priced tools at auto parts stores, swap meets, surplus stores, and reputable department stores such as Sears. Medium-priced tools work as well as the more expensive ones; they just don't feel as good and usually aren't guaranteed. I've gotten a lot of good, hard use out of **S-K Wayne** and **New Britain**, as well as **Stahlwille**, tools.

The really cheap brands (99 cents for a half dozen wrenches or screwdrivers) work once or twice, then break or bend—sometimes taking large hunks of flesh with them. Those bargain sets of 40 sockets and a ratchet wrench for $5-$10 you find at the discount stores also fall in this category. Watch out!

The large "Tool Sets" usually on sale at department stores *aren't* a good deal because you end up paying for (and hauling around) tools that you'll never use. But good plier and screwdriver sets can save you some money. It never hurts to have extra screwdrivers and pliers around.

When shopping for tools here are some things to consider in addition to price:

Wrenches: *Combination* wrenches have a "box end" on one end and an "open end" on the other. They're generally the most useful. Buy wrenches with 12-point box ends because they allow you to get the wrench on bolts and nuts in twice as many positions as 6-point box ends. Very handy in tight spots.

Most bolts and nuts on Subarus are 10mm, 12mm or 14mm. Having a selection of different lengths, shapes, and box end "offsets" of these sizes will make things easier. I like the way the box end of Stahlwille wrenches is attached: it's slightly offset and slightly angled so you won't scrape your knuckles as often. I get Stahlwille wrenches from my Mac Tool salesman.

Sockets: Buy six-point sockets—they're stronger than ones with 12 points. (You don't need the 12 points in sockets because the ratchet gives you an almost infinite option of angles for getting the socket onto the bolt or nut.)

Ratchets: For 3/8" drive sockets, ratchets with about 6" handles are the most versatile. As you become a tool aficionado you'll want one with a 3" handle for working in tight places and one with a 9" handle for added leverage. For ½" drive sockets, get a ratchet with a 12" handle.

Torque Wrench: Torque wrenches are a necessity for evenly tightening some nuts and bolts so they won't be too loose and unscrew themselves or so tight they break, strip the threads, or can't be removed the next time. The cheapest kind of torque wrench is a *beam type*. They're very accurate but when using them in certain positions it's hard to read the indicator needle. I prefer the *"clicker" type* that you set at the desired torque, then the wrench clicks when that torque is reached. To keep clicker types accurate, they must always be unwound to the lowest setting after use to relieve the tension on the spring inside. They should be checked and recalibrated occasionally (every six months to two years depending on use). How large a torque wrench do you need? Remove one of the front hub caps on your Soob. If there's a cotter pin through the axle nut, you'll need a torque wrench capable of tightening nuts to 154 ft. lbs. If there's no cotter pin through the nut and axle, but the edge of the axle nut is bent ("staked") into a groove on the axle, you'll need a least a 174 ft. lb. torque wrench.

Tools, Parts, and Books

PHASE 1 TOOL SET

The following list of tools and materials will get you through most of the procedures in this book. Again, you can buy 'em all at once, or just as you need them. A few special tools required for working on Subarus are listed at the end. Parts required are listed in the Tools and Materials list at the beginning of each procedure.

Safety Glasses
An absolute necessity if you value your eyesight. And who doesn't? Modern plastic ones are adequate and inexpensive.

Flashlight
One with a magnet attached to the side so you don't have to hold it. Or one small enough to hold in your mouth. (Sometimes you need three or four hands anyway, so why waste one holding a flashlight?) Check the batteries regularly.

Jack
The one that comes with the car is OK for changing flat tires but *don't* crawl under the car while it's being held up by that little thing. See Chapter 3, Safety.

Lug Wrench
One should have come with the car. If it's missing, find either an original type or an X type ("star-wrench") at a salvage yard or parts counter.

Combination Wrenches
6mm, 8mm, 10mm, 12mm, 14mm, 17mm, and 19mm. This is your basic wrench set. "Open end" at one end and 12-point "box end" at the other. It's nice to have a complete set of regular length wrenches plus longer 12mm, 14mm, 17mm and 19mm wrenches for added leverage on stubborn bolts and nuts. You can't have too many different lengths and shapes of 10mm, 12mm and 14mm wrenches.

3/8″ Drive Sockets
Same sizes as the combination wrenches. I urge you to get the 6-point type sockets.

3/8″ Drive Ratchet
Get a good one. I got my favorite ratchet in the 1960s when it cost only $12; the same ratchet now costs about $35 (which is probably too much). I'll tell you what it is, though—an **S-K Wayne #3870**. It's long and has the kind of swivel head I like!

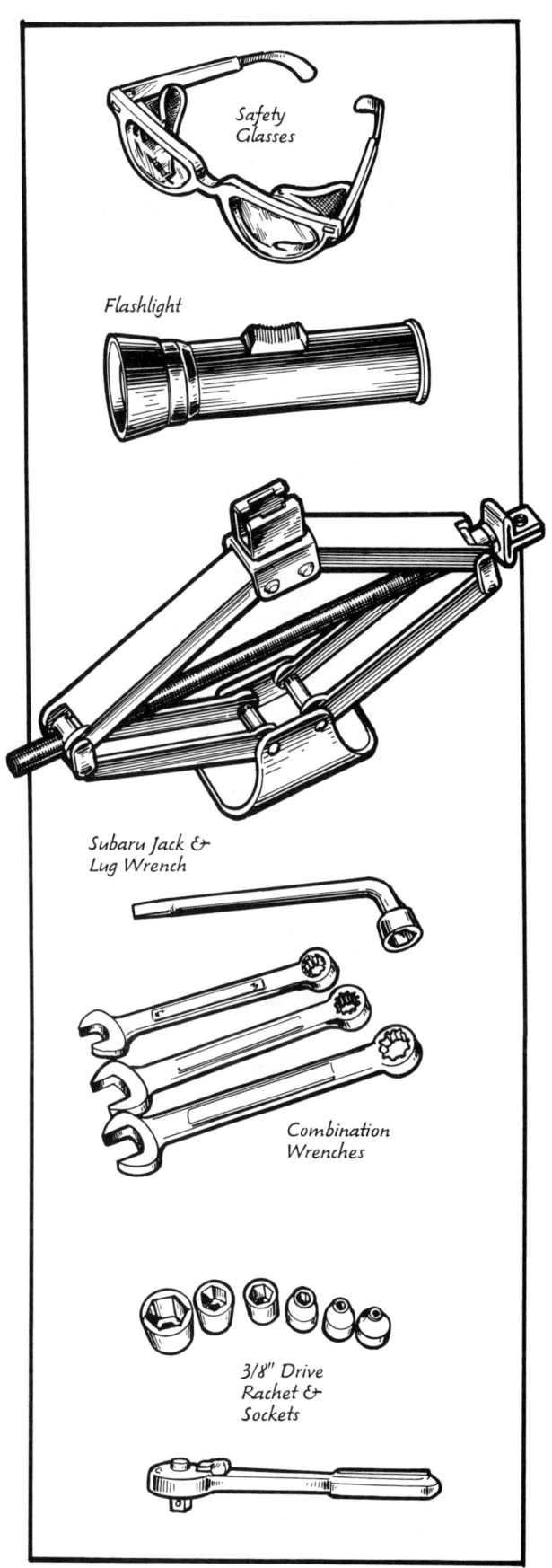

Safety Glasses

Flashlight

Subaru Jack & Lug Wrench

Combination Wrenches

3/8″ Drive Rachet & Sockets

48 Chapter 5

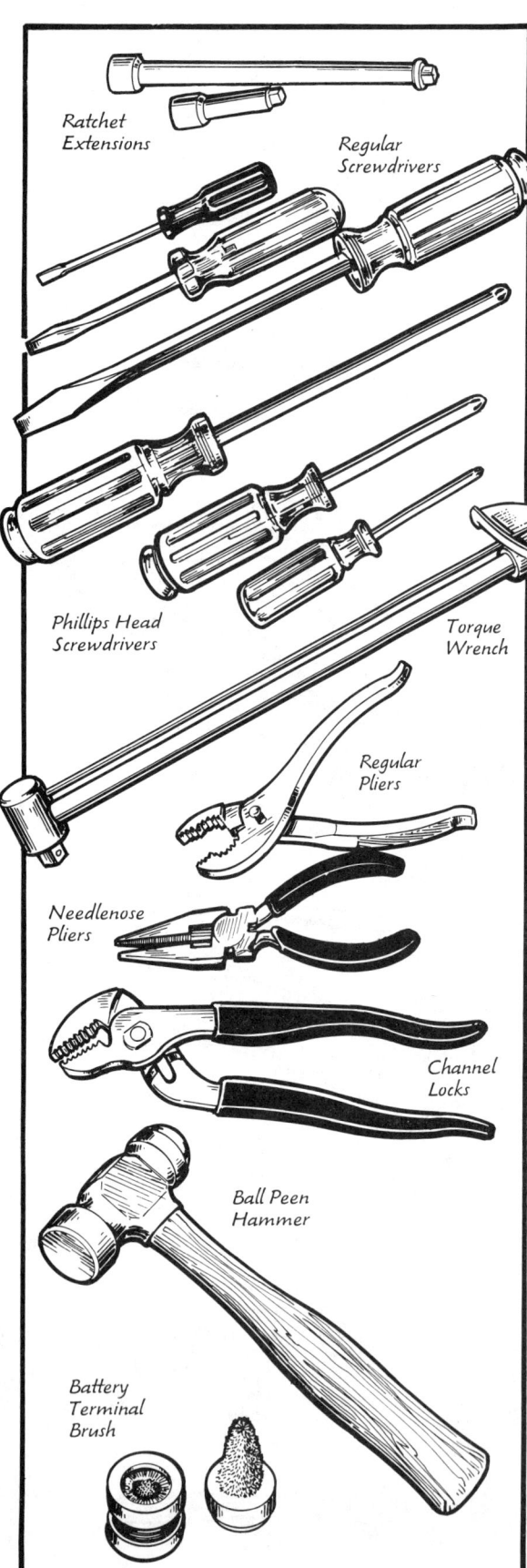

3/8″ Drive Ratchet Extensions
Several, ranging from 1″ to 12″. These make things easier to reach. They snap on between the ratchet and socket.

Screwdrivers
A variety of short, medium, and long ones with narrow and regular width blades. Get one giant one (16″-24″ long and strong).

Phillips Head Screwdrivers
Good quality small, medium, and large ones. The cheap ones wear out quickly and ruin the screws. These screwdrivers are for dealing with all those screws with cross-shaped slots in their heads.

Torque Wrench
See the *Torque Wrench* rap earlier in this chapter. It tells about the two kinds available.

Pliers
Regular and needlenose, and one set of large **Channel Locks**. Channel Locks are long-handled pliers with adjustable jaws.

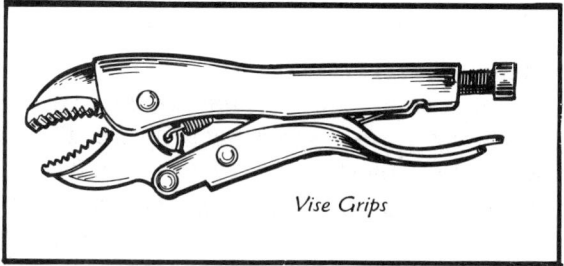

Vise Grips
One medium size (8″) with flat jaws. Vise Grip is a brand name of locking pliers. You'll learn to love this tool—it's like having an extra hand.

Ball Peen Hammer
A 12-16 oz. model. Carpenter's hammers are not safe for use on cars.

Battery Terminal Cleaner
The kind with internal and external wire brushes. These are handy, cheap, and readily available, but you can get by with a knife or the small wire brush mentioned later.

12 Volt Test Light
For finding shorts (electrical) and checking for "juice" in your wiring and electrical components.

Crescent Wrench
Handy when you can't find the wrench size you need. Get a 4″ and an 8″. Don't use them when the right-size combination wrench is available—they're not as safe and tend to round off the edges of nuts and bolts.

Pocket Knife
Swiss Army type with as many gizmo blades as you can afford. That corkscrew or bottle opener could save the day at a picnic.

Small Wire Brush
Get one about the size of a toothbrush. I've found good cheap ones in art supply stores.

GOOD Tire Gauge
Absolutely necessary for radial tires. The cheap pencil types don't stay accurate for very long.

Rags and Paper Towels
To clean your hands and tools, and to mop up spills. Worn out clothing, torn into 12″ squares, makes perfectly adequate rags.

½″ Drive Sockets
17mm, 19mm, 21mm, and 22mm. You'll need a 36mm socket to remove brake drums or discs. Again, go for quality 6-point sockets.

½″ Drive Ratchet or "Breaker Bar" and a 6″ Extension
For the ½″ drive sockets. Get a big one with about a 12″ handle. A breaker bar is a socket handle without a ratchet mechanism—it's wonderful on really stubborn bolts.

½″ to 3/8″ Adapter
So you can use the 3/8″ sockets on the ½″ ratchet, breaker bar, and torque wrench.

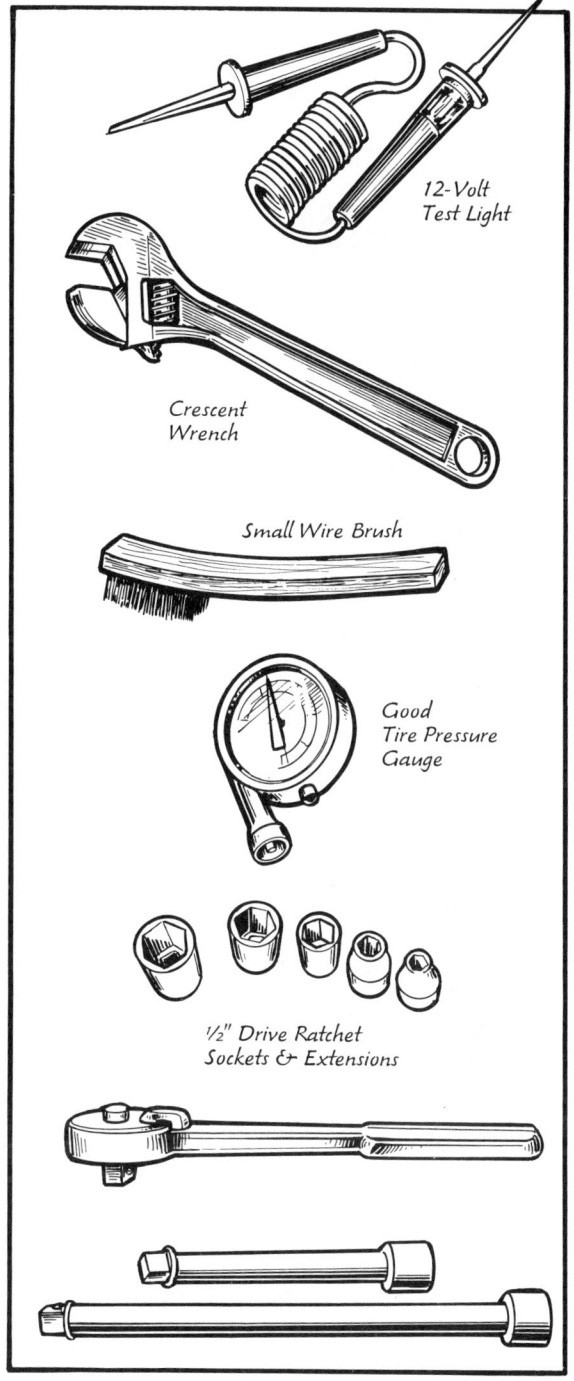

TUNE-UP TOOLS

These tools are used only when tuning the engine. Several more of them are illustrated in Chapter 7.

Spark Plug Socket
Right. It's for checking or changing the spark plugs. There should be a rubber boot inside to grab the spark plug.

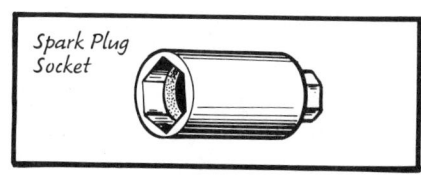

Feeler Gauges
The "Go-No Go" kind are the easiest to use. What they are and how to use them is explained in Chapter 7, Procedure 7, Step 4. If you have a breakerless distributor, also get brass feeler gauges.

Spark Plug Gapper
Bosch makes a really nice one. A cheap one will do, though.

Strobe Timing Light
For setting the ignition timing. The *inductive* kind are easiest to use. Avoid the cheapies, which are practically useless unless you live in a cave or mine shaft.

Jumper Wire
A jumper is a wire with an alligator clip on each end. You'll need one about 6" long.

Tach/Dwell Gauge
For setting engine idle speed and the points dwell on distributors with breaker points.

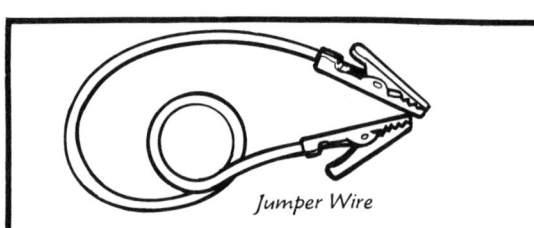
Jumper Wire

Compression Gauge
The kind that screws into the spark plug hole will eliminate the need for a helper. The cheaper kind that you just push into the hole is OK—if you have a Friend.

3/16" (5mm) Vacuum Hose
Get about 12"-18" of this rubber hosing. It's for checking vacuum-operated gizmos on the engine. Don't use the brake bleeding hose for this.

"Official" Valve Adjusting Tool
You can adjust the valves with a small (4") crescent wrench and 12mm wrench but it's a real pain. *OR* you can spring for a genuine Subaru valve adjusting tool that makes the job almost easy. As of this writing, Subaru sells them for about $25. Mac Tools sells them for about $45. The ones from Subaru fit a little loose on the adjusting bolt so you have to anticipate that the bolt will turn a little when you tighten down the 12mm nut. The Mac tool fits just right.

Ruler or Small Tape Measure
For measuring things like clutch and brake pedal "free play." Either inches or centimeters is OK.

File
A small, flat, hard steel one to file burrs off parts.

Magnet
The kind about the size of a pencil is adequate. Fancy ones have radio antennae type extension handles.

Mirror
Get a small one with a pivoting head, like the one your dentist uses.

PHASE II: OPTIONAL AND SPECIAL TOOLS

Consider getting these tools as need arises.

3/16" (5mm) Clear Plastic Tubing and Glass Jar
For bleeding the brake system (see Chap. 13). Suction tubing from hospitals works well.

Chisel
One with a sharp ½" to ¾" wide tip. Make sure it's one designed for use on steel. *Do not* use woodworking chisels: you'll ruin them, and probably your eyes too.

Small Chisel
A ¼" (or less) chisel to unstake the axle nuts on some models. If your axle nuts have cotter pins through them, you don't need this tool.

Cheater Pipe
A piece of pipe a couple of feet long that will fit over the handle of the ½" drive ratchet or breaker bar. It's for persuading extremely tight bolts or nuts.

Hacksaw and Blades (fine and coarse)
For when the going really gets tough.

Snap Ring Pliers (for circlips)
Wait to buy these until you definitely need them. If possible, get the kind that can convert to work on either internal or external snap rings. The kind with changeable tips of different sizes and shapes are the most versatile.

Volt/Ohm Meter
A *Volt/Ohm meter* (VOM) is very handy to have around. Radio Shack sells good cheap ones. Minimum requirements are listed in Chapter 10, Procedure 11. The procedure also tells you how to use one.

Piston Ring Compressor
For installing the pistons in the crankcase. Prices range from about $10 to $20.

6mm (3/16") Punch
For removing the DOJs.

Jumper Cables
For when the battery runs down because you left the headlights on.

Tow Rope
To tow a disabled vehicle.

Long Neck Funnel
To add oil to the transaxle or automatic transmission.

Syringe
To suck brake fluid out of the reservoirs when you change the brake fluid. Get the biggest one you can find.

Oil Suction Gun
You might need one to get oil into the rear differential on 4WD models.

Rubber Gloves
To keep your pinkies pink. Following are tools specifically designed for Subarus. You'll probably have to get them from the Subaru dealer or the Snap-on or Mac Tool truck.

Special Sockets for Retorquing the Cylinder Heads
You have to have these for retorquing the heads, for doing a valve job, or for an engine rebuild. One socket is a specially designed shallow socket on the end of a short extension. The length is critical due to limited space. The other socket is a shallow, thin-walled 17mm. You can make your own by grinding down the end of a thin-walled 17mm socket until there's room for the socket and torque wrench between the rocker arm bolts and car body.

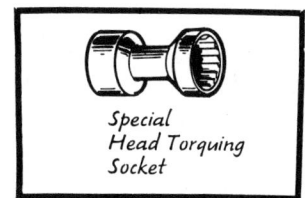

Special Head Torquing Socket

Disc Brake Piston Wrench
You might need this special tool to screw the pistons into the calipers. See Chapter 13.

Wrist Pin Puller
Sounds like something you'd find in a torture dungeon. They're expensive and you'll only use it maybe once every ten years for a ring and valve job or engine rebuild. Try to borrow or rent one, or hire a garage that specializes in Soobs to pull the wrist pins for you.

Special Tools for Adjusting or Replacing the Cam Belts on OHC Engines.
To adjust the camshaft belts, you'll need a Belt Tension Wrench (#499437000). To replace the camshaft belts you'll also need the following special tools; Tensioner Wrench (#499007000) and a Camshaft Sprocket Wrench (#499207000). If you have a manual transmission, you'll also need a Flywheel Stopper tool (#498277000), or if you have an automatic transmission, you'll need a Drive Plate Stopper tool (#498497000). These tools are shown in the procedure for adjusting and replacing the cam belts. And yes, you'll probably have to get these tools from the Subaru dealer.

PHASE III: DON'T LEAVE TOWN WITHOUT 'EM

Following is a list of tools and parts that should be considered part of the car. This survival kit will probably cover 90 percent of road emergencies (and several repair procedures). I roll them up in old towels and stash them under the front seats:

Jack and lug wrench (stashed in the engine compartment), small and medium *regular* and *phillips screwdrivers*, *pliers* (regular and needlenose), *feeler gauges, plug gapper, crescent wrench, 10mm, 12mm, and 14mm wrenches and sockets, ratchet, ratchet extension, spark plug socket, 12-volt test light, pocket knife, tire gauge, rags.*

Here's a list of spare parts that could save you hours of despair and a large towing fee. Most of them can be stashed on the spare tire: *ignition points and condenser* (if your car has them), *distributor cap* and *rotor*, a set of *spark plugs, spare fuses, drive belt(s)*, a quart of *oil*, one each extra *clutch and accelerator cables.*

GARAGE MATERIALS

The following materials are frequently needed for the maintenance and repair procedures. They're handy to have around to avoid trips to the parts store early Sunday morning.

Hand Cleaner
Get the kind with lanolin to keep your hands soft and lily white. *Ivory Liquid* dish detergent is a good substitute if you're caught dirty handed. Goop it on full strength, then wash it off. Incidentally, *Goop* is also a brand name of hand cleaner.

Rags and Paper Towels
Seems like you can never have too many rags around. Don't use fuzzy ones that might shed on things. Old towels cut up into small (12" square) pieces work well.

Catch Pan
To drain oil and antifreeze into. You can also use it for cleaning parts. Plastic ones are cheap these days. Get one that will hold at least five quarts.

Parts Cleaning Brush
Get a brush with long, stiff, fiber bristles. An old toothbrush is also very good for cleaning small parts.

Spray Cans of Cleaner
Berryman B-12 Carburetor Cleaner and *Solder Seal Brake Cleaner* are handy to have around. When sprayed on parts, they dissolve the crud so it runs off, then they evaporate without leaving a residue. Try not to breathe too much of the stuff and be sure to wear safety glasses to protect your eyes.

Tools, Parts, and Books 53

Penetrating Oil
Liquid Wrench, WD-40, and *Marvel Mystery Oil* all work well, but my favorite is *Sili Kroil* made by Kano Labs in Nashville, Tenn. It penetrates, then lubricates with silicone.

Wheel Bearing Grease
A small can of high-temperature wheel bearing grease is always handy to have around. You may even need it to grease the wheel bearings.

Cleaning Solvent
You can buy this by the gallon at some filling stations, parts stores, and machine shops. It's safer than using gasoline. *NEVER* use gasoline in a closed area or near heat or flame. In fact, it's best to use the same precaution with all cleaning solvents.

Drop Light
Get the kind that has a metal cage around the bulb (the plastic ones melt, then stink). Also good (but more expensive) are the fluorescent drop lights called "Sunlights."

Extension Cord
Get one with at least 14-gauge wire (12-gauge is even better). The length you need depends on how handily your wall outlets are located.

Silicone Gasket Sealer
A tube of the blue stuff works on nearly all gaskets except those exposed to gasoline.

Hydraulic Floor Jack and Jackstands
You can pick these up pretty cheap these days. They make working on your car a lot easier and safer. Jackstands are a *must* if you plan to crawl under your car.

Fire Extinguisher
The kind that puts out gasoline fires. Keep it handy and check it regularly. A small one, or two will do.

Conveniences and Odds 'n Ends
A role of soft tie wire (baling wire, machinist's wire). Pair of coveralls, stocking cap for long hair, low stool to sit on while you work, a large piece of cardboard or plastic to lie on, a few sheets of fine emery paper, plastic sandwich baggies, masking tape, rubber bands, indelible pen.

PARTS

When it comes to parts, Subarus seem to be the Rodney Dangerfields of the automotive world. They don't get no respect. It's getting a little better now, but it's still more difficult finding parts and accessories for your Soob than it is for the other major Japanese imports. Grumble, grumble.

Prices for Subaru parts vary so radically from store to store it's sometimes hard to believe. And the surprising thing is they're most likely the same brand! Store A might have good prices on some parts but not on others. The price markup in Store B might be exactly the opposite from Store A. And the same applies to the Subaru dealer parts department: some of their prices are the best you can find, while others are two or three times more than for the same part in the parts stores. A few phone calls or a little legwork can save you quite a bundle.

When trekking to the parts store, be armed with your Soob's *production date, vehicle identification number* (VIN), and *engine serial number.* These will maximize your chances of getting the right part for Sooby the first time. How to find these numbers is in Chapter 2.

If you get hung up for parts that aren't available in your area, call Mike at Mahneke Motors in Goleta, California at (805) 683-1885. They probably have the parts or can find and send them to you.

OTHER SOURCES OF INFORMATION

You should find a copy of the *Owner's Manual* stashed in the glove box. It has lots of little tidbits about your particular year and model. If yours has disappeared, get one from the Subaru dealer.

All *Subaru Workshop Manuals* from the Subaru dealer (except for '73, '74, and '79 models) cover engine removal, installation, and rebuilding. They also have complete wiring diagrams for each model of whatever year the manual was written for. And they all have more specifications about your Soob than you'd ever want to know. Like most automotive repair manuals, they assume you're an experienced mechanic and tell you *what* to do but don't give any clues as to *how* to do it. (Hopefully, this book fills the gap between what to do and how to do it.)

There are two Subaru workshop manuals for '72 models; one for the engine and one for the body (which includes brakes, suspension, steering, etc.).

The problem with the Subaru workshop manuals for '73-'77 and '79 models is that they only cover things that are different from the '72 models or the previous year models. To have a complete manual for your '77 Soob, you would have to buy each manual from '72-'77. That would be expensive.

The manual for '78 models is complete, but the '79 manual only covers changes from the '78 models.

The workshop manuals for '80-'84 models are pretty much complete for each year, except for '83 Turbo models. If you have an '83 Turbo, get an '84 manual because Turbos aren't covered in the '83 manual.

The official Subaru factory workshop manuals for 1985-1988 OHC models are divided into two volumes for 1985 models and four volumes for each year for 1986-1988 models. There are separate manuals for XT models. The volumes are divided into sections. Those you would probably find most helpful are Section 1, which covers tune-ups; Section 2, which covers most engine repairs; and Section 4, which covers suspension, steering, and brake systems. Unfortunately, these three sections are in three different manuals. 1985-1988 hatchbacks and 1985-1987 Brats must use the 1984 factory manuals. The manuals for 1985-1988 models are also available in Spanish.

In spite of all this, a Subaru workshop manual for your model is handy to have around. They have lots of pictures and cover things not included in this manual such as transmission and differential repair and replacing bumpers and door handles, etc.

For all of you Subaru fanatics, T-shirts, sweatshirts, and caps with the Subaru logo are available through the parts department at the Subaru dealer. The *Bentley Manuals* are pretty good. They have lots of photos but give rather abbreviated instructions. Unless you're quite experienced (mechanically speaking), you may find these other manuals don't give enough information.

SAFETY WITH TOOLS

Use your head! Not as a substitute for a 10-pound hammer but to select the correct tool for each job. Take the time to pick out the right wrench, extension, and so on, for the task. Wear your safety glasses when underneath the vehicle and wherever else called for to protect your eyes while working. Wear a painter's mask or respirator when dealing with dust, especially during brake and clutch jobs. Regardless of what else you might snort, keep the black brake and clutch powder out of your nose. That asbestos stuff is very nasty.

If you haven't worked with hand tools before, gradually get the feel of them. Make sure sockets and wrenches are fully on the nut or bolt head before you pull, and anticipate where your elbow or knuckles might land if a tool slips. Clean your tools after each procedure so you can look forward to fondling them the next time. Unless you've skipped ahead, you have already read my safety rap in Chapter 2. It's friendly—and essential. The John Muir legal staff wouldn't have you open your toolbox without it. I want you to make it through each one of the procedures without so much as a scratch. Thank you.

CHAPTER 6
HOW TO BUY A SUBARU

    The time to start shopping for any car is before you actually need one—preferably, even before you can actually afford one. The desire for a new (or newer) car combined with a wad of money in the pocket or a fat bank account creates a temporary "consumer insanity" in more people than would care to admit it. When bitten by the buy-a-car bug, rational, logical thinking people (like you and me) are often overpowered by irresistible impulses of emotion and impatience. I urge you to take your time and check out several Soobs before purchasing one. This will help ensure that you get a cherry or a peach rather than a lemon.

    Having to buy a car in a short period of time (like a day or two) adds pressure to a process that should be performed as leisurely as possible. You're more vulnerable to sales ploys such as, "Several people are interested in the car," and "This price is good today only; tomorrow the price goes up." *Don't* let the personality of the person selling the car influence your decision. High-pressure, sweet-talking salespeople who act like they'll commit suicide if you don't buy the car should be ignored. You're there to get acquainted with the car, not the person. It's your money, and the car you buy is probably going to be living with you for several years, so the better your choice, the more enjoyable your time together will be.

    If you're trading in a car, bear in mind that any spectacular offer you might get for it just represents a slice out of the dealer markup, which you may be able to get even without a trade-in. If you don't need to use it for a down payment, you'll probably be better off selling your old car yourself through the classifieds.

    While the car is under factory warranty, resist the urge to do the procedures in this book which are covered by that document until the warranty period is over. Repairs done by other than authorized service people may void the warranty.

    The place to start looking for a used car is in the classified ads of the local newspapers and newspapers of surrounding towns. If there's a college in the area, check the student newspaper. (Students tend to run out of money near the end of the term and often have to sell something fast.) Banks and credit unions sometimes have repossessed Subarus for sale. I bought a nice repossessed '81 Soob from a credit union for several hundred dollars less than I would have had to pay a private party or car dealer. Call your local financial institutions and see what they have.

Independent used car lots tend to charge more for cars than individuals selling their cars through the classifieds. Check them out though; they might have just what you're looking for.

New car dealers charge more for used cars than independent used car lots. The new car places usually do a little basic maintenance work and run a few tests on the used cars so they can offer some kind of warranty. If they don't think a car is worth guaranteeing, they either sell it cheaper "as is" or unload it cheaply to an independent used car dealer. Before buying a used car with a warranty, be sure you understand exactly what's covered. Sometimes the parts, sometimes the labor, and sometimes both are covered for a specific length of time. Some warranties cover everything on the car and some cover only the engine and maybe the transmission. Whatever they say is covered, be sure to get it in writing. Go through as many of the checks as possible in Procedure 3 in this chapter when considering any "as is" car.

You know your price range, right? Look at as many Soobs as you can within that range. Each will be slightly different in the way it looks, sounds, rides, handles, and performs. After driving a few, you'll develop a feel for Subarus. If you have time to make a few needed repairs to an otherwise sound car, you can probably save some money. If you don't have the time, then buying a car backed by a warranty might be best for you. If you're going to finance a used car, let the loan officer at your bank or credit union know about your plans ahead of time, so you won't have to go scurrying for a loan after you've agreed to buy the Subaru of your dreams.

Wear old clothes when checking used cars because you'll be crawling around on your hands and knees looking under the car. Have a rag handy for checking the oil and cleaning your hands. The owner may be more likely to lower the price for a person dressed in jeans, T-shirt, and old jogging shoes than for "Mr. Yuppie" in a three-piece suit.

Always have a notebook and pencil with you when checking a car. Write down the year, body style, color, license number, mileage on the speedometer, the owner's name and phone, the quoted price, accessories, and any obvious flaws (broken windshield, dented fender, oil leaks, etc). Before you leave, write down your impressions of the car (or give it a rating from 1 to 10). This will help you remember which car was which after you've looked at several. Don't shop for a car at night (for obvious reasons), while it's raining, or in the middle of a blizzard. Your attention will be divided between the car and how miserable you are. We'll get to the price later, but nine times out of ten, you'll end up paying less than the quoted price—if you follow a few simple rules of used car-buying etiquette.

I use four procedures when shopping for a car: (1) a looking, feeling, thinking procedure; (2) driving, listening, feeling, thinking procedure; (3) mechanical inspection procedure; (4) value assessment and bargaining procedure. The car must pass each procedure before qualifying for the next. If you're not sure how to check the vital fluid levels in Procedure 1, look at Chapter 7, Procedure 2. Here's how to perform the four procedures:

PROCEDURE 1: VISUAL PRE-PURCHASE CHECK

Condition: You're looking for a "pre-owned" Subaru to buy.

Tools and Materials: Time, a rag, daylight.

Remarks: Ignore pressure by the owner or salesperson.

Step 1. Visual Check of Everything.

Make a slow, thorough, visual inspection of the car, taking notes as you go. Are there dents or rust in the fenders or bumpers? Are there oil spots beneath the engine, transmission, and on 4WD models the rear differential? Is the underside of the car and the exhaust system dented and bashed, indicating hard off-road use? If so, the shock absorbers, engine and transmission mounts, and steering system will require a thorough check in Procedure 3 (if the car makes it that far). Check the windshield corners for signs of body metal fatigue. Bend over and sight along the fenders and door to look for waves in the metal that hint of accident repair. Check where rubber or chrome moldings fit to the body for paint marks—often a sign of repaired damage. You'll want to find out how extensive it was. See any little blisters in the paint? These often mean rust is lurking underneath. Now open the doors. Do they open and shut easily? A clunky, ill-fitting door is another sign of accident damage—or rough usage. Now look inside. Do the seats, dashboard, carpet, and headliner look like the owner took good care of the car? If the interior is funky and dirty, you can almost bet the mechanical parts have been neglected also.

Open the hood and prop it. Is the engine compartment covered with oil and mud? (If it's super clean, don't be too impressed. It may have been prettied up just for the sale.) Check the oil on the engine and differential dipsticks. If the oil is black and thick, you know the car has suffered from "deferred maintenance." Get some of the oil from the engine dipstick between your thumb and finger and squish it around. Gritty, dirty-feeling oil means the engine has more wear on it than the mileage might be telling you. If the engine oil looks like coffee with cream in it, or there are green droplets in it, there's water in the oil from a leaking head gasket (a major repair). Remove the oil filler cap and look at the inside of the cap and filler tube. White, frothy-looking stuff there is a sure sign of water in the oil. Rust inside the cap indicates a leaking head gasket or that the car was usually used for short trips to the market and the engine didn't have time to warm up properly.

If the car has an automatic transmission, pull out the transmission dipstick and give it a sniff. Does the oil smell burned? Automatic transmission oil should be light to medium red in color. Dark red, brown, or black oil means the oil and probably the transmission have been overheated and possibly damaged.

Is the brake fluid in the master cylinder reservoir(s) dark and dreary looking; or clean, clear, and fresh? If one of the reservoirs has less fluid than the other, there might be a leak in the brake system. We'll check it later.

If the engine is cool, remove the radiator cap and look down into the radiator for bright green antifreeze. Plain water or brownish-green coolant mean the cooling system hasn't been maintained properly. Stick your finger down into the radiator opening and feel around for cruddy deposits. Thick, oily slime means the cooling system has been neglected and/or a head gasket is leaking. If the slime is brownish, there may be rust in the radiator or water pump, a sign the system has been neglected.

Peek through the slots in the wheels at the brake disc (on some models the slots are too thin). The disc should look smooth and shiny with no large grooves worn in it. Grooves mean a brake job is needed.

Take a look at the tires, especially the front ones. Are they worn evenly across the tread, or is the tread thinner on the inside or outside edge? Uneven wear indicates an alignment is needed (no big deal, but mention it to the owner). Worn tires should be a consideration in what you'll offer for the car. If you need new tires right away, consider them in your personal accounting of what this baby's going to cost you.

If the car is the right model (station wagon, sedan, Brat, etc.) and you like what you've seen so far, take a closer look. How's the paint job? If the car is dirty, rub a small spot in the dirt with your finger to see if the paint is good enough to shine. Look inside the wheel wells, along the bottom edges of the doors, and around the windows for signs of rust. Any of those little bubbles in the paint that indicate rust is about to blossom forth? Rust is a four-letter word. If you find rust on the car, the price better be very attractive or you should quit looking at the car right now. Once this "cancer" sets in, it can be almost impossible to stop.

Step 2. Spiritual Check (don't skip it!)

Sit in the driver's seat for awhile, but don't start the engine. Put your hands on the wheel and close your eyes. Just sit and feel. Wiggle your butt around in the seat and soak in the car's vibes. Do you feel at home here? The owner or salesman will probably try to get you to start the engine—but don't, not yet. This will drive them crazy and that's OK.

Now stand back and look at the car again. Does it stand up with pride? Does it feel good to you from all angles? Walk around a bit and let the data you've obtained soak through to your subconscious. "Grok" the car. If you're lucky, you'll do all this without the owner or salesman fast-talking you from the sidelines; if not, tell him or her you want a little time alone with the car. Then take that important uninterrupted time. (By now the seller is really going bananas because you haven't yet started the engine.) If the car draws you back, you're ready for Procedure 2. Otherwise, find another Soob and start again.

PROCEDURE 2: TEST DRIVE

Condition: You've found a Subaru that merits further attention.

Tools and Materials: Time, Friend, a large parking lot, a deserted street, a bumpy road, a highway. Maybe a tire gauge.

Remarks: Unless you have a better than average memory, have Friend read the procedure to you while you test-drive the car. If you try to read and drive at the same time you might wreck the car and have to buy it regardless. Have Friend make notes as you go along about things that don't work or don't match my descriptions.

Step 1. Pre-Test Drive Inspection.

Ask if you can drive the car. Of course you can. You aren't going to buy a car without driving it.

Put the key in the ignition and turn it to the ON position but don't start the engine. Lightly rock the **steering wheel** back and forth. The wheel shouldn't move more than 1" before you feel resistance.

Check the warning lights on the dash. The **oil and charge lights**, the **handbrake warning light**, and the **seatbelt warning light** on later models should all be ON. Try the **turn signals** and see if the indicators on the dash flash at you. If the car is 4WD, push the clutch pedal down, then put the selector in the 4WD position and see if the **4WD light** on the dash comes on. Move the selector back to FWD (front wheel drive) and release the clutch. Toot the **horn**. If any of the electrical things don't work, make a note of it. Don't drive the car if the oil warning light didn't come on (unless there's an oil pressure gauge).

Press on the **brake pedal**. It should go down an inch or two and stop solidly. A soft, squishy feel means the brakes need to be bled. Keep that in mind on your test drive. The pedal should stop at least 2 inches from the floor. If it doesn't, the brakes are worn out or need an adjustment. We'll check them in Procedure 3.

If the car has a stick shift (standard transmission), press lightly on the **clutch pedal**. The pedal should go down about ½ inch before you feel resistance. Now push the pedal to the floor. It should go down fairly easily without binding or sticking in places (signs of a nearly worn out clutch cable). Shift the **transmission** through the gears. Does the gearshift lever feel firm? If it's mushy or sticky, problems may lie ahead.

If the car is an **automatic**, run through the gears and see if the lever slips into each notch properly. Shift to PARK. Does the lever stay firmly in place?

Try the seat adjustment. Does it slide smoothly forward and backward. Does the seatback recline and return properly? Have Friend try the passenger seat too.

Step 2. Check Cranking System and Throwout Bearing.

OK, here we go. Pull the handbrake ON, put the gearshift in Neutral or PARK, then turn the ignition key to START and listen to the sound of the starter. It should sound smooth and energetic. If it lugs and drags, the battery might be weak. A grinding, clunking sound means damage to the starter or the gears on the starter or flywheel. When the engine starts, turn it off and restart it a few times. A weak battery will poop out after four or five engine starts. Did you feel resistance when you pulled the handbrake on? If not, it may need adjustment (easy), or a new cable (big hassle).

Start the engine again and let it run. Lightly press the accelerator pedal a few times to get a feel for the engine. If the car is a manual shift, slowly press down and release the clutch pedal several times. A squeal or growl means the clutch **throwout** bearing is worn out (a clutch job is in order). Release the handbrake, put the car in gear, and head for the street.

Step 3. Check Suspension and Steering.

Find a bumpy road and feel how the car rides. Does every little bump nearly jar your teeth out and/or does the car continue bouncing after hitting each bump? If so, the **shock absorbers** are shot. Rear shocks are relatively inexpensive and easy to replace, but front shocks are expensive and a full day's work to replace. Hear clanks or clunks? Exhaust system or suspension parts could be loose or worn out.

How does the steering feel? Solid and positive; or does the car wander aimlessly back and forth? If the car wanders, pulls to one side, or is hard to steer, check the tire pressure (Chapter 7, Procedure 4, Step 2), then check the steering again. If the tire pressure was OK, some of the suspension parts may be out of grease and/or worn out.

Step 4. Parking Lot Tests.

Find a large parking lot where you can drive in circles. Slow down to about 5 mph and turn the wheel all the way in one direction. Do you hear clicks, clanks or clunks? Make a few circles in the other direction while listening. Noises while turning a tight circle that go away when you straighten the wheel indicate worn DOJs or CVJs (joints) on the front axles. DOJs are expensive and a nasty job to replace. CVJs are very expensive and a real hassle to replace.

Manual transmission models: While in the parking lot, make a few stop sign-type stops and starts. Does the car jerk forward no matter how slowly you release the clutch pedal? If so, there's oil on the clutch plate, the plate is nearly worn out, or there's a problem with the clutch cable. Do you hear a clunk when you take off or shift gears? Signs of worn DOJs, CVJs, U-joints on 4WD models, or worn engine and/or transmission mounts.

Stop the car and pull the handbrake ON. With the car in gear, press on the accelerator pedal lightly while slowly letting the clutch out. The engine should die quickly. If the engine keeps running with the clutch pedal out, a clutch job is imminent. Do this test only once so what's left of the clutch disc won't be worn away. If the car moves forward when you release the clutch pedal while the handbrake is on, the brakes are badly worn or in desperate need of adjustment.

Does the manual transmission shift into gear easily and stay in gear? Let's check it a little more. Be sure there are no cars behind you, then take off normally. Get up to about 15 mph in first gear and suddenly let up on the accelerator. The car should stay in gear. Now get up to about 35 mph in second gear and do the same thing. Find a place where you can back up. Put the car in reverse and get up to about 10 mph, then let up on the accelerator pedal. If the transmission jumped out of any gear, check that gear a couple more times to be sure. We'll check third and fourth gears in Step 6.

Step 5. Street Tests.

You probably have a pretty good idea how well the brakes work (or don't work) by now. Let's test them a little more. On a deserted street, get up to about 40 mph. Loosen your grip on the steering wheel so you can feel if the car tries to pull to one side. Now apply the brakes as you normally would. Does the car keep going straight? It should. If it veers to one side, the brake shoes or pads have brake fluid on them or are worn out. You can find out which in Procedure 3. Now get up to about 40 mph again, warn passengers that you're going to stop suddenly, then press hard on the brake pedal. The car should stop quickly without making grinding sounds or veering to one side.

If the car has 4WD, get on a straight road with the front wheels pointed straight ahead, push in the clutch, then shift the 4WD lever into the 4WD position. Does it shift smoothly? Except for the 4WD light on the dash, you shouldn't be able to tell *any difference* in the way the car handles or sounds when the 4WD is engaged. If the car has "dual range" 4WD, try both HIGH and LOW positions. The LOW position will make the engine turn faster (it's geared lower). Can you shift out of 4WD easily? On some Soobs it's easiest to shift out of 4WD while going at least 10 to 20 mph.

Step 6. Highway Tests.

Head for the open road. Cruise along for a few miles while getting a feel for how the car rides. Firm and solid feeling with no vibrations? If it seems to float and wallow along the road, the car may have worn shock absorbers. Does the steering wheel shimmy (vibrate and rock side to side)? The tires might just be out of balance (no big deal) or some of the suspension parts might be worn out (potential bigger deal). We'll check it further in Procedure 3. Subarus aren't blessed with an excess of power, but you should be able to pass cars without too much difficulty. Does it struggle to reach passing speeds? Does the engine run smoothly or does it stumble and sputter? We'll do further engine tests in Procedure 3.

Drive the car up a fairly steep or long hill with the gas pedal pushed to the floor. Release the pedal a little and listen to the sound of the engine. If you hear a light knock-knock-knock, the **connecting rod bearings** are worn. If you hear a *deep* knock-knock-knock, the **main bearings** are suspect. If you hear either sound (or both) the engine is in urgent need of a rebuild. A very good reason not to buy the car. Other signs of worn rod or main bearings: at idle the oil light flashes or the oil pressure gauge shows a very low reading (around 5-10 psi).

Manual transmission models: Get up to about 50 mph in third gear and release the gas pedal suddenly; then go to 55 mph in fourth gear and release the pedal. Both times the transmission should stay in gear. If the transmission jumps out of any gear, is difficult to shift into gear, or makes a whine or growl while cruising down the road, some expensive transmission work is needed. If you like everything else about the car, call a transmission shop and see how much they'll charge to rebuild a Subaru transaxle. If the car stayed in all the gears, shifts easily, and doesn't whine or growl, it's probably in good condition.

Automatic transmission models: When driving along at highway speeds, does the transmission shift easily into the passing gear when you floor the gas pedal? If not, a transmission shop should be consulted before purchasing the car. An adjustment won't cost much, but the problem may go deeper.

Does the transmission shift into high gear when you reach about 40 mph on level ground? If not, a small plastic **governor gear** on the side of the transmission might be worn out. The gear is relatively cheap and easy to replace, but if it's been worn out for a long time the engine and transmission have probably suffered from being over revved. The automatic transmission oil probably has a burned odor. Best to consult with a transmission shop.

Repeat any of the steps in this procedure that resulted in less than satisfactory performance, just to be sure. On the way back to the owner's house or the car lot, think about the tests you've just put the car through. Can you live with this car? Will it meet your needs? Did you detect any problems that need further evaluation by a professional mechanic? Will you be willing to put additional time and money into it to get it into safe and reliable shape? If you're still interested in the car, we'll check a few more things in Procedure 3, then try to determine what the car is worth in Procedure 4.

PROCEDURE 3: FURTHER MECHANICAL TESTS

To do Procedure 3, you'll need the car for a couple more hours. Work it out with the owner/salesperson. When buying a used Subaru, *always* check the engine compression, the distributor, the front shocks, and also the DOJs and CVJs if the parking lot test indicated they might be worn out. These are the things that are expensive to repair or replace. Also use this procedure to check out other things that didn't seem right during the road test.

Condition: You've found a Soob that passed the first two procedures.

Tools and Materials: Spark plug wrench, compression tester, phillips screwdriver, regular screwdriver, large screwdriver, flashlight, 12"-18" length of 3/16" (5mm) inside diameter vacuum hose, rags, Friend. A jack and jackstands are required for some of the suspension and steering checks. The tools required for checking the brakes are listed at the start of the appropriate procedures in Chapter 13: *Brakes*.

Remark: If you don't have the tools, the time, or the inclination to do the following mechanical steps yourself, I suggest you take the car to a garage that specializes in Subarus and have them do a "pre-purchase inspection" on the car. It takes about an hour, and they'll charge you accordingly. They should check the engine compression, distributor, brakes, suspension, steering, and exhaust system. They'll usually give you a written report of the test results and an estimate of what it would cost to fix the things that need fixing. You'll be able to use the figures in the bargaining process.

Step 1. Compression Test.

Always do a compression test before buying any used car. Chapter 7, Procedure 11, tells you how to remove and inspect the spark plugs, how to do a compression test, and how to evaluate the results.

Step 2. Check Distributor.

Subaru distributors are very expensive, easy to check, and frequently found to be worn out. It's certainly worth the effort to check it before buying the car.

On OHV models, Chapter 7, Procedure 5, Step 4, tells you how to remove the air cleaner so you can get to the distributor. While the air cleaner is off, look at the air filter (Chapter 7, Procedure 4, Step 3). A dirty, greasy air filter is an indication of poor maintenance.

Chapter 7, Procedure 9, tells you how to check the various parts in the distributor for wear.

Chapter 7, Procedure 5, Step 5, tells you how to install the air cleaner, if you removed it.

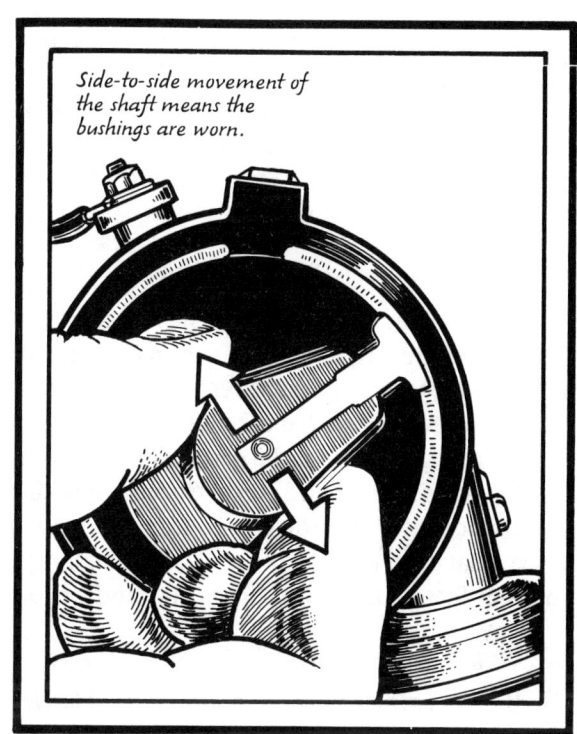

Side-to-side movement of the shaft means the bushings are worn.

Step 3. Oil Leaks.

It's usually difficult to determine the origin of oil leaks on the engine because the fan and wind blowing through the engine compartment scatter the oil everywhere. However, except for an oil leak between the engine and transaxle (the rear main oil seal), most engine oil leaks are fairly easy and cheap to fix. If the only leak seems to be at the rear of the engine, count on removing the engine to fix it. The clutch might also be ruined by the leaking oil.

It's easy to tell if and where the transaxle and the 4WD rear differential is leaking; look at both sides and the front and rear of the transaxle, and the rear differential if it's a 4WD model. If it's slightly greasy and dirty but dry looking, it's something to check regularly but doesn't need to be dealt with immediately. If you find a wet, juicy leak, it will have to be fixed by Subaru or a garage so get an estimate.

Step 4. Check Suspension and Steering.

If the steering wheel shimmies while driving, has more than 1″ of free play when parked, or the car handled or rode in a way that made you suspect the shocks are worn out, see Chapter 14, Procedure 1, to check the suspension and steering systems.

Step 5. Check Exhaust System.

Have Friend start the engine and repeatedly rev it up while you crawl along the side of the car listening for exhaust leaks. Hisses, ssshhhhs, and rumbles mean there's a leak. Exhaust system parts are expensive, so get an estimate from Subaru or a muffler shop as to what it'll cost to replace any leaking or damaged parts you find.

Step 6. Inspect Front Brake Pads.

From the test drive you have an idea of how the brakes work. If they didn't work too well, use this step to determine what the problem is and how much it will cost to fix it. Since the front brakes do most of the work and are the most expensive to replace, check them first. Then, if no problems are found up front, check the rear brakes. You'll find the listing of tools necessary to check the brakes at the beginning of the appropriate procedure in Chapter 13. Procedure 4 covers checking rear drum brakes, Procedure 6 for rear disc brakes, and Procedure 8 tells you how to check front disc brake pads and the discs.

If one of the brake fluid reservoirs had less fluid than the other or the brake pedal was spongy feeling and had to be pumped before the brakes would work, check the **calipers** (disc brake models) and the top of the **backing plate** (drum brakes) located just inside the wheels for signs of wetness. Wetness at these places indicates a wheel cylinder is leaking. If you find even slightly damp areas, the car is unsafe to drive until the brakes are checked out completely. You could be in for a brake cylinder rebuild and replacement of brake pads or shoes. Call Subaru or a garage to see how much the repair will cost. Use their "guesstimate" when negotiating with the seller, then fix it yourself for less than half of that amount using the procedures in Chapter 13.

Some tire shops and garages will do free brake inspections. If they tell you the brakes are in good condition, they probably are. If they tell you the car needs a complete brake job, use their word to help reduce the price of the car, then check them yourself before hiring someone to do it for you. With the right tools, brake jobs on Soobs are pretty easy.

Step 7. Further Drivetrain Checks.

See Chapter 7, Procedure 2, Step 10, to check the accordion-type **rubber boots** on the DOJs and CVJs. If any boots are torn or missing, get an estimate for replacing the DOJ or CVJ, because the unit is liable to be worn out due to the dirt that has entered through the broken boot. A torn boot should be replaced pronto. Chapter 15, Procedure 3, Steps 1 and 2, tell you how to check the DOJs and/or CVJs for wear.

If driving in circles in the parking lot or the start-and-stop test caused noises or clunks, or if the clutch chattered, grabbed, or slipped, see the troubleshooting guide at the beginning of Chapter 15. It will direct you to the proper procedure to diagnose the problem. Once you've figured out what's wrong, call Subaru or a garage to see what the repairs will cost. (If it's something you can fix, you can save the cost of the labor.) At any rate, consider these potential expenses in your decision—and in your bargaining position with the seller.

Step 8. Finish Up.

If there are any broken windows, dented fenders or bumpers, tears in the upholstery, and such, make a few phone calls to see what it will cost to have the repairs made. These figures may also come in handy when it comes time to haggle over the price.

Put back together everything you took apart then go for one more test drive. Think about the new information you discovered while doing the mechanical checks. Is this the car for you? If you still feel good about the Sooby you're driving, it's time to move on to Procedure 4 to determine what the car is worth and what the seller will take for it.

PROCEDURE 4: EVALUATION AND BARGAINING

Condition: You're still interested in the car!

Tools and Materials: Brain, poker face, pencil, paper, access to a National Automobile Dealers Association (NADA) used car Blue Book. Money, if you decide to buy the car.

Step 1. Determine the Car's Value.

Call a bank, your insurance agent, or a car salesman you trust and ask for the Blue Book value for the year and model of the car you're interested in. Many will actually let you browse through the book itself. Don't rely on the figure that the seller gives you; you want to check independent sources of information. The Blue Book gives the current wholesale and retail prices for used cars in your area. Extras such as air conditioning and low miles increase the value; high miles, poor body/interior condition, and tire wear lower a car's value. Three values are given according to the condition: poor, good, or excellent. Having done Procedures 1-3, you should have a good idea about which category this car belongs in.

Jot down the Blue Book figure for the car, then subtract dollars for damage and/or repairs that need to be made. Use the estimates you got from Subaru and/or garages even if you plan to do the work yourself. Now decide what you are prepared to pay. Carefully consider all the car's negative points as well as the things you like about the car (sun roof, sound system, good vibes, fuzzy dice hanging from the mirror, etc.). Even if this is the fourth car you've looked at and you really need wheels, don't rush! And you shouldn't feel obligated or pressured because everyone has been so patient while you checked the car out. Ignore any impatient remarks or restless pacing by the seller. You're now ready to bargain.

Step 2. Bargaining.

In this culture we're expected to haggle over real estate and car prices. Why not also in supermarkets, department stores, garages, and with the IRS? Anyway, put on your best poker face and start by offering the seller a few hundred dollars less than the asking price and less, of course, than you may ultimately be willing to pay. If the seller has a heart attack or spits in your face, you started a little low. Try again, a little higher this time. The seller will probably make a counteroffer a little below the asking price or try some pressure tactic like saying, "Several other people are interested in this car." On that point, you have to look sellers straight in the eye and decide whether they're B.S.ing or not. Who knows, maybe somebody really will be coming over right after lunch with cash in hand. Try another offer below the counteroffer. Try to stay below your estimated top figure. At some point you'll get the feel for when the seller is at his/her bottom dollar. If it's within your budget, shake on it. You've just bought a Subaru! Whew. OK, now look at Step 3. (If you can't get the seller down to your price range, it's back to the classifieds.)

Step 3. Now What?

Before handing over any cash, except for maybe a small "earnest money" check to hold the car, make sure the paperwork is in order. You need to know if there are any liens on the vehicle. Exchange your bread for a signed copy of the legal title to the car. Most individual sellers probably won't accept your personal check, but will take a cashier's check from your bank.

Now that the car is yours, you can take your time and thoroughly check the condition of everything on the car and make any necessary repairs. You'll then cruise around in your new wheels with a warm feeling of confidence rather than that anxious uncertainty about whether or not you can really trust it. To become intimately acquainted with your "new" Soob, do the 30,000-mile fluid change and the 12,000-mile tune-up in Chapter 7.

If the Soob you bought came with a warranty, have anything that breaks or goes bad fixed by the seller. You could violate the warranty agreement if you attempt repairs yourself. Make sure you're clear about the expiration date (or mileage) so that you can have as many things as possible fixed under the warranty terms. Dealers are generally not inclined to stretch them an extra day or an extra mile.

Chapter 6

CHAPTER 7

MAINTENANCE, LUBRICATION, AND TUNE-UP

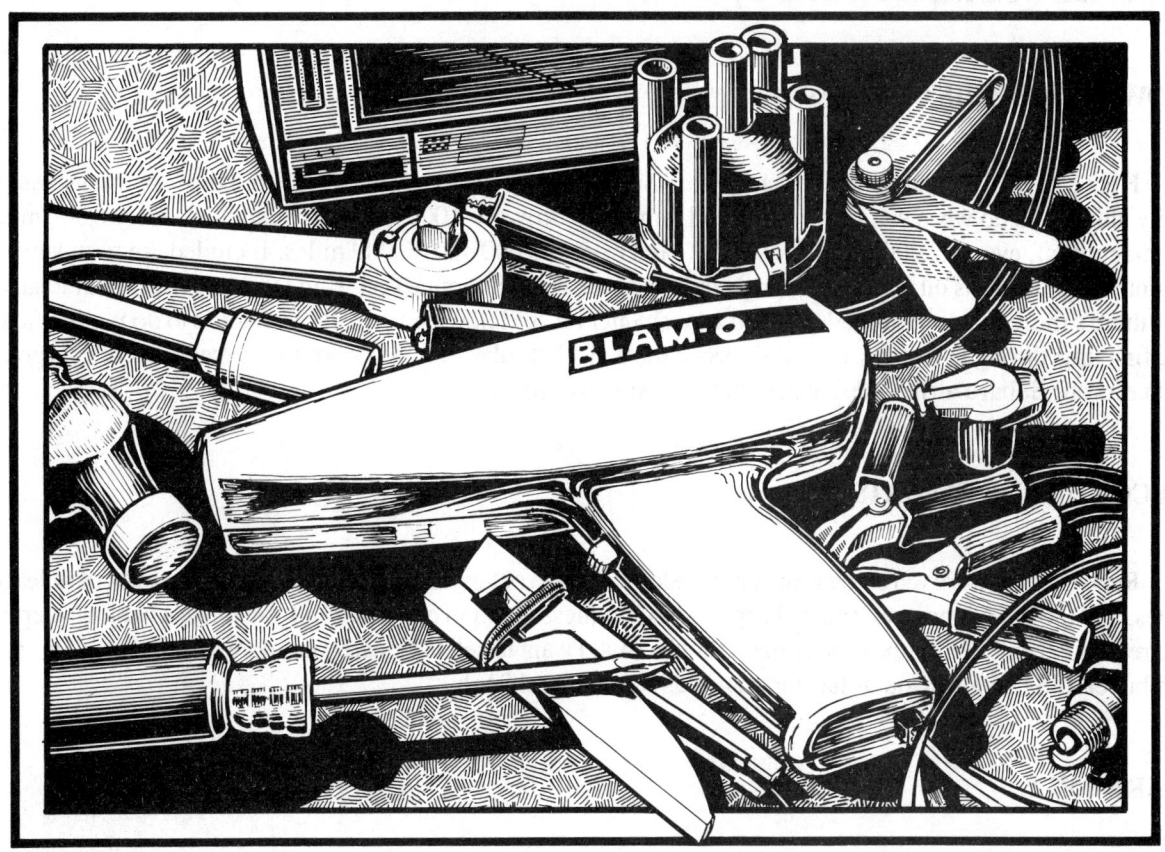

*"Translating words into actions is easy when you do it one step at a time. You are not going to intellectualize on these mechanical things, you are going to **do** them and that's different. The idea to grasp well here is one of Return. You are going to return the car to a position of well-being by adjusting or replacing certain things that have worn, been used up or been bounced out of alignment. As the I Ching says, 'Perseverance Furthers,' and that is your thing. Take your time and do each step completely before you even think about the next."*
—*John Muir,* How to Keep Your VW Alive

Welcome! You have arrived at the most important part of the show. This is the chapter that you will use more than any other in the whole book. It's the one that will keep your Subaru alive! That's what I promised up front and I know we can do it. Doing these maintenance procedures REGULARLY will keep your Soob in a high level of general health as well as put you in touch with the condition of your Soob, let you know what it needs right now, and what can wait for a while. (The "Telltale Graphic Monitor" on some later models will warn you when things like a stoplight bulb is burned out or the brake fluid level is low, but don't rely solely on it to warn you that something needs attention.) Often, while doing an oil change or tune-up, you'll notice something that could cause problems if not fixed right away. Look for loose bolts, oil leaks, broken or frayed wires, uneven wear on the tires, and other potential problems as you perform the maintenance procedures. If you notice something amiss, turn to the appropriate chapter and follow the repair procedures to remedy the problem as soon as possible. By staying in close touch with your Soob, you'll probably never have to call a tow truck on a rainy night.

A popular book in the early days of motoring, *Diseases of the Gasolene Automobile and How to Cure Them*, had this advice on maintenance: "When you buy an automobile, there is formed an unwritten agreement between you and the machine. You expect to receive certain benefits. It, likewise, exacts a penalty from you in direct proportion to your own demands." Thanks to modern chemicals and technology, the "penalty" isn't a direct proportion anymore. In fact, contrary to popular belief, newer cars are much easier to maintain and tune-up than older models. With the help of this chapter, an occasional penalty of a Saturday afternoon should give you years of carefree driving.

HOW TO USE THIS CHAPTER

Here's how I've organized this chapter for you. It goes by time and mileage. From the top: things you do daily, things you do when you stop for gas, and things you do every 3,000 miles (or 3 months), every 6,000 miles (or 6 months), every 12,000 miles (or yearly), and every 30,000 and 60,000 miles. Included are such key car maintenance items as oil and filter change and tune-up. You will notice that from the 3,000-mile maintenance on, there's more than one procedure to do at each interval, so allow yourself several hours to do it all, at least the first time through. You may need to set aside most of a Saturday. But, as I said, this is the chapter that's going to keep your Subaru alive—perhaps longer than you ever imagined.

RECORD YOUR EFFORTS

Record all the work you do on your car in the log at the end of this chapter. It's not easy to keep track of mileage, dates, and the little things you want to keep an eye on, unless it's all in one place and you make a habit of keeping the record current. When the time comes that you (may) want to sell your car, your log will very likely impress the buyer and bring you top dollar for your well-maintained Soob.

WARRANTY

If your car is still under warranty, let the Subaru dealer do the covered repair work. You've already paid for it in the purchase price of the car. If your car is less than five years old, and you don't have a copy of the warranty, ask a Subaru dealer for one. You might get a pleasant surprise. I sure did when Subaru replaced, free of charge, the worn-out distributor on a used Subaru I bought. This saved me $140 because it was covered under the "Extended Emission Control Warranty" for Subarus sold in California—five years or 50,000 miles, regardless of how many people had owned the car before me. It never hurts to check.

If a recurring problem isn't fixed to your satisfaction while the car is under warranty, don't wait until the warranty runs out to write a complaint. Later, if something major goes wrong on your car because the original problem was never properly solved by the agency, your written record may help you get it fixed by Subaru for no charge.

BODY MAINTENANCE

Take good care of your body and you'll enjoy life longer! The same applies to your Subaru. Wash it on top and underneath when it gets dirty (weekly, if you live where they salt winter roads) and wax it a couple of times a year. Waxing has been made pretty easy these days, thanks to modern chemicals and our lazy culture. Touch up little nicks and scratches with touch-up paint from Subaru and get fender-bender accidents fixed before rust has a chance to start. It's harder to get motivated to spend time and money on a mechanically sound car if it's filthy and funky looking. A good maintenance record will help you keep track of things and really dazzle a prospective buyer when it's selling time for the old Soob. When that time comes, the better it looks, the more it's worth and the easier it will be to sell.

WHY LUBRICATE?

Rub the palms of your hands together really fast for a few seconds and see what happens. Come on, don't be shy. Your palms get hot very quickly, right? Now imagine your hands moving 100 to 1,000 times as fast. The heat buildup would be unbearable. Now, if you're really into it, try rubbing your hands together with hand lotion, or even motor oil, on them. Amazingly, there's hardly any heat generated. The same situation goes on in your engine every time you start it. Pistons are moving up and down in cylinders, rods are spinning on the crankshaft, the crank and cam are spinning in the crankcase, and so on, and so on. As long as there's a thin film of oil between the moving parts, everything goes smoothly. If there's no oil, too little oil, or worn-out oil in the engine, those rapidly moving metallic parts overheat, then it's metal against metal. Soon the metal gets so hot it distorts and very quickly you have a warped, burned mess of Fried Subaru. Preventing heat and wear caused by friction is the main purpose of the oil in your engine. This, my friends, is called lubrication.

MY RAP ON OIL

Oil is truly the lifeblood of your engine. It not only reduces friction and wear but also helps cool the engine, helps form an airtight seal between the piston rings and cylinder walls, cleanses the internal parts, and counteracts the corrosive by-products of combustion. Therefore, the kind of oil used in your engine plays a major role in how long it will last.

Like most everything else, oil is made up of molecules. The difference between oils is in the ability of the oil molecules to form and continue to form a lubricating film under pressure and heat. The oil molecules that lubricate the longest are the best and usually the most expensive.

OIL QUALITY

To help sort out the various qualities of oil, the American Petroleum Institute (API) has developed a code that is stamped on the label of oils they have certified. Don't buy any oil that doesn't have the round API certification symbol on the lid or label. Here's how to read the code.

For some reason gasoline engines are designated "S" and diesel engines "C." The S and/or C is followed by the performance level of the oil—A to F for gasoline engines, A to D for diesels. Simply stated, SF is the best for gasoline engines and CD is best for diesels. Some oils are labeled both SF and CC or CD. That's the kind you want, even if your owner's manual says "SE or better." So when you buy oil be sure it has API service SF/CC or SF/CD somewhere on the label or lid.

RECOMMENDATIONS

Most major brands are rated SF and are certified to exceed car manufacturer's specifications. However, *Consumer Reports* found that almost one-fourth of the brands they tested didn't live up to their certification. Some of the brands that did and thus are recommended by *Consumer Reports* are:

VISCOSITY	BRANDS
5W-30	Mobil 1 and Pennzoil Multi-Vis
10W-30	Castrol GTX, Pennzoil P-Z-L Turbo Formula and Exxon Uniflo
10W-40	Castrol GTX
20W-50	None were tested.

To read more about the *Consumer Reports* tests and to see which brands of oil they recommend NOT using, hotfoot it down to your friendly neighborhood library and look up the February 1987 issue. In that same issue, they also report tests on oil filters, oil filter wrenches, and tire pressure gauges.

Oil companies use different base oils and additives, so it's best not to mix oils of different brands. If you have to mix brands in an emergency, change the oil and filter as soon as possible. If you choose a brand of oil that is readily available, or carry a spare can or two, you will probably never have to mix brands.

By far the cheapest way to buy oil is to pick it up when it's on sale by the case. Some hardware stores, discount department stores, even some drugstores, sell oil and filters at about half the price that gas stations and auto parts stores charge. It's the same oil, so go for the lowest price you can find for the brand you prefer.

I buy oil that comes in plastic screw-top containers because it's easier to store partial cans of oil without making a mess, and you can pour the old oil into the containers and haul it to the recycling center.

OIL ADDITIVES AND SUPPLEMENTS

Detergents are put in oils to dissolve burned molecules of oil, carbon, and other grunge that forms naturally inside the engine. As the oil is pumped through the engine, some of these contaminants in the oil are trapped in the oil filter while others stay in suspension until the oil and filter are changed. Most modern oils also have additives to retard corrosion and neutralize acids. Seems engines get indigestion too.

When you buy a quart of high grade oil, about 15 percent of it is additives, carefully blended so the oil will meet the standards of the API and the Society of Automotive Engineers (SAE). Don't waste your money buying oil supplements that are probably already included. In fact, adding supplements might upset the balance of ingredients in the oil and make it less efficient.

If you just bought a used Subaru, find out what kind of oil the previous owner used. If the car came off a lot, they might give you the prior owner's name, or you might find the brand of oil used written on a door sticker or in the Owner's Manual. If a detergent oil was used, you can switch to another brand of detergent oil, if you change both the oil and the filter. Non-detergent oil is rarely used these days, but if that's what is in the engine now, you should wait until after a rebuild to change to a detergent oil. The reason: non-detergent oil doesn't dissolve contaminants as they form. The crud just sticks to the parts on the inside of the engine. Changing to a detergent oil would suddenly get all that stuff in suspension and overload the oil with contaminants. When the mess gets pumped through the engine, it could plug oil passages and/or damage bearing surfaces. You can change from detergent oil to non-detergent without ill effect, but don't—there's no reason to.

OTHER OILS

Synthetic, "man-made" oils are supposed to extend the period between oil changes to about 15,000 miles, or one year. Sounds good, but even if the oil molecules maintain their lubricating properties for that long, there's bound to be a buildup of contaminants in the oil.

I've tried synthetic oils and enjoyed the freedom from oil changes. But I found that without the regular oil change every 3-6,000 miles, the overall maintenance of the car suffered. Things I normally do at oil change time were neglected for too long. Also, I discovered that places where there were very slight oil leaks tended to leak a lot more with synthetic oil. At $5 a can, the oil for even a slight oil leak gets very expensive. The cost of the five quarts of synthetic oil was very close to the cost of a year's supply of regular oil so I didn't save much money.

If you decide to use synthetic oil, use one that's readily available, carry a spare can or two, and promise your Soob you won't forget to do the regular maintenance procedures on schedule. Don't use synthetic oil just after an engine rebuild—the rings won't "seat" properly.

Also available are the "slippery" oils with graphite. These oils are more expensive than regular oil and don't last as long as synthetic, but it is are claimed they reduce engine wear. If you abuse your engine, it'll need all the help it can get, and slippery oil might be helpful. However, I don't recommend using an oil with graphite in an old engine that's burning a lot of oil because the graphite is a conductor and it might foul the spark plugs sooner than a regular oil. Again, don't use slippery oil just after an engine rebuild.

AVOID any oil labeled "Recycled," "Remanufactured," or "New oil blended with 100 percent recycled oil." The ecological idea is noble, but in reality oil molecules wear out, especially when subjected to high engine temperatures. Recycling or blending can never restore the molecules' lost ability to lubricate properly.

OIL FILTERS

Consumer Reports rated Fram filters best for filtering harmful grit out of the oil. Fram filters cost about a dollar more than most other filters, but they are probably worth it. Other filters that were slightly less efficient in the filtering test but that were comparable in their grit-holding capacity before becoming clogged were Lee, Purolator, and Sears.

VISCOSITY

Viscosity is a measure of how easily a liquid flows. Oil with high viscosity, such as S.A.E. 50, is thicker and doesn't flow as easily in cold weather. In extreme cold, oil with a high viscosity can get so sluggish it prevents the starter from turning the engine over fast enough to start. On the other hand, high viscosity oil maintains its lubricating ability at high temperatures, whereas low viscosity oil becomes too "thin" to do an adequate job as a result of the heat.

If you live in a climate where there are extreme changes in temperature, you want an oil that is thin enough to let you start the engine easily yet thick enough to lubricate at high temperatures. Multi-viscosity oils, such as 10W-30 and 10W-40, are ideal for these conditions. 10W-30 is the best grade to use except in very hot climates, where 10W-40 would be best.

If you happen to live where the temperature falls below -13°F (-25°C) and it's difficult to start the engine when it's cold, you can use 5W-30 oil if its service rating is SF. A word of caution, however. This

Recommended Engine Oil Viscosity

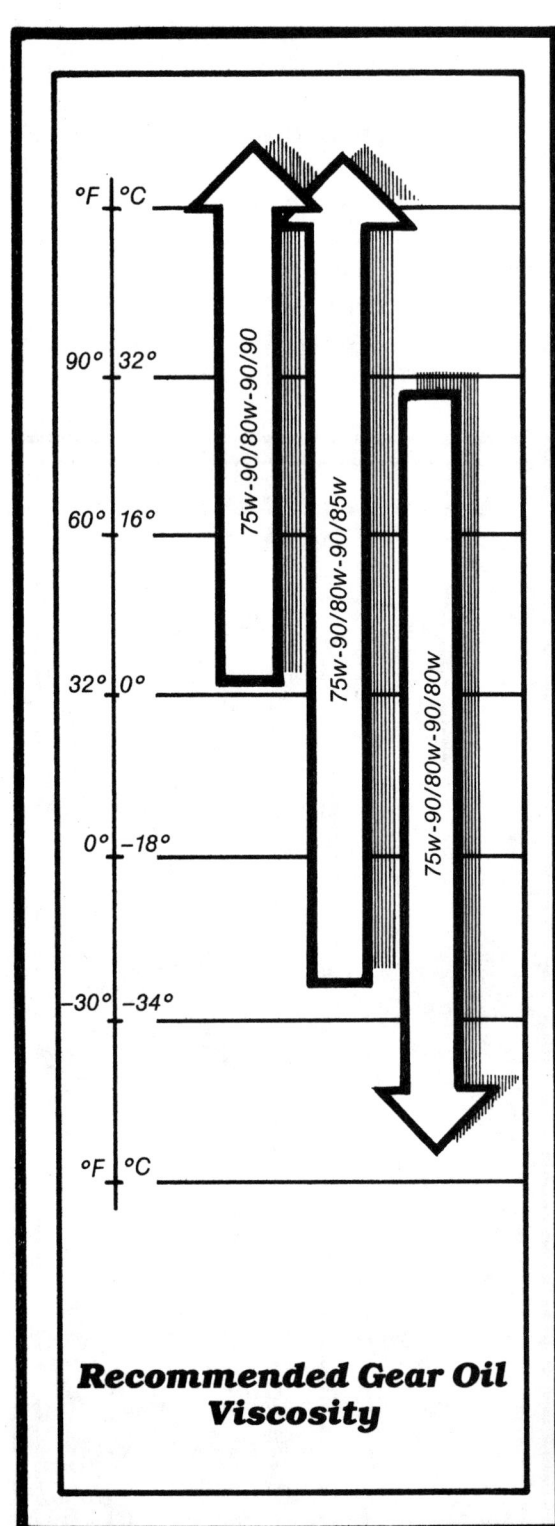

Recommended Gear Oil Viscosity

oil is not recommended for sustained high speed driving or for use in Turbo models, so change to one of the oils in the chart as soon as the weather warms up to a balmy 0°F (-18°C).

TRANSMISSION AND DIFFERENTIAL OIL (Gear Oil)

Gear oil for manual transmissions and differentials is thick and heavy and isn't exposed to the by-products (contamination) of combustion like engine oil is. Unless a seal breaks and lets contamination in, gear oil stays pretty clean. In fact, the latest Subaru factory maintenance schedules recommend changing the gear oil only if the vehicle has been used under severe conditions!

I use Castrol Hypoy C 80W/90 gear oil because it's a good multi-viscosity oil and it comes in a handy plastic container with a pour spout built into the lid. The pour spout eliminates the need for a funnel or suction-type filler for getting the oil into the transmission, differential, or rear differential on 4WD models. It's certified to meet the standards for Mack trucks, so I feel safe using it in my Brat. If you have a limited slip differential (LSD), you must use LSD oil in the differential. No, it isn't hallucinogenic!

Also available through off-road specialty shops is a synthetic gear oil called HPS. It is claimed to make transmissions, differentials, and transfer cases last longer and shift more smoothly. It costs about $12 a can. If you prefer to drive on goat trails and creek beds instead of roads, your Soob needs all the help it can get, so the super-stuff might be a worthwhile investment.

AUTOMATIC TRANSMISSION FLUID (ATF)

Like the gear oils, ATF doesn't get contaminated by combustion. But since it's subjected to friction and high temperatures, it should be changed at least every 30,000 miles. As with blood types there are different types of ATF. Some of these are Type A, Type F, Dexron, and Dexron II. '75-'84 Subarus are designed to use the Dexron type and '85 and newer models use Dexron II. Also like blood, other types shouldn't be mixed with the Dexron. Fortunately, Dexron is the most common type. Some brands recommended by

Subaru are Texaco Texamatic 6673 Dexron, Castrol TQ Dexron, Mobil ATF 220 and Shell ATF Dexron. If you have to add more than a quart every 6,000 miles, a seal or gasket is leaking and should be fixed right away. Power steering units also use the same kind of automatic transmission fluid.

ANTIFREEZE

Also vital to your engine's health is antifreeze. It keeps the water in the cooling system from freezing and breaking the radiator and/or engine. A mixture of antifreeze and water (called *coolant*) raises the boiling point of water so that even a very hot engine won't boil away its cooling fluid. Most antifreeze also contains rust and corrosion inhibitors that help keep the innards of the radiator and coolant passages in the engine clean and efficient. Be sure to use an antifreeze with an ethylene glycol base in your Subaru's aluminum engine. Phosphorous-based antifreeze can cause the aluminum to corrode.

Antifreeze should be changed at least every other year. I recommend replacing it every year. If you live in a climate with severe temperature changes, fresh antifreeze every fall gives you assured protection and peace of mind.

If you live in a very cold climate, either buy an antifreeze tester (cheap ones from Prestone and discount stores will do) or regularly have a service station check the freeze protection level of the coolant. Add more antifreeze if necessary. It's a good idea, although not always possible, to use distilled water when you fill or add water to the radiator. Distilled water doesn't have minerals or other impurities that can form deposits in the water passages.

Using plain water with no antifreeze allows corrosion and rust to form in the water passages of the radiator and engine. The buildup restricts the flow of coolant and thus reduces the efficiency of the cooling system.

Water is more efficient than antifreeze for cooling the engine, so using straight antifreeze isn't as effective as a mixture of the two. The proper mixture is at least 50 percent antifreeze to 50 percent water.

Antifreeze can be reused after you've drained it from the engine and radiator. It must be kept clean though, so straining it through a clean rag before pouring it back in is important. In Chapter 16, Capt. Quirk and Mr. Schpock will tell you more about the cooling system in your Starship Subaru.

TIRES and TIRE PRESSURE

If you're planning to keep your Soob for a long time, buying radial tires will save you money in the long run even though they're initially more expensive. Radials last longer, give you better gas mileage, and a better grip on the road so they're safer than bias ply tires. The only car I have with bias ply tires is my old '53 Chevy Bel Air that only gets driven on special occasions (like to the drive-in movies). I would have gotten radials for it but I couldn't find any with wide whitewalls.

I put over 60,000 miles on my last set of Michelin ZX radial tires, and they still had a lot of miles left on them when I sold the car. How did I do it? I kept them inflated properly, rotated them regularly, and kept the suspension and steering systems in good condition.

I consider the tire pressure listed in the Subaru Owner's Manual to be the minimum allowable pressure for radial tires. You'll find the maximum allowable pressure stamped on the sidewalls of whatever brand of tires you have. Running your tires at the minimum pressure will give you a softer, smoother ride, but inflating them to the maximum pressure or near the max will give you increased tire life, better gas mileage, and better handling. This is especially true of the P radials (the letter P will be stamped on the tire just before the tire size). You can experiment with the pressure between the minimum and maximum pressures until you find the right pressure for you. Just be sure both front tires and both rear tires are inflated to the same pressure. Inflate bias ply (non-radial) tires to the pressures in the chart in the Owner's Manual.

Rotate the tires at least every 6,000 miles. The more often the tires are rotated, the more evenly they will wear and the longer they will last. If the tires start wearing in funny patterns, go through Procedure 1 in Chapter 14 to check for worn steering and suspension parts that could be responsible for the uneven wear.

Have the front end alignment checked and the tires balanced by an alignment shop at least every two years. Do it more often if you do a lot of off-road driving or have a tendency to bash into curbs on the way home from parties.

Those of you who enjoy driving your Soob without the benefit of a road under it might want tubes in your tires so that rocks that find their way between the tire and rim won't cause deflated tires and egos. Be sure to use radial tubes with radial tires.

BUYING TIRES

The kind of tires and wheels you get for your Subaru should be determined by the kind of driving you want to do, not by how good they look, which I think is how most people choose tires. (No matter what those flashy white letters say, they won't do a thing for performance.)

All tires are somewhat of a compromise because none of them work "the best" in all situations. Street radials provide excellent traction and cornering on hard surface roads but just don't have the "bite" needed when the surface is soft. Combination tires are middle of the road, so to speak, and give acceptable performance on hard surfaces, as well as added traction when you leave the pavement. Genuine off-road tires for soft surfaces have large, aggressive treads with widely spaced tread lugs so they can get a good bite on whatever is available. On the highway, however, the off-road tires are noisy, rough riding, and wear out quickly. Fortunately, there is a wide variety of all three types available.

Here's what all those mysterious letters and numbers on tire sidewalls mean: Tires used to say 2 ply, 4 ply, etc. on the side, which told you how many plies (layers) of material were built into the carcass of the tire. Tires are now rated by "load range." Here's what the different load ranges mean: A=2 ply, B=4 ply, C=6 ply, D=8 ply, E=10 ply and F=12 ply. The higher the load range, the stronger the tire. Also, the higher the load range, the stiffer the tire, so heavy duty tires make for a rougher ride.

The government has developed a Tire Grading System (TGS) that is put on the sticker on new tires to help compare the countless brands and types of tires. Here's how to use the TGS:

Treadwear: This number gives you an idea of how much mileage to expect from a tire. The numbers are given in tens from 40 to 230. Unfortunately, the numbers don't relate to how many thousands of miles the tire will last; they are relative numbers, meaning that a tire graded 150 should give you 50 percent more mileage than one graded 100, and so on. But, as the old saying goes, the actual mileage you get will depend on how you drive and where you live.

Traction: Traction is graded A, B, or C and indicates the tire's ability to stop on wet surfaces. Tires graded A will stop on a wet road in the shortest distance. Tires rated C have poor traction, not the kind you want.

Temperature Resistance: This is also graded A, B, or C. Tires rated A run cooler than those rated B or C and therefore are less likely to blowout or have tread separation if driven over long distances at highway speeds.

Here are some more clues so you'll know what the letters and numbers on tires mean. A tire with 195/70SR-13, for example, is 195mm at its widest part (the cross section, not necessarily the tread width). The 70 is the tire's "aspect ratio," which means the tire's height is 70 percent of the width (thus it's a 70 series tire). The S means the tire is able to sustain a given high speed. No letter before the R is lowest, S is higher, H is higher still, and V is highest. The R stands for radial. And finally, the 13 stands for the diameter of the wheel in inches. Whew. So the tire size is designated by a combination of inches, millimeters, percentage, and some arbitrary letters. No wonder buying tires is a chore.

If you change to taller or wider tires, you'll probably want to change wheels. And there are hundreds of different styles to choose from. Three things must be considered when buying wheels: compatibility with tubeless tires, the wheel width, and the amount of offset (if any).

Compatibility: Any wheels will work if you plan to use tubes and tube-type tires. If you plan to use tubeless tires, be sure the wheels are made for tubeless tires.

Width: Generally speaking, the wheel width should be approximately two inches narrower than the cross-section of the tire. Be sure to ask the dealer if the tires and wheels you select are compatible.

Offset: Wheel offset refers to the relationship of the wheel center to the wheel rim. Negative offset means the rim of the wheel is moved inward making the car's track narrower. Positive offset means the rim is farther outward, giving the car a wider track, which will make the car corner better. Wheels with too much negative offset will probably rub on the brake calipers and/or tie rod ends. Too much positive offset can cause the tires to rub on the fenders and create greater strain on the wheel bearings and hubs.

MAINTENANCE SCHEDULES

How often should maintenance routines be done on your Subaru? Ask ten different mechanics and you'll probably get ten different answers ranging from a daily 30-minute ritual to "wait until something breaks, then fix it." Well, you won't find me wasting half an hour every day checking out my car, but you won't find me at the side of the road with my thumb out because I waited for something to break either. Preventive maintenance is the key.

When it comes to maintenance schedules, it seems like all car manufacturers are trying to outdo each other in the length of time between maintenance services. And since they are also extending the length of warranties, they must be convinced that modern lubricants and materials are capable of enduring longer periods between inspections and fluid changes. Here are my thoughts about the current recommended maintenance schedules.

How you use (or abuse) your car greatly affects how often the maintenance procedures should be performed. I'm very skeptical about regularly going 7,500 miles between oil changes. But I am satisfied that under *normal* driving conditions, good quality motor oil can withstand 6,000 miles between changes. If you drive your Soob under the *severe* conditions listed below, the oil and filter should be changed at least every 3,000 miles, or as soon as the oil starts looking dark and dirty.

The factory workshop manuals for '85 and newer models now recommend inspecting the front brake pads, brake lines, handbrake adjustment, clutch and hill-holder system, and the steering and suspension systems every 15,000 miles or 15 months. This sounds reasonable to me, except why not get on a yearly schedule and do these procedures every 12 months?

For 1985 and newer models, the factory manuals recommend that all engine tune-up procedures be performed at 30,000 miles or 30 months under normal driving conditions. I'm sure that materials and workmanship have improved, but I still recommend doing these basic service procedures at least every 12,000 miles or once a year. By spending one day a year inspecting the condition of critical parts and systems on your Soob, it will probably last longer, and you'll greatly reduce the chances of a breakdown on the highway. In other words, you'll be more in touch with your transportation. The choice is yours. If you decide to follow the factory schedule for maintenance service (it's in the Owner's Manual that's stashed in your glove box), you can use this manual to perform the recommended maintenance procedures, and you'll still be covered by their warranty.

At the start of this chapter I mentioned that it's easier to do tune-ups on the newer cars. Here's what I meant. With the advent of electronic "breakerless" distributors on late '70s models, and the introduction of the LED distributors on some '80s models, the most common cause of engine problems—the breaker points—was eliminated. Since there is essentially no contact between the parts in the new distributors, there's nothing to wear out or change that would cause the engine's performance to decrease. Checking the distributor now simply entails inspecting the distributor cap and rotor, a task that's much easier to do than programing a VCR or microwave oven. Since things in the distributor don't change, the ignition timing doesn't change. So if the engine seems to be running right, there's no need to check the timing on the later models. And the factory-sealed carburetors and fuel injection systems that were introduced in the early '80s have eliminated idle speed and mixture adjustments.

So what's left to do? Basically, simple things like changing the oil (still as messy, but as easy as it's always been), replacing the spark plugs (very similar to replacing the light bulb in a lamp), and checking things like wiper blades, brake lights, and vital fluids. So you see, newer cars really are easier to "work" on.

I've listed Minor and Major Massage procedures to do every 6,000 and 12,000 miles. Massaging your Subaru doesn't involve taking it to Madame Noogie's Massage Parlor. Massage means going over the whole car, checking things, lubricating things and looking for things that are broken, worn out, or that will be worn out before the next massage.

Here is my recommended schedule for performing the tune-up and massages.

SEVERE DRIVING CONDITIONS

The following conditions are considered to be **severe driving conditions**:
1. Driving up and down mountain trails, on dusty, muddy, or sandy roads.
2. Pulling trailers.
3. Making frequent short trips of less than five miles.
4. If you live where there are extreme temperatures (above 90°F or below 0°F).
5. Driving on roads that get salted when it snows.

If you frequently drive under these conditions, you should do Procedures 1 through 4 every 3,000 miles to replace the engine oil and oil filter, and to give your hard working Soob a minor massage. At 30,000 miles you should do Procedure 15 to replace the gear oil in the transmission and differerential, and the ATF if you have an automatic transmission. Remember, you can't change your oil too often!

If your car develops engine problems, run through the tune-up procedures in this chapter even if it hasn't been 12,000 miles since the last tune-up.

NORMAL DRIVING CONDITIONS

Get in the habit of doing Procedures 1 and 2 to familiarize yourself with your particular Soob's characteristics, idiosyncrasies, and appetite for the various vital fluids like oil, coolant, and brake fluid.

Under normal driving conditions follow the schedule listed below:

Gas-stop Fluid Checks	200-400 miles
Oil Change, Lubrication and Minor Massage	6,000 miles or 6 months
Engine Tune-up and Major Massage	12,000 miles or 12 months
Transmission, Differential Oil Change	30,000 miles
Parts Replacement	60,000 miles

Here's what the procedures for this chapter deal with:

Procedure 1.	Daily Sensory Check
Procedure 2.	Gas Stop Fluid Level Checks
Procedure 3.	Oil and Filter Change
Procedure 4.	Minor Massage
Procedures 5-13.	12,000 Mile or 12 Month Tune-up
Procedure 14.	Major Massage
Procedure 15.	30,000 Mile Transmission and Differential Oil Change
Procedure 16.	60,000 Mile Parts Replacement, Wheel Bearing and Axle Lubrication

Procedure 1, Step 1   Maintenance, Lubrication, Tune-up   **75**

Make it easy on yourself. Get on a schedule so you do the 6- and 12-month maintenance in the spring and fall while the weather is nice. My garage isn't heated or air conditioned. Is yours?

OK, enough verbiage—let's get on with the Procedures! Please read through each procedure before doing it so you'll understand what you are going to do and know what tools and materials are needed. Also, arrange for transportation in case you have to make an emergency run to the parts store. Have fun!

PROCEDURE 1: DAILY SENSORY CHECK

Condition: You want to stay in touch with your transportation so it will live a full healthy life.

Tools and Materials: Eyes, ears, nose, skin, brain.

Step 1. Use Your Senses.

Look for oil spots on the driveway or garage floor, know how your tires look when properly inflated, listen for new sounds when you start the engine and while you're driving. Be aware of different smells that usually indicate something is overheating, and use the seat of your pants and your hands on the steering wheel to notice new or different vibrations.

Make these simple sensory observations a habit whenever you're in or near your car. Mechanical problems are like diseases—the sooner they're detected, the easier and cheaper they are to fix.

If you've found anything that looks, sounds, or smells suspicious, better plan to deal with it pronto.

PROCEDURE 2: GAS STOP FLUID LEVEL CHECKS

Checking vital fluid levels when you stop to fill up on gas should be a regular habit. You might also find it useful to do these fluid checks at other times—like when you suspect you might be low on one or more of them.

Condition: Gas gauge is on or near empty; OR you believe OPEC needs another hit of your money.

Tools and Materials: Money, a clean rag or paper towel. You may need motor oil, Dexron or Dexron II ATF (automatic transmission fluid), a funnel, gear oil, DOT 3 or 4 brake fluid, radiator coolant (water/antifreeze), windshield washer fluid.

Remark: You don't have to carry engine oil, gear oil, transmission fluid, brake fluid and antifreeze to the station every time you go for a fill-up. Check the levels at home before you go or add the needed vital fluids when you get home. The important thing is to check them regularly and the gas stop interval will help you remember.

If you notice oil spots on the garage floor or driveway, check all fluid levels immediately—even if you still have a half tank of gas. If you have to add oil, fluid, or antifreeze at every fill-up or between fill-ups, a seal or gasket is probably leaking and should be fixed right away. Chapter 9: *Troubleshooting* will help you identify the source of the leak; then turn to the appropriate procedure to repair it.

Another Remark: There are three good reasons for filling the tank when you get gas instead of just adding a few gallons: (1) Water condenses in the empty part of the tank when the air temperature changes. The water can rust the tank and dilute the gasoline, causing the engine to run poorly. The fuller the tank, the less area there is for condensation. (2) Fill-ups provide a sensible interval, 200-300 miles, for checking things under the hood. (3) You can keep track of your gas mileage. Keeping track of gas mileage lets you know if something mechanical has changed, causing the gas mileage to get (usually) worse.

Step 1. Check Engine Oil Level.

Park on level ground with the engine OFF. Open the hood and prop it, then go to the right side of the car. The **engine dipstick** is at the top right rear of the engine on OHV models and at the top right front on OHC models.

The **differential and manual transmission dipstick** is on the right side about 8″ behind and slightly lower than the engine. Don't get the engine and differential dipsticks mixed up. (A friend of mine did and added three quarts of oil too many to the engine while checking the mysteriously unchanging differential dipstick!) On some '83 and '84 models with lots of accessories, like cruise control and power steering, you might need to remove the spare tire to locate the engine dipstick the first time. (It's kind of hidden below a black plastic thing.) Once you know for sure where it is, you can fish it out without removing the tire. Painting the end of the dipstick a bright color makes it easier to spot.

Dipsticks have a wire ring on the top for you to pull on. ('83-'84 Turbo models have a T-shaped rubber end.) Pull the dipstick out of its **tube** and wipe off the bottom end with a clean rag or paper towel. (A pant leg will do if you're wearing funky pants.) Stick the dipstick back into the dipstick tube as far as it will go. On the way in, don't brush it against anything dirty or you'll insert unneeded crud into your engine.

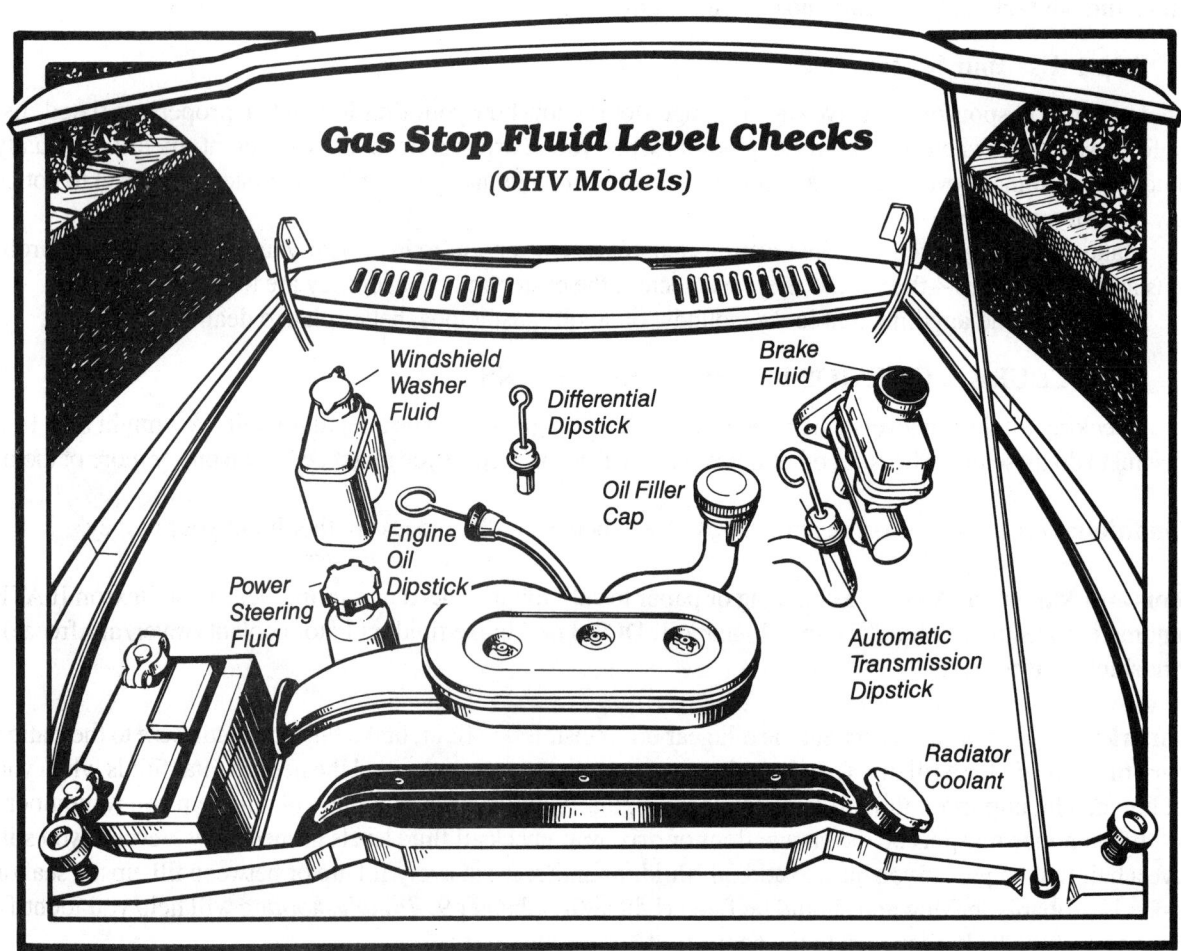

Pull out the dipstick again. The oil on the stick should stop somewhere between the two little holes in the dipstick. If the oil level is on or below the bottom hole, add one U.S. quart (0.95 liters) of oil. Use the same kind of oil you already have in your engine. After adding the quart, check the level again.

If the oil level is halfway between the two holes, add ½ quart and check the level again. Be careful not to add too much. If the oil is almost to the top hole, don't add any oil.

Oil is added to the engine through an **oil filler neck** that sticks up from the left rear side of the engine on OHV models and on the right front corner of the engine on OHC models. The oil neck has a **screw-type cap** that unscrews *counterclockwise*. Check the **gasket** that sits inside of the cap for cracks. Buy a new gasket if it's broken.

Procedure 2, Step 2   *Maintenance, Lubrication, Tune-up*   77

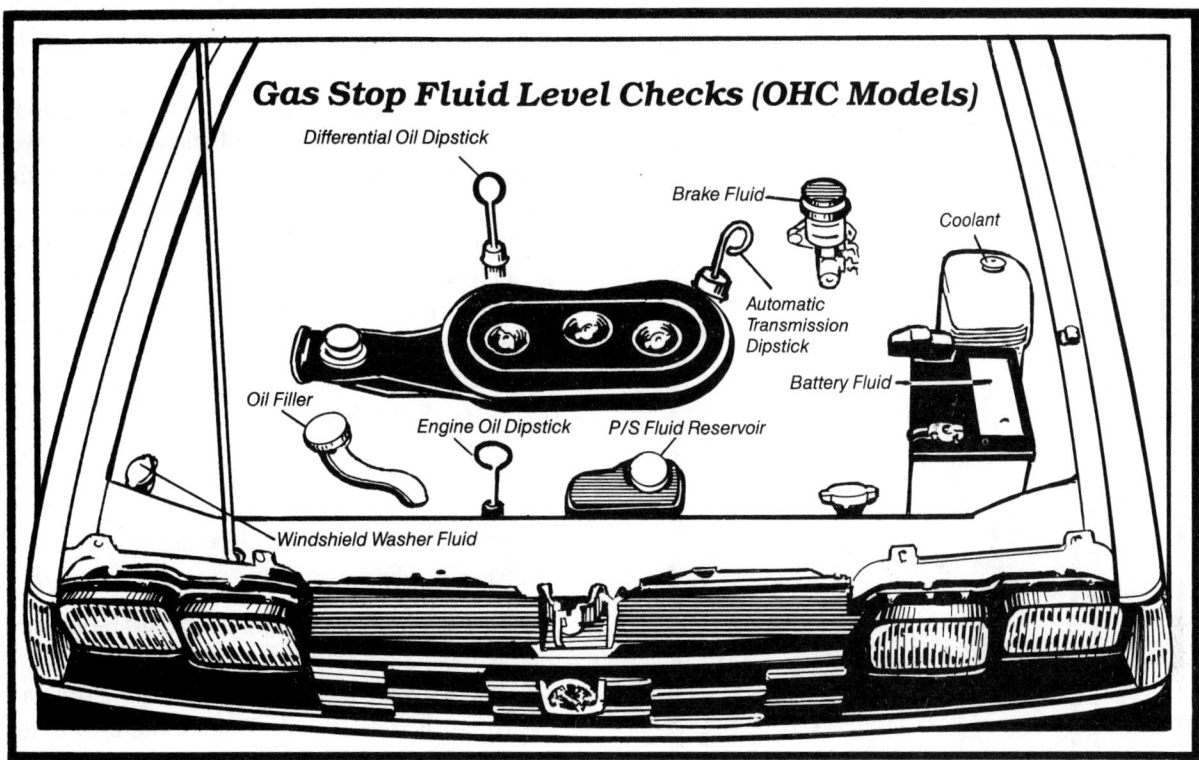

Milky-looking goo inside the oil filler cap means there's some water inside the engine where it shouldn't be. Water condenses inside the engine because of temperature changes. If you drive five to ten continuous miles every day or so, the moisture boils off and won't cause corrosion problems. Just driving around the block once or twice a week doesn't allow the engine to warm up enough to boil the water out of the oil. If you notice the milky goo even after a long drive, you should look in Chapter 9 for other symptoms of a leaking head gasket.

Step 2. Check Manual Transmission and Differential Oil.

The dipstick you'll find about 8" behind the right side of the engine is for checking the transmission and differential oil in cars with manual shift transmissions. It's only the differential oil dipstick for cars with automatic transmissions. Step 3 tells you how to check the automatic transmission fluid level.

Be sure you're parked on level ground and the engine is OFF. On some late models you'll need to remove the spare tire in order to reach the dipstick. Pull out the dipstick and wipe it off. Stick it back into

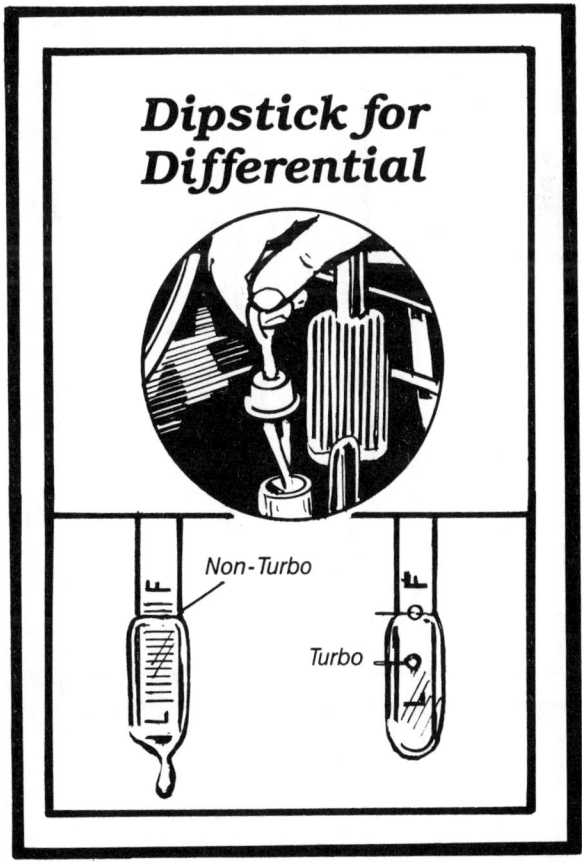

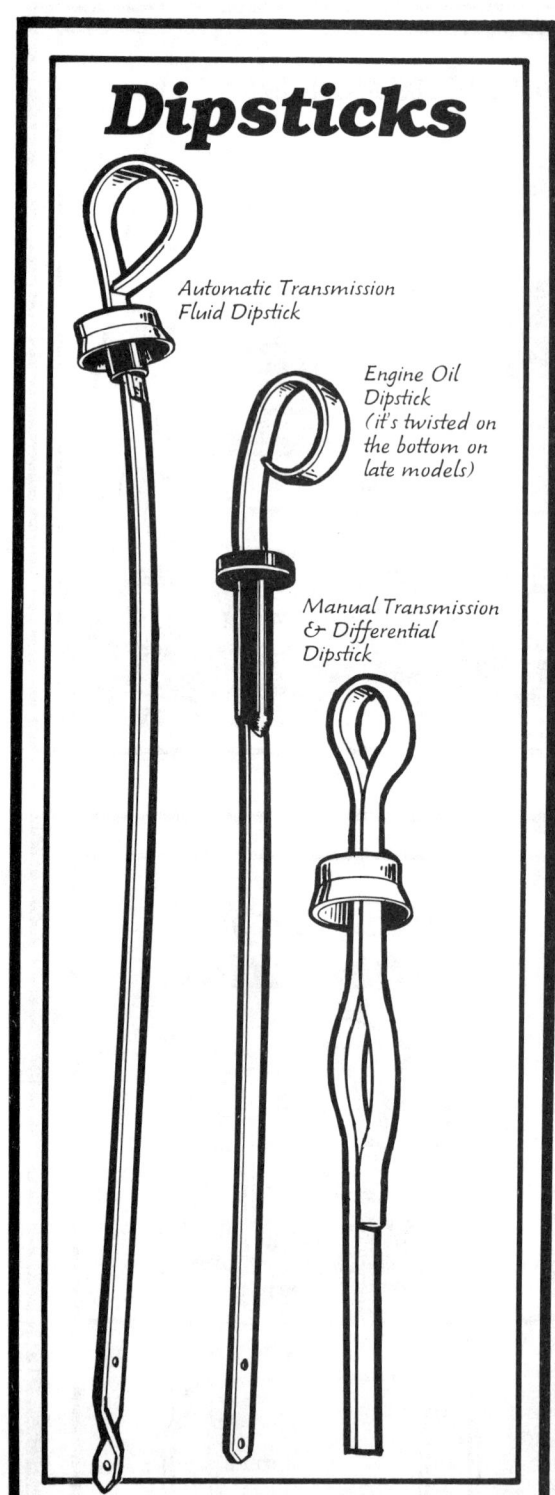

Dipsticks

Automatic Transmission Fluid Dipstick

Engine Oil Dipstick (it's twisted on the bottom on late models)

Manual Transmission & Differential Dipstick

the tube all the way, then pull it out and look at it. The dipstick has lines on it and an F, indicating the full level. A heavy line about eight lines down from the F line indicates ½ quart low. On '86 and newer Turbo models there are two holes near the bottom end of the stick. The top hole is the full mark and the lower hole is the ½ quart mark. If the oil level is below the heavy line or lower hole, add ½ quart of gear oil through the differential dipstick tube. You'll have to use a funnel to get the oil in if you're not using oil that comes in a pointed container (like Castrol). Check the oil level again. Add oil until the level is between the F mark and the heavy line. Be careful not to overfill it. Check the chart to see what grade oil to use.

If you don't have an automatic transmission, go on to Step 4.

Step 3. Check Automatic Transmission Fluid (ATF).

For this check, the transmission must be warmed up. Driving about five to ten miles will do it. Park on level ground, leave the engine running (or start it if you turned it off to do Steps 1 and 2). Put the handbrake ON and the gearshift lever in the PARK position. Find the **transmission fluid dipstick** located on the driver's side in the rear of the engine compartment near the **brake master cylinder**. Pull out the dipstick, wipe it off, put it all the way back in, then pull it out again. The level should be between the two little holes in the dipstick. The difference between the two holes is a little less than ½ quart. If the fluid is low, use a funnel to add a little **Dexron** ('75-'84 models), or **Dexron II** ('85 and newer models) transmission fluid through the dipstick tube, then check the level again. Be careful not to overfill it because too much fluid could cause a transmission seal to break. After checking for the last time, you can turn the engine OFF.

Step 4. Check Power Steering Fluid.

If you don't have power steering, go on to Step 5. Power steering fluid should be checked after the car has been driven a few miles to warm up the fluid. Check the level with the engine OFF. The **fluid reservoir** is a bulbous-looking black thing. On OHV models (except Turbos), it's on the right side of the engine, just behind the air cleaner. On '83-'84 Turbo models and OHC models, it's at the top front and center of the engine. Unscrew the reservoir cap *counterclockwise*. The dipstick is attached to the bottom of the cap. Wipe the little dipstick off and screw the cap back on. Remove it again and check the level. The fluid level should be somewhere on the lines above the arrow that points up from the word HOT. If the level is low, add about a teaspoon of Dexron II ATF. Then check the level again. Be careful not to overfill it.

Step 5. Check Drive Belt (fan belt, V-belt).

CAUTION: Be sure the engine is turned off!

A **drive belt** looks like a long piece of black licorice wrapped around some pulleys on the front of the engine. Soobs with air conditioning (A/C), and all '83-'84 Turbo models will have two drive belts. OHV non-Turbo models with A/C and power steering (P/S) will have three drive belts. OHC models will have one or two drive belts.

Put a finger on each drive belt about halfway between two of the pulleys and give a little push. If the belt moves more than ½" inward, it needs to be tightened. Replace the drive belt with a new one if it has cracks or frayed edges. Check both sides of all the belts. Drive belt too loose or worn out? See Chapter 10, Procedure 3, Step 1 to adjust or replace the drive belt(s).

Step 6. Check Brake Fluid Level.

Sticking out on the rear wall of the engine compartment, right in front of the driver's seat, is the **brake master cylinder**. '75-'82 Soobs have two small white plastic **brake fluid reservoirs** mounted on top of the master cylinder. On '83 and newer models, there is a single white plastic reservoir a little larger than a fist. Look for two lines on the side of the plastic reservoir(s) marked **MIN** and **MAX**. The brake fluid level in the container(s) should be somewhere between the two lines. You can see the fluid through the semi-translucent plastic.

If the level is low, wipe off the reservoir cap before removing it, then add fresh **DOT 3 or 4 brake fluid** until the level reaches the MAX line. Pour the fluid carefully and wipe up any drips—it's corrosive to paint.

Check both reservoirs if you have two. Be careful not to get dirt in the reservoirs—dirt plays hell with the little rubber seals inside. If brake fluid has to be added more than every six months, you probably have a leak in the hydraulic brake system. Chapter 13 covers brake diagnosis and repair.

Step 7. Check Windshield Washer Fluid.

Tucked somewhere in the engine compartment you will find a large (1-2 quart) white plastic container for the windshield washer fluid. On earlier OHV models, it will be in the rear corner on the driver's side, and on later OHV models, it's toward the rear on the passenger's side. On OHC models, it's tucked in the right front corner and you have to peek through a vertical, oval slot in the body to check the level. Don't confuse it with the smaller brake fluid reservoirs (look at the illustrations). Add **windshield washer fluid** and/or water when more than ¼ of the fluid is gone. Don't add plain water if you live where there's a chance it might freeze. Don't use engine antifreeze either because it will damage the car's paint.

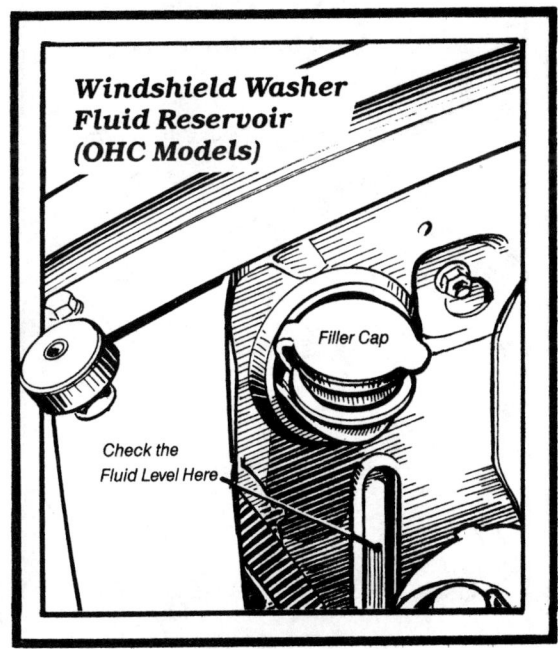

Chapter 7 Procedure 2, Step 8

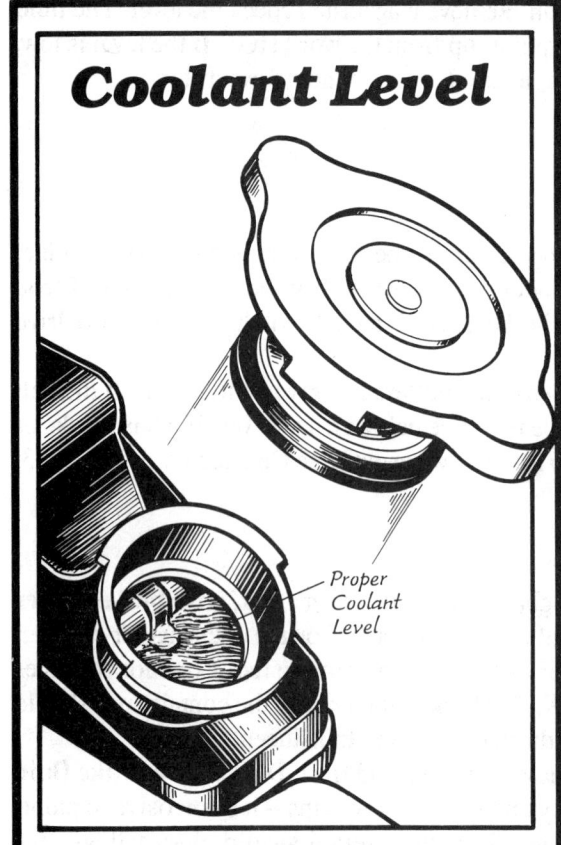

Coolant Level — Proper Coolant Level

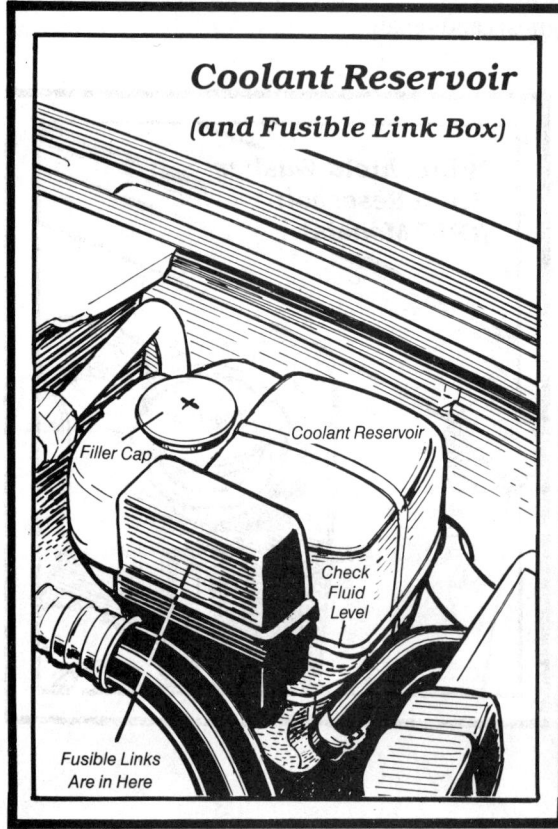

Coolant Reservoir (and Fusible Link Box) — Filler Cap, Coolant Reservoir, Check Fluid Level, Fusible Links Are in Here

Step 8. Check Radiator Coolant Level.

CAUTION: DON'T remove the radiator cap if the engine is hot. Wait until the engine has been off at least 5 minutes, then proceed with caution.

OHV models: The **radiator** is that big, black, flat, square thing in front of the engine. The **radiator cap** is on the top left (driver's) side of the radiator. If your radiator cap has a black button on it, push on the button before unscrewing the cap. Or, if your cap has a pop-top looking lever on it, lift the lever before you unscrew the cap. The button and lever are there to release pressure inside the cooling system before the cap is removed. No button or lever? Put a rag over the radiator cap before removing it.

To remove the cap, push down on it while you slowly unscrew the cap *counterclockwise*. If you hear a hissing sound, stop turning the cap until the hiss goes away, then slowly turn the cap a little more. The hiss means there's pressure inside the radiator and if you remove the cap suddenly, boiling hot coolant will shoot out of the radiator. Scary!

Once you have the cap off, look down inside the radiator. There's a little **horizontal metal plate** about 2″ below the opening. If the fluid level is below the plate, add coolant (water and antifreeze) until the fluid level reaches the plate. If the fluid level is up to the plate, the level is OK.

OHC models: A white translucent **coolant reservoir tank** is mounted to the inside of the left front fender. A rubber hose connects the tank to the radiator, just below the radiator cap.

To check the coolant level, locate two lines on the sides of the tank. The FULL line is in about the middle of the tank and the LOW line is near the bottom. You should be able to see the fluid level through the plastic. If the fluid level is between the two lines, don't add any coolant. If the level is below the LOW line and there's still some fluid in the tank, add coolant until it reaches the full line.

If the tank is empty, wait until the engine is cool, then follow the directions for OHV models above to carefully remove the radiator cap and check the coolant level in the radiator. Fill the radiator completely with coolant, install the radiator cap, then add coolant to the reservoir tank until it reaches the FULL line.

EVERYONE: If you have to add coolant at every gas stop check, there must be a leak in the cooling

Procedure 2, Step 9   *Maintenance, Lubrication, Tune-up*   **81**

system somewhere. Chapter 16 covers cooling system diagnosis and repair. It also has my rap on the ingredients of a good coolant.

Step 9. Check Tires.

Eyeball the tires. Check them with your **tire gauge** if they look low (Procedure 4, Step 2). If you have to add air to one or more tires at every fill-up, you have a slow leak that could become a fast one very suddenly. Get it fixed right away.

Step 10. Check DOJ and CVJ Boots.

Here's a five-second check that could save you hundreds of dollars! If a DOJ or CVJ boot breaks, it's no big deal as long as it gets replaced right away. A new boot, grease, and clamps cost around $20. However, if you don't notice that a boot has broken and you drive a few hundred miles, the grease gets slung out of the joint and dirt and crud gets in, which wears the joint out quickly. New DOJs cost around $100 and new CVJ/axle assemblies are almost $200 now. So it pays to check the boots every few hundred miles.

On most models you can see the black wavy rubber DOJ boots by looking down through the rear of the engine compartment. To check the CVJ boots and DOJ boots that you can't see from the top, kneel down in front of the car and look for the black rubber CVJ boots at the inside center of each wheel and DOJ boots at the inboard ends of the front axles. If any boots are torn, Chapter 15, Procedures 4, 5, and 6 tell you how to replace them. OK, that finishes the gas stop checks. Make a note to take care of anything you weren't able to deal with. After you've done these checks a few times, they'll only take a couple of minutes.

PROCEDURE 3: OIL AND FILTER CHANGE

This is the most basic of maintenance procedures and ESSENTIAL to long life for your vehicle. If this is your first time through, you may find it a little messy, but basically simple.

Also every 3-6,000 miles there are a series of checks and a rub-down that will keep your Soob lookin' good and running great. These are all in Procedure 4: Minor Massage.

Condition: 3,000 miles of severe use; OR 6,000 miles of normal use; OR it's been 300 miles since you rebuilt the engine; OR the TV is broken and you're looking for something to do.

Tools and Materials: Five quarts of oil (six quarts for 2700cc engines), new oil filter, new drain plug washer, a pan to catch the oil in, oil filter removal wrench, 17mm socket and ratchet or 17mm box end wrench, oil can spout or "church key," plastic containers to put the oil in for disposal, lots of rags or paper towels, a few old newspapers, safety goggles. *Optional*: rubber glove(s).

No filter wrench? Then you might need a long screwdriver, hammer, 10mm and 12mm wrenches, and patience.

Remarks: Something to lie on, like a large cardboard box flattened out or a sheet of plastic or garbage bag, isn't absolutely necessary, but it sure makes changing the oil a lot more comfortable. A rubber glove (white with sequins?) to wear while removing the drain plug is optional. The oil drain plug and oil might be warm, even hot, but not hot enough to give you a first degree burn.

Plastic oil drain pans are very cheap these days and they're also useful for cleaning parts in during repair procedures.

If the top or bottom of the engine and transmission are dirty or greasy, you can do yourself a real favor by first driving down to the car wash and hosing the crud off. (Procedure 5, Step 2, tells you what things to bring along in case the engine won't start immediately after its bath.) It is best, in any event, not to do this procedure in your new Calvin Kleins.

The oil will drain quicker, and more inner crud will flow out with it, if the engine is warmed up to normal operating temperature first. While draining the oil, be careful and don't accidentally grab one of those hot exhaust pipes on the bottom sides of the engine.

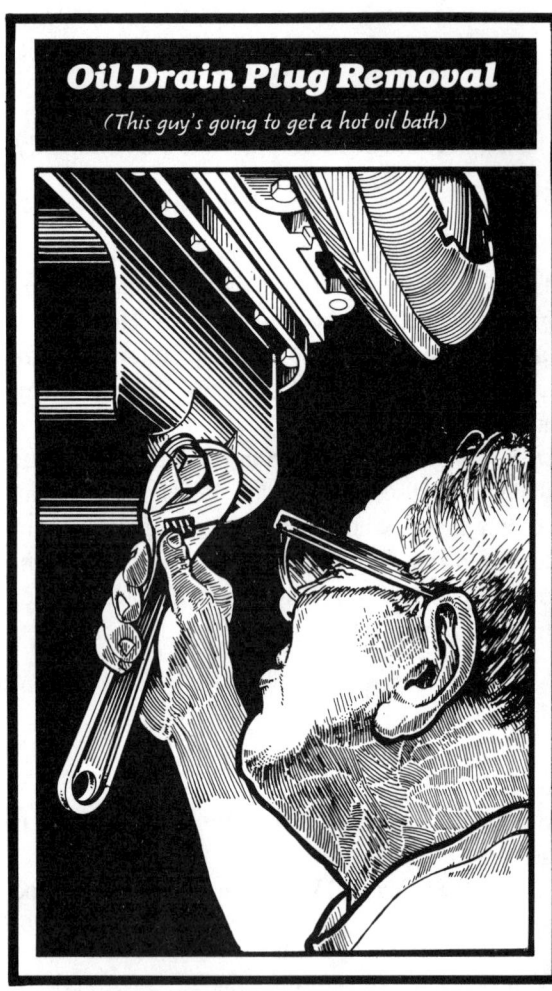

Oil Drain Plug Removal
(This guy's going to get a hot oil bath)

When you buy a new filter, check carefully that it's the right one for your car. It's a real disappointment, and an awful inconvenience, to discover that the new one won't fit once the old one is off the car.

It's also a good idea to be sure you can loosen the filter *before* draining the engine oil.

If you have a 4WD model, removing the skid plate makes the oil drain plug easier to get to. Most skid plates are attached with four or five 12mm bolts and are easy to remove and install. Some other skid plates consist of a large, flat sheet of heavy metal that nearly covers the entire bottom front of the car and is attached with 5.5mm allen head screws. If you don't have the correct allen wrench, try removing the screws with large pliers or Vise Grips. Unless you do a lot of off-road driving, you might want to leave the heavy skid plate off permanently.

Step 1. Drain the Oil.

Warm up the engine and park the car on level ground. No level ground? Then park so the front of the car is slightly higher than the back. Turn the engine off, set the handbrake, and block the two rear wheels so the car can't roll. Spread newspapers under the engine to catch stray drops of oil, then spread out a ground cover (cardboard, plastic, whatever) for yourself. Slide the **oil drain pan** under the engine. Put on your **safety goggles**, grab a rag or two, and crawl on your back under the front of the car with a 17mm socket and ratchet or a 17mm box end wrench. You'll have to use a box end wrench on 4WD models with skid plates.

The engine's oil pan is the black, bulbous-looking thing that covers the bottom of the engine. The oil drain plug is on the bottom of the pan. On 4WD models with a skid plate, there's a hole in the plate so you can get to the drain plug. It's more time consuming, but less messy, to remove the skid plate before draining the oil.

Put on your rubber glove (if you have one), then loosen the **drain plug** *counterclockwise* with the 17mm wrench. Remember, the oil that's about to come gushing out might be hot, so be ready to move your hand quickly. Don't worry if the plug and washer fall into the drain pan—you can fish them out after the oil cools off. When the drain plug first comes out, the oil will shoot toward the outside of the car. Locate the drain pan accordingly, then move the pan as the stream of oil subsides and moves toward the center of the car. On 4WD models, the oil will splash on the skid plate and drip from several places. If the plug and washer didn't fall into the pan, wipe them off with a rag and put them on the paper in a place where they won't get dirty or lost.

Step 2. Remove the Oil Filter.

When the oil coming out of the engine has slowed to a dribble, slide the drain pan to the front of the engine. Put a rag beneath the engine drain hole while you change the **oil filter**.

The oil filter is on the bottom front of the engine. It looks like an oil can that's gone to Weight Watchers for a while. Wipe the filter off with a rag so it won't be so slippery. Try loosening it with both hands.

OHV models: Turn the filter *counterclockwise* as viewed from the left side of the car (the front of the filter should turn toward the ground).

OHC models: Turn the filter *counterclockwise* as viewed from the right side of the car (the front of the filter should move up toward the top of the engine).

EVERYONE: Be sure you're turning it the right way. Keep your hand on the filter as it loosens up and starts to come off. If it falls off, it'll make a big mess. When the filter is off, pour the oil remaining in the filter into the drain pan. Toss the old filter in the trash.

If the filter won't turn, use an oil filter removal wrench if you have one (they sure make it easy). On Turbo models, be careful not to bend the two metal oil lines near the oil filter.

If the filter just won't budge, and you don't have a filter wrench, here's an old Jedi trick that works every time. It's very messy though. Be SURE you have the correct new filter with you. Get under the car and remove the four 10mm bolts that attach a metal plate to the car body directly below the oil filter on some early two wheel drive models, or the skid plate on four wheel drives (see Remarks). Stash the bolts where you'll find them. Next, take a long screwdriver and put the blade on the front of the filter, at least an inch away from where the filter screws onto the engine (watch out for those oil lines on Turbo models). Now drive the screwdriver clear through—

yes, through—the center of the filter with a hammer. This destroys the filter, but you're here to install the new one anyway. Now pull down on the screwdriver handle (OHV models) or push up on the handle (OHC models) and watch the filter loosen up. You may have to make two thrusts through the filter before you can unscrew it by hand. Sure is messy. Makes you want to run out and buy a filter removal wrench, doesn't it? Empty the filter into the drain pan, then wrap it in paper and toss it in the trash.

Step 3. Install the New Filter.

Use a clean rag or paper towel to carefully clean the **mounting surface** on the engine where the filter sits. Remove the **rubber seal** that went with the old oil filter if it's stuck on the engine. Take off the protective plastic cap from the new filter, if it has one. Now squirt a little oil on the new rubber sealing ring and spread it around with a clean finger. If you don't have an oil squirt can, just open one of the cans of fresh motor oil and use some of that.

Screw the new filter *clockwise* onto the threaded pipe on the engine. Be careful that no dirt gets into the filter or on the sealing ring. The filter should go all the way on just by turning it with your hand. If it's hard to twist after the first turn, unscrew it and try again. Don't force it. When you're sure it's going on straight, tighten it with your hand until the rubber sealing ring barely touches the smooth mounting surface on the engine. Now follow the directions that came with the filter and tighten it. No directions? Tighten it another ¾ turn with your hand. Don't use the filter removal wrench to tighten it. If the filter gets overtightened the rubber seal will break.

Put oil on the rubber ring before installing the Oil Filter.

Oil Pump

Oil Filter

Oil Filter Removal Wrench

Step 4. Put in Oil Drain Plug.

Find the oil drain plug (you might have to fish it out of the drain pan) and clean it off with a rag. Remove the old **washer** and install a new one. The old washer can be used again in a pinch if it isn't cracked or bent. Check the drain plug for stripped or flattened threads or rounded corners on the head. If it's getting funky, make a note to get a new one before the next oil change.

Plug and washer OK? Be sure there's a washer on the plug, then screw the plug *clockwise* into the oil pan. Use the 17mm wrench to get it good and snug but not so tight you won't be able to get it off the next time.

Install the metal plate and/or the skid plate if they were removed in Step 2.

Pull the newspapers, drain pan, tools, cardboard and yourself out from under the front of the vehicle.

Step 5. Refill Crankcase with Oil.

The oil capacity of Subaru engines is 3.7 quarts for 1600cc engines, 4.2 quarts for 1800cc engines, and 5.3 quarts for 2700cc engines. If you aren't sure which engine you have, look it up in the Numbers section of Chapter 2: *Orientation*.

Open the hood. The **oil filler cap** is on the top left (driver's side) rear corner of the engine on OHV models and on the top right front corner of the engine on OHC models. Wipe the cap off with a rag, then unscrew it *counterclockwise*. Wipe off the top of the appropriate number of cans then open one with your oil spout. No oil spout? Use a clean screwdriver or "church key" to poke holes on opposite sides of the top. (For you youngsters, a church key is what we called beer can openers before pop tops were invented.) Wrap a rag around the oil filler tube, just in case you miss the hole. It does take a little finesse to avoid dribbling oil on the engine. Are you sure you installed the drain plug?

Pour in 3½ cans (five for 2700cc engines), wait a few minutes, then pull out the oil dipstick. Wipe it clean, stick it all the way in, pull it out again, and check the oil level on the dipstick. Add oil a little at a time until it reaches the top hole on the dipstick. You'll have to look closely because it's hard to see clean fresh oil on the stick. Tilt the stick from side to side, and look for the reflection off the oil's shiny surface.

Screw on the oil filler cap, start the engine and let it run a few minutes. Turn the engine off, then check the oil level again. Since the new oil filter starts out empty, the level should have dropped about ½ quart. Add more oil until it reaches the top hole on the dipstick. Be careful not to add too much. Check the drain plug and oil filter for signs of a leak. A leaky filter or drain plug can quickly become a disaster.

Leftover oil can be stored in a clean plastic screw-top container and stashed in the trunk. If you don't want to carry oil with you, or don't have a plastic jug, put a plastic baggie over the top of the can and secure it with a rubber band, or use the plastic top from a one pound coffee can to keep dust and dirt out of the oil. Stash it where kids can't get to it.

Step 6. Clean Up.

Pour the used motor oil into the containers the new oil came in, if they are the plastic screw top type. Or use a plastic water, milk, or antifreeze bottle. Some filling stations or recycling plants will accept used motor oil. If this isn't possible, put the capped bottle in the trash. Never pour used oil down the drain.

The next morning, or after a short drive, look again for oil leaks. If you didn't tighten the oil drain plug or the oil filter enough, there will be a little oil beneath them. Tighten them if need be. If a leak continues after tightening, it's probably due to a bunged-up drain plug washer or oil filter rubber ring.

Step 7. Keep a Record.

Clean your hands, then record the oil and filter change in the log at the end of this chapter.

You're finished with the oil change, so let's move right on to Procedure 4 and give the ol' Sooby Doo a nice massage. The sensuous beast just loves its massage.

PROCEDURE 4: MINOR MASSAGE

Condition: Same as Procedure 3: 6,000 normal miles; OR 3,000 severe miles since the last massage.

Tools and Materials: Friend, tire pressure gauge, light source, maybe a 10mm wrench, safety glasses, maybe some or all of the vital fluids for your Soob. You may also need: new air filter element, PCV filter ('80 and newer carb models), distilled water for the battery.

Remarks: Park on level ground, handbrake on, engine OFF, for these steps.

Step 1. Gas-stop Checks.

Now that you're in your funky clothes (if they weren't, they are now) and your hands are no longer virgin to the feel of oil, do those Gas Stop Fluid Level Checks you may have been skipping (Procedure 2).

Step 2. Check Tire Pressure.

Please read the blurb on Tires and Tire Pressure in the first part of this chapter, then come back here to check your tires.

For an accurate reading, check tire pressure when the tires are "cold" (have been sitting still for at least 15 minutes). The warmer the tire, the higher the pressure. If you're parked so one side of the car is facing a hot morning or evening sun and the other side is shaded, the tires on the sunny side might read 5-10 lbs. more than the shady side. Don't let air out to lower the pressure—wait until that side is shaded, then check the pressure again.

To check the pressure, unscrew the **dust cap** from the tip of the **valve stem** (that little black rubber thing sticking out of the edge of the metal wheel). If there's no cap, it's not serious, but make a note to get one. Press your tire gauge firmly over the end of the valve and wiggle the gauge around a little until no air escapes. In other words, no hiss. Read the gauge, making sure you get the number right. On some gauges each line counts for 2 psi (pounds per square inch) of air. Pull the gauge off quickly and screw the dust cap back on. Check the air pressure in each tire, including the spare. If you have a T-type spare tire (the little skinny type), it should have about 60 psi. If you need air in one or more, truck on down and fill 'em up. If you've read my blurb on Tire Pressure, you know how much you want in each tire.

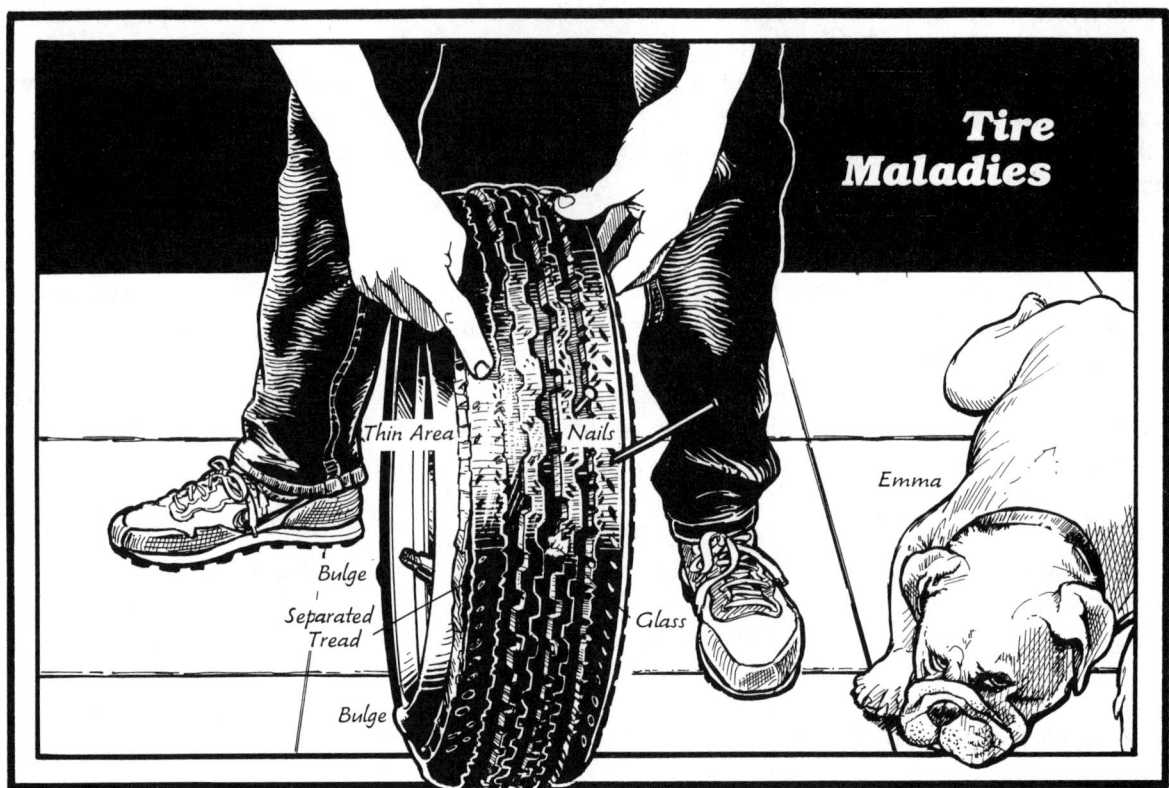

A loss of about 6 psi of pressure between gas stop checks means you have a slow leak that may turn into a fast one rather suddenly. It could be in the valve stem, the valve, the tire, or where the tire seals along the rim of the wheel. Get it fixed. A high speed blowout can kill you dead.

While you're checking the tire pressure, examine each tire's sidewalls and treads for cuts, lumps, nails, chunks of glass, armadillo parts, or anything (other than dirt or leaves) that isn't rubber. Is the tread getting a little thin?

If your tires start wearing more on the inner and outer edges than in the center of the tread, they are underinflated. If they wear more in the center of the tread than on the edges, they are overinflated. Adjust the tire pressure accordingly.

Rapid wear or scalloped-looking wear spots along the outer edge means some suspension parts are worn out or the front end is out of alignment. See Chapter 14 to check the suspension parts, then have the front end aligned by Subaru or an alignment shop.

Random spots of excessive wear on the tread indicate that the tire needs to be balanced, or the tire is defective. Have the tires checked and balanced by Subaru or an alignment shop.

Step 3. Check Air Filter.

CAUTION: When the air cleaner is open or off the engine, be very careful not to drop anything into the carburetor (carb models), or air filter housing, aluminum housing, or large rubber hose (fuel injected models). If something accidentally falls in, don't slash your throat, just be sure and fish it out before starting the engine.

Carburetor models: The air cleaner is that large, blue or black, flat thing sitting on top of the engine. The parts of the air cleaner are the **top** (or lid), a pleated paper **air filter element**, the larger bottom part called the **air filter housing**, and a **snout** that sticks out the right (passenger's) side of the housing. In 1980 the shape of the air cleaner changed from round to peanut shaped. First, take the lid off the housing.

'75-'79 carb models: Lift up on the bottom of the four clips located around the outer top edge of the air cleaner.

'80 and newer carb models: Unscrew the three wing nuts on the top of the air cleaner.

ALL carb models: Now you can lift the lid off the top of the housing. The pleated paper **air filter element** is inside, and it lifts right out too.

Fuel injected models: The air filter is inside a rectangular **air filter housing** located near the right (passenger's side) front corner of the engine compartment. A large round black rubber hose connects a squarish aluminum housing (the *airflow metering assembly*) to something on the engine (the *blower inlet elbow* on Turbo models, or the *throttle body* on non-Turbo fuel injected engines).

To check the filter, lift up on the bottom tab of the spring clips that attach the upper half of the air filter housing to the bottom half. Raise the upper half far enough to remove the rectangular, pleated **air filter element** from the housing. Note which side of the filter is TOP so you can install it the same way.

If you have difficulty raising the housing, use a screwdriver to loosen the large hose clamp that secures the large black hose to the housing. Slide the clamp farther onto the hose, then carefully pull the hose off the connection.

EVERYONE: Tap the filter element gently against a tire or your leg to remove any loose dirt. Now lift the filter element up to an unshaded light bulb or nuclear blast, whichever is handiest, and look through the paper pleats. Look for dark areas, indicating dirt or grime, and pinholes of light. The filter should be replaced if you see any holes or cracks in the paper pleats, or if the pleats are clogged with oil or dirt. Don't try to wash the filter because it's coated with a special viscous liquid that traps dirt. Washing removes the coating.

'80 and newer carb models: Look inside the oval air cleaner housing. On the rear corner closest to the driver's seat there's a small white PCV filter.

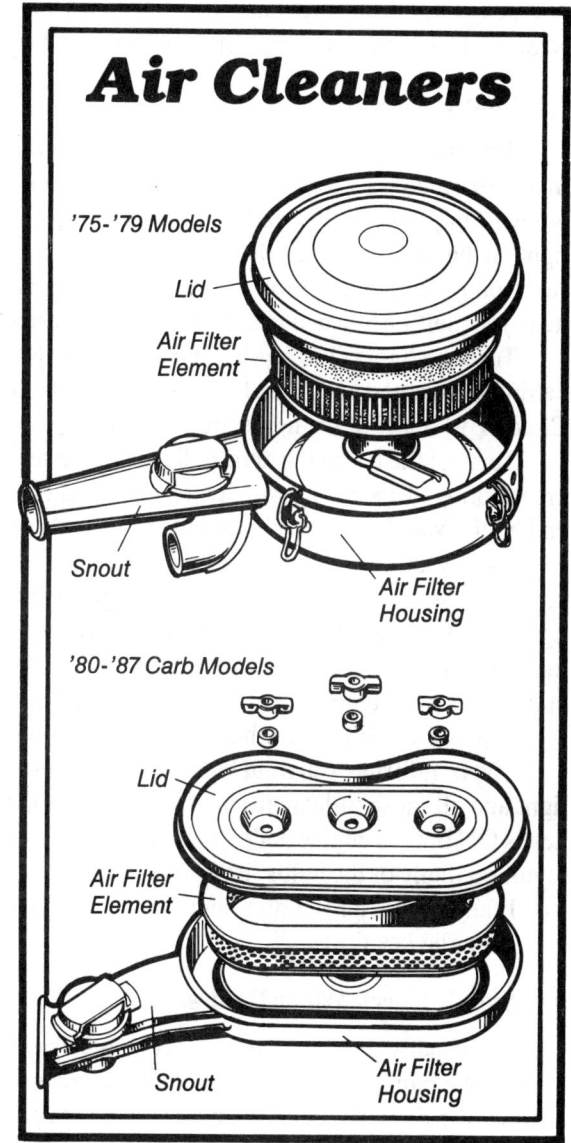

Air Cleaners

Pull up on the corners of the filter to remove it. If the filter is oily or dirty, use a spray can of carb cleaner to clean it or replace it with a new one. Wiggle the PCV filter down into the holder to install it.

EVERYONE: Wipe out the inside of the air cleaner housing with a clean rag. Set the pleated air filter on the rubber sealing ring. Is the lid clean too? OK, put it back on top of the air filter element. Depending on your model, install the wing nuts or clamp the lid with the spring clips.

Fuel injected models: If you disconnected the large rubber hose, carefully slip it onto its fitting on the aluminum housing. Run your finger all the way around the end of the rubber hose to be sure it's on properly and isn't kinked or cracked. Slide the large clamp into its groove on the end of the hose and tighten it with a screwdriver or 10mm wrench. Get it good and tight (the engine won't run if there's an air leak).

Step 4. Check Lights.

Turn the key to ON, but don't start the engine. Switch the headlights ON, set the handbrake, put the transmission in reverse, then walk around the car and see if the headlights, taillights, rear license plate light, and backup lights are working. Switch the headlights from low to high beam and check them again. Is the **high beam indicator** light on the dash working? Do the headlights burn equally bright on high beam? If not, the dim one's high beam function is kaput. Check the Third Eye (passing lamp) on some 4WD models. The switch is on the dashboard near your left knee when you're in the driver's seat. If you need to replace a light, refer to Chapter 10.

Turn the lights OFF but leave the key ON. Have Friend get in and pump the brake pedal while you stand behind the car and check the **brake lights**. Brake lights are very important and should be fixed right away. See Chapter 10 if any of the lights aren't working.

Turn on the **hazard warning light switch** and walk around the vehicle to see if all four turn signal lights are working. Turn the hazard switch OFF and check the left and right **turn signals**. Are they blinking, front and back? Watch the turn signal indicator lights on the dash, too, to be sure they're working.

To check the **dashboard lights**, set the headlight switch to the first position (parking lights). Most models have a rheostat so you can dim the dash lights (so they won't keep you awake while you're driving?). Turn the light switch *counterclockwise* to turn the lights up all the way (on '80 and newer OHV cars, and '82-'87 Brats, the brightness is controlled by a smaller knob on the end of the headlight knob). Shade the dash or do this check at night so you can tell if any bulbs are burned out. Turn the lights OFF.

If you have 4WD, shift the lever into 4WD to be sure the light on the dash warns you that you are in 4WD.

The **handbrake warning light** should come on when you pull up on the handbrake lever. The oil and charge light and all those little pictures in the "Telltale Graphic Monitor" on later models should be on anytime the key is ON but the engine isn't. (It's set up as an automatic check, but you have to tune your head to the display to notice if any of the bulbs have gone bad.)

If any of the lights didn't light up, look at Chapter 10.

Turn the key OFF.

Step 5. Check Wiper Blades.

You usually don't realize you need new wiper blades until you're late for an appointment and caught in the middle of a thunderstorm or blizzard. Then you notice the annoying blur or streak. Wiper blade refills are very cheap these days, so check them often and change them before they're so worn out they dangerously obscure vision or scratch the windshield. According to Murphy, of Murphy's Law fame, the blade on the driver's side always fails first. A good Boy Scout would probably always have a spare blade or two stashed in the trunk or engine compartment.

To check the blades, pull each wiper away from the windshield and feel along the sharp rubber edge for cracks, nicks, torn places, or limpness. If they pass this test, thoroughly clean the bugs off the glass, then use the windshield washer to squirt some water on the windshield. Now try the wipers to see if they leave streaks or miss some areas completely. Replace the blades if even a few streaks show up—a sign of impending failure. Don't forget to check the rear washer and wiper if you have one. Windshield washer doesn't work? See Chapter 10.

There have been so many different wiper blade styles over the years I can't specifically describe how to change them all. It's a simple operation once you see how it's done, so have the nice man at the parts store or an experienced friend show you how to change the blades the first time, if you can't figure it out.

Generically speaking, you usually squeeze the tabs on one end of the blade together, then pull the blade out of the wiper arm. Insert the rigid part of the new blade into the grooves on the wiper arm until the two prongs engage in the slots on the end of the wiper arm. That's it.

People who live where there's lots of (gasp) smog should check the wipers more frequently because smog attacks and quickly deteriorates rubber. The blades fall apart even if you never use them!

Step 6. Check Battery

CAUTION: Batteries give off a very explosive gas when the cells are open, so don't smoke anything while you check the battery. Don't connect or disconnect the battery cables while the cell caps are off. A spark could ignite the gas.

Wash your hands after touching anything on the battery. Touching your clothes right after handling battery parts will give them a religious experience—they'll become very holy the next time you wash them.

OHV models: The battery is located in the right front corner of the engine compartment.

OHC models: The battery is in the left front corner of the engine compartment.

EVERYONE: Put on your safety glasses, roll up your sleeves, and wipe off the top of the battery with an old rag so dirt can't fall into the battery cells. Throw the rag in the trash (don't use it on anything else) and wash your hands.

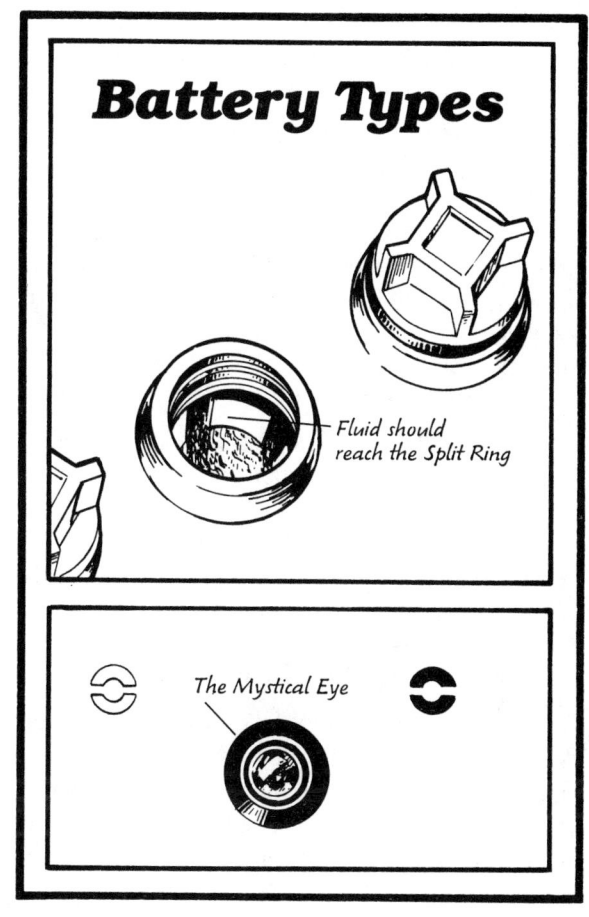

You have one of the four or so types of modern 12-volt batteries. Some have screw-on plastic caps (plugs), some use snap-off plugs that are often connected with two plastic bars, and some have broad, square plastic caps you have to pry off with a screwdriver. Some "maintenance-free" batteries have caps you can't remove. (Actually, on some maintenance-free batteries the filler caps are just hidden beneath the labels. You can peel back the labels and add distilled water if the level gets low.)

Unscrew the cell plugs in the top of the battery or pop the cell tops up carefully with a screwdriver, depending on battery style. Look into each hole. You should see a fluid in there. The fluid (*electrolyte*) level should be up to the level of the *split ring* (or about ¼" above the metal plates you can see down inside the battery). Check the level in each cell. If the electrolyte level is low, carefully add distilled water a little at a time, keeping your eyes well away from the top of the battery as you pour. A clean plastic funnel is helpful, but don't use a metal one. You can buy distilled water from a drugstore or grocery store. It's cheap. If none is available, use clean tap water, but don't make a habit of it. Do not add acid or any type of additive to your battery. It's dangerous and unnecessary. Don't overfill the cells. Install the cell caps, then wash your hands again.

If you have one of the new batteries with an *indicator light*, wipe off the sight glass and peer into the mystical eye. There should be something on the top of the battery that tells you what color the eye will be when the battery is fully charged or in need of a charge. Nothing on the battery? Generally the eye is blue if the battery is good. Red or white usually mean the battery needs a charge.

Check the **battery cables** where they attach to the two **terminal posts** on the battery. Wiggle each one with your hand to make sure they're on securely. Now look for corrosion at the cable ends. Is there white flaky stuff where the cables attach to the terminal posts? If the cables are loose, or there's corrosion on the terminals, look at Chapter 10, Procedure 1, to clean, then tighten the connections.

Always wash your hands after checking and/or servicing your battery. If any clothing touched the battery or cables, rinse it thoroughly in water right now. I'm serious about the religious experience mentioned at the beginning of this step. Most mechanics have a pair of Levis and T-shirt that are very holy.

Step 7. Check Front of Radiator for Trash.

Look through the grille to check the front of the radiator for leaves, sticks, paper, bugs, and Mopeds. If you see junk in there, remove the plastic grille (phillips head screws around the edges hold it on). Carefully brush the junk off the front of the radiator with a rag. The little vanes that make up the front of the radiator are very thin and fragile, so be gentle, darling. Screw the grille back on.

Step 8. Check Shock Absorbers.

Lower the hood if it's up, then bounce the car as hard and rapidly as you can by pushing down on a fender or bumper. It's especially effective if you step up on the bumper at each corner, and bounce the car with your full weight. Do this at all four corners of the car. If the car continues to bounce more than twice after you let go, the shocks are suspect. Look at Chapter 14, Procedure 1, for further shock absorber tests.

Step 9. Body Massage.

Rake out the beer cans, dirty diapers, and McDooDoo wrappers. Wash and wax the car, vacuum the interior, and clean the dash with a damp rag. Your Sooby will be so happy.

Step 10. Rotate Tires.

If 6,000 miles have passed beneath your Soob since the tires were rotated, look at Chapter 3, Procedure 1, and do it now.

Step 11. Clean Tape Heads.

Being a devout audiophile, I find it very irritating to try to listen to a tape deck with dirty playing heads. When the tape heads build up a layer of scum, the dynamic output range is narrowed considerably. Those brilliant high frequencies and low rolling bass lines disappear into a muddy sounding midrange. If the heads aren't cleaned and demagnetized occasionally, they start erasing high and low frequencies from the tape. After a tape is played on a dirty, magnetized tape head a few times, it will sound bad even on a good, clean tape deck. A dirty tape deck is much more likely to eat a tape (probably your favorite one) than a clean, well-maintained one. To protect your tapes, you have to keep your tape heads clean. Here's how.

You'll need: Long Q-tips and rubbing or denatured alcohol, and/or head cleaning and demagnetizing cassettes. You can order the cassettes from the address listed at the end of this step.

First, clean the heads with Q-tips and alcohol. Shine a flashlight into the **tape slot** and locate the head(s). You may have to hold the dust flap open with a finger. The head(s) will be either on a side or in the back, depending on where the exposed tape ends up when the cartridge is inserted in the slot. The heads look like tiny curved silver boxes with a couple of parallel lines across the surface. Dip a Q-tip in alcohol then rub it on the heads. Do this about three times. Clean all the levers and tape guides that you can reach with the Q-tip. Let the alcohol dry before playing a tape.

Second, demagnetize the heads. To demagnetize heads you need a rather expensive demagnetizing cartridge or wand, or a relatively inexpensive demagnetizing casette. You can also use the demagnetizer on your home stereo tape deck. Instructions for using the demagnetizer should come with it. If not, a stereo shop can tell you how to use it. If you only have a tape player in the car and don't want to spend the money for a demagnetizer, a car stereo shop will probably demagnetize the heads for a couple of bucks. It should be done at least once a year and more often if you use the tape deck a lot.

Although a good stereo system doesn't change the way your car looks or performs, it can make driving a lot more fun and can represent a significant investment of your hard earned cash. The only limit is the physical size of the stereo and your bank account; the combination of radios, tape decks, CD players, amplifiers, speakers, and so on, is almost endless. When buying a stereo system, the confusing part is how to rationally compare the features on comparably priced models. You need some cold hard facts and specifications that you can mull over while sitting by the fireplace instead of in a crowded showroom with several radios blasting and a hungry salesman breathing down your neck. Unfortunately, the choice is often made under these adverse conditions. I've walked out of several stereo stores suffering from total intellectual confusion.

Recently I've found a better way to shop for stereos. I highly recommend sending for the Crutchfield catalog listed at the end of this step. The catalog could qualify as a textbook about selecting and installing stereo systems because it explains what the different components do, which components will fit into your car without cutting any sheet metal, which ones require modification, which antenna to use, and most important, what all of those technical specifications mean. For example, which is best, a higher or lower number for the FM sensitivity rating of a radio? Answer: A lower number means the radio is more sensitive and will pick up weaker stations than one with a higher FM sensitivity rating! And at some time or other we've all wanted to know what "Wow and Flutter" really means. Crutchfield even has a toll free telephone hot line so you can call for help or advice.

I recommend getting the catalog and doing your homework about the specifications for the large number of brands and models they sell. You'll be able to narrow down the products that fit your needs and budget to a few makes and models. Then, if possible, go to your local stereo dealer to listen to those components and to compare the dealer's prices to those in the catalog. Go for the best deal.

The address is Crutchfield, 1 Crutchfield Park, Charlottesville, Virginia 22906. Or you can call (800) 336-5566 to order the free catalog.

Step 12. Record All Work in Log

Turn to the log at the end of this chapter and jot down the **date** and **mileage** for the procedures completed. Make notes about anything that still needs to be done or irregularities that need to be watched closely.

Have you remembered to install the drain plug and fill the engine with oil. More people than would admit it have forgotten to do this. Are the new filter and oil filler cap installed? Walk around the car with an eye to any loose ends or unfinished business.

OK, you're finished with the minor massage. I hope it was as good for you as it was for your Soob.

Step 13. Reward Yourself.

Depending on your slant on life—pour a stiff one, pop open a cool one, roll a fat one, chop a long one, chant a mantra, go for a jog, snuggle up to the mate and...whatever. The important thing here is to do something nice for yourself—you deserve it!

PROCEDURE 5: PREP FOR 12,000-MILE TUNE-UP, MAINTENANCE, AND MASSAGE

This procedure gets everything ready for you to launch into the tune-up activities (Procedures 6-13). There's nothing like doing a tune-up to give you a sense of mastery over the fate of your machine. Basically, you'll be refreshing and adjusting the engine. This means inspecting, replacing, and adjusting parts in the ignition system (distributor and spark plugs), checking internal condition of the engine, and adjusting the carburetor (on some models) for peak efficiency.

An oil and oil filter change is also part of the 12,000-mile maintenance, as are a few other checking, cleaning, and adjusting items which you'll find in Procedure 14, the 12,000-Mile Major Massage.

Condition: It's been 12,000 miles since the last tune-up; OR the engine isn't running like it should; OR you have an overwhelming urge to do some tinkering.

Tools and Materials: The first time you do this procedure all you need is a very small paint brush and a small bottle of white paint (model airplane paint will do).

The tools and materials required for the tune-up are listed at the beginning of each procedure. Read the conditions section of Procedures 6-13 to see which ones apply to your model. Make a list and round everything up the day before.

Remarks: Here's where you really start being a mechanic! Read through each procedure before you start. Take your time; do each step completely before moving on to the next. The first time through the 12,000-mile procedures could take most of a day. Take your time and enjoy it. After you've done it a few times and become familiar with the procedures, all of them will only take about 3 to 5 hours.

Remember, *right side* means the passenger's side and *left side* means the driver's side. *Rear* means toward the taillights, and *front* means toward the headlights. OK, let's do it.

Step 1. The Day Before.

Engine clean? If you want to make this a clean, warm, caring relationship, give the engine a bath. Step 2 will tell you what tools and materials to take to the car wash in case the engine won't start after its bath.

Round up all the parts you'll need for these procedures the day before you plan to do the work.

Park the car overnight at the spot where the operation will be performed because you can't start the engine before torquing the heads or adjusting the valves (not all models require this at every tune-up). And I've arranged the tune-up sequence so you do as many things as possible while the engine is cool.

Step 2. Wash Engine.

What's happening: Engine looks like it just crawled out of a sewer; OR you're trying to locate the source of an oil leak; Or you want to make the 12,000-mile maintenance a more pleasant experience.

You'll need: Several quarters, two large plastic bags (bread bags work well), tape or rubber bands, screwdriver, clean dry rags or paper towels, safety glasses, an old beach towel or blanket.

Remark: Unless you spring an oil leak or drive on a lot of muddy roads, you shouldn't have to wash the engine more than once a year. In fact, due to the sensitive, high-tech electronic gear, you shouldn't wash fuel injected engines until they get really dirty. Wear funky clothes to the car wash. To get the engine and transmission really clean top and bottom, you'll probably get covered with water, mud, and grease. Cover the seats with old towels or blankets to protect the upholstery from your wet, muddy body.

Once you're at the car wash, turn the engine OFF, open the hood and put a plastic bag over the **air intake snout** of the air cleaner on carb models (if there isn't a hose already connected to the end of the snout) and secure it with tape or rubber bands. If the spark plug wires are marked for position, pull them out of the distributor cap and cover the distributor with another plastic bag. Secure it with tape or rubber bands. If the wires aren't marked, cover the distributor as much as possible with a plastic bag and tape the edges together. Remove the spare tire if it's stored in the engine compartment.

Put on your safety goggles and use the water wand to wash the engine and transmission top and bottom, the engine compartment, inside the wheel wells, the rear differential (4WD), and all the suspension parts you can hit with the hot soapy water. Don't aim the high pressure nozzle directly at the alternator, distributor, or plastic electrical wire connectors. Rinse everything off with plain water, especially any grease and crud that got on the paint.

Remove the plastic bags and put the spare tire back in if you took it out. If you removed the spark plug wires, dry off the ends with a dry rag or paper towel and plug them into the distributor cap.

If the engine won't start after its bath, don't run the battery down trying to get it going. A little water is in the ignition system somewhere (usually the distributor). Remove the distributor cap (Procedure 9, Step 2) and thoroughly dry the inside of the cap and distributor with a clean, dry rag or paper towel. Some car washes have a hot air blower in or near the engine wash bay just for drying out the distributor. Install the cap with the notch on the edge of the cap fitting into the groove on the distributor. Snap the clips securely onto the cap or tighten the screws, depending on your setup. Dry the large and small wires connected to the coil. Presto, the engine should start. If it doesn't, check inside the distributor again. It doesn't take much water to short the electrical stuff in there and prevent the engine from starting.

Step 3. Remove Spare Tire (if it's in the engine compartment).

The day of the tune-up, park on a level surface, turn the engine OFF, and set the handbrake. Automatics in PARK. Open and prop the hood.

If you have already painted the timing marks on the flywheel, and you are not going to adjust the valves or check the ignition timing, you can skip down to Procedure 8 (OHC models) or Procedure 9 (OHV models).

If you need to paint the timing marks and/or you plan to adjust the valves and/or check the ignition timing, unscrew the large wing nut in the center of the wheel then remove the tire (and jack on '83-'84 Turbo models).

Step 4. Remove Air Cleaner (carb models only).

CAUTION: While removing the air cleaner (lid, filter, and housing) and once it's off, be very careful to not let ANYTHING fall into the opening of the carburetor! Cover it with a clean rag. If anything falls in there, be sure to fish it out before starting the engine.

The **air cleaner** is that big flat oval or round thing sitting on top of the engine. '75-'79 models have a *round* air cleaner, and '80-'87 carb models are *oval* (peanut-shaped). Remove the top of the air cleaner (Procedure 4, Step 3). Some late models have a black plastic **carburetor/distributor shield** snapped onto the front of the air cleaner. To unsnap the shield, grab it by the top corners and pull toward the front of the car until the shield pops out of the clips. Lift up to remove the shield.

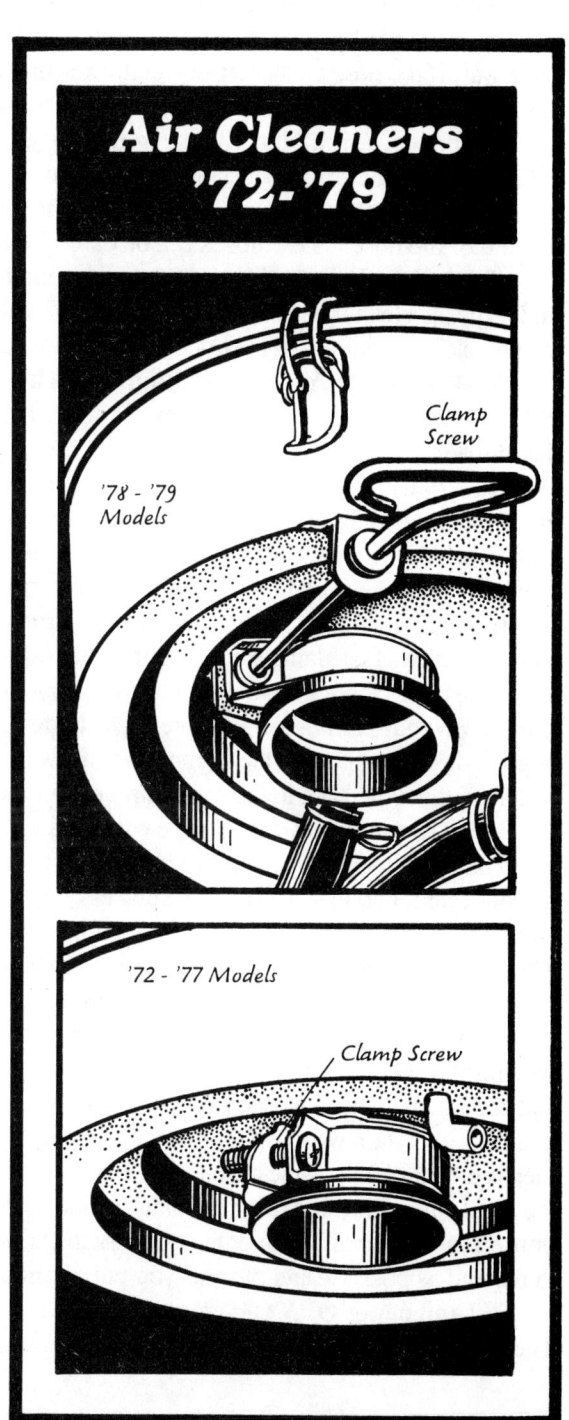

Attached to the bottom of the snoutlike air horn part of the air cleaner is a large, black or silver, flexible **hot air inlet hose**. To remove the hose, squeeze the two ears on the clamp and slide it down the hose. Grasp the hose as close to the air cleaner snout as possible and twist until it moves freely, then pull it off. It's fragile so squeeze gently. If the hose is torn or missing, make a note to get a new one.

'75-'79 models: Look on the right (passenger's) side of the air cleaner housing. There's a **black hose** about as big around as your thumb going from the bottom of the housing to the top of the valve cover on the right side of the engine. The hose might have a soft black rubber insulator around it, making it twice as thick as your thumb. Anyway, with one hand, squeeze the two metal ears of the hose clamp located near the *valve cover end* of the hose, then pull the hose off the valve cover with the other hand. Now look at the left side of the air cleaner housing. If there's **another hose** just like the one on the right side, disconnect it from the top of the left valve cover the same way. If the hose on the left side of the housing is short and goes to a black plastic **gizmo** with several other hoses connected to it, squeeze the clamp and disconnect it from the black plastic thing.

Disconnect a **small black hose** from the right rear of the air cleaner AND/OR a small hose coming out of the bottom of the air cleaner snout that connects either to the intake manifold or to a plastic T-fitting that connects it to two other hoses. Disconnect this hose at the manifold or T-fitting because it's difficult to get to the housing end of the hose. These hoses can be carefully twisted and pulled off.

'75 models: Is there still an **air pump** (a round thing about the same size and shape as the alternator) tucked under the air cleaner between the carburetor and alternator? If so, you'll need to disconnect the hose between the top of the air pump and the bottom of the air cleaner housing as you remove the housing from the carburetor.

'76-'79 models: You'll have a **thumb-size hose** on the left rear side of the housing that connects to a round little air injection muffler located about 3″ from the air cleaner. Squeeze the clamp and disconnect the hose from the muffler.

'75-'79 models: Remove the 10mm bolt on the left front side of the air cleaner housing, then gently lift up on the air cleaner to remove it. '75 models can now disconnect the hose to the air pump. Set the air cleaner in the back of the engine compartment where the spare tire goes, or take it out and put it on something clean. Don't lay it on the ground—it'll get dirty or stepped on.

If the air cleaner is stuck, stand on the right side of the car and look under the rear of the air cleaner for a clamp screw. The clamp screw secures the round clamp that holds the air cleaner to the top of the carburetor. Some have a thick wire sticking out with a loop on the end to turn. If you're not so lucky, there will be a phillips head screw that's almost impossible to see under the back of the air cleaner. Standing on your head helps. So might a flashlight. Loosen the clamp screw a few turns *counterclockwise*, then lift up on the air cleaner to remove it. Disconnect the hose to the air pump on '75 models.

If you're going to start the engine with the air cleaner off, like for a tune-up, use small phillips screwdrivers, small punches, pencils (break the lead off first), or tape to seal the ends of the small hoses (vacuum hoses) you disconnected, and in some cases the places on the engine where the small hoses were connected. (Don't worry about the larger thumb-size hose connections.) You can buy inexpensive rubber **vacuum line hose plug** sets. They're handy, but the substitute tools I suggested will do.

'80 and newer carb models: You have several hoses connected to the air cleaner, so keep track of the number of hoses you disconnect when removing the air cleaner. Write the number down and be sure they're all reconnected when you install the air cleaner. There are so many variations from model to model, depending on which engine and accessories you have, that I can't specifically describe each setup. Luckily the hoses are cut to precise lengths and bent in certain ways so they naturally end up right next to where they're supposed to connect when you set the air cleaner back on the carburetor. But you have to be sure you find and connect each hose when installing the air cleaner. The hose diagram on the inside of the hood will help (if you have one). Make your own diagram, or use a grease pencil, paint or tags to mark the hoses if you want. When removing the hoses grasp them as close to the end as possible and twist as you pull them off. Don't pull on the middle of the hoses.

'80 and newer OHV carb models: Look at the right rear corner of the air cleaner just behind the air snout. There will probably be two or three hoses laying in a bracket mounted to the corner of the air cleaner and another bracket on the air snout. Lift the hoses out of the brackets and push them away from the air cleaner. Disconnect the hose that goes from the air cleaner to the top of the right valve cover (it's about as big around as your thumb). Squeeze the ears of the clamp that's near the cleaner, and twist and pull the hose off. Right next to that connection there might be another thumb size hose to disconnect, and 1 to 3 pencil-size hoses. Some of the small hoses come out from underneath the air cleaner housing or snout so look carefully. It's easier to disconnect the small hoses from the engine end rather than from the air cleaner end. The small hoses don't have clamps, so grab them near the end and twist and pull them off.

On the front side of the housing near the air snout, there's probably a small hose that goes down to a gizmo on the engine. Pull and twist the hose off the gizmo. Some '82 and newer models also have another small hose connected to a tube on the bottom right front of the air cleaner. Pull the hose off the tube. Don't disconnect the hose going to the round thing on top of the air snout. It connects to the bottom of the air cleaner housing.

Move to the left rear side of the air cleaner. There should be a hose going from the air cleaner to a black plastic thing that has several other hoses connected to it. Squeeze the clamp and disconnect the hose from the air cleaner housing. '83 and newer models might also have a thumb-size hose to disconnect from the air cleaner housing. Check for other hoses that hook up to that side of the air cleaner. Find any? Label, then disconnect 'em.

OHC models: Find two thumb-size hoses on the left side of the housing. Squeeze the ends of the clamps together while you wiggle the hoses off the housing. There's a small round plastic thing with hoses attached to it near the left rear corner of the housing. Pop the small hoses for the little round thing out of the clip, then disconnect the medium size hose that's connected to the left rear side of the housing.

There's a small hose on the right front bottom of the housing to disconnect. There are two or three small hoses resting in clips on the rear side of the air cleaner snout. Don't disconnect the hoses, just remove them from the clip.

There are probably one or two thumb-size hoses on the right rear corner to disconnect. Look carefully for other hoses attached to the air cleaner hosing.

'80 and newer carb models: Now remove the 10mm bolts and washers on the left front and right rear corners of the air cleaner housing. Slowly lift the air cleaner off the carburetor while looking for any remaining hoses that need to be disconnected. When it's free, lay the air cleaner where the spare tire goes or on something clean (the spare tire?). Don't lay it on the ground because it might get dirty or stepped on.

If you're going to need to start the engine with the air cleaner off, plug the small, pencil-size hoses you disconnected or, in some cases, the places on the engine where the small hoses were connected. Don't worry about the thumb size hoses. To plug the vacuum lines (small hoses) use pencils (break the lead off first), small phillips screwdrivers, small punches, or tape. You can buy rubber vacuum line plug sets fairly cheap. They sure make it easy.

Step 5. Install Air Cleaner (carb models only).

Clean the air cleaner throat where it fits over the carburetor. Clean and check the rubber gasket on the carb where the air cleaner fits and replace the gasket if it's cracked or bent out of shape. Set the air cleaner housing on the carb and tighten the clamp screw on the back if you loosened it ('75-'79 models). Install and tighten the 10mm bolt(s) that secure the housing to the engine. Install the air filter, then the air cleaner lid. Screw on the wing nuts or 10mm nut or secure the lid with the spring clips depending on your setup. Reconnect all of the small vacuum hoses and the larger hoses going to the valve covers or to the plastic gizmo on the left side of the engine. Look for other thumb-size hoses you might have disconnected. Attach the large hot air intake hose to the bottom of the air snout. Pinch the ears on the clamp and slide the clamp to its original position, about 1" from the end of the hose.

Check again to be sure all the hoses are connected. Use the diagram under the hood (if it's there) if you're not sure where the hoses go.

Step 6. Mark Crankshaft Pulley and Timing Marks.

You only have to do this once. Skip this step if you painted the timing marks the first time you did a tune-up on this vehicle.

Be sure the handbrake is ON, the wheels are blocked, the gearshift is in NEUTRAL, and the ignition key is OFF.

Here's how you do it. First, remove the spark plugs (Procedure 11, Step 2). Next, put a socket and ratchet (usually a 19mm or 22mm) on the bolt in the center of the **crankshaft pulley**. That's right—down there at the front of the engine. See the big bolt head? Be careful not to bang the wrench against the delicate radiator. If you have air conditioning (A/C), you'll need to use a ratchet with a thin head in order to clear the A/C fan bracket. If you just can't get to the crank pulley bolt with the ratchet, use the nut on the *alternator pulley* to turn the engine. (You might have to press down on the alternator drive belt with one hand to increase the tension so the belt doesn't slip while you're turning the engine.)

Be sure the transmission is in Neutral, then use the socket and ratchet to rotate the pulley *clockwise* (as viewed from the front). This will turn the **crankshaft** and internal engine parts, including the **distributor shaft**. The rotor will also gradually turn until the brass tip points in the direction of the number one spark plug wire terminal of the distributor cap. The resistance you feel as you turn the engine is the compression in the cylinders. Turn the bolt a little, then look at the rotor tip, turn and look again—until it's lined up with the #1 spark plug wire when the dis-

Hood up? OK, look at the engine and locate the **number one cylinder**. It's the front one on the passenger's side. There's the #1 cylinder's **spark plug**, with a wire sprouting from it. Follow the spark plug wire to the **distributor cap** and note its location in relation to the other wires. The cylinder numbers might be stamped on top of the distributor cap. Also, on some models, the spark plug wires have numbers indicating which cylinder they're for. No numbers? Note the location of the #1 spark plug wire on the distributor cap.

Use a medium screwdriver or your thumb to pry open the spring clips that secure the distributor cap, or if your distributor cap is secured with a screw on each side, loosen the screws. Lift up on the distributor cap and see where the copper tip of the plastic **rotor** is pointing. Wherever it's pointing, you need it to point to where the #1 cylinder spark plug wire was when the cap was on.

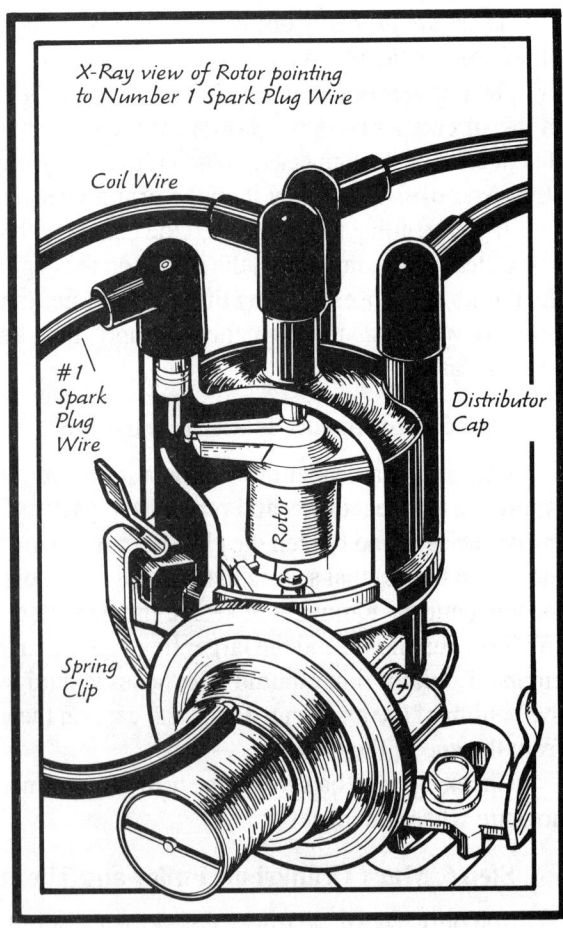

tributor cap is on the distributor body. Got it? OK.

OHV non-Turbo models and OHC models (except '87-'88 XT): On the rear of the engine there is a rectangular **timing hole** in the **flywheel housing** (that large, round piece of aluminum sticking up at the back of the engine). On OHV models it's on the right side and on OHC models it's near the top. The hole is about 1½" x 2". See it? If there's a rubber or plastic plug covering the hole, pull on the tab or pry on the plug to remove it.

Inside the hole you can see the face of the **flywheel** on manual transmission cars, or the **drive plate** on cars with automatic transmissions. For convenience I'm going to call them both the *flywheel*. The flywheel is bolted to the back end of the crankshaft. **Timing marks** are stamped in two-degree increments on the flywheel. You want to turn the engine with the ratchet until the line under the 0 on the flywheel is lined up with the tip of the little **triangle pointer** located on the bottom edge of the timing hole. If the light is dim, use your flashlight to find the marks. If you can't see the marks very well because the flywheel is rusty or dirty, wipe it off with a rag (lightly soaked in alcohol or solvent) or sand it a little with fine emery paper.

Paint a very thin white line over the line below the 0, then paint a vertical white line on the top front of the crankshaft pulley. Chalk will work, but you'll probably have to make new marks every time you tune-up the engine. Paint is permanent.

Now look at the sticker under the hood for the correct timing for your engine. No sticker? Look it up in the specifications table at the end of this chapter.

Rotate the engine *counterclockwise* (as viewed from the front) until the appropriate timing line on the flywheel matches up with the little pointer on the flywheel housing hole. Remember, each line means 2° and you should be to the RIGHT of the 0 line (as viewed through the hole). If you see a B stamped above the lines, you're on the right side. If you see an A, you're on the wrong side of the 0 line. Unfortunately, not all flywheels are stamped with an A (after) or B (before). If you've got 'em, they're helpful. Paint a thin line over the correct timing mark for your engine. Paint the triangle pointer while you're at it.

OHV models (except '83-'84 Turbos): Now rotate the engine *clockwise* with the ratchet 180° until the white line on the crank pulley is right at the bottom. Now look through the hole in the flywheel housing again for one long line. Clean the line if

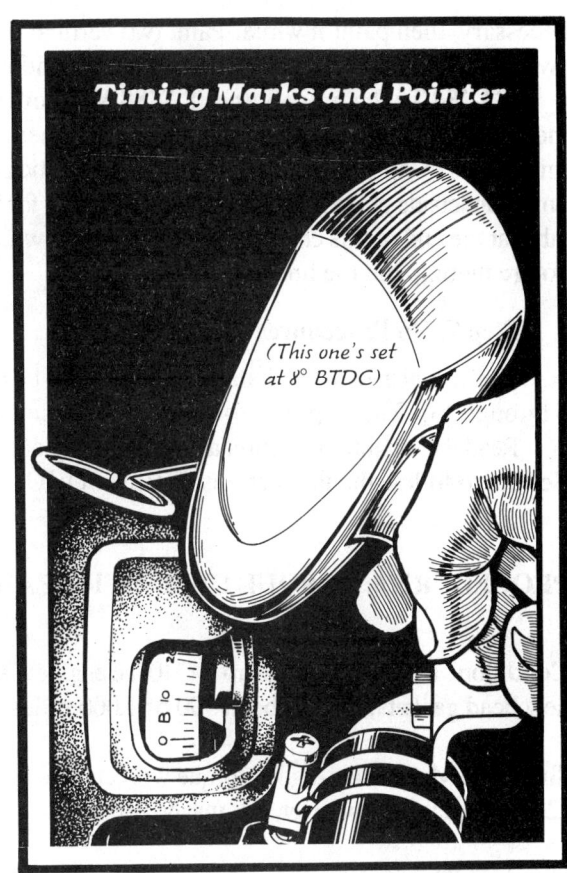

Timing Marks and Pointer

(This one's set at 8° BTDC)

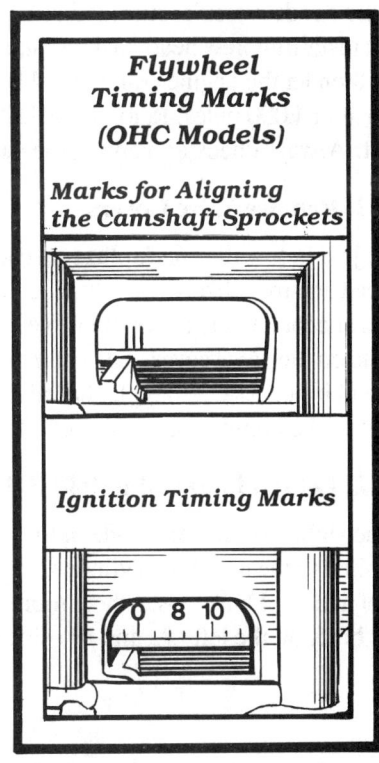

Flywheel Timing Marks (OHC Models)

Marks for Aligning the Camshaft Sprockets

Ignition Timing Marks

necessary, then paint it white. Paint two vertical lines on the top front of the crank pulley. OK, Picasso, put away the paint and brush. Remove the socket and ratchet from the pulley bolt.

'83-'84 Turbo models and '87-'88 XT models): The **timing plate** is bolted to the front of the engine on the driver's side of the crankshaft pulley. It's rather difficult to see, let alone get to. If you have large hands, you might need to tape the paint brush to a long thin stick or screwdriver to get to the timing plate. Look at the sticker on the underside of the hood for the ignition timing for your engine. If the sticker is missing, check the Specifications table at the end of this chapter. Paint a very thin white line over the appropriate line on the timing plate. While you're there, paint the line next to the 0.

Step 7. Do Procedures 6 through 13.

You've finished the preparations, now you'll be doing what mechanics generally call a tune-up (Procedures 6 through 13). The steps in Procedure 14 complete the 12,000-mile massage.

Read the conditions section at the beginning of each procedure to see if it applies to your year and/or model. Be sure to follow the instructions (OHV or OHC) for your engine.

PROCEDURE 6: TORQUE CYLINDER HEADS AND INTAKE MANIFOLD (OHV ONLY)

Condition: 12,000-mile tune-up on 1400cc engine; OR you suspect a head gasket is leaking; OR you just installed new head gaskets; OR it's been 300 or 1,000 miles since new head gaskets were installed.

Tools and Materials: A good torque wrench, two special sockets for torqueing the heads (see Chapter 5: *Tools*), 12mm wrench, screwdriver, oil, maybe two new valve cover gaskets and the little gaskets for the valve cover bolts.

Remark: This is a very important procedure for 1400cc engines—don't skip it! Leaking head gaskets seem to be the Achilles Heel of Subarus, especially on 1400cc engines. Usually, the head gaskets start leaking because the cylinder heads weren't retorqued at the proper intervals.

After installing **new** head gaskets, start the engine and let it warm up to operating temperature (about 10 minutes), then let the engine cool for 3-4 hours, then retorque the heads. Retorque them again after 300 miles, then again after 1,000 miles. Retorquing the heads on 1400cc engines once a year or every 12,000 miles will keep them tight. Always check and adjust the valves after retorquing the heads.

Step 1. Remove Valve Covers.

Look just below the spark plugs on each side of the engine for a **valve cover**. It's shaped like the top of a loaf of bread and most likely it's light blue like the air cleaner (a few are black). Squeeze the clamp on the rubber hose that's attached to the top of the valve cover, then pull the hose off. Tuck it out of the way. Unscrew the two 12mm bolts on the valve cover and gently pry the valve cover off. Use a screwdriver between the lip of the cover and the head if necessary. Wiggle the valve cover around until you find a space wide enough to pull the cover up and out of the engine compartment. Remove both valve covers.

Step 2. Loosen Intake Manifold Bolts.

On the right (passenger's) side of the engine, locate the three intake manifold mounting bolts. The **manifold** is bolted to the top of the cylinder head between the #1 and #3 spark plugs. Loosen the 12mm bolts about 60° (1/6 of a turn). Don't loosen them more than 60° or water might leak into the engine. *Don't* loosen the intake mounting bolts on the left (#2 and #4) side of the engine.

Step 3. Retorque Cylinder Head Nuts.

Do one side of the engine at a time. Look at the Torque Patterns illustration to find nut #1 for your engine. Use the long special socket on your ratchet to loosen the nut 60° (1/6 of a turn). Don't loosen it more than 90°. Squirt motor oil on the bolt and washer. Now tighten the bolt to its original position, then loosen it 60°. Do this five times, then use a torque wrench to torque the nut to 43 ft. lbs. on '75-'78 engines, or 47 ft. lbs. on '79 and newer OHV engines.

Follow the tightening sequence and repeat this process on each of the head nuts one at a time. Don't cheat on the sequence. You'll have to use the long special socket to retorque the #1 nut on all engines and nut #8 on '75 engines and nut #9 on '76 and newer OHV engines. Use the short special socket to retorque nuts #4 and #5. Either tool will work on the rest of the nuts. After torqueing the last nut (#9), check nut #1 again.

Now retorque the nuts on the other side of the engine. After both heads are torqued, torque the three intake manifold bolts on both sides of the engine to 15 ft. lbs.

Always check the valve adjustment (Procedure 7) after retorquing the heads. Fortunately, it's next on the agenda. Put the valve covers back on at the end of Procedure 7.

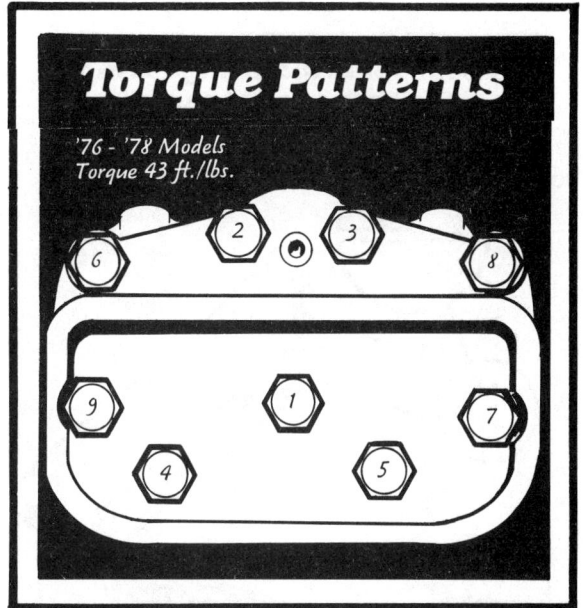

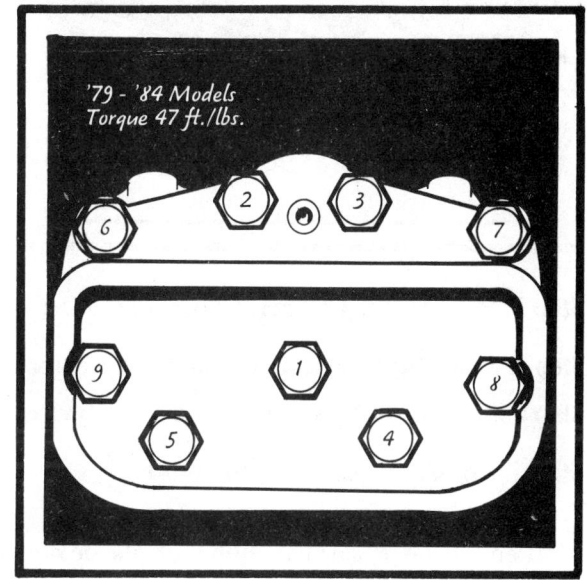

PROCEDURE 7: ADJUST VALVES (OHV MODELS ONLY)

On OHV engines with mechanical (solid) valve lifters, adjust the valves every 12,000 miles. Do it when the engine is cold (hasn't been started for at least four hours). The following models have mechanical lifters.

All '75-'82 models
All '83-'84 models with manual transmissions
The following models have hydraulic valve lifters so no valve adjustment is required.
All '83-'84 models with automatic transmissions
All '85-'88 models

EVERYONE: Just to be sure, look at the sticker under the hood. If the sticker says the valve clearance is 0, you have hydraulic lifters. If the sticker says Intake .010″, Exhaust .014″, follow this procedure to adjust the valves.

If you have hydraulic lifters, skip down to Procedure 8 (OHC models, or Procedure 9 (OHV models).

Condition: 12,000-mile tune-up; OR the valves sound noisy; OR you just torqued the heads.

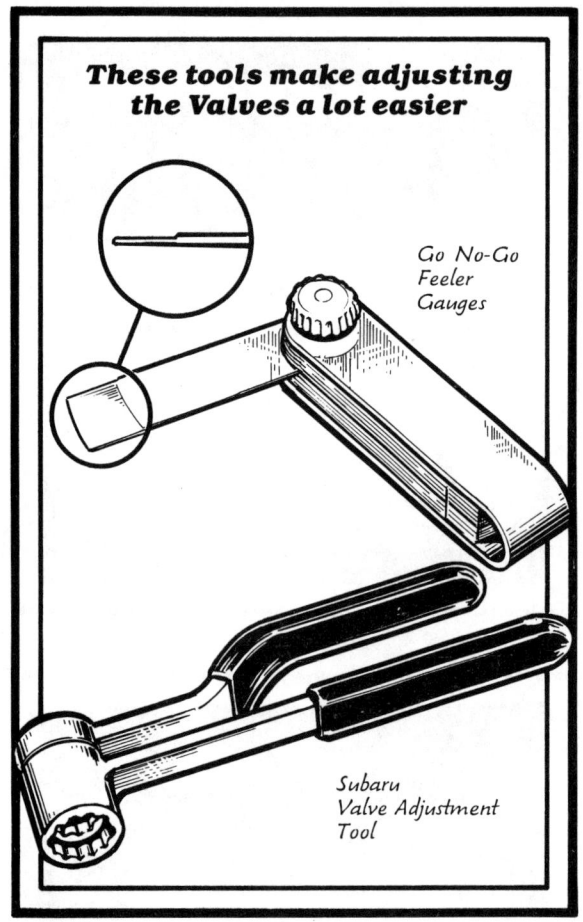

These tools make adjusting the Valves a lot easier

Tools and Materials: You'll need *either* a 12mm box end wrench and a 5mm open end wrench (these are hard to find and break easily—a 6mm wrench or a 4" adjustable crescent wrench will work), *or* a genuine Subaru valve adjustment tool (see Chapter 5: *Tools*). Also you'll need a feeler gauge with the correct blade sizes for your valve setting (Go No-Go feeler gauges are easiest to use), screwdriver, ratchet, and a 19mm or 22mm socket depending on the size of your crank pulley bolt, maybe two new valve cover gaskets and the little gaskets for the valve cover bolts.

Remark: Remember, the left side of the car is the driver's side, and the right side is the passenger's side. Front is toward the headlights and rear is toward the taillights.

If you are adjusting the valves on a 1400cc engine that has exhaust pipes attached to the front and rear of each cylinder head, the valve positions are reversed from the description below. Your exhaust valves are the outside valves and the intake valves are the two in the center of each cylinder head. Be sure you're adjusting the right valve.

Step 1. Remove Spare Tire.

If the spare tire is in the engine compartment, unscrew the large wing nut, then remove the tire.

Step 2. Remove Air Cleaner. (Procedure 5, Step 4.)

Step 3. Mark Flywheel and Crank Pulley. (Procedure 5, Step 6.)

Skip this step if you've already marked the flywheel and crank pulley. If you haven't done it, do it now.

Step 4. Adjust Valves For Cylinder #1.

Remove the valve covers (Procedure 6, Step 1).

Remove the rectangular **rubber or plastic plug** in the flywheel housing so you can see the **timing marks** on the flywheel (Procedure 5, Step 6). Now look at the distributor cap and find where the wire to the #1 spark plug goes into it. Mark this place with pencil, crayon, or paint on the edge of the body of the distributor. Remove the distributor cap (Procedure 9, Step 2). Turn the engine *clockwise* with the socket on the crank pulley until the rotor points to the mark you made on the outside of the distributor body. Now turn the engine just a bit to line up the *zero line* on the flywheel with the pointer on the flywheel cover. Be sure the rotor is pointing in the direction where the spark plug wire from #1 cylinder connects to the distributor cap when it's back on the distributor. The engine is now set at *top dead center* (TDC) firing position for cylinder #1. Now we're set to adjust the valves for the #1 cylinder.

Procedure 7, Step 4 — Maintenance, Lubrication, Tune-up

You'll be working on the right (passenger) side of the engine first. The intake valves are the two outside valves and the exhaust valves are the two middle valves. The valves for #1 cylinder are the two nearest the front of the car. (1400cc engines, see the Remarks section.)

To keep the following explanation simple, I'm going to use the numbers .010 (ten thousandths of an inch) for intake valves and .014 (fourteen thousandths of an inch) for exhaust valves. This is the correct setting for all '76 and newer Subarus with mechanical lifters. If you are adjusting the valves on a '75 Soob, the correct setting for your engine is .012 for the intake valves and .014 for the exhaust valves.

Your **feeler gauge** blades are the keys to successful valve adjustment. You're dealing with a slim gap between the **rocker arm** and **valve stem**. To set a valve to .010 (ten thousandths of an inch), adjust it so an .011 feeler gauge blade won't fit, but a .009 blade will. The same criteria applies for setting one to .014—adjust it so a .015 blade won't fit but a .013 will. This is where Go No-Go feeler gauges help. They combine two sizes on each blade. The tip is one size and the rest of the blade is another. For instance, .009 and .011, or .013 and .015. If the tip fits in the gap but the blade doesn't, the gap is set at whatever number is between the two sizes. They sure make adjusting valves a lot easier.

Get out the feeler gauge with the appropriate blades ready for action. Start with the front valve (intake). Slide the .010 feeler gauge blade (or the correct one for your intake valves) between the rocker arm and valve stem. Slip it in flat and straight—don't force it. If you're not sure where to stick the blade, push the top of the rocker arm in and out to see where it hits. It hits the valve stem sticking out of the center of the valve spring. The space between the valve stem and rocker arm is the distance we're checking.

If the .010 blade won't go into the gap, try a .009 blade. If it won't go, you have a *tight valve*. If an .011 blade falls through the gap, you have a *loose valve*. If the .010 blade slides through the gap with just a slight resistance to easy sliding, the valve is right. (If it seems OK but you want to make sure, try a .011 and a .009 blade. If the .011 blade won't go through and the .009 does, you know the adjustment is right.) Take your time. You can build up speed later but right now give yourself all the time you need. It might be useful to have a Friend who's used feeler gauges join you for the first try. Ask him to check your first valve and

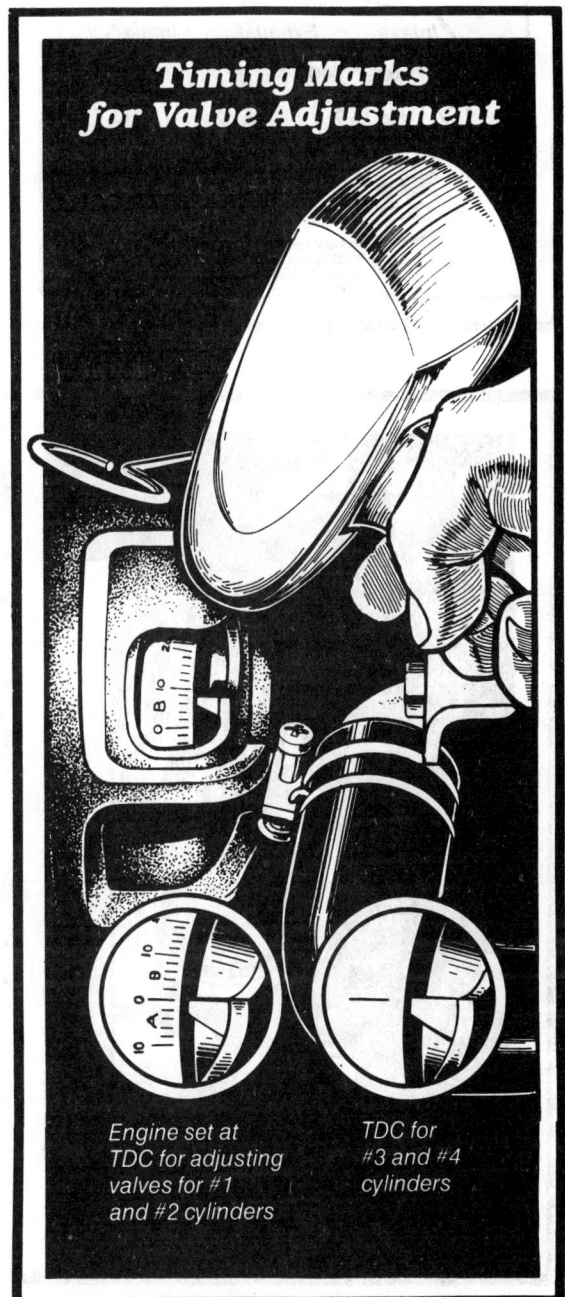

Timing Marks for Valve Adjustment

Engine set at TDC for adjusting valves for #1 and #2 cylinders

TDC for #3 and #4 cylinders

102 Chapter 7 Procedure 7, Step 4

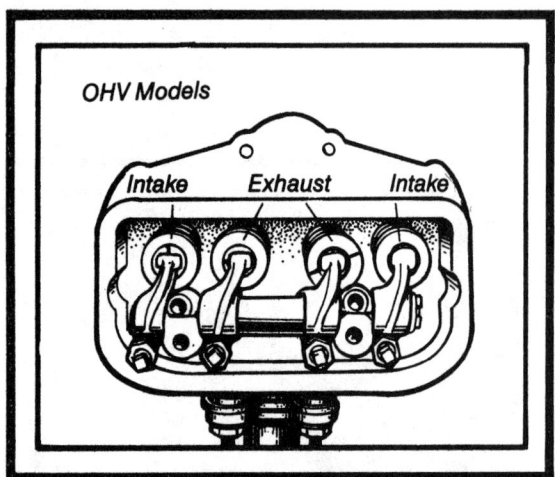

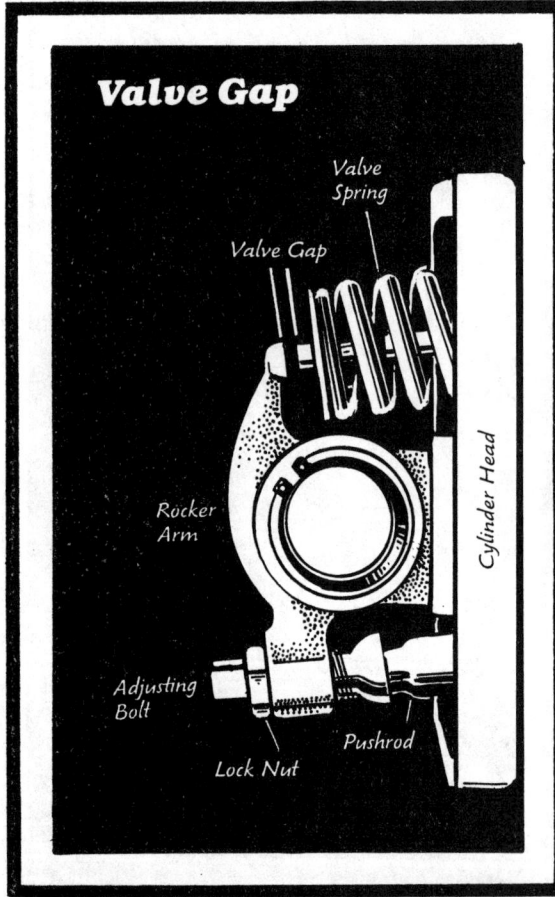

compare notes. You can actually *feel* the blade slipping with a slight pull between the two metal surfaces when the adjustment is correct.

Whether a valve is too tight or too loose, the procedure for changing the setting is the same: you change the position of the **adjusting bolt** in the bottom of the rocker arm. Turn the bolt *clockwise* to decrease the distance between the rocker arm and the valve, or *counterclockwise* to increase this clearance. Remember, *clockwise* is less, *counterclockwise* is more.

The adjusting bolt has a **locking nut** to hold it in position after it's been adjusted. The locking nut must be loosened (*counterclockwise*) before you can adjust the bolt to change the gap. You won't have to turn it far. Use your genuine Subaru valve adjusting tool, or the thinnest 12mm box end wrench you have, to loosen the 12mm lock nut. Make sure the wrench is secure on the nut because this is a place where skinned knuckles abound. If the nut doesn't come loose with one hand, use two (watch out for those skinned knuckles). One way to avoid skinned knuckles is to hold the wrench firmly with one hand while you use the free hand to tap (or pound) on the wrench to loosen the lock nut. When the nut is loose, hold it still with the wrench and move the adjusting bolt back and forth in the nut a few times to get the threads in a little better adjusting shape. Use the smaller handle on the Subaru tool, a 5mm or 6mm open end wrench or the small 4" crescent, to turn the adjusting bolt.

I have two methods for adjusting valve clearances. Which method I use depends on how easily the lock nut moves on the adjusting bolt. If the nut moves easily, I use the "Imprisoned Feeler Blade Method," but if the nut turns hard on the bolt I use the "Memorized Small Wrench Position Method." Sometimes I use a combination of both. (Small wrench means the short handle on the Subaru tool, the 5mm or 6mm open end wrench, or the 4" crescent wrench—whichever you're using. Big wrench means the longer handle on the Subaru tool or the 12mm box end wrench.)

Imprisoned Blade Method: After the lock nut is loose, put the big wrench on the lock nut and the small wrench on the adjusting bolt. Let the big wrench go and slip the proper feeler blade between the rocker arm and the valve. (If it won't fit, turn the bolt *counterclockwise* a little.) Now turn the adjusting bolt *clockwise* with the small wrench until it barely "imprisons" the blade by pinching it between the valve stem and the bolt. The blade can be moved, but offers resistance. Let the blade remain in the gap. Hold the small wrench in this position, let go of the feeler gauge and tighten the lock nut on the bolt. Now try the feeler blade again to see if you got it right. If the blade is too tight, back off on the lock nut, then the adjusting bolt, and do the adjustment again. Be sure you're not letting the small wrench move at all when you tighten the lock nut.

Memorized Small Wrench Position Method: This method is useful when turning the lock nut tends to turn the adjusting bolt also. The 12mm lock nut is loosened and the large wrench is on the lock nut, right? Let go of the large wrench and put the small wrench on the bolt and the feeler blade in place in the gap and tighten the bolt until the clearance seems right. The blade should be held gently in the gap's grip, as in the Imprisoned Blade Method. Memorize the position of the small wrench's handle at this point. Slip the feeler blade out. Now use the big wrench to turn the lock nut down on the bolt. Just before the lock nut reaches its seat on the rocker arm, *loosen* (*counterclockwise*) the adjusting bolt with the small wrench just a little so the lock nut will twist it *clockwise* to the memorized place when you tighten it down. You'll see the handle of the small wrench turn as you tighten the lock nut. First time through you'll need trial-and-error to determine how far you have to back off the adjusting bolt to get it to return to the memorized position when you snug down the lock nut. Be patient—you'll get it.

In both methods, snug the adjusting nut down tight and check the clearance again with the feeler blade(s). If it's correct, go on to the next valve. If it isn't, you're back where you started, so adjust it again. Remember that a little looser is better than a little tighter. It will take time and patience to get them right, especially the first time. Hang in there. The gaps are important so get them right.

When you're satisfied that the #1 intake valve is adjusted right, go on to the exhaust valve. That would be the second valve from the front. Use the appropriate feeler gauge blade and check and adjust the exhaust valve the same way you adjusted the intake valve. After the exhaust valve is adjusted, take a short break and give your back a rest. After you've been setting your own valves for a while and are familiar with them, the job will move quickly. Also, you'll find that there will only be one or two in the whole engine that need to be changed.

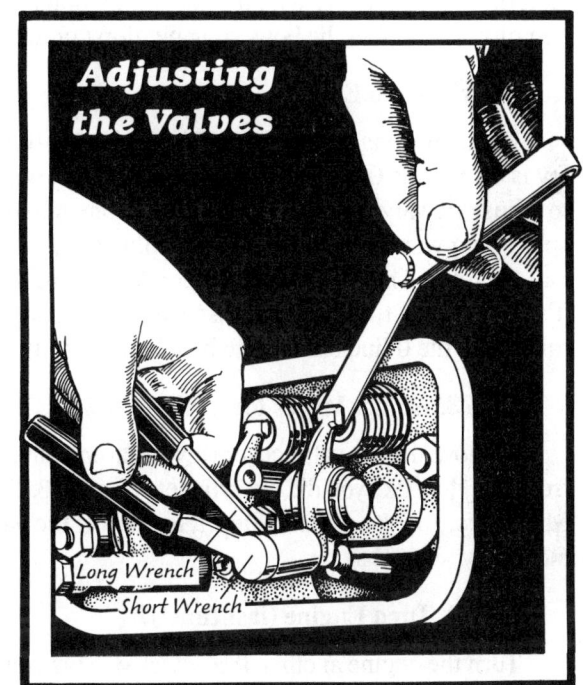

Adjusting the Valves

Step 5. Turn the Engine, Adjust Valves for Cylinder #3.

Cylinder #3 sits right behind #1 on the passenger side of the engine. Use the socket on the crank pulley to rotate the engine 180° (½ turn) *clockwise* (as viewed from the front of the car). The two white lines on the crank pulley will be on top after you rotate the engine. Now check the flywheel marks through the hole in the flywheel housing. The pointer on the flywheel housing must line up with the one long line on the flywheel. Use the socket on the crank pulley to get it right on. Now check the rotor inside the distributor. If it isn't pointing to the #3 spark plug wire post on the distributor cap, you turned the engine the wrong direction. Turn it until the rotor points to the #3 spark plug post and the line on the flywheel is lined up with the pointer on the flywheel housing.

Cylinder #3 is now in firing position—just where you want it. Now you can adjust the back two valves on this side of the engine. Look at the illustration again to be sure which is intake and which is exhaust. Be sure you use the right feeler gauge for each.

Check and adjust cylinder #3 intake and exhaust valves *exactly* as you did the cylinder #1 valves in Step 4. Don't hurry. Now that you've turned the engine you can no longer check the adjustment on the valves for cylinder #1.

Step 6. Install Valve Cover.

When all four valves on this side of the engine have been adjusted, you're ready to put the valve cover back on. Feel all the way around the surface on the head where the **valve cover gasket** fits. It must be smooth. Scrape off any remains of the old gasket with a knife, putty knife, or flat screwdriver. Leaving one little chunk stuck there could cause the gasket to leak and you'd lose oil. Unfortunately, pieces usually remain on the bottom center surface where it's most difficult to reach. Wipe off any gasket parts that fall on the valve springs, rocker arms, etc. If the gasket stayed on the head, check it with your finger for cracks or missing pieces. If you find any, replace the gasket. Wipe the inside of the valve cover clean and check and clean the surface around the edge where the gasket fits.

If you have white lithium grease or wheel bearing grease handy, lightly coat both sides of the valve cover gasket with the grease so it will be easier to remove the next time.

If the old gasket is still good, just bolt the cover on. If the valve cover looks like it's been leaking around the edge, or the old gasket got mangled when the valve cover was removed, slip a new gasket in the valve cover. Bolt on the valve cover with the two 12mm bolts. Use new valve cover bolt washers if the rubber part is broken or missing. Get the bolts snug but don't crank on them too hard.

Step 7. Turn Engine.

Rotate the engine another 180° *clockwise* with the socket and ratchet so the single line on the crank pulley is up and the 0 line on the flywheel lines up with the pointer on the flywheel housing. You're about ready to adjust the valves for cylinder #2, the front cylinder on the left (driver's) side of the engine. Now follow the spark plug wire from the front spark plug to the distributor cap. Slip the cap in place, then lift it off and eyeball the rotor. The rotor should be pointed toward the post where the cylinder #2 wire connects to the cap when it's on. (If it isn't, the engine was turned the wrong direction—turn it until the rotor points to the #2 wire terminal and the 0 line on the flywheel lines up with the pointer on the flywheel housing.)

Step 8. Adjust Valves for Cylinder #2.

Remove the left valve cover (if you haven't already) and check and adjust the valves for the #2 cylinder (the front two) just like you did for cylinders #1 and #3. Remember to use the chart for the correct intake and exhaust gaps. Refer to Procedure 6, Step 1, to take off the valve cover, and to Step 4 of this procedure to do the adjustment, if you need to.

Step 9. Turn Engine (last time!).

Turn the engine another 180° *clockwise* (as you face it) to line up the long single line on the flywheel with the triangle pointer. The two lines on the crank pulley will end up at the top. Cylinder #4 is right behind #2, so find the #4 spark plug wire and follow it to where it connects to the distributor cap. Again, slip the cap in place to see where the #4 spark plug wire connects to the cap, then lift the cap and see if the rotor is pointing to the #4 terminal. If it is, you're set to do the last set of valves; if not, you'll need to turn the engine so the rotor is aiming at the #4 terminal position and the long single line on the flywheel aligns with the pointer.

Step 10. Adjust Valves for Cylinder #4.

Adjust the rear two valves just as you did the others, then install the valve cover (Step 6). Remove the ratchet and socket from the crankshaft pulley and snap the distributor cap back on the distributor (Procedure 9, Step 9). Make sure all the wires are snugly in place. If you're continuing with the tune-up now, leave the air cleaner housing off (be sure to plug the vacuum lines). Leave the timing hole plug out, and the spare tire out.

If you've pooped out and decided to finish the tune-up later, put the air cleaner on (Procedure 5, Step 5), install the timing hole plug, and put the spare tire back in place. Make sure all tools, rags, and other materials are out from under the hood. Did you remove the wrench from the crankshaft pulley bolt? Turn the engine on and warm it up, then check to make sure the valve covers aren't leaking oil.

Congratulations, you have just completed the most tedious, back-breaking part of the tune-up! Now that

Procedure 8 — Maintenance, Lubrication, Tune-up — 105

the valves are correctly adjusted, only one or two, or maybe none, will have to be changed at the next 12,000-mile tune-up. Be sure and check them though. It's going to be easier and easier each time you do this procedure. Your friends will be amazed.

Now, on with the tune-up. Go to Procedure 9.

PROCEDURE 8: CHECK, ADJUST, REPLACE CAM BELTS (FOUR-CYLINDER OHC MODELS ONLY)

This procedure does not include adjusting or replacing the cam belts on six-cylinder engines. They have a hydraulic adjuster that automatically adjusts the belt tension.

The overhead camshaft belts consist of two belts; one that turns the camshaft on the right side of the engine and one for the camshaft on the left side. The cam belts run between **drive sprockets** on the **crankshaft** and **sprockets** on the front ends of the **camshafts**. The distributor is driven by a gear on the rear end of the left-side camshaft. The tension for each belt can be adjusted with a spring-loaded **belt tensioner**. The left-side belt is longer because it also turns an **oil pump drive sprocket** and goes around an additional toothed **idler sprocket**.

As the belts stretch and wear away, slack develops (especially in the longer left-side belt). Slack allows the belts to flap about and eventually break. Fortunately, it's always the longer left-side belt that breaks, which stops the distributor and thus stops the engine. Periodically checking the camshaft drive belts is cheap insurance against being left stranded in the middle of rush hour traffic.

Subaru recommends replacing the cam belts every 60,000 miles. Adjusting the belts, other than when new belts are installed, is not mentioned in the factory maintenance schedules. In reality, the belts usually require an adjustment sometime between 5,000 and 20,000 miles, and since the belts should only be adjusted once, the average time for replacement is around 40,000 to 50,000 miles.

It's a relatively easy job to adjust the belts but significantly more involved to replace them. Be sure to read through the entire procedure to see if you are up to the task before tearing into the engine.

Condition: Routine maintenance; OR strange noises are coming from the engine; OR a camshaft belt has broken.

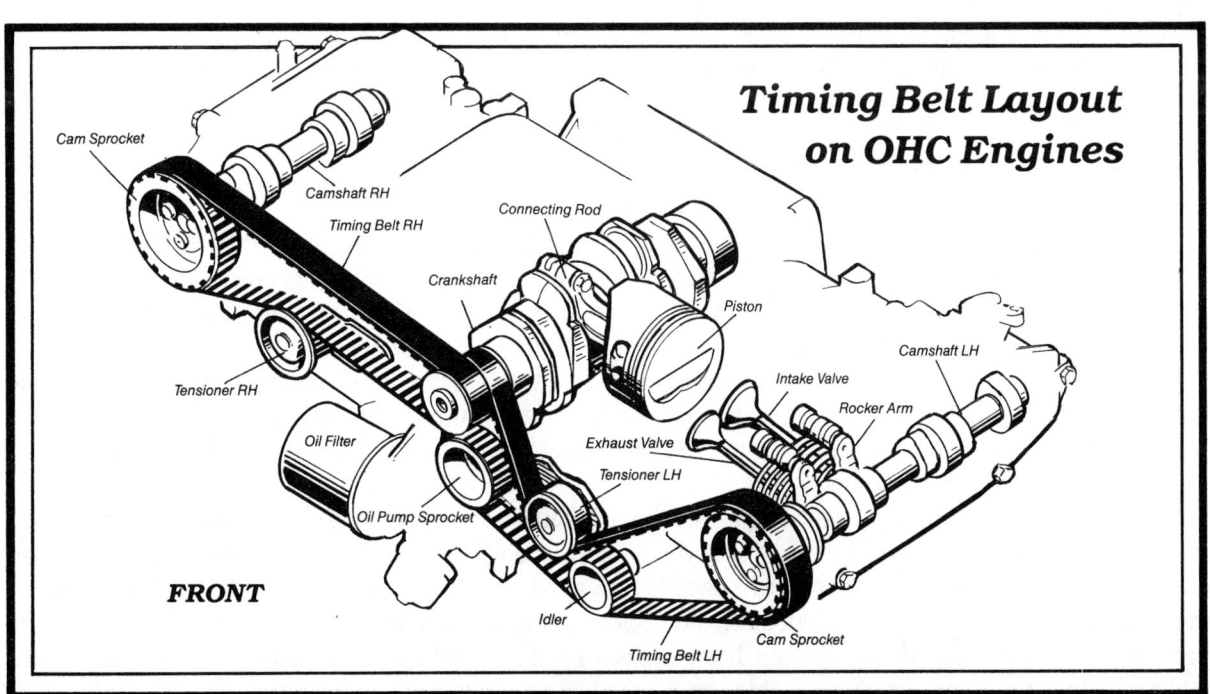

Tools and Materials: Friend, 10mm, 12mm, 14mm, 17mm deep socket, 19mm, and 21mm sockets and ratchet, torque wrench.

To adjust the belts, you'll also need the following special tools: a flywheel stopper CP for manual transmission models (Subaru part #498277000) or a drive plate stopper for automatic transmission models (Subaru part #498497000) and a belt tension wrench CP (Subaru part #499437000). See the Remarks section for alternatives to these expensive tools.

To replace the belts: Two new belts, a camshaft sprocket wrench (Subaru part #499207000), and a tensioner wrench (Subaru part #499007000).

Remarks: Remember, left side is the driver's side; right side is the passenger's side.

If you were to buy all of the special tools listed above, it would cost almost as much as hiring someone to do the work for you. However, the only tool you really have to buy is the belt tension wrench (#499437000). With a little ingenuity and perseverance, the alternate tools described in the steps can be substituted for the expensive factory tools.

Step 1. Check OHC Cam Belts.

To check the belts, all you do is open the hood, start the engine, then listen carefully on the left rear side and on both front corners of the engine. The cam belts are loose and should be adjusted if you hear a thwapping noise from the left rear corner, near the distributor, which sounds like marbles rattling around inside the distributor cap. The noise is from the drive gear on the camshaft slapping against the driven gear on the distributor shaft. This doesn't seem to cause any damage to the gears or cam box, but it's a definite warning that if the cam belts aren't adjusted or replaced soon, one will probably break and leave you stranded. If the belts have gone 40,000 miles or they've been adjusted once already, go ahead and replace them.

Another way to check for loose belts is to remove the distributor cap, then use a socket and ratchet on the crankshaft pulley bolt to move the crank back and forth, a few degrees in each direction. Watch the distributor shaft as you move the crank. There should be no delay between crank and distributor movement. The distributor is driven by the left-hand cam belt, and any looseness in the belt will delay distributor shaft movement.

If you hear a whine or high-pitched whirr from the front corners of the engine, the belts are adjusted too tight and they are putting excess pressure on the front cam bearings. You will probably only hear this noise right after adjusting the belts. It might not be noticeable at idle, so rev the engine a little and listen for it. If you hear the whine or whirr, adjust the belts again and don't add that extra little "just to be sure" tug on the torque wrench.

If you determine that the belts are loose, do Steps 2, 3, and 4 to adjust them. If the belts have been adjusted at a previous tune-up, or one has broken already, do Steps 2 and 5 through 9 to replace them.

Step 2. Remove Cam Belt Covers.

The engine should be cold when adjusting or replacing the cam belts.

First, let's clear some things out of the way so the cam belt covers are more accessible. Pull the hoses out of the holder on top of the fan shroud on the right rear side of the radiator. Disconnect the wires to the electric fan mounted on the right rear side of the radiator, then remove the four 10mm bolts that attach the fan shroud to the radiator. Pull the fan and shroud up and out of the engine compartment.

If you have air conditioning, remove the three or four bolts that attach the shroud to the left rear side of the radiator. Remove the four nuts that attach the rear of the vaned aluminum fan clutch to the pulley on the front of the water pump. (Don't remove the nuts that attach the fan to the front of the fan clutch.) Remove the fan and shroud from the engine compartment.

Cam belt replacers: To replace the cam belts, the crankshaft pulley must be removed. Loosening the crankshaft pulley bolt is sometimes very difficult, even if you have the special Subaru tool for locking the engine. If you are sure the cam belts need to be replaced, it would be a good idea to skip down to Step 5 now and follow the instructions for loosening the crankshaft pulley bolt before taking things apart any further. Once the crank pulley bolt is loose, come back and finish this step. If you can't loosen the crank pulley bolt, you'll have to buy the special tool for locking the engine or put everything back together and seek professional help.

Procedure 8, Step 2   *Maintenance, Lubrication, Tune-up*   **107**

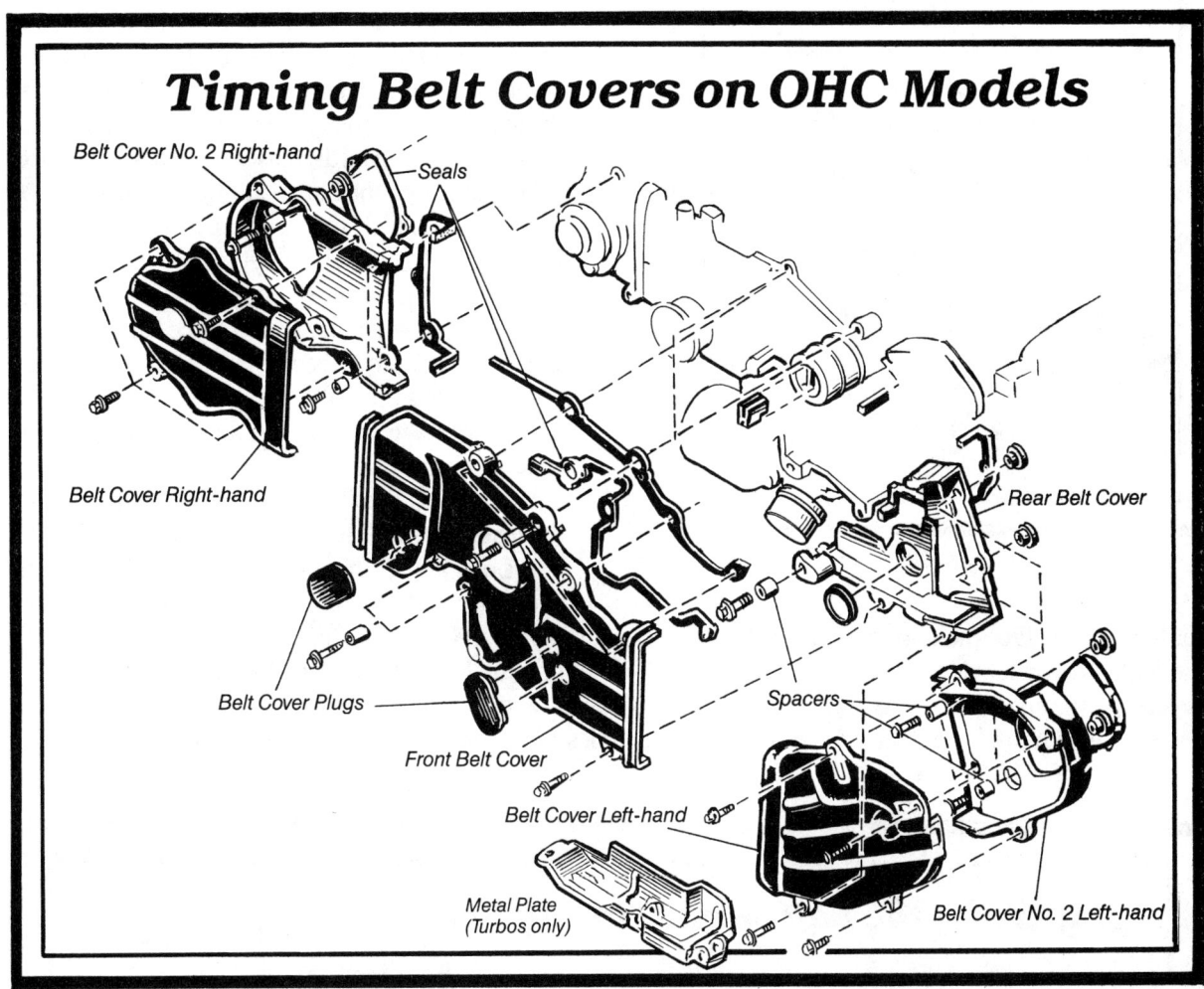

Timing Belt Covers on OHC Models

When replacing the cam belts, the drive belts for the alternator and air conditioner compressor (if you have A/C) and the water pump pulley must also be removed. Getting the drive belts and water pump pulley out of the way makes the bolts for the cam covers more accessible. So if you are here to replace the belts, loosen the water pump pulley nuts until you can turn them with your fingers, then remove the alternator and air conditioning drive belts (Chapter 10, Procedure 3). Now remove the water pump pulley. If you are replacing the belts, remove the crankshaft pulley also.

EVERYONE: Look at the "Timing Belt Covers" illustration for the location of the bolts that attach the left-hand, right-hand, and front covers to the rear covers. They are all 10mm bolts except the one at the bottom of the left-hand cover—it's a bolt and nut (you might need to remove it from under the car). As you remove the belt covers, pay close attention to the length of the bolts and spacers so you can reinstall them in the same places. Drawing a sketch or writing the sizes (short, medium, or long) on the "Timing Belt Covers" illustration will make reassembly a lot easier. While the covers are off, be very careful to not let oil, grease, antifreeze, or anything else get on the belts. Always clean your hands before touching the belts. OK, now remove the left-hand and right-hand covers. Remove the oblong rubber **belt cover plugs** from the front belt cover.

Cam belt replacers: Skip down to Step 5.

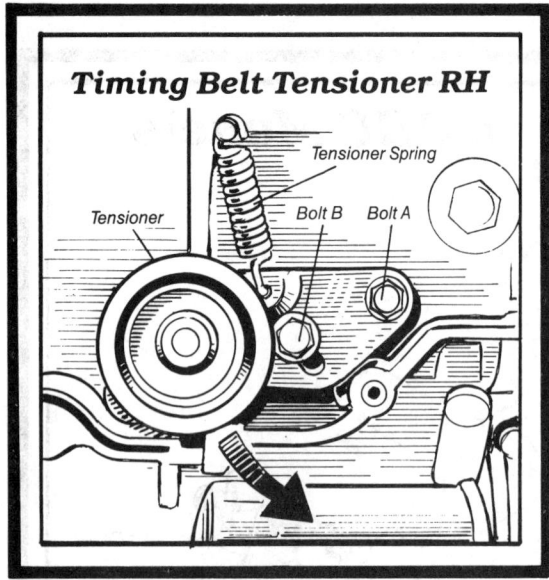

Step 3. Adjust Cam Belts.

Here's how the belt tensioners work. A strong spring pulls the tensioner toward the belt to eliminate slack. The spring isn't strong enough to maintain the tension while the engine is running, so the tension is adjusted, then the tensioner is locked in place. When adjusting the belts, a torque wrench is used to apply a specified amount of pull on the belt to eliminate all slack, but not enough pull to stretch (overtighten) the belt. While the torque wrench eliminates the slack, the tensioner spring forces the tensioner against the belt, then the tensioner is locked in place with two bolts. Got it?

Look at the illustrations for adjusting the left-hand and right-hand timing belts to locate the round **Tensioners**. If the front cover is still on the engine, the tensioners will be only partially visible.

Look at the illustration labeled "Timing Belt Tensioner RH" and find **bolt A** and **bolt B**. Remember that, as you face the engine, bolt A is to the right and above bolt B, and B is in the slotted hole. Now look at the illustration labeled "Raising The Left-Hand Tensioner" and locate **bolt C** and **bolt D**. Remember that, as you face the engine, bolt C is above and to the left of bolt D, and D is in the slotted hole. If the front belt cover is still on the engine, you'll have to peek through the holes in the lower part of the cover to see these bolts.

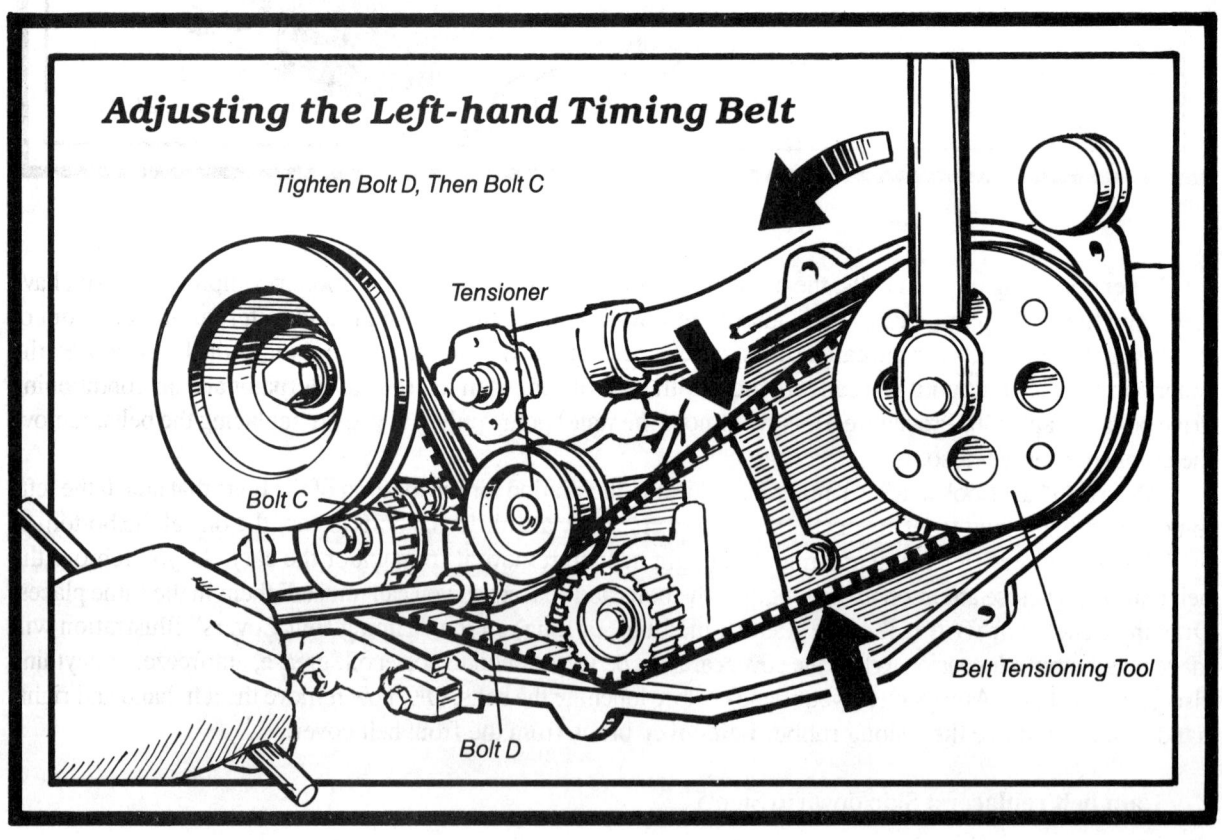

Procedure 8, Step 3 Maintenance, Lubrication, Tune-up 109

We'll adjust the left-hand belt first. Loosen bolts C and D about ½ turn *counterclockwise* (as viewed from the front of the car). Look at the illustration "Adjusting Left-Hand Timing Belt." Watch the tensioner while you squeeze the belt together where the arrows are pointing at the belt. (Your hands are clean, right?) The tensioner should be free enough to move a little. If not, loosen bolts C and D a little more.

Install the large round belt tensioner tool into the four holes on the left-hand camshaft sprocket. Set your torque wrench to 18 ft. lbs., if it's a clicker type. Fit the torque wrench onto the tool so the handle is pointing straight up. Put your socket and ratchet on bolt D so you can tighten it while holding torque on the cam sprocket.

Remove the rubber plug from the timing hole on the top rear of the engine. Use the Subaru flywheel stopper (manuals) or drive plate stopper (automatics) to lock the engine. If you don't have this tool, have Friend use a bent pry bar, a large screwdriver, or a *strong* punch to lock the engine. It's pretty easy to lock the engine while adjusting the cam belts. It's much more difficult to lock it while removing the crankshaft pulley bolt for belt replacement. Anyway, here's how you do it. Stick the bar or screwdriver through the timing hole at the top rear of the engine and engage the tip of the tool with the teeth on the flywheel or drive plate, or against a mounting bolt on the drive plate. On manual transmission models, you can also use a *strong* punch inserted into one of the holes around the edge of the flywheel. You might have to use a socket and ratchet on the crankshaft pulley bolt to turn the engine until one of the flywheel holes appears in the timing hole. Don't push the punch into the hole tightly before trying to lock the engine because if the punch should happen to break, it could be difficult to remove the part that's stuck in the hole. If this misfortune should befall you, don't start the engine until the broken punch is removed. A strong magnet might lift it out, or you might have to drill a hole in the punch, then use an easy-out to remove it.

If you are replacing the cam belts and you can't loosen the crankshaft pulley bolt by using one of the above methods, you can remove the starter for better access to the teeth in the flywheel or drive plate. See Chapter 10, Procedure 10, for starter removal and installation. Once the starter is off, wedge the bar or screwdriver between the aluminum bell housing and the teeth of the flywheel or drive plate.

OK, once the engine is locked, move the torque wrench handle in the direction of the arrow in the illustration (*counterclockwise*, toward the right side of the car) until it clicks or reads 18 ft. lbs. Hold the torque wrench there

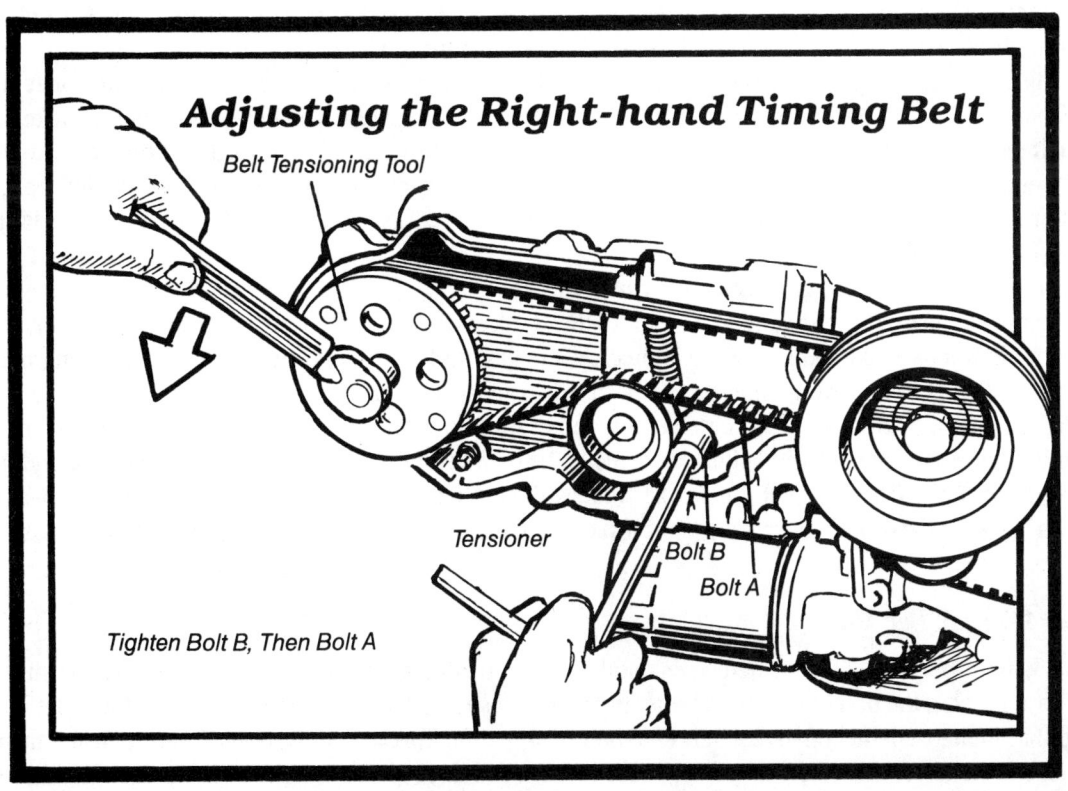

Adjusting the Right-hand Timing Belt

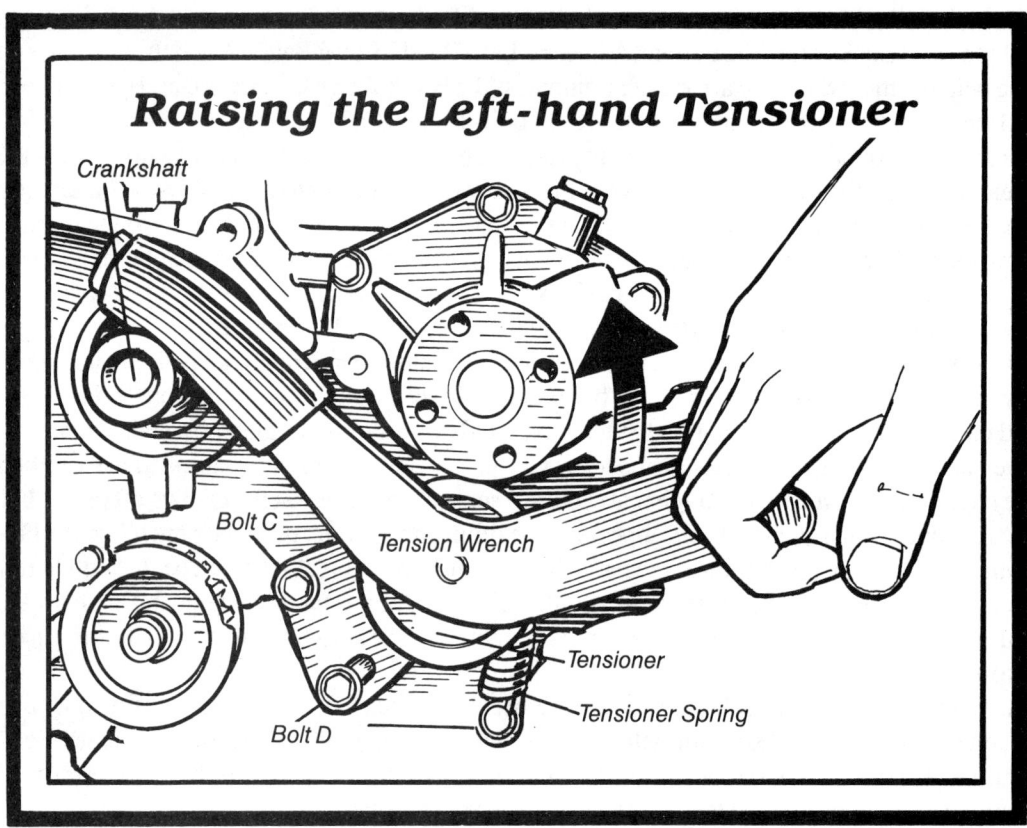

Raising the Left-hand Tensioner

without moving the handle while you (or Friend) snugs down bolt D (the lower bolt) and then bolt C (the upper bolt). After both bolts are snug, put the socket on the torque wrench and torque bolt D, then bolt C to 14 ft. lbs. Check both bolts again. The left belt is adjusted. Wasn't too hard, eh?

To adjust the right-hand belt, loosen bolts A and B about ½ turn, or until you can move the tensioner slightly by squeezing on the belt like you did on the left side. Set your torque wrench to 18 ft. lbs. (if it's a clicker), then fit the belt tension tool and torque wrench onto the right-hand sprocket. Fit a socket and ratchet onto bolt B. Lock the engine again, then turn the torque wrench *counterclockwise*, just like you did for the left belt, until it clicks or reads 18 ft. lbs. Have Friend snug down bolt B, then bolt A. Torque bolt B, then bolt A to 14 ft. lbs. Check both bolts again.

If you replaced the belts, go to Step 9 to finish the job.

If you only adjusted the belts and didn't remove the crank and water pump pulleys, or the front cover, remove whatever tools you used to lock the engine, then clear the fan, tools, rags, and stuff away from the engine. Start the engine and check for the thwapping sound near the distributor and for a whine or whirr from the front corners of the engine. If the distributor has quieted down and there's no whine or whirr coming from the front when the engine is revved up, the belts are adjusted correctly. If there's a thwapping, whining, or howling sound, adjust the belt tension again. If you can't eliminate the sounds, the problem could be worn-out belts or a worn-out cam box that is allowing the cam to move back and forth causing the distributor gear to tap against the cam box. You'll have to see the pros.

Step 4. Install Belt Covers.

Check the rubber seals for the belt covers and replace any that are torn, broken, or missing. Be sure there are no loose parts in the belt covers (like bolts, nuts, and washers) before installing them. If the front cover is off, install it, then install the left-hand and right-hand covers. On Turbo models, don't forget to install the metal plate on the bottom left side of the covers. It slides in from the side. Be sure all the bolts are installed and snug.

EVERYONE: If you have air conditioning, fit the A/C shroud over the water pump pulley while you install the vaned aluminum fan clutch onto the pulley. Tighten the nuts that attach the fan clutch to the water pump pulley. Install the fan shroud onto the rear of the radiator, then install and tighten the mounting bolts.

Install the electric cooling fan and shroud onto the right rear side of the radiator. Install and tighten the mounting bolts, then connect the electric wires for the fan. Fit the wires and/or hoses into the holder on top of the fan shroud.

Look for other things that were removed or disconnected during disassembly. Connect or install them. Clear all rags, tools, and beer cans from the engine compartment.

Now you can start the engine and enjoy the absence of the loose cam belt thwapping noise.

Let the engine warm up and check that the electric cooling fan kicks on. If it doesn't, check the electrical connection again.

Step 5. Replace Cam Belts.

Always replace the cam belts as a set. Never replace only one of the belts.

Remove the drive belts (Chapter 10, Step 3).

Remove the four 10mm nuts that attach the water pump pulley and pulley cover to the water pump. Remove the pulley and cover.

Remove the timing hole cover plug at the top rear of the engine. It's the hole where you check the ignition timing. Fit the special Subaru flywheel stopper or drive plate stopper tool into the hole. Use a socket and ratchet on the crankshaft pulley bolt to turn the engine *clockwise* (as viewed from the front of the engine). As you're turning the engine, wiggle the stopper tool so it engages with the drive plate or flywheel and locks the engine. If you don't have one of these tools, see Step 3 for alternative methods of locking the engine.

Now you can turn the crank pulley bolt *counterclockwise* to loosen it. The bolt might be pretty tight, so be careful where your hands will end up if the bolt breaks loose suddenly or the engine lock slips. Once the bolt is loose, remove the engine lock. Use the socket and ratchet on the pulley bolt to rotate the engine clockwise until the timing mark (a small dimple) in the left camshaft sprocket is aligned with the notch in the top of the rear belt cover (see "Aligning the Camshaft Sprockets" illustration). Look into the timing hole on the top rear of the engine. Three lines should be visible, and the centerline should be aligned with the tip of the triangle pointer (see the Flywheel Timing Marks illustration). Turn the engine, if necessary, to align the pointer and the centerline. Now remove the crank pulley while being sure that the dimple in the cam sprocket stays aligned with the notch in the belt cover and the centerline on the flywheel stays even with the pointer.

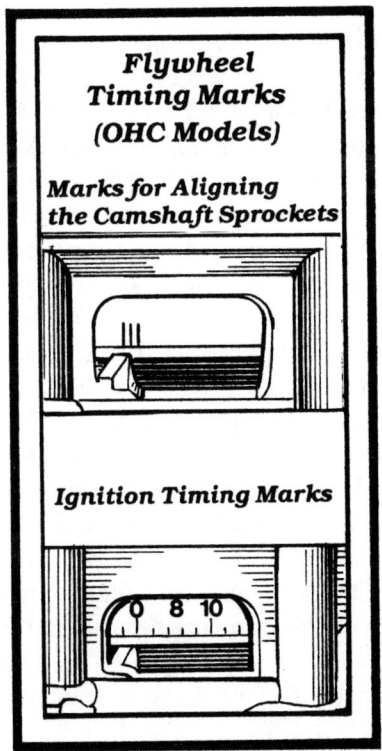

Disconnect the wiring harness from the oil pressure switch or gauge located at the bottom front of the engine.

Find the bolt on the right front side of the engine which attaches the engine oil dipstick tube to the engine. Clean around the tube where it fits into a lower tube (you don't want any dirt falling into the engine when you remove the dipstick tube). Remove the bolt, then wiggle the dipstick tube out of its holder. Cover the open tube with a clean rag to keep dirt out.

Turbo models: Remove the three bolts that attach the belt cover plate to the bottom left side of the cam belt covers. Slide the plate to the left to remove it.

EVERYONE: Remove the left- and right-hand belt covers (Step 2), then remove the front belt cover.

If you are going to use these cam belts again, use chalk or paint to make an arrow on the top outside surface of the belts to indicate which direction they turn. Since the engine turns clockwise, as viewed from the front, make arrows on the top surface of the belt pointing toward the left (driver's) side of the car.

The cam belts must be as slack as possible in order to remove them. To slacken the belts, the tensioner pulleys must be pulled away from the belts, then locked in that position by the tensioner adjusting bolts. While loosening the belts, you'll be struggling against the tensioner springs, which are trying to pull the tensioner against the belts to tighten them. Let's do it. Loosen bolts A and B on the right-hand tensioner (see illustration for "Adjusting Right-Hand Timing Belt"). Push down on the tensioner and hold it down while you snug the bolts to hold the tensioner in the down position.

Wiggle the right-hand belt off the cam sprocket, tensioner, and crankshaft sprocket. If you are going to use the belt again, stash it where it won't get dirty or greasy.

Loosen bolts C and D on the left-hand tensioner about ½ turn. Use the tension wrench to raise the left-hand tensioner (see the illustration), then snug the bolts down again. Wrap tape or a rag around the end of the wrench so it doesn't scratch the crankshaft.

If you don't have the tension wrench, look at the illustration for "Adjusting Left-Hand Timing Belt." Squeeze the belt together where the large arrows are pointing at the belt. This should raise the tensioner while you tighten the bolts to hold it in the up position. If this method doesn't work for you, use a strong, long screwdriver, broom handle, or hammer handle to pry the tensioner up while you tighten the bolts. Be careful not to scratch the crank or anything with your tool.

Now you can wiggle the left-hand belt off the cam sprocket, tensioner, crank sprocket No. 2, and the oil pump sprocket at the bottom front of the engine. Stash it somewhere clean if you are going to use it again.

The belts are liberated!

Step 6. Check Belts, Sprockets, Tensioners, Idler.

Belts: I assume that you are here to replace the cam belts, but just in case you want (or need) to use the old belts again, check them carefully for breaks, cracks, and any teeth that appear to be worn more than the others. If you find any of these things, or if there's any trace of cracks on the outside of the belts, replace them.

Sprockets: Check the teeth for chips, cracks, and areas that are worn more than others. If you find any of these things, replace the sprocket. To replace the cam sprockets, you'll need a tool like the one shown in the illustration to hold the sprocket while you loosen and tighten the mounting bolts. No tool? Stick two phillips screwdrivers or punches into two of the holes on the front surface of the sprocket, then use a long screwdriver or hammer handle between them to prevent the sprocket from turning.

Install the cam sprocket so the little timing mark (dimple) is toward the front of the car. Thanks to a little dowel pin in the end of the camshaft, the sprocket will only fit on the cam in one position, so it's impossible to install it incorrectly.

Tensioners: Spin the tensioner pulleys and listen for noise. Try to wiggle each pulley on its shaft. If you hear a rumble or scratchy sound, or if the pulley is loose on its shaft, replace the tensioner. Here's how. Just remove the tension adjusting bolts, then disconnect the tensioner spring. Connect the tensioner spring to the new tensioner, then install the two mounting bolts.

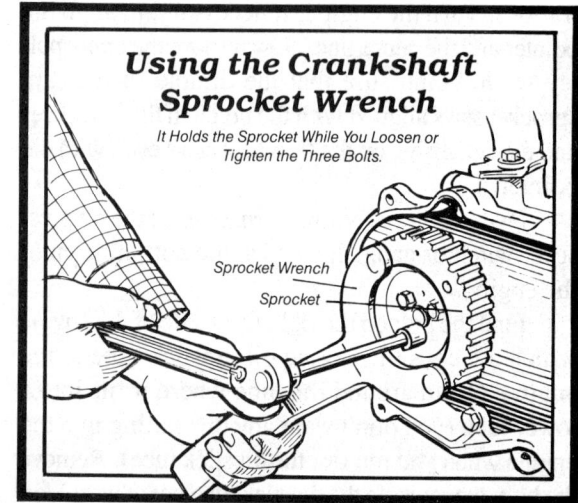

Using the Crankshaft Sprocket Wrench

It Holds the Sprocket While You Loosen or Tighten the Three Bolts.

Sprocket Wrench
Sprocket

Idler: The idler is that sprocket on the lower left side of the engine, just below the left belt tensioner. Check the idler the same way you checked the tensioners.

Step 7. Prepare to Install Cam Belts.

If both crankshaft sprockets came off the crank when you removed the cam belts, install sprocket No. 2 (see the illustration). It doesn't have a dowel pin. Then install crank sprocket No. 1 with the dowel pin facing the front of the car.

Check that the centerline on the flywheel is still aligned with the triangle pointer. If it isn't, slip the crank pulley onto the end of the crankshaft and install the pulley bolt. Use your socket and ratchet to slowly turn the engine until the middle line is even with the tip of the triangle pointer.

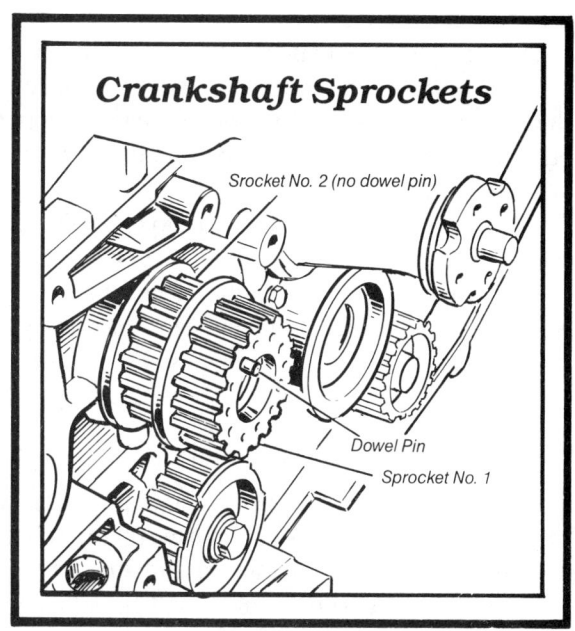

Now find the timing marks (little dimples) on the front surfaces of both camshaft sprockets. The dimples must be positioned so they are exactly beneath little notches in the rear cam covers (check the illustration). If the sprockets need to be turned, use the sprocket wrench, if you have one, or stick a couple of small phillips screwdrivers or punches into two of the holes on the front of the sprockets. Use a large screwdriver or hammer handle between the screwdrivers or punches to rotate the sprocket *clockwise* until the dimple is aligned with the notch. Align both cam sprockets.

Check that the right tensioner is down as far as it will go (bolt B should be at the top of the slot). The left tensioner should be as far up as possible (bolt D should be at the bottom of the slot). Check that bolts B and D are snug, then loosen bolts A and C ½ turn. See Step 3 if you aren't sure where these bolts are located.

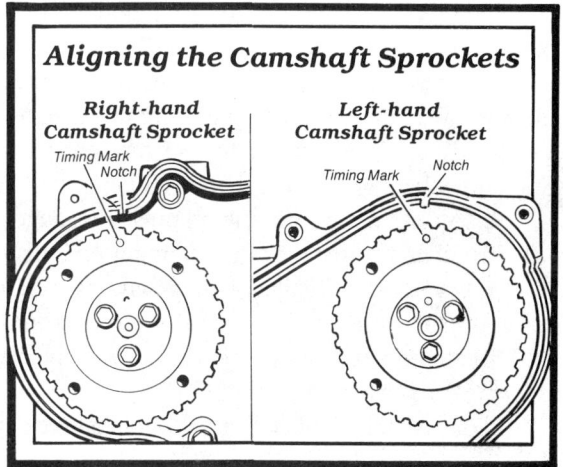

OK, everything should be set up for installing the cam belts. Leave the crank pulley on the crank because removing the pulley bolt now would probably turn the engine.

Step 8. Install Camshaft Belts.

Install the long, left-hand belt first. If you are using the old belt, find your arrow and install the belt so the arrow is pointing toward the left side of the car.

Slip the belt over the crank pulley and onto the crank sprocket and oil pump sprocket. Pull the top of the belt below the tensioner and slip the lower part of the belt under the idler sprocket. Now, keep tension on the belt while you fit it over the cam sprocket and wiggle it all the way on. Loosen bolt D ½ turn to allow the tensioner to press on the belt so it can't slip.

IMPORTANT NOTE: Whatever you do, don't skip the next paragraph.

Put your socket and ratchet on the crankshaft pulley bolt and rotate the engine one complete turn *clockwise* (as viewed from the front of the car). Watch for the three lines on the flywheel to come around again, indicating the engine has made one complete revolution. Align the middle line on the flywheel or torque plate with the triangle pointer on the timing hole, just like it was before.

Grab the shorter, right-hand belt. Remember, if you're using the old belt again, install it so the arrow on top is pointing toward the left side of the car. Check that the dimple on the right cam sprocket is still aligned with the notch in the rear cam cover. The dimple in the left-hand cam sprocket will be at the bottom now.

Slip the right belt over the crank pulley and onto the crank sprocket. Lift the bottom part of the belt onto the right belt tensioner. Hold tension on the bottom of the belt, next to the tensioner, while you slide it onto the right cam sprocket. When the belt is on the sprocket, loosen bolt B by ½ turn to allow the tensioner to press against the belt.

Now use the socket and ratchet to rotate the engine at least three full turns *clockwise*. This aligns the cam belts so the belt tension adjustment will be accurate.

Adjust the belt tension for the left belt, then the right belt as described in Step 3. After both belts are adjusted, turn the engine *clockwise* and recheck that the flywheel mark and the cam sprocket dimples are still aligned with the marks. Check the setting for the left belt, then rotate the engine one full turn and check the right belt. If the marks are off, remove the belt and try again.

Step 9. Finish the Job.

Use the socket and ratchet to rotate the crank *clockwise* while you insert the flywheel or torque plate stopper, or whatever tool you are using, into the timing hole to lock the engine. Once the engine is locked, turn the crank bolt *counterclockwise* to remove it. Pull the crank pulley off the end of the crankshaft. Be sure the rubber seals in the timing belt covers are in place. Check that nothing is in the front belt cover (like a bolt or washer), then install the front cover. Install and tighten the front cover bolts. Fit the rubber plugs into the holes on the front of the cover. Now install the left- and right-hand belt covers and tighten the bolts (Step 4).

Turbo models: Install the belt cover plate on the bottom left cam belt cover. It slides in from the side.

EVERYONE: Use whatever method worked for you to lock the engine, then install the crank pulley and pulley bolt. Torque the bolt to 75 ft. lbs.

Fit the water pump pulley and pulley cover onto the water pump, then install and snug down the mounting nuts. Wait until the drive belts are installed to tighten the nuts.

Round up the engine oil dipstick tube and put a little motor oil on the little rubber O-ring that's on the tube. Stick the tube into its hole, then install and tighten the mounting bolt. Insert the dipstick into the tube.

Reconnect the wire to the oil pressure gauge switch.

Install and adjust the alternator and A/C drive belts (Chapter 10, Procedure 3).

Now you can fully tighten the mounting nuts for the water pump pulley. The torque is only 7 ft. lbs., so be careful not to overtighten them or they might break.

Install the A/C fan shroud and fan, then the electric fan and shroud, then reconnect the electric wires. This is all covered in Step 4.

Look around for other things you might have disconnected or removed during disassembly. Connect or install them.

Start the engine and listen to the sound of silence. Let the engine run to check that the electric fans springs to life when the engine warms up. Congratulations. Job well done.

PROCEDURE 9: DISTRIBUTOR CHECKS

Condition: 12,000 miles have elapsed—tune-up time; OR engine is hard to start or running poorly.

Tools and Materials: To check the distributor cap and rotor, you'll need a medium screwdriver, a light wire brush (the wire bush on the end of a battery terminal cleaner will do), a clean rag, and a little solvent or rubbing alcohol.

To check the mechanical and vacuum advance mechanisms that are on some distributors you'll need a 12″ length of 3/32″ (5mm) vacuum hose, maybe a new advance/retard unit, needlenose pliers, and small phillips screwdriver. You may need penetrating oil.

Breakerless distributor models: You'll need brass non-magnetic feeler gauges (.008″-.020″), a medium screwdriver, and a phillips screwdriver. You may need your ratchet and 19mm or 22mm socket.

Remarks: Here's the kind of distributor you have, and which steps to follow to check it:
1975-1976 California models and 1975-1978 non-California models: You have a **breaker point-type distributor**. Instead of doing Step 5 in this procedure, you will need to do Procedure 10 while the distributor cap is off to check, adjust, or replace the breaker points.
1977 and newer California models and all 1979-1987 models (except 1986 SPFI, 1987 SPFI and MPFI and all 1988 OHC models): You have an "electronic" breakerless distributor. These little jewels are about 40 percent more efficient than the old breaker points-type distributors and require a lot less maintenance. Technology triumphs again! Do Steps 1-9 to check your distributor.
1986 SPFI models, 1987 SPFI and MPFI models and all 1988 OHC models: You have an **LED distributor**. Other than inspecting the distributor cap, rotor, and distributor bushings, there's nothing inside the distributor cap to check. So do Steps 1-4 for the checks, then do Step 9 to install the rotor and cap. When the cap is back on you can skip to Procedure 11.

Step 1. Get Ready.

Engine is turned OFF. Block the wheels, set the handbrake, then put the gearshift in Neutral and open the hood.
OHV carb models: Remove the air cleaner housing if it's on (Procedure 5, Step 4).
EVERYONE: Locate the **distributor**. It sticks up out of the top front of the engine on OHV models or up out of the top left rear corner on OHC models. It has five thick wires connected to the cap (seven on six cylinder models).

Step 2. Remove and Inspect Distributor Cap.

The distributor cap is attached to the top of the distributor with two **springy clips** or two **screws** on opposite sides of the cap. Use your fingers or a medium screwdriver to pry open the two springy clips, or loosen the two screws. Lift the cap up and rotate the bottom toward you so you can peek inside. Leave the wires attached to the cap.

Wipe off the outside and inside of the cap with a rag lightly soaked in solvent or alcohol (not the drinking kind). Eyeball the cap for cracks and chips. A typical crack is a faint jagged line, usually near the little **metal posts** inside the cap. Clean the four metal posts on the inside of the cap with a knife blade or wire brush. Check the little **carbon tip** hanging down inside the center of the cap. It's spring-loaded and should pop back out if you push in on it.

If the distributor cap is cracked, the carbon tip is broken or doesn't pop back out when you push on it, or if the metal posts inside the cap look burned and won't clean up, the cap should be replaced with

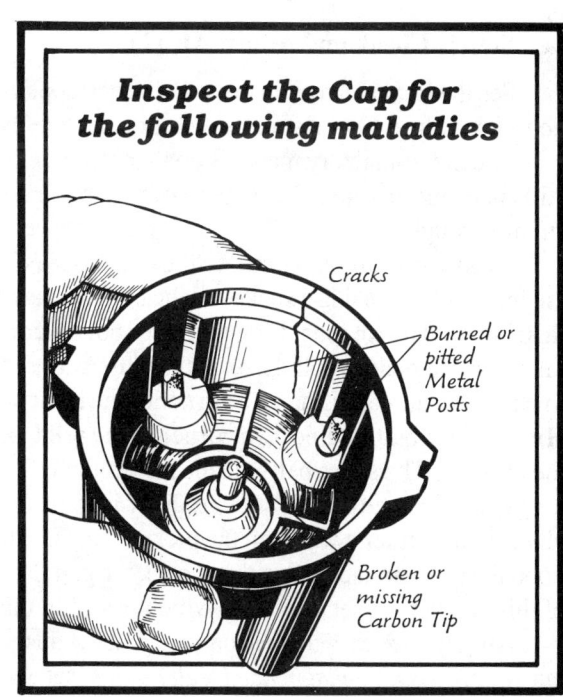

Inspect the Cap for the following maladies

Chapter 7 Procedure 9, Step 3

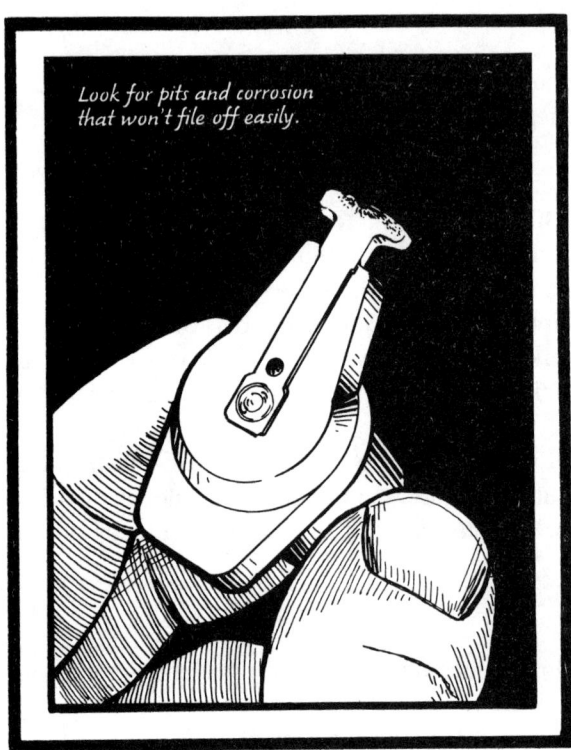

Look for pits and corrosion that won't file off easily.

a new one (Step 10). If the cap is kaput and you're going to replace it, replace the rotor also.

Step 3. Remove and Inspect Rotor.

Now look down into the distributor itself. The **rotor** sits at the center of it—a plastic thing with a metal tip. Look on the side of the rotor that's opposite the metal tip. If you have an LED-type distributor, you'll see a phillips screw there that you'll need to loosen in order to remove the rotor. To remove the rotor, just pull straight up on it. Check the copper end of the rotor for pitting, carbon tracks, and general funk (look at the illustration). Lightly clean the copper end with a fine wire brush. Don't use a file to smooth it. If the metal tip has deep pits or the metal is burned away on one edge, get a new rotor. Rotors and distributor caps work as a team so if one is replaced, replace the other one also.

Step 4. Check Distributor Shaft for Wear.

Grab the **distributor shaft** where the rotor fits and try to move it side to side. (You can also do this with the rotor installed as shown in the illustration.) If the shaft is loose in the distributor housing, the distributor shaft **bushings** might be wearing out. Ask Subaru or a garage for a second opinion. If the bushings are in fact wearing out, see Chapter 17 to remove the distributor, then take it to Subaru or an auto electric shop to have new bushings installed. Chapter 17 also tells you how to install the distributor.

Step 5. Check and Adjust Air Gap.

See the Remarks section to see if this step applies to your model. If you have a breaker points-type distributor, go to Procedure 10 to inspect, adjust, or replace the breaker points.

The Subaru factory manuals don't include this step as part of their periodic maintenance schedule. I would still check the air gap at least every two years, or sooner if the engine seems to lose some of its power or starts running rough.

To check the air gap, remove the opaque plastic dust shield in the distributor, if your's has one. Rotate the engine *clockwise* using a socket on the crank pulley bolt or alternator nut while watching what's going on in the distributor. The rotating thing with four pointy corners you see in there is the **reluctor**. The little black box is known as the **pickup coil**. Look at the illustrations to see which setup you have and where to put the feeler gauge to check the air gap. Line up a corner of the reluctor with the vertical metal line on the pickup coil or, on later Hitachi distributors, line up a corner of the reluctor with one of the metal blades located on opposite sides of the reluctor. The space between the reluctor and the pickup coil or blade is the *air gap*. About the only way the air gap can change once it's set properly is if the distributor shaft wears out. This would let the reluctor move closer to or farther away from the pickup coil. Be sure the ignition switch is OFF. Look at the sticker under the hood for your air gap setting then check the gap. No sticker? Look at the tune-up specifications chart at the end of this chapter, or set it to .014" which is within the correct range for all Subaru breakerless distributors.

Air gaps are easy to check and adjust because there's so much tolerance (clearance) to work with. Whip out your *brass non-magnetized feeler gauge* set and try different blades between the reluctor and pickup until you find one that slips through the gap with just a little resistance. If that blade thickness is between the tolerance figures for your engine, everything's cool and no adjustment is necessary. You can advance to Step 6. If

Maintenance, Lubrication, Tune-up

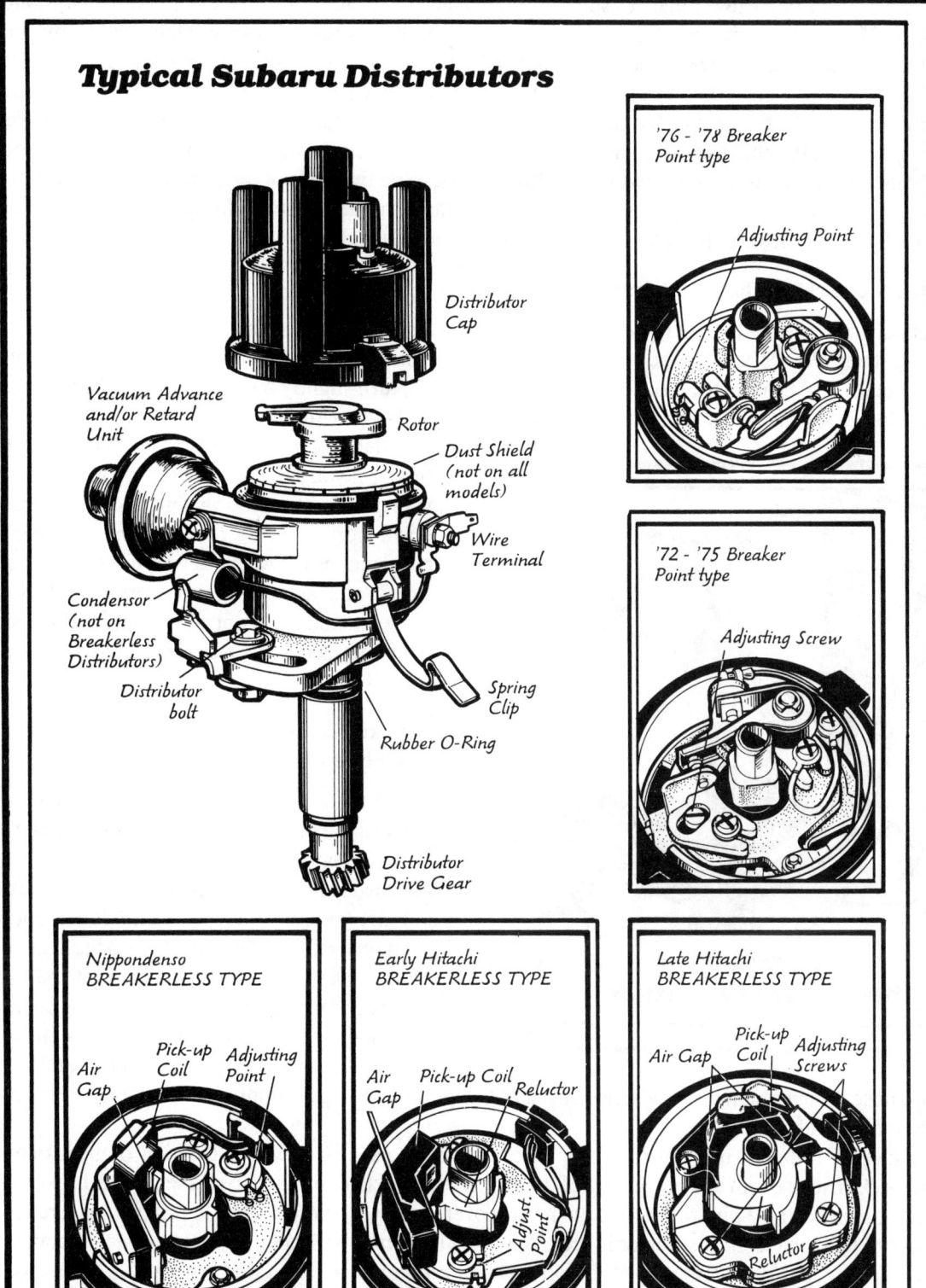

Typical Subaru Distributors

the air gap is wider or narrower than it's supposed to be, then make the adjustment. Here's how: **Nippondenso and Early Hitachi Distributors:** Slightly loosen the two phillips screws that secure the pickup coil. Put one corner of a screwdriver blade between the two little **nipples** on the distributor plate and the other corner of the screwdriver in the **slot** on the pickup coil plate. Move the pickup coil toward or away from the reluctor by turning the screwdriver a little, then tighten the phillips screws. Check the gap again. When the gap is within the tolerance figures, snug down the phillips screws one last time and you're finished. Easy, isn't it? **Late Hitachi Distributors:** Slightly loosen the two phillips screws that secure the blades on the sides of the reluctor. Move the blades to change the air gap. When the gap is within the specifications, tighten the two phillips screws.

EVERYONE: Always check the ignition timing if you adjust the air gap (Procedure 13).

Step 6. Check Mechanical Advance.

A faulty advance/retard unit or worn out or loose mechanical advance springs can make the car backfire, hard to start and idle, or have less power. To check the mechanical advance mechanism, grab the rotor and turn it *counterclockwise*. The distributor shaft it's mounted on will turn slightly but should spring back to its original position as soon as you release the rotor. If it does, skip down to Step 8.

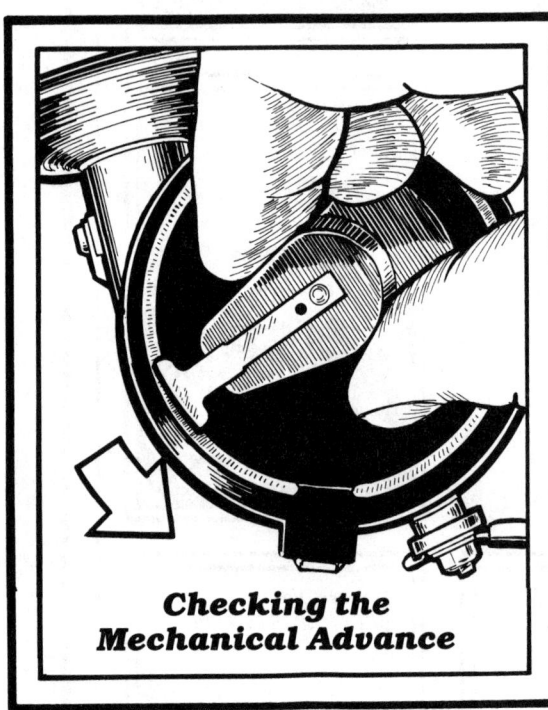

Checking the Mechanical Advance

If the rotor doesn't snap back to its original position or if you can't turn the rotor, either the springs in the depths of the distributor are shot or there's junk down there. Do Step 7 to see if the **circlip** is loose and jamming the works. If it isn't, it's the springs and we can't fix them. They're set very carefully to comply with emission control standards. Have Subaru or an auto electric shop check and replace the springs if need be.

Step 7. Check Vacuum Unit Arm in Distributor.

A little metal **arm** goes from inside the vacuum unit to a **pin** on the movable **distributor plate** inside the distributor. The points or pickup coil are also attached to this plate, depending on the type of distributor you have. When vacuum is present in the vacuum unit, it pulls or pushes on the arm and the plate moves, altering the position of the plate to advance or retard the timing. Depending on the year and model, some of the vacuum units are strictly advance units, some are retard units, and the ones with two hoses connected to them advance or retard the ignition timing depending on the vacuum condition in the intake manifold.

Remove the rotor and dust shield (if you have one) so you have an unobstructed view of the inside of the distributor. Locate the arm and pin and see if the arm is still attached to the pin or if the pin has broken off the plate. If the arm is off the pin, fit the hole on the arm over the pin. You might have to remove the screw(s) that attach the vacuum unit to the distributor in order to wiggle the arm over the pin. Look for a small groove around the pin near the top. Not all Subaru distributors have a *circlip groove*. If you find an empty groove, look for a loose *circlip* laying somewhere inside the distributor. If you're remarkably lucky, you'll find it. Examine the circlip; if it looks OK, slip it on the pin so it snaps into the groove. (Be sure the carburetor is covered so the circlip can't accidentally fly in there while you're trying to install it.) Replace the circlip if it's bent or slides onto the pin too easily.

If you removed the vacuum unit mounting screw(s), install and tighten it/them.

Step 8. Check and Replace Vacuum Advance/Retard Unit.

Disconnect the hose(s) from the round **vacuum unit** that's attached to the side of the distributor, then connect one end of a 12" to 18" long, 3/16" (5mm) inside-diameter hose to the unit. (If you don't have a hose handy, borrow one from someplace else on the engine. Be sure to put it back after checking the vacuum unit.) Suck hard on the other end of the hose while watching the inside of the distributor. The arm on the vacuum unit should move the distributor plate when you suck on the hose. If you have two vacuum hose connections on the unit, check them both. One connection should make the plate move *counterclockwise* and the other connection should make it move *clockwise*.

If the diaphragms in the vacuum unit are good, you should be able to suck on the hose, then cover the end with your tongue to hold the plate in its advanced or retarded position. If the diaphragm is broken and leaking, you'll have to keep sucking on the hose to keep the plate in the advanced or retarded position. Replace the unit if it won't hold vacuum.

If sucking on the hose doesn't move the plate, try moving it by pushing and pulling on the pin where the vacuum arm attaches or on the pin sticking through the points set. The plate should be free to move about ¼". Plate stuck? Squirt a little penetrating oil around the outer edge of the plate and let it soak awhile. Try moving the pin again. Sometimes a stuck plate can be loosened by repeatedly using penetrating oil and moving the pin. If the plate just won't loosen enough to move by sucking on the hose, the distributor needs to be rebuilt or replaced. If sucking on the hose didn't move the plate, but you could move it easily with your fingers, the vacuum unit is broken.

To replace a vacuum unit, remove the screw(s) that attach it to the distributor body. Pry the circlip (if you have one) from the pin with a small screwdriver. Don't let the clip fall through the hole in the distributor plate. Pull on the vacuum unit until it's almost out of the distributor housing, then wiggle the arm off the pin. While the vacuum unit is off see if the distributor plate moves easily by rotating it with the vacuum arm pin. If it doesn't, squirt some penetrating oil around the edge and work the plate back and forth until it moves freely. If it's stuck and won't loosen up, see Chapter 17 to remove the distributor. Take it to Subaru or an auto electric shop for repair.

To install the new vacuum unit, stick the arm of the new unit into the distributor and hook the arm over the pin. Push the unit into the distributor housing. If you have a circlip setup, snap the circlip into the groove on the pin (be sure the carburetor is covered with a rag). Install the screw(s) that attach the unit to the distributor and tighten them. Attach the hose(s) to the vacuum unit. If there are two hose connections on yours, be sure to hook them up the same as they were on the old one. Install the plastic dust shield if you have one, the rotor, and distributor cap.

If you are here from the ignition timing procedure because the line on the flywheel didn't move when you revved the engine, check the ignition timing again. The line should move now when you rev the engine.

Step 9. Install Rotor and Cap.

If you're going to check, adjust, or replace the points (Procedure 10), leave the cap and rotor off for now. Come back here to install the rotor and cap when you're finished.

To install the rotor, line up the flat spring on the inside of the rotor's hole with the flat spot on the distributor shaft. Push the rotor down while turning it until it locks into place. If your rotor has a set screw on the side, use a screwdriver to tighten the screw.

The bottom edge of the distributor cap has a **notch** in it that fits over a **tab** on the rim of the distributor body. When fitting the cap back onto the distributor, rotate the cap until it slips down on the tab. Hold the cap in position with one hand while you screw in the two screws (if yours has screws), or lift one of the springy clips up to the side of the cap. Press on the rounded middle part of the clip until the top snaps into the groove on the cap. Now fit the other springy clip the same way. If the springy clips won't fit, don't hammer on them; you haven't lined the cap up properly.

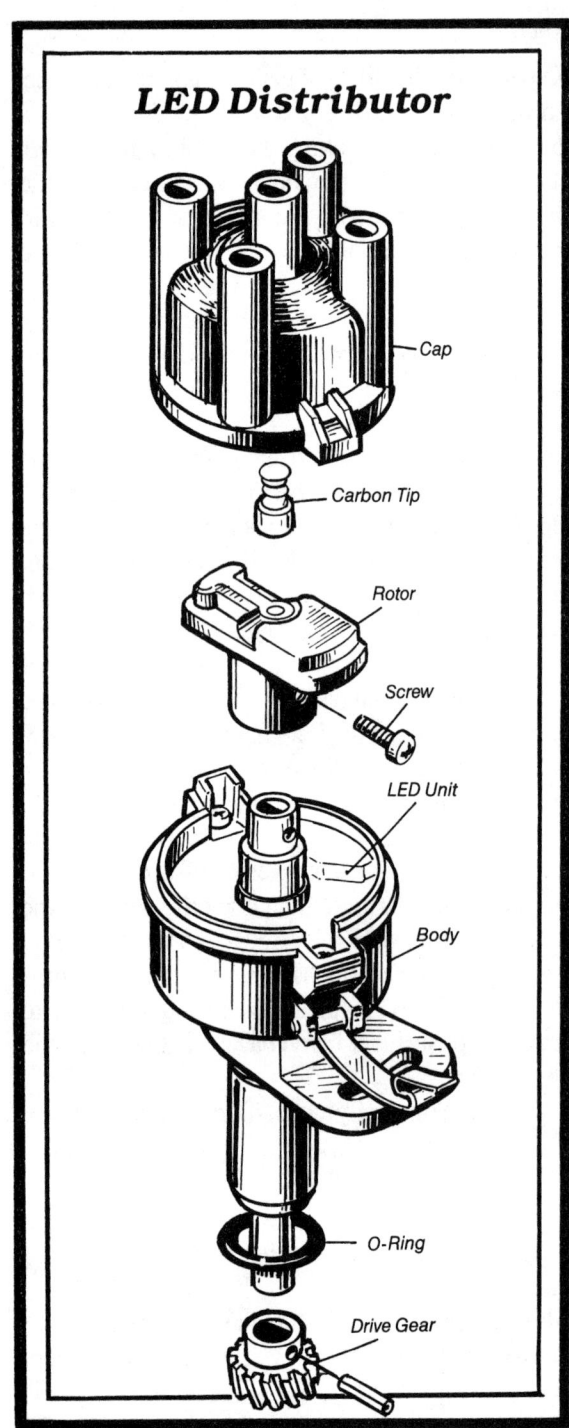

LED Distributor

Step 10. Replace Distributor Cap and Rotor.

This is only for you if you're putting in a brand new cap and rotor. Remove the cap and rotor from the distributor. Leave the five thick wires in the old distributor cap for the moment. If your distributor has a flat plastic dust shield, be sure it's in place before installing the rotor. Install the new rotor by lining up the **flat spring** inside the rotor's hole with the flat spot on the steel **distributor shaft** at the center of the distributor body. Push the rotor down on the shaft as far as it will go. It should fit snugly on the shaft. Snug down the set screw if your rotor has one.

Put the new cap on the distributor, lining up the notch on the cap rim with the tab on the rim of the distributor body. Snap the clips into place, or tighten down the screws.

OHV models: If you can't move the old cap far enough out of the way to install the new cap, release the #1 and #3 spark plug wires and the coil wire (the one that goes to the center of the distributor cap) from the white **plastic clip** on the right side of the engine. Now you should be able to fit the new cap onto the distributor.

EVERYONE: Transfer the spark plug wires one at a time from the old cap to the new cap so they don't get out of order. Just grab one close to the cap and twist it back and forth while you pull it straight out. The wires should end up in the same position on the new cap as they were on the old one. Think; go slow, one wire at a time. If the ends of the spark plug wires or the coil wire are corroded or dirty, use your wire brush to clean the ends before plugging them into the new cap. Push each one all the way into its hole on the new cap, making sure the **connector boot** is snugly over the nipple on the cap. Fit the spark plug and coil wires back into the plastic clip if you removed them.

PROCEDURE 10: INSPECT, ADJUST, REPLACE BREAKER POINTS

First, read the Remarks section of Procedure 9 to determine if you have any breaker points to inspect, adjust, or replace. If you have breaker points, read on.

Breaker points (usually just called *points*) are mounted to a flat **distributor plate** (also called a breaker plate) inside the distributor. As various components of the points wear away, the critical point gap changes, so you have to periodically adjust or replace the points set. This is a very important part of the tune-up, to ensure better engine performance, improved economy, smoother running, and increased longevity.

Condition: 12,000-mile tune-up time; OR engine is running poorly.

Procedure 10, Step 1 *Maintenance, Lubrication, Tune-up* 121

Tools and Materials: Medium screwdriver, medium phillips head screwdriver, feeler gauge, Tach/Dwell meter (if you can afford one), 10mm wrench or 10mm socket and ratchet, 19mm or 22mm socket and ratchet depending on the size of your crank pulley bolt.

Step 1. Inspect Points.

Block the wheels, set the handbrake, put the gearshift in NEUTRAL. Be sure the ignition key is OFF.

Release the **distributor cap** (Procedure 9, Step 2) and push it out of the way. The plastic **rotor** sits in the middle of the distributor body. Pull up on the rotor to remove it. If your distributor has an *opaque plastic dust cover* beneath the rotor, lift it out so you can see the points. Now put the socket and ratchet on the **crankshaft pulley nut** and turn the engine *clockwise*. (See Procedure 5, Step 6, if you need more detail). While rotating the engine with the ratchet, take a look at what's happening in the distributor.

Right next to the end of the distributor shaft is the **points set** (or *points*). There's a movable arm and a stationary arm. The movable arm has a little piece of fiber or plastic that rides on the turning **distributor shaft** (look at the illustration). The points open (spread apart, leaving a gap) as the squarish distributor shaft rotates its corners (called *lobes*) under the fiber or plastic block on the movable point arm. (I call the little block a **lobe rider**.) At the high point of each lobe the points are separated the maximum amount. When a lobe rotates past the lobe rider, the points close. The next lobe opens them again, and so on.

Some Subaru distributors have a *second* lobe rider mounted on a spring opposite the one that opens the points. It's called a **spring damper**. Don't confuse the spring damper with the points.

Using a screwdriver as a lever between the long, movable arm of the points and the distributor shaft, spread the points and have a look at the two small round **contact surfaces** on the end of the point arms. (This is where the points meet when they are closed.) They should be flat and smooth. Do either of the two surfaces have pits or small white deposits on them? Look closely. If so, they must be replaced. In days gone by, you could file the points smooth and keep using them. Today's points are made of such hard material that filing on them is a waste of time, except in an extreme emergency. It's just as quick and easy to replace the points as it is to file them.

Check the condition of the lobe rider for wear. If it's worn unevenly or worn down almost to the metal arm, you need new points. If your distributor has a spring damper, check it for wear the same way.

If the points are shot, go to Step 5 to replace them.

Points OK? If you don't have a dwell meter, go on to Step 2 to check the gap. If you have a dwell meter, move ahead to Step 3.

Step 2. Check Point Gap (no dwell meter).

The correct points gap is .020" for '75 models and .018" for '76-'78 models. Put the socket and

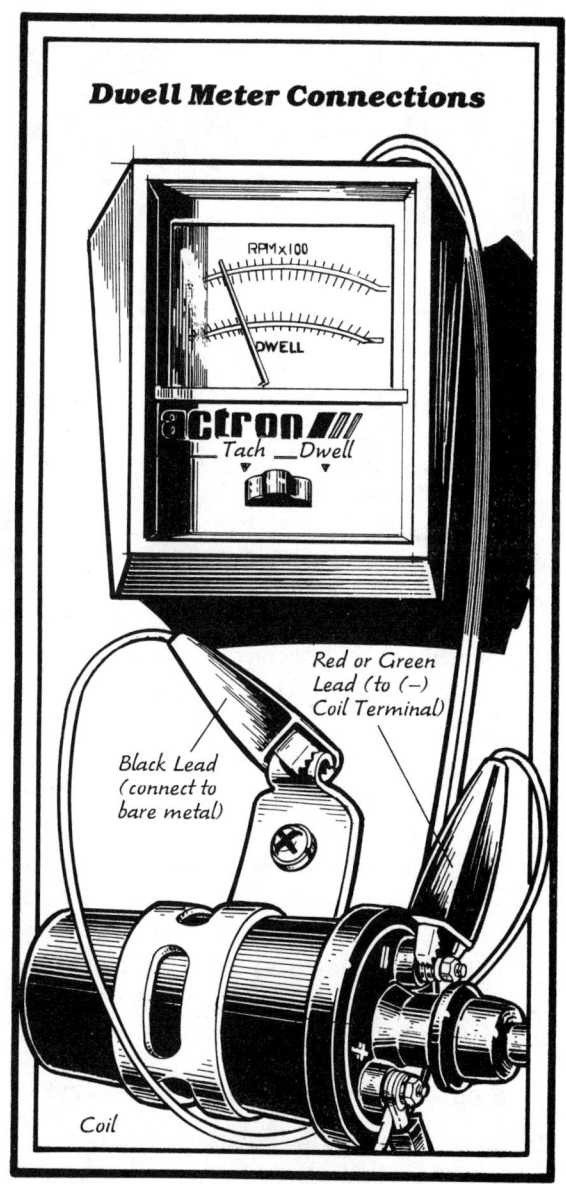

Adjusting the Points ('76-'78 Models)

ratchet on the crank pulley bolt and rotate the engine *clockwise* until the lobe rider is exactly on the corner of one of the lobes so the points are opened up as far as they'll go.

Whip out the appropriate **feeler gauge blade**, wipe it clean, then insert it between the end of the arm that moves and the end of the stationary arm—right between the two contact surfaces. Hold the blade parallel with the stationary arm. If you're lucky, the gauge will just barely fit between the two points without spreading them farther apart. A very slight resistance when you slip the gauge out means they're right on so you can skip to Step 6. If the blade won't fit, or if it fits with room to spare, the points need to be adjusted. Go to step 4.

Points are good? Install the opaque plastic dust cover, the rotor, and the distributor cap if they are off.

Remove the socket and ratchet from the pulley bolt.

Step 3. Check Point Gap with Dwell Meter.

Hook up your **dwell meter** according to the instructions that came with it. If the instructions disappeared the day after you got the gauge (mine usually do), try hooking it up this way: If there are two wires coming out of your dwell meter, connect the black wire to the negative (ground) terminal of the battery or to bare metal, and connect the other wire (could be red or green) to the negative (-) side of the **ignition coil**. If your meter has three wires, connect the black one to the negative battery post, the red one to the positive battery post, and the other one (green maybe?) to the (-) side of the coil. Switch the meter to the *four cylinder position* (eight cylinder position, if yours doesn't have a four cylinder position). Make sure the meter is set on the *Dwell* position if you are checking the points dwell, or to the Tachometer (Tach) position if you are checking the engine speed.

Clear tools, parts, rags and dwell meter wires away from the fan and drive belt(s). Set the meter in a secure position so it won't fall into the works. Remove the socket and ratchet from the crank pulley if they're still there. Be sure all the vacuum lines that were connected to the air cleaner are plugged. Take the rag off the top of the carburetor, then start the engine and let it warm up a few minutes. (Remember, you shouldn't run the engine in a closed garage.) The dwell meter should read between 49° and 55° on a four cylinder scale or between 24.5° and 27.5° on an eight cylinder scale. Since the point gap narrows as various components on the points set wear away, I set my points at the wide end of the range (49°-50°).

If the dwell reading is below 49° (24.5), the point gap is set too wide. A reading above 55° (27.5) means the point gap isn't wide enough. Either way it's points adjusting time. Not difficult, but you'll have to take the distributor cap off again. Turn off the engine and proceed to Step 4.

Step 4. Adjust Point Gap (if necessary).

Remarks: Changing the point gap also changes the engine timing so be sure to check the timing after adjusting the points (Procedure 13).

Procedure 10, Step 5   *Maintenance, Lubrication, Tune-up*   123

Back in the days when the most popular cars on the road were Model T and Model A Fords, people used a dime instead of a feeler gauge to set the points. Ah, the simple days of yore. (If you didn't have a dime could you use two nickels?)

Remove the distributor cap, rotor, and plastic dust shield. Use a socket and ratchet on the crank pulley to rotate the engine until the lobe rider is on the corner of one of the lobes again and the points are open as far as they can go.

The correct point gap is .020" for '75 models and .018" for '76-'78 models. There are two different point gap adjustment setups in Subaru distributors. If yours isn't covered under the description for your year, check the other setup. Someone might have changed distributors.

'75 models: The points are adjusted by turning a **screw head** located in an oval hole near the **stationary points arm**. To change the point gap, loosen the phillips mounting screw near the stationary point arm about ¼ turn. Now turn the screw in the oval hole *clockwise* to widen the gap or *counterclockwise* to narrow the gap. If you still can't make the stationary post move, slightly loosen the phillips screw on the other end of the points.

'76-'78 models with breaker point type distributors: Your distributor has two little **nipples** in the distributor plate near the **stationary point arm** and a **slot** in the shiny points plate right next to the two nipples. To adjust the points in this setup, loosen the phillips screw near the stationary point arm about ¼ turn. Insert one corner of a regular screwdriver blade between the two nipples and the other corner of the blade into the slot in the points plate. Turn the screwdriver slightly *clockwise* to make the points gap narrower. Turn it slightly *counterclockwise* to widen the gap. If the stationary arm won't budge, slightly loosen the phillips screw on the other end of the points.

EVERYONE: Be sure the lobe rider is on the corner of one of the lobes. If you're adjusting the points with a feeler gauge, narrow or widen the gap until the correct blade slides between the points with a very slight resistance. Keep the blade straight. When the gap is right, tighten both phillips head mounting screws (tighten the one furthest from the adjusting screwhead first), then check the gap again. Sometimes the gap narrows when the mounting screws are tightened. Try again, maybe anticipating a slight narrowing of the gap once the mounting screws are snug. When you're satisfied that the gap is correct, install the plastic dust shield, rotor, and distributor cap.

If you're using a dwell meter to set the points, *slightly* widen the gap if your reading was high, or narrow the gap if your dwell meter reading was low (Step 3). Now tighten the phillips mounting screws, doing the one farthest from the adjusting screwhead first. Put the plastic dust shield, rotor, and cap back on the distributor, snap it in place, start the engine and check the dwell meter reading again. Sometimes it takes a few tries. If it's not on the money, turn the engine off, remove the cap, and try again. Be patient and you'll get it.

When you have the point gap set so the dwell reads right on your meter, rev up the engine while watching the dwell meter. Here's how to rev (speed up) the engine without getting in the car and pushing on the gas pedal. Locate a thin **cable** next to the lower right side of the **carburetor**. It's right behind the distributor. The cable goes into a slot on the rounded top of a **throttle lever** that's attached to the carburetor. Put a finger under the bottom front of the throttle lever and lift up to increase the engine speed.

OK, now rev the engine while watching the dwell meter. If the needle wanders more than 10 degrees on the meter, the points are loose or the distributor shaft is worn. Turn the engine off again. Remove the cap and rotor and see if the points are securely mounted to the distributor. Tighten the two phillips mounting screws if they're loose. Try moving the distributor shaft front to rear and side to side. Just grab the end of it and wiggle. If the shaft moves significantly, the distributor needs new bushings or a military funeral. (See Chapter 17 for distributor removal and installation. Take the distributor to Subaru or an auto electric shop to see if they can install new bushings.)

You can move on to Step 6 if the points are good and the point gap has been set to correct specifications with either the feeler gauge or dwell meter.

Step 5. Replace Points and Condenser.

The points and condenser work as a team, so if you replace one half of the team, replace the other half too. If the engine's running, turn it off, then remove the distributor cap, rotor, and plastic dust shield (if you have one).

The points are held in place by two phillips head **mounting screws**. Loosen the two screws just enough to slide the set of points out of the distributor. Don't remove the screws completely—they might fall down into the distributor. Move the little ground wire that's attached to one of the mounting screws to one side as you slip the set out from under the loosened screws. Loosen the phillips screw or 8mm nut on the **wire terminal** on the outside of the distributor. Pull up on the wire coming from the points. The points are now liberated.

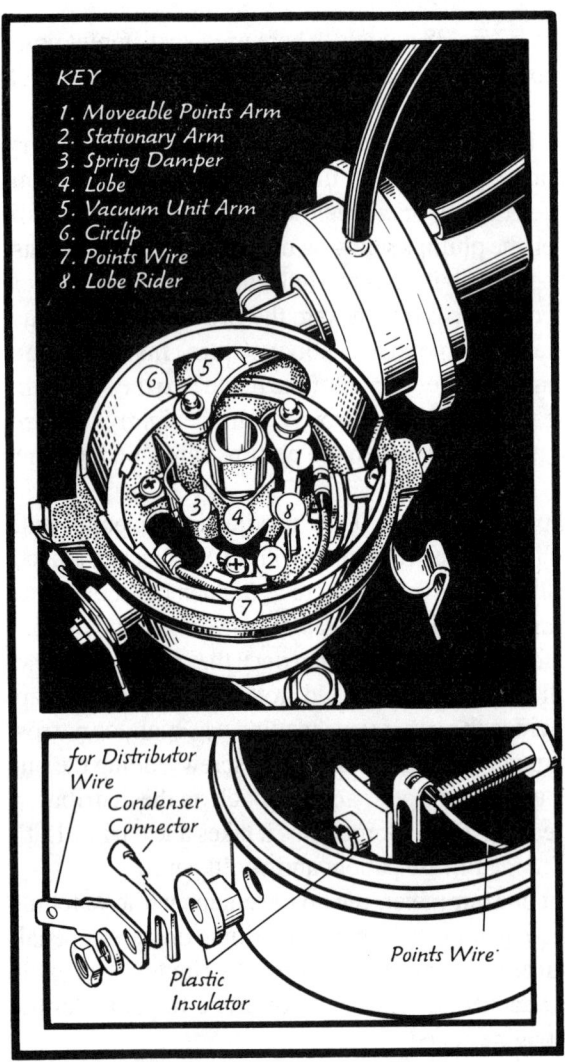

KEY
1. Moveable Points Arm
2. Stationary Arm
3. Spring Damper
4. Lobe
5. Vacuum Unit Arm
6. Circlip
7. Points Wire
8. Lobe Rider

for Distributor Wire
Condenser Connector
Plastic Insulator
Points Wire

The **condenser** looks like a small metal can about the size of a thimble with a wire coming out of one end. It's mounted to the outside of the distributor with a phillips head screw. Remove the screw. Slip the condenser wire off the terminal screw on the outside of the distributor. If the condenser wire has a washerlike loop on the end, you'll have to take the nut off. Be careful not to let the little wire terminal bolt fall into the distributor housing. You might need to hold the other end of the bolt with needlenose pliers while you remove the nut and lockwasher. Slip the condenser wire off the terminal, then put the washer and nut back on the screw so they don't get lost.

While the points are out, clean the inside and outside of the distributor with a rag dampened with alcohol or solvent, or spray it with some carburetor cleaner, then wipe it with a rag or paper towel. Clean the contact surfaces of the new points set with the alcohol or carb cleaner, or at least wipe them with a clean rag. New points sets are usually coated with oil to prevent corrosion. If not removed, the oil can cause arcing and premature burning of the contact surfaces.

If the new points set didn't come with a wire attached, you'll have to transfer the wire from the old point set to the new set. Loosen the phillips screw on the side of the old points and slide the wire out. Install it on the new points just like it was on the old points, then tighten the screw.

Slide the new points set into the distributor under the phillips screws and washers. Move the set around until the tab on the bottom goes into its hole on the distributor plate. Be sure the little ground wire is under the phillips mounting screw. Don't tighten the two mounting screws completely until the points have been adjusted, just snug them down a little. Put the new condenser in place on the outside of the distributor and attach it with its screw.

Slip the pronged end of the wire attached to the points onto the terminal on the inside of the distributor. Be sure the plastic insulation block is between the wire and the distributor housing. Slide the condenser wire onto the wire terminal on the outside of the distributor. Install the 8mm nut and washers, if they were removed, while pressing a finger or needlenose pliers against the other end of the bolt on the inside of the distributor. Tighten the nut or the screw depending on your setup.

Lubricate the distributor, Step 6, then go to Step 4 and adjust the point gap. Even if you have a dwell meter, you'll have to set the gap with a feeler gauge the first time around with a newly installed points set.

Procedure 10, Step 6   Maintenance, Lubrication, Tune-up   125

Step 6. Lubricate Distributor (breaker points-type only).

The distributor cap and rotor are off, right? Eyeball the end of the distributor shaft. If there's a **felt wick** in the top of the shaft, squirt four drops of any oil on the felt wick. If you bought new points, there was probably a small packet or capsule of grease in the package. Open the packet and put a small dab of grease on the distributor lobes, lobe rider, and spring damper if you have one. No grease packet? Use Bosch grease #64139 or High Temp wheel bearing grease. Just a dab about the size of a wooden match head or end of a Q-tip will do ya.

Adjust the points (Step 4) if you haven't already, then put on the dust shield, rotor, and cap. Snap the cap in place with its clips.

If you're doing a tune-up, move ahead to Procedure 11 to check the spark plugs and do a compression check.

PROCEDURE 11. CHECK SPARK PLUGS, DO A COMPRESSION TEST

Tools and Materials: Spark plug socket, ratchet, 3"-12" extension for the ratchet, light wire brush, spark plug gapper (gauge), antiseize compound. If you are going to do a compression check you'll need a compression gauge, paper and pencil, jumper wire (a piece of insulated wire with alligator clips on each end). Friend to help with compression test.

Remarks: Unless the engine starts running rough, and a tune-up doesn't cure the problem, you don't need to do a compression check until the car has 60,000 miles. After 60,000 miles it's a good idea to do a yearly compression check, and keep the figures, so you'll know if the internal engine parts are wearing out.

CAUTION! Never use Champion spark plugs in SPFI models.

Step 1. Warm Up Engine (maybe).

If you're going to do a compression test, you should first warm up the engine to operating temperature. Watch the TEMP gauge, and shut the engine off when the needle gets to the middle of the gauge.

CAUTION! If the engine has been warmed up or if you've just now parked the car, the spark plugs and nearby parts of the engine will be HOT!

Step 2. Remove and Inspect Spark Plugs.

First, number each spark plug wire with masking tape. On the passenger's side of the engine, plug **number 1** is closest to the right headlight and **number 3** is right behind number 1. On the driver's side, **number 2** is closest to the left headlight and **number 4** is behind number 2. On six cylinder models, plug **number 5** is right behind number 3 and plug **number 6** is right behind plug number 4.

Twist and pull on the heavy part of the plug wires where they fit over the spark plugs. Don't tug on the middle of the wire.

Clean around the spark plug so crud can't fall into the hole when the plug is removed. Use the spark plug socket, extension and ratchet to unscrew the spark plugs *counterclockwise*. For quick removal, loosen the plug a few turns with the ratchet, then snap the ratchet off and use your fingers and the socket to turn out the plug. Keep the spark plugs in order as you take them out so you know which cylinder they came from. On some models you'll have to use a long extension on the ratchet to reach through the air conditioner compressor bracket to get to the #2 spark plug.

The condition of the plugs can tell you a lot about the condition of various components of your engine. The **electrodes** consist of a central metal nubbin encircled by a white insulator, and the metal side wire that hooks over the top. The space between them is the spark plug **gap**. Spark plugs removed from a good, well-tuned '75-'78 engine will have a tan or light gray deposit on the electrodes. A light wire brush, like a battery terminal brush, will easily remove these deposits. Since '79-'84 engines run on unleaded gas, the central insulator should be white and the rest of the plug should be free of deposits.

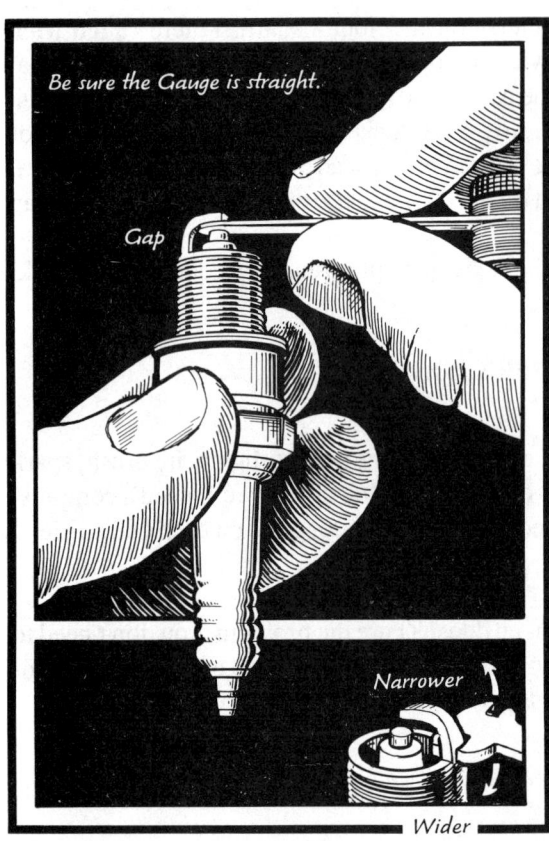

If the electrode end of the plug is covered with oily residue, the piston rings aren't sealing correctly, or a valve guide seal is worn out. A compression test, Step 3, will check the condition of the rings.

Electrodes that are burned away, with black or gray spots on the central insulator, indicate the engine is overheating. The ignition timing being advanced too far is usually the culprit.

Plugs with rounded center electrodes and tapered side electrodes are just plain worn out. The engine is probably fine.

Black, sooty deposits on the electrodes indicate the fuel/air mixture is too rich. Carb models should do Chapter 11, Procedure 13, to check the automatic choke. If the automatic choke is working, the carburetor might need adjusting. Procedure 12 will correct the problem on '75-'79 and '80 non-California models. '80 California and all '81 and newer models will have to go to the Subaru dealer or a garage that specializes in Subarus to have the carb adjusted or the fuel injection system checked.

Lots of white/gray deposits mean you buy cheap gas or use Gasoline Helper additives.

Bashed or mangled electrodes mean the plug is too long or there is something inside the cylinder that shouldn't be there. If the electrodes on all the plugs are bashed in, someone installed the wrong plugs. Replace them with the correct spark plugs for your engine. If only one plug is bashed and it has the same number printed on it as the rest of the plugs, there must be something in the cylinder. Get your flashlight and shine it in the spark plug hole while a Friend rotates the engine using the socket-on-the-crank-pulley method. See anything? Bits and pieces? If you do, try and fish 'em out with a magnet or piece of wire (chewing gum on a wire?). Be sure to do a compression test to see if any damage has been done to the piston or valves.

Step 3. Clean and Gap Spark Plugs.

If you are going to use these plugs again, clean the electrodes with a light wire brush. I use the end of a battery terminal cleaner. Scrape off heavy carbon chunks with a knife blade. Be careful not to chip the central insulator. After cleaning the plugs, blow the dust and crud from the space around the central insulator.

Before installing new or used spark plugs, check the gap and adjust it if it isn't .032" for '75-'80 models, or .040" for '81 and newer models. If you have an '81 or newer Soob, be sure you have the new type plug—just widening the gap on the old style plugs doesn't work (except in an extreme emergency). The gap is the space between the center straight electrode and the electrode hooked up and over the center of the plug. I have a *spark plug gapper*, one of those round things with wires all around it, to set mine—but you can do it close enough with any *feeler gauge*. Adjust the gap so the correct wire or feeler blade slides through the gap with a slight resistance.

The gap is changed by bending the outside electrode toward or away from the center electrode. Most spark plug gappers have a notch for changing the gap. Hook the notch over the outside electrode down close to the threads. Use the gapper as a lever to bend the electrode. If your gapper doesn't have a notch, the gap can be widened with needlenose pliers and narrowed by lightly tapping the electrode end on a piece of hard wood or clean metal. Check and adjust the gap until the proper wire or blade slips through the gap with just slight resistance.

Step 4. Compression Check.

Remove the spark plugs if they are still in the engine (Steps 1 and 2). All of the spark plugs must be removed so the starter can spin the engine fast enough to give you an accurate reading. The big wire connected to the center of the distributor cap is the **coil wire**. To avoid getting a shock from the spark plug wires while doing the compression test, pull the coil wire out of the center of the distributor. Clip one end of a "jumper" (a piece of insulated wire with alligator clips on each end) to the metal on the end of the coil wire and clip the other end of the jumper to a bolt or bare metal someplace away from the engine. This will ground the coil and keep you shock-free.

SPFI and MPFI models: You need to disconnect the fuel injection system so the engine isn't flooded with raw gasoline during the compression check. All that unburned fuel could damage the catalytic converter. Here's how to disarm the injector system:

On MPFI models, disconnect the electrical connectors from all four fuel injectors. The injectors are located right next to the spark plugs.

On SPFI models, locate the two connectors on the top front of the engine, right below and in front of the throttle body. Disconnect the two connectors.

EVERYONE: Get a piece of paper and write the numbers 1, 2, 3, and 4 across the top. Add 5 and 6 if you have a six cylinder engine. Have Friend set the parking brake, put the gearshift in NEUTRAL, press the clutch pedal and gas pedal to the floor, and hold them down until the compression test is completed.

Put on your safety glasses and screw the compression gauge into the spark plug hole of #1 cylinder. If your gauge doesn't have threads, press the rubber end into the hole as hard as you can and hold it there. Now have Friend crank the engine over (by turning the key to START) for about five seconds. Note where the needle on the gauge jumped to *first*, then the number it reached on the *last* engine revolution. Write these numbers below the number 1 on the paper. Pull out or unscrew the compression gauge.

Click the gauge back to zero and check the other cylinders the same way. Record the readings you get below the cylinder number on the paper. To keep things straight, go from one side to the other on the engine doing the test in numerical cylinder order. It's a good idea to go through the compression test twice for accuracy.

Step 5. Evaluation.

Look at your figures. These represent the pounds-per-square-inch (psi) of compression each cylinder is developing. If one number is substantially lower than the others (say, at least 20 psi lower), repeat the compression test for that particular cylinder. Be sure you pushed or threaded the tester fully into the spark plug hole. A hissing sound means the gauge isn't seated properly and you'll get an invalid (low) reading.

Fuel injected models: Reconnect the fuel injector connectors. Be sure they click securely into place.

EVERYONE: At sea level all the numbers should be:

MODEL	PSI
1975 and newer OHV non-Turbo	120-175
1983-84 Turbo	115-160
1985 OHC carb models	139-168
1986-87 OHC carb models	132-161
1985-87 MPFI non-Turbo	132-161
1985-88 Turbo	117-145
1986-88 SPFI	139-168

Subtract 2 psi for every thousand feet of altitude. When I do a compression test in Santa Fe, elevation 7,000 ft., I subtract 14 psi. In other words, slightly lower overall readings at high altitudes are OK.

If the readings for all the cylinders are within 20 psi of the lower figure in the chart, things are still OK for now, but you should do a compression test every time you perform the 6,000-mile maintenance.

If there is a difference of more than 20 psi between the highest and lowest reading, do the compression test again after driving the car a few miles. Sometimes when a spark plug is unscrewed, carbon flakes fall off the plug and get lodged between a valve and valve seat preventing the valve from closing completely. Driving the car will burn the carbon out. Don't forget to remove all of the spark plugs, even when you're just rechecking one cylinder.

If the reading is still low on the later test, something is amiss. Let's see if it's a **leaking valve** or **worn rings**. Squirt about four shots of motor oil (about a teaspoon) into the cylinder with an oil can or syringe (remove the needle first if it's that kind of syringe). Crank the engine over a few times to spread the oil around inside the cylinder, then do another compression check. If the number goes up by about 10 percent, chances are a piston ring is worn out or broken, a piston is cracked, or the cylinder wall is scratched, allowing compression to escape into the crankcase. You may need to **rebuild** the engine (Chapter 17).

If you don't get an increase in compression by squirting oil into the cylinder, a valve is leaking compression. (Carbon flake hopefully?) If the reading doesn't improve on a later test, it looks like a **valve job** is looming over the horizon, so think about doing it before taking off on a long trip (Chapter 17).

If the readings for two cylinders on one side of the engine are 20 to 40 psi lower than the cylinders on the other side of the engine, there is a possibility that the *head gasket* is leaking between the two low cylinders. Other symptoms of a blown head gasket are: the engine runs hotter than normal, water shows up on the engine dip stick and inside the oil filler cap and valve covers, and oil shows up in the radiator. See Chapter 9: *Troubleshooting* for more information about leaking head gaskets.

If two low readings are on opposite cylinders (#1 and #2, #3, and #4, or #5 and #6), the *camshaft lobes* or *valve lifters* might be wearing out and not opening the valves as far as they should.

If you want a second expert opinion on the internal condition of your engine, go to any well-equipped garage for a "leak-down" test. This checks for leakage between the valves and their seats, the piston rings and the cylinder wall sides, or the cylinder head and the crankcase. The test isn't expensive. It's a worthwhile investment, especially if your compression readings are on the 100 psi borderline or you suspect a blown head gasket.

Oh yes, your Friend can take his feet off the pedals now.

Step 6. Install Spark Plugs.

Clean and gap the spark plugs if you haven't already (Step 3). Smear a light coat of antiseize compound on the spark plug threads. Be careful; don't get any of the goo on the electrodes.

Screw each spark plug into the head BY HAND at least four complete turns. This will eliminate any possibility of getting them cross-threaded. (Incidentally, it makes no difference which plug goes in which hole, even if you're installing the used ones.) Tighten them the rest of the way with the spark plug socket and ratchet. They should be good and snug but not super-tight. The torque is about 15 ft. lbs. Connect the wires to the appropriate plug—you should feel them click into place. If you forgot to put number tapes on the wires and don't know which goes where, check the illustration on page 154.

Procedure 12, Step 1   Maintenance, Lubrication, Tune-up   129

If you did a compression test, remove the jumper wire and connect the coil wire to the center post on the distributor cap. Push it firmly into place.

PROCEDURE 12: ADJUST IDLE SPEED AND IDLE MIXTURE

Condition: Tune-up time; OR engine idling too slow or fast; OR rough idle; OR poor gas mileage; OR you just rebuilt the carb.

Tools and Materials: Long skinny screwdriver, tachometer, spray can of carb cleaner for carb models (see Chapter 5: *Tools*).

Remarks: Before adjusting the idle speed and/or idle mixture be sure the point gap or air gap (if you have it) in the distributor is properly adjusted (Procedure 9), and the engine is warmed up to operating temperature. Start this Procedure with the car parked on a level surface, handbrake ON, hood up, engine OFF.

1980 California and all 1981 and newer models: Checking the idle speed and idle mixture is not a part of the regular maintenance recommended by Subaru. So, if your car seems to be running well, you can skip this step.

CAUTION: Don't do this procedure in a closed garage! Exhaust fumes will take you off the tax rolls.

Step 1. Check Vacuum Hoses.

Inspect all the little rubber hoses in the engine compartment for cracks, holes, and loose connections. Replace any hoses that are cracked, stretched at the ends, or slide onto their fittings too easily.

Step 2. Clean Carburetor (carb models only).

Remove the air cleaner lid (Procedure 4, Step 3).

Break out your spray can of carburetor cleaner. If a little tube came with the can, insert the tube in the hole on the spray head. Use your finger or a screwdriver to hold the flat choke plate in the front part of the carb in a vertical position, then spray the inside of the carb with the cleaner. Let it soak a few minutes, then hit it again. Pay particular attention to the round brass jets and little holes. The inside of the carb should look clean when you're finished. Install the air cleaner lid.

Step 3. Connect Tachometer.

Follow the instructions that came with your tachometer or Tach/Dwell meter and hook it up. If the dog ate the instructions, look at Procedure 10, Step 3, Paragraph 1.

Step 4. Locate Idle Speed and Mixture Adjusting Screws.

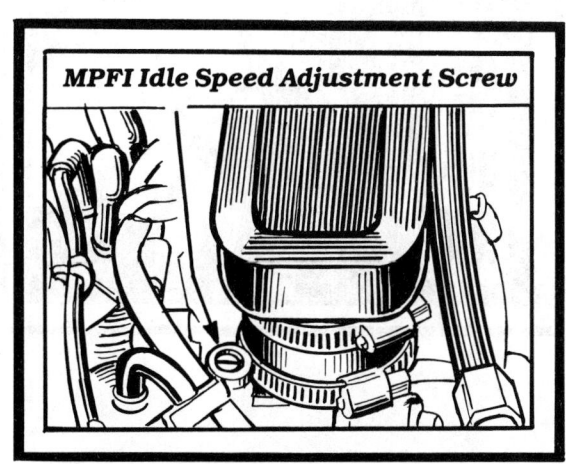

Look at the illustration for the location of the adjusting screws. All OHC models with carburetors have Hitachi carbs. If you have an '82 or newer OHV carb model and aren't sure whether you have a Hitachi or Carter/Weber carburetor, have Friend pump the gas pedal a few times while you watch the carburetor. You'll see a **cable** moving a rounded **lever** on one side. If the cable and lever are on the right (passenger's) side, you have a Hitachi carb. If the cable and lever are on the left (driver's) side, you have a Carter/Weber carb.

SPFI Idle Speed Adjustment Screw

Adjusting Screw

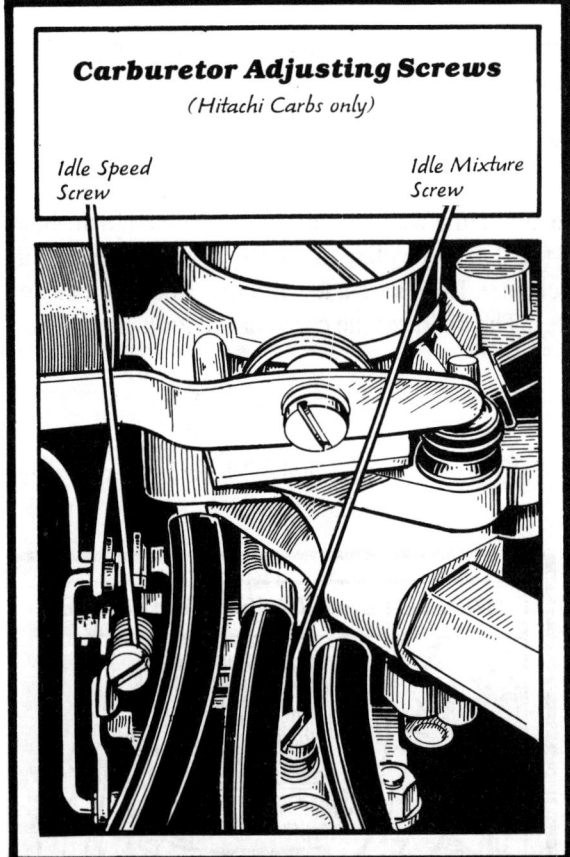

Carburetor Adjusting Screws
(Hitachi Carbs only)

Idle Speed Screw

Idle Mixture Screw

Idle Speed Adjustment Screw: Here's where to find it:

'75-'88 models with Hitachi carburetors: The screw is on the lower right (passenger's) side of the carburetor pointing toward the front of the car (see the illustration). The screw might have a thicker than normal head, which makes it easier to spot.

'82-'88 models with Carter/Weber carbs: The idle speed adjustment screw sticks out of a small round can on the lower left side of the carb. It points up toward the front of the car at about 45 degrees.

'83-'84 Turbo models: The idle speed screw is on the front of the **throttle body** which is in front of, and below the black metal thing on top of the engine that has SUBARU 4WD TURBO written on it. The idle speed screw is just in front of and below the letter "O" in TURBO.

SPFI models: The adjusting screw is on the top right (passenger's) side of the throttle body (see the illustration).

'85 and newer MPFI models: The adjusting screw is a large horizontal screw on the top rear of the throttle body assembly. The throttle body assembly is at the top center of the engine. The idle adjusting screw is just below where the large air intake hose connects to the top of the throttle body, except on XT models. On XTs, the idle adjusting screw is just above where the large hose connects to the rear of the throttle body. There might be a plastic plug covering the screw. Just pry the plug out of the hole to make the adjustment, then press it back in when you're through.

Idle Mixture Adjusting Screw: Here's where to find the mixture adjustment screw.

'72-'79 and '80 non-California models: There's an **idle *mixture* adjustment screw** on the bottom center of the front of the carburetor. If there's a little plastic cap on the mixture adjusting screw, pop it off. On some models the mixture adjustment screw is almost hidden behind three short vacuum hoses.

'80 California and all '81 and newer models: You only have a screw for adjusting the idle *speed*. The idle *mixture* adjustment screw is set at the factory, then plugged with a pin so you can't adjust it. The mixture is controlled by duty solenoid valves and vacuum switches. Dealing with these is out of our league.

Step 5. Adjust High Altitude Screw (carb models only).

If your Subaru is equipped with a **high altitude fuel enrichment screw**, it will be near the top left side of the carburetor pointing toward the left front fender. Not all Soobs have this screw, so if you can't find it don't worry about it.

If you live above 4,000 ft. altitude, screw the fuel enrichment screw on the top left side of the carb *clockwise* all the way in until it stops, then unscrew it *counterclockwise* six complete turns. If you live below 4,000 ft., just turn the screw in *clockwise* until it stops and leave it there. Sounds too easy doesn't it?

Step 6. Adjust Idle Speed.

'80 non-California models: Find the **secondary air cleaner.** It's mounted on the inside of the right front fender just in front of the brake master cylinder. It's the same color as the air cleaner and about the diameter of a 45 rpm record. Squeeze the clamp and pull the hose off the fitting. Use tape, a cork, or whatever to plug the open end of the hose.

'80-'82 models: Locate a small plastic **purge valve** in one of the hoses just behind the left side of the carburetor. That's the **purge hose**. Pull the hose off the engine side of the check valve and plug the end of the hose with a piece of tape or something.

'83-'84 carb models: Follow the bundle of small rubber hoses coming out from behind the left side of the carburetor to where three of them connect to three metal tubes on the inside of the left front fender. Pull the top hose off the tube and plug the end of the hose with tape or something. That's the **purge hose** you just plugged.

'85 and newer models: Locate the large round black evaporative canister. It's usually lurking in one of the front corners of the engine compartment and has about four small rubber hoses connected to fittings on the top. Near the edge of the canister top you'll see a small round **purge control valve** with two hoses connected to it. The fitting for the smaller of the two hoses is on top of the purge control valve. That's not the hose you're looking for. You want to disconnect the slightly larger hose that's connected to the side of the purge control valve. Cover the end of the hose with tape.

EVERYONE: A lot of good tach/dwell gauges have been eaten alive by the moving drive belt or fan, so please keep the wires away from the front of the engine. Block the wheels, set the handbrake, put the gearshift in NEUTRAL, start the engine and let it warm up for at least five minutes.

'81 and newer models: You need to warm up the O_2 (oxygen) sensor before setting the idle speed. Here's how: Rev the engine to 2,500 rpm for one minute after the five-minute warm-up. Now you can check and adjust the idle speed if necessary.

EVERYONE: Switch the gauge to *Tach* and read the engine rpm scale. (You might have to double the number on an eight cylinder scale if the gauge doesn't have a four cylinder scale.) Look at the sticker under the hood to see what the idle speed for your Soob should be. No sticker? Look up your idle speed in the **Carburetor Adjustment Table** in this chapter. If the speed indicated on the Tach matches the rpms on the chart, leave things be. If not, grab the skinny screwdriver and do the adjustment. Put the screwdriver in the slot of the **idle speed adjustment screw** and turn the screw *clockwise* to increase engine speed or *counterclockwise* to slow the engine down.

'80 California models and all '81 and newer models: Adjust the screw to the correct idle speed and you're through adjusting the carburetor. Reconnect the purge hose. Reconnect the rubber hose to the secondary air cleaner on '80 non-California models.

CARBURETOR ADJUSTMENT TABLE

'72-'79 and '80 non-Calif. models.:

1. Adjust carburetor so engine idles best (smoothest) at the RPM shown under A.

2. Turn the idle *mixture* screw in (clockwise) until engine speed is at the RPM shown under B.

YEAR		A	B
'72-'73		850	800
'74		850	800
'75	Manual	870	800
	Automatic	970	900
'76		980	900
'77-'78	Non-Calif.	930	850
	Calif.	990	900
'79	Non-Calif.	840	800
	Calif. Manual	910	900
	Calif. Auto.	930	900
'80	Non-Calif. Hatchback STD & DL, Sedan DL, Hardtop DL	840	800
	All other non-Calif. models	930	900

'80 Calif. and '81-87 models:

1. Plug the purge hose, then warm the engine up for five minutes.

2. On '80 Calif. models, disconnect and plug the hose to the secondary air cleaner.

3. On '81-'87 models, run the engine at 2,500 rpm for one minute after the five-minute warmup.

4. Adjust the idle to the rpm indicated in the tune-up specification chart at the end of this chapter.

5. Reconnect the purge hose. '80 models, reconnect the hose to the secondary air cleaner.

Step 7. Adjust Idle Mixture ('75-'79 and '80 non-California models only).

Put the screwdriver in the **idle *mixture* adjustment screw** (bottom center screw, remember?) and slowly turn it *counterclockwise* until the engine rpm just starts to drop. Slowly turn the screw *clockwise* until the engine reaches its highest rpm. You may have to turn the screw in and out a few times until you find the right spot. Got it? Now go back to the **idle *speed* adjustment screw** and adjust the engine speed to Figure A in the chart.

Now put your screwdriver in the *mixture* adjustment screw again (the one on your right) and screw it in (*clockwise*) until the engine rpm drops to Figure B in the chart. This setting will keep the carbon monoxide emissions within the legal limits. If the engine idles rough and you feel you just can't live with it, turn the screw *counterclockwise* slightly to add a little more gas. (You might not pass a smog test if you add the extra gas.)

If turning the idle mixture screw doesn't affect the engine rpm, check all vacuum lines and connections again for leaks. Turn the engine off and remove the mixture adjustment screw and look at it. Replace it with a new one if a groove is worn in the tapered needle end of the screw. Squirt some carb cleaner into the mixture screw hole before installing the pointed mixture screw. Are the carburetor mounting nuts tight? Check 'em with a 10mm wrench. Now start the engine and try adjusting the carb again (Steps 6 and 7). If you still can't change the rpm with the mixture adjustment screw, some passages in the carb are probably clogged. Remove the air cleaner lid and try squirting carb cleaner in all the holes inside the carb that you can reach with the nozzle. If you still can't adjust the idle mixture, the carburetor probably needs to be rebuilt. Turn to Chapter 11 for guidance and inspiration.

PROCEDURE 13: SET IGNITION TIMING

Models with breakerless or LED distributors: It isn't necessary to check the ignition timing unless the air gap has been adjusted or the distributor has been removed and reinstalled.

Condition: Tune-up time for models with breaker point-type distributors: OR the distributor has been removed; OR the engine isn't running right.

Tools and Materials: Stroboscopic timing light, tachometer, tape or two pencils or rubber vacuum line plugs, 10mm wrench. *Note*: It's best to use an *inductive type timing light* on cars with electronic or LED ignition, due to the increased voltage of these systems. *Optional*: A Friend would be handy.

Remarks: Changing the distributor points gap or air gap changes the ignition timing. Make the necessary adjustments to the distributor *before* checking the timing. Always check the timing *after* adjusting the points or air gap.

CAUTION: Keep the wires from the timing light and tachometer away from the front of the engine where they could get caught in the drive belt or fan. Remove the socket and ratchet from the crank pulley and the rag from the top of the carburetor (carb models) if they're still there. Be sure all tools are out of the way before starting the engine. If the air cleaner is off, install it before checking the ignition timing.

Step 1. Get Ready.

Warm up the engine to normal operating temperature. Turn the engine OFF and hook up the **tachometer** and **timing light**. (Procedure 10, Step 3, paragraph 1, explains how to connect a tach/dwell meter.) The dog ate the instructions for the timing light too? OK, connect the red lead wire to the positive (+) battery terminal and the black lead wire to the negative (-) battery terminal. These days most timing lights have an *inductive pickup connection* that clips onto the #1 spark plug wire. If the pickup has an arrow on it, make sure the arrow points *toward* the spark plug. If your light isn't of the inductive type, hook one end of a small spring (usually supplied with the light) to the end of the #1 spark plug. Fit the spark plug wire onto the end of the spring, then clip the lead from the timing light (usually blue) to the spring. Keep the wires away from the drive belt and fan—make sure they won't fall in there while you're working.

Carb models: Pull the vacuum hose(s) off the round **vacuum advance/retard gizmo** on the side of the distributor. If there are two hoses, mark them so you can't get them mixed up when you put them back on. Plug the hose or hoses with tape, rubber vacuum hose plugs, round punches, small phillips

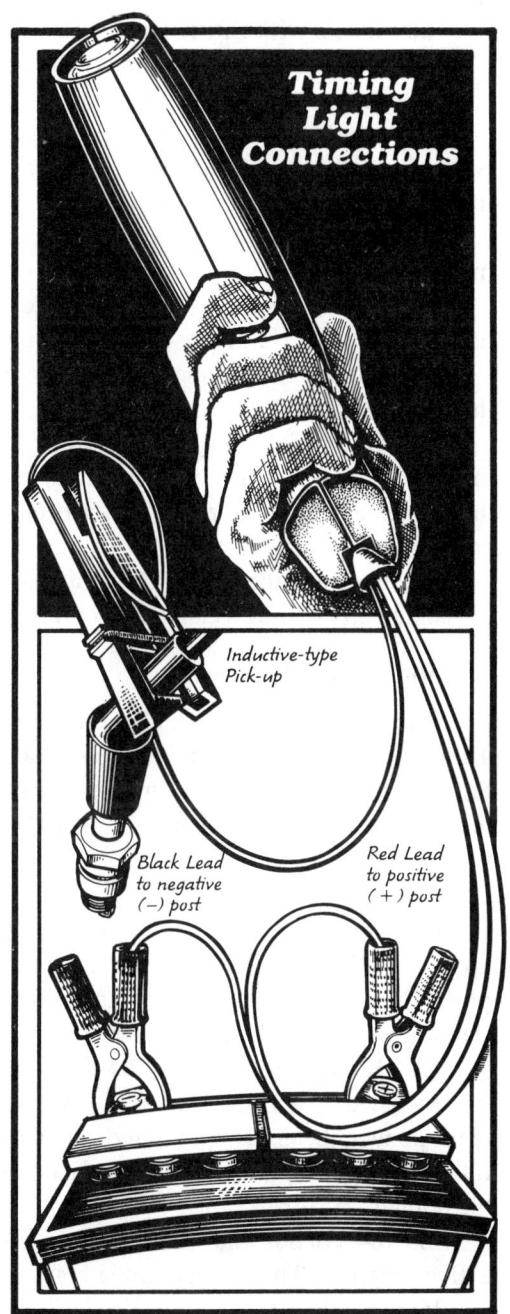

Timing Light Connections

Inductive-type Pick-up

Black Lead to negative (-) post

Red Lead to positive (+) post

screwdrivers, or pencils (break the lead off first so it can't accidentally get sucked into the engine).

EVERYONE (except '83-'84 Turbo models and '87 and newer XT models): Pop out the rectangular **rubber or plastic plug** located on the flywheel housing just behind the engine dipstick.

'83-'84 Turbo models and '87 and newer XT models: Wipe off the timing plate on the front of the engine.

'83-'84 Turbo models: Disconnect the **two-prong wire connector** beneath the coil.

'85-'86 Turbo models: Disconnect the large, round, black 8-pole connector between the distributor and the knock control unit. The connector is on the right side of the engine compartment, about halfway between the strut tower and the air cleaner housing. It's buried beneath other wires and stuff, so you'll have to dig to find it.

'86 models with SPFI: You have no vacuum hoses or wire connectors to connect or disconnect!

'87-'88 models with SPFI or MPFI: The throttle must be in the closed position to check the ignition timing, so keep your foot off the gas pedal.

Also, you must connect the green, T-shaped test mode connectors. One or two wires (probably brown) will be attached to each connector. Be sure to disconnect the test mode connectors after checking the ignition timing. Here's where the test mode connectors are located:

SPFI models: The test mode connectors are in the left rear corner of the engine compartment, near the brake master cylinder.

MPFI models except XT: The test mode connectors are under the dash, just to the left of the fuse box. You'll have to remove the large plastic panel around the fuse box to get to the connectors.

XT models: The test mode connectors are in the trunk, mounted to the bottom of the little shelf that holds the rear speakers.

EVERYONE: If the ignition timing needs to be adjusted, use a 10mm socket, long extension and ratchet to slightly loosen the distributor mounting bolt(s) located near the base of the distributor. If you haven't painted the pointer and timing mark on the flywheel, or the timing mark and pulley notch, do Procedure 5, Step 6, before going one step further.

When turning the distributor, grab it toward the *bottom end* away from the spark plug wires (less chance of accidentally getting a charge out of this procedure). Watch out for the drive belt(s).

Step 2. Set Idle Speed.

If you haven't checked the idle speed, do Procedure 12, Steps 1 through 6, for adjusting the engine idle speed. The correct speed for your engine is on the sticker under the hood, in your owner's manual, and beside the ignition timing in the Tune-up Specifications at the end of this chapter. After the idle speed is set come back here to *time the engine*. Don't do Procedure 12, Step 7 (adjust idle mixture), yet.

Step 3. Check and Adjust Timing.

Clear tools, wires, hoses, and stuff away from the fan and drive belt(s), then start the engine. Let it warm up to normal operating temperature. Aim the timing light at the hole in the **flywheel housing**, or the **timing plate**, depending on your model, and pull the trigger. Amazingly, the flywheel or crank pulley appears to be standing still while the engine is running!

EVERYONE (except '83-'84 Turbos and '87-'88 XTs): If the **white line** you painted to the right of the 0 line is lined up with the **triangle pointer** on the housing, the timing is right on. If the timing line is to the left of the pointer, the timing is *advanced* so rotate the distributor *counterclockwise* until the line matches the pointer. If the line is to the right of the pointer, the timing is *retarded* so rotate the distributor *clockwise* until the line matches the pointer.

'83-'84 Turbos and '87 and newer XTs: Each line on the timing plate is 5° on 1800cc engines, or 2° on 2700cc engines. The correct timing is 15° for '83-'84 Turbo models and 20° for '87 and newer XTs.

If the notch on the pulley is lined up with a number or line less than it should be, the timing is retarded so rotate the distributor *clockwise* until the notch is even with the correct line for your engine. If the notch on the pulley is lined up with a number above what it should be, rotate the distributor *counterclockwise* until it's even with the 15 ('83-'84 Turbos) or the 20 ('87 and newer XTs).

Procedure 13, Step 3 Maintenance, Lubrication, Tune-up 135

EVERYONE: When the pointer or notch and appropriate timing mark are lined up, tighten the bolt(s) at the base of the distributor. Put the timing light aside and adjust the engine idle speed if it changed (same as you did in Step 2), then check the timing again and adjust it if need be.

EVERYONE (except models with LED distributors): Have Friend rev the engine up a little while you watch the timing marks with the timing light. If a Friend isn't available, you can rev the engine by rotating the throttle lever on the bottom of the carburetor or throttle body (fuel injected models). As the engine speed increases, the painted timing line should move to the *left*—probably out of sight—if the **mechanical advance mechanism** in the distributor is working properly. If the line doesn't move, the mechanical advance isn't working and needs to be checked (Procedure 9, Step 6).

After the timing is set and the 10mm bolt is tightened, remove the plugs from any vacuum hose(s) you disconnected and reconnect them to the **vacuum advance/retard** unit on the distributor. Push the hoses on the same as they were to begin with.

On Turbo models, reconnect the two-pole connector under the coil ('83-'84) or the eight-pole connector ('85-'86 models). You can't check the timing with the hoses connected but that's how you check the ignition advance/retard unit. Here's how.

Rev the engine up while watching the timing marks with the timing light. Now the line on the flywheel should really move around when you rev the engine. If the line doesn't move to the left, the vacuum hose(s) are leaking (replace them), OR the hoses aren't connected to the distributor correctly (fix 'em), OR the vacuum/retard unit is broken (replace it, Procedure 9, Step 8), OR the movable plate in the distributor is stuck (see Procedure 9, Step 8).

If the line on the flywheel dances around and won't stand still at idle, the bushings in the distributor are probably worn. To be sure, remove the distributor cap and rotor, then move the distributor shaft side to side to see if it's loose. If you can move the shaft more than a slight amount, see Chapter 17 to remove the distributor. Take it to Subaru or an auto electric shop to have new bushings installed. Chapter 17 also tells you how to install the new or rebuilt distributor.

When the timing is correct for your model, check and adjust the idle speed again if it changed.

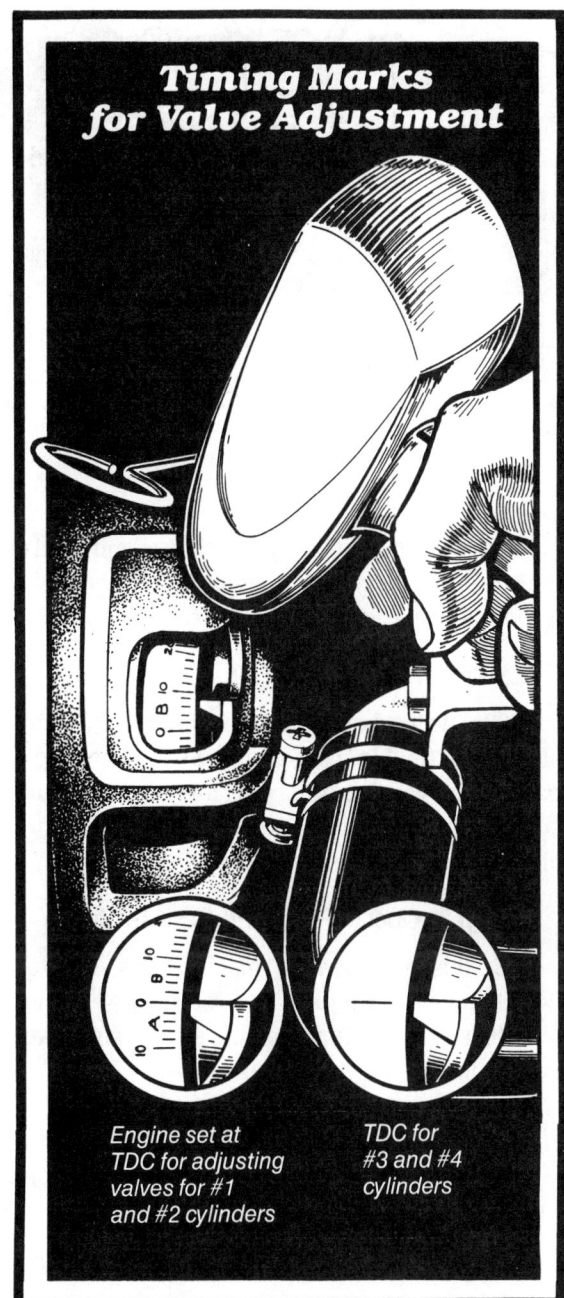

Timing Marks for Valve Adjustment

Engine set at TDC for adjusting valves for #1 and #2 cylinders

TDC for #3 and #4 cylinders

Loosen the Distributor hold-down bolt, then turn the Distributor clockwise to advance the timing, or counterclockwise to retard the timing. Don't forget to tighten the hold-down bolt.

Turn the engine off, unhook the timing light and tach/dwell meter, then install the plug in the flywheel housing hole (if that's where your timing marks are located).

EVERYONE: Reconnect any hoses you disconnected from the vacuum advance/retard unit on the distributor.

'83-'84 Turbo models: Reconnect the two-pole connector beneath the coil.

'85-'86 Turbo models: Reconnect the large 8-pin connector on the right side of the engine compartment.

'87 and newer SPFI and MPFI models: Don't forget to disconnect the test mode connectors.

PROCEDURE 14: MAJOR MASSAGE (12,000 MILE WRAP UP)

Except for an oil and filter change and fluid checks, you're finished with the engine. Steps 1 through 4 of the wrap-up refer you to other parts of the book. Most of these steps are fun to do, and they will make your Soob a continuing pleasure for you to drive. The tools and materials you will need for these are right in the step itself.

Step 1. Do Procedures 2, 3, and 4.

OK, we've done the critical mechanical procedures. Let's go back and change the oil and filter and check all the vital fluid levels. Steps 5 and 6 (coming up) can be done while the oil is draining, but don't forget to come back to screw in the drain plug and filter and put in the new oil. Hang in there, we're coming down the home stretch now. Remember, each time you do the procedures in this chapter they'll go easier and faster. Eventually most of them become a lot of fun!

Step 2. Check Front and Rear Brakes.

Do this step when you rotate the tires. Turn to Chapter 13, Procedure 8, to check the front brake pads. Every 24,000 miles do Chapter 13, Procedure 4, to check the rear brake shoes, except on the following models:

'85 and newer Turbo models and '87 and newer 4WD and/or Turbo XT models should do Chapter 13, Procedure 6, to check the rear brake pads.

Step 3. Adjust Rear Brakes.

Not all rear brakes are self-adjusting, so you need to adjust them every 12,000 miles. It's as easy as toast. Turn to Chapter 13, Procedure 1, to see if your model requires adjustment.

Step 4. Check Rear Differential Oil (4WD only).

Put on your safety glasses, spread out a piece of cardboard or plastic under the rear of the car, grab a ½" drive ratchet (3/8" drive won't do) and a rag and crawl under. The **rear differential** (pumpkin) is halfway between the two rear tires. There are two **plugs** in the back of it—the top one for checking and adding oil and the bottom one for draining oil. You're going after the upper plug.

Clean the area around both plugs with the rag so dirt won't fall into the hole when the plug is removed. Put the square part of the ratchet (the part where a socket usually goes) into the UPPER plug and unscrew it *counterclockwise*. It's probably pretty tight so you might have to hit the ratchet handle with your hand to pop it loose.

If the plug refuses to loosen, get out the jack and place it under the ratchet handle so the jack will force the handle *counterclockwise*. Put a rag on top of the jack so it's a little less slippery, then slowly crank up the jack until the plug breaks free. This is a little tricky—the ratchet handle can slip off the jack. Keep trying, go easy, and keep parts of your body well clear of where a slip might hurt them.

When the plug is out, use a clean pinky for a dipstick and gradually stick it into the hole, feeling down in there for oil. The level should be at or close to the bottom of the threads of the upper plug hole. If the oil is more than ¼" below the opening, add gear oil until it starts to run out of the hole. Look at the oil chart in this chapter to see what kind of gear oil to add. If you aren't using gear oil that comes in a plastic bottle with a pour spout, you'll need to round up a suction gun, refillable squirt-type oil can, or a large syringe (see Chapter 5: *Tools*). If it's not worth the hassle to you to get one of these, screw the plug in (see below), and take the car to a service station to have the oil put in.

Oil level OK now? Screw the plug back in and tighten it with the ratchet, but not so tight you won't be able to get it out the next time. Now pull the tools, oil can, plastic, cardboard, and yourself out from under the back of the car.

Use your finger for a dipstick to check Rear Differential Oil on 4WD models.

Step 5. Replace Antifreeze and Check Cooling System Hoses.

Condition: You live where the winters are harsh and it's been a year since the antifreeze was changed; OR you live in the banana belt where the livin' is easy, the cotton is high, your daddy's rich, your momma's good lookin', and it's been two years since you replaced the antifreeze.

Turn to Chapter 16, Procedure 3, and replace the antifreeze. Check the cooling system hoses and replace any that don't meet the Starship Subaru standards (Chapter 16, Procedure 2).

Step 6. Replace Fuel Filter.

Fuel filters get clogged with dirt, rust, and water and can eventually cut off the fuel supply to the engine. Turn to Chapter 11, Procedure 2, to change the fuel filter, then come back here and continue.

Step 7. Replace Brake Fluid.

Don't skip this step or you'll pay for it sooner or later. Brake fluid absorbs moisture that corrodes the mechanical and hydraulic parts of the brake system. Brake fluid is a lot cheaper than master cylinders, wheel cylinders, and disc brake calipers. Changing the brake fluid regularly will lengthen the life expectancy of the brake system and yours too, perhaps. Turn to Chapter 13, Procedure 3, and follow the directions for replacing the brake fluid.

Step 8. Check and Adjust Clutch (manual transmissions only).

Checking clutch pedal free play is as easy as eating ice cream. Adjusting the clutch is almost as easy. See Chapter 15, Procedure 1.

Step 9. Check Steering and Suspension Systems.

It only takes about ten minutes to thoroughly check the suspension and steering. Chapter 14, Procedure 1, tells you how.

Step 10. Check Emission Control Systems.

This is important! If parts of the emission control system become clogged, the engine won't run right no matter how well you tune it, and/or the engine can be damaged by the malfunctioning parts. The devices are easy to check and clean.

Look at Chapter 12: *Exhaust and Emission Control Systems*, Procedures 1-6, to check the emission control devices that apply to your Soob. Depending on the year and model you might be checking and cleaning the **Exhaust Gas Recirculation (EGR) Valve**, the **Positive Crankcase Ventilation (PCV) valve**, the **Air Injection System (AIS)**, the **secondary air cleaner** on '80 models, the **Evaporative Canister** and its filter, and the **Hot Air Control System**.

Step 11. Clean Up.

Pour all the old antifreeze and brake fluid into plastic containers and take them to the Hazardous Waste Dump. There isn't one in your neighborhood? Put them in the trash. Put the old oil in plastic containers and take them to a filling station or recycling center that collects used oil. If there isn't one, put the containers in the trash also.

Use a rag to wipe off all the tools that were used before putting them back in the tool box. Wipe up any oil that spilled on the floor with rags, then throw all the oily rags in an outside trash container (they *can* spontaneously burst into flames). Whew, one more step and we're finished.

Step 12. Record All Work in Log.

Record your valiant efforts in the log at the end of this chapter. Your Soob should now be in very fine running condition. Now do Procedure 4, Step 13. See you here next year!

PROCEDURE 15: CHANGE TRANSMISSION and DIFFERENTIAL OIL (30,000 MILES)

1975-1984 models: At 30,000-mile intervals, you'll do the regular 6,000-mile maintenance procedures, but don't add any transmission or differential oil—you're going to drain the old oil and replace it with new oil.

1985 and newer models: The Subaru manuals recommend replacing the automatic transmission fluid on 4WD models every 30,000 miles. On the other models they recommend replacing the gear oil every 30,000 miles and the automatic transmission fluid on all models every 15,000 miles ONLY if the car is operated under severe conditions. I think it would be a good idea to change the gear oil and ATF at least every 60,000 miles.

Condition: You just bought a Subaru with over 30,000 miles on it; OR it's been 30,000 miles since you last performed this maintenance; OR you feel like getting down and getting greasy.

Tools and Materials: If you aren't using gear oil that comes in a plastic squeeze bottle with a built-in pour spout (like Castrol or Valvoline), you'll need a **long neck funnel** for filling the transmission and differential, or a **suction-type oil filler**, which will work for the transmission and differential as well as the rear differential on 4WDs. You also need a catch pan, safety glasses, plastic bottles (at least two gallons) for disposal of the old oil, plus 17mm, 19mm, 21mm, or 22mm socket and ratchet or box end wrench depending on the size of your drain plugs, and rags or paper towels. Funky clothes aren't a bad idea either.

Automatic Transmissions Soobs: Get 7 quarts of Dexron for OHV models, or Dexron II-type ATF for OHC models, 2 quarts of gear oil for the front differential, and new gaskets for the transmission and differential drain plugs.

Manual transmission Soobs: Get 3 quarts of gear oil (non-4WD) or 4 quarts (4WD) and one new gasket for the drain plug.

4WD people: You also need a ½" drive ratchet and one quart of gear oil for the rear differential.

Remarks: Some gear oils, like Castrol and Valvoline, come in handy plastic bottles with a pointed pour spout. These containers make filling the differential easy—especially the rear differential on 4WDs.

Look at the oil viscosity charts near the start of this chapter to see which grade oil you should use. Brands of automatic transmission fluid that are recommended by Subaru are listed there also.

Step 1. Go for a Ride.

The transmission and differential should be warmed up to operating temperature before draining the oil. Go for a drive, at least 10 miles, then park the car on level ground and shut the engine OFF. Set the handbrake and block the wheels.

Step 2. Get Ready.

Spread out your ground cover on the driver's side, right behind the front wheel. Be sure the handbrake is on and the transmission is in gear or PARK. Slide the **catch pan** under the car. Grab your sockets and ratchet or box-end wrenches, and the new drain plug gaskets. Install safety glasses on your face, then squeeze your body under the car so your head ends up just inside the left front tire and your feet are pointed toward the rear tire. If you have a clearance problem, perhaps it's time to consider that last piece of cake or six-pack you had. If you just don't fit, jack up the car on the left side a little and put a jackstand under the frame (see Chapter 3). Be sure the car is resting solidly on the jackstand before crawling under. After removing the drain plug(s), take the car off the jackstand so the oil can drain completely, then jack it back up and slip the stands into position when you're ready to put the drain plug(s) back in.

You'll be unscrewing the plugs in the Steps ahead. After the drain plugs are out, come out from under the car and look them over. They have magnets built into them to trap tiny metal particles that wear off the gears. Hopefully, there aren't any large chunks of metal stuck to the magnet, which would indicate a chipped gear and potential trouble. Clean the plugs thoroughly with a rag before you attempt to screw them back in. If yours is a standard transmission vehicle, skip ahead to Step 5.

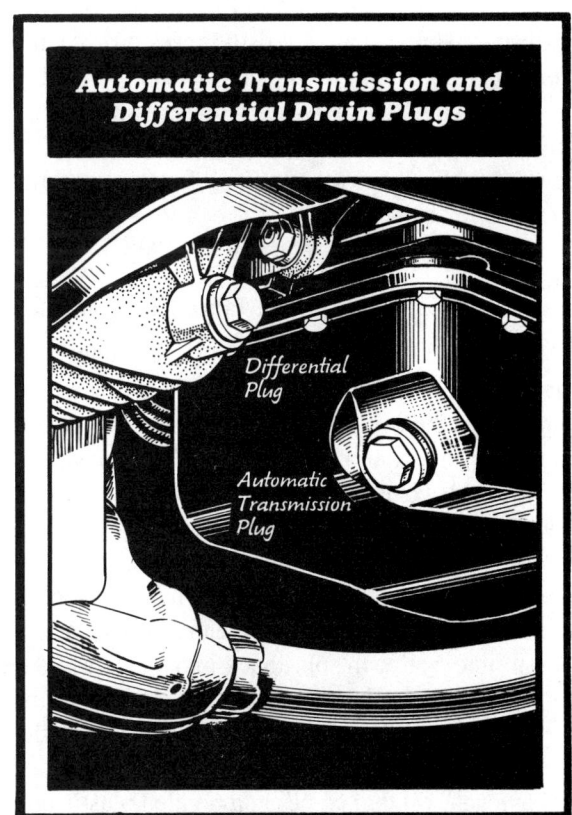

Step 3. Drain and Fill Automatic Transmission Fluid.

The **drain plug** for automatic transmissions is on the left front corner of the black bulbous thing hanging down behind the engine. One of the four sockets or wrenches fits the plug. Put the correct size wrench on the plug and unscrew it *counterclockwise*. When the plug is loose enough to turn by hand, scoot out from under the car as far as you can and remove the plug at arm's length. The oil will be *hot* as it gushes from the drain hole so you don't want any to splash in your face. Don't worry if the drain plug falls into the catch pan, you can fish it out with a magnet or your fingers after the fluid cools off, or retrieve it when you pour the old fluid into the disposal bottles. Let the oil drain for a few minutes.

Install a new drain plug gasket onto the drain plug, then screw the plug into the transmission. Tighten it down with the wrench, but remember who'll have to take it out next time. Now get out from under and find the **dipstick** for the automatic transmission located near the rear of the engine compartment on the driver's side. Remove the dipstick, wipe it with a clean rag, then put it in a clean place. Stick the small end of the **long, clean funnel** into the dipstick hole. Wipe off the tops of the new ATF cans with a clean rag. Open three cans and pour 2½ quarts into the transmission. Put the dipstick back in.

Be sure the handbrake is on and the gearshift lever is in the PARK position, and start the engine. Now check the fluid level with the engine running (Procedure 2, Step 3). Add fluid a little at a time until the level reaches the upper hole in the dipstick. The bottom hole on the dipstick means the level is a little less than ½ quart low. Be careful not to add too much fluid. When the transmission is full, put the dipstick in place and turn off the engine. Check beneath the car for leaks around the drain plug. Empty the drain pan into the disposal bottles, then go on to Step 4.

Step 4. Drain and Fill Differential (automatic transmission people).

The **differential drain plug** is about 4″ in front of the transmission drain plug. It sticks out of the side of the aluminum **differential case** and points toward the left front tire on most models. On some late models, it's on the opposite side of the differential from the one shown in the illustration. Put the catch pan beneath it. Use the correct socket or wrench to unscrew the plug *counterclockwise*. Again, back away so the oil won't splash in your face when you remove the plug.

Wipe off the drain plug with a clean rag and install a new gasket. When only one or two drops per minute are coming out of the drain hole, screw the plug back in and tighten it with the socket or wrench. Drag all the tools and catch pan from under the car. Take the jackstand out and lower the car if you jacked it up.

The differential dipstick is about 6″ behind and slightly lower than the top rear of the engine. The differential dipstick has lines on it and an F indicating the full level. A heavy line about eight lines down from the F line indicates ½ quart low. The differential dipstick tube is also the filler tube so stick a clean funnel in the tube if your gear oil isn't in plastic bottles with pointed caps.

Clean the tops of two cans of **gear oil**. Open the cans and pour one quart down the **differential dipstick tube**. The official capacity is 1.3 quarts, more or less. Check your owner's manual to be sure, or check the oil level with the dipstick and add oil from the second can a little at a time until the level reaches the F mark. Put the dipstick back in.

If you have 4WD, skip down to Step 6. No 4WD? Go to Step 7.

Step 5. Drain and Fill Manual Transmission and Differential.

Soobs with manual transmissions have one drain plug located in the bottom center of the aluminum differential case that drains both the transmission and differential. The plug is just in front of and above where the two exhaust pipes from the two sides of the engine merge together. On these models it's easier to get to the plug by crawling under the front of the car rather than the side. You shouldn't have to jack the car up, but if you do, be sure to block the wheels and use jackstands. Put the catch pan beneath the plug. You just warmed up the engine so watch out for those hot exhaust pipes.

Put the goggles on and don't let the hot oil splash in your face. Loosen the drain plug with the correct socket or wrench. When you can turn it by hand, unscrew it the rest of the way with your fingers. While the oil drains, wipe off the drain plug with a clean rag and install the new gasket. When oil is only dripping a couple of drops per minute, screw the plug back into the hole and tighten it with the socket or wrench. Slide the catch pan and tools out from under the car. Lower the car if you jacked it up.

Remove the **transmission/differential dipstick** (located about 8″ behind the engine dipstick), wipe it with a clean rag and lay it someplace clean. Stick the small end of the long funnel into the dipstick tube if you're not using a gear oil that comes in a pointed plastic container.

Clean the tops, then open three quarts of gear oil. It takes almost 3 quarts to fill non-4WD transmissions and just over 3 quarts for 4WD trannies. In either case, pour 2½ quarts down the funnel and check the level with the dipstick. Add oil a little at a time and keep checking until the oil level reaches the F mark on the dipstick. Late model Turbos have two holes in the bottom end of the dipstick. The upper hole means the differential is full and the lower hole means it's ½ quart low.

Step 6. Change 4WD Rear Differential Oil (4WD vehicles only).

Spread the ground cloth under the rear end of the car, then slide the drain pan between the rear wheels. Get a ½" drive ratchet with a long handle (you won't need a socket) and dive under. The **rear differential** is that big chunk of metal directly between the two rear axles.

The rear differential has **two plugs** facing the rear of the car. The top one is for checking and adding oil while the lower one is for draining the oil. Clean the area around the plugs with a rag, then use the square end (business end) of the ratchet to unscrew both plugs *counterclockwise*. Just insert the square part of the ratchet into the square holes in each plug. See Procedure 14, Step 4, if you have trouble removing the plugs. Always remove the top plug first to be sure you'll be able to get oil back in after draining the old oil.

When the oil is dripping out of the bottom hole only a couple of drops per minute, clean the plugs, screw the one with the magnet on it into the bottom hole and tighten it with the ratchet. Open a can of fresh gear oil and pour or pump it into the top hole until oil starts running out. It holds a little over ¾ of a quart. If the gear oil you bought came in a plastic bottle with a pour spout on the end, you shouldn't have any trouble getting the oil in the hole. If you bought oil in a regular can, you'll have to use a suction type gun to suck the oil out of the can and squirt it into the differential. Either way, when the oil starts running out of the filler hole, screw the plug in and tighten it with the ratchet. Wipe off any oil on the outside of the housing, then drag all the tools and catch pan from underneath the car.

Step 7. Clean Up.

Pour the old oil in plastic containers and give it to a service station or the nice people at the recycling center.

PROCEDURE 16: 30,000/60,000-MILE MAINTENANCE, LUBRICATION, AND PARTS REPLACEMENT

Condition: It's been 30,000 severe-type miles or 60,000 normal-type miles since the wheel bearings were inspected and/or greased. Although it's not part of the recommended Subaru maintenance schedule, the DOJs and CVJs on the axles will probably last longer if they are cleaned and repacked with fresh grease every 60,000 miles.

Confession: Since it's such a hassle, I confess I only get around to greasing my wheel bearings and axle joints when I have the brakes off and it's handy to get to everything. However, if you're in the habit of abusing your Soob on mountain goat trails or crossing rivers and streams frequently, check and grease the bearings at least every 30,000 miles. The Subaru manuals now recommend "checking" the grease in the bearings every 60,000 miles. To check the grease, remove the brake drums or discs, front and rear, and look at the grease around the wheel bearings. If there's white, yukky looking stuff around the bearings, or the grease looks thin and runny, turn to Chapter 14 to find how to grease the wheel bearings. Procedure 7 covers everybody's front wheel bearing lubrication and Procedure 9 covers non-4WD rear wheel bearings. Special tools are required to grease the rear wheel bearings on 4WDs so you'll have to have Subaru or a garage that specializes in Subarus lube them for you. The others you can do yourself.

Chapter 15 covers greasing the double offset joints (DOJs) and the constant velocity joints (CVJs) on the axles. Carefully inspect the rubber boots while greasing the axle joints and replace any that are cracked or torn.

On some models Subaru recommends replacing the emission control evaporative canister every 60,000 miles. Check your owner's manual to see if yours should be replaced. If it should, see Chapter 12, Procedure 5.

TUNE-UP SPECIFICATIONS 1975-88

If possible, use the tune-up specifications on the underside of the hood, or the specifications for your year and model in your Owner's Manual. If the underhood sticker and Owner's manual are missing, use the specifications listed below.

VALVE SETTING

	Intake	Exhaust
1975:	.012"	.014"
76-82:	.010"	.014"
83-84: OHV Manual	.010"	.014"
83-84: OHV Auto	0	0
85-88: ALL models	0	0

SPARK PLUG GAP

75-80:	.032"
81-88:	.040"

POINTS GAP

1975:	.020"
76-78:	.018"

POINTS DWELL

75-78:	49°-55°

AIR GAP

	MODEL	TRANSMISSION	AIR GAP
77-79:	All	Manual	.008"-.016"
	All	Automatic	.012"-.020"
80-82:	Non-4WD	All	.008"-.016"
	4WD	All	.012"-.020"
83-84:	HITACHI		.012"-.020"
	NIPPONDENSO		.008"-.016"
1985	Carb Models		
	California	Manual/Auto	.008"-.016"
	Non-Calif 2WD	Manual/Auto	.008"-.016"
	Non-Calif 4WD	Manual/Auto	.012"-.020"
1985	MPFI Non-Turbo	Manual/Auto	.008"-.016"
	MPFI Turbo	Manual/Auto	.012"-.020"
1986	Calif 2WD, 4WD	Manual	.008"-.016"
	Calif 4WD	Automatic	.008"-.016"
	Non-Calif 2WD	Manual	.008"-.016"
	Non-Calif 4WD	Manual/Auto	.012"-.020"
	Canadian	Manual/Auto	.012"-.020"
1987	Carb Models	All	.008"-.016"
1988	No air gap to check!		

ENGINE IDLE SPEED AND TIMING SPECIFICATION

YEAR	ENGINE	TRANSMISSION	TIMING	IDLE SPEED
1975:		Manual	8°	800
		Automatic	8°	900
1976:	ALL		8°	900
77-78:	Non-Calif.		8°	850
	California		8°	900
1979:	Non-Calif.		8°	800
	California		8°	900
1980:	All Calif.		8°	900
	Non-Calif. Hatchback STD & DL, Sedan DL, Hardtop DL		8°	800
	All other Non-Calif.		8°	900
81-83:	Non-Turbo	Manual	8°	700
		Automatic	8°	800
1984:	Carb 1600cc	4-speed	8°	650
		5-speed	8°	700
	Carb 1800cc	Manual	8°	700
		Automatic	8°	800
83-84:	Turbo Models		15°	800
1985:	Non-Turbo DL	4-speed	6°	650
		5-speed	8°	700
	GL	5-speed	8°	700
	GL	Automatic	8°	800
	GL-10	5-speed	6°	700
	GL-10	Automatic	6°	800
	XT	5-speed	6°	700
	XT	Automatic	6°	800
	Turbo	Manual	25°	700
		Automatic	25°	800
1986:	Non-Turbo	Manual	8°	700
		Automatic	8°	800
		SPFI	20°	700
	Non-Turbo XT	Manual	6°	700
		Automatic	6°	800
	Turbo	Manual	25°	700
		Automatic	25°	800
1987:	Carburetor	Manual/Auto	8°	700
	SPFI	Manual/Auto	20°	700
	MPFI	Manual	20°	700
		Automatic	20°	800
1988:	SPFI	Manual/Auto	20°	700
	MPFI	Manual	20°	700
		Automatic	20°	800

Chapter 7

CHECK:
- FRONT AND REAR BRAKES
- EMISSION CONTROLS
- SUSPENSION AND STEERING
- CLUTCH ADJUSTMENT
- CHECK REAR DIFF. (4WD)

REPLACE:
- ANTIFREEZE
- FUEL FILTER
- AIR FILTER
- SPARK PLUGS
- POINTS & CONDENSER
- DISTRIBUTOR CAP & ROTOR
- BRAKE FLUID

ADJUST REAR BRAKES
REWARD YOURSELF

30,000 MILE INTERVAL

REPLACE:
- MANUAL TRANS. & DIFF. OIL
- AUTO. TRANS. FLUID
- DIFF. OIL (AUTOMATICS)
- REAR DIFF. OIL (4WD)

LUBRICATE WHEEL BEARINGS
LUBRICATE AXLE JOINTS

60,000 MILE PARTS REPLACEMENT

REPLACE:
- DRIVE BELTS
- CAM BELTS (OHC MODELS)
- EVAPORATIVE CANISTER

NOTES:

MAINTENANCE LOG

3,000 SEVERE OR 6,000 NORMAL MILES

CHANGE OIL & FILTER
GAS STOP FLUID CHECKS
CHECK:
   TIRE PRESSURE
   AIR FILTER
   LIGHTS
   WIPER BLADES
   BATTERY
   RADIATOR FOR TRASH
   SHOCK ABSORBERS
   BODY MASSAGE
   ROTATE TIRES
   CLEAN TAPE HEADS
   REWARD YOURSELF

12,000 MILE INTERVAL

RETORQUE HEADS
ADJUST VALVES
SKIN KNUCKLES
CHECK, ADJ., OHC CAM BELTS
CHECK DIST. CAP & ROTOR
CHECK POINTS OR AIR GAP
ADJUST POINTS OR AIR GAP
CHECK VACUUM & MECH. ADVANCE
CLEAN & GAP SPARK PLUGS
CHECK AND ADJUST CARBURETOR
CHECK AND SET IGNITION TIMING
DO 3,000/6,000 MILE THINGS

Mileage

NOTES:

VITAL STATISTICS FOR MY SOOB

ENGINE TYPE:	POINTS GAP:	PARTS NUMBERS
ENGINE NUMBER:	POINTS DWELL:	SPARK PLUGS:
BODY NUMBER:	AIR GAP:	DISTRIBUTOR CAP:
PRODUCTION DATE:	SPARK PLUG GAP:	ROTOR:
ENGINE OIL	IGNITION TIMING:	POINTS SET:
BRAND:	VALVE SETTING	CONDENSER:
WEIGHT:	INTAKE:	AIR FILTER:
OIL FILTER:	EXHAUST:	FUEL FILTER:
(BRAND AND #)	IDLE SPEED:	PCV VALVE:
MANUAL		
TRANS./DIFF. OIL	TIRE PRESSURE	BRAKE FLUID BRAND:
BRAND:	FRONT:	(DOT3 or 4)
WEIGHT:	REAR:	
AUTOMATIC TRANS. FLUID	SPARE:	
BRAND:		

NOTES:

CHAPTER 8

DRIVING FOR ECONOMY AND LONGEVITY

This little chapter is about how to help keep your Subaru alive and efficient without even picking up a wrench or getting greasy. Driving for economy means more than just getting good gas mileage; it also includes saving on repairs that can be avoided if the car is driven correctly, making repairs promptly that would end up costing more if not done right away, and planning ahead so parts are purchased when they're on sale rather than being stuck with the full price on the day of the tune-up or repair. Getting into the habit of driving for economy and longevity will not only save you a bunch of money; you'll also become a safer driver because you'll be more aware of driving conditions. Driving will be more interesting because every time you drive your Soob you'll be challenging yourself to get the most possible value from your motoring dollar. Consider it a game played by the rules of physics where you can come out a winner.

GAS MILEAGE

Gas mileage alone isn't everything. As far as I know, Subarus have never won a major gas mileage test, so don't expect your Soob to get the same mileage as the cars at the top of the government's annual gas miser list. Subarus are, however, usually near the top of the list in overall economy when repair bills over a period of time are also tallied. Even a car that gets 50 miles per gallon (mpg) isn't economical to drive if it takes $50 a month to keep it on the road.

What kind of gas mileage do Subarus usually get? From talking with dozens of Subaru owners (and owning a few Subarus myself), I've deduced that with a manual transmission you should get 25 to 35 mpg on the highway and 20 to 30 mpg driving around town. Earlier models with 1600cc engines will probably get mileage close to the high end of the scale, while models with options like the 1800cc engine, 4WD, air conditioning, and power steering will probably be closer to the lower figures. Soobs with automatic transmissions usually get about 5 mpg less than models with stick shifts.

Here are a few good reasons to keep track of your gas mileage: 1. You'll know if something in the engine has changed, causing gas consumption to change (usually for the worse). 2. You'll know approximately how many miles you can drive on a tank of gas so you won't be as likely to run out. 3. You can use mileage calculations to see which brand of gas gives you the best mileage. 4. You'll find out if changing your driving habits as outlined below will really save you some money. (If it doesn't, drive how you've driven all along and don't worry about it.)

FACTORS AFFECTING ECONOMY

Tune-ups: No matter how you drive, your Soob won't perform as economically if the engine isn't operating at peak efficiency. Therefore, the single most important factor in getting good gas mileage is to keep the engine well tuned. Chapter 7 tells you the appropriate intervals for performing the various tune-up procedures.

Tire inflation: Keep the tires properly inflated to decrease the resistance (sluggishness) of the tires as they roll along the road. The higher the tire pressure, the better gas mileage you'll get. However, *don't* inflate the tires above the maximum pressure rating that's stamped on the tire just to squeeze out a few extra miles. It isn't safe.

Extra weight: Hauling around excess weight in the trunk can lower your gas mileage. It's time to tell your 350 lb. buddy to lay off those twinkies.

The carburetor: In order for your engine to perform satisfactorily under a wide range of conditions (such as cold weather, quick acceleration, or climbing hills), the carburetor has three devices built into it which operate only under certain conditions. The devices are the **choke**, the **accelerator pump**, and the **power system**. You have at least partial control over these devices, and the less you use them, the better gas mileage you'll get. Here's how they work and how you can control them to your advantage.

Choke: A richer (more gas to air) mixture is required to start a cold engine and keep it running until it warms up. A flap on the top of the carburetor called the *choke plate* makes this adjustment automatically. As the engine warms up, the choke flap is gradually opened. Since the engine uses more gas when the choke is "on" (flap closed), it makes sense to warm up the engine as quickly as possible. However, racing the engine or holding it at a very fast idle to warm it up causes excess wear on the engine parts. Driving warms up the engine more quickly than idling, so as a compromise between thoroughly warming up the engine at idle and wasting a lot of gas, or jumping into traffic before the engine is warmed up enough to run properly, let the engine idle just a short while—just long enough to get the oil flowing. Warm up the engine well enough to be able to drive conservatively in traffic without lugging or racing the engine; this should take about one to five minutes, depending on how cold it is outside.

Accelerator pump: When you push the gas pedal down suddenly (to pass a car or make a quick getaway after a bank robbery), the sudden rush of air into the engine would cause a temporary loss of power if it weren't for the accelerator pump. To keep the gas/air mixture in a proper ratio, the accelerator pump squirts an extra shot of gas into the engine when the gas pedal is pushed down quickly. If the gas pedal is pushed down slowly, the accelerator pump is not activated, so the slower and smoother you operate the gas pedal, the less extra gas you squirt into the engine.

Power system: The farther you press the gas pedal toward the floorboard during rapid acceleration—climbing steep hills, pulling heavy trailers, or racing—the more the power system in the carburetor is turned on. The power system allows more fuel to be drawn into the engine under these conditions. If you keep your right foot away from the floor and drive so you use the power system as little as possible, you'll save a lot of gas.

Brakes: It takes a certain investment in energy (i.e., gas) to get your car up to driving speed. Once you're cruising, less energy is required because you've gained some momentum from the initial investment. When you take your foot off the gas pedal, the car will coast for some distance without using much gas, and thus some of your initial investment is being repaid. To get the car back up to the desired driving speed, another investment is required to gain back the momentum. Using the brakes to slow the car not only wears out the brake parts but also quickly reduces the momentum you've achieved without getting the benefit of repayment by coasting. Staying aware of the traffic conditions ahead so you can slow down just by letting up on the gas pedal rather than having to apply the brakes allows you to get the most from the momentum you've already paid for. For example, when approaching stop signs, ease up on the gas pedal as soon as traffic will allow and let the momentum carry you close to the stop sign. This way you'll need to use the brakes a lot less. If you drive with a minimal use of the brakes, you'll save a lot of gas as well as wear and tear on the brake system.

Transmissions: The engine has an optimum rpm range that gives you the best economy, power, and longevity. This range is basically between 2,300 rpm and 3,700 rpm. Driving with the engine below this range is called "lugging" the engine, and driving with engine above the optimum range is called "over-revving." For economy driving, it's generally best to keep the rpms to the lower end of the range rather than the higher end. There are exceptions, though. For example, it's better to shift to a lower gear when going up a steep hill so the engine is turning easily at a higher rpm rather than lugging and struggling along at a lower rpm. The **tachometer** (if your model has one) enables you to keep the engine speed in the proper rpm range. If you don't have a tachometer, you can learn to regulate the rpms by the sound of the engine.

Manual transmissions: You can easily use the transmission gears to keep the engine within its optimum range under varying circumstances. While driving, don't rev the engine to the top of the rpm range between every shift; just rev it high enough so that when you shift up through gears, the engine will still be turning fast enough so it won't bog down or lug when you release the clutch. Shift up to higher gears as soon as you can without slowing the engine below the optimum rpm range.

Automatic transmissions: These are notorious for reducing gas mileage. Regardless of what the EPA says, if you have an automatic, count on getting about 5-10 miles per gallon less than your neighbor with the manual transmission.

The shifting in automatics is controlled by the engine speed, demands on the engine (going uphill or downhill, or carrying a heavy load), and the position of the gas pedal. The only economy driving tip I can give you about automatics is to let up on the gas pedal slightly when you feel the rpms are high enough to change to the next higher gear. This will cause it to go ahead and shift. Holding the pedal in one position tends to make the engine rev higher than I think is necessary. One good thing about automatics is that they shift into a lower gear by themselves whenever the engine is about to lug (which a lot of people don't do).

FACTORS AFFECTING LONGEVITY (and thus economy)

Stay on top of your Soob's overall condition and make necessary repairs or adjustments *right away*. Putting off things—like not tuning the engine when it starts running poorly or not having the front end aligned when the tires start wearing on the edges—tends to end up costing you more than if you attended to them right away.

When parking the car (especially on hills), set the handbrake *before* releasing the clutch pedal or putting the transmission in PARK. This way the car is held by the brakes (which are relatively inexpensive and easy to replace), and no strain is placed on the more expensive drive train parts that are involved when the engine and transmission are used to hold the car.

Buying a cheap **magnetic key** holder so you can hide a spare key under the bumper or fender can save you the time and expense of having a locksmith unlock your car on that fateful occasion when you absentmindedly lock the keys in the car or lose them while backpacking in the Pecos Wilderness.

Plan ahead when it comes to anticipated maintenance replacements (see Chapter 7). Buying tune-up and replacement parts (such as oil, filters, and brake shoes) when they're on sale at the local parts store can save you quite a lot of money over a couple of years.

Chapter 8

CHAPTER 9
TROUBLESHOOTING

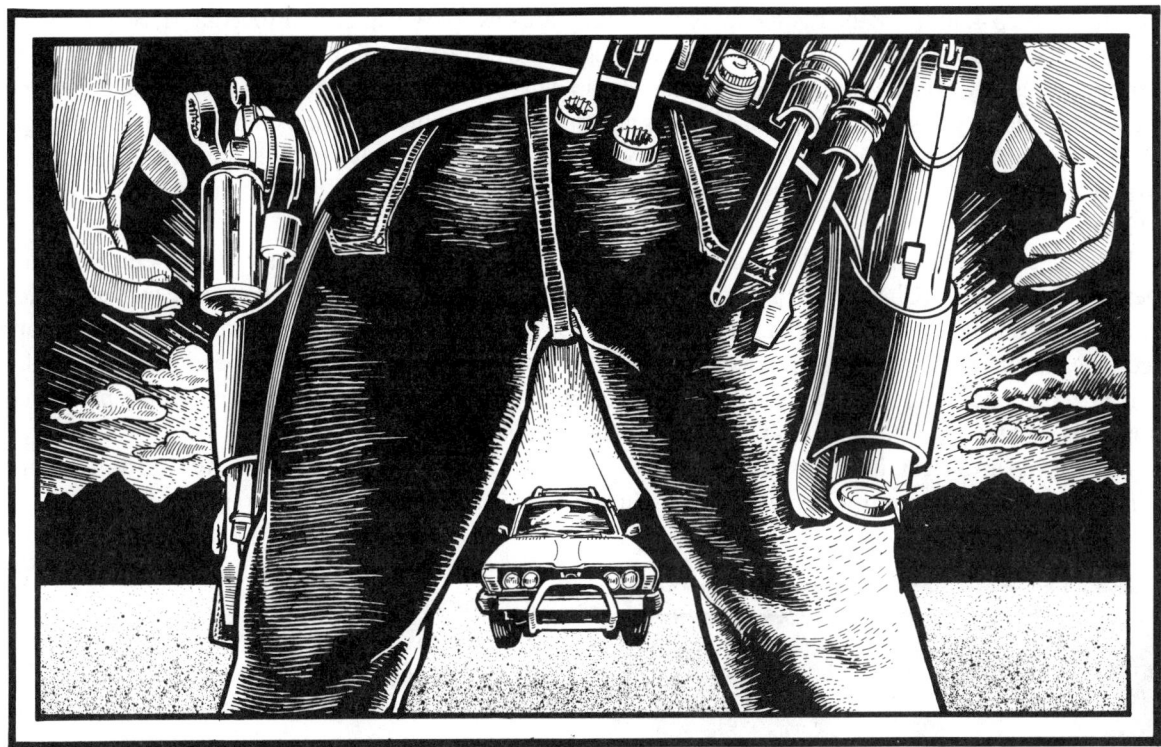

You are probably here because your Soob is misbehaving in one way or another, right? If you're stuck on the side of a busy road, you also have sweaty palms and a sick feeling in the pit of your stomach. Regardless of your present situation, *there's no need to panic*! Take one step at a time in a logical order, and you can probably diagnose the problem. Then either fix it on the spot (if you have the necessary tools and parts onboard), nurse it home, resign yourself to taking it to a garage or, in rare cases, call for a tow truck. At the very least, you'll know if the problem is serious.

This chapter lists some of the problems you are most likely to encounter and tells you the chapter and procedure covering how to fix them. To use this troubleshooting guide, find the section that applies to your problem (engine, brakes, noises, etc.), then locate the symptom that sent you here in the first place (engine won't start, brakes squeal, steering wheel vibrates, etc.). I'll either tell you how to fix it, direct you to the appropriate chapter and procedure in the book, or advise you to seek professional help. Often the diagnosis is the hardest part. If you can't identify the problem, take the car to Subaru or a garage for a professional diagnosis, which should cost little, provided you insist that it's just a diagnosis you want. Once the problem is diagnosed, read through the appropriate chapter and procedure, then you can decide if it's something you feel confident tackling or whether you'd rather have someone else fix it for you.

A friend who has owned dozens of cars offers this wisdom on car problems: "Whatever is wrong, it is rarely as bad as you first expect; only very occasionally is it far worse than you could ever imagine."

ENGINE PROBLEMS

1. Engine Stops and/or Won't Start.

    A. Starter doesn't turn the engine or turns it very slowly:
Turn the ignition key to ON and check the dashboard lights, headlights and horn.
    A1. Lights and electrical things DON'T work or just barely work (dim lights, etc.): See Chapter 10, Procedure 2, Step 4, to check the **fusible links**. If the links are OK, see Chapter 10, Procedure 1, Step 1, to check and add **battery fluid** and Step 3 in that procedure to clean the battery **terminal connections**. If you don't have the proper tools, try *gently* tapping on each cable clamp where it attaches to the battery (with the lug wrench, a rock, etc.), then try to start the engine. The tapping might temporarily make the connection good enough to start the engine. You might also try wiggling the ends of the battery cables where they attach to the engine and starter (Chapter 10, Procedure 1, Step 4). If the engine starts, clean both ends of the battery cables as soon as possible.

    If the electrical equipment still doesn't work after cleaning the terminals, the battery is **discharged**. You'll either need a jump start (Chapter 10, Procedure 1, Step 8) or you'll have to remove the battery (Chapter 10, Procedure 1, Step 7) and take it to a garage or service station to be trickle charged. Why did the battery lose its charge? Check the alternator **drive belt** and if necessary, tighten or replace it (Chapter 10, Procedure 3). If the drive belt is in good condition and properly adjusted, see Chapter 10, Procedure 1, Step 5, to check the battery condition and Chapter 10, Procedure 6, to check the charging system.

    A2. Lights and electrical things all work normally but the starter won't turn the engine: The problem is in the cranking system. Chapter 10, Procedure 9, tells you how to check the cranking system.

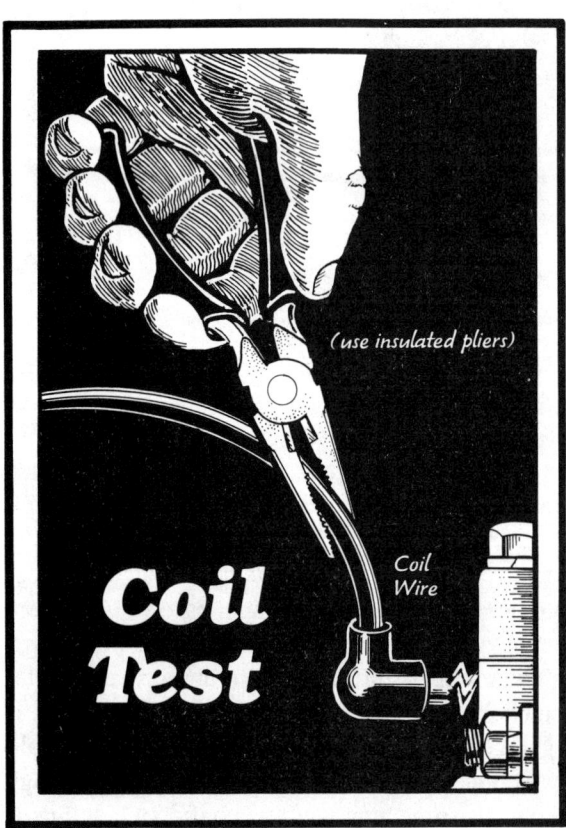

    B. Starter cranks engine normally but engine won't start:
To make the engine run, three elements are necessary: air, fuel, and a spark to ignite the fuel and air. Unless you live in a vacuum, there's plenty of air available, so let's check the other two.
    B1. Coil tests: Disconnect the coil wire from the distributor cap and test it for spark (Chapter 10, Procedure 12, Step 1). If a Friend isn't available to help you, just prop or tie the end of the wire close to bare metal someplace (away from the carburetor or fuel pump) where you can see it from the driver's seat. Then crank the engine with the key to START while you watch the end of the wire. If juice is getting to the end of the coil wire, you'll be able to see (and probably hear) a strong blue spark as you crank the engine. The ignition system is OK at least up to the distributor. Skip down to *B2.* to see if the spark is reaching the spark plugs.

    If there's no spark, check all of the **wire connections** on the end of the coil for tightness. Tighten them if necessary. Wire connections all tight? Check the **fusible links** (if your model has them) and the **fuse** in the fuse box labeled IGN (Chapter 10, Procedure 2). If you have a 12-volt test light, turn the ignition

Testing for Spark at Spark Plugs
(Be sure the Spark Plug is touching bare metal)

switch to ON, then attach one end of the test light to the small positive (+) wire post on the coil and touch the other end of the test light to bare metal. The test light should light up. If it doesn't, and the fusible links and fuses are all good, then the problem is probably in the **ignition switch**. Have Subaru or a garage check it for you.

B2. Spark plug wire test: Remove one of the spark plugs (Chapter 7, Procedure 11, Step 2). Connect the spark plug wire to the spark plug, then use a plastic- or wood-handled screwdriver or insulated pliers to hold the metal part of the spark plug against a metal part of the engine. Have Friend crank the engine while you watch for a spark across the electrodes on the end of the spark plug. If a spark intermittently jumps the gap, the ignition system is OK; skip down to *B4*. No spark across the spark plug electrodes? If the coil wire test was positive (there was spark at the end of the coil wire), but the spark plug test was negative (no spark across the spark plug electrodes), then the problem is in the **distributor**.

B3. Distributor checks: If there's a small wire terminal on the outside of the distributor, check the connection for tightness and tighten the little nut or screw if necessary. Remove and inspect the distributor cap and rotor (Chapter 7, Procedure 9, Step 2). Look for broken or loose wires inside the distributor.

Breaker points type distributors: If you have breaker points, do Chapter 7, Procedure 10, Steps 1 and 4, to inspect and adjust the points. If the points are adjusted correctly and open and close as you rotate the engine, rotate the engine so the points are closed (no gap). Turn the ignition switch to ON, then use a plastic- or wooden-handled screwdriver to push the movable arm of the **points set** away from the stationary arm. You should see a spark when the movable arm breaks contact with the stationary arm. No spark? Check the wire between the wire terminal and the points set and the little ground wire that connects the body of the distributor to one of the points set attaching screws. If either wire is broken or disconnected, reattach or replace it as necessary.

If there's still no spark when you move the points arm, the **plastic insulator** for the wire terminal bolt on the side of the distributor might be broken or missing, allowing the bolt to touch the distributor body. Replace the insulator if necessary.

Still no spark? It's time for professional advice.

Breakerless distributors: If the car starts OK when the engine is cold but won't start after it's warmed up, the **electronic pick-up unit** might be shot. Have Subaru or a garage check it and replace it for you if the unit is bad.

B4. Fuel tests: You're sure there's gas in the gas tank and you've checked the ignition system and you're sure electricity is getting to the spark plugs, right? OK. Do Chapter 11, Procedure 4, to see if fuel is getting to the carburetor. You'll be directed where to turn according to the results of the checks.

154   Chapter 9

2. Engine Starts OK, But Doesn't Run Right.

You can get the engine to start, but it isn't running the way you know it should. Symptoms are rough running, hesitation, lack of power, poor gas mileage, backfiring, and "pinging." Lack of power and/or poor gas mileage can be caused by any or all of the following problems.

A. Engine pinging: Pinging sounds like someone's in the engine compartment shaking a coffee can full of small pebbles. It usually occurs during rapid acceleration or when going up hills. What's happening is that the fuel/air mixture is being ignited in the cylinder before it's supposed to. The causes and cures are:

A1. Wrong fuel: The fuel octane is too low; use gas with a higher octane rating.

A2. Ignition timing: The ignition timing is advanced too far. Adjust it. Chapter 7, Procedure 13, tells you how.

A3. Faulty vacuum advance/retard unit: Check, and if necessary, replace the unit (Chapter 7, Procedure 9, Step 8). Not all models have these.

A4. Buildup of carbon in the combustion chambers: Check the automatic choke as described in *B4*. Also check the spark plugs and do a compression check to see if excess oil is getting into the combustion chambers (Chapter 7, Procedure 11).

B. Rough running: Your engine feels and sounds like it's not running on all its cylinders all the time. Often there's a drop in power and gas mileage. If the engine is missing (stuttering, fluttering), a general rule of thumb is that if the miss is regular and consistent, the problem is most likely in the ignition system. If the miss is irregular, or comes and goes, the problem is in the fuel system.

B1. Vacuum leaks: If the engine has suddenly started running like a three-legged dog, look for a **vacuum hose** that's come off its fitting. The open line will probably make a hissing noise when the engine is running. If you find the culprit, reconnect the hose, or replace it if it's cracked or stretched on the end.

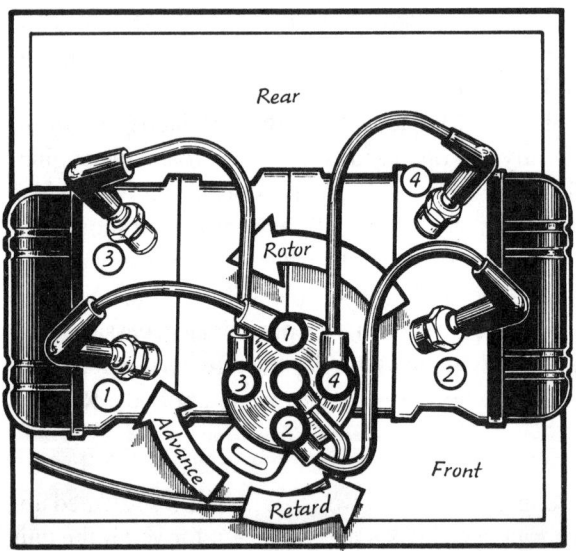

B2. Check spark plug wire connections, spark plugs, and engine compression: Are the spark plug wires securely connected to the distributor cap and spark plugs? Check 'em: push down on both ends of each wire. Remove the spark plugs and check their condition. Do a **compression test** while the spark plugs are out and evaluate the results. Directions for these checks are in Chapter 7, Procedure 11.

B3. Coil and coil wire connections: Check the coil and the wires attached to it (Chapter 10, Procedure 12). Replace the coil, or tighten the wires if necessary.

B4. Carburetor checks: For these checks you'll need to remove the air cleaner (Chapter 7, Procedure 5, Step 4).

Choke: To see if the choke is working, start the engine and let it warm up. When the engine is warmed up, the flat **choke plate** in the top of the carb should be in a vertical position.

If it isn't, feel for warmth in the round **automatic choke housing**. It's on the top right (passenger's) side of the carb (Hitachi carbs) or on the top left side of the carb (Carter/Weber carbs). (If you're not sure which kind of carburetor you have, see the rap at the beginning of Chapter 11: *Fuel Systems*.)

If the round choke housing doesn't feel warm after the engine has warmed up, the choke either isn't getting juice or the choke element inside the housing is shot. Follow the wire coming out of the housing to a **wire connection** and see that the wire is attached securely. If you have a 12-volt test light handy, check the wire for juice while the engine is running (Chapter 10, Procedure 5, Step 2). If there's no juice, locate and check the **choke fuse** (Chapter 10, Procedure 2, Step 3).

If the fuse and choke wire connection are both good, remove the three tiny screws and weird-shaped washers around the edge of the round choke housing. (Beginning in about 1980, some Hitachi carbs have rivets instead of screws. If your carb has rivets, you've done all the checking you can do; see the pros.) Put the screws and washers where they won't fall into the carb or get lost. Wiggle the choke unit out of its housing on the carb and check the **springs** inside. The flat spring should be concentric around the center post. If it's distorted and off-center, replace the choke unit. Check the small coiled wire inside the ceramic groove for breaks and distortion. Replace it if it's broken or doesn't fit neatly into the groove. Chapter 11, Procedure 9, Step 8, tells you how to reassemble the automatic choke.

Anti-diesel valve (Hitachi carbs only): The symptom of a faulty **anti-diesel valve** is the engine runs OK at high rpms but won't idle. Here's how to locate and check the anti-diesel valve.

The anti-diesel valve is a hexagonal, brass-colored, thumb-size gizmo sticking out of the front, left (driver's) side of the carb. It points toward the left headlight. Turn the ignition key to ON, but don't start the engine. Follow the wire coming out of the end of the valve to a wire connection. Disconnect the wires, then reconnect them while listening for a click from the anti-diesel valve. Try disconnecting/connecting the wires several times. If the valve clicks, it's probably working correctly. No click? See Chapter 11, Procedure 8, Step 8, to remove the valve, and Chapter 11, Procedure 9, Step 5, to install the new valve. On '80 and newer models, if your setup is such that the choke wire, anti-diesel valve wire, and a wire from another gizmo on the carb (the switch vent solenoid) all share a common plastic connector, you'll have to cut the old wire and splice the new wire to it. If you aren't sure how to splice electrical wires, see Chapter 18.

Other carburetor connections: Follow all other wires attached to the carburetor to where they connect to the **wiring harness**. Be sure the connection is clean and tight. Carter/Weber carbs have three electrical gizmos; Hitachis have one to three depending on the year and model.

C. Engine backfires: If your Soob occasionally makes loud explosions that cause nearby motorists to duck for cover, check the following systems as soon as possible or you run the risk of blowing the exhaust system apart.

C1. Idle speed: If the backfire only happens when you turn the ignition key OFF, the engine might just be idling too fast. Check and adjust the *idle speed* (Chapter 7, Procedure 12).

C2. Coasting by-pass system (decel system on '75-'80 models): See Chapter 12, Procedure 7, to check and adjust the *coasting by-pass system*.

C3. Anti-afterburning valve: See the rap at the start of Chapter 12, Procedure 8, to see if you have an *anti-afterburning valve* (AAV). If you have an AAV, continue to Step 1 to check and replace the valve (if necessary).

C4. Improper ignition timing: See Chapter 7, Procedure 13.

C5. Cracked distributor cap: See Chapter 7, Procedure 9.

C6. Faulty vacuum advance/retard unit: See Chapter 7, Procedure 9, Step 8.

C7. Crossed spark plug wires: Be sure the rotor is pointing to the #1 spark plug wire when the timing marks on the flywheel are aligned with the pointer (Chapter 7, Procedure 5, Step 6); then trace the wires going *counterclockwise* from the #1 wire on the distributor cap—the wires should go to cylinders #1, #3, #2, and #4 in order.

C8. Clogged EGR system: See Chapter 12, Procedure 1.

C9. Leaking or sticking exhaust valves: A

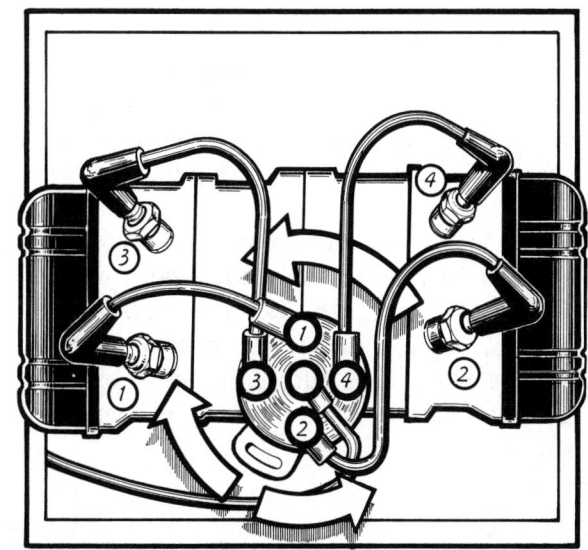

156 Chapter 9

compression test will tell you if the valves are leaking (Chapter 7, Procedure 11). An oil and filter change *might* prevent the valves from sticking.

C10. Leaking or worn out exhaust system: The engine normally creates some backfires, but you don't hear them because the muffler(s) muffle the sound. If the inside of the muffler(s) is worn out or there are leaks in the exhaust system, you'll hear these normal backfires.

D. Engine hesitates when accelerator pedal is pressed down suddenly: This symptom is called a "flat spot" and is usually caused by not enough fuel being pumped into the carb when the pedal is pressed down. Here's how to check the carb. If you have fuel injection, you'll have to see the pros.

D1. Check accelerator pump: Remove the air cleaner lid (Chapter 7, Procedure 4, Step 3). Hold the choke plate in the top of the carburetor in a vertical position with a finger or screwdriver so you can look down into the carb.

With the engine OFF and the choke plate in a vertical position, have Friend pump the gas pedal a few times while you peer into the barrel of the carb (the front one on Hitachi carbs). If Friend isn't available, you'll have to rotate the throttle arm on the side of the carb where the accelerator cable attaches. You should see a healthy stream of gas squirt into the barrel from a small brass nozzle each time the pedal is pushed down or the throttle arm is rotated. A weak, puny stream, or no gas at all, means the **accelerator pump nozzle** is clogged.

For Hitachi carbs, see Chapter 11, Procedure 11, to remove the carb top. Squirt lots of carb cleaner through the accelerator pump nozzle until it's clean. (See the large carburetor illustration in Chapter 11 to locate the nozzle.) If possible, borrow a set of carburetor jet cleaners to clean the nozzle. Chapter 11, Procedure 11, Step 4, tells you how to install the carb top and put everything back together.

For Carter/Weber carbs, you'll have to have Subaru or a garage clean the accelerator pump nozzle for you.

D2. Check mechanical and vacuum advance/retard unit on the distributor: If the accelerator pump in the carb is working correctly but there's still a flat spot, see Chapter 7, Procedure 9, to check the advance/retard mechanisms in the distributor.

3. Oil Warning Light Goes ON or Oil Pressure Gauge Drops to 0 while Engine Is Running.

A. STOP! Check oil level. Stop the engine as soon as possible and check the engine **oil dipstick** (Chapter 7, Procedure 2, Step 1). If the oil level is OK, skip down to Step B to check the oil pressure switch and gauge. If the oil level is low or you can't find any oil on the dipstick, don't drive the car until you add oil to the full mark. Start the engine to see if the light goes off or the gauge shows you have oil pressure. If the light stays ON, or the gauge remains at 0, turn the engine off immediately and skip down to Step B.

If adding oil solved the problem, look under the engine to see if you've developed a sudden oil leak. See Section 5 to fix any oil leaks you might find. No oil leaks? Slap yourself severely on the wrists, face, and the top of your head for letting the oil level get that low—and check the oil level more often from now on!

B. Check oil pressure switch (OPS): If you only have an oil pressure warning light on the dash (no gauge), the **OPS** will be screwed into the crankcase just to the right (passenger's) side of the oil pump. On models with an oil pressure gauge on the dash, the OPS is screwed into the bottom front of the oil pump near the oil filter.

Models with an oil pressure warning light: Turn the ignition key to ON, but don't start the engine. Disconnect the wire from the OPS and check the oil warning light on the dash. The light should be off when the wire is disconnected. If it's still on, there's a short in the wire someplace between the OPS and the gauge. See Chapter 10, Procedure 5, Step 3. If the light went off when you disconnected the wire, the problem is either a faulty OPS or the oil pump isn't pumping oil. Skip down to Step C.

Models with an oil pressure gauge: Use your jumper wire or round up about a 12" piece of electrical wire with ½" of insulation stripped away from the ends. Have Friend start the engine and let it idle. While Friend watches the oil pressure gauge, touch one end of the jumper (or wire) to the screw on the bottom of the OPS and touch the other end to bare metal. The needle on the gauge should go to the highest number. Quickly remove the wire. If the needle on the gauge didn't move, there's a problem with the gauge. Have Subaru or a garage check it for you. If the needle moved to the top end of the scale then moved back to zero when the wire was disconnected, the gauge is OK so the problem is either a broken OPS or there's no oil pressure. Do Step C to check the oil pressure. If the engine has oil pressure, replace the OPS (see Section 5 of this chapter). Step C will tell you what to do if there's no oil pressure.

C. Check oil pressure: To see if the **oil pump** is working, place a catch pan under the oil filter, then remove the filter (Chapter 7, Procedure 3, Step 2). Have Friend crank the engine for a few seconds while you watch for oil squirting out of the oil pump. If the engine starts, shut it off immediately.

If oil squirts out, the pump is working so the problem is a faulty OPS. The instructions for replacing the OPS are in Section 5 a little later in this chapter.

If oil doesn't squirt out of the pump (or just dribbles out), the pump parts are worn out or broken, the **oil pressure relief valve** in the pump is stuck or the **oil screen** in the oil pan is plugged. If you have an OHC model, it's time to see the pros. If you have an OHV model, see Chapter 17, Procedure 7, Step 4, to remove the oil pump and Chapter 17, Procedure 9, Step 4, to check it for wear. (You don't have to remove the engine to remove and install the oil pump.) Chapter 17, Procedure 19, Step 1, tells you how to install the pump. If the oil pump checks out OK, do the test below to be sure the screen in the **oil pick-up tube** isn't clogged.

If the oil pump checks out OK, the problem is either that the oil pick-up pipe is broken (unlikely) or the screen covering the end of the pipe is clogged with crud. Is there a big dent in the oil pan that might have broken the pick-up pipe? To see if the screen is clogged, round up a 12" to 18" length of 3/8" (10mm) outside diameter rubber hose. Then do the following while the oil pump is still off the car. Stick one end of the hose into the hole on the lower right side of the oil pump opening in the crankcase and blow into the other end of the hose. Be sure air isn't leaking around the hose. If you can blow through the hose, the screen on the end of the pipe isn't clogged. If you *can't* blow through the hose, the screen is clogged.

To unclog the screen, remove the rubber hose, drain the oil from the crankcase (Chapter 7, Procedure 3, Step 1), then squirt lots of carb cleaner into the hole where you stuck the rubber hose. Let the carb cleaner do its thing for a while, then use the hose to try blowing through the hole again. (Use compressed air if it's available.) Do this over and over until the screen is clear enough so you can blow easily through the hose, or until you decide the Dark Side has won. If the screen is still clogged, see the pros.

If you're successful in opening the screen, pour a quart of oil through the engine to flush out the carb cleaner, then follow the instructions in Chapter 17, Procedure 19, to install the oil pump. Install the oil drain plug and a new oil filter, then fill the crankcase with fresh oil (Chapter 7, Procedure 3, Steps 3-6).

Start the engine and see if you have oil pressure now. If not, see the pros.

4. Alternator Light Goes ON in Midflight

Pull off the road as soon as possible, and do the following:

A. Check alternator drive belt: Open and prop the hood and check the alternator drive belt (Chapter 10, Procedure 3). If the belt is broken, whip out your spare belt and install it (Chapter 10, Procedure 3). You do have a spare with you, don't you? If not, *don't* drive the car because the alternator drive belt also operates the water pump and without the water pump the engine will overheat quickly.

B. Check alternator wire connections and battery voltage: If the drive belt is OK, do Chapter 10, Procedure 6, Step 1, to check the wire connections on the rear of the alternator. If the wires are connected properly, do Step 2 to check the voltage across the battery. You'll be instructed what to do according to the results of the tests. If you don't have the tools to check the voltage, and the drive belt is intact and adjusted properly, you can still drive the car but the battery will discharge if you try to go too far. Turn off all electrical accessories to minimize the drain on the battery.

5. Engine Oil Leaks

To determine where the oil is leaking you might have to wash the engine (Chapter 7, Procedure 5, Step 2), then crawl under the car frequently to see where oil first appears.

If the engine seems to be leaking everywhere, check the thumb-size **positive crankcase ventilation (PCV) hoses** that attach between the valve covers and the air cleaner. These hoses relieve pressure that builds up inside the crankcase and if they get clogged with oil and carbon, the pressure will force oil out through the seals and gaskets. To check the hoses, disconnect one end at a time and blow through the hose. You should be able to blow through one end into the valve cover and into the air cleaner from the other end. I've seen a brand-new rebuilt engine leak badly because the fitting on the air cleaner was clogged where the hoses attach. Clean the hoses, valve covers, and fitting(s) on the air cleaner if necessary.

Here are the most common places for the engine to leak and how to fix them:

A. Valve covers (OHV models only): See Chapter 7, Procedure 6, Step 1, to remove the valve covers. Replace the **gasket** that fits between the cylinder head and valve covers as well as the rubber-coated **washers** on the bolts that attach the valve cover. Be sure there are no pieces of the old gasket stuck to the sealing surface of the cylinder head or valve cover before installing the valve covers. If the engine is cool, you might as well *adjust the valves* while the covers are off (Chapter 7, Procedure 7). Chapter 7, Procedure 7, Step 6, tells you how to install the valve covers.

B. Oil pressure switch (OPS): When the oil pressure switch starts leaking, it's like a kid with a runny nose; no matter how often you wipe it, within a few minutes there's big drop hanging down again. If you suspect the OPS is leaking, clean it thoroughly with a rag, then start the engine, and watch for the leak.

Before replacing the OPS, be sure the oil isn't running down the front of the engine from a leaking **front crank seal** or coming from a leaking oil pump. Checking the front crank seal is described in the next section.

On models with an oil pressure light on the dash, but *no* oil pressure gauge, the OPS is slightly larger than a 19mm socket and is screwed into the lower, front, right side of the crankcase just to the right of the oil pump. A wire is attached to the end of the OPS with a push-on connector. On models *with* an oil pressure gauge in the dashboard, the sending unit is round and screwed into the bottom of the oil pump near where the oil filter is attached. A wire attached to the bottom of the OPS with a phillips screw connects, with a push-on connector, to the wiring harness a few inches away. (For some reason, some models with an oil pressure gauge *also* have an OPS for an oil warning light installed in its normal position. Like an appendix, it's there but doesn't do anything.)

If the OPS is leaking, remove the skid plate on 4WD models, disconnect the OPS wire, then use large pliers (models with an oil warning light) or an open end wrench (models with an oil pressure gauge) to gently unscrew the unit *counterclockwise* as viewed from the wire terminal end. Put gasket sealer on the threads of the new OPS, then screw it into the crankcase or oil pump, depending on your model. Gently tighten it with the large pliers or wrench (depending on your setup). Don't squeeze too hard with the pliers or you might distort the new unit and cause it to leak. The threads on the OPS are tapered so you don't have to get it real tight, just good and snug.

C. Oil pump (OHV models only): First, be sure it's the oil pump that's leaking. The front crank seal is right above the oil pump and if it leaks the oil runs down on the oil pump. Use a spray can of carb cleaner and rag to thoroughly clean the oil pump and the crankcase between the oil pump and front crank seal. Start the engine and let it run awhile, then shut it off. Use a flashlight and small mirror (like the one your dentist uses) to check the area behind the crank pulley for signs of oil. If oil appears between the oil pump and crank seal, the crank seal is the culprit. Skip down to the crank seal section. If the area between the crank seal and oil pump stays dry but oil appears on the bottom of the oil pump, the oil pump is leaking.

Once you're sure it's the oil pump that is leaking, use a 10mm wrench to see if the four oil-pump mounting bolts are tight. They're small bolts, so don't crank on them too hard or they'll break. If the bolts are tight, the rubber **O-ring** between the oil pump and crankcase has probably become brittle and cracked, or one of the **oil pump gaskets** has broken. To replace the O-ring or gaskets, chock the rear wheels, then jack up the front of the car and put it on jackstands (Chapter 3: *Safety*). If there's a piece of sheet metal attached below the front of the car with four 10mm bolts, remove it. Remove the 12mm bolts or 5.5mm allen head screws that attach the skid plate on 4WD models. See Chapter 17, Procedure 7, Step 4, to remove the oil pump and install new gaskets. Be sure the two phillips screws that hold the two pump body pieces together are tight, then do Chapter 17, Procedure 19, to install the pump with a new O-ring. If the engine has a lot of miles on it, now would be a good time to install a new pump. Shop around for the best price.

D. Front crank seal (OHV non-Turbo models only): See the oil pump section above to determine if the front crank seal is leaking. To replace the crank seal, remove the drive belt(s) (Chapter 10, Procedure 3), then see Chapter 17, Procedure 3, Step 3, to remove the crank pulley and crank seal. You'll be directed to the seal and crank pulley installation procedures.

E. Rear crank seal: When the rear crank seal starts leaking, you'll notice oil dripping from the rear of the engine just in front of the transaxle. Oil leaking from the front crank seal, the oil pump, or the oil pressure switch will end up near the rear of the engine, so first be sure that none of these is the source of the oil leak. Another check for rear crank seal leaks is to remove the rubber or plastic plug from the timing hole just to the rear of the engine oil dipstick. With the engine off, stick a finger through the timing hole and feel for oil on the flywheel (manual transmission) or converter drive plate (automatic transmission). If oil is present, the rear crank seal is probably leaking.

Just to be sure, compare the smell of the oil dripping from the rear of the engine to the oil on the engine dipstick, the differential dipstick, and the automatic transmission fluid dipstick if you have an automatic transmission. (See Chapter 7, Procedure 2, if you aren't sure where the dipsticks are located.) If the dripping oil smells like the differential oil or the automatic transmission fluid, take the car to a transmission shop and have them check the leak and repair it (if it's the differential or automatic transmission that's leaking). If the oil drips smell like engine oil, it's time for some serious contemplation.

Since it's such an expensive or time-consuming job to replace the rear crank seal, weigh the inconveniences and expense of the oil leak (cost of the oil, messy driveway, insecurity about the engine oil level) against the cost and/or effort required to replace the rear seal (see how much a garage would charge to replace the seal and read the engine removal procedures in Chapter 17 to see if you're up to the task). Now you have to decide whether to live with the leak, or fix it. OHC models will have to see the pros. OHV models: If you want to do it yourself, here's how.

Since the bottom of the car is probably covered with oil from the leaking seal, do yourself a favor; go to a car wash and wash the top and bottom of the engine (Chapter 7, Procedure 5, Step 2) before removing the engine. You'll be glad you did, or sorry if you didn't. To replace the rear crank seal, see Chapter 17 to remove the engine from the car and to remove the clutch and flywheel (manual transmissions) or the drive plate (automatics). There are separate procedures in Chapter 17 for removing and installing the rear crank seal. Once the seal is replaced, install the flywheel and clutch assembly (manuals) or the drive plate (automatics). It's all in Chapter 17. Stick the engine back in the car, give it a good tune-up and you're finished. The ordeal is over.

6. Engine Overheats or Doesn't Warm Up.

If you're stuck at the side of the road with the temp gauge pegged on HOT and/or steam billowing from the radiator, see Chapter 16, Procedure 11. If your Soob is starting to run a little hotter than normal but you're not in an emergency situation, see Chapter 16, Procedure 10.

If it takes longer than you think it should for the engine to warm up or if it never fully warms up, see Chapter 16, Procedure 6, to check the thermostat.

7. Accelerator Pedal Goes to Floor but Engine Speed Doesn't Change.

See Chapter 11, Procedure 3, to check the accelerator cable and replace it if necessary.

8. Symptoms and Checks for Leaking Head Gaskets.

Some water normally condenses in the engine (especially in cold weather) but after the engine is driven and warmed up, the water boils away. If after driving several miles, you notice any of the symptoms listed below, retorque the heads on OHV models (Chapter 7, Procedure 6), and change the oil and filter. Drive the car 50-100 continuous miles and check for the symptoms again. If water is still evident in places where it shouldn't be, have a garage do a "leak-down" test for leaking head gaskets. It shouldn't cost much and is probably worth the money, just to be sure before removing the engine and taking it apart.

A: Symptoms of leaking head gaskets are: Water or white frothy looking stuff is evident inside the oil filler tube, oil filler cap, and valve covers; the engine oil becomes a light brown color (like coffee with cream); slimy oil is in the radiator; the engine might run slightly hotter than normal; the compression for two cylinders on one side of the engine is lower than for the two cylinders on the opposite side; you have to add coolant to the radiator frequently; you see water or antifreeze dripping from the bottom of the cylinder head(s) where they fit against the crankcase.

BRAKE PROBLEMS

1. The Handbrake Handle Comes Up Too High.
The handbrake cables need adjusting (Chapter 13, Procedure 15), the rear brakes need adjusting (Chapter 13, Procedure 1), and/or one of the handbrake cables is broken (Chapter 13, Procedure 16).

2. The Brake Pedal Feels Mushy and You Have to Pump on the Pedal to Stop the Car.
There's air in the hydraulic brake system; read the rap on brake problems in the first part of Chapter 13. You'll probably need to bleed the hydraulic brake system (Chapter 13, Procedure 2).

3. Brakes Squeal.

The friction surface of the brake shoes or pads might be worn out. First try to determine if the noise is coming from the front or rear of the car.

From the rear: If you have rear drum brakes, see Chapter 13, Procedure 4, to check the condition of the rear **brake shoes**. If you have rear disc brakes, see Chapter 13, Procedure 6, to check the **brake pads**. If you aren't sure which type of rear brakes you have, see the rap at the start of Chapter 13.

From the front: You have disc brakes up front; check the **brake pads** (Chapter 13, Procedure 8). If the pads are in good condition, squirting the front brake system with the garden hose when it starts squealing often solves the problem for awhile. This washes away the accumulated brake dust that seems to make the brakes squeal. Don't squirt the brakes while they're hot (within an hour of driving the car) or the rotors might warp. If the squeal returns, you might have semi-metallic brake pads, which naturally tend to squeal. If the noise really bothers you (it bothers me), change to regular brake pads (I did).

4. The Car Pulls to One Side When the Brakes Are Applied.

This means the brakes aren't adjusted correctly (or one side is sticking) or there's oil, grease, or brake fluid on the brake lining. See Chapter 13, Procedure 4, to check rear drum brakes, or Chapter 13, Procedure 6, to check rear disc brakes, or Chapter 13, Procedure 8, to check front disc brakes.

NOISES!

If your Soob has developed a noise alerting you that something's amiss, first determine if the noise is related to the *engine*, *drivetrain* (transaxle, axles, wheels), *suspension system* (shock absorbers, control arms, etc.), or *steering system* (ball joints, tie rods, steering gearbox, etc.).

1. Engine Noises.

If the sound is present when the engine is running but the car isn't moving, something on the engine is amiss. Here are some clues to tracking it down:

A. Squeals: If you hear a squeal when you first start the engine, then the noise goes away as the engine warms up, check the tension on the drive belt(s) (Chapter 10, Procedure 3), the *water pump* (Chapter 16, Procedure 4), and the distributor shaft for looseness (Chapter 7, Procedure 9).

If the squeal changes with the engine speed: If you have a breaker points-type distributor, the *lobe rider* might need a dab of grease (Chapter 7, Procedure 10, Step 6). Or the *alternator bearings* might be dry; have the alternator checked by Subaru or a garage. They might be able to install new bearings if the alternator is in good condition otherwise. If the alternator must be replaced, see Chapter 10, Procedure 7. You can do it yourself.

OHC models: If the cam belts are adjusted too tight, you'll hear a squealing, whining sound near the front of the engine.

B. Hissing sound: Check all the *vacuum hoses* in the engine compartment. Check the *spark plugs* to be sure they're tight. Check the intake manifold and carburetor *mounting bolts* for tightness.

C. Clicking sounds: A regular clicking sound that changes with engine speed is probably a loose valve. OHV models with mechanical valve lifters can adjust the valves (Chapter 7, Procedure 7). OHC models and OHV models with hydraulic lifters can have the valves adjusted by Subaru or a garage.

A clicking sound that changes with the speed of the car, but not necessarily the speed of the engine, may be in the wheel bearings or brakes. Try to determine which corner of the car it's coming from. Then search Chapters 13: *Brakes*, and 14: *Suspension* for solutions.

D. Knocking sounds: A regular metallic-sounding knock when the engine is decelerating is possibly a worn *connecting rod bearing*. A lower, hollow-type sound indicates worn *crankshaft main bearings*. Another symptom of worn rod and/or main bearings is low oil pressure (the oil warning light comes on at idle or the oil pressure gauge indicates lower than normal pressure). If you suspect worn rod and/or main bearings, I suggest getting a second opinion from the professionals before yanking the engine out.

Knocking noises from underneath that come and go are often from a loose exhaust system (Chapter 12) or possibly suspension parts (Chapter 14).

OHC models: A thwapping-type knocking sound from the area of the distributor means the cam belts are loose and need to be adjusted. The thwapping comes from the camshaft banging on the inside of the cam box. If the belts aren't adjusted soon, they are likely to break, leaving you stranded, distraught, and poorer. See Chapter 7, Procedure 8, to check and adjust the cam belts.

2. Steering and Suspension Noises.

You notice clunks, clanks, or bangs when you hit bumps or potholes in the road, or the car doesn't handle the way it used to. Chapter 14, Procedure 1, tells you how to check the suspension and steering systems. A knocking noise when the car is turned sharply might be a worn DOJ or CVJ. See the clutch, transmission, and driveshaft troubleshooting guide in Chapter 15.

SMELLS

There are usually two causes for a stinky, smelly engine: (1) the engine is overheating; (2) oil from the engine or grease from a torn axle boot is on the exhaust system.

1. Engine Overheating.

See Chapter 16, Procedure 10.

2. Engine Oil on the Exhaust System.

See Section 5 on engine oil leaks in this chapter. You'll be instructed where to turn for the solution.

3. Grease on the Exhaust System.

See Chapter 7, Procedure 2, Step 10, to check the axle boots (DOJs and CVJs). If an axle boot is torn, Chapter 15, Procedure 4, tells you how to replace a DOJ boot, and Chapter 15, Procedure 6, covers replacing CVJ boots.

ELECTRICAL PROBLEMS

If you're having trouble with electrical gizmos (such as lights, horn, radio, gauges, heater switch, etc.), start by doing Chapter 10, Procedure 1, Steps 1-5, and Procedure 5.

CLUTCH, TRANSAXLE, AXLESHAFTS, AND DRIVESHAFT PROBLEMS

There's a troubleshooting guide at the start of Chapter 15 that tells you how to identify the problem and where to turn to remedy it.

SHAKES, SHIMMIES, AND HANDLING PROBLEMS

If the car shakes and/or the steering wheel vibrates at certain speeds on the highway, or the car wanders from one side of the road to the other, see Chapter 14, Procedure 1, to check the steering and suspension systems. If no problem is found, have the front end alignment checked and the tires balanced.

If the car pulls to one side of the road, it's most likely that the *air pressure* in one of the tires on that side of the car is low. If the car pulls to one side *only* when you apply the brakes, you could have a leaking *wheel cylinder*; see Chapter 13 for diagnosis and cure.

164 *Chapter 9*

CHAPTER 10
THE ELECTRICAL SYSTEM

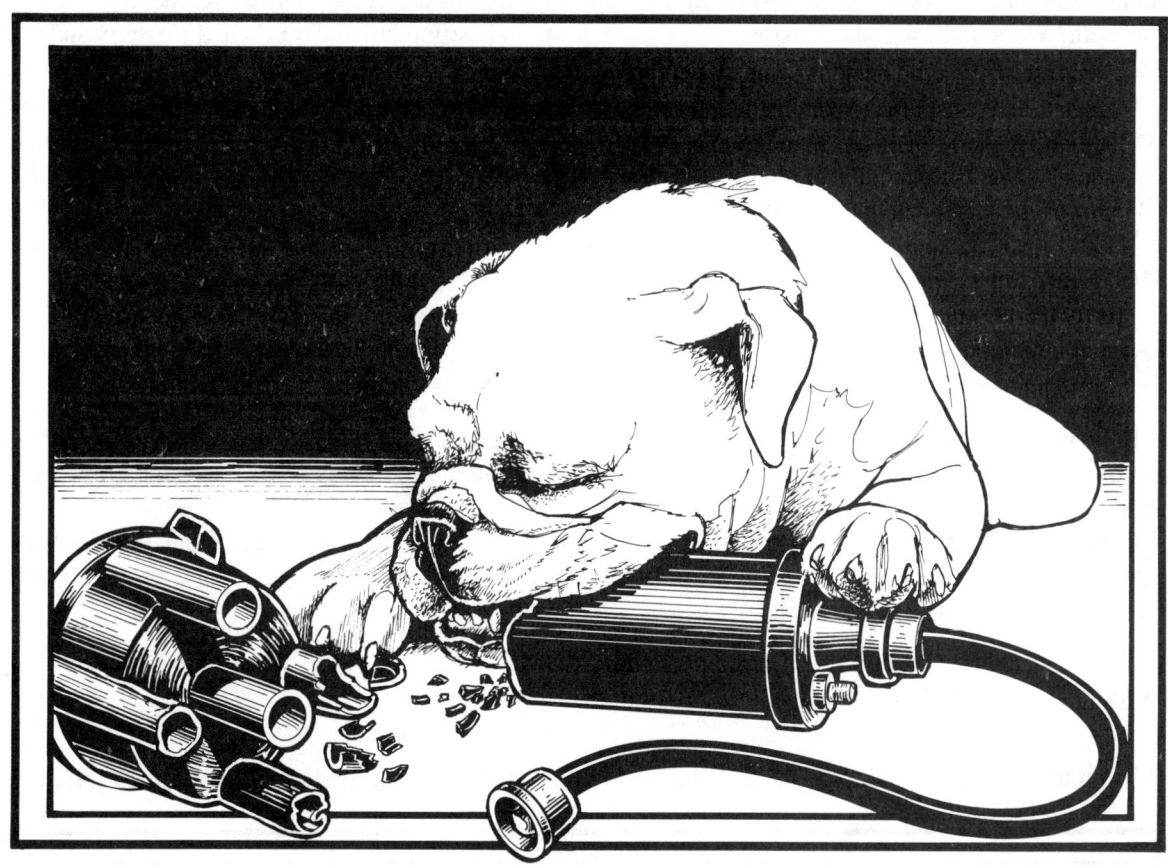

This high-charged chapter is about your Soob's electrical system. First off, we're going to see how electricity stored in the battery is used to start the engine and ignite the fuel/air mixture to make the engine run and how the alternator "generates" electricity to keep the battery fully charged so it can supply electrical energy to the various electrical components such as lights, horn, and wipers.

I freely admit that I don't completely fathom the theory that electrons dancing merrily from one atom to another is what makes a light bulb light, a horn beep, or an electric motor turn. It's been explained to me in countless high school and college courses over the years and I could always pass the tests, even if I didn't really "grok" it. The theory is relatively simple, but if something's invisible, I'm skeptical. I consider electricity a first-water mystery and relate to it as "controllable magic." Sounds as reasonable to me as dancing electrons.

Furthermore, I think the reason most people, including electricians, refer to electricity as "juice" is because they, too, have trouble relating to the dancing electron theory. Imagining something *tangible* flowing through the wires is psychologically easier to digest, so throughout this chapter I'll be calling electricity "juice."

Anyway, I've found over the years that you don't need to know anything about electrons (or believe in them) to keep your car's electrical system working. All you need to grasp is the concept that an electrical circuit makes a complete circle (like a hula hoop). If the circle is complete, the electrical gizmos will work; if the circle is broken, they won't. Just think of a circle whenever a circuit is mentioned and you won't have much trouble understanding the electrical wonders of your Soob. Simple enough? OK, with a circle in mind, I'll elaborate.

WHAT ARE THE NECESSARY ELEMENTS IN AN ELECTRICAL CIRCUIT?

Four elements are necessary for an **electrical circuit** to work: (1) a source of juice like a **charged battery**; (2) a **"hot" wire** to carry juice from the **positive battery post** to the component; (3) a **component**—such as a light bulb or horn—in the circle that resists (slows) the flow of juice; and (4) a **"ground" wire** to carry juice from the component back to the **negative battery post** to complete the circuit. Why do you need the resisting component? Without the resistance to the flow of juice, it would flow too fast and overheat the battery and wires in the circuit.

Now let's add a **switch** to break the flow of juice in the circuit when we want to turn the component off (in other words, break the circle). And let's add a **fuse** to protect the wires, components, and battery in case of a problem (such as a **"short,"** which happens when the resistance is bypassed, or an **overloaded circuit**). Now we have a complete circuit, just like all the ones in your Soob.

What follows is an explanation of the two most common electrical problems—"shorts" and overloaded circuits.

SHORTS (SHORTCUTS) AND OVERLOADED CIRCUITS

If the juice takes a shortcut from the positive battery post back to the negative post without going through a component to slow it, it's called a "short." Shorts cause the battery and wires to overheat, melt, and maybe start a fire. The battery might even explode. Nasty.

Circuits can occasionally be overloaded by turning on too many components at the same time. The wires are designed to handle the load, but once in a while there's just too much going on. Again, the wires may overheat or damage may be done to the battery.

FUSES AND FUSIBLE LINKS

To protect the wires, components, and battery when a short or overload condition occurs, **fuses** and **fusible**

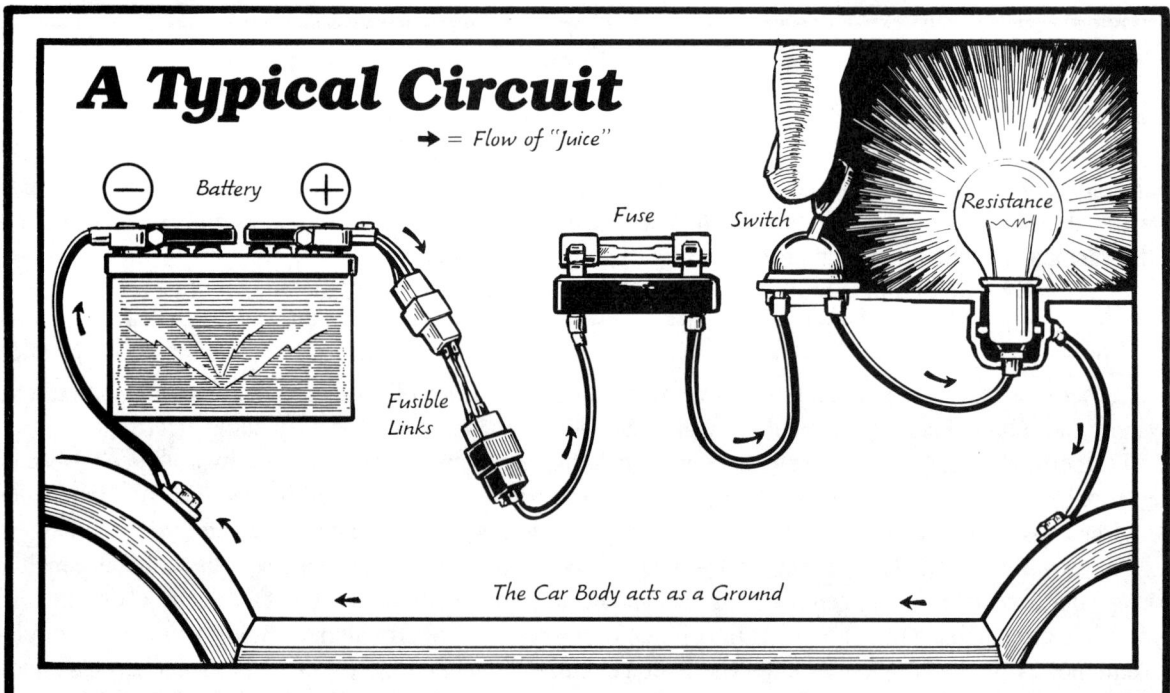

links on '78 and newer models are installed in each circuit, with one exception—the cranking circuit. Fuses and fusible links are made of lighter, more fragile material than the wires and components in the circle. They're designed to melt and break if more juice is flowing through the circuit than the wires or components can handle.

A TYPICAL CIRCUIT (CIRCLE)

Let's follow the juice all the way around a circuit (circle) to see how it works. We'll take a taillight for example and start and end the circle at the battery. (Turn the **headlight switch** ON to complete the circle and start the juice flowing.) Starting at the positive (+) battery post, juice flows through a wire to the **fuse box** (on '75-'77 models) or to **fusible links** and then to the fuse box (on '78 and newer models). From the fuse box, the juice goes through a wire to the light switch. For convenience, the taillight switch, parking light switch, and headlight switch are all incorporated into the **headlight switch** so they all go on by pulling or turning just one knob instead of three. Switches simply cause an open place in the circle when you want to turn the component off.

From the light switch, the juice goes through a wire to a **bulb** on the rear of the car. The wire passes the juice to the bulb through a **contact** (metal point) on the bottom of the bulb. Inside the bulb, the juice flows through a tiny wire called a **filament**, which you can see inside the glass globe of the bulb. Since the filament is a smaller wire, it resists the flow of juice. This *resistance* makes the filament get so hot it glows brightly, creating light. After squeezing through the filament, the juice moves on to the large metal part of the **bulb base**, which passes the juice to the metal **bulb socket**.

Now, here's a nifty part. The juice still has to get back to the battery to complete the circle, but instead of using another wire to carry the juice back to the battery, the car body is used to do it. This is called a **"ground,"** and all circuits work this way on their return run to the battery. In the case of our light circuit, here's how: the bulb socket either touches the body itself or is connected to it with a wire. The juice flows through the metal body, finally meeting the point where the negative battery cable is attached to the body (and/or engine). It flows through the cable to the negative battery post and thereby completes the circuit (circle).

With all that electricity in the body, how come you don't get zapped when you touch the car? Because the voltage is so low (12 volts) and it's in the form of **direct current (DC)**, you can touch both posts of the battery at the same time and not even feel the full 12 volts of DC current coursing through your body. The coil and spark plug wires however should be left alone when the engine is running because the ignition coil hops the 12 volts up to about 30,000 volts!

ELECTRICAL SYSTEMS IN YOUR SOOB

Your Soob has four separate electrical systems with four distinct jobs: the **charging system**, the **ignition system**, the **cranking system**, and the **accessory** (everything else) **system**. The four systems have one important common component: the *battery*. They also share the battery cables and the "ground" (body), so they are interrelated. Let's take it from the top and go through them one by one.

CHARGING SYSTEM

Main parts of the charging system are the **battery**, the **alternator**, the **voltage regulator**, and the wires that connect them.

You know the battery, the big box with two posts sticking out of the top and plastic **filler caps** on top so you can add water (except on maintenance-free batteries). The battery *stores* electricity so you can start the engine, play the radio or tape deck while parked in Lover's Lane, and operate any of the other electrical gizmos even if the engine isn't running.

How the battery stores electricity is another first-water mystery. Anyway, here's what they told me in school: inside the battery, the interaction between a water/sulfuric acid-based fluid called electrolyte and a series of metal plates creates a form of chemical energy that becomes electricity when you need it. That's why it's important to have enough water in your battery.

When the engine is running, a **drive belt** from the **crank pulley** turns the **alternator**, which then "generates" electricity. (This is very much like the generators at a power plant, like Hoover Dam or Three Mile Island.) The fresh juice travels through a wire to the **voltage regulator**, then to the battery, and on to supply the electrical needs of the engine and accessories. Excess electricity is stored in the battery for use when the engine isn't running.

Why the voltage regulator? The alternator is capable of generating more electrical volts than the battery can handle. Limiting the excess is the job of the voltage regulator. When the battery is fully charged (has taken on all the juice it can handle), the voltage regulator shuts off the juice supply from the alternator until more is needed. When the supply in the battery drops, the regulator allows more to come through from the alternator.

CRANKING SYSTEM

The only function of the *cranking system* is to spin the engine fast enough for it to start. Here's how it's done. The *positive battery cable* is attached directly to a part called the **starter solenoid** that's mounted on an electric **starter motor**. When you turn the **ignition key** all the way over, juice is sent from the battery to the *ignition system* (for the spark plugs) and to the solenoid on the starter motor. When the solenoid is energized by juice from the battery, it does two things: it pushes the **starter gear** on the end of the **starter motor shaft** into teeth on the outside of the **flywheel** of the engine and also starts the starter motor spinning. The starter motor thus turns the flywheel, and the flywheel turns the engine to get it started.

IGNITION SYSTEM

The **ignition system** provides a large spark to each **spark plug** at just the right time to ignite the fuel/air mixture in the cylinders. The main components of the ignition system are the **ignition switch, coil, distributor, spark plugs,** and the wires that connect them. When the ignition key is turned on, 12 volts of juice goes from the battery to the coil. The coil boosts the 12 volts up to about 30,000 volts (WOW!), then sends the super-juice through a **high tension wire** to the center of the **distributor cap**. Inside the distributor, **breaker points** on earlier models, a **reluctor and pickup coil** on some later models, or a **light emitting diode (LED)** on other late models, act as switches to turn the juice on and off. This happens quickly: it goes on each time a spark plug is supposed to fire. The rotor sequentially directs the hopped-up electrical charge to the right spark plug through **high-tension spark plug wires**. There's more about the ignition system in *Chapter 4: How a Subaru Works*, and in *Chapter 7: Lubrication, Maintenance and Tune-up*.

THE ACCESSORY SYSTEM

The **accessory system** includes the **battery, ignition switch, and other non-engine related gizmos like lights, heater, horn**—and the wires that connect the battery to these components. This system includes everything electrical that isn't related to the cranking, charging, and ignition systems, with the exception of the battery and ignition key switch, which all the systems share.

Procedure 1, Step 1   *The Electrical System*   **169**

LET'S GET ON WITH IT

The following procedures cover maintenance, diagnosis, and repair of the electrical things on your Soob. When special tools or expertise are required, I'll refer you to your local Subaru dealer or an auto electric shop for the repair. ***To avoid expensive accidents, please disconnect the negative battery terminal when I tell you to.*** Thanks.

PROCEDURE 1: BATTERY MAINTENANCE, CHECK, AND REPLACEMENT

Condition: Routine maintenance; OR you've been referred here from another chapter; OR you need to replace your dead battery.

Tools and Materials: Safety glasses, 10mm or 12mm wrench depending on your battery clamps, distilled water, battery terminal cleaning brush or something abrasive like emery cloth or sandpaper, maybe a large screwdriver or battery terminal puller, maybe a box of baking soda, maybe a new battery. To check the battery condition, you'll need a 12-volt test light or a volt/ohm meter (VOM). To charge the battery, you'll need a battery charger (I recommend a 4 to 6 amp "trickle" charger). Depending on the problem you may also need: a new battery hold-down bracket, battery tray, bracket rods, battery cables, rags, jumper cables.

CAUTION: The electrolyte fluid in batteries is mostly sulfuric acid which can do a bad number on your eyes, clothes, or any cuts or scratches you might have on your hands. Wear safety glasses and don't get any of the fluid or white flaky stuff from the battery on your clothes (they'll end up full of holes the next time you wash them). Wipe off tools you've used on the battery before putting them away. Throw rags used for cleaning the battery or tools in the trash so you can't accidentally grab one to wipe your brow or blow your nose. *Always* wash your hands after messing with the battery or its cables.

Remark: With proper maintenance a good battery should last at least three to five years. I've had batteries that lasted eight years!

Step 1. Check and Add Battery Fluid.

Safety glasses on? Lift the hood. Look at Chapter 7, Procedure 4, Step 6, to check the fluid level in the battery and add some if necessary.

Step 2. Clean Battery.

If the battery is dirty or has white flaky stuff around the *terminal posts* where the cables connect, use a solution of baking soda and water and an old rag to remove the crud. Be sure the caps are on snugly when you do this, so as not to contaminate the electrolyte. The baking soda neutralizes acid that's around the battery so it isn't so caustic. When the battery's clean, be sure and rinse the battery and the area in the car around it with lots of fresh water. Throw the rag in the trash immediately.

Step 3. Disconnect and Clean Battery Terminals.

Normally the *negative (-) terminal* is the one closest to the front of the car. The *positive (+) terminal* is toward the rear of the car. To be sure, look for a + or - stamped on or near the round battery posts. There's a picture of a battery somewhere nearby.

Use a 10mm or 12mm wrench (depending on your clamps) to loosen the nut on the end of the bolt sticking through the end of the **battery cable clamps**. Remove the negative (-) clamp from the battery first, then the positive (+) clamp. If the clamps are stuck, twist them side to side and/or put a large screwdriver in the slot where the bolt goes through and twist it to spread apart the end of the clamp. *Don't pry up on the clamp to remove* *it because the post might pop out of the battery.* If the clamp still refuses to budge, you'll need a battery terminal puller. But patience and the above method will usually do the trick.

Once the clamps are off, use a battery terminal brush, sandpaper, emery cloth, wire brush, or a knife to clean the two posts on the battery and the inside of the cable clamps until they're bright and shiny. If the clamp bolts are funky or the inside of the clamps won't clean up, you can either replace the clamp on the end of the cable or replace the entire cable.

When you're done, place the clamp back on the correct post, wiggle it down until it's snug, then tighten the nut on the clamp bolt with your wrench. Put the positive (+) clamp on first, then the negative (-) one. Don't force them. If one won't go on, spread the ends of the clamp apart a little more.

Step 4. Clean or Replace Battery Cables.

If you're here because the battery checked out OK but the starter still doesn't crank the engine very fast, or the lights don't shine as bright as they should, check both ends of both battery cables for looseness, funk, and corrosion. Replace the cables if the clamps are funky and can't be cleaned, or if the clamp bolts are broken, stripped, or mangled, or if the cable itself is corroded where it attaches to the ends.

There's a *cable* and a *wire* attached to both battery cable clamps. If you're replacing a cable, be sure the new cable has a little wire just like the one on the old cable attached to its clamp.

First, disconnect the negative (-) battery clamp from the battery (Step 3). The negative cable goes from the negative battery post to the engine, where it's attached to the *cylinder head* or *intake manifold*. The little wire attached to the negative cable clamp attaches to the body with a screw or bolt. The positive (+) cable goes from the positive battery post to a terminal post on the *starter solenoid*. The little wire attached to the positive cable clamp goes to the *fuse box* ('75-'77 models) or the *fusible links* ('78 and newer models).

To clean or replace the negative (-) battery cable, detach the cable from the battery post and follow it to where it bolts to the engine. Make a note if other things are attached to the engine with the same bolt. Remove the bolt (probably 12mm). If it's a cleanup job, clean both sides of the cable end and the bolt with a wire brush or sandpaper. Clean the terminal post if you haven't already done so. Follow the smaller wire from the cable clamp to where it's bolted to the body (probably in front of or beside the battery). Remove the bolt or screw and clean the end of the wire just as you cleaned the large cable.

If the cable is terminally funky and you're going to replace it, pull the old one all the way out now and install the new one. Connect the cable end to the engine with the bolt, then torque the bolt to 15 ft. lbs. Bolt or screw the end of the little wire to the body. Don't connect the clamp to the battery until after you've cleaned or replaced the positive cable.

To get to the other (starter solenoid) end of the positive (+) cable you'll need to remove the spare tire, if it's in the engine compartment. Disconnect the negative (-) cable clamp from the battery post if you haven't already. Now follow the cable from the positive battery terminal to where it connects to the solenoid on the starter motor. Peel back the **rubber boot** covering the cable end, then remove the 12mm nut and washer that secures the cable to the solenoid. Clean the cable end with a wire brush or sandpaper and the threaded post on the starter solenoid with a wire brush.

Disconnect the positive battery clamp from the battery post, then clean the battery post and cable clamp (unless you're replacing the cable). Step 3 tells you how. If you're here to replace the cable, disconnect the small wire that's attached to the fuse box or the fusible link (depending on your setup). Now you can pull the old cable out and install the new one.

Slip the cable end onto the starter solenoid post, then install and tighten the washer and nut. Pull the rubber boot over the starter solenoid post. If you replaced the cable, attach the small wire on the cable clamp to the fuse box or fusible link. (See Chapter 18 if you need to splice the new wire to the old one.) Wiggle the positive cable clamp onto the positive battery post, then tighten the clamp bolt with the 10mm or 12mm wrench.

Now attach the negative clamp to the battery (Step 3). Install the spare tire if you removed it.

Step 5. Check Battery Condition.

If your battery seems tired, if it has to be charged frequently, or if the engine sounds like it's struggling to turn just fast enough to start—don't rush out to buy a new battery before you check the old one. The problem might not be the battery.

First, check the fluid level in the battery and add some distilled water if need be (Step 1), then clean and check the battery terminals (Steps 3 and 4). Try driving the car to see if the battery will charge up now.

If you have a **Volt/Ohm meter** (VOM), set the meter to 15 DC volts. Touch the *red* (+) probe from the meter to the *positive* (+) battery terminal and the *black* (-) probe from the meter to the *negative* (-) battery terminal. The meter should read about 12 volts with the engine off. If it's less than 12 volts, either the battery is worn out or the alternator isn't charging it the way it should. Do Procedure 6 to see if the battery is getting a charge from the alternator. If the charging system checks out OK, come back here and finish this step.

If you don't have a VOM, or if you checked the battery and charging system with a VOM and everything checked out OK, check the *cranking system* (Procedure 9). You don't need a VOM to check this.

If the cranking system is good, take the car to an auto electric shop or garage and have them check the *specific gravity* of the battery fluid, the *voltage* and *amperage* of the battery, and do a "load test" to see how much reserve cranking power the battery has. These tests only take a couple of minutes, and shouldn't cost much. If the battery, charging and cranking systems all check out OK, you should run through Procedure 5, Step 3, to check for electrical shorts.

Step 6. Charge the Battery.

Naturally, you'll need a battery charger to do this step. Small ones are usually available at reasonable prices from auto parts stores or department stores.

Before charging the battery, disconnect both cables from the battery posts (Step 3) to protect the various components in the charging system. This is especially critical on Turbo models to protect the delicate electronic fuel injection system. Check the fluid level in the battery and add some *distilled water* if need be (Chapter 7, Procedure 4, Step 6). Leave the filler caps loose while the battery is being charged.

It's best for the battery to charge for 5 to 8 hours with a 4-6 amp "trickle" charger, rather giving it a 1-2 hour "quick" or "booster" charge at 8-10 amps. Never charge the battery with more than 10 amps. Follow the instructions that come with the charger to give your battery a full charge. All Soobs are 12 volts, so the switch (if yours has one) should be at the 12-volt position on the charger. Do not plug in the charger or turn it on until *after* you hook it up to the battery. Attach the red clamp to the positive (+) battery post and the black clamp to the negative (-) battery post. When you're ready to disconnect, turn the charger off (or unplug it) before detaching the clips to the battery.

After the battery is charged, tighten the filler caps, then reconnect the cable clamps. Tighten the clamp nuts with your 10mm or 12mm wrench.

If the battery becomes weak again within a few days, do the battery check (Step 5), the charging system check (Procedure 6), and the cranking system tests (Procedure 9) before buying a new battery.

Step 7. Replace the Battery.

To give your new battery its best shot at a long and happy life, replace the battery **hold-down bracket, battery tray, cables** and/or **clamps** if they're corroded and funky.

Remove the negative and positive cable clamps from the battery posts (Step 3). Remember that the negative cable should come off first. Remove the two 10mm nuts you'll find around the top edge of the battery—the ones that secure the *battery hold-down bracket*. The **rods** beneath the nuts are hooked into slots on the little shelf that holds the battery or to the body behind the battery. Push down on the rods to unhook them, then lift off the hold-down bracket.

Carefully lift the battery out of the engine compartment, keeping it level so the acid (electrolyte) can't spill. Hold it away from your clothes as you lift it out. Don't set the battery on the fender or anything you don't want full of holes. If the battery hold-down bracket is corroded and funky, replace it with a new one (available at Soob or parts stores). Clean the old one if it's still in good condition. A solution of baking soda (Arm & Hammer soda bicarb) and water really does a good number on corrosion. Use the solution to wash the plastic battery tray (if there is one) and the shelf where the battery sits. Rinse them with lots of fresh water and old rags. Toss the rags in the trash.

Set the plastic tray (if yours has one) on the battery shelf in the engine compartment. Set the fresh battery on the shelf with the negative (-) post toward the front of the car. Fit the hold-down bracket on the battery top, hook the bottom ends of the bracket rods in the slots on the shelf, then fit the top ends of the rods through the holes in the hold-down bracket. Install the washers and 10mm nuts and tighten them. (You may find it convenient to secure the rod closest to the fender loosely with its nut before you work with the other rod.) Now clean, then reconnect first, the positive, then the negative cable clamps to the battery posts (Step 3). Snug the clamp nuts with your wrench.

You may be able to turn the old battery in for some $$. If not, give it to a service station or car dealer. Be careful while handling it because it still contains acid! Don't set it on the seats while transporting it—put it in a box and carry it in the trunk.

Step 8. How to Use Jumper Cables to Get a Jump Start.

You'll need a set of **jumper cables** for this step. Avoid cheap ones that will come apart or fail you when you need them most. Good ones have a solid, heavy feel to them.

If your battery is too weak to start the engine, or you're being a good Samaritan and helping someone else start their car, follow this sequence to safely connect and disconnect the jumper cables.

Park the car with the good battery close enough so the jumper cables can easily reach from the "live" battery terminals to the "dead" battery terminals. If you have to stretch the cables, there's a good chance one of the cable ends will touch something you don't want it to touch. Be sure the car bodies (or bumpers) aren't touching.

One of the jumper cables will be *red* and one *black*, or at least the handles will be red or black. First, connect one end of the red jumper cable to the positive (+) terminal of the live battery, then connect the other end of the red cable to the positive (+) terminal of the dead battery. Now connect one end of the black cable to bare metal on the alive car and the other end to bare metal on the dead car. The bumpers are a good place to connect the black cable. The reason you don't connect the black cable to the negative battery terminals is because of the sparks that usually fly when the last connection is made. Since batteries are known to give off an explosive gas, you sure don't want to take a chance of igniting any gas that might be lurking around the top of the battery.

Start the car that has the live battery and rev it up a little. Then attempt to start the car with the dead battery. If it doesn't crank strongly, either the jumper cables are a little loose (wiggle them where they connect), or a clamp on one of the dead car's battery cables is loose or corroded, which could be your problem in the first place. When the dead car starts, disconnect the black cable first, then the red cable.

Thank the chap who helped you. Buy him (or her) a brew, if camaraderie has developed over the cables—and it usually does. If it was your Soob that needed the jump start, turn to Procedure 1, Step 5 to check the battery when you get home.

PROCEDURE 2: CHECK AND REPLACE FUSES AND FUSIBLE LINK

Condition: An electrical component (lights, heater, etc.) isn't working. If several components aren't working, start by checking the fusible links (Step 3). If nothing electrical is working, check the battery, battery cables, and clamps (Procedure 1).

Tools and Materials: Maybe new fuses, and maybe a 12-volt test light or Volt/Ohm Meter (VOM).

Remarks: You can't always tell whether a fuse is good or bad just by looking at it. The little flat wire you can see in the glass part of the fuse might look perfect, but be burned or broken near the end where you can't see it. When checking fuses, always start by trying a new fuse. You can check fuses with a VOM to see if they're good (Procedure 11).

'75-'81 models: While you're in the fuse box, take a quick look at all the other fuses. The wire in the fuse tends to bend with age, then break due to vibration. Replace any fuses whose inside wire looks bent.

CAUTION: The correct fuse amperage (15, 25, etc.) for the different electrical circuits is stamped on the fuse box cover, or on a piece of paper inside the fuse box. When replacing fuses, always use new ones that are of the correct amp rating. You'll find the amp rating stamped on the metal ends of the fuse. In an emergency you can replace a burned fuse with one of a lesser amperage rating—just be sure and replace it with the correct fuse as soon as possible. *Don't* substitute tinfoil for a fuse because expensive electrical components could be damaged very quickly! It's dangerous, too.

Step 1. Locate and Check Fuses in Fuse Box.

'75-'77 models: The fuse box is just behind the battery in the engine compartment.

'78 and newer models: The fuse box is near your left knee when you're driving the car. It's under the dash near the hood release knob.

'75-'79 cars and '77-'81 Brats: To open the fuse box, press in on the ends of the cover while pulling it away from the box. The tabs on the ends of the cover are different sizes so the cover can only fit on the box one way. There's a little clip in each end of

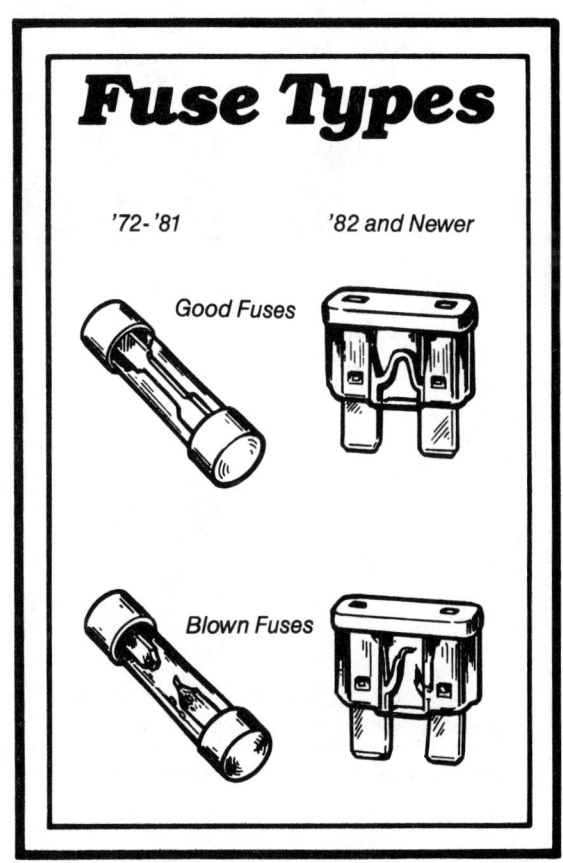

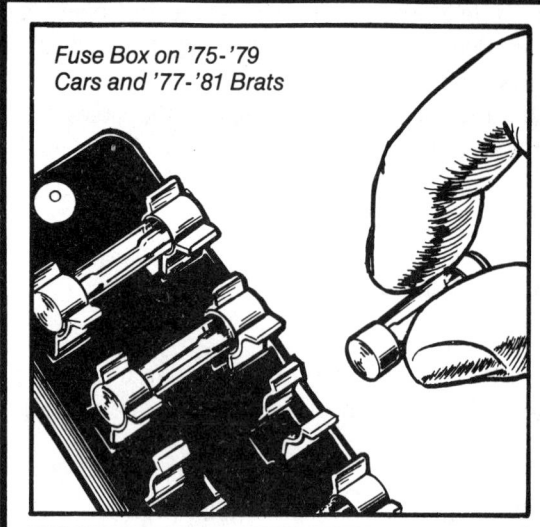
Fuse Box on '75-'79 Cars and '77-'81 Brats

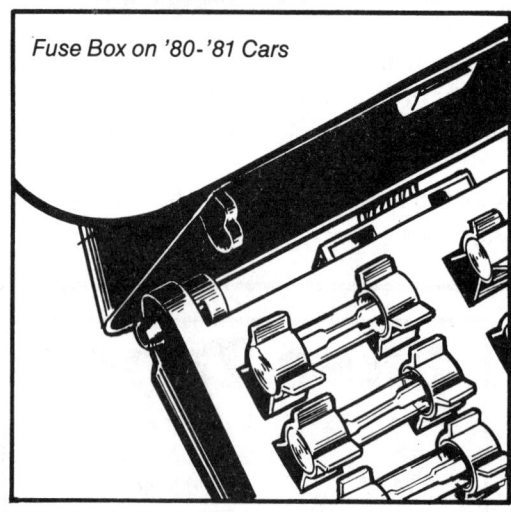
Fuse Box on '80-'81 Cars

Fuse Box on All '82 and Newer Models
Fuse Tweezers
Tweezer Holder

the cover to hold spare fuses. It's wise to always have one 15 amp and one 25 amp stashed in the cover.

'80 and newer cars and '82 and newer Brats: Press down on the top edge of the fuse box. The lid is hinged and will swing down.

'80-'81 models (except Brats): A fuse holder will also swing down when you open the fuse box. There should be a spare 15 amp and a 25 amp fuse sticking up out of two small holes between the two rows of fuses.

'82 and newer models: There are rows of colored fuses and a tweezerlike fuse puller/installer inside the box. Yours will be similar to the one in the illustration. Spare fuses should be lurking in the corners of the cover, or in the fuse box (see the fuse chart in or on the cover for their location). To change a fuse, pull the tweezer thing out and use it to remove and install the fuses in the holder.

EVERYONE: The proper fuse amperage and a list of the components on each fuse circuit are stamped on the fuse box cover or on a printed paper inside the fuse box. If you're missing the cover or paper, get a new one from Subaru.

Find the circuit on the list for the component that's not working. Remove the fuse for that circuit from the holder and insert a new one. (You probably have a new fuse stashed in the box somewhere.) Turn on and check the component to see if it works now. If it does, throw the old fuse away and go merrily on your way. Replace the spare fuse you used with a new spare as soon as possible. If the component still doesn't work, do Step 2.

Step 2. Check Fuse Holder for Juice.

If the component still doesn't work after installing a new fuse, you'll need a 12-volt *test light* or a *VOM* to see if juice is getting to the fuse.

If you have a VOM, set it to 15 DC volts. Turn both the *ignition key* and the *component* you're checking ON and touch the red (+) probe of the VOM to one of the two clips that holds the fuse ('75-'81 models) or to one of the tiny slots near the end of the fuse ('82 and newer models). Ground the other probe by touching it to bare metal (not the other fuse clips).

Test both fuse clips or both slots depending on your setup. The test light should light or the VOM should register about twelve volts on one of the clips. If you get juice on both ends of the fuse, the fuse is good and the component is getting juice—so the problem is either in the component itself or in the wire between the fuse box and the component. See Procedure 5 to check the various components. If you get juice only on one side of the fuse, the fuse isn't carrying the juice. Try another fuse.

If there's no juice to the fuse box, there's a problem in the wire between the battery and fuse box (see Procedure 5), or the fusible link is burned (see Step 4).

Step 3. Locate and Check Other Fuses.

Radio fuse: The radio might have an *extra fuse* in the wire (usually red) going from the fuse box to the radio or in the radio itself. If the radio isn't working and the fuse in the fuse box checked out OK, you'll have to dig around under the dash to find a long, opaque plastic *in-line fuse holder.* If you find one, press the ends of the holder toward the center while twisting one end counterclockwise. The holder will come apart, letting its fuse drop out. Put a new fuse of the proper amperage (or less) in the holder, align the little tab with the slot, press the ends of the holder toward the center, then twist one end clockwise. If the radio still doesn't work, head for a radio repair shop.

Air conditioner fuse: There's usually a fuse in a **white plastic holder** on the right side of the engine compartment just to the rear of the *ignition coil*. On some models, it's in a **clip** on top of three little boxes. Check it the same way you do the radio fuse, or use a 12-volt test light or VOM.

Additional fuel pump and automatic choke fuses:

'76-'81 models: There are two fuses (5 or 10 amp) in separate fuse holders tucked under the dash. These fuses are part of a circuit that shuts off the juice for the automatic choke and the fuel pump when the engine stops, even if the ignition switch stays on. It's a safety measure to help prevent fires in case of an accident. On **'76-'79 models**, the fuse holders are white and located in the corner below the glove box in front of the passenger's seat. On **'80-'81 models**, the fuse holders are dark blue and located in the tangle of wires just above the fuse box. You might have to cut a piece of black tape that's wrapped around the holder before you can open it. To check these fuses hold the two tabs on the ends of the holder while lifting the tab in the center. The holder will open like a little jewelry box. Pull the fuse and wires out of the holder, then pull the fuse out of the connectors on the ends of the wires.

'76-'79 models: Insert a new fuse of the same amp rating between the connectors.

'80-'81 models (except Brats): If the choke fuse is blown, Subaru says to replace it with a 15 amp fuse even if the blown fuse was 5 or 10 amp. Replace the fuel pump fuse with one of the same amperage as the original.

EVERYONE: Fit the fuse and wires into the holder and close the lid. Check the wires for juice if the new fuses didn't solve the problem (Procedure 5, Step 2).

Step 4. Check and Replace Fusible Link(s) ('78 and newer models only).

A fusible link is really just a high-tech fuse. There are *two* wires in the link on '78-'81 models and *three or more* wires on '82 and newer models. Except for the juice for the starter motor, all current flowing from the battery goes through the fusible links. If the current flowing through one of the wires in the link is higher than it should be, the fusible metal in the wire melts and breaks the circuit to protect the wires and electrical components on that circuit— just like a fuse **'78-'81 models:** The fusible link is located just to the rear of the battery. The *smaller wire* attached to the positive (+) terminal clamp goes straight to a plastic connector on one end of the link. The link itself consists of two red or green cloth-

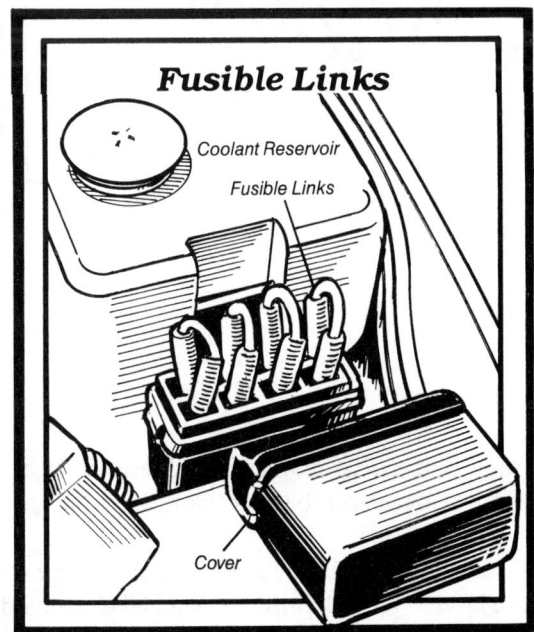

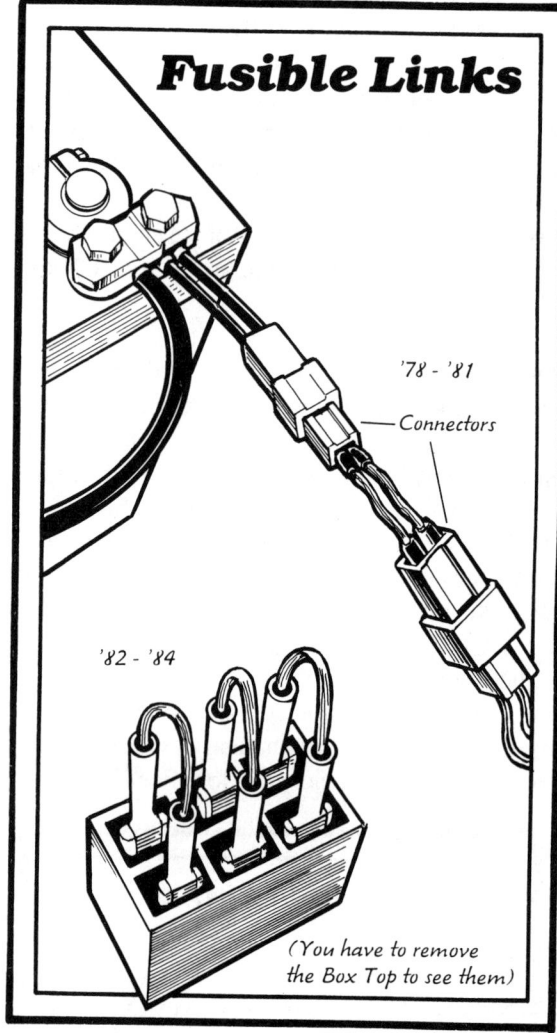

Fusible Links
'78 – '81 — Connectors
'82 – '84
(You have to remove the Box Top to see them)

covered wires with a plastic connector on each end. To check the wires in the link, feel along the cloth on each wire to see if the wire is still intact. Sometimes the cloth will be burned and black at the point where the wire melted. The fusible link is a unit, so if one of the wires is burned or broken you have to replace them both. Be sure the new link has the proper rating for your year and model.

To replace the fusible link, separate the plastic connectors on each end of the two wires by pulling them apart. Connect the plastic connectors onto the ends of the new link the same as they were on the old link.

'82 and newer models: The fusible link wires are in a little plastic box near the positive (+) battery terminal. To get to the links, pry out on the bottom of the gray plastic lid, then wiggle the lid off the box. The links are colored cloth-covered wires arching up out of the box. To check the wires in the links, feel along the cloth for breaks in the wire. If you find a break in the wire or the cloth looks burned, the link is broken. Buy a new one with the same color cloth (rating) as the old one.

To replace a broken link, just pull on the rubber part of the link where it disappears into the little box. Remove both ends. Then insert the ends of a new link into the two slots. Install the cover.

EVERYONE: If the new link blows (breaks) right away, there's a problem in one of the components in the circuit controlled by that link. Procedure 5 tells you how to trace faulty components.

PROCEDURE 3: CHECK, REPLACE, AND/OR ADJUST DRIVE BELT

People used to call drive belts "fan belts." Once upon a time, they just drove the fan, water pump, and generator (predecessor of the alternator). Today, they drive lots of things, but no longer the fan in many cases! Be sure the engine is off when you deal with the belts. Everyone should do Step 1, then go to the specific belt step that concerns you.

Condition: Drive belt(s) are too loose, too tight, worn out, or broken; OR the drive belt(s) have to be removed in order to take off the alternator, water pump, or other engine parts.

Tools and Materials: 12mm wrench, a large screwdriver (or broom handle, long ratchet handle, etc., to use as a lever). '83–'84 Turbo models and OHC models also need a 12mm socket, short extension, and ratchet. To adjust the power steering belt on OHV models, you'll need a 10mm wrench, large pliers, and a rag.

Remarks: After three or so years of use, drive belts can break suddenly regardless of how good they look. I recommend that you make a habit of replacing the drive belt(s) every three years, or at least carry a spare belt and the tools to change it. On top of the spare tire is a good place to stash a spare belt.

Adjusting and changing drive belts is easy on models without air conditioning and/or power steering. If you have these accessories, read the appropriate Step and look for the adjusting method that applies to your Soob. If you aren't sure which bolts to loosen, or where to place the lever to pry on the alternator, air conditioner compressor, or idler pulley, you might want to have a garage show you how to change and/or adjust the belts the first time.

'75 4WD models: See Step 6 to adjust or replace the drive belt for the belt driven fan.

OHV models with air conditioning and/or power steering: You'll have to remove the air conditioning (A/C) and/or power steering (P/S) drive belts before you can remove the alternator drive belt.

OHC and '83-'84 Turbo models: Do Step 1 to check the condition and tension of the belts, then skip down to Step 5 to change and/or adjust them.

Step 1. Check Condition and Tension of Drive Belts.

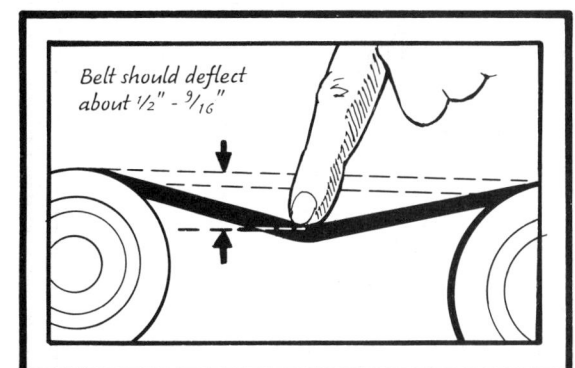

All drive belts are located on the front of the engine. So, with the engine turned off, open the hood and peer down there.

Look at the outer edges of the drive belt(s) for signs of fraying (little threads of material will be unraveling from the belt). Now twist the belt 180° so you can see the inner side of the belt. Look for cracks, tears, or missing chunks. If you see any of these maladies, the belt should be replaced now.

To check the *belt tension*, push down on the belt midway between two of the pulleys. (It's best to check it between the two pulleys that are farthest apart.) Subaru says to use 22 lbs. of pressure. You'll have to guess how hard you're pushing (or maybe use a fisherman's spring scale and pull on the belt with 22 lbs. of force) while you measure the distance the belt deflects. To make things simple, use two fingers and push a bit harder than you push a doorbell. A new belt should deflect about ½" and a used belt about 9/16".

Loose belts tend to squeal and don't turn the components (such as the alternator) as fast and efficiently as they're supposed to. Belts that are overtightened are hard on the bearings inside the components and can cause them to fail prematurely. I think just a little too loose is better than a little too tight. When you install a new belt, always check the tension again after running the engine for about 15 minutes, to see if the new belt stretched a little.

Step 2. Replace and/or Adjust Alternator Drive Belt on OHV Models (except '83-'84 Turbo models).

The alternator is attached by *two brackets* to the engine. Locate an "ear" on the front side of the alternator that points toward the left front fender. The 12mm bolt screwed into the ear is the **drive belt tension adjustment bolt**. Notice how the adjustment bolt goes through a long, curved **slotted bracket**. There's one long or two short bolts going through ears on the opposite side of the alternator that allow the alternator to pivot.

Replace drive belt: Loosen, but don't remove the bolts that attach the alternator to the brackets on the engine. Push the alternator down until the adjusting bolt hits the bottom of the slot in the outer bracket. Slip the belt off the alternator pulley, water pump pulley, crankshaft pulley, and the belt-driven fan and air pump pulleys (if you have them).

Fit the new drive belt over the same pulleys, then pull up on the alternator with your hand to hold tension on the belt while you lightly snug down the adjuster bolt with the wrench. Now go on and adjust the belt to the proper tension. If the old belt still looks pretty good, stash it on the spare tire for emergency service.

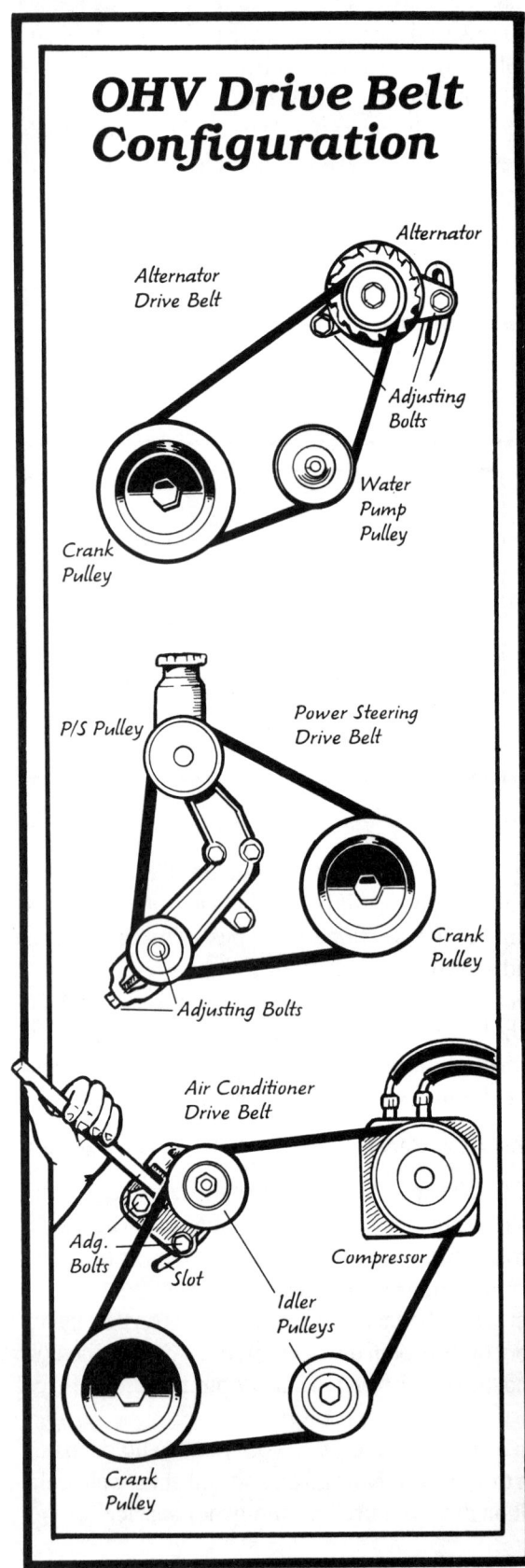

OHV Drive Belt Configuration

Adjust drive belt: Slightly loosen the 12mm tension adjusting bolt and the pivot bolt(s) if you haven't already.

If you have a late model Soob, look for a bolt and nut on top of the slotted bracket. If you have this bolt and nut, turn the nut clockwise to tighten the belt or counterclockwise to loosen it. When the tension is right (see Step 1), tighten the bolt in the slotted bracket and the pivot bolt. Too bad it isn't this easy on all models.

If you don't have a bolt and nut on top of the slotted bracket, slide a large screwdriver, broom handle, or ratchet handle (or whatever you're using for a lever) below the alternator so the end is on the top of the engine. Be sure you're not smashing any hoses, tubes, wires, or other parts, with the end of the lever. Now pull up on the lever to raise the alternator and tighten the drive belt. Loosen the adjuster bolt a little if it's too tight. Pull up on the lever with one hand while you check the tension on the belt with your other hand. Get the tension so the belt will deflect about 9/16" (used belt) or ½" (new belt) when you push on it midway between two of the pulleys. Step 1 tells you exactly how to check belt tension. When the belt is tight enough, keep the pressure on the lever while you tighten the adjuster bolt with a 12mm wrench.

To loosen a too-tight belt, you can usually just push down on the belt between two of the pulleys after you loosen the two bolts. This will pivot the alternator toward the engine slightly.

Check the belt tension again (see the illustration) and tighten or loosen it if necessary. When the tension is right, tighten the pivot bolt(s). New belts quickly stretch a little, so if you installed a new belt, check the tension again after running the engine for about 15 minutes. Turn off the engine and tighten the belt if need be.

Step 3. Replace or Adjust Air Conditioner Drive Belt on OHV Models (except '83-'84 Turbo models).

There have been so many different air conditioner setups, I can't specifically describe each one. Luckily, however, there are basically only two methods for replacing or adjusting the A/C drive belt. You'll have to determine which type you have and follow the appropriate directions. Good luck.

One style/method, which I'll call the **slotted bracket type**, is very similar to replacing or adjusting the alternator drive belt. The **air conditioner compressor** is mounted to a slotted bracket on the engine. Moving the compressor up or down in the bracket tightens or loosens the drive belt. The other style/method, which I'll call the **idler pulley type**, relies on a **movable pulley** to tighten or loosen the drive belt.

Slotted bracket type: To adjust the drive belt, loosen the bolts that go through the slots in the bracket and into the compressor. Use a large screwdriver (broom handle, etc.) as a lever to pry up on the compressor to tighten the belt. When the belt deflects about ½" when you push on it between two of the pulleys, hold tension on the belt with the lever while you tighten the bolts in the slots.

To replace the drive belt, loosen the bolts that go through the slots and into the compressor, then push down on the compressor so it slides down in the slots far enough to allow you to lift or pull the belt off the pulleys. Wrap the new belt around the pulleys; be sure the belt is in the groove of both the crankshaft and compressor pulleys. Adjust the belt tension as described above.

Idler pulley type: You'll see that the A/C drive belt goes around the *crank pulley*, the *A/C compressor* pulley, and one or two smaller pulleys. One of the small pulleys might be in a bracket near the top center of the engine and the other one in a bracket below the compressor on the lower left front side of the engine. You might have one of the small pulleys or both. One of these small pulleys can be moved to tighten or loosen the drive belt.

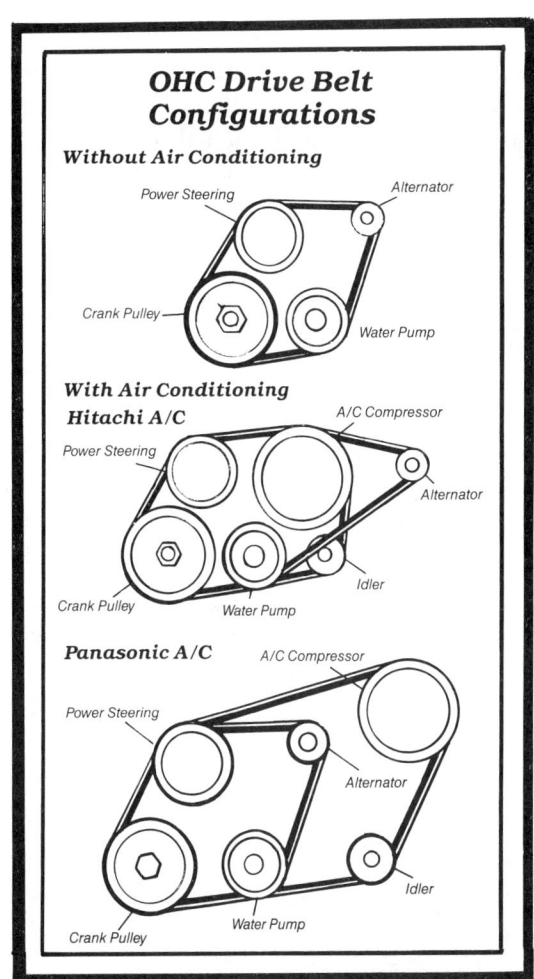

There are two types of movable idler pulleys. Here's one type:

Some late models have a vertical 14mm bolt and lockwasher in a bracket just behind the upper idler pulley. If you have this bolt, turn the bolt *clockwise* to tighten the belt or *counterclockwise* to loosen it. If you're replacing the belt, loosen the bolt far enough that you can slip the belt off the pulleys, then install the new belt. Tighten the bolt until the tension is correct. Check the tension again after running the engine for about 15 minutes. Why aren't all belts this easy to adjust?

The **offset bracket** type has a small pulley mounted on a bracket in such a way that when the bracket is rotated the pulley will increase or decrease the drive belt tension. The bracket is attached to the engine with two bolts. One bolt is in a slot so the bracket can rotate. To figure out which pulley is offset, look for a slot in the small idler pulley mounting bracket(s). When you've found it, slightly loosen the two bolts in the bracket. To tighten the belt, use a large screwdriver (broom handle, or whatever) as a lever to pry the pulley bracket toward the outside of the belt. Hold tension on your lever and check the deflection. When the belt deflects about ½" as you push on it between two pulleys, tighten the bolts in the pulley bracket. Check the tension again after tightening the bracket bolts, and adjust it again if necessary.

To replace the belt, loosen the bolts in the idler pulley bracket, then push on the pulley to loosen the belt. Slide the belt off the idler pulley(s), compressor pulley, and crank pulley. Install a new belt around the same pulleys and adjust the tension as described above. Check the tension again after the engine has run about 15 minutes.

Step 4. Replace and/or Adjust Power Steering Drive Belt on OHV Models (except '83-'84 Turbo Models).

The drive belt for power steering (P/S) goes around the crankshaft pulley, up over the pulley for the **P/S pump** (located on the top front right side of the engine), then down around a small pulley mounted on a long **slotted bracket** near the bottom front right (passenger) side of the engine. The belt tension is adjusted by moving the small pulley up or down in the slotted bracket.

It's easiest to get to the adjusting bolt from underneath, so remove the flat piece of sheet metal below the small pulley and bracket (four 10mm bolts attach it to the body). Now crawl under the front of the car with a 12mm wrench, large pliers, and a rag.

Find the small **plastic cap** on the front of the small pulley in the slotted bracket. Put a rag over the cap, then squeeze it with large pliers and it will pop off. Now loosen the 12mm bolt in the center of the pulley about two turns counterclockwise (as viewed from the front of the car). The bolt head at the bottom end of the long bracket is the **adjusting bolt**.

If you're replacing the belt, turn the bolt head (adjusting bolt) a couple of turns counterclockwise (as viewed from the bottom end of the bracket). Now see if the belt will slip off the pulley. Keep turning the bolt counterclockwise and pulling on the belt until you can pull the belt off. If the belt doesn't loosen, use a hammer or screwdriver handle to tap the head of the bolt toward the bracket.

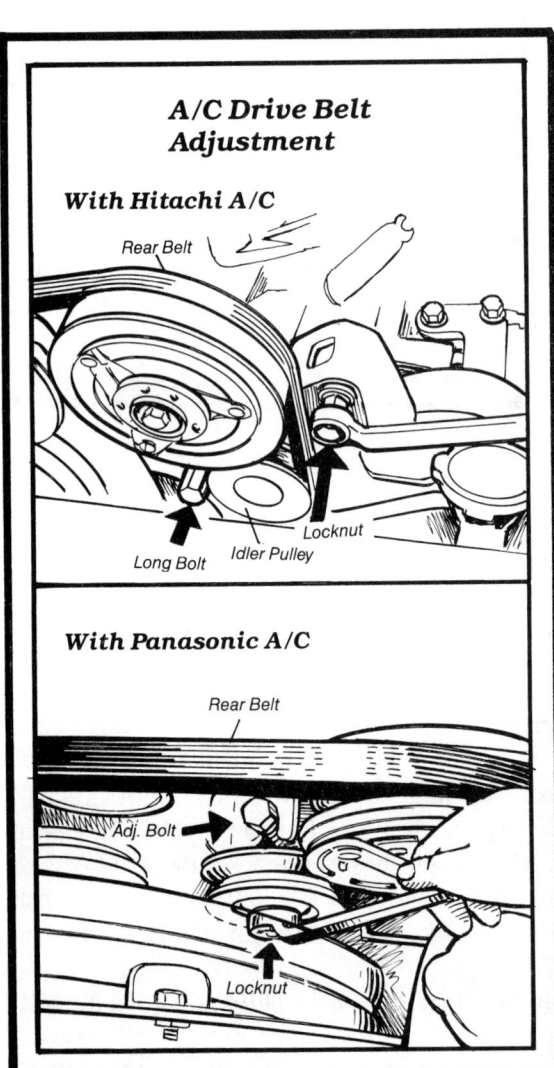

Pop the carburetor/distributor shield off the front of the air cleaner, then remove the old belt from the pulleys. Slip a new belt over the crank pulley, over the pump pulley, then over the small adjusting pulley.

To adjust the belt tension, turn the adjusting bolt clockwise until there's about ½" to ¾" deflection when you press on the belt halfway between the adjusting pulley and the pulley on the power steering pump. When the deflection is correct, tighten the bolt in the center of the adjusting pulley with a 12mm wrench. If you just installed a new belt, check the belt adjustment again after the engine has run for 10-15 minutes. Now coat the edge of the plastic cap with oil or grease (you can use a little oil off the dipstick), then pop it in place on the pulley. Rotate the cap a little to be sure it's securely attached. Install the sheet metal piece to the bottom of the car with its four bolts, and the carburetor/distributor shield if you removed it.

Step 5. Replace and/or Adjust Drive Belts on OHC and '83-'84 Turbo Models.

These models have two drive belts that work in tandem for the air conditioning compressor, water pump, and power steering pump. The front belt (closest to the radiator) drives the alternator so I'll call it the **alternator belt**. The rear belt (closest to the engine) drives everything but the alternator. I'll call it the **compressor belt**.

Adjust alternator belt tension: Loosen the 12mm bolt in the slotted bracket located near the bottom front of the alternator. Now slightly loosen the long 12mm pivot bolt that goes through the two ears on the top of the alternator.

OHC models with Panasonic air conditioning: If you have Panasonic air conditioning, the A/C compressor will be mounted on the left side of the alternator.

Slip a large screwdriver (broom handle, etc.) below the alternator and pry the alternator upward with one hand while checking the belt tension with the other. (Be sure the end of the screwdriver isn't resting on anything fragile while prying on the alternator.) When the tension is correct, tighten the 12mm bolt in the slotted bracket. Release the tension on the screwdriver, then check the tension again. If it's still correct, tighten the long pivot bolt.

'83-'84 Turbo models and OHC models with Hitachi air conditioning: If you have a Hitachi air conditioner, the A/C compressor will be mounted on the right side of the alternator.

Insert a large screwdriver between the alternator and air conditioning compressor. Using the *black bracket* above the compressor for a pivot point, push the screwdriver handle toward the center of the engine. On Turbo models, be careful to not pry against the brass-colored pipe that might be attached to the top of the bracket. Hold pressure on the screwdriver lever while you check the belt tension. There should be about ¼" to ⅓" deflection when you push on the belt midway between the crank pulley and the power steering pump pulley. When you have the tension right, tighten the 12mm bolt in the slotted bracket. Check the tension again. If it's still right, tighten the 12mm pivot bolt on top of the alternator.

Replace/install alternator drive belt: If you have air conditioning, look at the illustration of the pulser. If your model has a pulser, remove the two bolts that attach it to the A/C compressor. You'll need to lift it up slightly in order to remove and install the drive belt(s).

'83-'84 Turbo models: Remove the two 10mm bolts that attach a small **fan shield** to the top left (driver's) side of the radiator.

EVERYONE: Loosen the 12mm adjusting and pivot bolts (see Adjust Belt Tension section above). If you have power steering, slightly loosen the two 10mm bolts on top of the power steering fluid reservoir. Lift up on the reservoir while you remove the belt from the compressor and power steering pump pulleys. Remove the belt from the other pulleys, then carefully slip it under the bottom front of the fan that's attached to the engine. Be careful of the radiator as

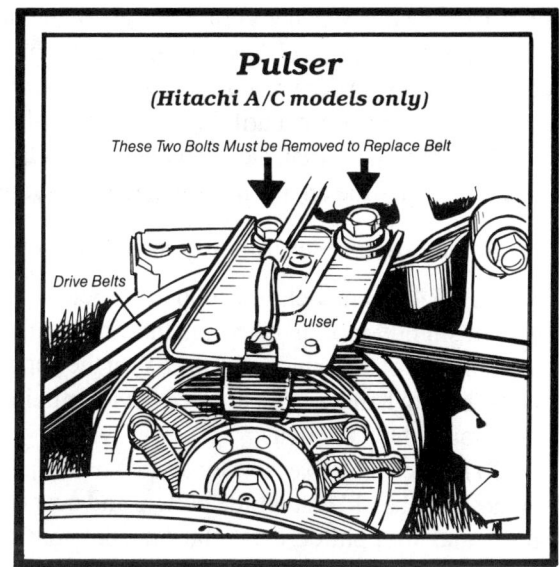

you slide the belt up between the fan and radiator to remove it from the car. Unless you're also replacing the compressor belt, you're ready to put on the new alternator drive belt.

Slide the new belt down between the fan and radiator until it clears the fan. Now you can fit the belt onto all the pulleys. Adjust the belt tension and tighten the two 12mm adjusting bolts on the alternator. If your model has power steering and/or a pulser, install and tighten the two bolts on the pulser and the two bolts on the power steering reservoir. If you removed a part of the fan shield, reinstall it on the radiator and tighten the two bolts.

Be sure to check the belt tension again after running the engine for about 15 minutes. New belts quickly stretch a little. Tighten the belt again if need be.

OHC models without air conditioning: Loosen the 12mm bolt and pivot bolt (see adjusting the alternator belt above). Push down on the alternator to loosen the drive belt. Now you can remove the belt.

To install the drive belt, thread it over the pulleys, then adjust the tension as described above in the adjustment section.

Dealing with the compressor drive belt: First remove the *alternator drive belt* (earlier in this step). Look at the A/C drive belt adjustments illustrations to see which type air conditioner you have. An intelligent, intuitive person like yourself knows that you should follow the appropriate instructions below. So I won't have to mention it.

Hitachi-type A/C: Find a 12mm bolt between and below the alternator and air conditioning compressor. Use a 12mm socket and short extension to loosen the bolt a couple of turns. There's another 12mm bolt with a long head sticking out of the engine farther to the right, below the compressor. Use a long 12mm box end wrench to loosen it a couple of turns. Push the small *idler pulley* between the two bolts up toward the compressor until you can slip the belt off the pulley. Remove the old belt from the car the same way you removed the alternator belt. Fit the new belt onto all the pulleys, then adjust it. Here's how.

There are two ways to adjust the belt tension. If you have a deep 17mm socket, you can do #1 below. No deep socket? Do #2.

1. There is a 17mm nut behind the left (driver's side) bolt that you loosened to remove the belt. Fit your deep 17mm socket onto the nut and turn it *counterclockwise* to tighten the belt. Check the tension on the belt and when it deflects ¼" to ⅓" tighten the bolt on the right—the one with the long head. Check the tension again and adjust it if need be. When the tension is right, tighten the 12mm bolt in front of the 17mm nut.

2. Position a large screwdriver so its shaft is against the battery side of the compressor pulley and the tip is on the crank pulley side of the idler pulley. Use the screwdriver to lever the idler pulley down and away from the compressor. Check the belt tension between the crank pulley and power steering pulley. When the belt deflects ¼" to ⅓", hold tension on the belt with the screwdriver while you tighten the bolt with the long head. Check the tension again. When it's correct, tighten the other 12mm bolt.

Panasonic-type A/C: Loosen the lock nut in the center of the idler pulley a couple of turns. Now turn the adjustment bolt until the belt is loose enough to remove from the pulleys. Fit the new belt over the pulleys, then turn the adjustment bolt until the belt deflects about ¼" to ⅓". Tighten the lock nut. Easy as toast, right?

EVERYONE: Install the alternator drive belt (above). New belts quickly stretch a little. So be sure to check the tension after the engine has run about 15 minutes. Adjust the belts if necessary.

Step 6. Replace and/or Adjust Belt Driven Fan ('75 4WD Models).

On '75 4WD models a second drive belt turns a fan mounted to the front of the engine. To adjust the belt tension, slightly loosen the bolt in the slotted bracket just below the small idler pulley on the lower front left (driver's) side of the engine, and the bolt at the upper end of the long idler pulley bracket. Use a lever (long screwdriver, broom handle, etc.) to force the idler pulley toward the left side of the car. Hold tension on the pulley while you tighten the bolts.

To replace the drive belt, loosen the two adjusting bolts, then push the idler pulley toward the center of the engine. Slip the old belt off the pulleys and over the front of the fan. Fit the new belt onto the crank pulley, fan pulley, and idler pulley, then adjust the belt tension as described above. Check the belt tension after running the engine for about 15 minutes and adjust it if necessary.

PROCEDURE 4: REPLACE LIGHT BULBS

This procedure covers all kinds of light bulbs. If a headlight is your problem, do only Step 1. If it's one of the other light bulbs, read Step 2, then go to the Step that deals with your particular bulb. Turn the ignition key and light switch OFF when replacing bulbs. If the hazard (emergency) or turn signal lights and the indicator light on the dashboard light up but don't flash, see Step 10 to replace the flasher unit(s).

Condition: One or more of the lights aren't working; OR the turn signals or hazard lights won't flash.

Tools and Materials: Phillips screwdriver. Maybe new bulb(s), new flasher unit, a wire brush, and a flashlight.

Remarks: If lights on both sides of the car are out, check the fuses before changing the bulbs (Procedure 2, Step 1). The little owner's manual for your car shows the location of all the bulbs and tells you how to replace them, kind of. If you still have the book, take a look at it.

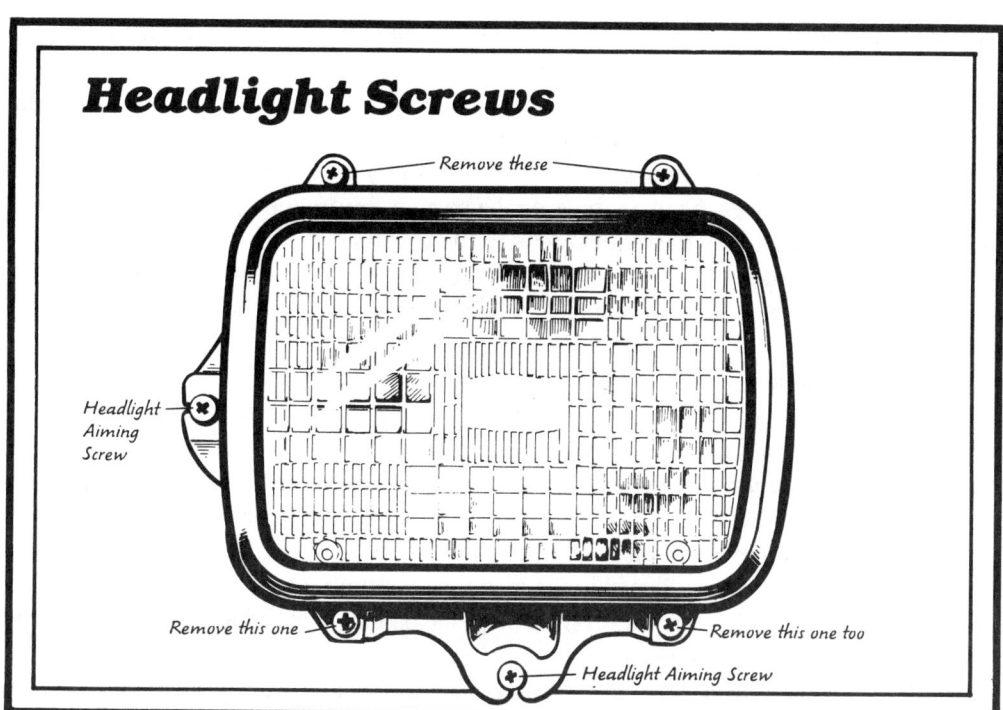

Step 1. Replace Headlight (and parking and turn signal bulbs on some '80 and newer OHV models).

Before buying a new headlight, check the fuses (Procedure 2, Step 1) and the connection on the back of the headlight bulb. Headlights are expensive these days, especially for the late models, so be sure the headlight is dead before buying a new one. Most parts stores won't let you return electrical parts even if you bring them back unused and virginal.

Here's how to check the electrical connection on the headlights: Open and prop the hood, then locate an *electrical connector* on the engine side of the nonworking headlight. You'll see the backs of the headlights poking back toward the engine compartment on either side of the radiator. Wiggle the connector off the back of the headlight, clean the three flat metal **prongs** on the back of the headlight with a wire brush, then wiggle the connector back onto the prongs. Now try the headlights. If the headlight still doesn't work, you probably need a new one.

OHC GL models (except XTs): You have the super-duper extra large headlights with small halogen bulbs: To replace the halogen bulb, look in the engine compartment for the rear end of the headlight assembly. There's a large round collar at the rear center of the headlight. An electrical connector is mounted behind the collar. Press down on the plastic strip that's on top of the electrical connector, then pull the connector rearward and off. Twist the collar counterclockwise until it unlocks, then pull it out of the headlight assembly. There's the little halogen bulb. Replace the bulb, then fit the collar back onto the assembly and turn it clockwise until it locks in place. Reconnect the electrical connector and you're finished.

EVERYONE (except OHC GL models and XTs): To change a headlight bulb, the grille and

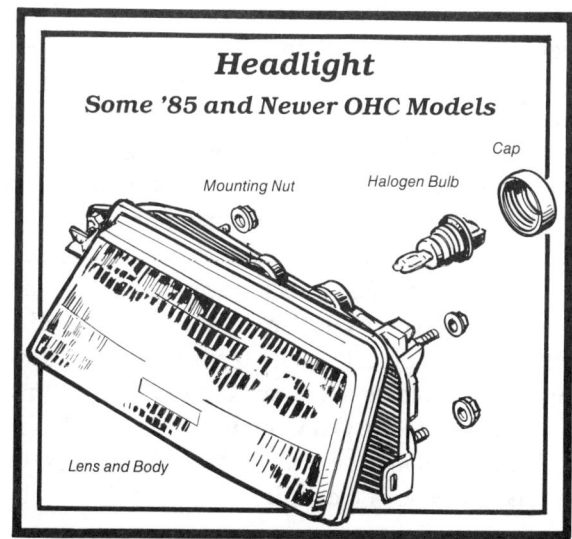

maybe a piece of plastic molding around the headlight(s) has to be removed. This is done from the front of the car. It's easy because they're held on only by phillips screws. Here's how.

Remove the phillips screws around the edge of the grille, then pull the top of the grille out slightly and lift up to remove it. If the parking lights are mounted in the grille, gently lower the grille and let it hang by the wires.

'75-'77 and '80 and newer OHV models (except '80-'81 Brats): Now you need to remove another molding that's around the headlight. Remove the two screws on the corners toward the center of the car (if they weren't removed with the grille screws), then the other screws in the molding.

'80 and newer OHV models with one headlight on each side: Remove the screw in the top of the outer turn signal lens and the screw beneath the parking light lens that's sandwiched between the headlight bulb and the turn signal lens.

'82 and newer OHV models with two square headlights on each side: Remove the screw above the white parking light lens and the screw on the bottom of the molding on the side of the car. Don't mess with the screw directly below the headlight bulb(s).

'80 and newer OHV models: Pull the molding out far enough to remove the parking light and turn signal sockets from the rear of the light holder assembly. Turn the sockets counterclockwise (as viewed from the rear of the holder), then pull them out of the holder. Lay the holder aside. If you're here to replace the parking light or turn signal bulb, do it now, then skip down to the reassembly.

'85 and newer OHC DL models (except XTs): Remove the phillips screws that attach the grille, then remove the grille. Lay it where it won't get stepped on.

XT models: Here's how to change the bulbs in your fancy retractable headlights. Set the headlights in the OPEN position. There is a plastic panel on the inboard side of the headlight assembly that must be removed so you can get to the headlight cover screws. Remove the bolts that hold the plastic panel to the body, then remove it.

Remove the four screws from each side of the headlight assembly. The top two attach the lid, so be careful that it doesn't fall off and get scratched when you remove the screws. When all eight screws are out you can remove the headlight cover.

EVERYONE: Now that the decorations are off, you'll see several phillips screws around the edge of the headlight. *Two* of the screw heads will be larger than the others (three smaller screws on round headlights or four smaller screws on square headlights). *Don't mess with the two larger screws, they're adjusters used only for aiming the headlight.* Remove the three or four smaller screws and pull the metal *retainer ring* and headlight out of the **headlight cradle** (socket). On round headlights, you only need to loosen the screws a few turns, then rotate the retainer ring counterclockwise to remove it. You'll see how the screw slots are bigger at one end so the ring can lift off. The headlight will lift right out into your hands.

Disconnect the *electrical connector* from the back of the old headlight. It just pulls straight out (use both hands so you don't put too much tension on the wires). Then plug the electrical connector onto the new headlight. Look for TOP stamped on the front of the new headlight. Insert the bulb into the cradle so TOP is, you guessed it, at the top. The bump(s) on the back of the light fit into the slot(s) on the cradle. If the new bulb isn't marked TOP, orient the light so that the bump(s) fit into the slot(s). Hold the headlight in place with one hand while you install the metal retainer ring and tighten the three or four phillips screws. Remember, don't touch the two adjusting screw heads. If your headlights are the round type, slip the retainer ring over the light, aligning the big part of the slots over the mounting screws. Turn the ring counterclockwise, so that the narrow part of the slots tucks under the screw heads. Then tighten the mounting screws.

'75-'77 models: Install the plastic molding around the headlight with its phillips screws.

'80 and newer OHV models (except '80-'81 Brats): Fit the parking light and turn signal sockets into the rear of the molding, then turn them clockwise (as viewed from the rear of the molding) to lock them into place. Attach the molding to the car with the four phillips screws.

'78 and newer OHV models and OHC DL models (except XTs): If there are tabs on the bottom of the grille, fit them into the holes on the body. Be sure they're all in place, then install and tighten the phillips screws around the edge of the grille.

XT models: Fit the headlight cover in place and install the phillips screws. Now install the lid and secure it with the phillips screws. Install the plastic panel on the inboard side of the headlight.

EVERYONE: If you accidentally messed with one or both of the larger phillips screw-heads that aim the headlights, or you don't think the headlights are aimed correctly, have Subaru or a garage adjust the headlights. It's faster and easier for them to do it. The car has to be on level ground a specified distance away from a headlight aiming target.

Here's how the headlight aim is adjusted in case you're desperate and have to do it yourself. Screw the large phillips screw-head on the side of the headlight clockwise to aim the headlight more toward the side the screwhead is on. Turn it counterclockwise to aim the light more in the opposite direction to the side the screw is on. If there's a large phillips screw-head above the headlight, turn it clockwise to aim the headlight higher, or counterclockwise to lower the aim. If the large screw-head is below the headlight, screw it clockwise to lower the beam, or counterclockwise to raise the beam.

Step 2. How to Replace Light Bulbs (except headlights).

The rest of the steps in this procedure (3 through 9) tell you how to get to the different bulbs by removing the **lenses** or the **bulb holders**. This step explains how to replace the bulb after you've gotten to it. So find the step below that relates to your particular dead bulb, then return here.

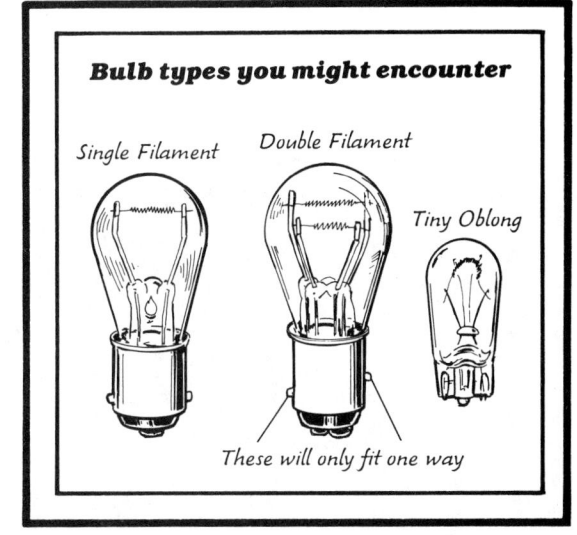

Once the lens is off or the bulb holder is removed, you'll see either a **small round bulb** or a **tiny oblong bulb**.

Replace round bulbs: Tail lamps and parking lights are typical of the round-bulb style. To remove a round light bulb, push in on the bulb and gently turn it counterclockwise until it stops, then lift it out. It should come out easily. If it won't, push and turn again—you may not have turned it far enough.

To install a new round bulb, align the two little bumps on the sides of the metal part of the bulb with the little grooves in the bulb socket. Push in on the bulb until it touches bottom, then hold pressure on it and turn it clockwise to lock it into place. Bulbs with two filament wires have to be installed in a certain position because one of the bumps on the side is farther from the end than the other. Try the bulb one way and if it won't go into the socket all the way, pull it out, turn it around 180° and insert it again. It'll turn and lock into place this time.

Replace tiny oblong bulbs: To remove a tiny oblong bulb, just wiggle it out of its holder.

To install a new tiny oblong bulb, align its flat bottom with the slot in the socket, then wiggle it in.

EVERYONE: After replacing a bulb, test the light with the switch to see if it works. If the light still doesn't work, see Procedure 5.

If you removed a lens to replace the bulb, clean off the inside of the lens as well as the shiny reflector behind the bulb with a rag. Then carefully fit the rubber gasket (if you have one) and lens in place and secure them with the phillips screws.

If you removed a bulb holder, fit it into the hole so the tabs on the sides of the holder fit into the slots in the hole, then push on the holder while turning it clockwise to lock it into place.

Step 3. Front Light Bulbs (except headlights).

The front lenses are easy to remove on most models; just unscrew and remove the phillips screws, then carefully pull the lens off. (You want to be careful, so as not to tear up the rubber gasket that may be between the lens and the body.) If you can't find any phillips screws in the lens, you'll have to remove the **headlight molding** to get to the bulbs. Step 1 tells you how to remove the headlight molding. Changing the bulb is explained in Step 2.

Step 4. Bulbs in Side Marker Lights.

OHC models: The front side marker lights are built into the front light bulb assembly (see Step 3), and the rear side marker lights are built into the rear light assembly (see Step 6).

OHV models: Most models have **side marker lights** mounted on the sides of the body near the front or rear or on the side of the bumper; yellow in the front, red in the rear. On some **'80 and newer OHV models**, the rear side marker lights are mounted in the side of the *rear combination light assembly* (see Step 6).

To remove side marker lenses that are not mounted in the headlight or taillight assembly, unscrew the two phillips screws in the lens, then carefully pull the lens off the car. Replacing the bulb is explained in Step 2. The bulbs are usually the tiny oblong type.

Install the lens with the two phillips screws, then try the light switch to be sure the light works. If it still doesn't work, see Procedure 5.

Step 5. Brake Lights.

If the brake lights aren't working, check the *fuse* (Procedure 2, Step 1) and the *bulbs* (Step 6 in this procedure). If the lights still won't work when you step on the pedal, look at Chapter 13, Procedure 14, to check the *brake light switch*.

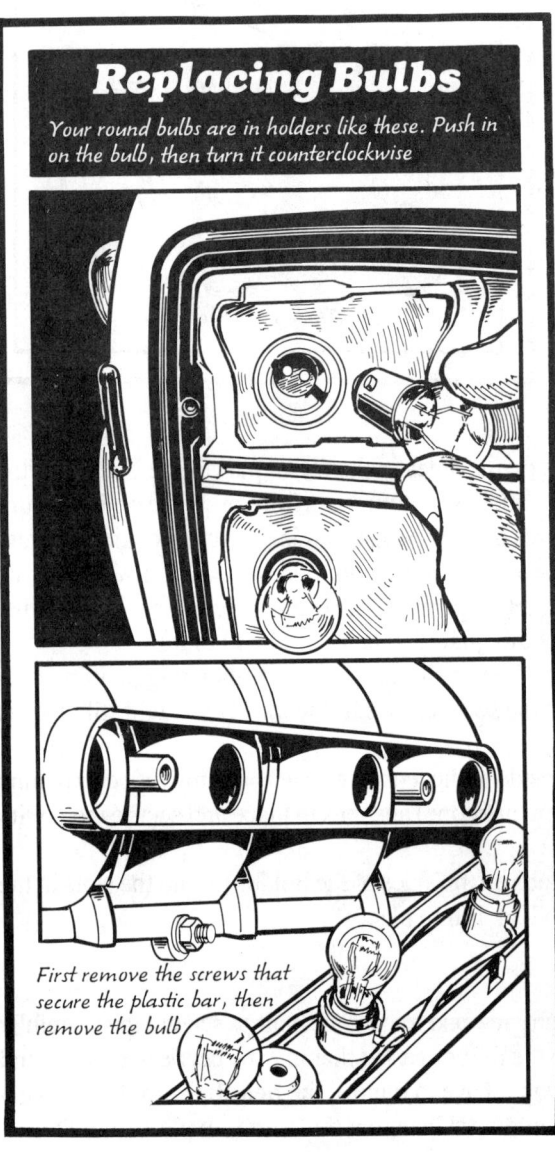

Step 6. Rear Lights.

The bulbs for the brake lights, taillights, turn signals (and sometimes the backup lights and side marker lights) are all in what's called a **rear combination light assembly**. The backup lights have a white lens, the brake lights and taillights are red, and the turn signal lens is red or yellow depending on the year and model.

OHV Sedans, Coupes, Hardtops, Hatchbacks: The bulbs are removed from inside the trunk. On **Hatchbacks** and **'80-'84 Coupe GLF models**, you'll have to remove an inner body panel or piece of cardboard to get at the bulbs. To remove the plastic panel on Hatchbacks, use a thin screwdriver to gently pop out the round panel fasteners located around the edge of the panel.

On some models each bulb has a *separate holder* mounted in the combination light assembly. Turn the holder counterclockwise (as viewed from inside the car), then pull the holder out. On other models, the bulb holders are all in a long *plastic bar* across the combination light assembly. Remove the two or three screws securing the plastic bar, then pull the bar away from the light assembly to expose the bulbs. How to change the bulbs is explained in Step 2 of this Procedure.

Hatchbacks and Coupe GLF models: Install the panels you removed. On Hatchbacks, align the holes in the panel and body then use your thumb to press the fasteners back into place.

OHV Station Wagons and Brats: The lens is held in place by a metal ring around the outside of the lens, or by phillips screws through the lens itself. On some models you'll have to open the rear gate to get to some of the screws.

'75-'79 Station Wagons and '77-'81 Brats: Remove the phillips screws, then carefully pry the lens away from the combination light assembly and lay it aside. Now you can replace the bulb (Step 2). Check the bulb to see that it works. Before putting everything back together, clean the inside of the lens and the reflector. Be sure the rubber gasket for the lens is in place, then fit the lens on the assembly and install and tighten the screws.

'80-'84 Station Wagons and '82-'87 Brats: Remove the phillips screws, then carefully pull the lens and combination light assembly away from the body. A rubber mounting pad may come out with it. Each bulb has a separate holder mounted in the rear of the combination light assembly. Find the holder

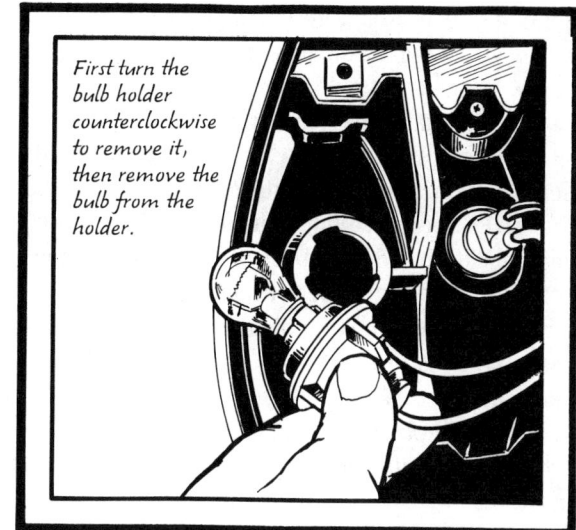

First turn the bulb holder counterclockwise to remove it, then remove the bulb from the holder.

that matches the location of the nonworking bulb, twist the bulb holder counterclockwise (as viewed from inside the car) until it stops, then lift it out. See Step 2 of this procedure to change the bulb.

Fit the rubber mounting pad, combination light assembly, lens, and metal ring (if yours has one) in place on the body. Install the phillips screws and tighten them. If the light still doesn't work, see Procedure 5.

OHC models: Bulbs located in the rear combination assembly are replaced from inside the car. Look for a plastic panel in front of the light assembly.

Station wagons: There's one large panel in each rear corner. Remove the panel and you'll see three plastic bulb holders. Push on the holder while turning it counterclockwise to remove the holder. See Step 2 to replace the bulb(s). Align the tabs on the bulb holder with the slots in the rear light assembly, then push on the holder while turning it clockwise to lock it in place. Install the plastic panel.

Sedans and 3-Door models: There are two panels, one large and one small, on each side of the car. The smaller outer panel contains the bulbs for the turn signal and side marker and the larger panel covers the back-up and stop/taillight bulbs. Remove the panel and you'll see the bulbs. See Step 2 to replace the bulbs, then install the panels.

Step 7. Replace Rear License Plate Bulbs.

Whenever the headlights are on, the license plate light should go on too. In some places the cops may stop you if it's not working.

If there are two phillips screws in the license plate lens, remove the screws securing the lens and pull the lens off to expose the bulb. If there are no phillips screws in the lens, remove the bulb holder from inside the car by turning it counterclockwise until it stops, then pull it out. On **Hatchbacks** and **Coupe GLF** models you have to remove a trim panel to get to the bulb (see Step 6). Step 2 tells you how to change the bulb.

Install the bulb holder or the lens, depending on your setup, then switch on the lights to see if it works now. If not, see Procedure 5.

Step 8. Dash, Warning, and Indicator Light Bulbs.

OHC models: The instrument cluster must be removed to replace the bulbs. Better let the experts do it.

OHV models: You'll need a flashlight and maybe a phillips screwdriver to locate the instrument panel illumination bulbs and the bulbs for the *warning lights* (brake, oil, charge, etc.) and *indicator lights* (high beam, turn signals, 4WD, etc.).

If all of the dash lights are out, the problem is probably a blown fuse, a broken headlight switch, or a faulty ignition switch. Rotate the headlight switch knob counterclockwise to check if the dash lights aren't just dimmed all the way down by the rheostat. If some of the dash lights work, you probably have one or more burned-out bulbs. Burned-out bulbs in the back of the instrument panel are fairly simple to replace. See the Other Dash Lights section in this step to replace bulbs not located behind the instrument panel.

'80 and newer OHV cars and '82-'87 Brats: You have to remove some phillips screws securing a plastic panel that covers the bottom left side of the dash below the instrument panel to get to the bulbs.

OHV models: With a flashlight in hand, wiggle into a position (probably uncomfortable) so you can peek under the dash and at the back of the instrument panel. Through the wires you'll see several *short knobs* all turned at about a 45° angle. Determine which knob is closest to the unlit area of the instrument panel or to the non-functioning warning or indicator light. Grasp the little knob and turn it counterclockwise (as viewed from the back of the instrument panel), then pull it out. It'll come out easily. With this little unit in hand, crawl out from under the dash. Wiggle the small bulb out of the knob. If it doesn't look burned out, you may have pulled out the wrong knob and bulb. Check the dash lights again to make sure you've got the culprit.

Take the bulb with you when you buy a new bulb. Some of the bulbs are small and some are downright tiny. Insert the new bulb into the knob, then crawl under the dash again and stick it in the hole and rotate it until you feel the tabs on the knob fit into the notches on the instrument panel. Push in on the knob while twisting it clockwise to lock it into place.

Other dash lights: On some models there are other illumination lights behind the heater/vent/air conditioner/fan controls. To get to these bulbs, the plastic panels (and maybe the radio and tape deck) have to be removed. I can't describe how to remove all of the variations used over the years, but here's a general description. Pay close attention to how everything comes apart so you'll know how to put it all back together. If your setup doesn't fit the description and it looks bewildering, seek professional help.

Locate the phillips screws that attach the panel around the controls to the dashboard. Some of them are cleverly hidden so they're almost impossible to find. Remove the screws, then gently try to pull the panel away from the dash. If you can't pull the panel out far enough to get to the bulbs, see if other panels need to be removed or if the radio is holding the panel. If it's the radio, pull the radio knobs off, then remove the nuts hidden under the knobs. You'll need a small crescent wrench or a pair of pliers. Try the panel again. If you still can't pull the panel out far enough to reach the bulbs, seek guidance from Subaru or a garage.

If you're successful in reaching the bulbs, see the Step 2 in this procedure to change them. Now put everything back together in the reverse order of removal.

Step 9. Other Light Bulbs (dome, glove box, etc.).

Dome light: The interior dome light on the ceiling is covered by an opaque plastic lens. Look for a Fuji symbol (∧) or a dash mark (-) on the lens. Turn the lens until the symbol or dash mark is aligned with the switch knob, then pull down to remove the lens. If there's no symbol or dash mark on the lens, just turn the lens while gently pulling down until it pops off.

The bulb is tube-shaped with pointed metal ends that fit into the holes in two springy clips. To remove the bulb, push it toward one of the ends until the other end can slip out of the clip. The bulb will fall out now. Insert one end of the new bulb in one of the clips and push on it while pushing the other end of the bulb into the other clip. Be sure the pointed bulb ends are in the clip holes. Now put the lens back on. Align the Fuji symbol or dash mark (if your lens has one) or the small tab on the lens with the switch knob and push the lens into the holder. Turn the lens to lock it into place. Move the switch to see if the light works. If the light works with the switch but not when the door opens, either the switch is in the wrong position (try all three positions) or the switch in the door opening is broken. If the light doesn't work in any switch position, see Procedure 5.

Spot lights: Use a very thin screwdriver or knife blade to pop the lens off the light. See Step 2 to replace the bulb(s). Hold the lens in position while you push on the center. You'll feel it click into place.

Glove box light and trunk light: Not all models have these lights. Twist the plastic lens to remove it. See Step 2 in this procedure to change the bulb (probably the tiny oblong type). Then fit the tab(s) on the lens into the groove of the holder and twist the lens to lock it into place.

Step 10. Check and Replace Turn Signal and Hazard Light.

Flasher Unit (OHV models only). OHC models: The flasher unit is buried beneath the dash where only trained technicians dare to tread. Let them replace it for you.

OHV models: The symptoms of a defective flasher unit are: The turn signal lights go on when the turn signal lever or hazard switch is turned on, but the lights flash very slowly, very quickly, or not at all. It's a good idea to buy the new flasher unit before digging around under the dash so you'll know what you're looking for. If you have separate turn signal/hazard light units ('75-'82 models), replace the one that has the same part number as the new part, or replace one, then the other until you find the defective unit. (I've substituted a General Motors flasher unit #SF 552 for the turn signal unit when I couldn't find the correct Subaru unit.)

If the turn signals work on one side of the car, but neither the lights nor the indicator light on the dashboard work for the other side, the turn signal switch might be broken. Have Subaru or a garage check and replace it for you.

'80 and newer OHV cars and '82-'87 Brats: Remove the phillips screws that secure the plastic panel to the bottom of the dash in front of the driver's seat, then remove the panel.

'75-'82 models: There are two small round flasher units mounted in a *white plastic clip* under the dash. One is for the turn signals, the other is for the hazard (emergency) system that flashes all four turn signals at the same time. The flasher units are about the same diameter as a size D flashlight battery, but only about half as long. The white clip is attached to the left side of the clutch pedal bracket ('75-'79 cars and '77-'81 Brats), or attached straight above the hood release cable ('80-'82 cars and '82 Brats). An *L-shaped two-wire connector* is attached to each flasher unit.

'83 and newer OHV models: The flasher unit is a small box-like gizmo with a plastic *three-wire connector* attached to one end. The unit is attached with a screw to the clutch and/or brake pedal bracket. A triangle with an arrow on either side might be stamped on the unit.

OHV models: Peek up under the dash and locate your type of flasher unit(s). Remove the phillips screw that secures the unit ('83 and newer OHV models), or pull the units out of the plastic holder (everyone else). Pull the plastic wire connector off the unit, then fit it onto the new flasher unit. It will only fit one way. Now fit the unit back into the holder, or attach it with the mounting screw. Turn the ignition key to ON (don't start the engine), then try the turn signals or hazard lights to see if the problem is solved. If everything's working properly, turn the key OFF. If there's still a problem, see Procedure 5, or seek professional help.

'80 and newer OHV cars and '82-'87 Brats: Attach the plastic panel to the bottom of the dash.

PROCEDURE 5: HOW TO DIAGNOSE NON-ENGINE ELECTRICAL PROBLEMS

This deals with electrical failures or gremlins not related to the way the engine starts or runs. If the engine has cranking or charging problems, go to Procedure 6 or Procedure 9 later in this chapter.

Condition: An electrical component isn't working; OR the battery loses its charge; OR a fuse keeps blowing (breaking); OR anything amiss that seems like it may have an electrical source.

Tools and Materials: A 12-volt test light or Volt/Ohm meter (VOM), maybe new fuses, light bulbs, or whatever component you're checking, maybe a 10mm or 12mm wrench to disconnect the negative battery terminal. Also: sandpaper or knife for cleaning contacts, a piece of wire about 12" long for testing "ground," some extra fuses to help locate shorts, electrical tape for patching shorts.

Remarks: Most problems with the electrical system are due to a blown fuse, a poor wire connection, or a worn-out component (bulbs, etc.). Very seldom is a broken wire the problem.

If you've never used a Volt/Ohm meter (VOM), or need a refresher course, see Procedure 11.

Step 1. Check Fuses.

Start by locating the fuse box and the fuse for the component that isn't working (see Procedure 2). Replace the fuse for that component with a new fuse, then try the component to see if it works. Don't forget to turn the ignition key to ON if the component is switched by the ignition system. If the fuse blows within a few seconds after installation, see Step 3.

Is yours a headlight problems? Some models have three fuses that affect the headlights: One fuse for the high beams or right headlights, a separate fuse for the low beams or left headlights, and a master fuse that controls all the headlights and a few other lights. Check all three fuses if you have them (Step 3).

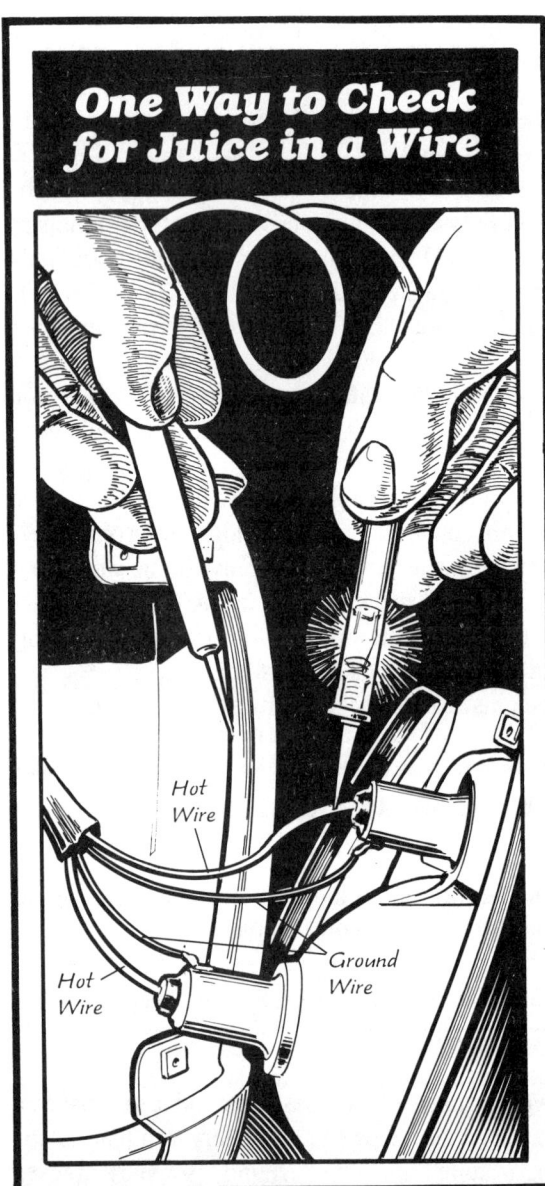

Step 2. Check for Juice and Ground at Component.

All electrical components receive their supply of electrical energy from the *positive* (+) terminal of the battery. The electrical energy (juice) arrives at the component through an insulated wire, passes through the component to make it light, beep, pump, or whatever it was designed to do, then returns to the negative terminal of the battery through the car body and frame (the "ground"). This circuit must be completed for electrical things to work. Here's how to see if there's juice getting to the component through a wire, and if there's a good ground connection so the juice can get back to the battery.

Light bulbs: Remove the lens and bulb (Procedure 4), then come back here to check for juice and ground connection.

The juice for light bulbs gets to the filament inside the bulb through small brass or aluminum contact(s) inside the bulb socket that touch a metal contact (or contacts) on the bottom of the bulb. The contacts inside the socket and on the bottom of the bulb have to be clean and free of crud and corrosion for the bulb to work properly. Be sure the ignition key and light switch are OFF, then use sandpaper, a knife, or a small screwdriver to clean the contact points in the bulb socket and on the end of the bulb then try the bulb again. On small round bulb setups, also clean up the metal walls of the socket and sides of the bulb holder. If the light still doesn't work, see if there's juice to the contact(s) in the socket and if the socket is grounded. (See Check for Juice and Check for Ground, just ahead.)

On some lights, the bulb socket and/or its mounting screw(s) touch the car body and act as the ground to return the juice to the battery. Other light sockets have a wire (usually black) that runs from the socket to a part of the body to provide the ground. Check to see that the wire is firmly attached at both ends.

Other components: There's usually a wire connection on or near the electrical component (windshield washer motor, windshield wiper motor, fuel pump, etc.) that supplies the current to make the thing work. To complete the circuit there's either a wire connecting the component to the body, or the component itself is mounted to the body, which provides the ground directly. Get out your test light or VOM.

Check for juice: Turn the ignition switch and the component's switch ON. If you have a VOM, set it to 15 DC volts. Disconnect the wire that supplies current to the component. Touch one probe of the test light or the red (+) probe of the VOM to the wire and touch the other probe to bare metal. Test both contacts if there are two. If none of the wires to the component lights the test light, or moves the VOM needle, there's no juice getting to the component. If the fuses are good, the problem is probably in the switch. The switches are usually complicated and difficult to get to, so I suggest you take the car to Subaru or a garage and have them check the switch.

If more than one wire goes to the component and one of the wires has juice but the other one is black and doesn't have juice, check the black wire to see if it's a ground wire. Its other end will attach to bare body metal somewhere. Here's more about grounding.

Check for ground: If there's juice to the component but it still won't work, maybe the component isn't grounded properly. Again, first turn the ignition and the component switch ON. You'll need a VOM or a piece of wire to test the ground. Set the VOM to RX 10, then touch one probe to the component's metal body or to the black ground wire that didn't have juice in it. Touch the other probe to bare metal. The needle should swing over to 0 ohms if the component is properly grounded. No VOM? Install the bulb if it's a light you're checking. Check again that the component is switched on. Touch one end of a piece of wire to the metal part of the bulb socket, or to the metal body of whatever thing you're checking. Touch the other end of the wire to bare metal. If the bulb lights up or the component works, the thing itself is good but it isn't properly grounded.

If that's the case, turn off the switch and remove the mounting nuts, bolts, or screws that attach it to the car body, or follow the black wire from the component to where it attaches to the body and detach it. Use sandpaper or a wire brush to clean the place where the screw, nut, bolt, wire, and/or socket touches the body. Make it shiny. Now attach the light socket or component to the body, turn on the switch, and see if the problem is solved.

If the component is getting juice and is grounded properly but still doesn't work, the component is probably bad. Replace it with a new one.

If the component isn't getting juice or you can't get it grounded, you'll have to seek professional help.

Step 3. Checking for Shorts.

A short means the juice is taking a short cut back to the battery before going through the component. How? A break in the insulation (the wire's plastic sheath) allows the wire to contact the body or frame of the car and this completes the circuit. Without the resistance in the component to slow the flow of juice, the juice flows so fast it overheats the wires and blows the fuse for the circuit. If new fuses blow within a few seconds after you install them, you have a major short for sure. A minor short can slowly drain the battery over a period of a few days without blowing the fuse.

Check for a minor short: Put your safety glasses on, then disconnect the negative (-) terminal of the battery (Procedure 1, Step 3). Turn the ignition switch and all electrical components OFF, then gently touch the negative battery clamp to the negative battery post while watching for a small spark. If you see a spark, you have a short in some circuit somewhere. Now to find the short. Go to the fuse box (see Procedure 2, Step 1, to locate it) and pull out one of the fuses, then try the ground-clamp-to-negative-post-test again. Still sparks? Put the fuse back in and try another fuse. Try each fuse like that until you find the circuit that *doesn't* cause a spark when the fuse is removed. The short is in that circuit. Put the fuse back in, then read the next section.

Identify faulty component: If you have a major short, the fuse will blow immediately or very soon after the faulty component is turned on. It might take several ones to locate the problem so be sure you have several new fuses handy. Disconnect the components on the problem circuit one at a time. Then do the spark check (for minor short) or install a new fuse (for major short). Keep disconnecting components, then testing one at a time. When you find the component that doesn't cause a spark or blow a fuse when it's disconnected, you'll know the short is in that component or the wiring to that component. Note the color of the wire(s) to the component, then follow that wire until it disappears into a large bundle of wires taped or wrapped together (the **wire harness**). If you find a bare place in the wire, tape it with plastic tape. Look for a wire running from the fuse box that's the same color (**color code**) as the one to the component and check it for bare places. Reconnect the component and try the ground-clamp-to-negative-post spark test, or install another new fuse, to see if the short is eliminated.

If you can't find a break or bare place in the wire, the short is either in the component itself or in the wiring where you can't find it. It's time to seek professional assistance.

PROCEDURE 6: CHECK CHARGING SYSTEM (ALTERNATOR, VOLTAGE REGULATOR)

The **red alternator (charge) light** on your dashboard is the key to checking your charging system. If the battery's completely dead, it won't go on—you'll have to first charge the battery or jump-start the car with jumper cables. When you turn the ignition key ON, the alternator light turns on, so you know the bulb's OK. As soon as the engine starts it turns OFF and should stay off if the charging system is OK. It's the charging system that operates everything electrical while the engine's running and is designed to keep the battery full of juice to run accessories while the engine's off, and to start your car in the morning.

Condition: The red alternator light stays ON while the engine's running; OR the battery needs recharging every few days.

Tools and Materials: Volt/Ohm meter (VOM) or 12-volt test light. If you don't have these, you'll need a 10mm or 12mm wrench to remove the positive battery clamp.

Remarks: If the red charge light goes OFF when the engine is running, but the battery needs frequent recharging, do Procedure 5, Step 3, to see if it's a *minor short* that's draining the battery.

Step 1. Check Electrical Connections.

Check the connections on both ends of the battery cables to be sure they're clean and tight (Procedure 1, Steps 3 and 4). Check the alternator drive belt for tightness (Procedure 3, Step 1). Check the electrical connections on the alternator (Procedure 7, Step 1) and voltage regulator (Procedure 8, Step 2). Disconnect the wire connections, clean them with a wire brush, then reconnect them. Now see if the red alternator light on the dash goes out with the engine running. If there's a voltmeter in the dash, the needle should go to about 14 volts when the engine is revved above idle. Still a problem? Read on.

Step 2. Check Voltage Across Battery.

Checking with VOM or test light: Start with the engine off. If you have a VOM, set it at 15 DC volts. Touch the *red* probe to the *positive* (+) battery terminal, and the *black* probe to the *negative* (-) battery terminal (or touch the probes of the test light to the battery terminals). The VOM should read about 12 volts or the test light should light up. Now start the car and read the meter again. If the battery is too weak to start the engine, use jumper cables to fire it up (Procedure 1, Step 8).

Evaluation: With the engine revved above idle the VOM should read about 13.5 to 14.5 volts, or the test light should glow brighter than at idle. In other words, there should be a slight increase in voltage when you rev the engine a little above idle.

If the voltage is slightly higher (up to 14.5 volts), the battery is probably the problem since the alternator and voltage regulator are supplying the proper voltage.

If the voltage is *too high* (above 14.5), the voltage regulator isn't functioning properly and the battery cells in the battery might be burned out due to constant overcharging. Replace the voltage regulator (Procedure 8) and have the battery checked.

If the voltage is *too low*, there's obviously a problem with the alternator and/or the voltage regulator, but it's difficult to determine which one is bad. You need an **ammeter** to test the amperage output of the alternator, including an amperage output test with the voltage regulator bypassed. Since it's probably cheaper to have the alternator/voltage regulator checked by a garage than to buy a good ammeter, I suggest you have a garage determine which component is bad. You can replace either of them yourself and save some money.

PROCEDURE 7: REMOVE AND INSTALL ALTERNATOR

Condition: Alternator needs replacing; OR you need to remove the alternator for engine rebuild or some other repair procedure.

Tools and Materials: One 8mm and two 12mm wrenches, masking tape, and pen. Maybe a new or rebuilt alternator, if your old one has died. You'll also need a large screwdriver (or lever) to tighten the drive belt after installing the alternator.

Remarks: Brand new alternators from the manufacturer are pricey. Fortunately for you, rebuilt alternators can be found at parts stores and are generally about as reliable as new ones. They usually cost about half as much as replacement ones from the factory.

Step 1. Disconnect Electrical Wires.

Disconnect the clamp from the negative (-) battery post on the battery (Procedure 1, Step 3).

If there's a *plastic wire connector* plugged into the rear of the alternator, wiggle it out. Or, if there's a plastic wire connector a couple of inches from the alternator for the bundle of wires coming from the rear of the alternator, wiggle the connector apart. Use masking tape and a pen to label the *small single wire(s)* attached to the rear of the alternator with the letter or number stamped on the alternator next to where the wire attaches. Now remove the nut (probably 8mm) and washer that attaches the single wire(s) to the alternator. Stash the nut and washer so they won't get lost.

Step 2. Remove Alternator.

Remove the *drive belt* (Procedure 3, Step 2), then remove the *belt adjustment bolt* from the *slotted bracket*. There should be a flat washer and a lockwasher on the bolt. Stash them where they they won't get lost. Now unscrew the *pivot bolt(s)* while holding the nut(s) on the rear surface of the bracket. (The nuts are probably attached to *spark plug wire looms*.) When the nuts are off the bolts, support the bottom of the alternator with one hand while you remove the pivot bolt(s). Now you can lift the alternator off the engine. Stash the pivot bolts with the adjustment bolt and washers.

Step 3. Install Alternator.

If you have *two* pivot bolts, hold the alternator so the *two ears* on one side of the alternator are on the front sides of the *inner bracket*. If you have one long pivot bolt, the ears on the alternator go on the outside of the bracket. The pulley should be toward the front of the car. From the front, slide the pivot bolt(s) through the alternator ears and the bracket holes. Screw the bolt(s) into the nut(s) until they're lightly snug. Fit the drive belt onto the alternator pulley. Be sure it's also in the groove on the crank pulley, water pump pulley, the fan pulley (if you have a belt-driven fan), and the air pump pulley on '75 models. Now pull up on the alternator so there's enough tension on the belt to hold it in the pulleys. Be sure there's a lockwasher, then a flat washer on the adjustment bolt. Fit it through the slotted bracket and into the ear on the alternator, and screw it in. See Procedure 3, Step 2 to adjust the drive belt tension.

Step 4. Attach Wires.

Now plug the plastic wire connector into the rear of the alternator or reconnect the two plastic wire connectors. (Due to the shape, the connectors will only fit one way.) Finally attach the wire or wires that are held in place with the small nut(s). If there's more than one wire, your label will tell you where each one attaches. Slip the wire, washer, and nut over the stud and snug it down with your wrench.

PROCEDURE 8: REPLACE VOLTAGE REGULATOR ('75-'81 only).

Condition: You, or your garage, have determined the voltage regulator has reached the end of a long, high-charged life.

Tools and Materials: New voltage regulator; phillips screwdriver or 10mm wrench depending on your setup; 10mm or 12mm wrench depending on your battery clamp nut.

Remarks: Voltage regulators tend to outlive the car so be sure yours is bad before replacing it. The voltage regulator is built into the alternator on 1982-1984 models so you can't replace it separately.

Step 1. Detach Battery Cable.

Disconnect the negative (-) battery cable from the battery (Procedure 1, Step 3).

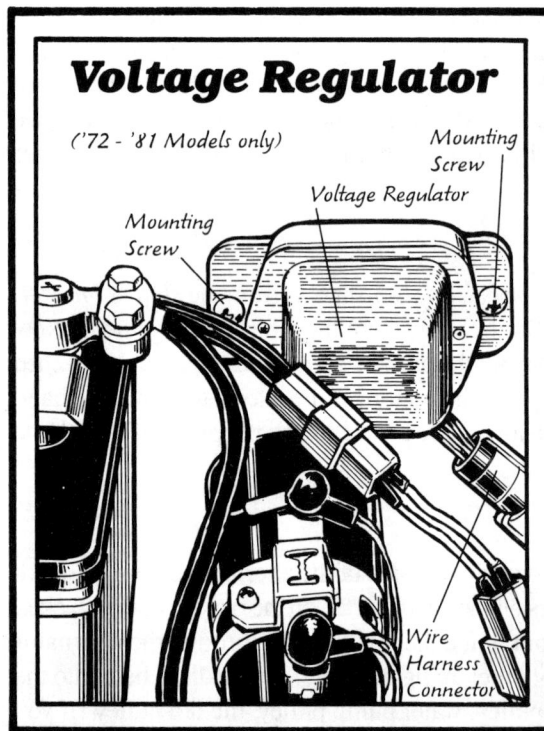

Step 2. Remove Regulator.

The voltage regulator is attached to the side of the engine compartment just to the rear of the battery. It's approximately 3" x 3" and has a bundle of wires coming out of it. Some models also have a separate single wire sprouting from the regulator that attaches to a single wire connector.

Remove the phillips screws or 10mm bolts that attach the voltage regulator to the car. Follow the bundle of wires to a plastic connector. On some models you have to squeeze two tabs on one end of the bundle connector while pulling on the ends of the connector to separate it. If there's a single wire attached to the regulator, follow it to a connector, and gently pull on the wire on each side of the connector to disconnect it.

Step 3. Install New Regulator.

Position the new regulator the same way as the old one. Notice that the ends of the plastic wire connectors are shaped so they can only fit together one way. Align the connectors, then press them together until they lock in place. Reconnect the single wire if you have one. Attach the new regulator to the car with the screws or bolts and tighten them. Connect the negative battery clamp and tighten its bolt, and you're finished.

PROCEDURE 9: CHECK CRANKING SYSTEM (STARTER MOTOR, SOLENOID, IGNITION SWITCH)

The starter solenoid is mounted on the starter motor. Its function is to engage a little gear on the starter motor with teeth on the flywheel of your engine. Thus engaged, the starter then cranks the engine around to get it started. The solenoid or starter can be replaced separately by Subaru or an auto electric shop. The cable from the positive (+) battery terminal mounts at a post on the solenoid. For simplicity's sake, I'll sometimes refer to the solenoid/motor combo as "the starter."

Condition: The engine won't turn over when the ignition switch is turned to START; OR you can hear the starter engage but it won't turn the engine; OR the engine turns over too slowly to start.

Tools and Materials: A screwdriver or insulated pliers; for some '80 and newer models you will also need about 12″ of heavy insulated wire.

Step 1. Check Battery.

First, let's be sure the battery is delivering a good supply of juice to the starter. Turn on the headlights and see if they shine brightly. If not, check the battery connections (Procedure 1, Steps 3 and 4). If that doesn't make the headlights bright, check the battery (Procedure 1, Step 5). Now try to start the car. If you still have problems, move on to Step 2.

Step 2. Check Ignition Switch Wire to Starter.

The battery and cables are in good shape, right? Remove the spare tire if it's in the engine compartment.

Follow the positive (+) cable from the battery to a **terminal post** on the starter solenoid. Right next to the terminal post, there's a *small wire* from the ignition switch attached to the rear of the starter with a push-on connector. Wiggle the ignition wire off the starter. It should be tight. If the wire came off easily, use pliers to gently squeeze the little grippers on the sides of the connector so it will fit tightly on the starter. Put the wire back on the starter and see if your problem is solved. If it is, secure the spare tire in its place and consider yourself lucky. Problem still not solved? Then let's check the starter solenoid and motor.

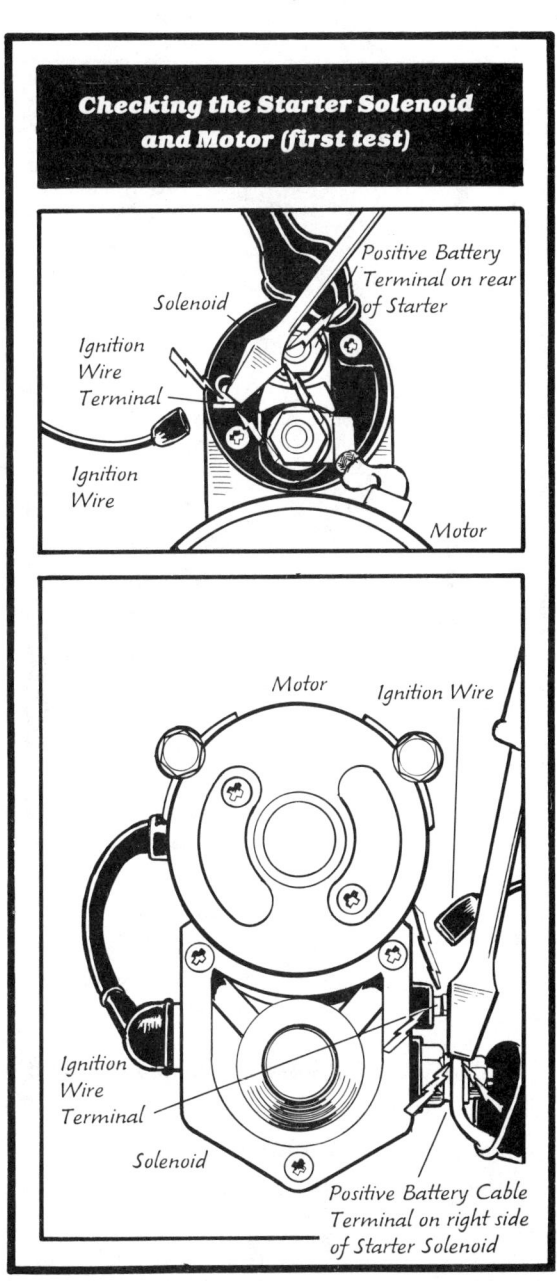

Checking the Starter Solenoid and Motor (first test)

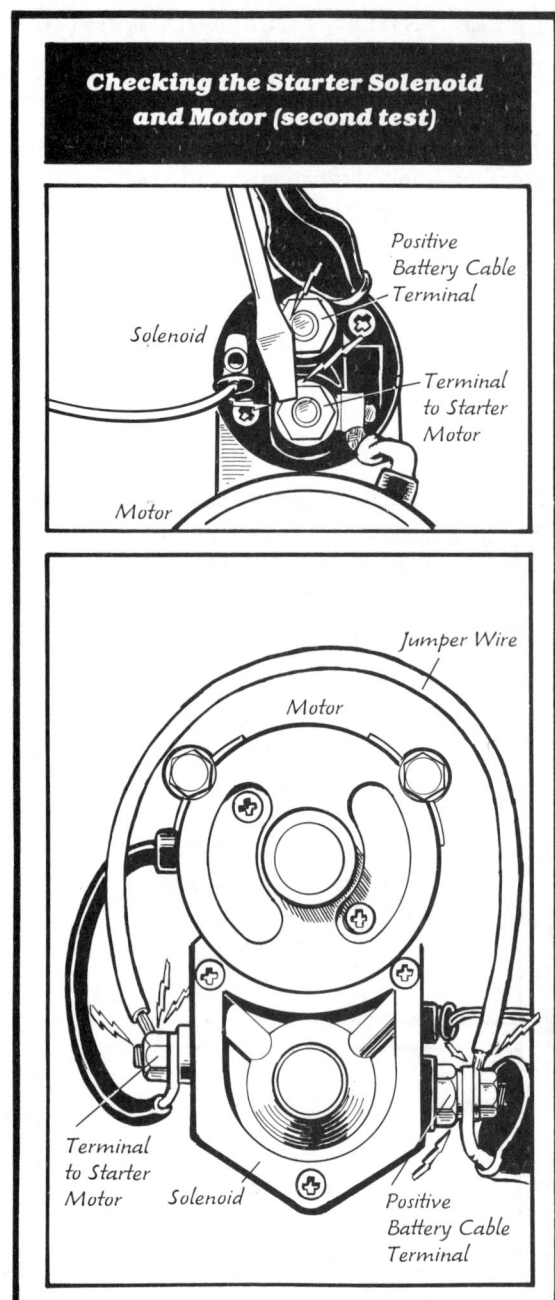

Step 3. Check Starter Solenoid and Motor (first test)

Set the handbrake, then put the gearshift in NEUTRAL (manual transmission) or PARK (automatics). Be sure the ignition key is turned to OFF. Caution: Be sure tools, rags, neckties, long hair, etc., stay away from the drive belt(s).

Now you need to get juice from the positive (battery cable) terminal post on the starter to the little flat post on the starter where the ignition switch wire connects. You can do this with a screwdriver, insulated pliers, or a piece of insulated wire. First, peel the rubber boot back so the end of the battery cable is exposed where it attaches to the starter. Then disconnect the small ignition switch wire to the starter (Step 2).

Make a metal connection between the battery cable terminal on the starter and the ignition wire terminal on the starter. Touch *only* those two points with your jumper (pliers, etc.). Don't worry, you won't get a shock if you follow the instructions. If the starter rapidly turns the engine, the starter motor and solenoid are both good. The problem must be in the ignition switch. Have Subaru or a garage replace the switch for you. Put the boot back over the battery cable end.

If the starter didn't turn the engine over, or turned it very slowly, do Step 4 to further check the starter solenoid and motor.

Here's a note you may find useful. You can use this step to start the engine even if the ignition switch is bad. Connect the little ignition wire to its terminal on the starter, turn the ignition key to ON, then go back under the hood and use your jumper to connect the terminal post and ignition switch terminal on the starter. Quickly remove the jumper when the engine starts.

It used to be easy to start (borrow, steal) cars even if you didn't have the key by installing a jumper wire from the positive battery terminal to the coil, then using another jumper wire from the battery cable terminal post to the ignition switch terminal on the starter—the same as you do when checking the starter solenoid. You can't use this method any more because on modern cars you must have the key to unlock the steering wheel. Bah, foiled again.

Step 4. Check Starter Solenoid and Motor (second test)

There's another nut on the starter like the one securing the cable from the battery. On all **'75-'79 models** and some **'80 and newer models**, the second nut is right below the battery cable nut. On some **'80 and newer models** it's on the opposite side of the starter and covered with a rubber boot. To check the starter motor, you need to get juice from the battery cable terminal on the starter to the other nut. You can use a screwdriver blade or pliers for a jumper if the nuts are right next to each other, but you'll have to round up a piece of heavy insulated wire if the nuts are on opposite sides of the starter.

Be sure the handbrake is set and the transmission is in NEUTRAL (manuals) or PARK (automatics). Connect the two large nuts with your jumper. The starter motor should whir like an electric motor without turning the engine. If it doesn't, the starter motor has problems.

It's time for an evaluation. If the test in Step 3 was negative (jumping from the battery cable terminal post to the ignition wire post didn't turn the engine), but jumping from the battery cable post to the other nut on the starter made the motor whir, then the solenoid is either bad or the starter is hung up in the flywheel. Let's hope it's just hung up. If the starter isn't hung up in the flywheel, you'll need to remove the starter (Procedure 10) and have the solenoid replaced by Subaru or a garage.

If the starter motor didn't whirr when you connected the battery cable post to the other nut on the starter, the motor is kaput. Procedure 10 tells how to replace the starter.

Step 5. See If Starter Is Hung Up in the Flywheel

Check both starter motor mounting nuts and tighten them if they're loose. A loose starter can easily get hung up in the flywheel.

Manual transmission models: CAUTION: If you happen to be stuck on a hill, either have Friend sit in the car with one foot ready to stomp on the brake, or do the automatic transmission routine, below. Anyway, stand on the uphill end of the car while you rock it back and forth.

Put the gearshift in 4th, take your foot off the clutch pedal, then release the handbrake. Now open and prop the hood. Push on the front of the car to rock it back and forth while watching the engine drive belts. If the engine (belts) turns a little, the starter isn't hung up. If the engine doesn't turn, rock the car a little harder while listening for a satisfying clunk. A clunk means the starter just broke free and the engine should turn now. No clunk? Then you'll have to remove the starter (Procedure 10). Be sure and read the EVERYONE section of this step.

Automatic transmission models: Set the handbrake, then put the gearshift lever in NEUTRAL. Use a socket on the crankshaft pulley nut to turn the engine *clockwise* (Chapter 7, Procedure 5, Step 6, tells you how). If the engine won't turn, remove the starter (Procedure 10), then try to turn the engine again. Read on.

EVERYONE (who has removed the starter): Once the starter is off, try to turn the engine with whatever method you were using (car rocking in gear or socket on the crankshaft pulley). If the engine still won't turn, the GOOD news is that the starter is probably OK. The BAD news is that something inside the engine is locked up so an engine rebuild or replacement seems imminent. And, brethren, that is BAD news.

If the engine turns after the starter is removed, the starter motor is probably bad. Take it to an auto electric shop to see if they can salvage it. If you have to buy a new or rebuilt starter, shop around because the price can vary radically from store to store.

PROCEDURE 10: REPLACE STARTER (MOTOR AND SOLENOID)

Fortunately, Subaru starters are simple and relatively easy to take off and put on. This is another part which can be replaced by a quality rebuilt one for much less than it would cost for a new one. Call Subaru and several parts stores for starter prices, then call an auto electric shop to see how much it would cost to rebuild your old one. Sometimes you can trade your old starter in on a new or rebuilt one and save some money. Be sure and ask.

Condition: Starter appears to be dead; OR you wish to examine your starter at close range.

Tools and Materials: 10 or 12mm wrench to disconnect battery, 14 or 17mm wrenches depending on the size of your starter mounting bolts, and maybe a new or rebuilt starter.

Step 1. Get Ready

Disconnect the negative (-) battery terminal (Procedure 1, Step 3). Remove the spare tire if it's in the engine compartment.

Step 2. Disconnect Wires from Starter

Wiggle the small ignition switch wire off its post on the rear of the starter. Peel the rubber boot away from where the battery cable attaches to the starter. Remove the 12mm nut and washer, then lift the end of the cable off the post. Tuck it out of the way. Stash the nut and washer where they won't get lost.

Step 3. Remove Starter

If the starter is on the top center rear of the **flywheel housing**, it's attached with a 17mm nut and lockwasher on each side. Early models with the round solenoid directly on top of the starter motor are a cinch to remove. On later models the solenoid is kind of on the side of the starter motor, making it a little more difficult to reach the nut on the driver's side. Due to the limited space, a 12-point 17mm box end wrench is almost a necessity to remove this nut.

If the starter is mounted on the driver's side of the flywheel housing, it's attached with a 17mm nut and lockwasher toward the bottom and a 14mm bolt, nut and lockwasher on the top. You'll have to hold the nut on the end of the bolt with a wrench while unscrewing the bolt. The top mounting bolt is also one of bolts that attach the engine to the transmission. On some models it's easiest to remove the bottom bolt from beneath the car with a socket, long extension, and ratchet.

Remove the two mounting nuts, or nut and bolt (whichever you have), then wiggle the starter toward the rear of the car. Be careful to not bang the starter against the small metal brake lines on the firewall. Now thread the starter through the lines and wires and out of the engine compartment. Kind of heavy, isn't it?

Step 4. Install Starter

Thread the starter through the lines, wires and cables in the engine compartment and into position on the flywheel housing. Fit the starter over the mounting stud(s), then push the bolt through the starter and flywheel housing if yours is that type. Put it through the same way it came out. Install the two lockwashers and nuts and tighten them.

Step 5. Connect Wires and Finish.

Connect the battery cable to the starter terminal post with the nut and lockwasher, and slip the rubber boot over the connection. Then fit the ignition switch wire snugly onto the small post. Be sure the cable and wire are on tight. Reconnect the negative (−) battery terminal and tighten the clamp nut. Put the spare tire back in its place if you removed it.

PROCEDURE 11: HOW TO USE A VOLT/OHM METER (VOM)

Small Volt/Ohm meters are readily available, and relatively inexpensive, at your local electronics store. (Is there a town in the world that doesn't have a dear old Radio Shack?) You don't need a big fancy one to check out your Soob. Just be sure it will measure at least 15 volts DC and has an OHM scale.

Condition: You need to check the voltage of the battery; OR you're checking the charging system; OR you're checking for juice at the fuse box or one of the electrical components; OR you're checking a fuse or wire to see if juice can go from one end to the other (continuity check).

Tools and Materials: A Volt/Ohm meter (also called a VOM).

Remark: The VOM you have may look different from the one illustrated, and use slightly different names or symbols for the various scales, but they all measure the same electrical phenomena: AC and/or DC *volts*, and resistance in *ohms*.

A good VOM will test a number of things, but I'm going to limit the explanation to things that are applicable to your Soob: *Volts, Continuity,* and *Resistance.* **Caution:** The VOM is a very sensitive instrument and you should just touch the probes lightly to whatever you're testing, so you can quickly see if you have the dial set at the wrong scale (the needle will jump all the way across). Setting the VOM to the wrong scale can burn it out. Never test for continuity or resistance on anything that's plugged in to a battery or wall outlet. If you're testing voltage and have the VOM set to DC volts and the needle takes a dive to below zero, you have the *wrong polarity* so switch the probes around...that is, put one where the other was. Don't try to check the voltage of the large spark plug or coil wires with a VOM; you might fry the meter.

Step 1. Set Up Volt/Ohm Meter

Most Volt/Ohm meters require one or two small flashlight batteries. Be sure yours has good batteries before using it to do tests on your Soob.

Untangle the two wires for the VOM. You'll notice that the plastic insulator on one end of each wire is longer than the one on the other end. The longer insulator end is called a **probe** and the shorter insulator end is called a **jack**. Plug the jack for the red wire into the positive (+) **V-Ω-A hole** on the meter. Now plug the jack for the black wire into the negative (-) **COM hole** on the meter.

Step 2. How to Measure Voltage

Set up your VOM according to Step 1. Since your Soob has a 12-volt DC electrical system, set the selector knob on the VOM to the next higher DC volt setting above 12 volts (probably 15 volts DC). (Your VOM might say DC V, Volts DC, etc.) Now to find the proper scale on the meter for your setting. Look at the column of numbers under the DC on the right side of the meter. Find the number that corresponds to your selector knob setting (probably 15). The numbers to the left of that number on the same row are the ones you use to read the voltage of the component being checked. Look at the illustration of my VOM on page 171 (if you don't have one handy) so you'll know what I'm talking about. In the illustration, the selector knob is set at 15 DC V (volts) and the needle is showing 12 volts (two lines to the right of the 10).

To check the voltage in the battery, touch the *black* probe to the *negative* (-) battery terminal and the *red* probe to the *positive* (+) battery terminal. If the battery has any juice in it, the needle on the meter will move to the right telling you how many volts the battery is putting out. If it's less than 12 volts, the battery needs a charge. Doing this test with the engine running should give you a higher reading, like about 13.5 to 14.5 volts, if the alternator and voltage regulator are working properly. If your readings are different, see Procedure 6.

To see if there's juice in any wire on your car (except spark plug and coil wires), turn the ignition switch and the switch for the component being tested ON. Touch the red probe to the metal on the end of the wire and the black probe to bare metal on the car body or engine. The VOM should show 12 volts. If it doesn't, the wire or component isn't getting any juice or is shorted out, or there may be a loose connection.

Step 3. How to Check for Continuity.

CAUTION: This is not a test to see if the battery or a component is getting juice. Turn the switch to whatever you're testing OFF or disconnect the negative (-) battery cable clamp to be sure it's not getting juice. Use this test to see if juice is *capable* of flowing through a wire, fuse or ground connection.

Set up your VOM as described in Step 1. Turn the selector knob to the RX10, RX100, or RX1K position in the OHMS section. To adjust the VOM, touch the metal ends of the two probes together. The needle should swing toward the zero (0) on the right side of the OHMS scale on the meter. If the needle doesn't point to the 0, turn the *Ohms adjust knob* until the needle points to the 0.

Now you can test wires, fuses, paper clips, your body, etc., to see if electricity can flow from one probe, through whatever you're testing, to the other probe. To check continuity in a fuse, you must remove it from its receptacle. Touch a probe to each end of the fuse. If the needle swings to zero, the fuse is OK; if it stays at *infinity*

(∞), the fuse is blown. Use the VOM in the same way to test for continuity through any wire or component, touching the probes to the opposite ends of the electrical connector (juice path) you want to test.

Let's play with the VOM for a while. With the selector knob set at the RX1K position, touch the two probes together. The needle goes to 0 so there's no resistance to the flow of electricity and you have continuity. Check a paper clip, belt buckle, or anything metal that isn't connected to a source of electricity. If the needle goes to the 0 on the OHMS scale, you have continuity. If the needle doesn't move, there is no continuity or you're testing something that's nonconductive (incapable of carrying electricity). If the needle moves part way toward the 0 and stops, electricity is capable of flowing through the object, but there's a resistance to the flow (see Step 4).

Step 4. Test for Resistance

Some wires and electrical gizmos on your Soob are designed to have a certain amount of resistance to the flow of electricity. For instance, the coil and spark plug wires on most Soobs have a built in resistance factor to help eliminate electrical static on the radio. The wires work fine as long as the resistance is within a prescribed range, but when the resistance becomes greater than it's supposed to be, the current flowing through the wires to the coil or spark plug(s) will be insufficient to "fire" the plug efficiently.

If you're handy with a VOM and have the Subaru workshop manual for your model, you can check the resistance of almost every wire and electrical component on the car, then compare your meter readings to the specifications in the manual. Space just doesn't allow me to include all the specifications for all the years and models. Anyway, here's how you use a VOM to check wires for resistance: Set up the VOM as described in Step 1. Now set the selector knob at RX1K. The R stands for resistance (to the flow of electricity), the X means times (as in multiplication), and the 1K stands for 1000. Touch the probes to the palm of your hand about 1" apart. Don't worry, you won't get zapped. If you have a sweaty palm, the needle will move just a little. A dry palm probably won't move the needle. Now lift off the probes, lick your palm and try again. The needle will probably move to about 200 on the OHMS scale. Multiple 200 times 1000(1K) and you get 200,000 ohms resistance in 1" of wet palm skin. If the probes are clean and you haven't used them on a battery, touch the probes to your tongue and see what the resistance is. There's probably less resistance on your tongue than your sweaty palm because more moisture is present (water is a good conductor).

I'm trying to figure out a way to use a VOM to measure the resistance of my kid to taking out the trash and making his bed. If anyone knows how to do this, please write me.

PROCEDURE 12: CHECK AND REPLACE IGNITION COIL

Condition: 12,000-mile tune-up; OR you're here from Chapter 9.

Tools and Materials: To check the coil: Friend, insulated pliers or a wooden spring-type clothes pin or thick rag, maybe a 12-volt test light. To replace the coil: Phillips screwdriver, 8mm and 10mm wrenches.

Remarks: The ignition coil is a black cylinder about 5 inches long. It's located just to the rear of the battery. There might be a white ceramic gizmo (a ballast resistor) and/or a small box (the control unit for electronic ignition) mounted piggyback on the coil. A thick wire connects one end of the coil to the center of the distributor cap. One or more smaller wires are attached to posts on each side of where the thick wire connects to the coil.

Step 1. Check Coil.

Engine OFF. Pull the thick center wire (the coil wire) from the top of the distributor cap. Roll the rubber boot away from the end, then hold the wire with insulated pliers, a wooden clothespin, or a thick rag. Don't use your bare hands; the results could be painfully shocking. (In an emergency you can use two plastic handled screwdrivers like chop sticks to hold the wire.) Have Friend put the transmission in neutral and turn the engine over with the key while you hold the end of the coil wire about ¼" (6mm) away from any *bare* metal surface **except**

the carburetor or fuel pump! A hot blue-white spark should jump from the tip of the wire to the bare metal (the ground). If the spark is a weak sickly orange, the coil is shot and must be replaced. A strong but yellow spark that can jump the gap indicates the coil is going around the bend toward old age but will last a while yet.

If there's no spark at all, check the two small posts on either side of where the large wire plugs into the end of the coil. Are the small wires securely attached to the posts? Wiggle them to be sure. Turn the ignition key to ON, then touch one end of a 12-volt test light to the positive (+) wire post on the coil. (It's usually marked with a + and is the one closest to the front of the car.) Touch the other end of the test light to bare metal. The test light will light up if the coil is getting juice. No juice? The ignition circuit isn't being supplied with electricity. Check the fusible links (if your model has them) and the ignition fuse (usually marked IGN) in the fuse box (Procedure 2). If the fuses are good but no juice is getting to the coil, the ignition switch is suspect. Have Subaru or a garage check it and replace it for you, if broken.

If the coil is getting juice but a spark didn't jump the gap from the coil wire to ground, pull the coil wire out of the end of the coil and check the wire and its socket for corrosion. Use a wire brush to clean them if need be. Is the socket on the coil cracked or chipped? If so, replace the coil. If you have a VOM check the coil wire for resistance to see if it's broken (Procedure 11).

Evaluation: If the coil is getting juice, isn't cracked or corroded, and the coil wire is in good condition but no spark will jump the gap, the coil is kaput. Step 2 tells you how to replace it.

Step 2. Replace Coil.

Disconnect the clamp from the negative (-) battery post (Procedure 1, Step 3).

Before removing the old coil, transfer the wires one at a time from the old coil to the same position (+ or - terminal) on the new coil.

A large flat clamp around the center of the coil holds it in place.

'75-'77 models: Use a phillips screwdriver and 10mm wrench to loosen the long thin bolt going through the top of the clamp. Slide the old coil out of the clamp and insert the new coil. Tighten the phillips clamp screw while holding the nut with a 10mm wrench. Check the electrical connections to be sure they're tight.

'78 and newer models: Remove the two phillips screws that attach the coil clamp to the car's body. Note any other things that are held in place by the two screws. When the clamp is free, use a phillips screwdriver and 10mm wrench to loosen the long thin clamp bolt that goes through the clamp beneath the coil. Slide the old coil out of the clamp and install the new one. Hold the clamp nut with a 10mm wrench while you tighten the phillips clamp screw. Position the coil clamp on the car body, then install and tighten the two phillips mounting screws. Be sure anything else held in place by the screws is securely attached.

EVERYONE: Reattach and tighten the clamp on the negative (-) battery post. Do the spark jump test again to see what a good spark looks like. Fit the coil wire back into the center of the distributor.

PROCEDURE 13: CHECK AND REPLACE SPARK PLUG WIRES

Eventually the insulation in the spark plug wires wears out, the wires break, or the connections on the ends get broken. It's an easy and satisfying job to replace them.

Condition: Spark plug wires are worn out or broken.

Tools and Materials: To check the wires: a Volt/Ohm meter. To replace the wires: new set of wires.

Remarks: If possible, buy a set of spark plug wires that are designed for Subarus. (NGK makes nice Subaru spark plug wires.) The wires in generic "one size fits all" four-cylinder replacement sets are generally much longer than necessary. When installed they look awful and are frequently in the way while you are working on the engine.

Step 1. Check Spark Plug Wires.

Set up your VOM to check for resistance (Procedure 11, Step 4). The knob should be at set at RX1K. Remove the distributor cap (Chapter 7, Procedure 6, Step 2).

Disconnect the #1 spark plug wire from the #1 spark plug. Stick one of the VOM probes into the *spark plug end* of the wire so it's touching the metal end. Now touch the other probe to the *metal post* inside the distributor cap that corresponds to the #1 spark plug wire. The needle on the meter should move toward the zero end of the scale.

OHV models: If your Soob has *resistor spark plug wires* (and most of them do these days) the needle will stop at around 4 or 5 on the scale. Multiply the number on the scale by 1,000 (RX1K) to see how much resistance is in the wire and distributor cap. With resistor wires you should have about 4,000-5,000 ohms resistance. If the resistance is more than 15,000 ohms or the needle doesn't move (wiggle the probes around to be sure), the wire is shot. Non-resistor wires should have 0 (zero) resistance.

OHC models: The resistance for the coil and spark plug wires should be within the following values:

	Carb models	MPFI	SPFI
Coil wire	2.33-2.54	2.33-5.67	2.43-5.67
Wire #1	9.10-21.24	9.58-22.36	8.38-19.56
Wire #2	2.99-6.97	2.99-6.97	2.99-6.97
Wire #3	8.14-19.00	9.58-22.36	7.90-18.44
Wire #4	2.41-5.62	2.41-5.62	2.41-5.62

EVERYONE: Check all four spark plug wires the same way. If any wires are defective, replace all of them (see Remarks). Step 2 tells you how. Install the distributor cap (Chapter 7, Procedure 9, Step 9).

Step 2. Replace Spark Plug Wires.

Arrange the new spark plug wires according to length. Replace the wires one at a time so they don't get mixed up. Be sure the wires are securely fastened in the plastic holders (looms) on the engine. This would be a good time to use tape and an indelible marking pen to label each end of the wires with the appropriate cylinder number. A new coil wire usually comes with spark plug wire sets. Install it if you have it.

PROCEDURE 14: FIX HORN

The horn is an electromagnetic noise-making device. Here's how it works. A "hot" wire from the positive (+) battery post goes through the fuse box to a wire terminal on the horn. The ground wire, to complete the circuit, runs from another wire terminal on the horn up through the hollow steering rod to the horn button. Pushing on the horn button touches the end of the ground wire to bare metal completing the circuit and the horn goes BEEP. If your horn ever starts to blow without your consent and keeps blowing, the ground wire is shorting out somewhere between the horn and button. To stop the racket, disconnect the two wires from the horn. Or if one of your horns is located behind the grille, remove the horn fuse so you don't have to listen to it while you're removing the grille to get to the wires. Be sure to reinstall the fuse after disconnecting the wires because other electrical things are probably also on the horn circuit.

Subaru horns are about the size and shape of small pancakes. They're round (about 4″ in diameter), thin, and have two wires attached with push-on connectors. Some Subaru models have only one horn (high tone), but most have two (high and low tone). Thus some Soobs are hornier than others. The horns have migrated around over the years so here's a directory to find them:

'75-'79 cars and '77-'81 Brats: The horns (high and low tones) are in the engine compartment mounted on the front of the left strut tower.

'80-'82 cars and '82 Brats: A high tone horn is behind the grille next to the left headlight. If your model has two horns, a low tone horn is just in front of the battery.

'83 and newer OHV models: A high tone horn is in the engine compartment just to the rear of the left headlight. If your model has two horns, a low tone horn is behind the center of the grille.

OHC models: There is a horn mounted behind each headlight assembly. On XT models, the horn is behind the front bumper.

Condition: Horn doesn't work; OR the sound of the horn has changed indicating one horn isn't working.

Tools and Materials: Depending on the problem you might need some or all of the following: sandpaper or wire brush, new horn fuse, 12-volt test light or VOM, two lengths of wire, Friend, new (or used) horn(s).

Remarks: If the sound of your horn has changed, one of the horns has quit working (if you have two) or the horn adjustment has changed (see Step 4).

You can probably find a used horn in a salvage yard and save some money. Be sure the horn has the same high or low tone as your old one.

Step 1. Check Fuse, Wire Connections, and Mounting Nut.

Check the fuse for the horn (Procedure 2, Step 1) and replace it if necessary. Try the horn now. Still not working? If one of your horns is behind the grille, remove the phillips screws around the outer edge of the grille to remove it. Set the grille someplace where it won't get stepped on. If your horns are behind the headlight assembly, you'll have to remove the headlight bulbs and the cradle they are mounted in. On XT models, you have to remove the front bumper to get to the horns.

Locate the horn and wiggle the wires off each connection. Use sandpaper or a wire brush to clean the wire terminals. Reconnect the wires, then try the horn again. Still not working? Tap the horn with a small hammer or screwdriver handle. Sometimes the plate which vibrates inside the horn and makes the noise gets stuck, and the tapping just might free it. Try the horn again. Still won't beep? Have Friend repeatedly push and release the horn button while you touch the horn(s). If the horn is getting juice you'll feel and probably hear a click. If the horn clicks you can skip down to Step 3 to hot wire the horn. No click? Do Step 2.

If the horn is loose in its bracket, the adjusting screw in the rear of the horn might be too far out of adjustment for the horn to work. Here's how you adjust the screw. Use a crescent wrench to remove the large nut that attaches the horn to the bracket, then pull the horn away from the bracket. Disconnect the wires to the other horn (if you have two) so you'll know which horn you're listening to. Use your fingers or a screwdriver to gently turn the large screw into the horn (clockwise) until it stops. Don't force it in. Try the horn button while turning the large screw counterclockwise ½ turn at a time until it's all the way out. If the horn works when the screw is in a certain position, adjust the screw so the horn is loudest, then fit the screw through the hole in the mounting bracket. Install and tighten the large nut without allowing the screw to turn. You might need Friend to hold the horn while you hold the screw with a screwdriver in the slotted end while tightening the nut. Reconnect the wires to the horn(s). Install the grille if you removed it.

Step 2. Check for Juice at Horn.

Use a 12-volt test light or VOM (set at 15 volts DC) to check the two wires that attach to the horn (Procedure 5, Step 2). One of the wires should light up the test light or show about 12 volts on the VOM. If there's juice in one of the wires, skip down to Step 3. No juice? Check the fuse holder for the horn fuse to see if there's juice on both sides of the fuse (Procedure 2, Step 2). If there's no juice at the fuse holder, the wire between the battery (or fusible links) and fuse box is broken. If there's juice on both sides of the fuse holder when the fuse is installed but there's no juice at the horn connection, the wire between the fuse box and horn is broken. Procedure 5, Step 3, tells you how to trace wires in search of a short. If you can't locate the problem, have Subaru or a garage deal with it.

Step 3. "Hot Wire" Horn.

The is the final check to see whether the horn is broken or there's a problem in the wiring.

Reconnect only the horn wire with juice to its terminal on the horn. Leave the other wire disconnected. Strip about ½" of insulation from the ends of a piece of wire that's long enough to reach from the open horn terminal to bare metal on the car body or engine. Hook one end of the wire to the open wire terminal on the horn, then touch the other end of that wire to bare metal. If there's no sound, try reversing the two wires on the wire terminals of the horn. Ground the wire again. Still no sound? The horn is shot and must be replaced (Step 4). If hot wiring the horn made it toot, the horn is OK but the wiring from the horn to the button on the steering wheel is defective. Go through Steps 1 and 2 again, or take the car to Subaru or a garage.

Step 4. Replace Horn(s).

If the horn you're replacing is behind the grille, remove the phillips screws around the edge of the grille and lift it off. Set it someplace where it won't get stepped on.

The horn is attached to a flat metal strap that is bolted to the car body. Disconnect the wires from the wire terminals on the horn, then use a 12mm wrench to remove the bolt from the flat metal strap. The horn is now liberated.

Position the new (or used) horn the same as the old one, then install and tighten the mounting bolt. Attach the wires to the terminals on the horn. Push the horn button to be sure it's working. BEEP! BEEP!

Now install whatever you had to remove to get to the horns.

CHAPTER 11
FUEL SYSTEMS

Every time you buy gas for your car and drive it, you're committing a political act. You're turning *MONEY* into *POWER*, and isn't that what politics is all about? However, by using simple physics rather than politics, your car makes the conversion in a more predictable, rational, and efficient manner. Here's how it works on a Subaru.

CARBURETOR, FUEL INJECTION, AND TURBO SYSTEMS

The gasoline in the **tank** is pumped to the engine through metal and rubber **fuel lines** by an **electric fuel pump**. On its way to the engine, the gas passes through a replaceable **fuel filter** which removes rust, bugs, and other debris that could clog the system. '82 and newer carburetor models have an additional replaceable **vapor separator**.

The liquid gasoline pumped to the engine is flammable and will burn easily and quickly, but just being flammable won't make the engine run. The stored energy in the gasoline must be mixed with the air drawn in through the **air cleaner** in a precise ratio to create an **EXPLOSIVE** mixture. On carb models, the **carburetor** accomplishes this feat with jets, venturi tubes, floats, float bowls, and other tiny parts. Fuel injection models have electronically controlled **fuel injector(s)** that squirt a precise amount of fuel into the cylinders relative to such things as engine speed, throttle position, engine temperature. See Chapter 4: *How A Subaru Works*, for a complete explanation of how fuel and air are combined into an explosive mixture.

Your carburetor (carb for short) or fuel injection system are very delicate and sensitive instruments, yet they can work well for many years, forever maybe, if proper maintenance procedures are followed. Besides things like a five-pound sledge hammer, dirt and rust are their two main enemies. Dirty air and/or fuel can clog the tiny passages inside the carburetor or injection system and cause the fuel/air ratio to get out of whack so the car won't run well, or at all. By inspecting the *air* and *fuel filters* frequently, and replacing them when they become contaminated, you can extend the life of your fuel system indefinitely.

ORIENTATION: WHICH SETUP DO YOU HAVE?

All '75-'81 models and '85 and newer OHC carb models have Hitachi carbs. '82 and newer OHV Soobs have either a Hitachi or a Carter/Weber carburetor, or a Turbo/fuel injection setup. '85 and newer fuel injected models have Single Port Fuel Injection (SPFI) or Multi Point Fuel Injection (MPFI). Some MPFI models also have a Turbocharger (Turbo).

Here's how to tell the difference between a Hitachi and a Carter/Weber carburetor. Remove the air cleaner (Chapter 7, Procedure 5, Step 4), then have Friend get in the car and pump the gas pedal while you watch the sides of the carburetor. On one side you'll see a cable rotating a rounded lever. If the lever is on the right (passenger's) side of the carb, you have a Hitachi carb. If the lever is on the left (driver's side), you have a Carter/Weber.

If you have fuel injection, the air cleaner housing will be located in the right front corner of the engine compartment. Models with Single Port Fuel Injection have a throttle body on the top center of the engine. It looks a lot like a carburetor. On Multi Point Fuel Injection models you'll see a fuel injector with a fuel line and electric wire connector sprouting from its top mounted near each spark plug. MPFI will probably be prominently displayed somewhere in the engine compartment.

If you have fuel injection, and still aren't sure which type you have, see the Year and Model Variations section of Chapter 1, and/or look at the sticker on the underside of the hood.

HITACHI CARBURETORS

On Hitachi-equipped Soobs, there are two vertical holes, called **barrels**, going through the carburetor, one right behind the other. Since there are two barrels, you have what's called a *two-barrel carb*. The slightly smaller barrel closest to the front of the car is the *primary system* (sometimes called the 1st stage). It operates when starting the engine and while driving under light to moderate conditions. When you push the gas pedal more than halfway to the floor (or "put the pedal to the metal") the larger rear barrel, called the *secondary system* (second stage) of the carb comes into action. This allows you to drive economically on the smaller primary system until you need the power to pass a car, drive up a steep hill, or do something silly like race a Porsche, when more fuel and air (power) are needed.

'80 California Soobs, all '81-'82 models, and all '83-'84 California carb models and non-4WD, non-California models (whew!) have electronically controlled carburetors (ECCs) to help reduce harmful exhaust emissions. ('83-'84 4WD non-California and Canadian Soobs don't have electronically controlled carbs.) On models with ECCs, the fuel mixture is regulated by a small *computer* (the "brain") located under the dashboard in front of the driver's seat (it's behind the driver's seat only on '81 Brats). Here's how it works. Signals from sensors on the engine and exhaust system go to the brain where they are analyzed, then the brain sends signals to *duty solenoids* that regulate the air/fuel ratio (duty ratio) in the carburetor.

Fuel Systems 207

CARTER/WEBER CARBURETORS

The Carter/Weber carb is an electronically controlled one-barrel carb. Sensors on the engine and exhaust system send signals to a computer ("brain") located under the dashboard in front of the driver's seat. The brain analyzes the signals from the sensors, then sends signals to a duty solenoid valve that adjusts the air/fuel ratio of the carb for different driving conditions (idle, acceleration, etc.). Procedure 12 tells you how to remove and install Carter/Weber carbs. I haven't included a Carter/Weber rebuild for two reasons: (1) there aren't that many around, and (2) they seem very durable and seldom cause problems.

FUEL INJECTION SYSTEMS

I'll describe how the fuel injection systems work even though how to repair them isn't covered in this manual. Tune-up and lubrication of fuel-injected and Turbo models is included in Chapter 7. If you suspect something is wrong with the Turbo or fuel injection system, take the car to Subaru or a garage that specializes in Soobs. Here's how the systems work.

Single Port Fuel Injection (SPFI): This system utilizes a single **fuel injector** mounted inside a **throttle chamber**, which is bolted to the top center of the intake manifold, just like a carburetor. In fact, it looks a lot like a carburetor. The volume and density of air being drawn into the engine is measured by a **Hot-and-Cold wire system** located in the **airflow meter**, which is mounted on the engine side of the air cleaner housing. The **cold wire** measures the temperature of air flowing into the engine, then sends this information to the **hot wire**. The hot wire, also located in the airflow meter, measures the amount of air flowing through the meter by utilizing the heat transfer phenomenon between the incoming air and the hot wire (heating resistor). In other words, the more air flowing in, the more it cools the wire. The hot wire sends an electric signal to the computer to let it know how cool it is and thus how much air is being drawn into the engine. The computer also receives electronic signals from other sensors that tell it such things as throttle position, coolant temperature, exhaust oxygen content, crankshaft angle, engine rpm, if the starter is in operation, if the air conditioner is on, and if the transmission is in gear. As the signals are received, the computer calculates the optimum amount of fuel needed by the engine, then sends a signal to the fuel injector, telling it how much gas to squirt into the engine.

Multi Point Fuel Injection (MPFI): This system has four **fuel injectors** mounted in the cylinder heads or intake manifold near the intake valves (six injectors on six cylinder engines). A **hot-wire system**, similar to the hot and cold wire system used on SPFI models, measures the volume of air passing through the airflow meter, then sends the information in the form of an electrical signal to the computer. The computer incorporates the airflow data with information from other sensors such as throttle position, coolant temperature, crankshaft position, engine rpm and exhaust oxygen content, then sends signals to the fuel injectors to let them know how much gas to squirt into each cylinder.

SPFI and MPFI: The computer for the fuel injection systems can "learn" the driving habits of the owner and react to them, as well as automatically compensate for wear of various components within the system. Although these high-tech systems sound complicated, in terms of efficiency, reliability, and exhaust emission control, fuel injection is a great improvement over a carburetor.

TURBOCHARGERS

Turbochargers are available on certain models that also have MPFI. The turbo unit (turbocharger) is driven by the engine's exhaust gas. Basically what a turbocharger does is force the fuel and air mixture into the cylinders ("packs" it), rather than relying on atmospheric pressure and vacuum created by the pistons to fill the cylinders. Here's how the turbo works.

On its way to the exhaust pipe, the exhaust gas passes through a **turbine housing** causing a windmill-like **turbine wheel** to spin. The turbine wheel is attached via a shaft to a **compressor impeller** located in a separate **compressor housing**. The compressor impeller sucks air through the air cleaner and forces it through the **throttle body** and into the cylinders. As engine speed increases, more exhaust gas is created so the turbine automatically turns faster to meet the engine's demands. The turbine wheel/compressor impeller speed varies between approximately 20,000 and 130,000 revolutions per minute! Servicing the turbo unit should be left to the professionals because a misadjusted turbo can quickly ruin the engine.

ECS: HIGH-TECH SELF-DIAGNOSING CAPABILITY ON FUEL INJECTED MODELS

Starship Subarus with fuel injection have an onboard computer called the **Electronic Control System (ECS)** that is capable of diagnosing problems in the electrical sensors and components related to the fuel injection systems.

I'll explain how the ECS works because it's so fascinating (to me anyway) and is probably an indication of how high-technology gizmos will be involved in automotive diagnosis in the future. Before long our cars will probably speak to us when something is wrong. (Can you imagine getting in your Soob, turning the ignition switch on and hearing a voice say, "Not now, darling, I have a headache.") To do these checks yourself, you'll need the Subaru workshop manual for your year model so you can look up the code number for the various components. Here's how the ECS works.

If there's a problem in one of the electrical sensors or components, the ECS light on the dash goes on. To locate the problem, two "test mode" wire connectors must be snapped together, which puts the ECS system into its test mode. The unit checks the performance of all components related to the fuel injection system, then blinks a Morse code signal for any faulty components that it detected.

The *ECS diagnosing light* (it's also the exhaust 02 monitoring light) is on the black box right below the steering column. I call the black box the "brain" but Subaru calls it the **SPFI Control Unit** on models with SPFI or the **Electronic Controlled Gasoline Injection (EGI)** system on MPFI models.

This high-tech stuff is nifty, eh? It's great for identifying which system has a problem, but it doesn't tell you which part of the system is broken—whether it's the electrical component, the wiring for the component, or maybe even the ECS unit itself. The Subaru workshop manuals devote pages and pages of flow charts to diagnosing the various engine electrical systems using a volt/ohm meter and dwell meter. If you're electrically inclined, buy the workshop manual for your year and model, let the ECS diagnose which system is malfunctioning and follow the flow charts. Otherwise, have Subaru diagnose the problem and replace the faulty part for you.

EVAPORATIVE CONTROL SYSTEM

An elaborate **Evaporative Control System** has been added to the fuel system to help your Soob meet smog control standards. This system simply captures gasoline fumes before they evaporate into the atmosphere, then either returns them to the gas tank where they condense to a liquid again or allows them to be sucked into the intake manifold of the engine so they can be sucked into the cylinders and burned. Except for inspecting the rubber hoses and checking the **charcoal canister** for cracks and changing its filter occasionally (Chapter 12), the system is pretty much maintenance-free and rarely causes problems. Isn't that nice?

CARBURETOR PROBLEMS

If your Soob starts misbehaving suddenly, or dies and won't start no matter how much you beg and plead with it (or cuss at it), follow the troubleshooting chart in Chapter 9. You will be referred back here at the appropriate time.

The fuel system is easy to check, so before tearing into the carburetor or fuel injection system because the engine doesn't run right, go through Procedures 1, 2, 4 and 6 in this chapter, to do some simple tests to locate the problem. Do a carburetor rebuild or replace the carburetor only as a last resort.

If it's determined the carburetor is faulty, the carburetor can be removed, then rebuilt ('75-'79 models) or replaced with a new or factory rebuilt unit. Procedures 7 and 10 tell you how to remove and install Hitachi carbs. Procedures 8 and 9 tell you step-by-step how to rebuild a '75-'79 Hitachi carb. If you're broken down in the boonies and determine the carburetor is the problem, Procedure 11 tells you how to remove the carb top and check the **needle valve and seat** (the most likely cause of your problem). Procedure 11 also includes a "quicky" rebuild for those of you who don't feel up to a full-scale rebuild. If you're looking for more power, see Chapter 18, Procedure 2: *High Performance Parts*.

Rebuilding your carb will require relaxed determination and attention to detail. It'll take at least a full day counting mental health breaks. Don't try to rebuild the thing the night before a Monte Carlo rally; wait until you have peace and quiet...and time. The work is really more like fine watch repair than car repair, and you'll need an uncluttered, clean place in which to work.

In case you're interested, in Chapter 4: *How A Subaru Works*, there's a great (in my opinion) description of how the carburetor atomizes (mixes) the fuel and air as they pass through the barrels. There's more about the electronically controlled carburetors in Chapter 12: *Exhaust and Emissions Control Systems*.

CAUTION! FIRE WARNING: When doing anything with the fuel system, be aware that a spark could turn your Soob into a large black ugly mess. When I tell you to disconnect the battery, please do so; this will eliminate sparks made by accidentally touching live wires to metal. Please read Chapter 3, and keep a fire extinguisher handy.

PROCEDURE 1: CHECK AND REPLACE AIR FILTER

Condition: Regular 6,000-mile maintenance; OR you just went through a Texas-type dust storm; OR your engine seems sluggish and the gas mileage has taken a nosedive.

Tools and Materials: Maybe a new air filter element, '75 models require a 10mm wrench.

   Step 1. Do It.

Turn to Chapter 7, Procedure 4, Step 3, to check and/or replace the air filter element.

PROCEDURE 2: CHECK AND REPLACE FUEL FILTER (All Models) AND VAPOR SEPARATOR ('82 and newer OHV models).

Condition: Regular 12,000-mile maintenance; OR fuel isn't getting to the carburetor; OR the fuel in the gas tank is contaminated.

Tools and Materials: Maybe a new fuel filter, maybe a new vapor separator ('82 and newer OHV models). Depending on the clamps, you will need either a regular or phillips screwdriver, or pliers, and a rag or two.

To check the filter on '82 and newer models and converted '81 models (see Step 1) you'll need a jack and jackstand. To change the filter on these models you'll need Vise Grips and an extra rag.

Remarks: If it's been 24,000 miles since you replaced the filter, don't bother checking it, replace it.

CAUTION: The smoking lamp is OUT. Keep smokers busy making sandwiches or something while you replace the fuel filter. **Fuel-injected models:** Release the pressure in the fuel system before changing the filter (Step 4).

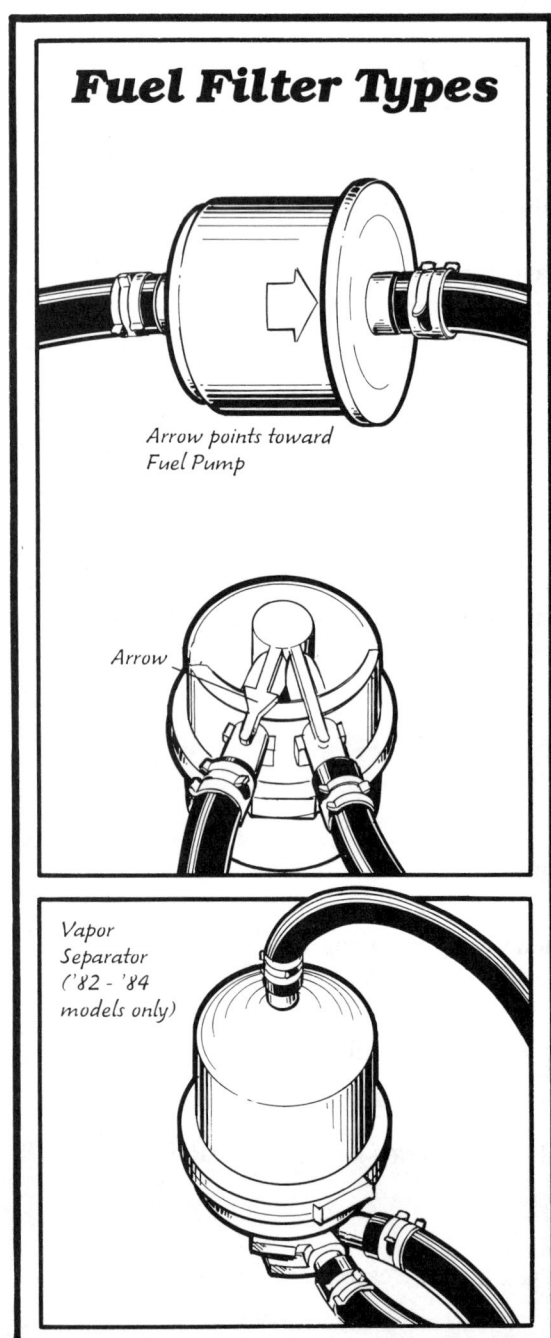

Arrow points toward Fuel Pump

Arrow

Vapor Separator ('82 - '84 models only)

Step 1. Locate and Check Fuel Filter.

Look at the fuel filter illustrations so you'll know what you're looking for. Be sure the ignition key is OFF.

'75-'79 models and '80 Brats: The fuel filter can be found on the shelf in the right rear corner of the engine compartment.

'80-'81 models (except Brat): The filter is in the left rear corner of the engine compartment.

Converted '81 models: If you have an '81 and can't find the filter, don't panic; it's been moved to the bottom of the car just in front of the left rear wheel.

Carb models '82 and newer, '81-'87 Brats: The fuel filter is located under the car in front of one of the rear wheels.

Fuel-injected models: The filter is in the left rear corner of the engine compartment. It's a soup-size metal can with a hose attached to each end. Since it's metal you can't see inside to check it, so just replace it at least every 24,000 miles. Skip down to Step 4 to replace the filter. Be sure to release the pressure in the system before removing the hose clamps!

Carb models: To check the fuel filter, pull it out of its clip-type holder and look through the plastic for signs of dirt and crud, especially on the bottom. If you see any dark residue or little chunks of stuff in the gas, replace the filter (Step 2). If the filter is clean, snap it back into the holder. You can't check a metal fuel filter—just replace it every 12,000 miles, or sooner if you suspect it's dirty. You can replace the metal filters with plastic filters except on fuel-injected models.

Step 2. Replace Fuel Filter (carb models only).

Before removing the old filter, make a mental note or draw a picture of which hose connects to the *outlet* end of the filter. You'll see an *arrow* pointing to the outlet tube. The hoses must connect to the same places on the new filter. Have some rags handy to mop up any spilled gas. After replacing the filter, start the engine and check for gas leaks. Replace the clamps or hoses if they're cracked, leaky, or broken.

Fuel filter in engine compartment (except fuel-injected models): Depending on your type of hose clamps, loosen them with a regular or phillips screwdriver or pliers. Just do the two clamps right next to the filter. On the wire type where you need pliers, just squeeze on the two tabs and slide 'em back with the pliers. Slide the clamps away from the filter a few inches. Hold the filter while you twist the hoses off the connections. Put the hoses on the new filter (be sure the arrow is pointing toward the hose that runs to the fuel pump), then slide the clamps to the end of the hoses where they used to be, and tighten them if they're screw type. Tighten them snug but not so tight you risk breaking the clamps. Push the filter into the holder clips. Start the engine and check for leaks.

Fuel filter under car: Put the gearshift in 1st or PARK, set the handbrake, chock the front wheels, jack up the rear end of the car and put it on jackstands. Put your safety glasses on, grab the new filter, your Vise Grips and several rags, then crawl under the car. Find the filter and note where the two hoses attached to the filter go. One hose from the filter goes to the *fuel pump* and the other hose goes to a metal pipe from the *gas tank*. Put a few folded layers of a rag over the hose between the filter and gas tank pipe, then use your Vise Grips to pinch the hose closed a few inches from its end. Be sure the rag is between the grips and hose, protecting the hose from the teeth in the Vise Grip jaws and don't set the Vise Grips any tighter than necessary.

Once the fuel line is pinched, loosen the two hose clamps at the filter and slide them away from the filter a couple of inches. Locate your body so your face isn't under the fuel pump. Gasoline in the eyes, ears, or mouth is a big league bummer so work at arm's length. Twist the hoses off the old filter. Slide the hoses on the new filter (be sure the arrow on the new filter is pointing toward the hose going to the fuel pump), then slide the clamps into position and tighten them if they have screws. Squeeze the tabs on the other type to free it so it can slide. Release the Vise Grips, remove the folded rag, then slip the filter into its holder.

Wipe up any gas that spilled, slide out from under the car, then lower the car to the ground. Start the engine and check for leaks around the filter and where you clamped the hose.

Step 3. Replace Vapor Separator (converted '81 models and '82 and newer OHV models).

The **vapor separator** is located in the left rear corner of the engine compartment. It looks a lot like a fuel filter except it has a third hose connection attached to the domed top. Replace it when you replace the fuel filter.

Pull the vapor separator out of its holder. Loosen the three hose clamps and slide them out of the way. Note where each hose goes, then twist and pull them off the old separator. Put the hoses on the new separator, slide the clamps into their original position, and tighten them if they have tightening screws. Fit the separator into its holder, then start the engine and check for leaks.

Step 4. Replace Fuel Filter on Fuel-Injected Models.

Fuel filters for Turbo models are very important to the long life of the fuel-injection system. If you neglect the filter, you'll pay for it later in injectors.

Since the fuel system is under high pressure, you have to release the pressure before removing the fuel filter hoses. If the ends of the hoses or hose clamps are getting funky, replace them with new ones while you're changing the filter. Be sure to get *high pressure* fuel line hoses.

Before removing the fuel filter, first set the handbrake, put the gearshift in PARK, block the front wheels, jack up the *right rear* corner of the car, then lower it onto a jackstand. Put on your safety glasses and slide under the rear of the car. The fuel pump is shaped like a short tube of sausage and is mounted

Fuel Filter for Fuel Injected Models

in front of the right rear wheel. It's on a little square shelf on cars, and mounted to the frame on Brats. Follow the wires coming out of one end of the pump to a wire connector. Disconnect the pull-apart-type connector.

Slide out from under the car, be sure the gearshift is in PARK, then use the ignition key to crank the engine for at least five seconds. If the engine starts, let it run until it dies. You've now released the pressure in the fuel line. Turn the key OFF. Now you can replace the fuel filter. Be sure you're using a fuel-injection filter; the plastic ones can't withstand the pressure and will burst!

Pull the filter out of its holder. Loosen the screws on the clamps and slide the clamps out of the way. Twist and pull the hoses off. Install the hoses onto the new filter just as they were on the old filter. The curved fitting on the Turbo filter goes toward the *rear* of the car. Fit the filter into the holder and check that the hoses aren't kinked. Slide the clamps to their original positions and tighten them.

Crawl under the car again and reconnect the wire to the fuel pump. Crawl out and lower the car, then start the engine and check for fuel leaks around the filter.

PROCEDURE 3: CHECK AND REPLACE ACCELERATOR CABLE

The accelerator cable is the vital link between the gas pedal and the carburetor. It consists of a woven wire cable inside a thicker black *cable housing*—the whole works is usually just called the accelerator cable.

Condition: Engine will start and idle, but won't speed up when you step on the gas pedal.

Tools and Materials: Maybe a new accelerator cable, 10mm open end wrench, medium phillips screwdriver, regular pliers, and a flashlight. Some models require an 8mm wrench.

Remark: Before buying a new cable, check the old one to see if it's broken or has just come loose. If it's loose, we can probably reconnect and/or tighten it. If it's broken, remove it and take it with you to the Subaru parts department when you buy a new one.

Step 1. Check Accelerator Cable.

Carb models: Remove the air cleaner (Chapter 7, Procedure 5, Step 4).

EVERYONE: Check the illustration to see where and how the cable is attached to the carburetor. Open your hood up and compare. You'll notice that the cable on '75-'79 models is clamped to the **throttle arm** (lever) with a nut or screw and on '80 and newer models the cables are hooked to the throttle arm with a little metal cylinder.

First, let's see if the cable is still correctly and firmly attached to the carb (or *throttle plate* on fuel injected models). Pull on the exposed wire cable between the **cable housing clamp** and the throttle lever.

'75-'79 models: If the wire cable end is just loose in the clamp at the bottom front of the throttle lever, adjust the cable, then tighten the clamp (Step 7).

EVERYONE: Is the cable in the groove of the throttle arm? If it isn't, slide the cable through the gap beside the metal tab on the outer edge of the throttle arm and into the groove. Check the gas pedal to see if you get some action now. If the end of the cable is broken off, or if the cable comes completely out of the black cable housing when you pull on it, the cable is broken and has to be replaced (Steps 2-8). However, if the cable only slides out of the housing a few inches then stops, it might still be intact but just unhooked from the gas pedal. Look under the dash at the top of the gas pedal to see if the end of the cable is still hooked into the slot. It's the same type connection as the '80-'84 carb connection—a little metal cylinder hooked into a slot. Connect it if it's unhooked (Step 5).

Check the black cable housing where it's clamped to a bracket on the engine and also where it goes through the firewall. The housing has to be clamped securely or the accelerator cable can't work properly. See Step 5 for the firewall clamp and Step 6 for the clamp on the engine.

Step 2. Disconnect Accelerator Cable from Throttle Arm.

'75-'79 models: On the right side of the throttle arm, hold the **clamp nut** the cable sticks through with a 10mm wrench while you loosen the phillips screw or 8mm nut that pinches the cable. Loosen it just enough so you can pull the cable out.

'80 and newer models: Rotate the top of the throttle arm toward the rear of the car (carb models), or toward the front of the car (fuel injected models). Hold it there while you align the wire cable with the slot in the side of the throttle arm. Slide the little metal cylinder on the cable's tip out of the throttle arm. You can disconnect one end of the *throttle return spring* if it's in your way.

Step 3. Release Cable Housing from Bracket.

'75-'79 models: Remove the phillips screw and clamp that secures the cable housing to the *bracket* a few inches behind the carb.

'80 and newer models: The cable housing is bolted to a *bracket* on the engine a few inches behind the throttle arm. Hold the metal part of the cable housing with pliers while you unscrew the 10mm nut on the front side of the bracket. Pull the cable housing toward the rear of the car until the cable can slide up through the slot in the bracket.

Step 4. Remove Accelerator Cable and Housing.

'75-'79 models: Use pliers to remove the *spring clip* that attaches the cable housing to the firewall in the engine compartment.

'80 and newer models: The cable housing is attached to the firewall with a *plastic clip*. From inside the car, use needlenose pliers to squeeze the sides of the clip so you can push it through the firewall and into the engine compartment.

EVERYONE: Look for the end of the cable inside the car under the dashboard. A flashlight helps. It's at the top end of the metal lever part of the gas pedal. Pull on the cable until you can line up the wire cable with the slot in the side of the lever. Slide the metal cylinder tip out of the lever.

'75-'79 models: Pull the cable housing through the firewall from inside the car.

'80 and newer models: Pull the cable housing through the firewall from the engine compartment.

Step 5. Attach Cable End to Gas Pedal Lever and Cable Housing to Firewall.

CAUTION: Don't kink or bend the new cable and housing during installation. A bent cable will bind in the housing causing premature wear and a scary, sticking accelerator.

'75-'79 models: From inside the car, push the cable housing through the hole in the firewall. If it won't go through the hole, try the other end. From the engine compartment, use pliers to insert the spring clip into the groove on the cable housing.

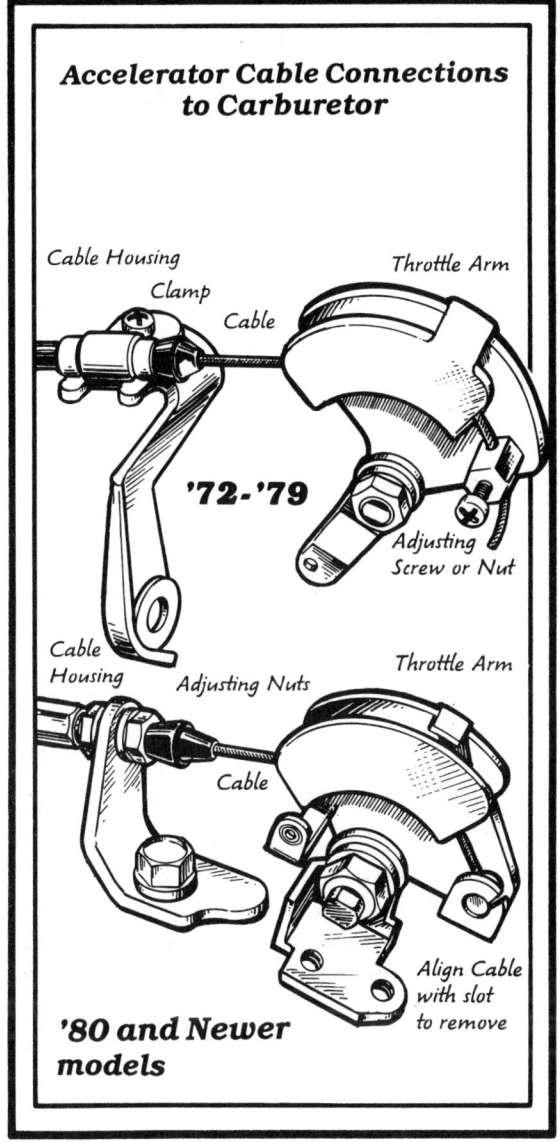

Accelerator Cable Connections to Carburetor

'80 and newer models: From the engine compartment, push the cable end with the black plastic clip through the hole in the firewall. Align the clip with the hole, then push it in until it locks into place.

EVERYONE: To attach the cable end to the gas pedal lever, align the wire cable with the slot in the pedal lever and insert the metal cylinder cable tip into its hole on the lever. Pull the cable toward the front of the car.

Step 6. Attach Accelerator Cable Housing to Bracket.

'75-'79 models: Thread the cable to the bracket on the engine so there are no sharp bends. Lay the metal end of the housing on the bracket. Install the clamp on the housing so the end of the clamp fits into the slot on the bracket, or so the tab on the clamp hangs over the rear edge of the bracket, depending on your clamp type. Install the phillips screw and tighten it.

'80 and newer models: Thread the cable housing to the bracket so there are no sharp bends. Install one 10mm nut onto the housing end, or unscrew one of the nuts off the cable end if there are two there. Slide the cable through the bracket slot, then pull forward on the housing so the threaded part goes through the bracket hole. Screw the other 10mm nut onto the cable housing but don't tighten it yet.

Step 7. Attach Accelerator Cable to Carburetor Throttle Arm.

'75-'79 models: Thread the cable through the groove in the throttle arm and into the little hole in the *clamp nut*.

'80 and newer models: Rotate the top of the throttle arm toward the rear of the car (carb models), or toward the front (fuel injected models). Hold it there while you thread the cable into the groove on the throttle arm. Align the cable with the slot in the arm, then slide the little metal cylinder on the end of the cable into the hole on the throttle arm. Let the top of the throttle arm rotate to the idle position. Be sure the cable stayed in the groove. Reconnect the throttle return spring if you unhooked it.

Step 8. Adjust Accelerator Cable Tension.

When properly adjusted, the cable should have about 1/8" slack ("give") when you push on the cable between the cable housing and throttle arm (see illustration). Before adjusting the cable tension, set the choke plate in the top of the carb to the OFF (vertical) position. If it flips back to the ON (horizontal) position while adjusting the cable tension, reset it to the OFF position. Here's how:

Carb models: Rotate the top of the throttle arm toward the rear of the car and hold it there while you reach into the top of the carb with a finger and push down on the front edge of the flat **choke plate** covering the front half of the opening. Hold the plate in a vertical position while you let go of the throttle arm. The choke plate will stay in the vertical position unless you rotate the throttle arm. If the choke plate flips closed while you're adjusting the cable, repeat this paragraph to set it in the horizontal position again.

'75-'79 models: Use pliers to pull the accelerator cable through the clamp nut, and hold it with a little tension. Now adjust the cable so it has about 1/8" of slack ("give") when you push down on the cable between the throttle arm and the housing clamp. (There's an illustration of this somewhere nearby.) When the slack is right, hold the 10mm nut on the throttle arm while you tighten the phillips screw or 8mm bolt.

'80 and newer models: The adjustment is made with the two 10mm nuts on the end of the cable housing. Screw the rear nut forward (turn the top of the nut toward the right fender) to tighten the cable and remove slack, OR screw the front nut toward the rear (turn the top of the nut toward the left fender) to loosen the cable and add slack.

To adjust the slack, first decide whether the cable is too loose or too tight and which nut you need to move to make the adjustment. Now screw the other nut a few turns away from the bracket and out of your way. Hold the smooth unthreaded metal part of the cable housing with pliers while you turn the nuts—you don't want the housing to get twisted. When the slack is correct, tighten the other nut against the bracket.

Step 9. Do This and That.

Carb models: Install the air cleaner (Chapter 7, Procedure 5, Step 5).

EVERYONE: Start the engine and let it warm up. Press the gas pedal a few times to be sure it operates smoothly. If it sticks, the housing is kinked or the wire cable is bent inside the housing. Can you see the problem? Remove the cable and install it again.

Check the idle speed and adjust it if need be (Chapter 7, Procedure 12, Steps 3-6). If the engine won't idle slow enough by adjusting the idle speed adjustment screw, give the cable a little more slack (Step 7), then set the idle speed.

PROCEDURE 4: CHECK FUEL SUPPLY AT CARBURETOR (Carb Models)

Condition: You were sent here from Chapter 9 because your car won't start, or starts but runs poorly.

Tools and Materials: Friend, 10mm wrench, pliers, rag, maybe a regular screwdriver or phillips screwdriver depending on the kind of fuel line hose clamp that's on the carburetor, 12-ounce beer or soft drink can with the top removed. **CAUTION:** There is a possibility that some gasoline will run out of the fuel line when you disconnect it from the carb. Place a rag under the connection to catch the gas. *NO SMOKING.*

Step 1. Remove Air Cleaner. (Chapter 7, Procedure 5, Step 4)

First, peek under the left side of the air cleaner for the round sight glass on the left side of the carb. A flashlight helps. If you can clearly view the sight glass, it won't be necessary to remove the air cleaner.

Step 2. Check Float Bowl for Gas.

Wipe off the little round *sight glass* on the left side of the carb and check the fuel level in the bowl. You'll see a round dot in the center of the glass. If fuel is in the bowl, you can see a horizontal line indicating the level. No fuel? Start the engine if possible, or crank it with the starter for about ten seconds. Turn the key to OFF. The electric fuel pump should fill the float bowl up to the dot on the sight glass. Still no fuel? Go to Step 3. If you can see fuel in the float bowl, the line should go through the dot on the glass, or at least be very close to the dot. If the fuel level is more than 1/16" (1.5mm) above or below the dot, do Procedure 11 to change the *float level*. If the fuel is at the proper level, let's see if the fuel pump is supplying a sufficient amount when the engine is running.

Step 3. Test for Fuel Supply at Carb.

CAUTION!: A spark near an open container of gas can cause a fire. While doing this test, hold the pop or beer can as far away from the engine as possible. If you have a jumper wire (a piece of insulated wire with alligator clips on each end), disconnect the coil wire from the top center of the distributor cap, clip one end of the jumper wire to the metal tip of the coil wire and clip the other end to bare metal away from the can. The **fuel supply hose** is on the top left rear corner of the carb. '80 and newer models have a Y connection with a smaller *fuel return hose* attached next to where the fuel inlet hose attaches to the carb (see illustration). Put a rag under the fitting to catch any gas that might dribble out of the hose.

Disconnect the fuel supply hose from the carb. It's attached with a *clamp* that you unscrew with a regular or phillips screwdriver, or a *clip* that you squeeze with pliers. Loosen the clip or clamp and

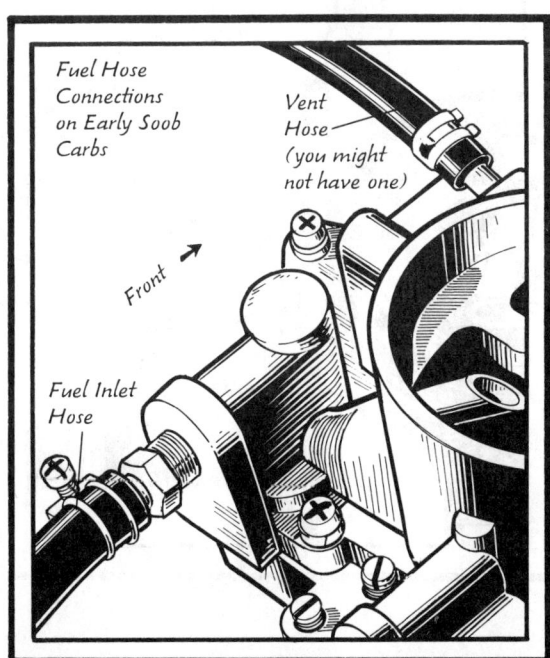

Fuel Hose Connections on Early Soob Carbs

Vent Hose (you might not have one)

Front

Fuel Inlet Hose

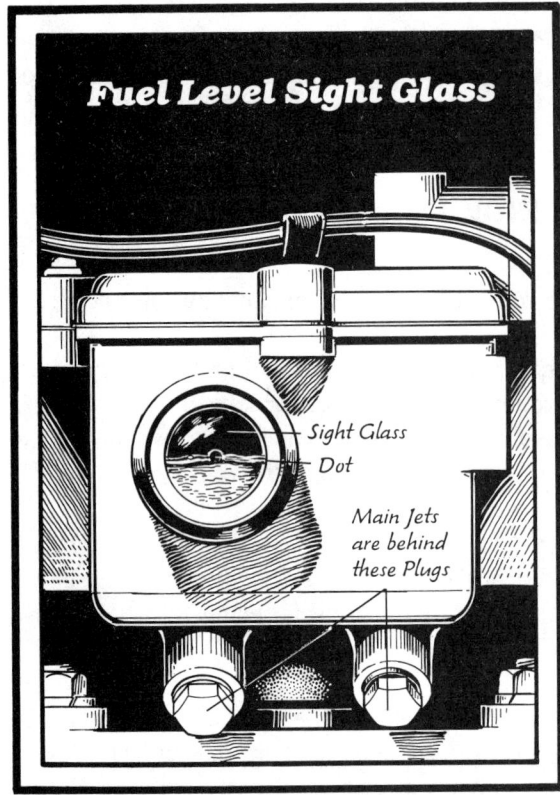

Fuel Level Sight Glass
- Sight Glass Dot
- Main Jets are behind these Plugs

Fuel Hose Connections on Late Hitachi Carbs
- Fuel Return Hose
- Switch Vent Solenoid
- Fuel Hose
- Vent Hose

slide it away from the carb. Grab the hose close to the fitting on the carb and twist and pull it off. Cut the top off a 12-ounce beer or pop can and stick the hose into the can.

Have Friend pull the handbrake ON and put the transmission in PARK or neutral. Hold the hose in the can while Friend turns the key ON and cranks the engine for ten seconds (time it with your digital watch). Have Friend turn the key to OFF. Measure the gasoline in the can. There should be between 1″ and 2″ of gas in the can. If there is, the fuel supply is sufficient so the problem isn't the fuel pump. Skip to Procedure 7. If there is less than 1″ of gas in the can, not enough fuel is being pumped to the carb. See Procedure 2, to check the *fuel filter* and *vapor separator* (if you have one). If they appear to be OK, let's check the fuel pump. Remove the jumper wire (if you used one) and reconnect the coil wire to the distributor cap. Reconnect the fuel hose to the carb, then slide the clamp back to its original position over the fitting and tighten it (if it's that kind). Install the air cleaner if you removed it (Chapter 7, Procedure 12, Step 8).

PROCEDURE 5: CHECK AND REPLACE FUEL PUMP

Condition: Fuel supply at carburetor is insufficient; OR loud clacking noises are coming from the direction of the fuel pump when the engine is running.

Tools and Materials: To *test* the fuel pump you'll need a regular or phillips screwdriver, or pliers, depending on the type of clamps you have, 12-volt test light or VOM meter, wire brush, emery cloth, a 12mm wrench. Maybe a new fuel pump. To *replace* the fuel pump you'll need a new fuel pump and 10mm and 12mm wrenches.

Remarks: Subaru fuel pumps tend to outlive the car, so be sure the fuel pump is dead before replacing it. If you're not sure how to use a Volt/Ohm meter, look at Chapter 10, Procedure 11.

Step 1. Locate Fuel Pump.

Look at Procedure 2, Step 1, and find the *fuel filter*. The arrow on the filter will point to the hose that connects the filter to the fuel pump. Follow the hose a few inches and you'll run right into the pump. The fuel pumps on all '75-'79 models, '80 Brats and fuel-injected models are round and about the size of a large frozen orange juice can. '80 and newer carb model fuel pumps are square and only slightly larger than the fuel filter.

The fuel pump on converted '81 models and all '82 and newer models is mounted under the rear of the car, just in front of the gas tank.

Converted '81 models: A bit of detective work may be necessary to locate the fuel filter and pump on converted '81 models. The fuel filter and pump both might be in the engine compartment, or both might be under the car, or the filter might be located under the car and the pump in the engine compartment. There also might be a vapor separator in the engine compartment (the same as '82 and newer OHV models). Good Luck!

Fuel-injected models: The fuel pump is located under the car in front of the right rear wheel.

Step 2. Check Electrical Stuff.

'75-'82 models: Check the **fuse** for the fuel pump (Chapter 10, Procedure 2). If all is well in Fuseville, let's see if the juice is getting from there to the fuel pump.

EVERYONE: If your fuel pump is located under the car, put the car in gear (or PARK), set the handbrake, chock the front wheels, jack up the rear of the car and put it on jackstands. If yours is in the engine compartment, there's no need for those preparations.

Turn the ignition key to ON. Disconnect the wire(s) going to the fuel pump. Use a test light or VOM meter to check for current in the wires you disconnected from the fuel pump (*not* the wire(s) coming *out* of the pump). Insert one probe of the test light or the red probe from the meter into one of the wires (there's only one wire on '75-'79 models and '80 Brats), then touch the other probe to bare metal. Test both wires if you have two. One of the wires should light the test light, or the VOM should read 12 volts. It does? Then the pump is getting juice. No juice? First trace the wire back, looking for a broken or bare spot where it may have shorted out. If there's just one wire going to the pump, locate a little *ground wire* that has one end attached to the fuel pump body with a screw (usually on the front) and the other end secured by one of the fuel pump mounting bolts. Release each end of the wire and clean the wire and its attaching place with a wire brush, or emery cloth. Reattach the wire and check for juice again. Got some? Lower the car and start the engine to see if the fuel pump is working now. If not, do Step 3.

Step 3. Replace the Old Fuel Pump with the New.

Wear safety glasses and be careful; the *no smoking* rule applies. Put a rag down or have one handy to catch any gas drips.

'75-'79 cars and '77-'80 Brats: First, disconnect the wire to the fuel pump. Loosen the fuel line hose clamps or clips and slide them away from the pump. Unscrew the two 12mm mounting bolts that attach the fuel pump to the car body and the pump comes right off. If the new pump you're installing doesn't have a black ground wire attached to the pump with a screw, remove the one from the old pump and attach it to the new pump in the same position as it was on the old pump. Slip the other end of the ground wire onto one of the mounting bolts, then set the new pump in position and install and tighten the two mounting bolts. (The ground wire should be under the front bolt.) Be sure there's a *flat washer* between the bolt head and the rubber grommet on the pump.

Fit the fuel hoses onto the new pump, then position and tighten the hose clamps over the connection. Reconnect the electrical wire. If you don't remember which hose goes where, the one from the fuel filter goes to the *bottom* fitting on the pump and the hose to the carburetor connects to the *top* fitting. Start the engine and check for leaks.

'80-'81 (except Brats): Disconnect the wire connector to the fuel pump. Now remove the two 10mm bolts that attach the brass-colored **fuel pump bracket** to the top rear of the left (driver's side) strut tower. This will let you lift the bracket up so you can loosen the hose clamps and slide them away from the pump. Pull the hoses off the fittings on the pump. Now remove the two 10mm nuts that attach the pump to the bracket, then slide the pump off the bracket.

If the new pump doesn't have **rubber grommets** in the mounting tabs, use the ones from the old pump, or get new ones if the old ones are funky. Fit the mounting tabs of the new fuel pump into the grooves on the grommets so the thicker side of the grommet is on the bracket side of the pump. Orient the pump so the large nut-looking thing with the fuel line sticking out is on the left (driver's side) of the car. Be sure there's a *flat washer* on top of the grommet before you put the nut on. Attach the pump to the bracket with the two nuts and tighten them. Attach the fuel hoses to the new pump and position the clamps over the connections. In case you've forgotten, the hose from the fuel filter goes to the fitting on the left (driver's) side of the pump. The hose on the right side of the pump should go to the carburetor. Now attach the fuel pump bracket to the car body with the two 10mm bolts. Reconnect the wires and you're finished.

'82 and newer carb cars, '81-'87 carb Brats, and converted '81 cars: Chock the front wheels, set the handbrake, put the transmission in gear or PARK (if yours is automatic), then jack up the rear of the car and put it on jackstands.

If the fuel pump is on a little **shelf**, remove the 10mm bolts that attach the corners of the shelf to the brackets on the body, then lower the shelf. Disconnect the electrical wire connection to the fuel pump. Pinch the hose between the fuel filter and car body (*not* the hose between the fuel filter and fuel pump). Use Vise Grips lightly applied, wrapping the hose with a rag first to protect it from cuts. Now, working at arm's length, loosen the hose clamps, slide 'em back, and twist the hoses off the fuel pump.

Fuel-injected models: Release the pressure in the fuel system just as you do when changing the filter (Procedure 2, Step 4). OK, the car is up on jackstands and the *fuel pump wire* is disconnected. Now locate the fuel hose attached to the pump on the opposite end from where the electrical wires stick out of the pump. Use Vise Grips and a rag to pinch the fuel hose between the fuel pump and car body (see *fuel filter under car* in Procedure 2, Step 2). Use a screwdriver to loosen the hose clamps on each end of the pump and slide them back; then working at arm's length, twist and pull the hoses off the pump.

EVERYONE: Remove the mounting bolts or nuts that attach the fuel pump to the bracket or shelf.

To install the new pump, be sure the rubber grommets are in place on the pump mounting tabs (the thicker side of the grommet goes toward the bracket or shelf). Install the new pump onto the bracket or shelf and secure it with the nuts or bolts. Connect the fuel hoses to the pump and position and tighten the clamps. Remove the Vise Grips and rag, then reconnect the electrical wire connector. If the pump is mounted on a shelf, fit the shelf into the brackets, then install and tighten the mounting nuts or bolts. Lower the car, start the engine, then check for fuel leaks.

PROCEDURE 6: CHECK FOR WATER IN THE GAS TANK ('75-'79 Station Wagons and Brats and All '80 and Newer Models)

Condition: The car sputters and flutters, you've already checked the ignition system and fuel supply, and everything else seems OK; AND/OR you've noticed water in the fuel filter.

Tools and Materials: Clear glass jar, large crescent wrench for '75-'79 models, 12mm wrench for '80 and newer models, rags, goggles.

Remarks: There are commercial products called "fuel conditioners" available that you pour in the gas tank to remove small traces of water. You might want to try a can of the stuff before doing this procedure. If the fuel conditioner doesn't work, do this procedure to drain the gas from the bottom of the tank. If you have a '75-'79 Sedan or Coupe, trying the fuel conditioner is all you can do without removing the fuel tank from the car.

CAUTION! Fire Hazard: Don't light any matches, rub two Boy Scouts together, think about former lovers, or do anything that could create a spark while draining gas from the tank. Have a **fire extinguisher** nearby and ready.

Step 1. Get a Gas Tank Specimen.

Locating the bottom of the gas tank requires a bit of detective work on your part. Look at the bottom rear of the car for a large, black, contoured sheet metal tank. The **drain bolt** is in the lowest section of the tank.

Tie strips of rags around your wrists so gasoline can't run down your arm and into your armpit when you remove the plug. Seriously, gasoline irritates delicate bare skin so wash your hands, arms and any place touched by gasoline with soap and water after obtaining your specimen. Put on your safety goggles.

Now crawl under the car and clean the area around the drain bolt with a rag. Loosen the drain bolt with the wrench while holding the jar under the drain bolt to catch the gas. You don't need to remove the plug. When you have a couple of inches of gas in the jar, quickly tighten the drain plug. Crawl out from under the car without spilling the gas.

Step 2. Diagnosis Please, Doctor.

Clean gasoline is normally a transparent reddish-orange color. Water in the gas will turn it a milky off-white color, or form round beads or blobs in the bottom of the jar. Remember that water is heavier than gas, so it will be on the bottom. See anything besides clean fresh gas? If not, be sure the drain plug is tight, then lower the car if it's on stands. If the gas is milky looking or has blobs in the bottom of the jar, drain the rest of the gas from the tank and stash it in metal screwtop containers. Take it to the recycling center or a filling station for disposal. Replace the *fuel filter* and *vapor separator*, if you have one (Procedure 2). Install the drain plug and tighten it, then fill the tank with fresh gas.

PROCEDURE 7: REMOVE HITACHI CARBURETOR

You'll be using this one if you're going to replace or rebuild your Hitachi carburetor (people with Carter/Weber carbs should go to Procedure 12). Rebuilding a carburetor essentially means taking it apart and cleaning it, then putting it back together with new gaskets, new accelerator pump and so on. Most of the critical parts are accessible by simply removing the top of the carb while it's still on the engine so you might want to run through the quicky carb check and clean (Procedure 11) before yanking the carb out by it roots.

Condition: You've done the 12,000 mile tune-up and checked all the things in Chapter 9: *Troubleshooting*, and have come to the conclusion your carburetor needs to be rebuilt or replaced.

Tools and Materials: 10mm and 19mm wrenches, phillips and/or regular screwdriver, notebook and pencil, masking tape, indelible pen. You'll need a tachometer to adjust the carb once it's back on the engine.

Remarks: If you decide to buy a rebuilt carb from a parts store or Subaru, be sure the rebuilt carburetor has the same part number stamped on the top left rear corner as your old carb. Shop around for the best deal; prices can vary radically from store to store.

If your engine compartment is dirty, nasty, greasy, and filthy, give it a bath (Chapter 7, Procedure 5, Step 2). You don't want any junk to get in the manifold when the carburetor is off. Always cover the hole in the manifold left by the departed carb with a clean rag or paper towels.

Before removing the carb, draw a simple diagram of the vacuum hose(s) and electrical wire connection(s) for your setup. As you disconnect the hoses and wires, label them A, B, C, and so on, with masking tape and indelible pen. *This is important!* It's impossible for me to describe what goes where on every year and model, but this is something you can (and must) do yourself. Before disconnecting anything, refer to the hose layout diagram under the hood (if you have one) to see if the hoses are presently connected correctly. Now, with masking tape, notebook, and pen at hand, you can begin to remove the carburetor.

Step 1. Disconnect Negative (-) Battery Terminal (Chapter 10, Procedure 1, Step 3).

Step 2. Drain Coolant from Engine Block.

Look at Chapter 16, Procedure 3, Step 5, to locate the **engine block drain plugs** (they're in the bottom of the cylinder heads). You only need to remove one of the plugs, so remove the one in the right (passenger's side) cylinder head since it's most accessible. When the coolant has stopped draining, install and tighten the drain plug. Be sure it has an aluminum washer.

Step 3. Remove Air Cleaner (Chapter 7, Procedure 5, Step 4).

Step 4. Remove Fuel Inlet, Return, and Vent Hose(s).

Locate the rubber **fuel line hose** on the top rear left (driver's) side of the carburetor. The other end of the hose is connected to the fuel pump or vapor separator depending on your year and model. Put a rag below where the hose connects to the carb, loosen the clamp and slide it back, then pull the hose off the carburetor fitting. If the carb fitting is Y-shaped and has another smaller **fuel return hose** connected to it, loosen the clamp and remove that hose also.

If a **vent hose** is connected to the top left front of the carb, release the clamp (if there is one) and pull the hose off the fitting.

Step 5. Disconnect Dashpot, Servo Diaphragm, Secondary Diaphragm Hoses.

If you have one or two small round things (choke diaphragms) mounted in a bracket on the right rear of the carb, disconnect the hose from the fitting on the right (passenger's side).

If there's a small round thing in the center of the back of the carb (the *servo diaphragm*) and/or a round thing on the top right rear corner (the *choke diaphragm*) label the hose(s), then pull them off the fitting. Some late models have two hoses so label them *top* and *bottom*.

'80 and newer models: If there's a large round thing mounted to the right rear corner of the carb at an angle, disconnect and label the hose. That's the **secondary diaphragm** that controls the secondary throttle valve.

Step 6. Disconnect Choke.

'75 and newer models: Locate the electrical wire for the automatic choke coming out of the round **automatic choke housing** on the top right side of the carb. Disconnect the wire at the connector a few inches from the choke housing. On late models, other wires may be connected to the choke wire at a white plastic connector. Push on the sides of the white connector and separate the two halves.

Step 7. Disconnect Hoses from Front of Carb.

There might be anywhere from zero to four vacuum hoses attached to the front of the carb that go to the front of the *intake manifold* and/or to small metal pipes below the intake manifold. Pull the hoses off the carb fittings but leave them attached to the manifold and/or the metal pipes. The hoses reconnect in the same order, left to right, so it's hard to get them mixed up. Draw a simple picture of your hoses if they're different from the ones in the illustration.

Step 8. Disconnect Anti-Diesel Valve.

If you have a thumb-sized gizmo known as the **anti-diesel valve** sticking out of the front left corner of the carb and pointing toward the left headlight, follow the wire from the gizmo to a wire connector. It might share a connector with the choke wire. Disconnect the wires. Use a 19mm open-end wrench or crescent wrench to slightly loosen the valve but don't remove it from the carb yet.

Emergency and Quicky People: On '81 and newer models you'll need to *carefully* unscrew the anti-diesel valve without damaging the wire. When it's off, pull the pointed plunger out and stash it where it won't get lost.

Step 9. Disconnect Accelerator Cable.

See Procedure 3, Step 2, in this chapter to disconnect the accelerator cable from the lower right side of the carb.

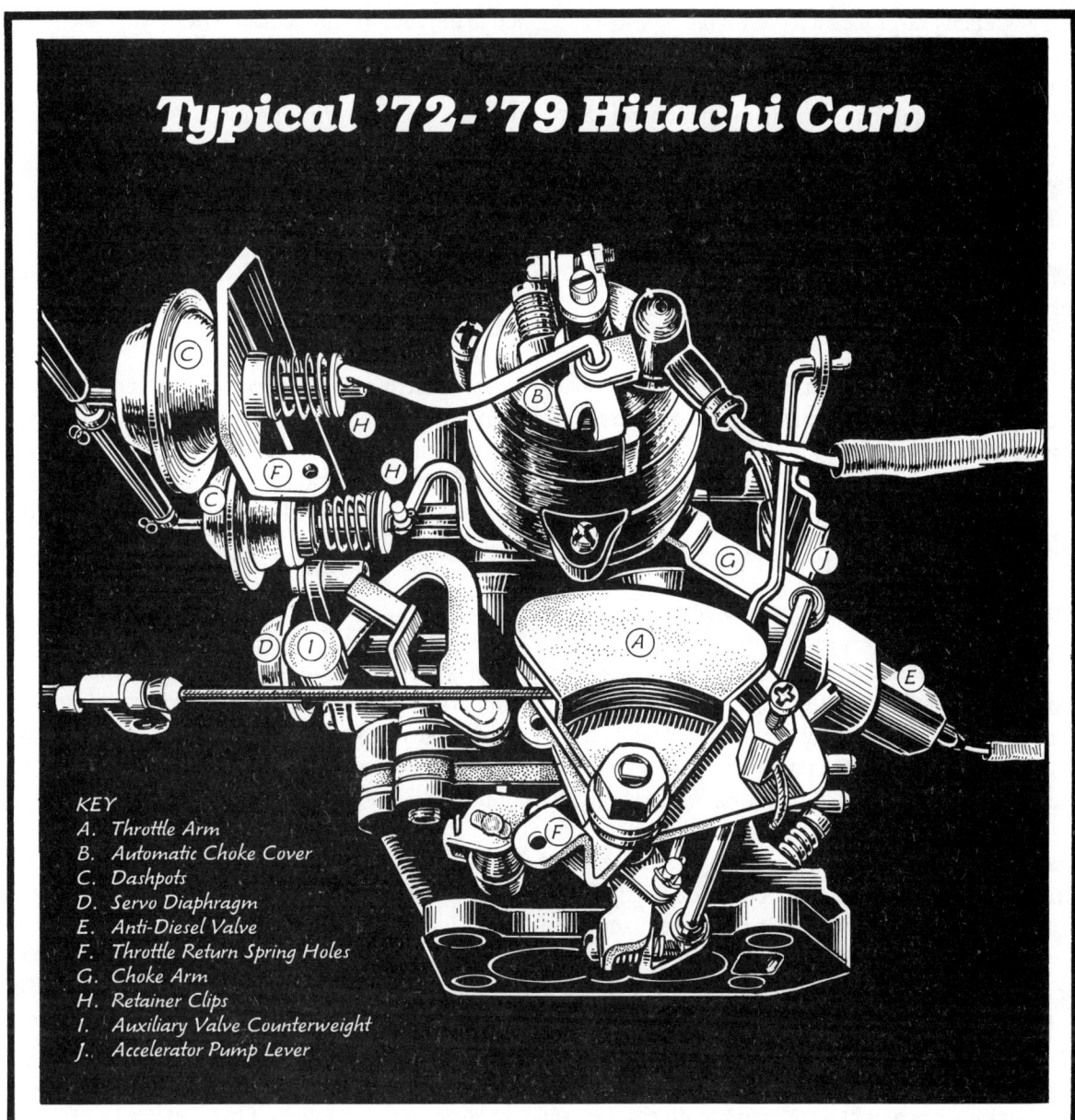

Typical '72–'79 Hitachi Carb

KEY
A. Throttle Arm
B. Automatic Choke Cover
C. Dashpots
D. Servo Diaphragm
E. Anti-Diesel Valve
F. Throttle Return Spring Holes
G. Choke Arm
H. Retainer Clips
I. Auxiliary Valve Counterweight
J. Accelerator Pump Lever

Step 10. Disconnect Other Stuff.

You may have some, all, or none of the following hoses and wires to disconnect from the carb. A hose or two on the top left rear corner (from the *duty solenoid valves*). A hose attached horizontally just below the large screw at the top front center (from the *slow duty solenoid valve*). A hose or two attached to the left rear corner (*altitude compensator* or *duty solenoid*).

Emergency and Quicky People: Only disconnect hoses connected to the top of the carb.

Step 11. Remove Carburetor.

Check all around your carburetor to see if there's anything else hooked to it that would prevent lifting it off. All clear? Proceed.

Have a few clean rags or paper towels handy to wipe up the coolant that might leak out of the manifold when the carb is removed. Unscrew (*counterclockwise*) the four 10mm bolts on the bottom corners of the carb (a long skinny wrench makes it easier). If there's a bracket attached to the round brass-colored *EGR valve* on the back of the manifold, remove the two 12mm nuts and washers and remove the bracket if it's in your way. Lift the carb straight up to remove it. Watch for any wires or hoses still connected to the carb. Once the carb is off, hold it over a can and tilt it so the fuel in the float bowl can drain out the *fuel inlet fitting*. You're now ready to take it apart (Procedure 8), or put on a new or rebuilt one (Procedure 10). If you're replacing the carburetor, you might want to consider installing a high performance Weber carb (see Chapter 18, Procedure 11).

PROCEDURE 8: DISASSEMBLE, CLEAN, AND INSPECT HITACHI CARBURETOR ('75-'79 Models Only)

This procedure does not include rebuilding '80 and newer Hitachi carbs. They are more complicated than the earlier carbs and put together so as to discourage rebuilding by amateurs like us. If you've rebuilt a few carbs before, with a little ingenuity and the instructions that come with a rebuild kit, you can probably follow this procedure and rebuild an '80 or newer Hitachi. It's up to you, but don't blame me if you run into problems.

However, the '75-'79 Hitachi carb is relatively simple and straightforward, and together we can rebuild this baby.

Condition: The carburetor needs to be rebuilt.

Tools and Materials: Safety glasses, maybe a magnifying glass; 10mm, 12mm, and 19mm wrenches; needle-nose pliers; medium phillips screwdriver; very small, small, and medium regular screwdrivers; carburetor cleaner (see Remarks), spray can of carb cleaner, a medium screwdriver with a notch in the blade (see the illustration), carburetor rebuild kit for your carburetor, one can or tray labeled "Tiny Parts" and another can or tray labeled "No Soak," rags, knife or razor blade, an old toothbrush, time, and patience.

Remarks: If you carefully record the *jet numbers* in the circles next to the jets' name in the jet location illustration, you'll know where to put them during reassembly. All the jets will have different numbers stamped on them and most of them will fit in only one place!

Before you start rebuilding your carb, get a large can of *liquid carburetor cleaner*—large enough to soak the carburetor body and various parts in once it's all apart. (Get the kind that comes with a strainer basket in the can.) Carb cleaner is rather expensive (it will probably cost more than the carb rebuild kit) but you can also use it to clean things like wheel bearings and nuts and bolts, when doing other repair procedures. It's handy to have around. If you don't have a place to store it or can't afford it, you might find a garage that will clean the carb parts for you and blow them out with compressed air for a couple of dollars. Or get at least two (three to be sure) cans of *spray carburetor cleaner*. It works almost as well as the large cans of carb cleaner. Have at least one can handy for giving the parts a final shot of "clean" before assembling them.

Get a couple of one pound coffee cans or medium-size bread pans and label one TINY PARTS and the other one NO SOAK. I'll tell you which can to put the parts in as you remove them. Parts that don't go in the TINY PARTS or NO SOAK cans can go in the carb cleaner strainer basket. No strainer basket? Label another coffee can STRAINER BASKET.

You'll need a *notched screwdriver* to remove one of the jets. You can either buy one or file a notch in one of yours (see the illustration).

If you disassemble the carburetor and find it full of crud/water, check the gas tank (Procedure 6). After rebuilding or replacing a carb, always install a new *fuel filter* (Procedure 2) and check the *air filter* (Chapter 7, Procedure 4, Step 3) before you start the engine.

Take your time during both disassembly and reassembly so you'll be absolutely sure you're keeping track of everything. There may be variations I don't cover, especially in the "little stuff," but these should be fairly straightforward and logical and my instructions will serve as a guide to removing any unmentioned oddball parts your carb may have.

Step 1. Remove Little Stuff.

Most carb rebuild kits come with new cotter pins and gaskets, but hold on to the ones you remove until you're sure you have new ones. Emergency people here from Procedure 11, be sure and save everything!

Get the Tiny Parts and No Soak containers handy. If you have a can of liquid carb cleaner, pull the strainer basket out of the carb cleaner and set it on a rag.

Remove the **throttle return spring** that's between the **throttle arm** (*lever*) and the bottom of the **dashpot bracket** (early models) or a bracket on the right front corner of the carb. If there's a small *spring* attached between the inner side of the throttle lever and a short lever from the choke housing, remove it. Put the springs in the strainer basket.

The long piece of metal going across the top front of the carb is the **accelerator pump lever** (or just *pump lever*). If there's a large coiled *spring* between the pump lever and carb, use a small screwdriver to flip the hooked end of the spring off the top of the pump lever. Now loosen the large screw that attaches the pump lever to the carb body. Watch for a flat washer and lockwasher that are on the carb side of the pump lever. Remove the screw, washers, and spring and put them in the Tiny Parts can. If your pump lever has a *pin* on the left (driver's side) end, pull the pump lever away from the carb until the pin is out of the accelerator pump shaft. The right (passenger's) end of the pump lever is attached to a crooked *rod* which is in turn attached to the inside of the throttle arm.

Rebuilders: Carefully rotate the pump lever so it comes off the hooked end of the rod. Leave the other end of this rod attached to the throttle arm shaft. Put the liberated pump lever in the strainer basket.

Emergency and Quicky People: Rotate the lever to the right (passenger's) side of the carb so it's out of the way.

EVERYONE: The round thing attached to the right side of the carb top is the **automatic choke housing** and cover. There's a lever sticking out of the lower front inside of the choke housing that I'll call a **choke arm**. Use needlenose pliers to remove the tiny cotter pin and washer from the end of the rod that's attached to the choke arm. Pull the end of the rod out of the choke arm. Put the tiny washer and cotter pin in the can for Tiny Parts.

Now look at the top rear of the carb. If there's a bracket attached to the top rear or top left of the carb body with two or three phillips screws, remove the screws and lockwashers. If there are no round **dashpots** on the bracket, remove the bracket and put it in the basket. If there are two dashpots on the bracket, the outer pot has a *spring* and retainer washer held onto its shaft by a small *rod* coming from the outside of the *choke housing cover*. Press the retainer and spring on the outer dashpot shaft toward the bracket while you pull the choke rod out of the dashpot shaft. Put the spring and retainer washer in the can for Tiny Parts. Now rotate the outer pot on the bracket toward the bottom of the carb until the rod attached to the inner pot can slide out of its holder on the carb. Put the dashpots and bracket in the No Soak can.

Step 2. Remove Carburetor Top.

Remove the phillips screws on the top of the carb body. There are five altogether, but you might have already removed two of them with the bracket. Everything that would keep you from lifting the top off should now have been removed or disconnected.

Carefully pry the carb top off the carb body. If the carb is off the engine, keep the carb body upright after the top is off so some little pieces won't fall out and get lost. Try to remove the top without tearing up the **main gasket** (carb top gasket) so you can use it to match with a new gasket (or reuse it if you don't have a new gasket). Be careful with the black plastic thing that hangs down into the carb body. That's the **float**. Once the top is off lay it down bottom side up so the float isn't damaged.

Emergency and Quicky People: If the carb is still on the engine, skip ahead to Step 3.

Rebuilders: Be sure to do the next paragraph.

Remove the spring sticking out of the large hole near the front of the carb body. In some cases, the accelerator pump plunger may be sitting on top of this spring. Now hold your hand across the front of the body to catch a couple of pieces that will drop out as you tilt the carb body upside down toward your hand. Presto! A little *BB-size ball* and a small *pointed hexagonal shaft* will fall into your hand. Put the spring, BB ball, and pointed shaft in the Tiny Parts can.

Step 3. Remove Float Needle Valve.

Now set the detached top of the carb upside down on your work surface, and we'll take out its innards. The metal arms on one end of the float are attached to two *posts* on the carb top with a straight *pivot pin*. Gently lift up on the float to see where it pivots. Pull the pin out with your fingers, then lift the float off the carb top. Put the pin with the Tiny Parts and the float with the No Soak pieces.

In the carb top next to the two posts that hold the float pivot pin, is the brass **needle valve**. This is the valve that shuts off the gas when the fuel in the float bowl reaches the proper level. Use a 10mm wrench (early models) or screwdriver (later models) to unscrew the needle valve. Save the *gasket* for the needle valve. There's probably a tiny **brass** screen in the needle valve hole. Turn the carb top over and dump the screen in your hand. Put the needle valve, gasket, and screen in the Tiny Parts can.

Here's how the needle valve works. The fuel pump pumps fuel through the fuel lines into the *float bowl* in the carb body. As the fuel level rises, the float also rises because it's hollow and floats on top of the fuel like a rubber ducky. When the fuel in the float bowl reaches a certain level, the little *tab* between the float arms presses on the *pin* sticking out of the needle valve. The pin in turn pushes a pointed *shaft* into the **fuel inlet line** so no more fuel can enter the float bowl.

If you were referred here from the Emergency Procedure, or you're a curious carb rebuilder, use a small screwdriver or your fingernails to pry the tiny *wire clip* off the pin end of the needle valve. Be careful so none of the very tiny things inside the needle valve fall into dirt or gravel. You'd be up the creek without a needle valve. Inside the needle valve is a very, very tiny *spring* that fits inside the larger hollow end of the pin. The larger end of the pin and spring fit inside a hollow *square shaft* that has a pointed end. That's the needle!

Rebuilders and Quicky people: There should be a new needle valve in the kit; see if you can find it. Got it? OK, lay the old one aside and put the new one back in the kit for now. Go on to the next step.

Emergency people: Lay the small parts on a clean rag so they won't get lost. Look in the *needle valve housing* for dirt and crud that could prevent the needle from seating in the hole or cause it to stick in the hole. Check the pointed end of the needle to see if a groove has worn in the tapered part. If you're stuck on the side of the road, all you can do is clean the needle valve parts, put it all back together and hope you solved the problem. Emergency people go to Procedure 9, Step 1.

Step 4. Remove Accelerator Pump and Rubber Boot.

Hold the carb top upside down. The **accelerator pump** is mounted in a rubber boot near the front edge of the carb top and has a spring wrapped around the shaft. (Don't confuse it with the long skinny shaft sticking up from the center of the carb top.) Pull the accelerator pump out of the rubber boot, then use a small screwdriver to push the edge of the rubber boot through the opening in the carb top. Put the pump and boot in the No Soak can. At this point you can lift the main gasket (carb top gasket) off the carb top mating surface, if it's been hanging on there.

The accelerator pump does just what its name implies; it pumps a small shot of fuel into the carb when you want to accelerate.

Step 5. Remove Choke Housing Cover (except '81 and newer models).

The **choke housing** is that round thing on the right side of the carb top. Remove the three phillips head screws and funny triangular-shaped washers around the edge. Gently pull the **choke cover** off and look inside. You'll see a flat spiral-shaped piece of metal wrapped around a center post. Now look a little deeper into the cover until you see a brass-colored spring inside a porcelain groove. Are the coils of both springs evenly spaced and round? If they're lopsided, uneven, or broken, you need a new (or used) choke cover. Make a note to get one. The function of the springs is explained in Step 14. Put the choke cover in the No Soak can.

Step 6. Remove Jets from Carb Top.

Use the jet illustration to record the numbers of the two small brass *jets* called the **primary and secondary slow air bleed jets** screwed into the bottom of the carb top. Now use a small screwdriver to remove the jets. Take

Fuel Systems

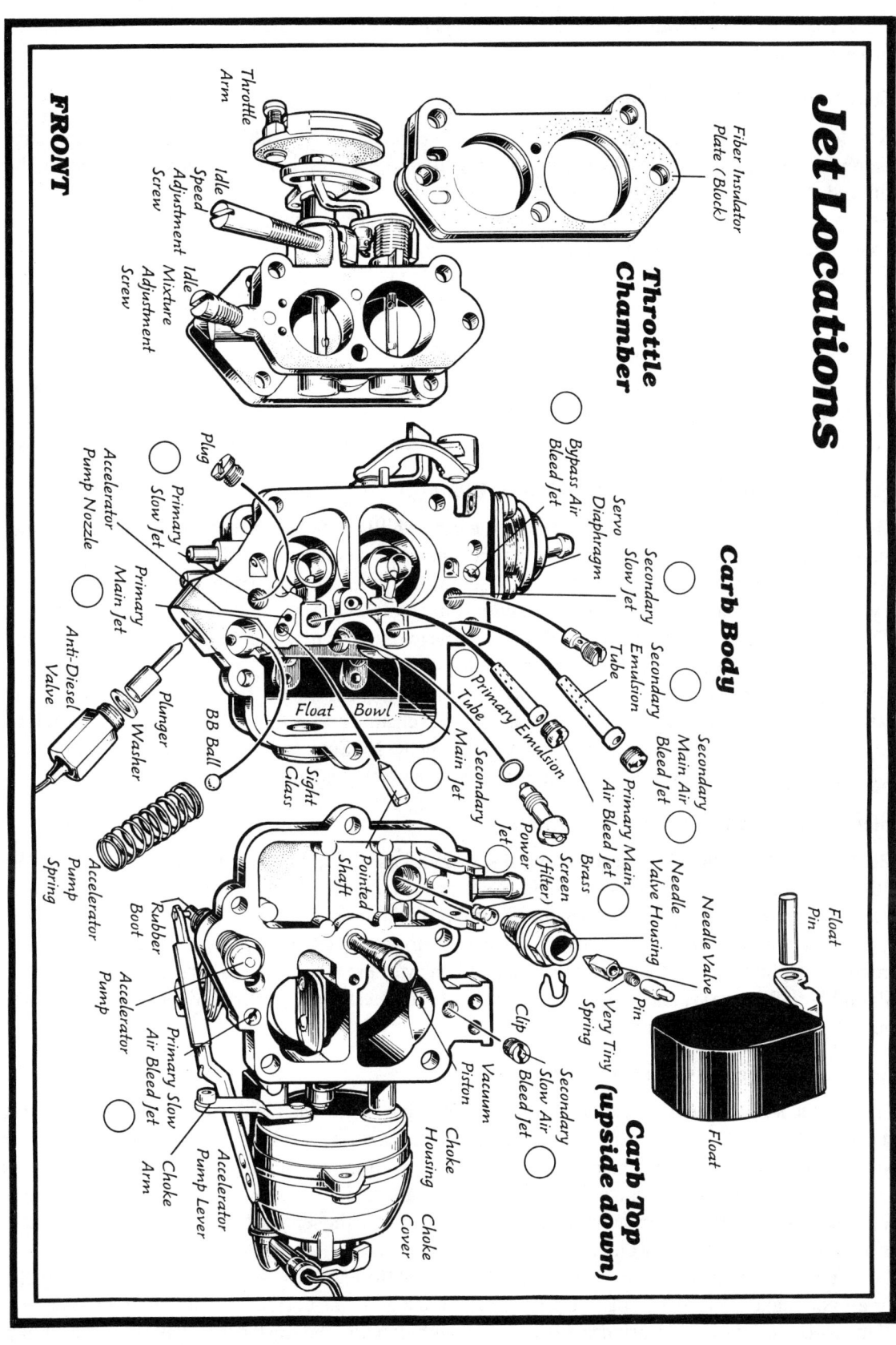

the time to find the right screwdriver; these jets get bunged up easily. Put them both in the strainer basket. Lay the carb top aside for now.

Step 7. Remove Servo Diaphragm.

Now look at the carb body, right side up. If there's a *round diaphragm* attached to the rear of the carb with three screws, remove the screws and carefully pull the *diaphragm shaft* out of the body. If there's a rubber *O-ring* around the shaft, save it to compare to a new one.

Besides preventing the carb from becoming pregnant, this **servo diaphragm** allows more air to enter the carburetor when the car is coasting or decelerating. The leaner (more air relative to fuel) mixture reduces HC (hydrocarbon) emissions. Check the *rubber tip* on the end of the shaft. If it's cracked, ragged, or anything but smooth and flat, replace the servo diaphragm. Set the servo diaphragm and its three screws in the No Soak can.

Step 8. Remove Anti-Diesel Valve, (if you have one).

Use a crescent or 19mm wrench to unscrew the thumb-size thing sticking out of the left front side of the carb, if it's there. That's the **anti-diesel valve**. Pull the pointed *plunger* out of the valve so it doesn't get lost. Stash the valve and plunger in the No Soak can. The function of the anti-diesel valve is explained in Step 14.

Step 9. Separate Carb Body from Throttle Chamber.

Turn the carb body upside down and remove the large phillips head screw and its toothed lockwasher. Be careful not to damage the screw because it has a very important vacuum hole drilled through it. Turn the body right side up now and remove the two large phillips screws on the throttle arm (right) side of the body. On some carbs you can't get a straight shot at the screws with your screwdriver so you'll have to press hard while turning. If the screws get mangled during removal, make a note to round up new ones before reassembly. Put all three screws in the basket; keep their lockwashers on so they don't get mixed up.

Now pry the carb body away from the **throttle chamber** just beneath it. There are *two gaskets* and a fiber **insulator plate** (block) between the carb body and throttle chamber. Carefully pull the fiber block and gaskets off the carb body and/or throttle chamber and put them in the No Soak can. You may have to wiggle the fiber block and gaskets off a hollow dowel pin on one side; go easy so you don't snap the block.

Step 10. Remove Idle Adjustment Screws.

Remove the short **idle mixture adjustment screw** and its **spring**. The screw sticks out of the front center of the throttle chamber at about a 45° angle. Some are covered by a plastic cap, with a groove for inserting your flat screwdriver. You may need to pop the cap off to get the screw out. Now look at the tapered needle end of the screw. If you find a groove worn into it, make a note to get a new mixture screw. A new one *should* come with rebuild kits, but I haven't found a kit that supplied one yet. Put the screw and spring in the strainer basket.

Rebuilders: Remove the long **idle speed adjustment screw** and **spring** on the throttle arm side of the throttle chamber. Put them in the strainer basket.

Step 11. Remove Jets from Carb Body.

Look at the *jet location illustration*. You'll notice a circle beside each of the jet names in the illustration. If you carefully record the number of each jet in the circle next to its name in the jet illustration before removing it, you'll have no trouble installing them in the correct position during reassembly. Luckily, each jet in your carb will have a different number stamped on it. If you have jets located differently than the ones in the illustration (there were slight variations over the years), make a circle where the jet is located, then make a circle for the jet number. Joe, the illustrator, won't mind.

I won't bore (or confuse) you by explaining what each of the jets does. Suffice it to say that they meter out fuel or air and that each jet has a specific purpose and must go in the correct position in order to do its job.

If the carb is off the engine, arrange the throttle chamber, body, and top the way they are in the jet location illustration before removing the jets.

There are a few hidden jets. Here's how to find them: Look carefully for numbers on all the plain looking brass screws on the top of the carb body. If there's a number on it, it's a jet so write the number in the circle before removing it. No number on the screw? Then it's a *plug*, so remove the plug to get to the jet that's *under* the plug. Write all the jet numbers in the circles, then use a screwdriver to remove the jets. Be sure the blade of the screwdriver fits into the slots on both sides of the jet. On the small jets that may be below the surface, use a screwdriver that's narrow enough to clear the threads in the bore. Don't remove the two **main air bleed jets** just yet. They're located in the rectangles near the center of the carb. Put the jets you removed in the strainer basket.

Quicky People: Find the two **main air bleed jets**, record the numbers, then remove the jets. You won't be able to remove the emulsion tubes so skip the EVERYONE paragraph.

Rebuilders: There are two **emulsion tubes** hiding beneath the two main *air bleed jets*. The main air bleed jets are located in the rectangles between the *float bowl* and the *main nozzles*. You need to know which emulsion tube goes in which hole so don't remove both jets at the same time. Write the numbers of the two main air bleed jets in the circles in the illustration, then remove *one* of the jets. Turn the carb body upside down and catch the tube that will fall out. Count the holes on one side of the tube and write the total in the appropriate circle. Now remove the other jet and emulsion tube, count the holes on that tube and write the number of holes in the circle. If one or both of the tubes are stuck in the carb body, hold the body upside down over a rag or paper towel and tap the sides of the body with a screwdriver handle.

If the tube(s) still won't fall out, you'll need to find a gas station or someone with an air compressor to blow 'em free. You'll have to put the main jets and plugs back in if you've already removed them. Hold a finger over the emulsion tube hole so the tube can't fly across the street (into a weed patch where it will never be found), then put the end of the air compressor nozzle against the hole in the bottom of the float chamber below the stuck emulsion tube and pull the trigger. It might take awhile but the tube should eventually come out. If it still won't budge, try blowing it out again after soaking the body in the carb cleaner for a while or after spraying carb cleaner around it.

Quicky People: You can't reach the main jets while the carb is on the engine so skip the next paragraph. Just move on down to the EVERYONE paragraph.

Rebuilders: The main jets are located below the sight glass on the side of the carb body. You'll have to remove the two 12mm brass *plugs* to see them. If there's a thin metal *lock plate* around the plugs, pry it off with a small screwdriver. Save the copper *washers* off the plugs so you can match new ones to them or reuse them if you don't have new ones in the rebuild kit. Use a small screwdriver to unscrew the jets . Record the jet numbers on the illustration as you remove them. Use the right flat screwdriver so you don't score the threaded bores.

EVERYONE: Use the special screwdriver with a notch in the end to remove the **power jet** that's screwed into the little shelf in the float chamber. Toss it in the strainer basket.

Check the carb body and top for other jets. If you have more, draw their location on the jet location illustration and record the number the same as you did for the other jets. Put all the jets and their plugs in the strainer basket.

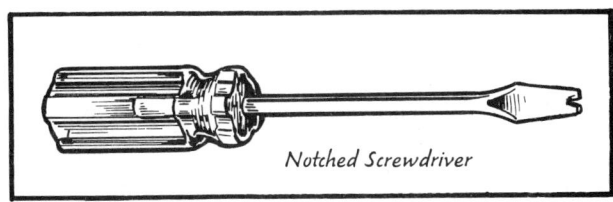
Notched Screwdriver

Step 12. Cleaning.

Quicky People: If you have a new gasket for the carb top, use a rag or paper towel to mop up any gas left in the float bowl. If you don't have a new gasket, leave the gas in the bowl—you might need it later. Shoot spray carb cleaner in all the holes in the carb body and top. Wait a few minutes and spray them again. Clean all the parts in the cans with a toothbrush and carb cleaner.

Rebuilders: If you don't have a can of carb cleaner to soak the parts in, use an old toothbrush and a can of spray carb cleaner to clean *spotlessly* the parts in each can except the No Soak can. Also clean the carb body, top, and throttle chamber. Be sure you're in a well-ventilated area because the fumes are pretty strong. Wear a respirator or dust mask if you have one, and/or take a break every few minutes and get some fresh air.

Have a can of carb cleaner to soak the parts in? Put the following parts in the cleaner: the throttle chamber, carb body and top, and the strainer basket with all the jets and screws. *Don't* put the parts in the Tiny Parts and No Soak cans in the cleaner. These include the float, choke cover (the part that has the springs in it), accelerator pump, dashpots (diaphragms), gaskets, fiber insulator, the BB ball or the tiny washers and cotter pins (they might get lost). Soak everything else (except the carb body) for at least two hours. You should not soak the carb body for more than two hours because the *sealing ring* for the *sight glass* might deteriorate. If possible, try to prop or hang the body in the cleaner with a piece of wire so everything except the sight glass is in the cleaner; leave it there until you're ready to take the other parts out.

While the parts are soaking, clean up your work area. Wipe up the grease and crud, then spread clean rags, newspapers, or paper towels on the workbench. Wash your hands.

When the parts have soaked for at least two hours, pull them out of the cleaner and rinse them thoroughly with clean solvent or water. Use an old toothbrush (*not* a wire brush) to remove the large chunks of crud on the outside of the large pieces. Soak the parts in the cleaner longer if they don't look brand new.

If you have access to an air compressor, blow everything dry. Pay particular attention to the holes in the jets and all the holes in the throttle chamber and carb body and top. No air compressor? Dry the large parts with a clean rag and lay them in the sun to dry. When they've dried, squirt spray carb cleaner in all the jet holes, and all the holes and passages in the throttle chamber, carb body, and top. You'll have to move the butterfly valves back and forth in order to see all the tiny holes in the **throttle chamber barrels**. Lay the parts on clean fresh rags, newspapers, or paper towels.

Step 13. Fondle the Parts.

Quicky People: Since your carb isn't completely apart, you'll just have to vicariously enjoy some of the fondling that's about to take place.

Rebuilders: Now that all the parts are clean and naked in front of you, it's an opportune time to fondle them and find out what they do. Let's start by arranging them in a logical order. Orient the carb body and top the way they are in the jet location illustration. Now set the *throttle chamber* top side up to the left of the carb body so the throttle lever is on the left.

There are two holes, called **barrels** going through the carburetor throttle chamber, body, and top. Since there are two barrels, you have what's called a *two-barrel carb*. The slightly smaller barrel closest to you is the front barrel when the carb is on the engine. It's the *primary* (sometimes called the 1st stage) part of the carb that operates when starting the engine and while driving under light to moderate conditions. When you push the gas pedal more than halfway to the floor (or put the pedal to the metal) the larger rear barrel, called the *secondary* part (2nd stage) of the carb, comes into action. Pick up the throttle chamber with your right hand and rotate the top of the throttle arm toward you. Now slowly rotate the top of the throttle arm toward the rear. Watch the two round plates in the throttle chamber move as the throttle arm rotates. The round plates you're moving are called **butterfly valves** (or *throttle valves*). When the butterfly valves are fully open they are vertical in the throttle chamber so the maximum amount of fuel and air can be sucked into the engine. You can see that the *primary butterfly valve* opens about halfway before the larger *secondary butterfly* starts to open. This allows you to drive economically on the smaller primary system until you need the power to pass a car, drive up a steep hill, race a Porsche—times when more fuel and air (power) are needed. You step down on the gas and the larger secondary system kicks in.

There's another butterfly valve called the **auxiliary valve** located in the secondary barrel of the carb body. It's attached by a shaft to a sickle-shaped arm with a round *counterweight* on the end on the outside of the carb body. The function of the auxiliary valve is to keep the secondary system from operating when the engine is running slowly under a heavy load. In this condition, if the intake air could pass through both the primary and secondary sides of the carburetor at the same time, the air flow in the barrels would become slow and the fuel in the barrels wouldn't be *atomized* (mixed with air) sufficiently, resulting in a loss of power instead of gaining power. The counterweight (or the *secondary diaphragm*) holds the auxiliary valve closed until the engine is turning fast enough to create enough vacuum to pull the valve open.

The round gizmos hanging in the barrels of the carb body are the **primary and secondary main nozzles**.

When the engine is running, gas is sucked out of the float bowl, through jets, and through the small brass tubes in the middle of the main nozzles. This is where the gas is atomized (mixed with air) as the air rushes through the barrels.

Now look in the front barrel of the carb top where there's one more butterfly valve called a **choke plate**. This butterfly is operated by the *choke mechanism*, be it automatic or manual. When the engine is cold, a *richer* fuel mixture is required to get the engine started and enable it to run until it warms up. Richer means more fuel relative to the amount of air in the fuel/air mixture. On '75-'84 models, when the engine is cold the flat spiral spring in the choke cover pulls the choke plate (butterfly) closed. The closed choke butterfly changes the mixture by restricting the amount of air drawn into the carb. When the engine is running, electricity passes through the small brass-colored spring in the choke cover causing it to heat the inside of the choke housing. The heat causes the large flat spring to expand (unwind its spiral) which allows the butterfly shaft to move the butterfly to the open position, so the engine gets a *leaner* (less fuel relative to air) mixture.

There's more information about how the carb works in Chapter 4: *How A Subaru Works*.

Step 14. Inspect Everything.

Quicky People: Again, you'll just have to do the best you can since your carb isn't completely apart.

Rebuilders: Now that all the pieces are clean, let's give them an inspection that even the IRS would envy. If you find something that doesn't look right to you, take the part to Subaru or a garage for their opinion. Give all the parts one more shot of spray carb cleaner as you inspect them, just to be sure everything's copacetic. Be sure to wear safety glasses when spraying. I know from experience how much that stuff burns when it gets on the eyeballs. Let's go through our audit, part by part:

Throttle chamber: Grab the throttle chamber and rotate the throttle arm to see that everything operates smoothly. Do the butterfly valves open to a vertical position when you rotate the throttle arm? The secondary butterfly valve (the larger one) should snap shut completely when you release the throttle arm. If it doesn't, there's a problem with the *spring* wrapped around the end of the shaft. One end of the spring hooks over the arm on the shaft end, and the other end sticks into a hole on the outside of the throttle chamber.

Use a razor blade or sharp putty knife to carefully scrape off any traces of old gasket material you find on the top or bottom.

Squirt some spray carb cleaner into all the holes in the throttle chamber, especially the tiny ones inside the primary barrel. You'll have to open the primary butterfly valve (the smaller one) to see some of them.

If everything looks good, lay the throttle chamber aside.

Carb body: Now pick up the carb body and carefully inspect it for cracks. Examine the holes that things screw into for stripped or damaged threads. Check all the holes and passages for dirt and blockage. Squirt spray carb cleaner into all the holes and passages to make certain they're open. (If the spray can comes with a little tube, attach it to the nozzle to reach down into those tiny places.) Pay particular attention to the brass *accelerator pump nozzle* (see illustration).

Clean the inside and outside of the *sight glass* with spray carb cleaner and a clean rag or paper towel. Be sure it's clear or you won't be able to check the float level.

Grab the counterweight and rotate it back and forth to check the *auxiliary butterfly shaft* for smooth operation. Set the carb body aside.

Carb top: Pick up the carb top, turn it over, and press on the end of the spring-wrapped *rod* sticking out of the bottom. This is the **vacuum piston** that activates the *power valve*. The *spring* should pop the rod back out when you release it. To be sure it's clean, squirt some spray carb cleaner around the rod where it goes into the carb top while pumping on the rod. The rod movement should be smooth. Squirt some cleaner in the two *jet holes* on either side of the bottom surface of the carb top.

Check the *choke butterfly shaft* for smooth operation. (You may have to hold the arm sticking out between the choke housing and carb top in a certain position so it doesn't interfere with the choke shaft. Experiment a little and you'll find the position.)

Examine the holes in the two metal arms that hold the float in position. The holes should be round, not oval or egg shaped.

Everything look good? Set the carb top aside.

All that other stuff: Examine the holes in all the jets to see that they're clean. Squirt some spray carb cleaner through the holes.

If you have a *servo diaphragm*, wipe off the hose fitting with a paper towel, then suck on the fitting. The rubber tipped plunger should retract into the round housing. Suck, then put your tongue over the hole to see if the diaphragm holds vacuum. If you have to keep sucking to keep the plunger retracted, the diaphragm in the housing is broken. Inspect the rubber pad on the end of the plunger for wear. The end should be smooth. If the diaphragm is broken or the rubber pad is funky, get a new servo diaphragm.

Check the two *dashpots* mounted in the long bracket (if you have them) the same way you checked the servo diaphragm. Suck on the hose fitting on the end to see if the plungers retract. If they do, see if they hold vacuum when you suck and put your tongue over the hole. If the plungers don't retract or won't hold vacuum, replace the dashpots. They come as a complete assembly.

Check the black plastic *float* and its metal *bracket* for cracks. The holes in the bracket should be round. If they're oval, replace the float. Inspect the *float pivot pin* and replace it if there are grooves worn near the ends.

Clean the fiber *insulator block* that fits between the throttle chamber and carb body. Carefully use a razor blade or knife to remove traces of old gasket material on both sides. Use spray carb cleaner and a paper towel to clean the holes. Check the block for cracks and replace it if you find any.

Check the tiny *brass filter* that was behind the needle valve. Gently pull on the ends to straighten it. Look for tears or holes in the screen.

If you have an *anti-diesel valve* (that thumb-sized gizmo attached to the front of the carb with a wire sticking out of the end), pull the pointed *plunger* out of the valve. Now look inside the valve for a thin spiral *spring*. The spring has to be centered in the hole to do its job. If it isn't, try to center it with a small screwdriver. Insert the large end of the pointed plunger into the valve. Push gently on the pointed tip to see if the plunger pops back out. If it does, all's well. If it doesn't, you'll have to mess with the spring some more or replace the valve. Check the wire where it disappears into the valve. Is it broken or frayed? If it is, replace the valve.

Here's why you have an anti-diesel valve. Sometimes a hot engine can continue to run even after the ignition key is turned off. How? The temperature in the cylinders is hot enough to ignite residual fuel in the cylinders. This sucks more fuel through the carb and the engine continues to run like a diesel engine; heat rather than a spark is igniting the fuel. With an anti-diesel valve, a pointed plunger inside the valve closes an opening (the *primary slow passage*) in the carburetor so no more fuel can be sucked in when the key is off. Without fuel, the engine can't "diesel."

Now we're ready to put the whole mess back together. Go slowly, and double- or triple-check each jet's number and location before installing it.

PROCEDURE 9: ASSEMBLE HITACHI CARBURETOR

Condition: You have a table covered with spotlessly clean carburetor parts and you're dying to get it all back together to see if works; OR you're doing a quicky rebuild and/or you're in an emergency situation and need to install the parts you removed.

Tools and Materials: Same as Procedure 8, maybe plus a small metric ruler.

Remarks: Make sure your hands are surgically clean. Arrange everything neatly on your workbench so the different parts are easy to find. When installing the jets, needle valve, plugs, etc. in the carb body and top, get them good and snug but don't crank on them so hard you damage the slots in the jets or strip the threads in the carb body or top. *Carefully* check the jet numbers and locations to be sure they're right before installing each jet.

Emergency people will have to reuse the old parts.

Step 1. Assemble Carb Top.

Emergency People: Do the steps applicable to you (install the needle valve and float).

Rebuilders and Quicky People: Arrange the *throttle chamber*, *carb body*, and *carb top* the way they are in the jet location illustration. Let's take it from the top.

Carb top upside down on the bench? OK, let's go. Find the primary and secondary *slow air bleed jets*. Use a small screwdriver to screw them into the appropriate holes in the carb top.

If you had a small round brass *filter screen* under the needle valve, find it and straighten it if it's squished. Drop the filter into the needle valve hole. It should fit over the round dowel at the bottom.

Find the new *needle valve* in the rebuild kit. See if the pin pops back out when you push on it and that the little spring clip holding the pin is securely in its groove around the holder. Find a new *round gasket* that just fits over the threaded end of the needle valve. Slide it on. Hold the carb top firmly on the bench while you screw the needle valve in. Tighten it with a 10mm wrench or screwdriver depending on your type of needle valve.

Find the new *accelerator pump* and *rubber boot* in the rebuild kit. Insert the grooved end of the boot into its hole from the outside surface of the carb top (yep, you'll have to turn it over). If necessary, gently push the boot through the hole with a small screwdriver. Turn the carb top on its back again. Rotate the boot until it fits neatly in the hole. Insert the accelerator pump rod through the rubber boot from the float side (bottom) of the carb top. The small end of the boot fits into a small groove encircling the pump rod.

Gather the *float* and its *pivot pin*. Hold the float so its bracket arms are on the outside of the float posts on the carb top. The tab (*float seat*) between the two arms should be straight above the needle valve pin. Align the holes in the arms and posts and slide the pivot pin in so its ends extend equally on both sides. Now gently press down on the float. It should pop up when you release it.

Step 2. Adjust Float Level.

Emergency People: If you don't have a metric ruler handy, skip down to Step 7.

Rebuilders and Quicky People: If you checked the float level in the sight glass before removing the carb and it was right on the dot, skip this step. If you didn't check the float level before disassembly or if it was more than 1/16" above or below the dot, adjust the float level. Here's how:

Get your little metric ruler handy. Checking the float level is a bit awkward, but you can do it. The carb top should be upside down on the table with the float side toward you. Gently lift the float until the tab on one of its bracket arms touches the mounting post. Slowly lower the float while watching the end of the needle valve pin. Measure the distance between the float and the rim of the carb top just as the pin touches the central tab (float seat) on the float bracket. Yes, you'll probably need to look at the illustration. If the measurement you get isn't approximately 10.5mm (7/16" or just a tad over 3/8"), you'll need to bend the float seat up or down. It's easy if you pull the float pin and remove the float. Use needlenose pliers to slightly bend the float seat up or down, then install the float and measure again. Keep checking and changing until you've got it.

Measuring the Float Level
(Hitachi Carb)

Raise Level
Lower Level

Step 3. Assemble Carb Body.

Quicky People: Follow the Rebuilders' instructions to install the parts you removed.

Rebuilders: Set the carb body right side up on the workbench. Insert the primary and secondary *emulsion tubes* into their holes in the carb body. Be *sure* each is in its correct hole. Now install the primary and secondary *main air bleed jets*. Tighten them snug with a screwdriver, but don't use so much force you strip 'em.

Install the *power valve* with a new gasket into its hole on the shelf in the float chamber. Use the notched screwdriver to tighten it.

Install the *primary slow jet* into its hole and tighten it with a skinny screwdriver (*not* one that will scrape the threads in the hole). Now install the primary slow jet plug and tighten it.

Install the rest of the jets on the top of the carb body and tighten them with a screwdriver. Remember to go by the numbers.

Turn the carb body over and install the primary and secondary *main jets*. Be sure you get each in its right hole, then tighten them both with a small screwdriver. Find new gaskets for the *main jet plugs*, and slip them on. Install the plugs and tighten them with a 12mm wrench. (Put the *lock plate* on the plugs if you have one. Press the teeth over the plugs with a screwdriver after the plugs are tightened.)

If you have a *servo diaphragm*, install a new O-ring (if your diaphragm had one) then fit the rubber-tipped shaft into the hole on the rear of the carb body. Rotate the triangular mounting plate so the three screw holes are aligned with the holes in the carb body. Install and tighten the three small phillips screws and lockwashers.

Step 4. Attach Carb Body to Throttle Chamber.

Quicky People: Skip this step.

Rebuilders: Find two new gaskets that match the shape of the fiber *insulator plate*. There should be a hole in the gaskets wherever there's a hole in the insulator.

The carb body is upside down, right? Orient one of the new gaskets so all the holes match the holes in the bottom of the carb body. Be sure a hole in the gasket fits over the hollow *dowel* sticking out of primary end of the carb body. Now install the fiber *insulator block*, then the other gasket. All the holes match up? Good.

Find the large, long *hollow phillips screw* and its toothed lockwasher, and the other two short fat phillips mounting screws and their regular lockwashers. Put the lockwashers on the screws then lay them someplace close. Grab the *throttle chamber*, turn it upside down, then set it on the bottom of the carb body so all the holes line up. (You might have to wiggle the lever on the auxiliary butterfly shaft a little so it clears the throttle chamber. Be sure the two rods attached to the throttle arm shaft are sticking out in front and clear of everything and have not slipped between the throttle arm shaft and the secondary shaft on the carb body.) Everything lined up? The insulator plate should be neatly and evenly sandwiched between the throttle chamber and carb body (slip it into place with your fingers if it isn't quite there yet). With the whole "sandwich" upside down, insert the long hollow phillips screw into the hole between the two butterfly valves in the bottom of the throttle chamber. Screw it in until it's lightly snug but don't tighten it yet. Turn the carb over and install the two fat mounting screws into their holes on the throttle arm side of the carb body. Tighten them with a phillips screwdriver (yes, you'll have to angle it in there). Now turn the carb over again and tighten the hollow phillips screw.

Step 5. Install Anti-diesel Valve (if yours has one).

Be sure there's a thin gasket on the valve, then screw it into the carb body. Tighten it with a 19mm or crescent wrench.

Step 6. Install Tiny Drop-in Parts.

Quicky People: Install the parts named in this step now if you removed them.

Rebuilders: Turn the carb body right side up. Look in the rebuild kit for a new **accelerator pump inlet valve** (a BB-size ball). If there isn't one, you'll have to reuse the old one. Drop the ball into the large accelerator pump hole in the top front of the carb body. That's right, just drop it in. Jiggle the carb around until the ball falls into the small hole at the bottom. Now find the *spring* that's bent so one end of the wire forms a U shape across the end of the spring. Insert the U-shaped end of the spring into the accelerator pump hole where the little ball lives.

Here's another drop-in part. Look in the Tiny Parts can and find the **accelerator pump outlet valve** (injector weight). It's a short solid hexagonal shaped shaft with a pointed end. Drop it into the hole between the accelerator pump hole and the primary main air bleed jet. The pointed end goes down.

Set the carb body aside for now. Remember that those little pieces are just lying in the carb body now and you'll have to catch them if you turn the carb upside down for some reason.

Step 7. Install Carb Top on Carb Body.

Emergency People: The old gasket might have shrunk and wrinkled while you were cleaning the needle valve. If it did, carefully soak it in whatever gas is left in the float bowl, then try to install it.

Rebuilders and Quicky People: Find a new *carb top gasket* in the kit that exactly matches your old one. Compare the holes and the shapes of the gaskets carefully. Set the new gasket on the carb body so all the holes line up. Check 'em carefully. If they didn't line up, you'll have to fetch the right gasket. Take the gasket off and set it aside for now.

Go to the carb top, which should be upside down. Remove the float again and slip the new gasket onto the carb top. (Don't try to stretch it around the float!) Do all the holes match? Be sure the gasket fits around the outside of the rubber accelerator pump boot. Install the float.

Hold the gasket in place with your fingers while you turn the carb top over and align it with the carb body. Guide the accelerator pump and float into their holes as you gently lower the top onto the carb body. Wiggle it a little to be sure it's seated. Install the longest top-mounting screw into the hole on the top front of the carb right next to the choke housing. (One early version has a single dashpot bracket that mounts beneath this long screw. If that's you, install the bracket at this time, as well as the two bracket mounting screws that fit into the right side of the carburetor body.) Install mounting screws and lockwashers in the holes next to the accelerator pump and above the sight glass. Snug the screws with a phillips screwdriver. (On later models, you'll install the two rear screws later with the dashpot bracket. If you have an earlier model with no rear dashpot bracket, install the two rear screws now.)

Step 8. Assemble Automatic Choke.

There should be two rods still attached to the throttle arm shaft. Lift the shorter, straighter rod up to the lever attached to the bottom front of the choke housing. Fit the end of the rod through the hole in the lever, then install the tiny washer and cotter pin you stashed in the Tiny Parts can. There might be a new cotter pin in the rebuild kit you can use. Bend the cotter pin around the shaft. If you didn't remove the choke cover, skip down to Step 9.

The *choke cover* is clean, right? Hold it next to the choke housing so the words CLOSE and OPEN are at the top. The hook on the end of the flat spiral spring in the cover has to hook the little lever sticking out of the choke housing. Here's how to do it: Before fitting the cover to the housing, rotate the cover *clockwise* about 90° (¼ turn). Now fit the cover between the three ears on the housing. Push on the cover while you rotate it *counterclockwise* until the short line on the edge of the cover is aligned with the short line just to the left of the long line on the housing. Hold the cover in that position while you install and tighten the triangular washers and phillips screws. The washers are slightly bowed so install them with the convex side toward the screw head.

Step 9. Install Rear Bracket to Carb Top.

If you don't have two dashpots mounted in the bracket that attaches to the top rear of the carb, install the bracket with the two remaining mounting screws. Snug them down, then tighten all five of the carb top mounting screws. (A few versions may have no bracket here at all—just put in the screws and tighten them all.)

If you do have *two dashpots* mounted in a bracket, grab them. Look in the Tiny Parts can for the spring and retainer washer that go on the outer dashpot shaft. Lay them nearby and handy.

The hooked end of the rod attached to the pot in the middle of the bracket has to hook into the slot of the small brass-colored arm hanging down between the carb top and the choke housing. It's rather difficult to see.

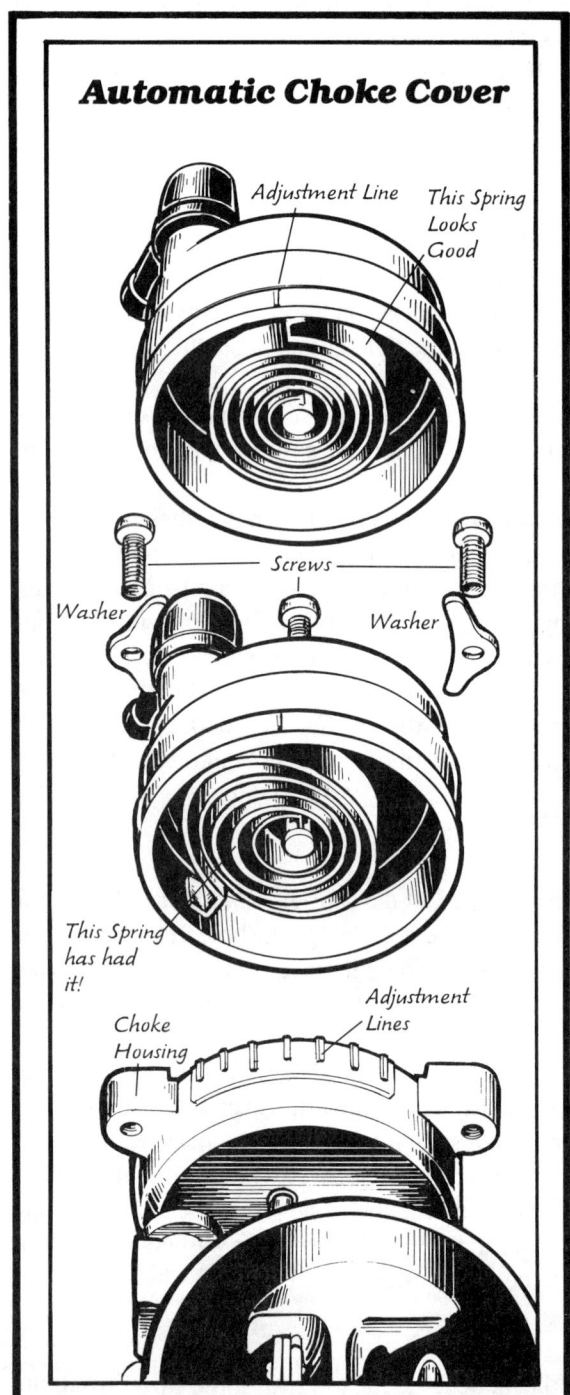

Automatic Choke Cover

Pick up the carb and turn it so the rear is toward you. The choke cover and housing will be on your right. Hold the carb in your left hand and the dashpots and bracket in your right hand. Hold the bracket up to the carb in its installed position, then rotate the bracket *clockwise* until you can hook the end of the rod into the slot in the little arm. Now rotate the bracket *counterclockwise* into position on the rear of the carb. Set the carb down. Install the spring, then the washer, onto the outer dashpot shaft. The little tabs on the retainer washer fit inside the spring. Pull the washer toward the dashpot while you fit the end of the rod that's dangling from the carb top through the hole in the dashpot shaft. Install the two remaining mounting screws and washers through the bracket holes and into the holes on the carb top. Snug the two screws, then tighten all five top-mounting screws.

Step 10. Install Accelerator Pump Lever.

Remember the *accelerator pump lever*? It's a strip of metal with two or three small holes in one end, a small pin sticking out of the other end, and a large hole toward the pin end.

Set the carb so the front is toward you. Lift the *long crooked rod* attached to the throttle arm shaft up toward the choke housing. Stick the hooked end through the small hole that's second from the end in the pump lever. Insert it from the pin side of the lever. Wiggle and rotate the rod through the hole until you can stick the pin on the other end of the lever through the hole in the *accelerator pump shaft* that's sticking up out of the top of the carb. You might have to rotate the accelerator pump shaft so the pin can slip into the hole.

Look in the Tiny Parts can for the *pump lever screw* (it's the one with the big head), a flat washer, a lockwasher and large round *pump lever spring* (some very early models don't have a spring). Pull the pin on the lever back out of the accelerator pump shaft. Stick the large screw through the large hole in the lever. Wiggle it until the shoulder on the screw fits snugly in the lever hole. Hold it there while you slip the flat washer, then the lockwasher, onto the screw. The spring (if you have one) has a hook on one end and a 90° bend on the other. Put the spring on the screw so the hooked end is next to the bottom of the pump lever pointing straight down. The other end should be pointing toward the carb. Now try to hold the screw in the lever, and the washers and spring on the screw, while you guide the pin on the lever back into the hole in the accelerator pump shaft. Be sure the 90° end of the spring ends up on the carb top right next to the rubber boot. Screw the large screw into the carb with your fingers. You'll probably have to push down on the accelerator pump shaft to align the screw and its hole on the carb. If the pump lever slipped off the screw shoulder, wiggle it back on and hold it in place while you finish tightening the screw with a screwdriver. Is the 90° end of the spring next to the rubber boot and the hooked end hanging down below the lever? You should be able to wiggle the lever a little even after the screw is tightened. Check it. Is the pin engaged in the hole in the accelerator pump shaft? If anything's amiss, remove the screw and start over. Everything's where it should be? Good.

Now you need to get the hooked end of the spring over the top of the pump lever. Slide a small screwdriver between the pump lever and spring on the choke side of the screw. Put the end of the screwdriver in the hooked end of the spring and, using the screw as a pivot point, push the screwdriver handle to your right. When the hook is even with the top of the lever, press it against the lever with your finger while you pull the screwdriver out of the spring. The end of the spring will hook over the top of the lever. The other end of the spring should be on the carb top near the accelerator pump boot. Check it.

Step 11. Whew! Finish the Job.

Find the *throttle return spring*. It has a hook on each end. Hook one end of the spring in the hole on the lever sticking out on the bottom of the throttle arm, then hook the other end in the hole on the bottom of the dashpot bracket or choke housing, depending on your setup.

If you have a single dashpot carb with the dashpot bracket mounted on the throttle arm side of the carb body, now's the time to attach the dashpot's little rod to its hole on a lever on the throttle arm. A cotter pin locks it into place.

Slip the short coiled spring onto the pointed *idle mixture adjustment screw*. Now install the screw into the hole on the front of the throttle chamber. Gently screw it in until it stops. Now unscrew it *four* complete turns. We'll do the fine adjustment with the engine running. (If your mixture screw has a plastic top with a tab, the tab may not clear the carb body as you screw it in. Use pliers to gently pull the top off; then push it back on once the screw is in place.)

Find the long *idle speed adjustment screw* and spring. Fit the spring onto the threaded end of the screw, then screw the screw into the threaded hole in the throttle chamber just above the throttle arm shaft. It goes in at about a 45° angle, just like the mixture screw. Screw it in until the end barely touches the tab on the throttle arm shaft. You'll have to do a final idle adjustment with the engine running.

The carb is now assembled. Or should be. Any loose screws or springs left in the cans? Some may be old ones you have replaced with new, or extras. Turn the carb around to see if everything's secure and the throttle arm rotates back and forth smoothly. If it's all together, you're ready to put the carb back on the engine.

Quicky People: You'll be doing some Procedure 10 stuff, starting with Step 2.

PROCEDURE 10: INSTALL HITACHI CARBURETOR

Condition: You've removed the carb for whatever reason and now you want to put it back on; OR you're installing a new or rebuilt carb; OR you did a quicky rebuild.

Tools and Materials: 10mm wrench, phillips and/or regular screwdriver, knife or putty knife or razor blade, new carburetor mounting gasket. (Quicky people won't need the gasket or razor blade.)

Step 1. Attach Carburetor to Intake Manifold.

Emergency and Quicky People: Skip this step.

Rebuilders: Stuff a clean rag or paper towel into the hole in the manifold where the carburetor fits so pieces of the old gasket can't fall into the engine. Use a knife, putty knife, or razor blade to scrape all traces of the old *carburetor mounting gasket* off the intake manifold. Be sure the surface is absolutely smooth. A little solvent will help get off the last of the crud. Remove the rag or paper towel from the hole. Remove any traces of dirt or gasket that might have fallen in there.

Find a new mounting gasket that matches the old one. Fit it over the four studs sticking up on the manifold, making sure the holes match perfectly. Now set the carb on the four mounting studs. Remember, the adjusting screws are on the front, and the round choke housing on the side of the carburetor top goes toward the passenger's side of the car.

Here's where your patience will be tested: Put a lockwasher (or whatever was under the nuts) and a 10mm nut on each stud, then screw the nuts down as far as you can with your fingers. Use a 10mm wrench to tighten them evenly in a diagonal pattern (first one corner, then the far opposite corner, then back to the other side, etc.). Go around a few times until all four nuts are snug.

Step 2. Connect Vacuum Hoses and Wires to Carb.

Connect the vacuum hoses and/or rubber plugs to the front of the carb. They might go like this as you face the carb: the left hose to a fitting hiding under the carb top just above the idle-speed adjustment screw; one or two hoses or rubber plugs to fittings on the front center of the carb; the right hose might go to a fitting sticking out of the top left (driver's side) of the carb. Late models have hoses that attach horizontally to the front and/or rear of the carb. Refer to the illustration or your sketch to be sure. There may also be a diagram under your hood. You'll need all the help you can get. Persevere.

Connect the *fuel inlet hose* to the fitting on the top rear corner of the carb, then position and tighten the clamp. Attach the *fuel return hose* and the hose to the *switch vent solenoid* (if you have them) the same way.

If your carb has dashpots, connect the vacuum hoses to the dashpot(s) on the rear of the carb.

Attach the *accelerator cable* to the throttle arm (Procedure 3, Step 7).

Connect the *automatic choke wire* to the wiring harness. If you have them, connect the *anti-dieseling valve wire* and the *switch vent solenoid valve wire* to the wiring harness.

EVERYONE: Be sure the vacuum hoses are securely attached to the intake manifold, metal pipes or whatever. Check for any loose hoses or wires; Reconnect them if you find any. It's like a puzzle; it's not done till the last piece is in place.

Step 3. Do This and That.

EVERYONE: Reconnect the negative (-) battery cable clamp (Chapter 10, Procedure 1, Step 3).

Rebuilders: Add coolant to the radiator and be sure to check the coolant level again after the engine has warmed up (Chapter 16, Procedure 1, Step 2).

Step 4. Adjust Carb.

Install the air cleaner (Chapter 7, Procedure 5, Step 5), then start the engine. It will take a few seconds for the fuel pump to fill the float bowl, so don't panic. You might have to screw the *idle speed* adjustment screw in (*clockwise*) a little to keep the engine running at first (Chapter 7, Procedure 12).

Once the engine will idle, check the *fuel level* in the sight glass on the left side of the carb. If the level is more than 1/16" above or below the dot, you'll need to remove the carb top and adjust the float level (Procedure 11).

Fuel level is right on? OK, let the engine warm up to normal operating temperature, then adjust the *idle speed* and *idle mixture* (Chapter 7, Procedure 12). If the engine won't idle slow enough after unscrewing the idle adjustment screw, give the accelerator cable a little more slack (Procedure 3, Step 7).

Check the coolant level again and add some if it's needed (Chapter 16, Procedure 1, Step 2).

Go for a test drive. Does the car accelerate properly and idle as it should? Sit back and wallow in the pride of your accomplishment.

PROCEDURE 11: EMERGENCY! OR QUICKY CARB CLEAN AND/OR REBUILD (Hitachi Carbs Only)

Carburetor problems can often be cured without a full-scale carb rebuild. Step 1 might solve your problem. The rest of the procedure is for people who merely need to adjust the float level, or for those unfortunate souls who are broken down at the side of the road with a stuck needle valve (open or closed), or for lazy people (like me) who are in the mood for just a "quicky" rebuild. It might solve your problem with less hassle, but it's not a complete job, mind you, so you won't qualify for the Carburetor Rebuilding Merit Badge. If all this fails, you'll have to remove the carb and do a complete rebuild.

For people who need to adjust the float level or are in an emergency situation, and have been referred here from other procedures and steps in this chapter, read the **Emergency People** instructions, then do the step using whatever tools and ingenuity you have available. Basically what you'll be doing is removing the top of the carburetor, adjusting the float level (if necessary), and checking the needle valve assembly for dirt.

People here for a quicky, read the special instructions in the procedures and steps designated **Quicky People**, then follow the **Rebuilders** instructions also. You'll be removing the top of the carb, then removing and cleaning the accessible jets and replacing the gaskets and needle valve assembly.

Condition: You're stranded on the side of the road and suspect the carburetor is the culprit—gas is pouring out around the top of the carb, or there's no gas visible in the sight glass on the side of the carb; OR the engine isn't running right and you want to do a quicky carb clean and/or rebuild.

Tools and Materials:
 Emergency People: You'll need a 10mm wrench, phillips screwdriver, and pliers. Some clean rags would be helpful (handkerchief, tie, socks, etc.). If you just happen to have a spray can of carb cleaner, you are truly blessed.
 Quicky People: I'm assuming you aren't in an emergency situation and can round up a few parts and supplies before you start.
 For Step 1, you'll need a spray can of carburetor cleaner and maybe a 10mm wrench to remove the air cleaner top. To do the quicky rebuild, you'll need all the tools and materials listed in Procedure 8 *except* the 12mm wrench and the big can of carb cleaner (you'll use spray cans). If possible, have a carb rebuild kit handy.

CAUTION: Be careful not to drop anything into the carb while you're working on it. If something does drop into it, try to fish the part out with a magnet, or remove the carb if you can't get it out otherwise.

 Step 1. Quicky Carb Clean.

 Emergency People: If you don't have a spray can of carb cleaner, skip down to Step 2.
 Emergency and Quicky People: One day on the way home from work, my Brat decided it would only run at idle or full throttle, with nothing in between. What a frantic ten miles of driving just to get home! All the way I was thinking for sure I'd be up late that night rebuilding the carb instead of going to a beach party I had been looking forward to for weeks. In desperation I yanked off the air cleaner and doused the inside of the carb with carb cleaner. I must have used half a can of the stuff. When I started the engine it coughed, sputtered, belched a cloud of blue smoke that nearly brought out the fire department, then smoothed out and purred like a kitten. My evening wasn't ruined after all, thanks to the "mechanic in a can." Maybe you'll be just as lucky. There's only one way to find out.

Remove the 10mm nut or the three wingnuts on the *air cleaner top*, or flip up the retaining clips around the edge depending on your setup. Lift the air cleaner top off the housing, then remove the *air filter element*.

Put the little tube that comes with it in the nozzle of the carb cleaner can and spray the inside of the carburetor. Let it soak a few minutes then spray it some more. Stick the tube into the holes in the rear of the carb and give them a good shot. Look for small round brass screws to squirt. Use your finger or a screwdriver to hold the flat choke plate in the front half of the carb straight up and down so you can clean the front part of the carb. If you have a clean rag handy, use it to wipe away as much crud as possible from inside the carb.

Now try to start the engine. If it starts it'll probably belch out a huge cloud of blue smoke. That's the carb cleaner burning off so don't worry. Just be sure you're not in a closed garage. Try revving the engine with the gas pedal. Is your problem solved? If so, put the air filter in the housing, put the air cleaner top on and secure it with the 10mm nut, wingnuts, or clips. Go for a test drive to be sure you've eliminated the problem. If your Soob still doesn't run right, let's dig a little deeper for the solution.

Step 2. Tap Carb Top to Free Needle Valve.

EVERYONE: Remove the air cleaner (Chapter 7, Procedure 5, Step 4). Look at the **sight glass** on the left (driver's) side of the carb. If the fuel level line in the glass is near the top or bottom of the glass, use a wrench or the handle of a screwdriver or hammer to tap on the top of the carb near the fuel inlet. Tap, don't bash! The tapping might free the *needle valve*, if it's stuck. Tap the carb a few times, then start the engine if possible. If the fuel level in the sight glass returns to the dot in the middle, you may have solved the problem. Replace the needle valve as soon as possible to avoid future emergency situations (and possible ulcers).

If there doesn't appear to be any gas in the float bowl after tapping the carb top, check the *fuel supply* (Procedure 4). If fuel is getting to the carb and tapping the top didn't solve the problem, do Step 3.

Step 3. Remove Carb Top, Clean Needle Valve, Adjust Float Level.

EVERYONE: To remove the carb top, do Procedure 7, Steps 1, 3, 4, 5, and 6. Do Step 8 if the wire for the *anti-diesel valve* is connected to the choke wire. Do Step 10 but disconnect *only* the hoses attached to the top of the carb. Do Procedure 8, Steps 1, 2, and 3, to disconnect the **carb top** from the body, remove the **float**, and check the **needle valve**.

If you don't have a new gasket for the carb top, leave the gas in the float bowl. You might need it to soak the old gasket in later. If you have a new gasket, clean the inside of the float bowl with a clean rag or paper towel.

Step 4. Install Carb Top.

Emergency People: After the needle valve is cleaned and the float is adjusted, go to Procedure 9, Step 1, to start putting the carb back together. You'll need to do the following steps in Procedure 9: 1, 2, 7, 9, 10, and 11.

Procedure 10, Steps 2 and 3, will get everything reconnected. Hopefully the problem is solved and you can drive off into the sunset with a satisfied smile. If not, I offer you my sympathy. It's complete rebuild time, so call for a tow or a miracle.

Quicky People: In Procedure 8, you can do any of Steps 4-14 (except Step 9) that you feel needs doing. The more steps you do, the better your chances of having a healthy carburetor. To put things back together, read Procedure 9 and do the steps that are applicable to you.

Do Procedure 10, Steps 2, 3, and 4, to get everything reconnected, the engine running, and the carb adjusted.

Hopefully your problem has been solved. If not, a carb rebuild or replacement is necessary (Procedure 7).

PROCEDURE 12: REMOVE AND INSTALL CARTER-WEBER CARBURETOR

Condition: Your Carter-Weber carb needs to be rebuilt or replaced.

Tools and Materials: 10 and 12mm wrenches, phillips screwdriver, masking tape, indelible marking pen, rags.

Remarks: Use masking tape and pen to label the fuel and vacuum hoses before disconnecting them.

Step 1. Get Ready.

Do Steps 1 through 3 in Procedure 7. These preliminaries are the same as for the other carburetor.

Step 2. Disconnect Fuel Hoses.

The fuel **inlet and return hoses** are attached to a Y-shaped fitting on the left rear corner of the carb. The larger hose is the inlet hose. Label the hoses, then use a phillips screwdriver to loosen the clamps. Now disconnect the hoses.

The **vent hose** is attached to a bracket near the left front corner. Label the hose, squeeze the hose clamp and slide it away from the end of the hose, then pull the hose off the fitting.

Step 3. Disconnect Electrical Things.

There are two electrical *harness connectors* on the right side of the carb near the round automatic choke housing. Separate the two connectors. They're shaped differently so you don't need to label them.

Step 4. Disconnect Vacuum Hoses.

Label, then disconnect the small hose for the vacuum advance unit on the distributor from the bottom front of the carb. Now label and disconnect the vacuum hose for the *EGR valve* from the round gizmo on the rear of the carb. See any additional vacuum hoses? If so, label them for location and disconnect them.

Step 5. Disconnect Accelerator Cable.

See Procedure 3, Step 2, to disconnect the accelerator cable from the throttle arm on the carb.

Step 6. Remove Carb.

Remove the 10mm nuts and lockwashers on the bottom front and rear of the carb, then gently pull the carb off the intake manifold. Check all around and disconnect and label any hoses or wires that might still be attached to the carb. Remove the **fiber insulator plate** from the intake manifold or the bottom of the carb; it may be stuck either place. Cover the hole in the intake manifold with a clean rag or paper towel.

Step 7. Prep for Installing Carter-Weber Carb.

Use a knife or razor blade to carefully remove traces of the old gasket from each side of the fiber insulator plate. Scrape the old gasket from the carb mount on the intake manifold, then remove the rag or paper towel. Remove any gasket parts that may fall into the manifold. Now install a new **carb mount gasket**, then the *insulator*, then another carb mount *gasket* onto the manifold. Be sure all the holes are aligned.

Step 8. Install Carter-Weber Carb.

Fit the carb onto the manifold, then install and tighten the 10mm lockwashers and nuts on the bottom front and rear of the carb.

Connect the accelerator cable to the throttle arm (Procedure 3, Step 7).

Reconnect the two electrical harness connectors.

Connect the hose from the vacuum advance unit to the bottom front of the carb.

Connect the hose from the EGR valve to the round thing on the rear of the carb.

Connect the hoses for the fuel inlet and return to the Y fitting on the left rear corner.

Connect the vent hose to the vent solenoid valve on the front of the carb and tighten the clamp. Attach the bracket to the top of the carb with the 10mm bolt.

Connect any other hoses that you disconnected from the carb.

Step 9. Do This and That.

Reconnect the battery cable (Chapter 10, Procedure 1, Step 3).

Add coolant to the radiator (Chapter 16, Procedure 1). Be sure to check the coolant level after the engine has been warmed up, then cooled off.

Install the air cleaner (Chapter 7, Procedure 12, Step 8). Start the engine and let it warm up, then adjust the *idle speed* (Chapter 7, Procedure 12, Steps 1, 3, 4, and 5).

Have Subaru or a garage set the idle mixture and adjust the fast idle mechanism for the automatic choke.

PROCEDURE 13: CHECK AUTOMATIC CHOKE (Carb Models Only)

Start this procedure when the engine is cool. Read Procedure 8, Step 9, for an explanation of how the automatic choke works. It's the same principle on Hitachis and Carter-Webers.

Condition: It's hard to start the engine on cold mornings; OR the engine starts but won't idle; OR the engine starts easily but runs poorly and the gas mileage is down.

Tools and Materials: 10mm wrench, maybe a phillips screwdriver, maybe a file and pop rivet gun and rivets if yours is a 1980 or newer model.

Step 1. Remove Air Cleaner.

Remove the air cleaner, then plug the vacuum lines that were connected to the air cleaner (Chapter 7, Procedure 5, Step 4).

Step 2. Check Position of Choke Plate.

With the engine off and cold, push the accelerator pedal to the floor one time and release it. This should set the choke to its horizontal ON position.

Now look in the top of the carb. On Hitachi carbs the **choke plate** (butterfly valve) should be covering the front half of the opening in the top of the carb. On Carter-Weber carbs the choke plate should cover the entire opening. If it does, skip to Step 4. If the choke plate isn't in the horizontal ON position, do Step 3.

Step 3. Remove Choke Cover and Check Springs.

If the choke plate isn't covering the opening, the choke isn't working. See if you can move it with your fingers or a screwdriver. If it's stuck, squirt a little penetrating oil on both ends of the **choke plate shaft** inside the carb opening, then squirt some on the shaft that connects the choke plate and the round choke housing on the right (passenger's) side of the carb. If you can't free the choke plate, do Step 5 to remove and check the choke cover.

Step 4. See if Choke Opens.

Clear tools, rags, and stuff away from the drive belts and fan(s), be sure the vacuum lines are plugged, then start the engine. As the engine warms up the rpms will increase. Tap the accelerator pedal occasionally and see if the engine slows to idle. It should. The choke plate should gradually open to a vertical position as the engine warms up. If it doesn't, feel the round *choke housing* on the right (passenger's) side of the carb. It should be warm. If it isn't, see if the *wire* to the choke is connected. Wire OK? Then check the *fuse(s)* for the choke (Chapter 10, Procedure 2, Steps 1-3). If all's well in Fuseville, see if there's juice in the wire at the connection to the choke (Chapter 10, Procedure 5, Step 2). If there's juice getting to the choke wire but the choke housing doesn't warm up, the little *heater wire* inside the choke cover is probably kaput. Do Step 5 to remove and install the choke cover.

Step 5. Remove, Check, and Install Choke Cover.

'72-'79 models: Remove the three screws around the perimeter of the round plastic *choke cover* and their little triangular washers (Procedure 8, Step 5).

'80 and newer models: If the choke plate is stuck and you can't free it or the choke housing isn't heating up, you'll have to remove the phillips screw at the bottom of the round choke cover (right side of the carb), then file the *two rivets* off the top corners. (Don't let the metal filings fall into the carb.) You'll need a pop rivet gun and a couple of pop rivets to reinstall the cover, or hire someone to rivet it for you. If you aren't up for it, put the air cleaner on and take the car to Subaru or a garage and have them check the choke for you.

EVERYONE: Lift off the cover to see if the springs inside are broken or bent. The *flat spiral-shaped spring* should be wound evenly around the center post and the small brass spring should be neatly tucked into the ceramic groove. If the springs look good, try to move the choke plate again. If it moves now or if the springs are distorted and weird, get a new choke cover. If the choke plate is still stuck, have Subaru or a garage check it for you.

To install the choke cover, see Procedure 9, Step 8. If you filed off rivets to remove the cover, install the bottom screw then pop new rivets into the top two holes (or have Subaru or a garage rivet it for you). If you're installing a new choke cover and the old choke wire is permanently connected to other wires, you'll need to cut the old wire and splice on the new choke wire. See Chapter 18, Procedure 10, to splice the wire.

Install the air cleaner (Chapter 7, Procedure 5, Step 5).

PROCEDURE 14: CHECK AND REPLACE ANTI-DIESEL VALVE (Hitachi Carbs Only)

Condition: The engine will start but won't idle. It will run as long as you pump the gas pedal or keep the engine running at high speed.

Tools and Materials: 10mm and 19mm wrenches, maybe a new anti-diesel valve.

Remark: Early Hitachi carbs don't have an anti-diesel valve. Check the description in Step 1.

Step 1. Check Anti-Diesel Valve.

Remove the air cleaner (Chapter 7, Procedure 5, Step 4).

The anti-diesel valve is a thumb-sized, six-sided gizmo sticking out of the front left (driver's) side of the carb. It points to the left front headlight and has a wire coming out the end.

Follow the wire from the valve to a wire connection. Disconnect the wire, then turn the ignition switch to ON but don't start the engine. Now connect the wire from the anti-diesel valve to the connector while listening for a *click* at the valve. Do it several times. If you hear a click, the switch is working but the spring inside might be bent. Do Step 2 to remove the valve and check the spring and plunger. If you don't hear a click when connecting the wires, use a 12-volt test light or Volt/Ohm meter (VOM) to check the wire for "juice" at the connector (Chapter 10, Procedure 5, Step 2). If there's juice going to the anti-diesel valve wire but the valve doesn't click when you connect the wires, the valve is kaput. Step 2 tells you how to replace it. If there's no juice in the wire where the valve wire connects, the wire is broken somewhere between here and the battery. Follow the wire until it disappears into a bundle of wires. Follow the bundle as far as you can while checking for breaks. Check the wires around the fuse box for breaks. If you find a broken or frayed section of wire, splice it (Chapter 18, Procedure 9). Can't find a break? You'll have to have Subaru, a garage, or an auto electric place locate the problem.

Step 2. Remove and Install Anti-Diesel Valve.

Disconnect the wire to the anti-diesel valve, then use a 19mm wrench to remove the valve *counterclockwise* as viewed from the front of the car. (If the wire for your anti-diesel valve wire is attached to a connector with other wires and doesn't disconnect separately, go ahead and unscrew the valve; the wire will twist enough to get the valve out.) Don't lose the thin copper *gasket* (washer). Pull the pointed **plunger** out of the valve. Is the plunger dirty or bent? Is the tiny **spiral spring** inside the valve crooked or missing? Replace the valve if the plunger is bent or the spring is crooked or missing. If the plunger and/or the inside of the valve are dirty, clean them, then install the valve and see if it works. Still no luck? Replace the valve.

To install the valve, insert the fat round end of the plunger into the valve. Be sure there's a thin copper washer on the threaded end, then screw the valve into the carb. Tighten the valve *clockwise* with a 19mm wrench, then connect the wire. If you're replacing the valve and the wire is directly connected to other wires with no handy local connector, you'll have to cut the wire and splice it (Chapter 18, Procedure 9).

Install the air cleaner (Chapter 7, Procedure 5, Step 5).

Chapter 11

CHAPTER 12
EXHAUST AND EMISSION CONTROL SYSTEMS

This chapter is basically about *waste*; what to do with the leftovers after the good stuff has been removed. The problem has plagued humanity for years, from human waste to nuclear waste. If it isn't dealt with properly, we all suffer from the resulting pollution. Other than furtive protestations, you and I can't do much about nuclear waste, but we can help reduce air pollution by keeping our cars well-tuned and the *emission system* in good working order.

Automotive exhaust fumes contain *hydrocarbons* (HC), *carbon monoxide* (CO), and nitrous oxides (NOx) that react chemically in sunlight. These chemicals form inside the engine when gasoline is burned, then get pumped through the *exhaust system* and into the air. Since the '60s, car manufacturers (under pressure from environmentalists and the government) have been using a trial and error process to develop ways to reduce these harmful exhaust emissions. The first steps were rather simple, but in recent years, they've developed into complex systems controlled by electrical and vacuum devices. Sure enough, since emission control laws went into effect, the amount of pollution pumped out of exhaust pipes has dropped significantly. Here's how the miracle is accomplished.

EMISSION CONTROL SYSTEMS

Some mechanics (and would-be mechanics) blame emission control devices for poor gas mileage, decreased power, premature engine failure, acne, hemorrhoids, famine, and floods. The truth is, emission control devices rarely cause the problems they're frequently blamed for. A good, thorough tune-up (which includes some emission control maintenance) will usually remedy most engine performance problems.

If the engine still runs poorly after a tune-up or there's a sudden decrease in gas mileage, first check all vacuum hose and wiring connections under the hood. A poor connection is the most frequent cause of problems. When disconnecting hoses, pull on the end, not the middle, of the hose. When disconnecting wires, pull on the connector, not on the wire. Label all hoses and electrical connections before disconnecting them and double check that they're reconnected correctly when the job is finished. Even Subaru mechanics often label and recheck, due to the multitude of variations from year to year and model to model. If you have one, use the sticker under the hood for reference.

Your Soob uses a combination of systems to make it one of the cleanest running machines on the road. I'll start by describing the various systems and the years they were used. You might want to use a yellow marking pen to highlight the systems that apply to your particular year and model so you won't have to read through all the systems. I'll also tell you which components in the systems you can check at home and which ones require special tools or expertise to diagnose or replace.

Here are a few precautions to follow to avoid damaging some of the emission control devices: Use only unleaded fuel in '79 and newer models. Avoid coasting with the car in gear and the ignition off. (The unburned fuel being sucked through the engine will coat the catalyst on some models and ruin it.) Be careful not to bang against electrical devices while working on the engine. Also, prolonged engine idling can cause the exhaust system to overheat and possibly damage the exhaust system (maybe even start a fire).

CRANKCASE EMISSION CONTROL SYSTEM

When the fuel is ignited in the cylinders, some of the burned gas (called *blow-by gas*) squeezes past the piston rings into the crankcase. As the engine runs, the blow-by gas builds up pressure inside the crankcase which must be relieved or it will blow out the engine seals and gaskets. Back in the old days, the pressure was released through a pipe directly into the air. Nowadays, the gas is recirculated through the engine to be burned again, then passed to the exhaust system.

On early Soobs, the two hoses connected to the tops of the valve covers carry the blow-by gas to the air cleaner where it's sucked into the carb and burned again. Starting in '77 on some models and in '79 on all models, a gizmo called a **positive crankcase ventilation (PCV) valve** was added to allow fresh air from the air cleaner to be sucked into the crankcase to mix with the blow-by gas before being sucked into the intake manifold.

On '77-'79 models, you can tell if you have a PCV valve by looking at the hose connected to the top of the left (driver's side) valve cover. If the hose connects directly to the air cleaner, you don't have a PCV valve. If the hose connects to a plastic elbow, the hose on the other end of the elbow connects to the PCV valve that's screwed into the intake manifold. A smaller hose attached to the side of the elbow connects to the air cleaner. The hoses attached to the top of the valve covers and the PCV valve need to be checked and cleaned periodically. Procedure 2 tells you how.

EXHAUST EMISSION CONTROL SYSTEMS

Depending on the year and model, the exhaust emission control system utilizes vacuum and electrical devices, temperature sensors, revolution counters, and timers to reduce the pollutants pumped out of the exhaust pipe. Here's how some of these gizmos work:

Vacuum: When the engine is running, the pistons create a vacuum on the intake stroke which draws the fuel/air mixture from the carburetor, through the intake manifold, and into the cylinder to be burned on the next combustion stroke. It's the same principle as filling a hypodermic syringe; pulling the plunger away from the needle end of the syringe creates a vacuum that sucks the fluid into the syringe. In the case of your Soob, you have four plungers (the pistons), one inlet like the syringe's needle (the carburetor), four syringes to be filled (the cylinders), and a manifold to connect the four syringes to the single needle.

Exhaust and Emission Control Systems

The difference between the hypodermic needle and your Soob is that the opening in the carburetor can be opened or closed by pressing or releasing the accelerator pedal. When the accelerator pedal is pressed down, the throttle valve (butterfly) in the bottom of the carburetor opens and allows the fuel/air mixture to be drawn in easily. When the accelerator pedal is up and the throttle valve in the carb is closed, the pistons still try to suck the mixture through the carb, but can't as well as they might because the opening is partially closed, so a *vacuum* is created.

The amount of vacuum in the cylinders and intake manifold varies relative to the position of the butterfly valve in the carburetor; there's *low vacuum* when the throttle valve is open (accelerating, cruising, heavy load), and *high vacuum* when the throttle valve is closed (decelerating, idling, light load). The variation of vacuum in the *intake manifold* just beneath the carburetor is used to regulate several engine and emission control components to increase the engine's efficiency and decrease nasty emissions.

Some examples of vacuum operated emission control devices are the *vacuum advance or retard unit* on the distributor, the *Exhaust Gas Recirculation* (EGR) system, and the *coasting bypass* (deceleration) circuit in the carburetor. Some of the vacuum gizmos are controlled by other gizmos like these:

Thermovacuum valves open or close vacuum passages between the intake manifold and various vacuum-controlled devices depending on the coolant temperature or the temperature of the intake manifold.

Thermoswitches turn electrical and vacuum devices on or off depending on the temperature of the coolant or the intake manifold.

Timers determine how long some of the electrical and vacuum devices will be on or off after the ignition switch is turned on.

Now that you know the principle of how some of the various emission control devices work, here's a list of the components and how the principles are applied to reduce exhaust emissions.

'75-'76 models: A simple *hot air induction system* is used to vary the air temperature entering the carburetor. The function of the hot air system is explained later in the '77-'84 hot air induction section.

'75-'80 models: A **coasting bypass system** (also called the *deceleration system*) operates when the car is decelerating or coasting along easily. Here's how it works. A **vacuum control valve** is mounted on the top right side of the intake manifold (it's on the front center of the manifold below the carb on '76 models). This valve operates in conjunction with the **carburetor** and a small round **servo diaphragm** on the rear of the carburetor. When the car is decelerating, higher than normal vacuum is created in the intake manifold. The increased vacuum overpowers a spring inside the vacuum control valve and opens a **poppet valve** which allows the vacuum to operate the servo diaphragm. The servo diaphragm opens the **bypass passage** in the carburetor and allows more air to be drawn into the bottom of the carb. The added air makes the air/fuel ratio *leaner* (less gas relative to air), and thus reduces the amount of gas being burned during deceleration when gas isn't needed anyway. Procedure 7 tells you how to check and repair the coasting bypass system.

'75-'80 models: A **vacuum retard unit** is mounted on the side of the *distributor*. When the car is decelerating, higher vacuum is created in the intake manifold. The increased vacuum causes the vacuum retard unit on the distributor to retard the *ignition timing*, which promotes the combustion of unburned fuel. See Chapter 7, Procedure 9, to check and/or replace the vacuum retard unit.

'75-'76 California cars and all '77 and newer models: On carb models, an **exhaust gas recirculation (EGR) valve** is mounted to the rear of the intake manifold just below the carb. A metal *EGR tube* connects the *exhaust port* of the #3 cylinder and the intake manifold. On fuel-injected models, the EGR valve is on the top left side of the intake manifold and the EGR tube connects the intake manifold to the exhaust port of the #4 cylinder. Here's how the EGR system works.

When the engine is decelerating, a vacuum hose from the intake manifold opens the EGR valve and allows some exhaust gas to be drawn into the intake manifold to be recirculated through the combustion chambers. The recycled exhaust gas lowers the combustion temperature in the cylinders which reduces the formation of nitrous oxides (NOx).

Over a period of time, the passages for the EGR system can become clogged with carbon and the EGR valve can get stuck. Procedure 1 tells you how to check, clean, and replace the EGR components.

'75 models only: An **air pump** was added to inject **"secondary air"** into the exhaust ports of the cylinder heads when the car is decelerating. In the exhaust ports, the secondary air promotes recombustion of unburned hydrocarbons and carbon monoxide. A *check valve* is installed between the pump and cylinder heads to prevent exhaust gas from flowing back into the pump.

An **anti-afterburning valve (AAV)** is attached between the air pump and intake manifold. The AAV allows the air pump to pump air into the intake manifold when the car is decelerating to prevent "backfiring."

The air pump is mounted between the carburetor and alternator and turned by a *drive belt*. The air pump was only used on '75 models. Such a short life. Maintenance and repair of the air pump is in Procedure 3. The anti-afterburning valve is covered in Procedure 8.

'75 California models only: A small round **dashpot** was added to the carburetor to prevent the throttle arm from snapping to the idle position when the accelerator pedal is released suddenly. The dashpot allows the throttle arm to return to the idle position slowly. The theory behind the dashpot is that if the throttle valve closes suddenly, the combustion in the cylinders will be incomplete, resulting in increased unburned hydrocarbon emissions. Procedure 10 tells you how to check, adjust, and replace the throttle dashpot.

'76 models only: The vacuum control valve was moved from the top right side of the intake manifold to a plate (*vacuum modulator cover*) on the front of the intake manifold just below the carburetor. Due to special tools and expertise required, you'll have to have a Subaru garage check and adjust the vacuum control valve.

'76-'79 models: A **vacuum modulator** is bolted to the bottom front center of the intake manifold. It's sort of triangular-shaped and has vacuum hoses connected to the top and right side. The modulator is a thick aluminum plate with channels machined into it to connect various vacuum ports. The function of the modulator is to reduce the number of hoses required to operate the various vacuum devices. No maintenance is required for the modulator, but I always clean mine when I rebuild the carburetor.

'76 and newer models (except '81): A pumpless **air injection system (AIS)** replaced the air pump used on '75 models. In this system metal tubes connect the exhaust ports of each cylinder to a **reed valve** which in turn connects to the engine *air cleaner* ('80 models have a separate "secondary" air cleaner for the air injection system). When vacuum in the exhaust system is high (deceleration, low engine speed, light load), the reed valve opens to allow "secondary" air from the air cleaner to enter the exhaust ports. The secondary air promotes oxidation of residual hydrocarbons and carbon monoxide before they're pumped through the exhaust system and into the atmosphere. When vacuum in the exhaust ports is low (high speed, heavy load), the reed valve closes the passage to the air cleaner so exhaust gas can't be sucked into the air cleaner. Procedure 3 covers AIS maintenance and repair.

'76-'80 models: An ignition timing **advance unit** was added to the *retard unit* on the *distributor*. When there's low vacuum in the intake manifold (acceleration, heavy load), the advancer advances the ignition timing to give the engine a little more power. The retard unit retards the timing when there's high vacuum in the manifold (deceleration, idle). Chapter 7, Procedure 10, tells you how to check the advance/retard unit and how to replace it if it's broken.

'76 and newer models: Stainless steel **exhaust port liners** were added to the cylinder heads to promote better oxidation of residual hydrocarbons (HC) and carbon monoxide (CO). There's no maintenance required for the liners.

'77 and newer carb models: A **hot air control system** is incorporated into the *air cleaner snout* to reduce hydrocarbon emission when the engine is cold. When the air temperature in the engine compartment is below 100°F, a flap in the snout closes the opening so hot air is sucked into the air cleaner through the large **hot air intake hose** that connects the air cleaner snout to an **air stove** on the right exhaust pipe. When the temperature is 100-127°F the flap in the snout starts opening so both hot and cold air can be sucked into the air cleaner. Above 127°F, the flap opens fully so cool air only is sucked into the air cleaner. Besides reducing hydrocarbon emissions in cold weather, the hot air control valve helps the engine warm up quickly and prevents carburetor icing. Procedure 6 covers maintenance and repair of the hot air control system.

'79 California models: In my opinion, this is when "high tech" emission controls began appearing. A **timer** and two **solenoid valves** control the *vacuum advance/retard unit* on the distributor to reduce exhaust emissions when starting the engine. Here's how the setup works. When the ignition switch is turned on, a *timer* causes two things happen: (1) the timer tells **Solenoid Valve I** to release the vacuum going to the advance unit on the distributor to the atmosphere so the advancer won't work; (2) the *timer* tells **Solenoid Valve II** to change the vacuum source for the retard unit on the distributor from the carburetor to the intake manifold. When 130 seconds have elapsed, the timer turns off so the vacuum advance works normally and the vacuum source for the retard unit becomes the carburetor. The two solenoids are in a bracket mounted to the *thermostat housing* on the engine. You'll have to have Subaru or a garage check the solenoids and timer for you.

'80 models: The **air injection system (AIS)** used is basically the same system used since '76, but a separate air cleaner was added. It's about the diameter of a 45 rpm record, painted the same color as the engine air cleaner, and mounted on the left side of the engine compartment near the brake *master cylinder reservoirs*. It should be checked periodically for dirt (Procedure 4).

'80 all California models, all automatic transmission models, and all manual transmission models *except* non-California Hatchback standard and DL, Sedan DL, and Hardtop DL models: A *timer* and *solenoid valves* similar to those used on '79 California models (described above) were used. A 245-second timer is on automatics and a 130-second timer is on cars with manual trannies.

'80 manual transmission non-California and Canadian Hatchback standard and DL models, Sedan and Hardtop DL models: An **anti-afterburning valve (AAV)** is mounted on the top left side of the intake manifold to inject air into the manifold when the engine is decelerating. Procedure 8 covers AAV check and replacement.

'80 California models: The *carburetor idle mixture* is set at the factory, then a **tamper-proof pin** is installed on the carburetor so you can't change the idle mixture (without removing the pin, at least).

'81 models: The *air injection system (AIS)* used on '76-'80 models changed to an **air induction system**. Here's how it works: A gizmo called **"thermo-vacuum valve (II)"** is screwed into the intake manifold to monitor the coolant temperature. When the coolant is cool, the valve allows air to be sucked into the intake manifold to provide a "leaner" mixture (less fuel to air ratio) which reduces carbon monoxide emissions while the carburetor choke is on. When the coolant temperature reaches 114°F, the valve closes, cutting off the air induction. Have Subaru check the thermo-vacuum valve.

'81 and newer models (except models with LED distributors): Only an ignition timing *advance unit* is used on the distributor. The retard unit was dropped. See Chapter 7, Procedure 10, to check the vacuum advance unit. A **tamper-proof pin** prevents changing the idle mixture of the carburetor on all models. An exhaust gas analyzer must be used to properly adjust the idle mixture within emission control limits. The day of "tuning by ear" is over.

Some 1981 and newer models: A **three-way catalyst** is added to the exhaust system to reduce hydrocarbon (HC), carbon monoxide (CO), and nitrous oxides (NOx) emissions. It's mounted where the two exhaust pipes from the engine merge together. The catalyst is a compound of platinum (Pt) and rhodium (Rh); a thin coating of the compound covers an oval-shaped honeycomb made of porous ceramics. The catalyst permits simultaneous *oxidation* and *reduction* to reduce exhaust gas emissions. (See your high school chemistry book for an explanation of oxidation and reduction.) An **oxygen (O_2) sensor** screwed into the catalyst monitors the ratio of oxygen in the air compared to the oxygen in the exhaust gases. Have Subaru check the O_2 sensor for you.

'81 and newer carb models: On most models an **electronic "brain"** and an **Electronically Controlled Carburetor (ECC)** were added so the fuel/air ratio could be changed automatically according to varying conditions. On '81s the brain is called an **Electronic Control Unit (ECU)** and on '82 and newer models it's called an **Electronic Control Module (ECM)** because a few more components were added to the system. To simplify things I'll just call both systems **"the brain."**

The brain is mounted under the dash in front of the driver's seat (it's on the wall behind the driver's seat on '81 Brats). Here's what it does: The brain receives signals from various emission control devices on the engine like *thermosensors, solenoid valves, vacuum switches, revolution control sensor* ('82 and newer models), and the *oxygen sensor* on the *exhaust catalyst*. According to the signals it receives, the brain sends signals to **duty solenoids** (two on Hitachi equipped cars, one on cars with Carter/Weber carbs) which control the fuel/air mixture of the electronically controlled carburetor (ECC). As you can see, some things are getting very complicated and beyond our ability to deal with at home.

If you're handy with a Volt/Ohm meter and dwell gauge, you can buy the workshop manual for your year, then follow the diagnostic flow charts to track down problems in the electrical emission control devices. I don't want to discourage you, but there are eight pages of flow charts for '81 models, 14 pages for '82 models, 22 pages for '83 models, 31 pages for '84 models, and more pages than I can count on '85 and newer models. If you're not up for it, take the car to Subaru and let them diagnose the problem, then replace the faulty component yourself. Most of the components are easy to replace.

'82 and newer carb models: An all-new **Air Injection System (AIS)** returns after a one-year absence. The new system injects air into the exhaust pipes instead of the exhaust ports in the cylinder head as the old system did. The **air suction valve** for the AIS is mounted on the lower right rear corner of the engine on some models, and on both lower rear corners on other models. When there's high vacuum in the exhaust system, the air suction valve (ASV) allows air from the air cleaner to be sucked into the exhaust pipe(s). On its way from the air cleaner to the exhaust pipe the air passes through a rubber hose into a black softball-size **plastic muffler** that muffles the exhaust noises, then through the ASV, then through an air suction pipe and, finally, into the exhaust pipe. The "secondary" air promotes oxidation of hydrocarbons and carbon monoxide in the exhaust gas and thus decreases the emissions.

Depending on the model, the new AIS system is controlled by a *timer*, a *solenoid valve*, a *thermosensor*, and *the brain*. Under certain vacuum and temperature conditions the brain tells the air suction valves to not allow secondary air to be injected into the exhaust pipes. Due to the control mechanisms, servicing and repair of the new AIS should be left to Subaru or a garage that specializes in Soobs.

Fuel-injected models: An efficient electronically controlled **fuel injection system** is used instead of a carburetor. There's more about the fuel injection and Turbo systems in the rap at the start of Chapter 11: *Fuel Systems*. Repair of the Turbo and/or fuel injection system is beyond our means.

'83 and newer models: An *Electronic Control System (ECS)* is added to monitor the "brain" and several of the emission control and fuel system devices on the engine and exhaust system. When the ECS detects a problem in one of the emission control or fuel system devices, the *ECS light* on the dash comes on and a small light on the "brain" indicates in Morse code which system is misbehaving. There is more about the ECS system in Chapter 11.

If you're electronically inclined, you can buy the shop manual for your year, then using pure Vulcan logic, follow the flow charts to check the devices in the malfunctioning system with a Volt/Ohm meter and dwell gauge.

EVAPORATIVE EMISSION CONTROL SYSTEM

Unburned gasoline is very volatile and causes pollution if allowed to evaporate into the air. The **evaporative emission control system** on your Soob captures the gas fumes before they have a chance to evaporate into the air, then either sends them back to the gas tank (where they condense into liquid again) or sends them to the carburetor to be burned. On '77-'84 models, a coffee-can-size black **canister** in the engine compartment serves as a holding place for the vapors until they're sent to the tank or carb. If you've ever wondered why the gas pump nozzles in California are so weird, it's because they capture the vapors that are displaced by the gas as you fill the tank. The vapors go through a separate hose to the station's tanks where they condense to liquid gas again. Hmmm.

The evaporative emission control system is mainly composed of rubber and metal lines to carry the vapors from the engine to the gas tank or canister, and from the canister to the engine. A few *check valves* are in the lines to prevent the vapors from flowing the wrong direction. There's not really much that can go wrong with the system, so checking the rubber lines and canister periodically is the only maintenance required. Procedure 5 tells you how to check and replace the canister and/or canister filter.

PROCEDURE 1: EGR VALVE: CHECK, CLEAN, REPLACE

Condition: Routine maintenance; OR you were sent here from Chapter 9.

Procedure 1, Step 1 *Exhaust and Emission Control Systems* **249**

Tools and Materials: To check the valve: 18" to 24" piece of 3/16" (5mm) inside-diameter vacuum hose. To remove and clean the valve: new EGR valve gasket, 10 and 12mm wrenches, maybe a sharp screwdriver, and spray can of carb cleaner. If the EGR pipe has to be removed, you'll also need a 17mm open-end wrench (and patience to get it back on).

Remarks: The EGR valve should be removed and inspected at least every 30,000 miles. On '80 and newer carb models it's easiest to remove the PCV valve while the EGR valve is off, so coordinate your efforts accordingly.

On '75 and '76 California models and some '85-'86 models, an EGR warning light in the speedometer housing lights up every 25,000 miles ('75-'76 models) or 60,000 miles ('85-'86 models). When the light comes on, be sure to check the EGR system. Here's how to turn the warning light off:

'75-'76 Calif. models: Reach behind the speedometer and flip the *little black switch* to turn the EGR warning light OFF. It's on the passenger side of the large white housing on the backside of the speedometer.

'85-'86 models: Remove the plastic panel on the lower left side of the dashboard. Remove the screws that attach the fuse box, then pull the fuse box away from the dash. Dig around amongst the wires behind and above the fuse box until you find a blue connector plugged into another connector. There should be a green connector nearby that's just like the blue one, except that it isn't connected to anything. Disconnect the blue connector and plug in the green one where you disconnected the blue one. Install the fuse box and plastic panel.

CAUTION: Don't soak the EGR valve in solvent or degreaser because the diaphragm will be damaged.

Step 1. Check EGR Valve Operation.

Remove the spare tire if it's in the engine compartment.

'82 and newer carb models: There might be a flat white plastic **heat shield** covering the rear part of the engine behind the carburetor. The shield is held in place by *clips* on the intake manifold. If you have a heat shield, note where it's attached, then wiggle it toward the rear of the car to remove it.

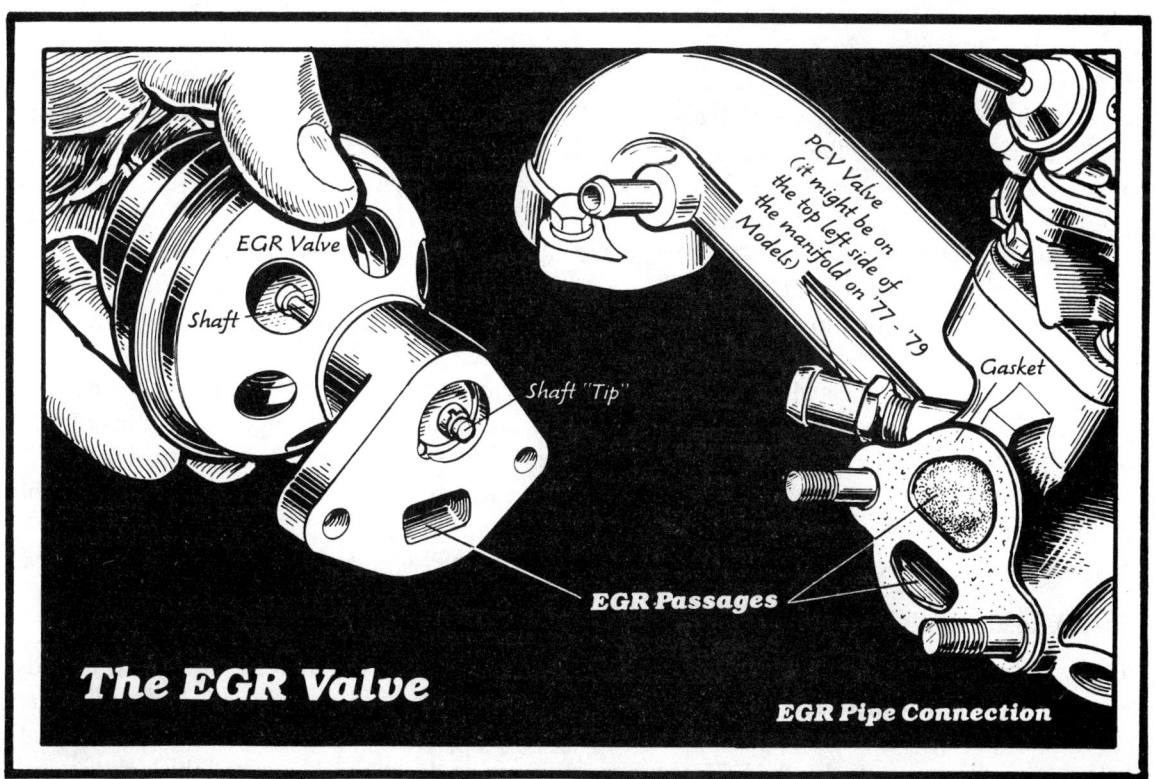

EVERYONE: The EGR valve is a round, brass-colored thing about 3″ in diameter. On carb models, it's mounted to the rear of the intake manifold just below the carburetor, and on fuel-injected models, it's on the rear side of the intake manifold, near the center. A small rubber vacuum hose is attached to the side of the valve. On some models, a thumb-size hose from the anti-afterburning valve connects to the base of the valve.

To see if this valve is working, start the engine and let it warm up to normal operating temperature. Due to a timer on some '83 and newer models, the engine has to run for at least eight minutes before you can check the EGR valve.

Look through an opening on the EGR valve body so you can see the thin **shaft** in the center. The shaft should move toward the rear of the car when the engine is revved up to 3,000-3,500 rpm, then return forward when the throttle is released. If the shaft moves, you know the valve is working. If the shaft doesn't move, see Step 2.

To be sure the passages aren't plugged with carbon, disconnect the small rubber *vacuum hose* from the round brass-colored valve and connect your test hose to the fitting. With the engine at idle, suck on the open end of the test hose you attached to the valve. If, while sucking on the hose, the engine begins to idle roughly or dies, you know the passages are open and the EGR system is working properly. Sucking on the hose opens the valve and allows exhaust gas to be sucked into the combustion chambers. At idle speed the engine can't handle the high concentration of exhaust gases so it stumbles or dies.

If the shaft didn't move when the engine was revved up, or the engine didn't stumble or die when you sucked on the hose, remove the EGR valve to clean and inspect the valve and passages (Step 2).

Step 2. Remove and Clean EGR Valve.

The EGR valve is mounted to the intake manifold with two 12mm nuts and lockwashers. Before removing it, make a note of other things held in place by the two nuts (accelerator cable bracket, wire connector brackets, etc.).

Disconnect the rubber hose(s) from the EGR valve, then remove the two 12mm nuts and washers and other things held in place by the nuts. Wiggle the EGR valve off the mounting studs.

If the shaft didn't move when testing the valve in Step 1, press on the end of the shaft where it sticks out of the valve to see if it moves. If it does, connect the piece of hose to the valve and suck on it. If the shaft doesn't move when you suck on the hose but moves when you press on it with your finger, the diaphragm is broken and the valve must be replaced.

If the shaft is stuck, use a small screwdriver to clean the carbon away from the tip and out of the rectangular hole in the valve. Set the valve so the shaft tip is sticking up, then squirt penetrating oil around the tip and into the hole and let it soak awhile. Keep working at it until the shaft moves freely when you suck on the hose. If the shaft refuses to loosen, buy a new EGR valve. If you get the shaft to move smoothly, test the valve with the rubber hose as described in the previous paragraph.

Dig the carbon chunks out of the EGR holes in the intake manifold with a small, sharp screwdriver until the passages are clean and smooth. Pull the chunks out of the manifold so they can't get sucked into the cylinders.

The upper hole in the manifold connects the EGR valve to the EGR pipe. If the EGR shaft moved but the engine didn't stumble or die when you sucked on the hose in Step 1, or if the hole in the manifold is severely clogged, remove the EGR pipe and check it for clogging. It's attached with 17mm fittings to the intake manifold and one of the cylinder heads. Some models have a *heat shield* attached to the pipe with 10mm bolts. If you have a shield, loosen the bolts and slide the shield out of the way so you can loosen the upper pipe fitting. When the pipe is off, tap it with a small hammer and run a piece of stiff wire (like a coat hanger) through it to loosen the chunks of carbon. Blow through the tube to be sure it's clear.

If you have an '80 or newer carb model, remove and check the PVC valve before installing the EGR valve.

Step 3. Install EGR Valve.

Everything clean and working smoothly? Install the EGR pipe if it was removed (be sure the threads are started correctly before tightening it with a wrench). Tighten the heat shield around the EGR pipe (if you have one) or it will rattle and buzz. Install a *new gasket* onto the manifold, then fit the EGR valve onto the studs. If there were other things attached to the EGR valve, install them on the studs, then install the lockwashers and

nuts and tighten them. Connect the hose(s) to the valve.
   '82 and newer models: Install the white plastic *heat shield* if you have one.
   EVERYONE: Install the spare tire if you removed it.

PROCEDURE 2: CHECK AND CLEAN PCV (Positive Crankcase Ventilation) VALVE.

This procedure only applies to some '77-'78 models and all '79 and newer models.

Condition: Routine maintenance; OR you were sent here from Chapter 9.

Tools and Materials: To check the valve: a phillips screwdriver or pliers depending on your clamp, Friend, a finger. To remove and clean the valve: a 19mm open-end wrench, maybe a crescent wrench, a spray can of carb cleaner, wire brush.

Remarks: Subaru says to clean the PVC valve every 30,000 miles. To be sure, I clean mine at every 12,000 mile tune-up. It ain't hard.

Step 1. Check PCV Valve.

Remove the spare tire if it's in the engine compartment.
   '77-'79 models: The PCV valve is on the top right side of the *intake manifold*. A black rubber **hose** from the top of the left valve cover will eventually lead you to it. Use a phillips screwdriver to loosen the hose clamp, then pull the hose off the PCV valve.
   '80 and newer carb models: The PCV valve sticks out of the rear of the *intake manifold* at about a 45° angle just to the left of the EGR valve. Use pliers to squeeze the two ears on the clamp together, then slide the clamp away from the valve. Pull the hose off the valve.
   Fuel-injected models: The PCV valve sticks out of the left side of the large aluminum lump on the rear of the intake manifold. Use pliers to squeeze the ears of the clamp together, then slide the clamp away from the valve. Pull the hose off the valve. Fuel-injected models won't run if any part of the PCV system is opened (including the oil filler cap!) so you'll need to have Friend start the car while you hold a finger over the end of the PCV valve *and* the open end of the hose.
   EVERYONE: Start the engine and cover the end of the PCV valve with a finger. Rev the engine a little several times (by rotating the *throttle arm* if you don't have a Friend inside the car) while you feel for suction on your finger. If your finger isn't sucked, or it's been 30,000 miles since you cleaned the valve, you'll need to remove the valve (Step 2). If the valve seems to be working and you aren't going to remove it, reconnect the hose and set the clamp in place.
   The **cap** on the *oil filler neck* is also an integral part of the PCV system. Unscrew the cap and check the *gasket*. Replace it if it's stiff, cracked, or broken.

Step 2. Remove and Clean PCV Valve and Hoses.

Remove the hose attached to the PCV valve if you haven't already (Step 1), then use a 19mm open-end wrench to unscrew the valve (*counterclockwise* as viewed from the hose end). On some models there's a **fitting** between the PCV valve and the manifold. If you have a fitting, hold it with a crescent wrench while you unscrew the PCV valve.
   When the valve is out, shake it to see if it rattles. If it doesn't rattle, replace it with a new one (they're pretty cheap). If the valve rattles, spray carb cleaner into it and let it soak; do this several times.
   While you're at it, check the **thumb-size hoses** attached to the top of the *valve covers* for clogging. Remove them from the engine, then tap them with a wrench or hammer to loosen any carbon that might have collected on the inside. Run a piece of wire (like a straightened coat hanger) through the hoses to be sure they're clean. Put the hoses back on the engine.

Step 3. Install PCV Valve.

Clean the threads on the PCV valve with a wire brush, then screw the valve into the intake manifold and tighten it with a 19mm wrench. Not too tight. Fit the hose onto the valve and secure it with the clamp.

'80 and newer models: Install the EGR valve if it's off (Procedure 1, Step 3).
EVERYONE: Install the spare tire if you removed it.

PROCEDURE 3: CHECK, CLEAN, REPLACE AIR INJECTION SYSTEM (AIS)

This procedure only applies to '75-'80 models.

Condition: Routine maintenance; OR you're here from Chapter 9.

Tools and Materials: To check the AIS: Friend, maybe a phillips screwdriver. To clean or replace AIS components: 10mm, 12mm, and 14mm wrenches, phillips screwdriver, maybe carb cleaner or solvent, knife or razor blade, feeler gauge to check reed valves and reed valve gaskets (Step 3).

Step 1. Check Air Injection System.

'75 models: The **air pump** looks a lot like an alternator only it doesn't have vanes around the pulley. It's located between the alternator and carburetor. When the bearings in the air pump wear out the pump will growl, grumble, and/or squeal. Step 2 tells you how to replace the pump.

To see if the air pump is working, loosen the *hose clamp* on the **hose** attached to the rear of the air pump and slide it away from the pump, then pull the hose off the fitting on the air pump. Have Friend start the engine and rev it up a few times while you hold a finger or thumb over the hose and feel for vacuum. You should feel

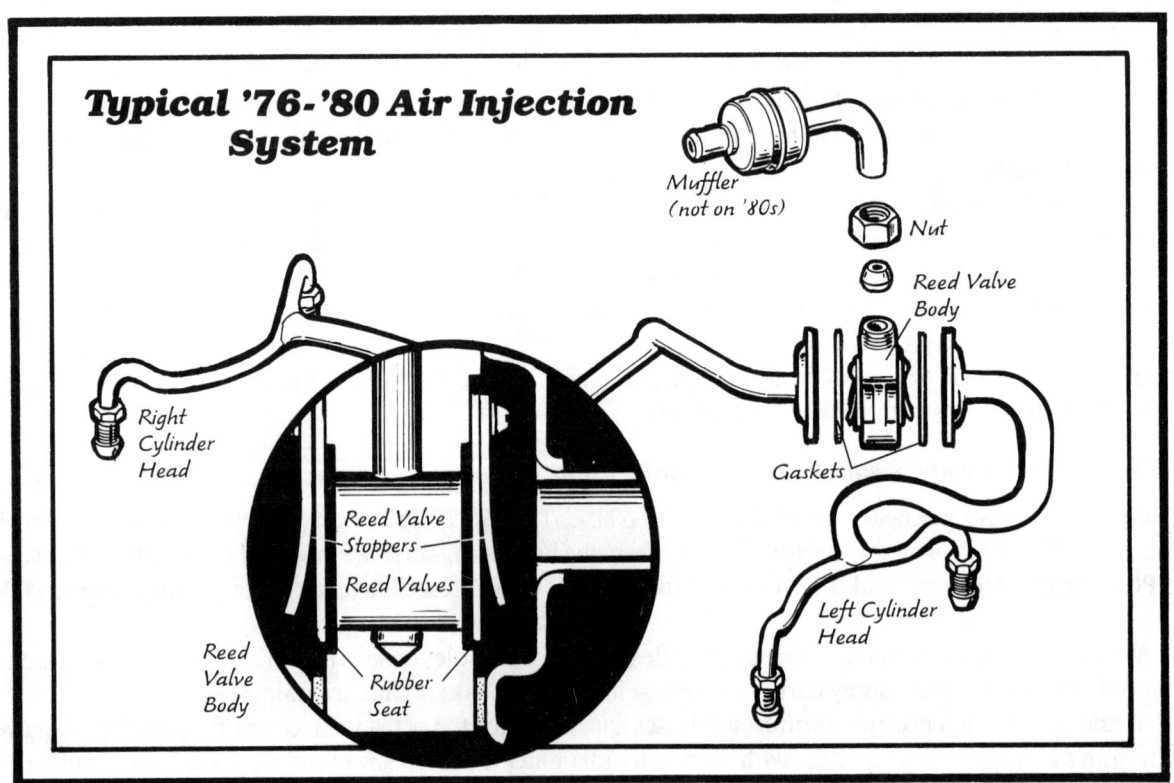

the hose sucking on your finger, not pressure trying to blow your finger off the hose. If you feel pressure, the *air injection valve* needs replacing (Step 3).

Now put your finger over the fitting on the rear of the air pump and have Friend rev the engine a few times. You should feel air pressure against your finger. You do? The pump is working; reconnect the hose and clamp to the pump. No pressure? Check the hose between the air pump and air cleaner for clogging and clean it if necessary. If the hose is OK, the air pump is shot and not pumping air. Step 2 tells you how to replace it.

'76-'79 models: There's a small round **muffler** for the AIS located behind and to the left of the air cleaner. A rubber hose connects the muffler to the bottom of the air cleaner. Disconnect the hose from the front of the muffler.

'80 models: A **secondary air cleaner** for the AIS is located on the left side of the engine compartment near the brake master cylinder. It's round and painted the same color as the engine air cleaner. Disconnect the hose attached to the front of the secondary air cleaner.

'76-'80 models: Have Friend start the engine and rev it up a few times while you hold a thumb over the muffler fitting where the hose was attached ('76-'79 models) or over the end of the hose you disconnected from the air cleaner ('80 models). You should feel a little suction on your thumb. If there's no suction and/or there's air pressure coming out of the fitting, the **AIS reed valves** need to be cleaned and checked. It's easy, see Step 3. If the fitting sucked your thumb, the AIS is working so reconnect the hose(s).

Step 2. Replace Air Pump ('75 models only).

New air pumps cost over $200 now so it would be worth your time to look around for a used one. If the pump bearings are worn out and the noise is driving you crazy and you can't find a used one or can't afford a new one, remove the pump from the engine and plug the hoses that were attached to the pump with corks or rubber plugs. You'll have to use a shorter drive belt to turn the alternator and water pump (a belt for '76 Soobs might work). The car will work fine, but keep in mind that you could get busted in some states for tampering with the emission control system.

To remove the air pump, take off the air cleaner (Chapter 7, Procedure 5, Step 3), then disconnect the hose from the rear of the air pump. Loosen the alternator drive belt (Chapter 10, Procedure 3, Step 2).

4WD models: Loosen the bolt in the *slotted bracket* below the belt-tension-adjusting *idler pulley* (see Chapter 10, Procedure 3, Step 2). Push the small pulley toward the crankshaft pulley, then remove the drive belt for the engine-driven fan.

EVERYONE: Remove the four bolts around the edge of the air pump pulley. Carefully wiggle the air pump and bracket off the engine without smashing it against the carburetor.

To install the air pump, wiggle it into position on the engine, then insert the long mounting bolt through the bottom right hole in the *air pump bracket* (the one closest to the distributor), the bracket on the engine, then through the mounting ear on the air pump. Push the bolt through the ear at the rear of the engine bracket and screw it in a few turns. Now install the other three bolts through the bracket. Two of the bolts screw into the air pump and one of them attaches the alternator to the bracket. Tighten the three pump mounting bolts but not the alternator mounting bolt. Install and adjust the alternator drive belt (Chapter 10, Procedure 3, Step 2). If you have 4WD, install the drive belt for the fan and adjust the tension (Chapter 10, Procedure 3, Step 2). Attach the hose to the rear of the air pump and tighten its clamp, install the air cleaner, and you're finished.

Step 3. Clean and Inspect AIS Reed Valves.

This step applies only to '76-'80 models. Be sure new gaskets for the reed valve assembly are available before taking it apart. If you suspect the AIS system on your '82-'84 model is misbehaving, have Subaru check and repair it.

'76-'80 models: The **reed valves** are located in a square **reed valve housing** on the top left rear corner of the engine. A pipe attached to the top of the housing connects to a small round *muffler* on '76-'79 models or to a rubber hose connected to a pipe on the *secondary air cleaner* on '80 models. Disconnect the hose attached to the muffler or pipe, then use a crescent wrench to unscrew the nut on top of the housing to remove the muffler or pipe. Follow the pipe coming out of the front of the square housing to see if it's attached to the *oil filler tube*.

If it is, remove the 10mm bolt to free it. The pipe coming out of the rear of the housing branches into two pipes that are attached to the top of the left cylinder head with 14mm nuts. Unscrew the nuts and lift up on the pipes. The one under the alternator is a bit difficult to reach.

Remove the four 10mm bolts on the reed valve housing, then carefully pull the housing apart. Be very careful with the thin metal pieces (reed valves) attached to each side of the thick center part (the *valve body*). Use carb cleaner or solvent to carefully clean the thin reed valves, the rubber seat behind the valves, the curved reed valve stoppers, the passages, and the muffler or pipe that attaches to the top. Use a knife or razor blade to remove all traces of the old gasket from the mating surfaces of the valve housing and the square plates attached to the pipes on the engine.

Use a feeler gauge to measure the gap between the tip of the reed valve and the rubber seat. If the gap is more than .008" (.2mm) replace the valve. Inspect the valves for cracks and warps, and the rubber seat for cracks, indentations from the reed valve, and looseness in the valve body. Replace the whole valve body if any abnormalities are found.

To assemble the reed valve assembly, use new gaskets on each side of the valve body, and fit it between the two plates so the fitting for the muffler or air cleaner pipe is at the top. Install and tighten the four 10mm bolts, then fit the pipes into the top of the left cylinder head and tighten the 14mm nuts. Install and tighten the 10mm bolt that attaches the pipe to the oil filler (if you removed it). Install the muffler or pipe to the top of the reed valve assembly and tighten the nut with a crescent wrench. Attach the rubber hose from the air cleaner to the muffler or pipe, depending on your setup.

PROCEDURE 4: CHECK AND REPLACE SECONDARY AIR CLEANER ('80s Only)

Condition: Routine maintenance.

Tools and Materials: 10mm wrench, maybe a new secondary air cleaner.

Step 1. Do It.

The secondary air cleaner on 1980 models is on the left side of the engine compartment. It's blue, like the air cleaner, round, and about the size of a 45 rpm record.

To check this air filter, disconnect the hose from the front, then lift straight up to remove the air cleaner. Remove the two 10mm nuts and bracket from the rear, then pry the front away from the back (it's stuck pretty tight sometimes). The air filter element is attached to the rear part. If it's only dirty on the side near the air intake opening, you can rotate it 180° and use it again. If more than a small part is dirty and oily, or if the pleated filter element is torn, replace it with a new one.

To assemble and install the secondary air cleaner, fit the back part with the filter element into the front so the two bolts fit through the holes. Now hold the air cleaner so the tube on the front is pointing down. Install the two rubber washers on the bolts, then fit the bracket onto the bolts so the rounded top end of the bracket is up. Install the two nuts and tighten them. Fit the tabs on the sides of the air cleaner bracket into the slots of the bracket on the car, then push down on the air cleaner. Attach the hose, secure it with the clamp and you're finished.

PROCEDURE 5: INSPECT AND/OR REPLACE EVAPORATIVE CANISTER AND/OR REPLACE FILTER ('77 and Newer Models Only)

Condition: Regular 60,000-mile maintenance; OR you smell gasoline but can't find a leak.

Tools and Materials: New canister filter, maybe a new canister, 10mm wrench, a phillips screwdriver or pliers depending on the type of clamps on the canister hoses (some of the hoses don't have clamps), masking tape, and pen to mark the hoses.

Remark: Check your Owner's Manual to see when your canister should be replaced. Step 1 tells you how to remove and install it.

Step 1. Inspect Canister, Replace Filter or Canister.

The **canister** for the evaporative emission system is big, black, round, and has 3 to 5 hoses connected to the top. It's located in one of the corners of the engine compartment. Label the hoses on the canister, then pull them off. Loosen the bolt or screw in the bracket holding the canister ('82-'84 models have a clip to flip), then pull the canister out of its holder and out of the engine compartment.

Inspect the canister and replace it if it's cracked and/or blistered, or if your Owner's Manual tells you it's time to replace it.

To replace the filter, carefully remove the old filter from the bottom. It's hard to remove without tearing it to shreds so go slowly. The smaller the pieces, the more difficult it is to remove them.

Carefully insert the new filter into the canister. Gently push and pull it into position. Be sure it completely covers the bottom of the canister.

Fit the canister into its holder and tighten the clamp. Inspect the hoses that attach to the canister for cracks and replace any that are funky. Attach the hoses to the canister with the clamps and you're finished.

PROCEDURE 6: CHECK AND REPAIR HOT AIR CONTROL SYSTEM (Carb Models Only)

There are two ways for air to enter the air cleaner housing: cool air can enter through the end of the *air cleaner snout*, or hot air can enter through the large **hot air intake hose** connected to the bottom of the snout. The other end of the large hose is connected to an **air stove** on the front of the right exhaust pipe. Determining which way air enters the carburetor is what the **Hot Air Control System** is all about.

To promote efficient combustion and minimize exhaust emissions, the temperature of the air drawn into the carburetor should be between 100° and 127°.

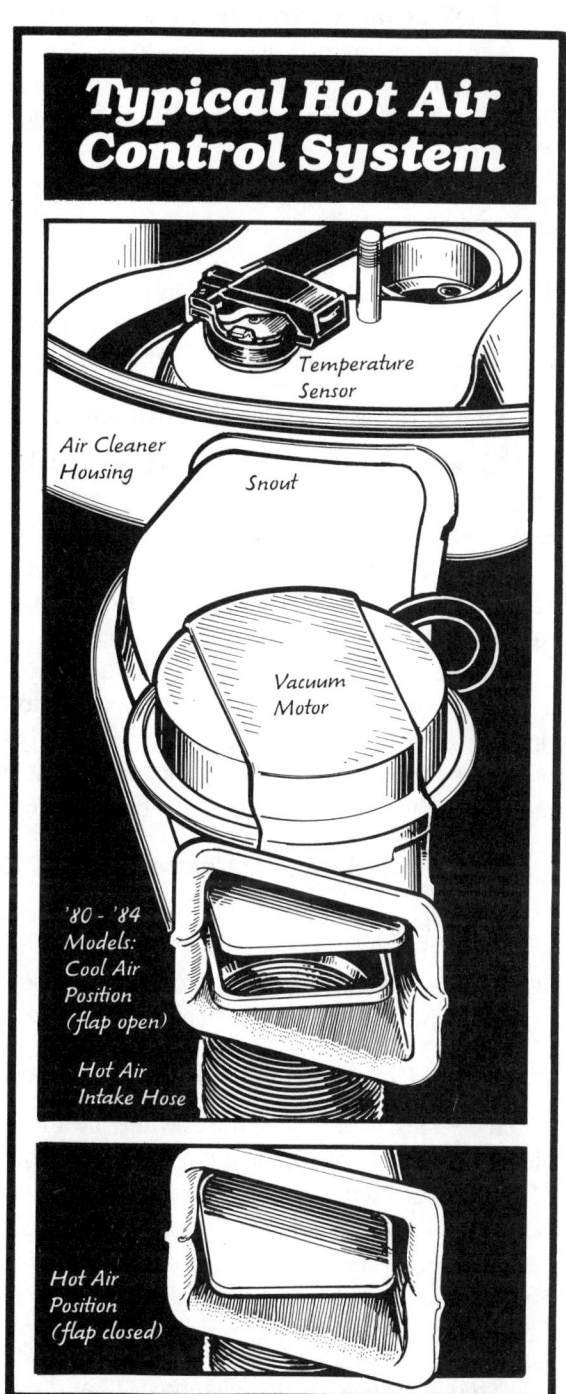

Drawing warm air into the carb in cold weather also shortens engine warm-up time and helps prevent carburetor icing.

'75-'76 models: There's a simple system for controlling the temperature of the intake air. You can set a lever on the air cleaner snout to the "winter" position so only hot air is drawn into the carb, or to the "summer" position so only cool air is drawn in.

'77 and newer models: There are two simple gizmos to control the air temperature automatically: a **vacuum motor** and a **temperature sensor** that controls the vacuum motor.

The hot air control system is easy to check and should be inspected at every 12,000-mile/12-month tune-up. You probably wouldn't notice a malfunction of the system in hot weather, but in cold weather the engine might use more gas, lose power, stall easily, or hesitate when you want to accelerate.

Condition: Periodic maintenance; OR the carburetor has been icing up or the car runs poorly and balky during cold weather.

Tools and Materials: '75-'76 models: maybe pliers or screwdriver to remove the hot air intake hose. '77 and newer models: a small mirror and flashlight, an 18"-24" piece of 3/16" (5mm) vacuum hose, maybe a new hot air intake hose, vacuum motor, or temperature sensor.

Step 1. Inspect, Replace Hot Air Intake Hose.

Check both ends of the hot air intake hose that connects the bottom of the air cleaner snout to the air stove on the front of the right exhaust pipe, or to the top of the catalytic converter. If the hose is torn, crushed, or missing, replace it with a new one.

To remove the hose, squeeze the ears on the clamp and slide it away from the end of the hose. Grab the hose as close to the end as possible (over its fitting) and gently twist until it's loose, then pull the hose off the fitting. Remove both ends the same way.

Before installing the hose, slide both clamps onto the hose a few inches, then carefully *enlarge* the ends a little with your fingers. It's made of heavy tinfoil so it bends easily. Now align one end the hose with the fitting and gently slide it on while rotating it slightly back and forth. If the end of the hose gets crimped or caught on the tube and messed up, remove it and straighten it with your fingers. When the hose is on the fitting, squeeze the ears of the clamp and slide it to about ½" from the end. Do the other end the same way.

Step 2. Check Hot Air Control System ('75-'76 models).

Do Step 1 to check the hot air intake hose. Hose OK? Now look at the **lever** on the front side of the air cleaner snout. Set the lever in the "winter" (UP) position when the *average ambient air temperature* (what the average of night and day temperatures outside have been running lately) is *below* 59°, or in the "summer" (DOWN) position when the ambient air temperature is *above* 59°. Simple, eh?

Step 3. Check Vacuum Hoses ('77 and newer models).

It's easiest to check the hoses while the air cleaner is off. If you're here from the tune-up chapter, the air cleaner is already off. If the air cleaner is still on, remove it (Chapter 7, Procedure 5, Step 4).

A rubber vacuum hose connects the round *vacuum motor* on top of the air cleaner snout to a *temperature sensor fitting* on the bottom of the air cleaner housing. Another vacuum hose (right next to the hose from the vacuum motor) connects the temp sensor to the *intake manifold* or to a *T-fitting* in another vacuum line. Check both hoses for cracks and breaks and see if they fit tightly on the fittings. Replace them if they're damaged or fit loosely.

Step 4. Check Vacuum Motor ('77 and newer models).

Do this step with the engine turned OFF.

'77-'79 models: Release the four clips around the top of the air cleaner and remove the lid and air filter. Set the air filter on something clean. Look into the snout from the air filter side. A *round flap* should be covering

Procedure 6, Step 5   *Exhaust and Emission Control Systems*   257

the hole in the bottom of the snout where the hot air intake hose connects. In this position the flap is in the **cool air position**.

    OHC carb models: Peel the rubber hose off the end of the air cleaner snout so you can peek into the snout.

    '80 and newer models: The flap in the end of the air cleaner snout should be open (horizontal). This is the **cool air position**.

    EVERYONE: Disconnect the rubber vacuum hose from the round vacuum motor on top of the snout. Attach a piece of 3/16" (5mm) vacuum hose to the motor, then suck on the open end of the hose.

    '77-'79 models: Sucking on the hose should raise the round flap away from the hole in the bottom of the snout. This is the **hot air position**.

    '80 and newer models: Sucking on the hose should move the flap to a vertical position and close the opening in the snout. This is the **hot air position**.

    EVERYONE: If the flap doesn't return to the cool air position when there's no vacuum applied to the vacuum motor, the flap is stuck. If sucking on the hose didn't change the position of the flap from the cool air position to the hot air position, the diaphragm in the vacuum motor is broken or the flap is stuck in the hot position.

    If the flap moved to the hot air position when you sucked on the hose, suck on it again and hold vacuum in the hose while you quickly cover the end of the hose with your tongue. The flap should stay in the hot air position for at least 30 seconds. If it doesn't, there's a leak in the vacuum motor diaphragm. Step 6 tells you how to see if the flap is stuck and how to replace the vacuum motor if it's shot.

Step 5. Check Temperature Sensor ('77 and newer models).

The engine must be cool and the vacuum motor must be operating correctly (Step 4) to test the temperature sensor. With the engine turned OFF and cool, the flap in the air cleaner snout should be in the *cool air position* (see Step 4).

    If you're here from the tune-up, see if the flap is in the cool air position, then check the temperature sensor after the engine is tuned, everything's back together and you've gone for a test drive. It takes several minutes for the temp sensor to warm up so don't waste your time waiting for it.

    '77-'79 models: Install the air filter and air cleaner lid if you removed them. You'll need to use a mirror and maybe a flashlight to see the flap inside the snout while checking the temperature sensor.

    EVERYONE: Start the engine and see if the flap moved to the hot air position. If it did, check it occasionally to see if it gradually changes to the cool air position. Depending on the air temperature, it might take up to 20 minutes to change.

    If the flap doesn't move to the cool air position, and the vacuum motor and hoses are all in good condition and connected properly (you checked them in Steps 3 and 4, didn't you?), there's a problem in the temperature sensor (see Step 7).

Step 6. Replace Vacuum Motor.

The vacuum motor is attached to the air cleaner snout with a **flat strap**. The vacuum motor shaft hooks into a slot on the flap to move it.

    Disconnect the vacuum hose from the vacuum motor, then remove the two screws on top of the air cleaner snout. Hold the vacuum motor down while you gently lift up on the screw end of the flat strap until it clears the motor. Lift the strap out of the slot on the snout and set it aside. Carefully lift up on the vacuum motor while tilting it toward the rear of the snout. You'll have to wiggle and tilt the motor to disengage the shaft from the flap. When the motor is out, notice that the hole in the snout and the matching one on the bottom of the vacuum motor are square.

    While the motor is out, check the flap with your finger to see if it moves freely. If it sticks, the snout is bent or the flap shaft is bent. If you can't straighten things so the flap moves smoothly, you'll have to replace the air cleaner housing. Look for a used one and check its vacuum motor (Step 4) before buying it.

    To install the vacuum motor, hold it so the hook on the shaft is pointed toward the rear of the snout. Insert the shaft into the snout and fit the hook into the round tab on the flap. Gently push and pull on the motor while watching the flap to be sure the shaft is engaged. When you're sure, wiggle the motor down so it fits into the square hole on the snout. Hold it there while you insert the end of the strap into the slot on the snout. Press the strap over the vacuum motor, then install and tighten the two screws. Reconnect the vacuum hose. If you're replacing the temperature sensor, go on to Step 7. Otherwise, install the air cleaner (Chapter 7, Procedure 5, Step 5).

Step 7. Replace Temperature Sensor.

Remove the lid and air filter and set them someplace clean. Look inside the air cleaner for a small plastic gizmo on the snout side of the carburetor. That's the **temp sensor**. Make a note of how it's oriented so you can install the new one the same way. Now look at Chapter 7, Procedure 5, Step 4, to remove the air cleaner housing.

Follow the hose from the vacuum motor to where it connects to the temperature sensor on the bottom of the air cleaner. There's another hose connected right next to the hose from the vacuum motor. Make a note about which hose goes where, then disconnect both hoses. You might have to use a small screwdriver to pry the metal clips away from the hoses as you remove them. The temp sensor is held in place by the clip around the two metal *vacuum tubes*. Pull outward on the two clip arms to release the clip, then slide the clip off the metal tubes. Now pull the temp sensor out of the air cleaner. There should be a rubber gasket between the sensor and the air cleaner. If it's stuck to the air cleaner, leave it there; if it's torn or funky replace it.

Install the new temp sensor into the air cleaner housing so it's oriented the same as the old one. Be sure the rubber gasket is in place. Hold the sensor in place with one hand while you fit the clip over the vacuum tubes on the bottom of the air cleaner. When the clip is on as far as you can get it with your fingers, press on the sides with a screwdriver until the sensor is held tightly in place. Reconnect the vacuum hoses to the sensor, then install the air cleaner housing, air filter and lid (Chapter 7, Procedure 12, Step 8).

PROCEDURE 7: CHECK AND ADJUST COASTING BYPASS SYSTEM ('75-'80)

There are two components in the coasting bypass system: a **servo diaphragm** on the rear of the carburetor that's controlled by a **vacuum control valve** (also called a *decel valve*) mounted to the right side of the intake manifold. Basically, the coasting bypass system allows more air to be drawn through the carburetor while coasting and/or decelerating (creating a leaner mixture), thus reducing the amount of gas being burned. The vacuum control valve has a rubber plug covering the adjustment screw. The rubber plug faces the front of the car on '75-'79 models and the right front fender on '80s.

'76 models: Your setup is different. The vacuum control valve is mounted to the front of the intake manifold below the carburetor and there's no servo diaphragm on the back of the carb. It takes two vacuum gauges and a special tester to adjust the valve. If your Soob backfires or the engine surges while you're cruising down the road, have a Subaru dealer adjust the deceleration valve for you.

Condition: You were sent here from Chapter 9 (engine backfires or surges); OR routine maintenance; OR excessive fuel consumption.

Tools and Materials: Friend, 18"-24" of 3/16" (5mm) vacuum hose, maybe small regular and phillips screwdrivers, maybe a new vacuum control unit and/or servo diaphragm, maybe a small swatch of paper.

Remarks: This procedure should be performed after the engine has been tuned. If you don't have any friends or none are available, you can rev the engine by rotating the *throttle lever*. Here's how: Locate a thin cable near the lower rear of the carb. Follow the cable to the arc-shaped throttle lever on the side of the carb. To rev the engine, rotate the top of the lever toward the rear of the car.

CAUTION: Don't turn the adjustment screw in the air control valve more than two turns in either direction.

Step 1. Check and Replace the Servo Diaphragm.

Locate the small round servo diaphragm on the rear of the carburetor (see the carburetor illustrations in Chapter 11). Disconnect the vacuum hose, then connect a piece of 3/16" (5mm) vacuum hose to the fitting. Suck on the open end of the hose, then quickly cover the end with your tongue. Does your tongue stick there by vacuum suction? If the diaphragm won't hold vacuum, it's broken and should be replaced. If it holds vacuum, it's good, so remove the test hose, reconnect the vacuum hose, then skip to Step 2.

To replace the servo diaphragm, remove the air cleaner (Chapter 7, Procedure 5, Step 4). Loosen, but don't remove, the two screws that secure a *bracket* to the top rear of the carburetor. Disconnect the vacuum hose from the servo diaphragm, then remove the three small screws that attach it to the rear of the carburetor and wiggle the servo diaphragm off.

If the old servo diaphragm had a rubber O-ring around the part sticking into the carb, be sure the new servo diaphragm also has one. Install the new servo diaphragm onto the rear of the carb so the three screw holes are aligned (it will only fit one way). Install and tighten the three mounting screws, then reconnect the vacuum hose. Tighten the two screws for the bracket on the top rear of the carb, then install the air cleaner (Chapter 7, Procedure 5, Step 5).

Step 2. Check, Adjust, and/or Replace Vacuum Control Unit (all except '76 models).

Remove the air cleaner lid (Chapter 7, Procedure 4, Step 3). Start the engine and let it warm up to operating temperature. Have Friend rev the engine up to around 3,000-4,000 rpm, then quickly release the accelerator pedal (see Remarks if a friend isn't available). When the accelerator pedal is released, there should be a slight delay, then you should hear a fizzing, sizzling noise coming from the carburetor while the engine is decelerating. Try it several times if you don't hear the fizzing sound at first. Still no fizzing? Pry the rubber cap off the vacuum control valve, then use a very small screwdriver to turn the small screw inside the valve *clockwise* about ¼ turn. Rev the engine again and listen for the fizz. Continue revving and adjusting until you hear the fizzing sound after a slight delay when the engine is decelerating. Don't turn the adjusting screw more than two turns.

If you hear the fizzing noise when the engine is idling, turn the adjusting screw *counterclockwise* slowly just until the noise goes away (not more than two turns). Now go through the above paragraph just like everyone else, to adjust the vacuum control.

If you can't adjust the vacuum control valve so you hear the fizzing sound and you've checked the servo diaphragm and it's good, replace the vacuum control valve. Here's how: Label the vacuum hoses before disconnecting them from the valve, then remove the two 10mm bolts and washers that attach the valve to the manifold. Attach the new valve to the manifold with the two 10mm bolts, then reconnect the vacuum hoses. Adjust the valve so it fizzes (first paragraph this step).

PROCEDURE 8: CHECK ANTI-AFTER-BURNING VALVE (AAV)

The following Soobs have an anti-afterburning valve (also called an *anti-backfire valve*): '75 models, '80 models (except Hatchback STD and DL, and manual transmission Sedan and Hardtop non-California and Canadian models), and '83-'84 non-California 4WD and all Canadian models. For '85

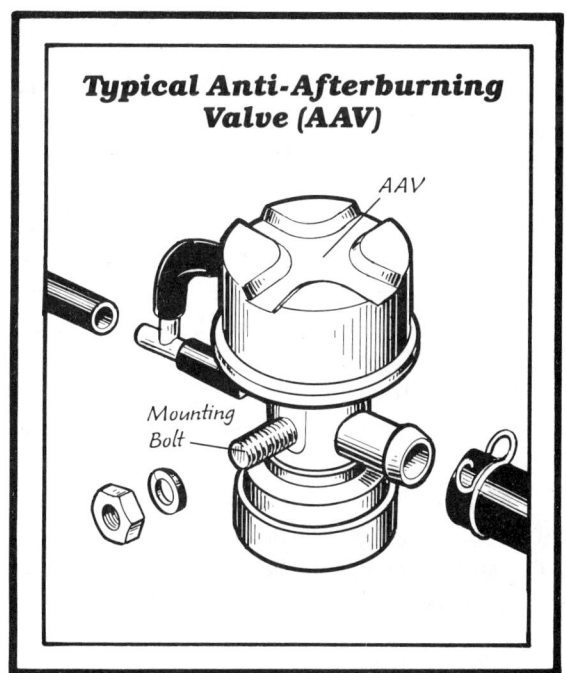

Typical Anti-Afterburning Valve (AAV)

and newer models, look at the emission control sticker on the underside of the hood. If you see a gizmo labeled AAV, you have one.

The valve allows a little extra air to be drawn into the intake manifold when the engine is decelerating. The extra air prevents "backfiring."

Condition: You were sent here from Chapter 9 (engine backfires when decelerating); OR regular maintenance.

Tools and Materials: To check the valve: a small piece of paper, Friend. To replace the valve: 10mm or 12mm wrench depending on the model.

Step 1. Check and Replace AAV.

'75 models: The round brass-colored AAV is mounted to the top left side of the intake manifold. It has two vacuum hoses that connect it to the intake manifold and one vacuum hose that connects it to a fitting on a pipe. Here's how to find the connection on the pipe: Follow the hose coming out of the back of the *air pump* to where it attaches to a pipe. (The air pump is that round thing between the alternator and carburetor.) Follow the pipe to the other end and you'll see a small hose from the AAV connected to the side of the pipe. The rear end of the pipe points downward and is connected to the *air injection valve* with a rubber hose.

To check the AAV, first disconnect the hose from the AAV where it attaches to the pipe. Start the engine and let it idle while you put your finger over the end of the hose. You shouldn't feel any suction from the hose. If you feel suction on your finger, the valve is bad and should be replaced. Now, while you hold your finger over the end of the hose, have Friend rev the engine to about 3,500 rpm and release the throttle quickly. You should feel vacuum in the hose (it should suck your finger) while the engine is decelerating. If it does, the AAV is operating correctly. If it doesn't, check the two hoses that connect the AAV to the intake manifold for clogging and tight-fitting connections. If the hoses are clear and attached tightly, the AAV is shot and should be replaced.

To replace the AAV, label the hoses so you know where they go, then disconnect them. Remove the bolt that attaches the AAV bracket to the engine, then pull the valve off the engine. Remove the nut that attaches the AAV to the bracket. Insert the bolt on the new AAV into the hole on the bracket, then install and tighten the nut. Fit the bracket onto the engine, then install and tighten the bolt. Connect the vacuum lines to the new AAV.

'80 models: The anti-afterburning valve (AAV) is mounted on the top left side of the intake manifold. Use the sticker under the hood to see if the vacuum lines to and from the AAV are attached correctly and are in good condition.

'83-'84 Non-California 4WD and Canadian models: The AAV is located in the left rear corner of the engine compartment next to the white plastic *fuel vapor separator*. Use the sticker under the hood to see if the hoses are attached correctly and are in good condition.

'80 and '83 and newer models with AAVs: To check the valve, hold a small piece of paper under the valve while Friend revs the engine up to about 3,000 rpm, then quickly releases the accelerator pedal. If the valve is working correctly, the paper will be sucked toward the bottom of the valve. Try it several times to be sure. If the paper isn't sucked toward the valve, the valve isn't working and should be replaced. Here's how.

If there isn't a sticker under the hood showing where the vacuum hoses connect, label the hoses then disconnect them from the AAV.

'80 models: Remove the nut that attaches the AAV to the bracket on the manifold, then pull the valve off the engine. Fit the bolt sticking out of the new AAV into the hole in the bracket, then install and tighten the nut. Reconnect the hoses.

'83 and newer models with AAVs: Remove the two bolts that attach the brass-colored AAV bracket to the *strut tower*. Move the AAV and bracket far enough away from the strut tower to remove the nut that attaches the AAV to the bracket. Be sure there's a rubber grommet in all three of the bolt holes in the bracket, then attach the new AAV to the bracket with the nut. Attach the bracket to the strut tower with the two bolts. Reconnect the hoses.

PROCEDURE 9: CHECK AND REPLACE ALTITUDE COMPENSATOR ('80 California Models Only)

'80 California Soobs have an *altitude compensator* in the engine compartment that varies the fuel/air ratio according to the altitude. To test the compensator you need to know the approximate elevation where you're doing the testing.

Condition: You've tuned the engine and it still doesn't run right, so you're checking everything you can check.

Tools and Materials: 18″ to 24″ of 3/16″ (5mm) vacuum hose, maybe a new altitude compensator.

Step 1. Do It.

The altitude compensator is located near the right rear corner of the engine compartment and has three rubber hoses attached to it. Label the bottom two hoses "front" and "rear," then disconnect them. Check the two bottom hose fittings on the compensator one at a time by connecting your vacuum hose, then gently blowing into the hose. Here's what to look for:

At 1,640 ft. or lower elevation, you shouldn't be able to blow air into either fitting on the compensator. Between 1,640 ft. and 5,905 ft. you should be able to blow air into the compensator with some resistance. The higher the altitude, the easier it should be to blow. Above 5,905 ft., the compensator is wide open and air should pass smoothly through both fittings. If your results were different than this description, the compensator is suspect.

To replace the altitude compensator, label the three hoses, then disconnect them. Remove the three screws that attach the compensator to the bracket. You might have to remove the three screws that attach the bracket to the car in order to get to the front compensator screw. Remove the compensator from the bracket, then install the new one and attach it with the three screws. Attach the bracket to the car if you removed it, then reconnect the three hoses.

PROCEDURE 10: CHECK, ADJUST, REPLACE THROTTLE RETURN DASHPOT ('75 Models Only)

Condition: You were sent here from Chapter 7 or 9 because the engine idle speed is too high.

Tools and Materials: Small ruler or tape measure, 12mm wrench, maybe a new throttle return dashpot.

Step 1. Locate, Check, and Adjust Throttle Return Dashpot.

Warm up the engine to operating temperature, turn it OFF, then remove the air cleaner (Chapter 7, Procedure 5, Step 3). Look down the front half of the carburetor top to see if the carburetor **choke plate** (butterfly valve) is in a vertical position. (If it isn't, see Chapter 11, Procedure 13, Step 2). If the choke plate is vertical, the choke is working properly, so you're set up to check the **throttle return dashpot**.

If you aren't sure what the dashpot looks like, have Friend press on the gas pedal (engine OFF) while you watch the right side of the carburetor. When Friend presses on the gas pedal a cable rotates an arc-shaped *throttle lever* on the lower right side of the carb. When the pedal is released, the bottom edge of the throttle lever presses against a *pin* sticking out of a small round can. The can is the dashpot. The pin should slowly retract allowing the lever to return gradually to the idle position. Got it?

Lift the throttle lever away from the dashpot. Press lightly on the dashpot pin with a finger. The pin should slowly (with resistance) retract into the dashpot as you press. If the pin is stuck or offers no resistance, replace the dashpot. If the pin retracts slowly, quickly remove your finger from the pin to see if it pops up. If the pin doesn't pop up to its original position, replace the dashpot.

To check the dashpot adjustment, set a small ruler on the dashpot so you can measure the distance the lever moves the pin. Raise the throttle lever until it clears the pin, then slowly lower it until it barely touches the pin. Position the bottom of the ruler at the bottom edge of the lever. Now let go of the throttle lever, wait a few seconds, then check the position of the bottom edge of the lever on your ruler. The lever should have moved .024″(6mm). That's almost exactly ¼″. Measure it a couple times to be sure. If your measurement was different, loosen the *locknut* on the bottom of the dashpot mounting screw where it screws into a mounting bracket sticking out of the intake manifold. Screw the dashpot *clockwise* into the intake manifold until the pin clears the throttle lever. Now slowly turn the dashpot *counterclockwise* until the pin barely touches the throttle lever. Each complete *counterclockwise* revolution of the dashpot will raise it .004″ (1mm), so turn the dashpot six complete turns counterclockwise and it will be set just right. Hold the dashpot in that position while you tighten the locknut. Start the engine and see if the idle speed is correct. If the engine still idles too fast, do Step 2 to replace the dashpot.

Step 2. Replace Dashpot.

To replace the dashpot, loosen the locknut on the bottom of the stubby dashpot mounting shaft. Hold the throttle lever up out of the way while you unscrew the dashpot *counterclockwise* to remove it. If there isn't a locknut on the mounting shaft of the new dashpot, screw the locknut from the old dashpot onto the shaft. Screw the new dashpot into the threaded hole in the intake manifold until the pin clears the throttle lever. Now adjust the dashpot (Step 1).

THE EXHAUST SYSTEM

The exhaust system serves two basic functions: silence and safety. It stifles the noises made by all those little explosions in the cylinders, and carries the burned gases from the engine to the rear of the car so they don't go into the passenger compartment. A noisy, leaky, worn-out exhaust system is not only embarrassing and irritating, it's downright *dangerous*. One of the by-products of burning gasoline is carbon monoxide. This is an odorless gas that first makes you sleepy, then as you doze off, it kills you. Dead. It's a method of choice for those bent on suicide, but I presume you're not one of them. The lethal potential of carbon monoxide poisoning is the main reason it's wise to keep your exhaust system in shape.

Starting in 1980 on some models, and '81 on all models, a **catalytic converter** (*cat*) was added to the exhaust system to help reduce noxious exhaust emissions. The cat is made of special metals that convert most of the carbon monoxide in the exhaust gas to harmless carbon dioxide and water. Models with a cat must use unleaded fuel because lead coats the special metals and renders them ineffective.

The exhaust system on all non-Turbo Soobs is essentially the same. The exhaust gases created in the cylinders rush past the exhaust valves into the **exhaust pipe assembly** (sometimes called the *exhaust manifold*) that is bolted to the cylinder heads. The pipes from each of the two cylinder heads merge into one pipe beneath the car, just to the rear of the engine compartment. The catalytic converter (on models that have 'em) is inside the "Y" where the two sides merge. The whole Y-shaped works is one piece called the **exhaust pipe assembly**. The exhaust moves along into the **muffler/tailpipe assembly**, then into the air (and everybody's lungs).

On Turbo models the section of the exhaust pipe assembly bolted to the bottom of the left cylinder head goes across the bottom front of the engine to the right cylinder head. This front pipe assembly then curves upward to where it bolts to the bottom of the *turbocharger*. The rear exhaust pipe assembly, bolted to the rear of the turbocharger, carries the exhaust gas rearward to the muffler/tailpipe assembly, the same as on non-Turbo models. Metal and asbestos **gaskets** fit between these components to prevent leaks.

The rear end of the exhaust pipe assembly is securely bolted to an **exhaust pipe bracket** that's attached to the frame. On all models the exhaust pipe assembly, pre-muffler, and muffler/tailpipe assembly are attached to the body with **rubber cushions** which dampen vibrations. On some models the rear end of the tailpipe is bolted to a rubber **tailpipe hanger** that's attached to the frame.

Replacing most exhaust system components is relatively straightforward. Here's how you do it.

Procedure 11, Step 1   *Exhaust and Emission Control Systems*   **263**

PROCEDURE 11: REPLACE EXHAUST SYSTEM COMPONENTS

Condition: Your Soob sounds like an angry truck and you're getting hostile stares from fellow motorists, OR; you smell exhaust fumes inside the car. Holes may be visible in the exhaust pipe and/or muffler/tailpipe.

Tools and Materials: Safety glasses, penetrating oil, 10mm, 12mm, and 14mm wrenches and sockets, ratchet, a long extension for the ratchet is sometimes handy, new exhaust gaskets, a block of wood, maybe new exhaust pipe(s), muffler/tailpipe, head pipes. I recommend using new nuts, bolts, lockwashers, and flat washers when replacing exhaust components. At least have a few handy because, due to the heat and rust they're subjected to, exhaust nuts and bolts tend to break easily when you remove them. You might need a hacksaw to remove some of the rusted bolts.

Remarks: Replacing exhaust system components is a cinch nowdays. Why couldn't it have been that easy when I was a teenager?

If you're planning to keep the car for several more years, check out the muffler shops that give a lifetime guarantee on their mufflers. The slightly higher price may save you money in the long run.

You can probably find exhaust system components cheapest at local parts stores or through mail order catalogs.

CAUTION: Don't try to work on the exhaust system while it's hot; let things cool down for 20 minutes after you shut the engine off.

Step 1. Chock, Jack, and Block.

Depending on the location of the component you're replacing, you might need to jack up the front or rear of the car. See Chapter 3: *Safety*, on how to do it safely. Be sure to use jackstands!

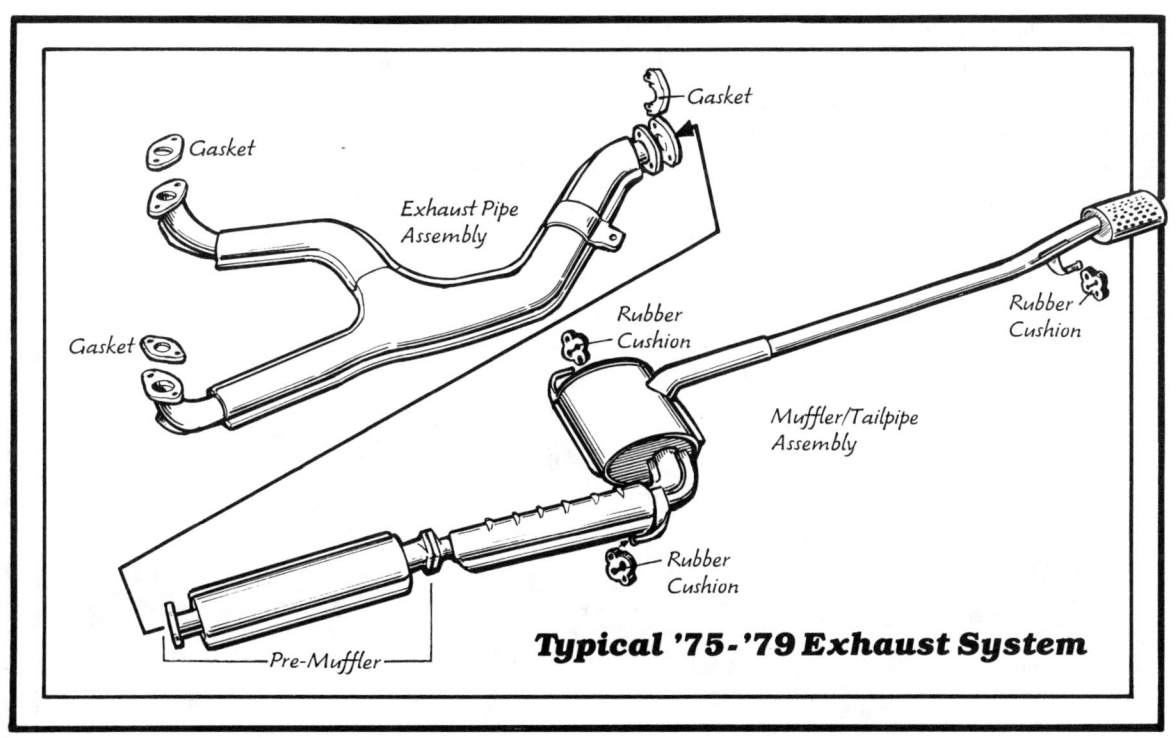

Typical '75-'79 Exhaust System

Step 2. Replace Exhaust Pipe Assembly and/or the Gaskets between the Cylinder Head and Exhaust Pipe (non-Turbo models).

Turbo Models: If there's a problem with the exhaust pipe assembly on your Turbo model, take it to the pros.

EVERYONE (except Turbo models): Depending on your size, you might need to jack up the front of the car (skinny people probably won't need to). Try replacing the gaskets without jacking the car up (it's quicker and safer). If you just don't fit, put the car in gear or in PARK, chock the rear wheels, jack up the front of the car and put it on jackstands (Chapter 3: *Safety*). Since the exhaust pipe assembly is a one piece unit, you should replace both cylinder head exhaust gaskets even if only one is leaking. Safety glasses on? Continue.

Start by removing the flat piece of sheet metal (*splash shield*) below the right exhaust pipe connection (it's attached to the front and side of the body with four or five 10mm bolts). Now disconnect the large *hot air inlet hose* from the front of the right side of the exhaust pipe assembly. Just slide the clamp away from the end of the hose, then put your hand around the hose end and gently twist to break it free from the fitting. The hose is usually stuck, and if you try to pull it off without twisting it first, the hose will tear. Pull the hose off the fitting.

'81 and newer models: If you're removing the exhaust pipe assembly, disconnect the wire attached to the *oxygen sensor* on the top front of the exhaust pipe assembly where it merges together. Just grab the rubber boot (not the wire) and wiggle it off. Be careful not to bang anything against the sensor—it's delicate and expensive.

'76 and newer models: The hot air intake hose was connected to an *air stove* which is attached to the right front of the exhaust pipe assembly. On OHC models the air stove is on top of the catalytic converter—that large lump where the two exhaust pipes join. On some models, the stove is simply a tube welded to the exhaust pipe. On other models, the stove consists of two pieces of sheet metal wrapped around the exhaust pipe and attached with two or three 10mm bolts. The kind of air stove that wraps around the exhaust pipe must be removed so you can get to the exhaust pipe mounting nuts on the bottom of the cylinder head. To remove the air stove, remove the 10mm bolts below the hot air hose fitting, then spread the two halves of the stove apart until you can unhook the tabs from the slots on the top and remove the two halves.

Squirt some penetrating oil on the two nuts and studs that attach each side of the exhaust pipe assembly to the bottom of the cylinder heads. Use a 14mm socket on a long extension to remove the nuts.

If you're just replacing the gaskets, on some models you can pull the exhaust pipe assembly down far enough with your hands to remove the old gaskets and slip the new ones in. If there's a raised edge on the gaskets, it goes toward the pipe and the smooth side goes toward the cylinder head. Don't pry on the exhaust pipe assembly with anything or you might damage the pipe assembly or yourself.

If you're removing the exhaust pipe assembly to replace or repair it, or you can't pull it down far enough with your hands to replace the gasket, you need to remove a bolt or two that attach the rear end of the exhaust pipe assembly to the car. Follow the assembly rearward to where the pipes merge together (the crotch). Go just a little farther and you'll see where the rear end of the exhaust pipe assembly is bolted to a bracket. Place a board

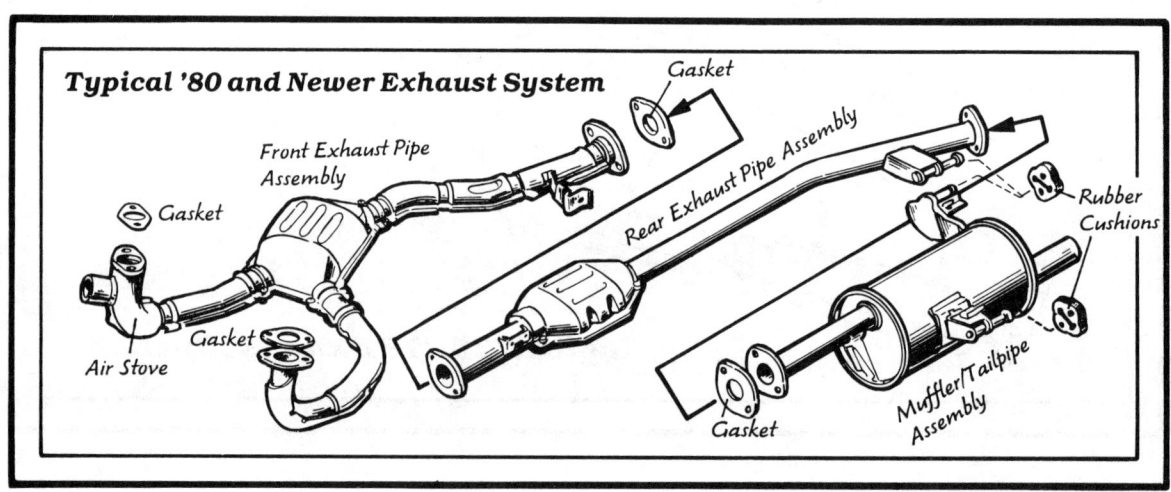

on top of your jack and slide it under the crotch. Raise the jack so it supports the weight of the pipe assembly (it's heavier than it appears).

If you're removing the exhaust pipe assembly, remove the two bolts that attach the rear end of the exhaust pipe assembly to the pre-muffler or rear exhaust pipe assembly (see illustration). Now remove the 12mm bolt(s) from the bracket. On '75 models there's also a *retaining bracket* that attaches the left side of the assembly to the bottom of the transmission. Remove the two 12mm bolts. If you're removing the exhaust pipe assembly, carefully lower the jack all the way, then drag the works out from under the car.

If you're just replacing the gaskets, slowly lower the jack until you can remove the old gaskets and slip new ones in. Don't lower the jack any farther than necessary. If the gaskets have a raised edge on one side, the raised side goes toward the exhaust pipe and the smooth side goes toward the cylinder head.

Now that the new gaskets are in, raise the jack (if you're using one) or push up on the exhaust pipe so you can get the nuts started. Once the nuts are started, you can remove the jack. Torque the exhaust pipe nuts to 20 ft. lbs. Install and tighten the exhaust pipe bracket bolt(s) if you removed them.

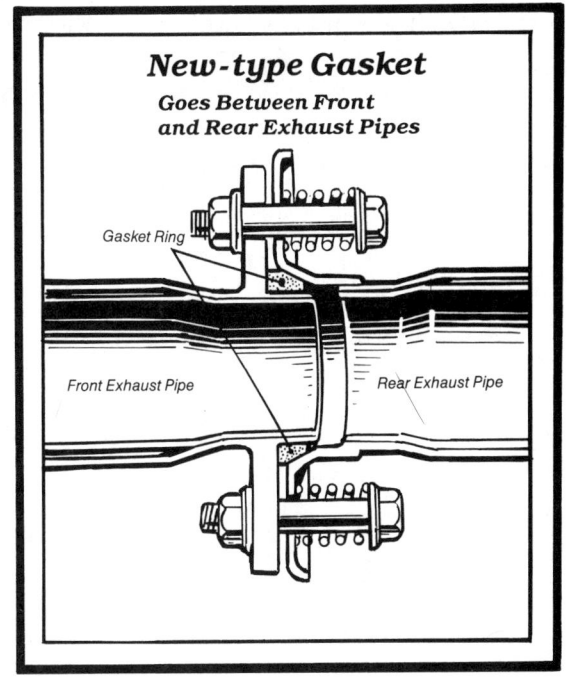

'75 models: Don't forget to install and tighten the two bolts that attach the assembly to the transmission, if you removed them.

Clean the air stove with a rag if it's oily, greasy, and funky. Wrap it around the right side of the exhaust pipe assembly and engage the tabs in the slots. Wiggle it into position so you can install and tighten the 10mm bolts. Reconnect the hot air inlet hose and secure it with the clamp. Install the splash shield and secure it with the 10mm bolts. Lower the jack if it's still holding anything up under there. Remove the jackstands and lower the car if you jacked it up.

Step 3. Replace Exhaust Pipes and/or Muffler/Tailpipes.

Chock, jack, and block the rear end of the car (Step 1).

To replace the muffler just unbolt it from the rear of the exhaust pipe assembly or pre-muffler and unhook the **rubber cushions** from the brackets on the muffler. If the end of the tailpipe is bolted to a **rubber hanger**, remove the 12mm bolt that attaches the tailpipe to the hanger. Now the muffler/tailpipe assembly can be removed. On 4WD models you'll have to thread the pipe over the rear axle shaft. Inspect the rubber cushions and tailpipe hanger (if you have one) and replace them if they're cracked, funky, or missing.

To install the new muffler/tailpipe, thread the pipe on the front of the muffler into position (over the rear axle shaft on 4WD models). Fit the rubber cushions over the hooks on the muffler, then install a new **gasket** between the muffler flange and exhaust pipe (or pre-muffler) flange. Install and tighten the bolts and nuts. If you have a *tailpipe hanger*, install and tighten the bolt. Lower the car, start the engine and check for leaks around the gasket. Do this *outside*, where exhaust fumes won't zap you. Tighten the bolts a little more if necessary.

To replace the rear exhaust pipe assembly or pre-muffler, remove the bolts, nuts, washers (and springs on late models), just to the rear of the rear exhaust pipe bracket, which attach the rear exhaust pipe or pre-muffler to the front exhaust pipe assembly. If you want to raise the car for access, be sure to use jackstands to support the car. Remove the bolts that attach the rear exhaust pipe assembly or pre-muffler to the muffler/tailpipe assembly. Now you can remove the exhaust pipe or pre-muffler.

To install the new rear exhaust pipe assembly or pre-muffler, fit it into place using new gaskets on each end, then install and tighten the bolts, washers, nuts, and springs (on late models). Lower the car and start the engine. (Don't do it in an enclosed space.) Feel around both gaskets for leaks. Tighten the bolts a little if necessary.

CHAPTER 13

BRAKES

"The ability to stop is often more important than any other capability—humans, cars, what-have-yous. Do a good slow solid job on your brakes."
—John Muir

HOW THEY WORK

Your Subaru has two brake systems that work independently of each other—a **hydraulic system** and a **mechanical system**. The hydraulic system is operated by applying pressure on the brake pedal with your foot. This pressure ends up activating the brakes on all four wheels. The mechanical system is operated by pulling up on the "emergency" **handbrake lever** located between the front seats. Only the front brakes are activated by the mechanical handbrake system.

Let's go through the hydraulic system first. When you push on the brake pedal with your foot (ear, nose, or whatever), a rod attached to the pedal is moved into the **master cylinder** which is bolted to the firewall in the engine compartment. The rod pushes against two **pistons** located inside the master cylinder. The pistons are fitted with rubber seals which form an air- and fluid-tight seal against the smooth walls of the master cylinder. When the plungers are forced forward by the rod attached to the brake pedal, pressure is created in the fluid in the master cylinder. It's like a hypodermic syringe: a plunger forces fluid into a hollow metal tube. The **brake lines** are hollow metal tubes that carry the hydraulic pressure to **wheel cylinders** at each of the four wheels.

268 *Chapter 13*

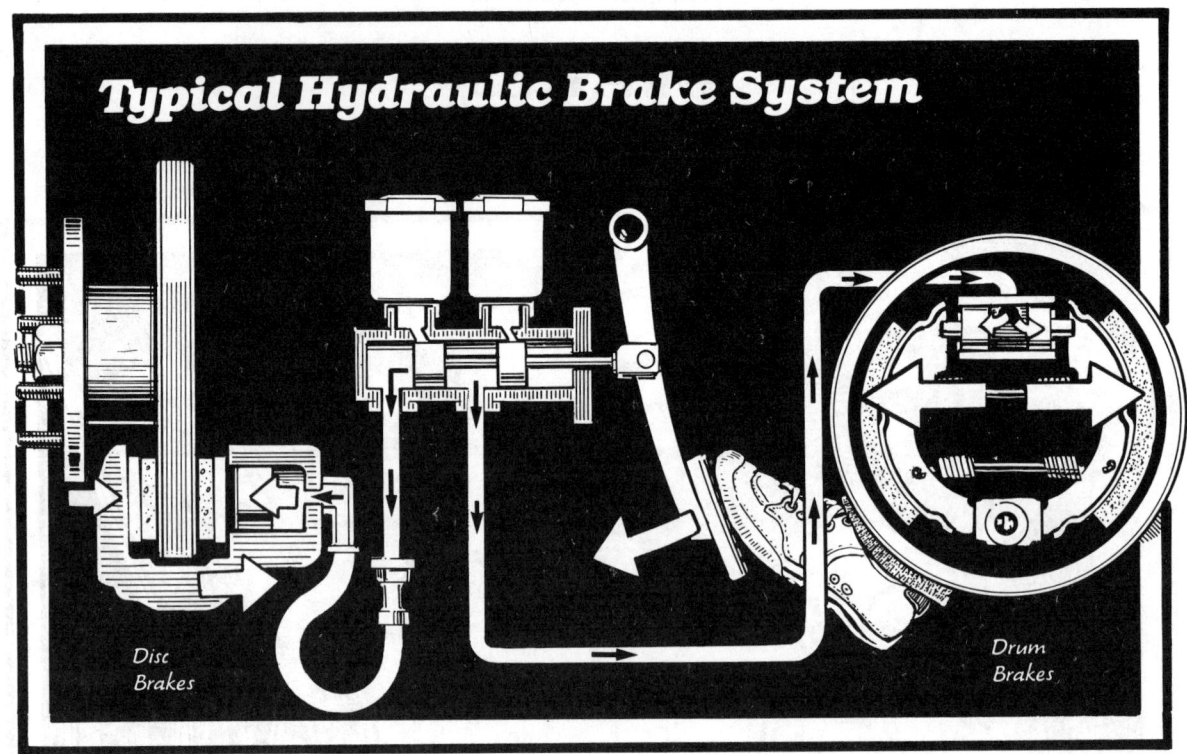

These wheel (or "slave") cylinders are bolted to brackets near the end of each axle. A short rubber **brake hose** takes the place of the metal lines near each wheel, allowing the wheels to move up and down and the front wheels to turn right and left.

There are two types of brake systems used on Subarus—**drum brakes** and **disc brakes**. Some 1975 models have drum brakes up front. Replacing the brakes on these models is not covered in this manual. You'll have to find the first edition of this manual, or write to me at John Muir Publications and I'll send you the instructions. All 1976 and newer Soobs have front disc brakes and all models until 1985 have rear drum brakes. Starting in 1985, OHC Turbo models and some non-Turbo XTs have disc brakes on the rear. I'll describe how the drum-type works first:

When the hydraulic pressure reaches a rear wheel cylinder, it forces two plungers inside the wheel cylinder to move outward against the tops of two **brake shoes**. The shoes are hinged at the bottom and secured to a **backing plate** by a pin. The brake shoes move outward and contact a heavy steel **brake drum** bolted to the wheel. Friction created by the brake shoe rubbing against the rotating brake drum makes it harder for the wheel to turn, thus slowing the car. This is happening at all four wheels at the same time. The plungers in the wheel cylinders are fitted with rubber seals to form an air- and fluid-tight seal, just like the master cylinder. **Brake springs** attached between the two brake shoes pull the shoes back away from the brake drum when the pressure is released from the brake pedal.

DISC BRAKES

Disc brakes derive their name from the shape of the strong metal **disc** bolted onto the front driveshaft which rotates along with the wheel. Bolted to the front axle housing is a **"floating caliper"** which surrounds the disc. **Pads** mounted inside the calipers will contact the disc when the brakes are applied. Machined into the caliper body is a **wheel cylinder bore** which houses the **brake piston**. When you press the brake pedal with your foot, hydraulic pressure goes out to the wheel cylinder where the piston is forced outward, pushing the inside brake pad against the inside surface of the disc. Since the caliper "floats" (can shift slightly), pressure applied to the inside brake pad moves the caliper body away from the inside of the disc and draws the outside pad against the outer surface of the disc. Thus the disc is squeezed from both sides, which slows and stops the wheel. Disc brakes are very efficient and are used on all four wheels of most high performance and racing cars. For example, all 1985 and newer Subarus with Turbo engines, as well as models with the six-cylinder engine, also have rear disc brakes. Since the front brakes supply most of the stopping power, they wear out faster than the rear brakes, so inspect them regularly.

Front disc brakes have been standard on GL and GSR coupes since 1972. For some reason sedans and station wagons were denied the nifty, efficient disc brakes until 1976, when all Subarus imported to the U.S. came with front disc brakes. In 1980, Subaru changed from Bendix calipers to AD calipers on all models except Brats. Brats got the AD calipers in '82. A thicker, ventilated disc was introduced on '83 4WD station wagons with automatic transmissions. All models after mid-1983 have the thicker ventilated discs.

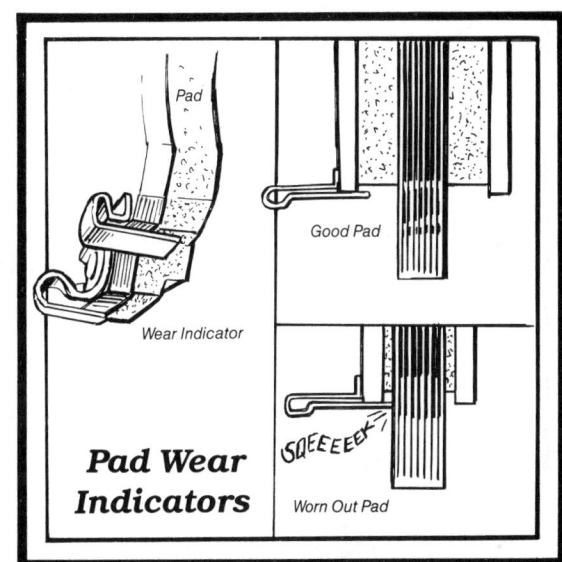

Pad Wear Indicators

Disc brakes seem to have a natural tendency to squeeeeel even when the pads and discs are in good condition. That's the trade-off we make: noisier but more efficient disc brakes, rather than quieter but less efficient drum brakes. The disc brake pads on **'80 and newer cars and '82-'87 Brats** have a built in **wear indicator** that *makes* the brakes squeal when the pads are nearly worn out. If your pads and discs are in good condition but tend to squeal, try squirting them with the garden hose occasionally to wash the accumulated brake dust off the pads. *Don't* do this while the discs are hot from a recent drive; the discs might warp.

When buying replacement pads for disc brakes, often you can choose between regular pads that are quieter but wear out faster, or hard pads that tend to squeal more but last longer. The choice is yours.

Except for screwing in the caliper pistons, changing the brake pads and removing the caliper for repair or replacement is a breeze with either the Bendix or AD system. Rebuilding the calipers, especially AD calipers, is very tedious and difficult and should be left to the professionals.

OTHER PARTS OF THE BRAKE SYSTEM

All 1975 and newer Subarus (except for 1975 two-door sedans) have a **master vac** unit. It's located between the brake pedal and master cylinder. The pretentiously named master vac uses vacuum from the engine to reduce the amount of pressure needed on the brake pedal to stop the car.

Since 1972 all Subarus sold in the U.S. have *tandem* master cylinders. This means there are two separate hydraulic circuits in the master cylinder body. The primary circuit operates the right front and left rear brakes. The secondary circuit operates the left front and right rear brakes. If a seal in the master cylinder or wheel cylinder of one of the circuits breaks, the other circuit still provides 50 percent of the normal braking action. It's like having a safety net.

Until 1979 a **brake failure switch** was incorporated into an octopus-looking brake line *junction block* on the firewall behind the engine. When the pressure in one of the hydraulic circuits on these cars is less than the pressure in the other circuit, a red light on the dash lights up. This is the same light that reminds you that the handbrake is on. In 1979, Subaru changed to a **low-brake-fluid warning** system (Brats got this system in '78).

270 Chapter 13

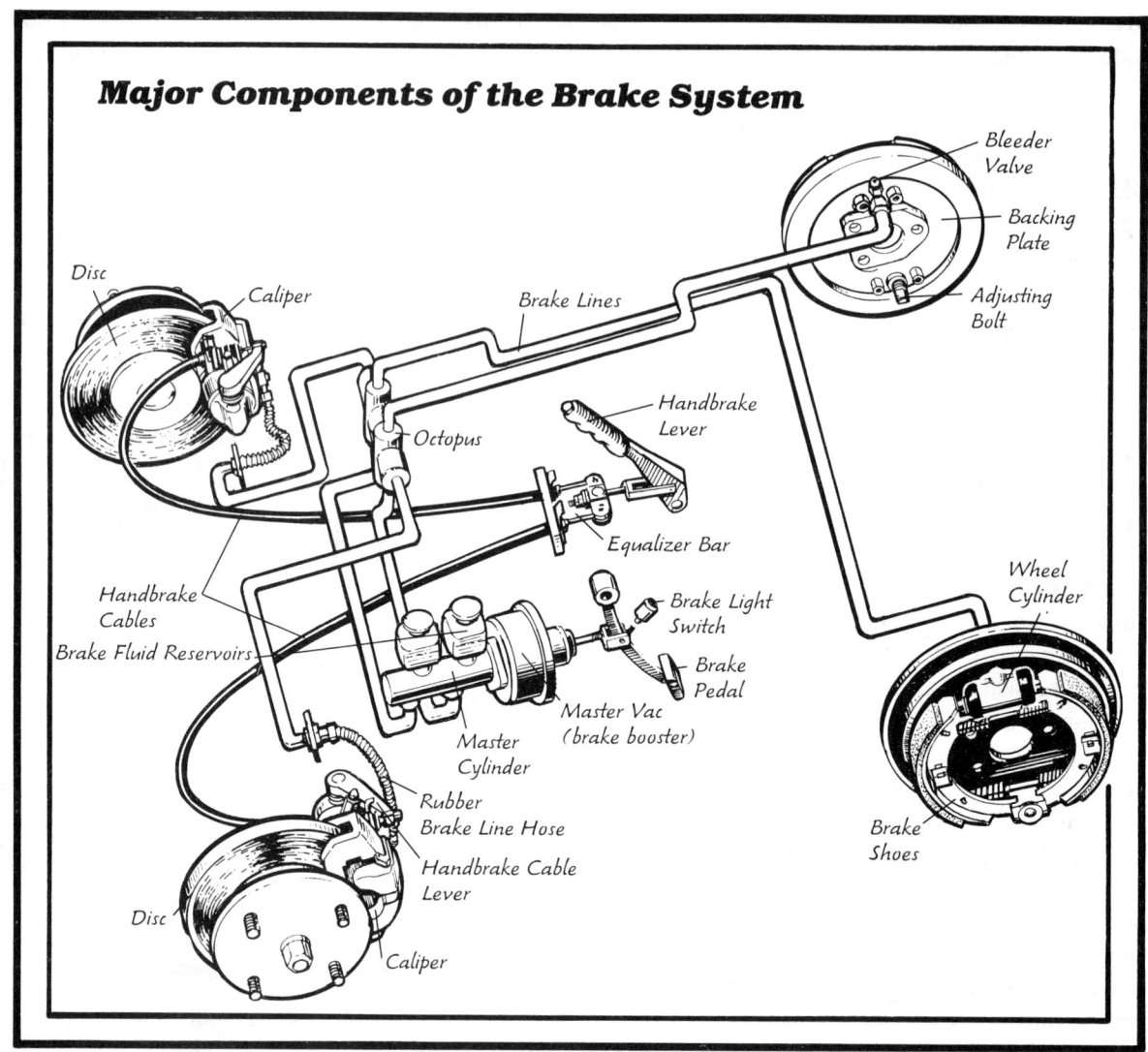

Each brake fluid reservoir cap has a switch that lights the brake warning light on the dash if the fluid level is low.

Here's how your outside **brake lights** work: A switch for the brake lights is mounted to a bracket near the top of the brake pedal. When the pedal is pushed away from the switch the rear brake lights light up.

BRAKE ADJUSTMENT

When there's friction, there's also wear and tear. Naturally it's best to have one surface (the cheaper one) wear out before the other. That's why replaceable *asbestos compound* brake pads and brake shoe linings are softer than the metal discs and drums they rub against. Eventually, the brake pad and shoe linings wear thin and have to be replaced.

For the brake system to operate at maximum efficiency, the brake shoes and pads must ride as close to the drums and discs as possible. The front brakes on all models are self-adjusting, so no manual adjustment is necessary. The rear brakes on all OHC Turbo models and all XT6 (six-cylinder) models are discs, so they don't require manual adjustment. The rear brakes on all OHC 4WD models are self-adjusting drum brakes, so they don't require periodic adjustment. Nice for us lazy people.

Brakes   271

The following models have rear drum brakes that must be manually adjusted every 12,000 miles to compensate for wear: all OHV models, 1985 and newer four-cylinder, non-Turbo, non-4WD (2WD) models. Procedure 1 tells you how to do it.

HANDBRAKE SYSTEM

The **mechanical handbrake system** (also called the emergency or parking brake) works when you pull up on the **brake lever** between the front seats. The lever pulls on two **cables** that are attached directly to the front brake shoes (or calipers) and applies those brakes. When you park, set the handbrake before releasing the clutch (manual transmission cars) or before putting the automatic shift lever in PARK. This way no strain is put on the drivetrain and things last longer. If you're ever cruising down the road and (gulp!) the brake pedal goes to the floor when you press on it, DON'T PANIC. Just keep the button on the handbrake lever pressed in and gently use the handbrake lever to slow you down. It's unlikely this will ever happen to you, thanks to the dual master cylinder.

BRAKE PROBLEMS

All brake shoes, disc pads, and rubber seals in the master cylinder and wheel cylinders are mortal, like you and me, and will eventually wear out due to normal usage. Keeping the system filled with fresh fluid and adjusting the rear shoes regularly (if yours require adjustment) will prolong the brake system's life (and maybe yours), but sooner or later you'll encounter one or more of the following problems.

If the brake pedal feels solid, but goes to within three inches of the floor before any resistance is felt, the brake pads or shoes aren't making contact against the discs or drums as quickly as they should. Try adjusting the rear brakes (Procedure 1). If that doesn't help, inspect the front and rear shoes or pads for wear (Procedure 4 for rear shoes, Procedure 6 for rear pads, Procedure 8 for front pads).

Squeals, growls, and rumbles coming from the wheels when the brakes are applied means the asbestos compound has worn through and the metal part of the shoes or pads is contacting the drums or discs. Very bad. This causes scratching or scoring which can quickly ruin the expensive drums and discs. **1980 and newer models** (except '77-'81 Brats) have a wear sensor built into the pads that squeals at you (a cry for help!) when the pads are almost worn out. If you hear this plea for attention, check the pads.

If the brake pedal feels spongy, mushy, or has to be pumped a few times before any resistance is felt, air is in the hydraulic system. Since air can be easily compressed, the pressure applied to the system by pumping the brake pedal merely causes the air pockets to get smaller (compressed) and thereby undermines the hydraulic fluid's job of forcing the wheel cylinder plungers outward to move the brake shoes or pads.

Air can enter the system if the brake fluid level in the master cylinder reservoir gets too low, when the hydraulic system is opened for inspection or repair, or when a seal in one of the wheel cylinders wears out. Check the fluid level in the master cylinder reservoir and top it up if necessary (Procedure 2, Step 2). Look on the inside of each wheel and around the master cylinder for any signs of wetness (signs of an opening in the system that would let fluid out and air in). But don't do this on a rainy day. If no leaks or wet spots can be found, adjust the rear brakes (if yours require manual adjustment), then bleed the system (Procedure 2). Check the pedal again for firmness. Problem solved? Congratulations. If no leaks were found and the pedal is still mushy after bleeding the system, the master cylinder seals are probably incapable of holding pressure in the system. The master cylinder needs to be rebuilt or replaced (Procedure 12).

If you find a damp-looking area on the inside of a wheel or backing plate, check the smell of the wet spot to see if it's brake fluid. How? Get some of the goo on your finger and compare the aroma to an open can of brake fluid. Don't give it a taste test because brake fluid is poison. Smell the same? If so, a wheel cylinder rebuild is in order (Procedure 7). On drum brakes, it's best to rebuild or replace both rear wheel cylinders even if only one side is leaking. If a caliper is leaking, also take the caliper on the opposite side to Subaru or a garage and have them both rebuilt. Back to the smell test—if the smells don't match, the wet spot could be from a neighborhood dog. Wash your hands and make a note about what to do to that dog the next time you see him.

A leaky master cylinder is easy to spot because it's sticking out of the firewall or master vac in the engine compartment in plain view. Carefully check all the brake line connections at the master cylinder and the brake line **junction block** for leaks. The junction block is located on the firewall behind the engine on '75-'79 cars and '77-'81 Brats, and below the master cylinder on '80 and newer cars and '82-'87 Brats. Make sure the clamps on the bottom of the brake fluid reservoirs are snug, and check the reservoirs for cracks.

If the master cylinder is leaking, don't try to rebuild it yourself. Take it to an expert! It is vital that the job be done perfectly. Procedure 12 tells you how to remove and replace the master cylinder.

Always adjust the rear brakes (if yours are adjustable) before bleeding the system and always bleed *all* the wheels, even if the pedal seems firm after bleeding the first wheel or two. It's worth the effort.

Dragging brakes can affect your car's performance in several ways: decreased gas mileage, engine overheating, and dangerous wheel lock-up when the brakes are applied. To check for dragging brakes, park on level ground with the gearshift in NEUTRAL and the handbrake OFF. You should be able to push the car without much effort. If you can't, jack the car up one wheel at a time, then check the turning resistance on each wheel. The handbrake has to be off to check the front wheels so be sure to block the rear wheels.

If you find that one or more of the brakes is dragging on your **'81 and newer Soob**, check the **hill-holder system** if you have one (Procedure 17).

If you don't have a hill-holder, or that wasn't your problem, jack up the car at the wheel that's dragging and put it on jackstands. If the wheel has drum brakes, remove the brake drum (Procedure 4) and check for broken return springs and linings that have come off the metal part of the shoes. If it's a disc brake wheel, remove the wheel and check the caliper and brake pads to see if they are free to move in the holder (Procedure 8, Steps 1 and 2). Check the handbrake cable lever on the caliper to see if it's sticking and holding the front brakes on (Procedure 8, Step 5).

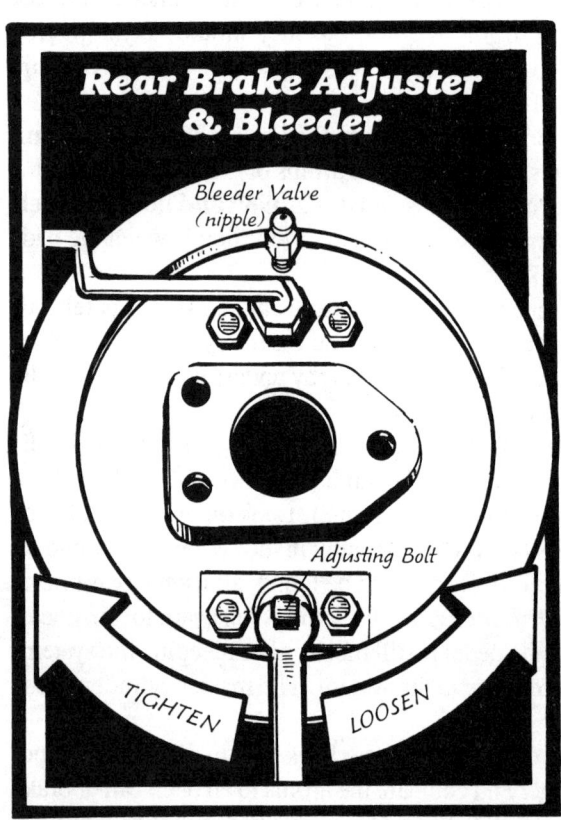

If all looks well at the brakes, or all the brakes are dragging, the master cylinder might be holding residual pressure after the brake pedal is released. Rebuild or replace the master cylinder (Procedure 12).

Since almost every brake procedure involves jacking up the car, please read the safety precautions in Chapter 3.

PROCEDURE 1: ADJUST REAR BRAKES

This procedure is for all OHV models and OHC non-Turbo, non-4WD models (except six-cylinder models).

Condition: Your car doesn't stop as well as it used to; OR the pedal goes over halfway to the floor before resistance is felt; OR it's been 6,000 miles since the rear brakes were adjusted; OR you're tired of sticking your foot out the door and dragging your foot to stop the car.

***Procedure 1, Step 1**   Brakes*   **273**

Tools and Materials: Safety glasses, jack, jackstands, blocks for the wheels, can of penetrating oil, a 6mm open-end wrench or small crescent wrench. **'75 models** also require a 14mm box-end wrench.

Step 1. Chock, Jack, and Block.

Park on level ground, put the car in 1st gear (manual transmission) or PARK. Set the handbrake, and put chocks in front of and behind the front wheels. Place the jack under the jack point in front of a rear wheel and raise the car until the wheel is off the ground. Block the car up with a jackstand in case your jack fails (Chapter 3).

Step 2. Adjust.

Put on your safety glasses and crawl under the rear of the car. Look behind the wheel at the round **brake backing plate** attached to the outer end of the rear axle. Except for the very top and bottom, it's pretty much covered by the **suspension arm.** The backing plate serves as a bracket for the brake components and prevents dust and moisture from entering the mechanisms.

Look at the bottom of the backing plate for two short bolts with nuts on them. Between the short bolts is a longer threaded bolt with a square head on the end. This is the **brake adjusting bolt.** Squirt some penetrating oil on the threads of the adjusting bolt. If there is a nut on the adjusting bolt right next to the backing plate, loosen it a couple of turns with the 14mm box-end wrench. (If there's no nut, don't worry about it; Subaru quit putting them on in '76.)

Put the 6mm or crescent wrench on the square end of the bolt and turn it *clockwise* as far as it will go. You'll feel the bolt get tight then loose, tight then loose, as you turn it. Here's what's happening: On the other end of the bolt, there's a four-sided wedge that sits between the bottom of the brake shoes. Screwing the bolt in spreads the shoes and thus moves the brake linings closer to the drum. When the bolt is screwed in as far as it will go, unscrew it *counterclockwise* 180° (half a turn). This leaves about .004″ to .006″ (0.1 to 0.15mm) clearance between the lining and the drum. Spin the tire while you rock the wrench back and forth a little. Leave the bolt set in a position where the tire spins freely. Tighten the 14mm nut if there is one (hold the bolt head with the wrench if it turns with the nut). Spin the tire with your hand to see that it rotates freely. If it seems to drag, loosen the adjusting bolt 90° (quarter of a turn) and spin the wheel again. A very light scraping sound when you rotate the wheel is normal. Easy, isn't it?

Repeat this step to adjust the other rear brake.

PROCEDURE 2: BLEED BRAKES

The purpose of bleeding the hydraulic system is to eliminate all air bubbles and air pockets in the system. This is accomplished by forcing brake fluid into the system from the master cylinder and forcing air and water out through the **bleeder valves.** Seems like blood should squirt out but it never does.

Check the fluid level in the master cylinder reservoir(s) frequently while you're bleeding the brakes (Step 2). Never let the fluid go below the MIN line. If the level gets too low, air will get pumped into the system and you'll have to start all over.

Bleed the brakes in this order:

OHV models: Bleed the master cylinder, then the left rear, then the right front, then the right rear, and finally the left front.

OHC models: Start with the left front wheel, then bleed the right rear wheel. Bleed the right front, then the left rear.

Read all the way through the brake bleeding steps before you do them. They go too fast to thumb through while you're under the car.

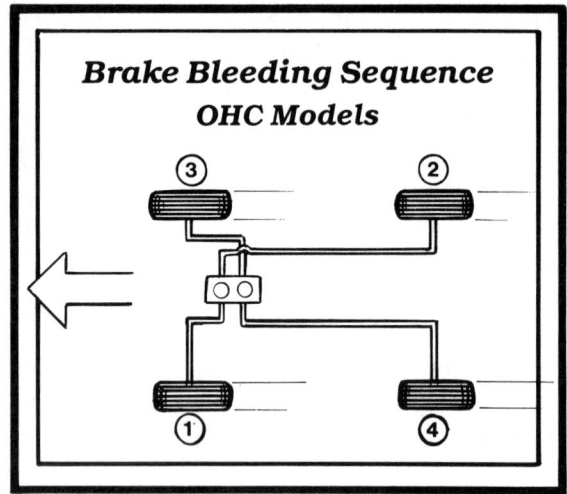

Condition: Brake pedal feels spongy or mushy and it takes a few pumps on the pedal before any braking action occurs; OR some part of the hydraulic system has been opened for inspection or repair.

Tools and Materials: Pint of DOT 3 or 4 brake fluid, small glass jar with lid, at least 18" of 3/16" inside diameter clear plastic hose (old suction tubing from a hospital works well), 8mm and 10mm box-end wrenches, safety glasses, jack, jackstands, a Friend who can hear and is willing to follow your instructions. My son has been helping me bleed brakes since he was 3 years old.

Remarks: Wear safety glasses while you bleed the brakes and be careful not to get any brake fluid in your mouth—it's extremely poisonous. Use the glass jar to catch the used brake fluid, then properly dispose of it. Brake fluid also ruins paint; if any gets on the car, wipe it off immediately and wash the spot with warm soapy water.

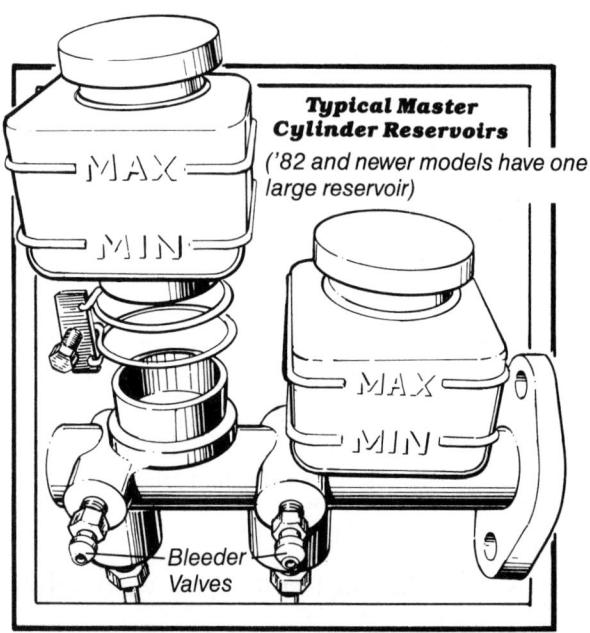

CAUTION!: Brake fluid is like a magnet for moisture in the air. An open can of brake fluid can become contaminated within a few minutes on a humid day. So keep the can of brake fluid tightly sealed and the reservoir caps on except when adding fluid.

Don't reuse fluid pumped out during the bleeding process. It's become aerated (full of minute bubbles) and thus useless.

If you're stuck on the road, you can bleed the brakes without the glass jar or plastic hose. Hold a rag over the end of the bleeding nipple to keep the fluid off the tires and out of your eyes. Do it this way only in a real pinch.

Step 1. Adjust Rear Brakes.

See Procedure 1 to see if your model requires periodic rear brake adjustment. If it does, always adjust the rear brakes before bleeding the brake system.

Step 2. Check Brake Fluid Level.

The **brake fluid reservoir(s)** is on top of the master cylinder. To keep dirt out of the brake fluid, clean the cap(s) and reservoir(s) with a rag before removing the cap(s). Lay the cap(s) someplace clean and cover it with a clean rag or paper towel. Look for two lines on the side of each reservoir marked MIN (minimum) and MAX (maximum). Fill the master cylinder reservoir(s) to the MAX line with fresh DOT 3 or 4 brake fluid, then put the reservoir cap(s) on.

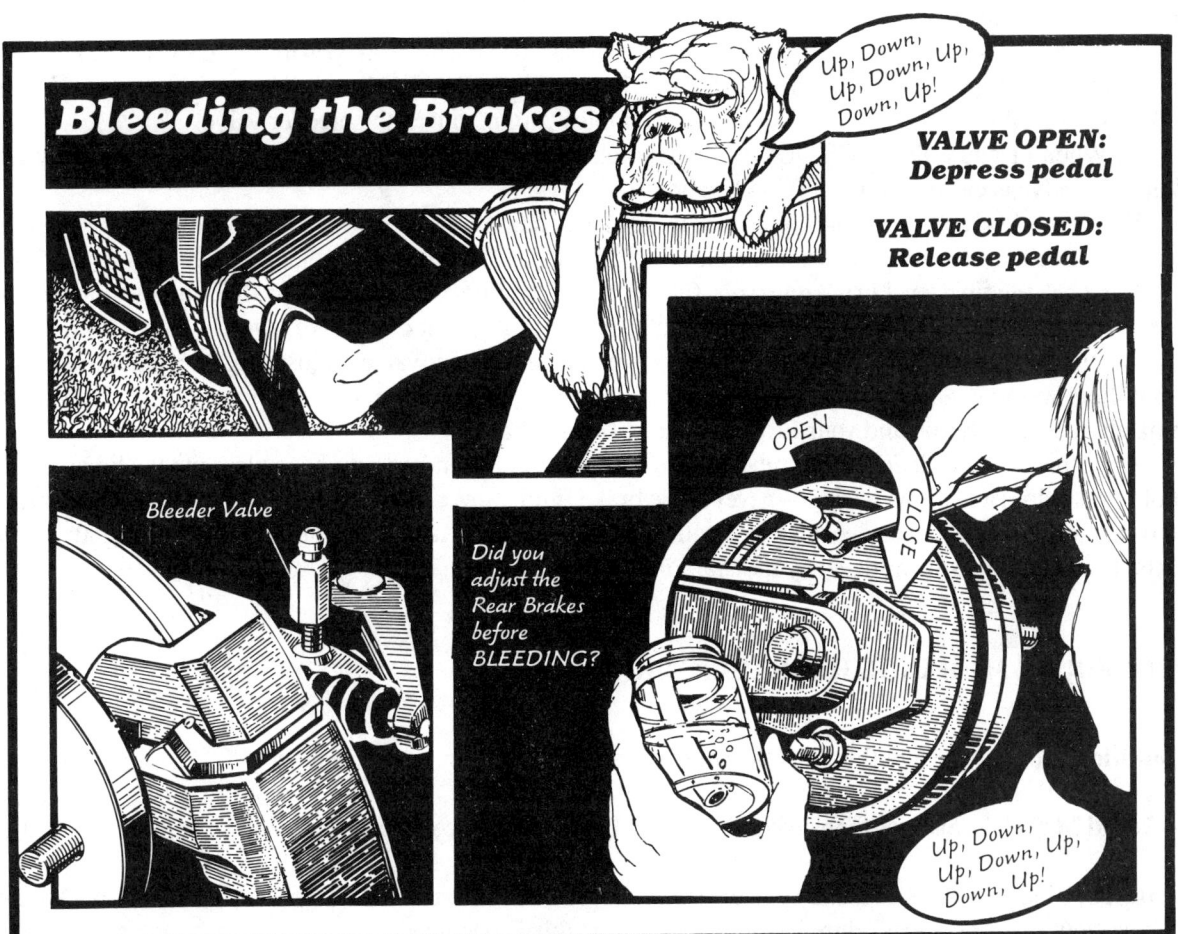

Step 3. Locate Bleeder Valves

Bleeder valves look like hollow bolts that screw into the wheel cylinders. They tend to be rather fragile, so be sure you use a box-end wrench when loosening and tightening them. Open-end wrenches quickly round off the corners and leave you unable to bleed!

OHV models: There are two bleeder valves on the side of the master cylinder. Bleed the rear one first, then the front one.

EVERYONE: The bleeder valves for drum brakes are near the top of the brake backing plate, and rather difficult to reach. Removing the wheels makes the job a lot easier, especially the first time through.

On disc brakes the bleeder valves are located near the top rear of the calipers. With difficulty they can be reached by turning the wheels opposite the side of the car you're working on. Again, it's easier to reach the bleeder with the wheel off—especially the first time.

Step 4. Bleed 'em.

Put on your safety glasses. Find the bleeder valve and peel off the **rubber cap**, if there is one. Position the box end of an 8mm wrench (10mm on the master cylinder) over the bleeder valve so the valve can be opened *counterclockwise* at least ¼ turn. Slip one end of the clear plastic hose over the end of the bleeder valve nipple and stick the other end of the hose into the glass jar. Pour about one inch of fresh brake fluid into the jar and check to see that the end of the tube is submerged in the fluid.

Bleeding the brakes is a team sport, so you and your Friend should read and practice the next five sub-steps at least once before bleeding the brakes for real.

A. Friend slowly pumps the brake pedal about 10 times then, while holding his or her foot firmly on the pedal, yells, "READY!"

B. When you yell, "DOWN," Friend presses on the brake pedal while you open the bleed valve ¼ turn (counterclockwise). Friend's foot forces the pedal to the floor and HOLDS IT DOWN. When it hits the floor Friend yells, "IT'S DOWN." You'll watch fluid and air bubbles coming out of the bleeder valve.

C. When Friend yells, "IT'S DOWN," you quickly close the bleeder valve by tightening it (clockwise). When the valve is closed, yell, "UP" at Friend.

D. Friend slowly lets the pedal come up to its normal position, then yells, "IT'S UP." If the pedal is released while the bleeder valve is open, air or used fluid will be sucked into the system. Don't panic, just repeat A-E.

E. Check the fluid level in the reservoir, fill it to the MAX line, then repeat steps B-E until no bubbles can be seen coming out of the bleeder valve. It might take two times, or it could take several.

When you're sure all the bubbles are gone, make sure the bleeder valve is closed tight, replace the rubber cap if there was one, and wipe up any fluid that might have spilled. Move on to the next wheel and try not to think about how silly you and your Friend sound to the neighbors.

After the master cylinder (OHV models) and all four wheel cylinders have been bled, put the lid on the jar of old brake fluid and throw it away—never reuse brake fluid. Never store anything but brake fluid in a brake fluid can; someone might accidentally use it with bad to fatal results. Keep spare cans of brake fluid tightly sealed so the fluid can't be contaminated by moisture in the air.

PROCEDURE 3: CHANGE HYDRAULIC BRAKE FLUID

Condition: You just bought the car; OR you're doing the 12,000-mile maintenance.

Tools and Materials: Same as for bleeding the brakes (Procedure 2) except three pints of brake fluid will be needed.

Remarks: This procedure is usually performed in shops with a machine called a *pressure bleeder*, but we can do it without one. Read Procedure 2 before performing this Procedure.

Brake fluid absorbs water, which hastens the demise of the wheel cylinders and master cylinder. Changing the brake fluid regularly will save you money in the long run and make your car safer to drive—a nice combination.

Step 1. Drain Master Cylinder Reservoirs.

If there are two wires coming out of the top of the reservoir cap(s), follow the wires to a connector located a few inches from the reservoir(s) and disconnect the wires.

Clean each master cylinder reservoir cap to prevent dirt from falling into the reservoir, then remove the cap and little *strainer basket* inside the reservoir. Store the cap(s) and strainer(s) in a clean, safe location while you change the brake fluid.

OHV models: Locate the two master cylinder bleeder valves on the side of the master cylinder. Remove the dust cap from one of the bleeder valves, put a 10mm box-end wrench on the valve, then slip one end of 3/16" inside diameter clear tubing over the nipple. Stick the other end of the tube into a jar or can.

Open the bleeder valve and have Friend slowly pump the brake pedal while you watch the fluid level in the reservoir. When the fluid level reaches the aluminum part of the master cylinder, tell Friend to hold the pedal down while you tighten the valve. Be sure to leave a little fluid in the master cylinder.

OHC models: Don't add any fluid to the reservoir while you bleed the left front wheel until there is only a little fluid left in the reservoir. Don't completely empty the reservoir.

EVERYONE: Clean the strainer(s) with a clean rag, then install it/them in the reservoir(s). Fill the reservoir(s) with fresh brake fluid.

OHV models: Bleed both nipples on the master cylinder the same way you did in Procedure 2. After going through substeps A-E a few times, the fluid flowing through the tube will be clear and no air bubbles should be seen. Have Friend hold the brake pedal down while you tighten the bleeder valve and install the dust cap.

OHC models: Bleed the left front wheel just like you did in Procedure 2 until the fluid in the tube looks clean and clear and has no air bubbles in it.

Step 2. Bleed Wheel Cylinders.

Bleed each wheel cylinder in the sequence described in Procedure 2. Start with fluid in the master cylinder reservoir at the MAX line and bleed each wheel cylinder until the fluid is at the MIN line. Keep filling the reservoir and bleeding the wheel cylinder until the brake fluid flowing through the plastic hose is clear and has no bubbles in it. It will probably take 3-4 reservoirs of fluid for each rear wheel and 2-3 reservoirs for front wheels. Be sure to tighten the bleeder valves and install the rubber dust caps.

Fill the reservoir(s) to the MAX line with fresh brake fluid, then install the cap(s). If there are wires coming out of the cap(s), be sure they are securely connected to the wiring harness.

If you removed any wheels, install them and snug down the lug nuts. Lower the car and torque the lug nuts to 72 ft. lbs. Lower the hood and be sure it's latched securely. Record the brake fluid change in the log at the end of Chapter 7. Thanks.

PROCEDURE 4: REMOVE BRAKE DRUMS OR DISCS, CHECK REAR DRUM BRAKES

This procedure tells you how to remove and install the brake drums to inspect or replace the rear brake shoes, or how to remove the disc on models with disc brakes. If you only need to check the brake pads on models with disc brakes, see Procedure 8.

Condition: You just bought the car; OR you're doing the regular maintenance; OR strange noises are coming from the rear of the car when the brakes are applied; OR the drums or discs must be removed for repair or replacement.

Tools and Materials: Everyone will need the following tools: Safety glasses, a dust mask or respirator to protect you from the nasty carcinogenic brakedust, ruler or small tape measure (to measure the brake shoes), jack, lug wrench, jackstand(s), rags or paper towels, newspapers, large pliers, medium screwdriver, hammer, 10mm and 14mm wrenches. Depending on how tight the axle nuts and drums are on, you might need a cheater bar, penetrating oil, and a brake drum puller. Additional tools for the various years and models are listed below.

'75-'78 front discs and 4WD rear drums: 36mm socket, ½" drive ratchet or breaker bar, 175 ft. lb. torque wrench, 3/16" chisel, wire brush, and some oil (any kind). Maybe new axle nuts.

'79 and newer front discs and 4WD rear drums: 36mm socket, ½" ratchet or breaker bar, two new cotter pins, 154 ft. lb. torque wrench, wire brush, some oil (any kind).

All non-4WD (2WD), rear brakes: You'll need two new lock plates for the rear axle nuts.

Remarks: CAUTION! WARNING! When you remove a brake drum, disc or caliper, wear a surgical mask or respirator and **DON'T** breathe any of the black brake dust. Before removing the brake drums or discs spread a newspaper under the wheel to catch the dust. As you remove the drums or discs, dump the accumulated dust onto the newspaper then fold the newspaper so the dust is safely wrapped inside. Secure it with a rubber band or piece of string and put it in the trash, then put a fresh newspaper under the wheel. After handling brake parts, wash your hands before eating or smoking anything.

DON'T press on the brake pedal while a drum or disc is removed. The pistons will shoot out of the wheel cylinder and you'll have a nasty mess to clean up.

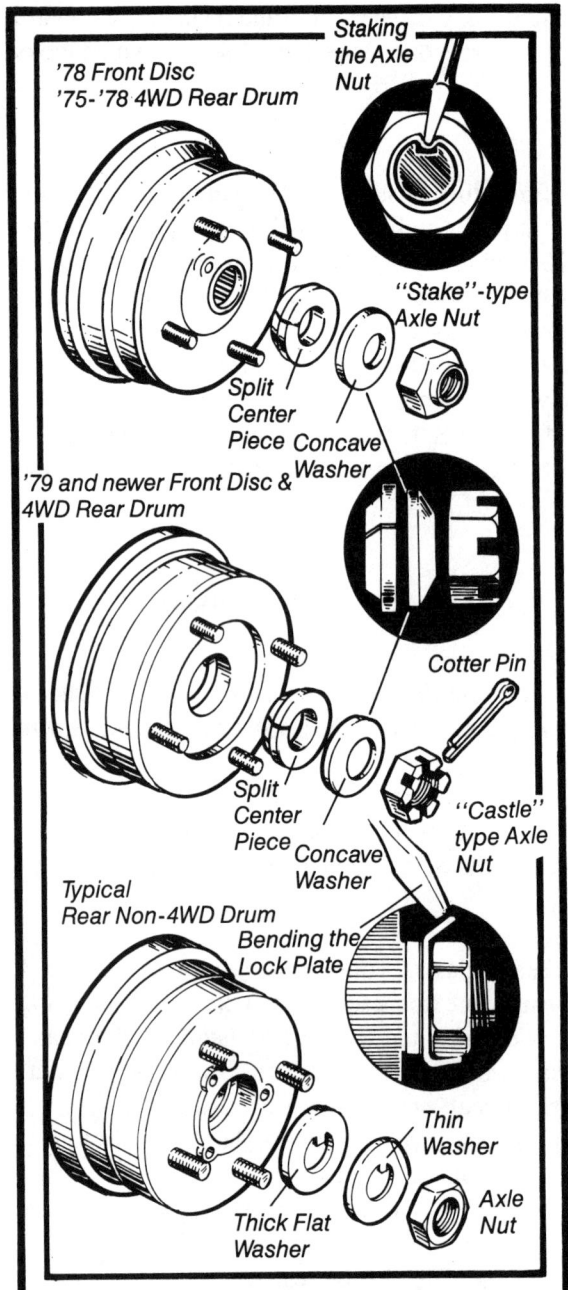

Step 1. Remove Brake Drum or Disc.

Park on level ground, put the gearshift in 1st or PARK, put chocks in front of and behind the wheels on the opposite end of the car you're going to check. If you are removing the front discs, release the handbrake (OFF). Remove the 14mm hubcap bolt or pry off the hubcap with a screwdriver, depending on your setup. Loosen the lug nuts counterclockwise about one turn.

'75-'78 non-4WD rear drums: Jack up the car and put it on jackstands. Remove the wheel. Unscrew the three 10mm bolts on the **brake drum cap** (that bulbous little thing in the middle of the brake drum) and remove the cap. Be careful when you remove the cap so you don't tear the gasket under the cap. If the gasket is stuck to the drum and isn't torn or broken, leave it there. Replace it with a new one if it gets garbaged.

'79 and newer non-4WD rear drums or discs: Jack up the rear end of the car and put it on jackstands. Remove the wheels. There's a bulbous drum cap in the center of the brake drum that you pry off with a screwdriver. Here's how: Put a thin screwdriver blade between the brake drum or disc and the little ridge around the cap. Tap lightly in the groove all around the cap until you can pry the cap off. Replace the rubber O-ring on the cap if it breaks.

All non-4WD rear drums: Once the drum cap is off, you'll see that a big flat **lock plate** has been bent over one side of the axle nut to keep it from turning. Pry the lock plate away from the axle nut by lightly hammering a small screwdriver or chisel between the nut and plate. Straighten the plate enough so it won't interfere with removal of the large axle nut. Remove the axle nut with large pliers, then pull off the thin lock plate and thick washer that's right behind it. Wiggle the drum until the **wheel bearing** slides out enough to grab with your fingers. Remove the bearing and put it somewhere clean. When you install the bearing, be sure it goes back on the same wheel. Support the weight of the drum, then pull straight out on the drum to remove it. Dragging the drum off the axle can damage the grease seal on the inside of the drum.

Front disc brakes and 4WD rear drum or disc brakes: If there's a cotter pin sticking through the axle and axle nut, straighten the pin with pliers then tap it out of the axle. No cotter pin? Locate the groove in the axle where the axle nut has been bent ("staked") down into the groove to lock the nut in place. Tap a 3/16" wide chisel into the groove under the staked portion of the nut until the end of the nut is round enough to clear the threads on the axle.

Put the 36mm socket and ratchet on the nut so you can push down on the handle to loosen the nut *counterclockwise* about ½ turn. These nuts are hard to crack sometimes, so you might have to put a foot on the ratchet handle (keep one foot on the ground) or slide a *cheater bar* (a 2 to 3 foot long piece of pipe) over the ratchet handle for added leverage. Be sure you're turning the nut *counterclockwise*.

When the axle nut is loose, jack up the car and put it on jackstands. Remove the lug nuts and wheel. Remove the axle nut. Remove the big **flat washer** and the **split center piece**. Pull straight out on the drum or disc to remove it. If it's stuck, see the next paragraph.

Stuck drum or disc: Here's an old Jedi trick that usually works on tight drums or discs. Squirt some penetrating oil on the axle splines and around the split center piece and let it soak for a few minutes. Be sure your safety glasses are on, then put the sharp end of a chisel in the groove between the drum and center piece and tap it with a hammer. Do this all the way around. Once the center piece pops out, the drum can usually be removed. If the drum still won't come off, the Dark Side has won and you'll have to borrow, buy, or rent a drum puller.

Step 2. Inspect Brake Shoes.

OK, now that the brake drum is off, check the **brake shoes** and the **wheel cylinder** at the top of the backing plate for any signs of wetness—an indication that the wheel cylinder is leaking fluid. A slight leak will make the brake dust darker right around the cylinder. A bad leak will coat everything with brake fluid. If any fluid is present, the wheel cylinder must be rebuilt or replaced (Procedure 7). Replace the brake shoes if any brake fluid or grease is on the linings.

Removing the split center piece if it's stuck

Use a ruler or tape measure to measure the brake lining where it looks the thinnest—don't include the metal part of the shoe. If the lining of the rear shoes is 1/16" or less, the shoes should be replaced (Procedure 5).

Use a clean, non-oily finger to check the surface of the brake lining and the contact area inside the brake drum. Both surfaces should feel almost smooth with no large ridges or grooves worn in them. If the linings and drum are real groovy, the shoes should be replaced and the drums turned (machined), Procedure 5.

Measure the Brake Lining in the thinnest place. Don't include the metal Brake Shoe in the measurement (this one looks plenty good).

Check the rubber **brake hoses** for cracks, worn, split, or bulging spots. To find the rubber hoses for the rear brakes, follow the brake line forward from the top of the backing plate to the top of the **torsion bar**. There it is. Replace the hoses if any of the aforementioned abnormalities exist (Procedure 11).

If the shoes, drums, and wheel cylinder are OK, go on to Step 3 and install the drums, then do Step 4 to tighten the axle nuts.

Step 3. Install Brake Drums or Discs.

Non-4WD rear drums or discs: Check the wheel bearings for dark blue or black spots on the rollers and races. If the bearings aren't bright and shiny they should be replaced (Chapter 14, Procedure 9). Clean the outside of the rubber **grease seal** that's on the inside of the drum or disc with a rag. Don't let the dirt fall into the wheel bearing hole. If the seal is cracked or you can see a thin metal spring hanging inside the seal, or if the spring was pulled out of the seal by the inner wheel bearing, you need to replace the seal (Chapter 14, Procedure 9). Seal OK? Get a dab of grease from inside the drum or disc and smear it on the grease seal lip.

Hold the drum so your fingers won't get squished between the drum or disc and the backing plate—ouch! Line up the hole in the drum or disc with the axle and carefully slide it onto the axle. Keep the axle centered in the hole so the seal doesn't get damaged by the wheel bearing. Push the drum or disc over the axle as far as you can. It helps to wiggle the drum or disc slightly while pushing on it. Wipe the **outer bearing race** in the drum or disc with a clean rag, then slide the wheel bearing onto the axle with the larger part of the bearing to the outside. Slide the thick washer onto the axle with its tab in the groove. Install a new lock plate on the axle with the tab in the groove and the flat edge hooked over the flat part of the thick washer.

Screw the axle nut on and torque it to 36 ft. lb., if you have a torque wrench and the proper size socket handy. Otherwise, use the large pliers to get the nut good and snug, but not real tight. Rotate the drum forward and backward several times to seat the bearings. Now turn the nut counterclockwise so the edge of the nut moves about 1/8". Rotate the drum with your hand to see if the drum turns freely. There should be a little drag but not much. If it's hard to turn, loosen the axle nut just a bit more and check it again. When it turns smoothly, try moving the drum side to side and up and down. If any looseness is felt, tighten the axle nut slightly and check it one more time. When the drum rotates smoothly with no looseness in the bearing, use the large pliers to bend the lock plate over one of the flat sides of the axle nut. Squeeze the lock plate so it touches the entire side of the nut.

'75-'78 non-4WD rear drums: Install the brake drum cap and gasket (if it came off the drum) and tighten the three 10mm bolts.

'79 and newer non-4WD rear drums or discs: Install the rubber O-ring onto the bulbous cap. Press the cap into its hole on the brake drum, then use a hammer or screwdriver handle to tap it in until the little ridge touches the drum all the way around.

All non-4WD rear drums: Install the wheel and snug the lug nuts. If you don't have auto-adjusting brakes, adjust the brakes (Procedure 1).

All non-4WD rear discs: Go back to Procedure 6, Step 4, to install the caliper holders and calipers.

All front discs and all 4WD rear drums: Clean the round center part in the middle of the inside of the brake drum with a rag. That's the surface the wheel bearing seal rides on. Clean the splines on the axle and inside the drum with a wire brush, then give them a very light coat of oil. Wipe off any excess oil with a rag. Hold the drum up to the axle and wiggle it until the splines engage, then gently push the drum all the way onto the axle.

If you used a screwdriver or chisel to loosen the split center piece, smooth off any rough spots with a file. Slip the split center piece onto the axle and into the drum or disc. The large washer is slightly cone shaped. Fit it onto the axle so the raised center part is toward the outside.

Screw the axle nut onto the axle so the tapered staking lip ('75-'78 models) or the slots for the cotter pin ('79 and newer) is to the outside. Snug it down with the 36mm socket and ratchet.

DRUM BRAKE PEOPLE: Put the wheel on the drum and snug the lug nuts. Lower the car then torque the lug nuts to 72 ft. lbs. Look at the illustration in Chapter 3 for the tightening sequence.

DISC BRAKE PEOPLE: Do Procedure 6, Step 5, to install the rear caliper holder or Procedure 10, Step 8, to install the front caliper holder.

EVERYONE (except non-4WD rear drums or discs): When the wheels are back on and the car is off the jackstands, don't forget to come back here to do Step 4 to tighten the axle nuts.

Step 4. Tighten Axle Nuts on Front Disc, 4WD Rear Drum or Disc.

OK, the brakes are all back together and the lug nuts have been torqued to 72 ft. lbs., right? If not, do it. If your axle nut is the kind that was staked into the groove on the axle shaft, torque the axle nut to 174 ft. lbs., then "stake" the edge of the nut into the groove with a hammer and large screwdriver. Be sure the staked part of the nut reaches the bottom of the groove. If the axle nut has been staked so many times there's nothing left to stake, replace it with a new nut. Install the hubcap.

Those of you with a castle nut and cotter pin setup, torque the axle nut to 145 ft. lbs. then see if a gap in the axle nut lines up with a hole in the axle. If it does, slip in a new cotter pin and bend the ends of the pin around the axle nut. If a gap in the nut doesn't line up with a hole in the axle, tighten the axle nut a little farther until the cotter pin can slide through the hole in the axle. Bend the ends of the cotter pin around the axle nut. Install the hubcap.

PROCEDURE 5: REPLACE REAR BRAKE SHOES

This procedure is only for models with rear drum brakes.

You can buy new brake shoes from Subaru, or rebuilt ones from auto parts stores. The rebuilt units seem to work as well and last as long as new ones, so call around for prices and go for the best deal.

Condition: Groans, growls, or squeals come from the rear of the car when the brakes are applied; OR the brake linings are 1/16" or less; OR a wheel cylinder has taken a leak on the brake linings.

Tools and Materials: Jack and jackstands, Phase 1 tool kit, new set of brake shoes for both rear wheels, safety glasses, dust mask or respirator, needlenose pliers, medium screwdriver, catch pan, can of brake cleaner or solvent, rags, old newspapers, baggies, rubber bands or tape, wheel bearing grease or antiseize compound.

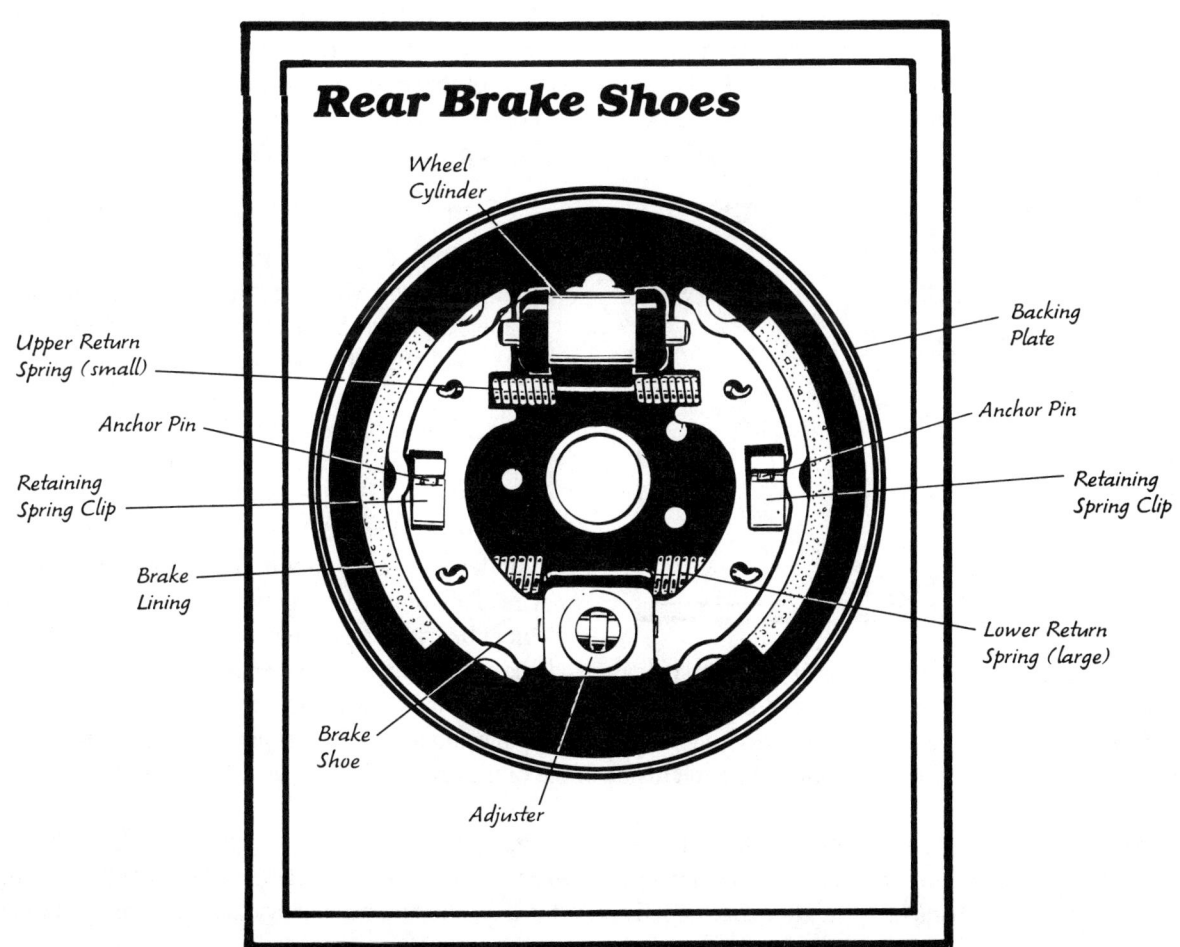

Remarks: Read **Caution! Warning!** in the Remarks in Procedure 4.

Remove and replace the brake shoes on one wheel at a time so you can use the other side for reference when assembling the shoes.

Step 1. Remove Rear Brake Drums (Procedure 4, Step 1).

Step 2. Identify Rear Brake Components.

The top ends of the brake shoes fit into slots in the **wheel cylinder pistons**. The bottom of the shoes fit into slots on the **brake adjustment mechanism** (non-auto-adjusting models), or the brake shoe anchor (auto-adjusting models). Two brake shoe **return springs** keep the shoes pulled away from the drums until the brakes are applied. An **anchor pin** sticks through the backing plate and the center of the shoes, and is held in place by a **retaining spring clip.**

Step 3. Remove Rear Brake Shoes.

Non-auto-adjusting models: Unscrew (counterclockwise) the **brake adjusting bolt** on the back of the backing plate several turns (Procedure 1, Step 2).

EVERYONE: Safety glasses and respirator on? Spread out some newspapers under the side you're working on. Locate the retaining spring clips half way between the top and bottom of each shoe. Grab the little flattened anchor pin sticking out of the center of the clip with pliers. Turn the pin 90° in either direction until the flat part of the pin lines up with the slot in the clip. The clip will pop off when they're aligned. Put the clip aside, then push the pin through the hole in the brake shoes.

There are three bolts on the backing plate—two toward the front of the car and one toward the rear. Put a medium screwdriver blade against the front of the lower front bolt. Pry against the bottom of the front brake shoe with the screwdriver while pulling out (toward you) on the bottom of the brake shoe with your other hand. When the bottom edge of the shoe is out of the slot, release the tension on the screwdriver and let the shoe come over the outside of the adjuster or anchor. Pull the bottom of the other shoe out of the adjuster or anchor with your hand. Using both hands, slide both shoes down and out of the slots in the wheel cylinder. Your shoes are off. Ah, doesn't that feel better? Lay the old shoes on the newspaper as a unit with the springs still attached.

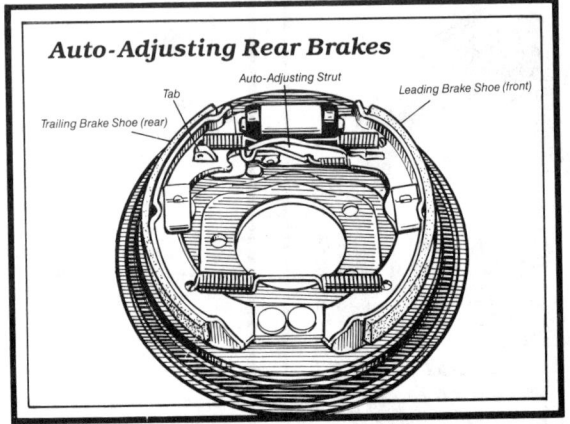

Step 4. Clean and Inspect Brake Parts.

CAUTION!: Protect the rubber parts on the wheel cylinder and the wheel bearings from solvent, brake cleaner, and dirt. Stash the new shoes somewhere safe and clean until you're ready to install them.

If you are replacing the shoes because the wheel cylinder leaked on them, rebuild or replace the wheel cylinder (Procedure 7) before installing the new shoes. Replace springs and clips that are broken or bent.

Non-4WD models: Put a baggie over the wheel cylinder and secure it with rubber bands, tape, or wire. This would be an opportune time to repack the wheel bearings (see Chapter 14, Procedure 9).

4WD models: Slide a baggie over the wheel cylinder and one over the axle and wheel bearing housing located in the center of the backing plate. Secure the baggies with rubber bands, tape, or wire.

EVERYONE: Put a catch pan or rags under the backing plate and use brake cleaner, or a rag or stiff brush soaked in solvent, to clean the backing plate and inside of the brake drum. If you're using solvent, dry them off with a clean rag.

Remove the baggies and put a very light coat of wheel bearing grease or antiseize compound on the *six bumps* on the backing plate where the shoes rub. Two are near the wheel cylinder, two are near the adjuster at the bottom, and one is next to each anchor pin. Now use a small screwdriver to smear a little grease or antiseize compound

Procedure 5, Step 5   Brakes   283

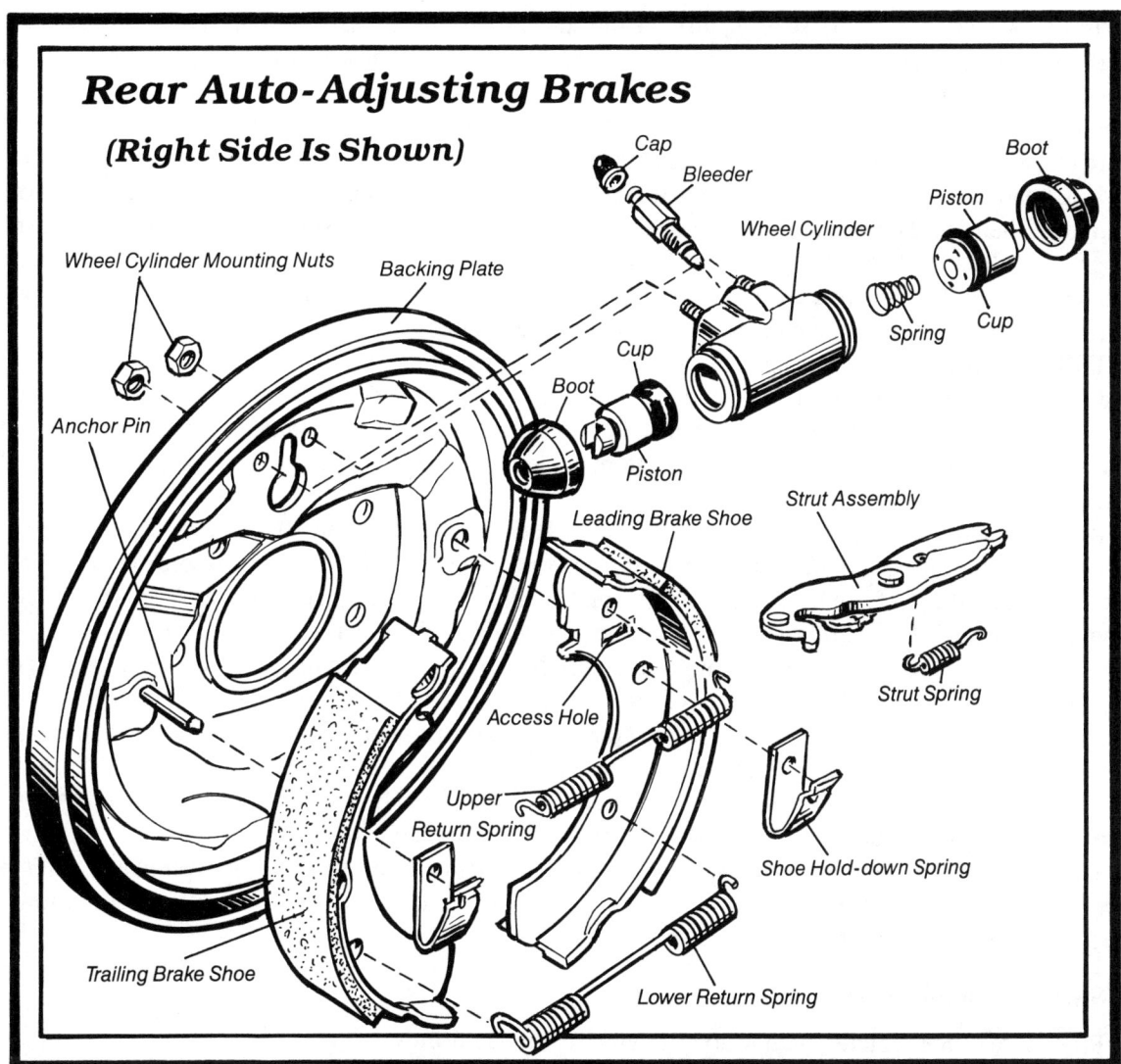

Rear Auto-Adjusting Brakes (Right Side Is Shown)

in the slots on the ends of the wheel cylinder and adjuster or anchor where the ends of the brake shoes fit. Wipe off excess grease with a rag.

If the friction surface of the brake drums has grooves, scores, or ridges, you should get them smoothed out by having them "turned" by a machine shop, parts store, garage, or Subaru dealer. If the grooves are too deep, the drum will have to be replaced. You might find a good used one at a junkyard and save some $$.

Step 5. Install Brake Shoes.

Clean and dry your hands before handling the brake shoes.

The old shoes are on the newspaper with the springs still attached, right?

Shoe replacers: If you are replacing the shoes, break out the new ones and put one on each side of the old shoes. Position them so they are exactly like the old shoes. If the shape of the metal part of the new shoes doesn't match the old, the parts store gave you the wrong shoes. Put the old shoes in a paper sack and take them, along with the shoes they gave you, back to the store to get the right ones.

Shoes match? OK, the new shoes are laying on the outside of the old shoes. On auto-adjusting models, the auto-adjusting strut is between the two shoes, near the top. Look at how the strut is attached to the front shoe with a spring hooked through the rectangular access hole. Unhook the end of the spring in the access hole.

To remove the shoe-return springs, turn the old shoes so the inside metal part is facing up and the lining part is on the newspaper. Unhook the springs from one shoe at a time. Replace the old shoes with the new shoes in the same position. Hook the ends of the springs through the appropriate holes in one new shoe, then twist the shoe so the lining is toward the outside. Replace the other old shoe the same way. Be sure the springs are secure in their holes. The smaller spring goes at the top of the shoes and the heavier spring goes at the bottom.

If you have auto-adjusting brakes, be sure the short end of the strut spring is inserted in its hole on the bottom of the strut, then use pliers to insert the longer end of the spring into the access hole on the front shoe, just like it was on the old shoe. The notch on the front end of the strut fits into the notch on the metal part of the brake shoe. The little lever on the rear end of the strut goes in the access hole on the rear shoe. Pull the lever toward the front shoe while you fit it into the access hole on the rear shoe.

EVERYONE: Lift the shoes up to the backing plate while pulling outward on them to keep the springs in place. Slide the top part of the rear shoe into the slot on the wheel cylinder and the bottom of the rear shoe into the slot on the adjuster. Pull the top of the front shoe into the slot of the wheel cylinder, then use the screwdriver blade against the bolt head again to lever the bottom of the front shoe into the slot on the adjuster. Check that the springs are properly in place.

Retrieve the *anchor pins* if they've fallen out of the backing plate, then push them toward you through the holes in the backing plate and brake shoes. You might have to use a screwdriver because there's not much room back there. Hold the pin from behind the backing plate while putting the clip on the pin. Align the slot in the clip with the flat end of the pin. Press against the clip with pliers until you can grab the pin with the pliers. Turn the pin 90° so it fits securely in the groove of the clip. Now install the clip on the other shoe. Tap the ends of the shoes up or down until the very tops of the shoes are even with the top of the wheel cylinder.

If you have auto-adjusting brakes, check that the notch on the front of the strut is still engaged in the notch on the front shoe, and the lever is engaged in the access hole on the rear shoe.

Slide the drum onto the axle and over the brake shoes. Watch those fingers—if they get caught between the brake drum and backing plate, you'll be running around like a moth on dope!

The ends of the shoes may have to be tapped up or down with a hammer or screwdriver handle until they are centered. If the drum refuses to fit over the shoes, loosen the brake adjusting bolt some more, or move the little lever on the auto-adjusting strut farther forward.

Step 6. Install Rear Brake Drum.

Procedure 4, Step 3, tells you how to install the rear brake drums.

Non-auto-adjusting brakes: Adjust the brakes after the drums and wheels are on, but before you lower the car off the jackstands.

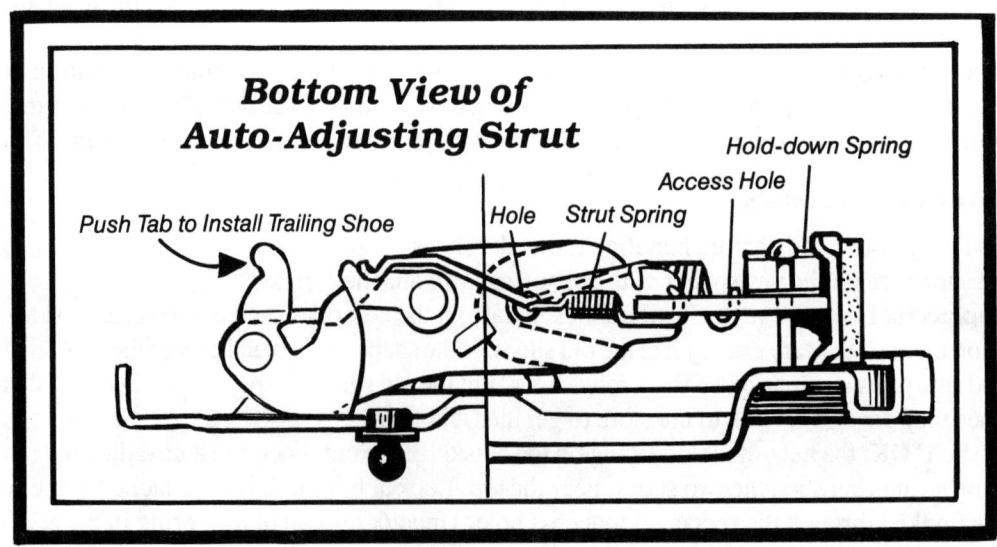

Auto-adjust models: After the drums and wheels are on, lower the car to the ground, then pump on the brake pedal several times. This adjusts the rear brake shoes.

EVERYONE: This would be a good time to change the hydraulic brake fluid if it hasn't been changed recently (Procedure 2).

Don't forget to torque the lug nuts to 72 ft. lbs. after lowering the car to the ground.

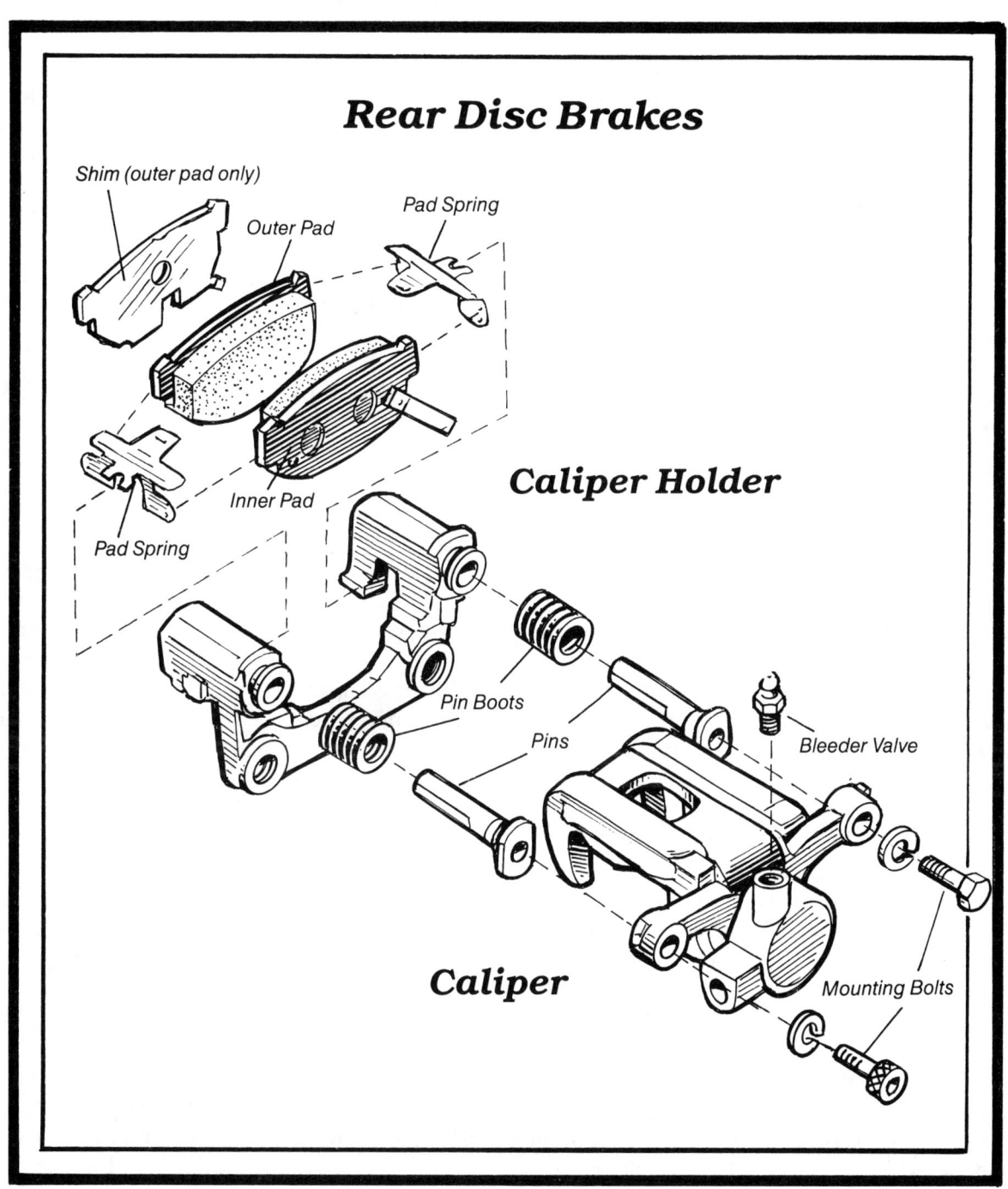

PROCEDURE 6: CHECK AND REPLACE REAR DISC BRAKE PADS, REMOVE AND INSTALL REAR CALIPERS AND DISCS

This procedure is for 1985 and newer OHC Turbo models and XT6 models.

Condition: Routine maintenance; OR the rear pads are worn out; OR the caliper is leaking; OR you hear a growling sound from the rear of the car when you step on the brakes; OR you need to remove the caliper and/or the disc.

Tools and Materials: Jack and jackstands, Phase 1 tool set, maybe new brake pads, safety glasses, dust mask, small wire brush or old toothbrush, spray can of brake cleaner, two pieces of string or wire at least 18" long.

If you remove the caliper, you'll also need a 10mm flare-nut wrench and the brake bleeding tools listed in Procedure 2.

2WD models: If you remove the disc, you will need two new axle-nut lock plates.

4WD models: If you remove the rear disc, you'll also need a 36mm socket, a large ratchet or breaker bar, a torque wrench that goes to 145 ft. lbs., and two new cotter pins for the axle nuts.

Remarks: Read the rap about brake pads at the start of Procedure 9. Take your time on this procedure—if possible, do one side at a time so you can look at the other side for reference.

CAUTION: Wear a dust mask or respirator while working on the brakes, and don't breath any of the black brake dust. Don't press on the brake pedal while the caliper is off the pads—you'll have a nasty mess to clean up.

Step 1. Chock, Jack, and Block.

Park on a hard, level surface, put the transmission in 1st gear (manual) or PARK (automatics). Set the handbrake, and put chocks in front of and behind the front wheels.

4WD models: If you are going to remove the disc, you'll need to loosen the axle nuts before jacking up the rear end of the car. Follow the instructions in Procedure 4, Step 1. When the axle nut is loose, come back here to remove the brake pads, caliper, caliper holder and disc. Leave the handbrake ON while working on the rear brakes.

EVERYONE: Loosen the lug nuts for the rear wheels, then jack up the rear end of the car and put it on jackstands. Remove the rear wheels. If you are here to replace the brake pads or remove the caliper or disc, tie one end of a piece of string or wire to the upper end of the coil springs that surround the rear shock absorbers. You'll use the string or wire to hold the caliper up once it's released from the caliper holder.

Step 2: Inspect Rear Brake Pads, Disc, and Caliper.

Do Procedure 8, Steps 2, 3, and 4 to identify the brake components and check the pads and disc. If everything is OK, skip to Step 6 to put everything back together. If the pads are worn out, and/or the disc is grooved, do Step 3 below to remove and install the pads. If the caliper is leaking, do Steps 3 and 4 below. If the disc needs to be removed, do Steps 3, 4, and 5 below.

Step 3: Replace Rear Brake Pads.

The caliper is attached to the inboard side of a heavy metal caliper holder with two bolts, one near the top and one near the bottom. The upper bolt is also a pivot pin. Remove the lower bolt and rotate the lower end of the caliper up and away from the disc. Tie the string or wire to the bottom of the caliper to hold it up out of your way. Wiggle the pads, one at a time, away from the disc until they are out of the holder. The outer pad has a thin shim clipped onto the outer metal part of the pad. If you are replacing the pads, remove the shim. The inner pad has a wear indicator tab mounted on the bottom end.

Look at the thin metal pad springs (clips) in the caliper holder where the ends of the pads fit. Remove one of the clips and clean it with a rag and a squirt of brake cleaner. Carefully inspect the clip for cracks and worn areas. Get new clips if you find any cracks or worn spots, or if the clip is bent. Install the clip back into the caliper holder. Remove and inspect the other clip, then fit it back into the holder.

Inspect the caliper for signs of wetness which would indicate a leak. If the caliper is leaking, or you need to remove the caliper in order to remove the disc, do Step 4.

If you are installing the old pads, you won't need to push the piston into the caliper. So skip the next paragraph.

If you are installing new pads, you'll need to push the large round piston located in the center of the caliper as far into the caliper as you can. If you can't push it in, loosen the bleeder valve screw about one turn, then push the piston in. Be sure to tighten the bleeder valve after the piston is pressed in. If you still can't get the piston in, remove the caliper (Step 4) and take it the Subaru dealer or a garage and have them press it in for you.

Fit the shim onto the metal side of the outer brake pad. If the shim is loose on the pad, remove it and bend the tabs a little so they grip the pad securely.

Here's how to install the pads: Wiggle the pads into the holder so the tabs on the ends fit into the clips in the holder. If necessary, wiggle them around a bit until they fit flush against the disc. The wear indicator(s) should be at the bottom of the pad.

Untie the end of the caliper and guide it down and over the pads. Install the lower mounting bolt and tighten it to 16-23 ft. lbs. Skip down to Step 6 to finish the job.

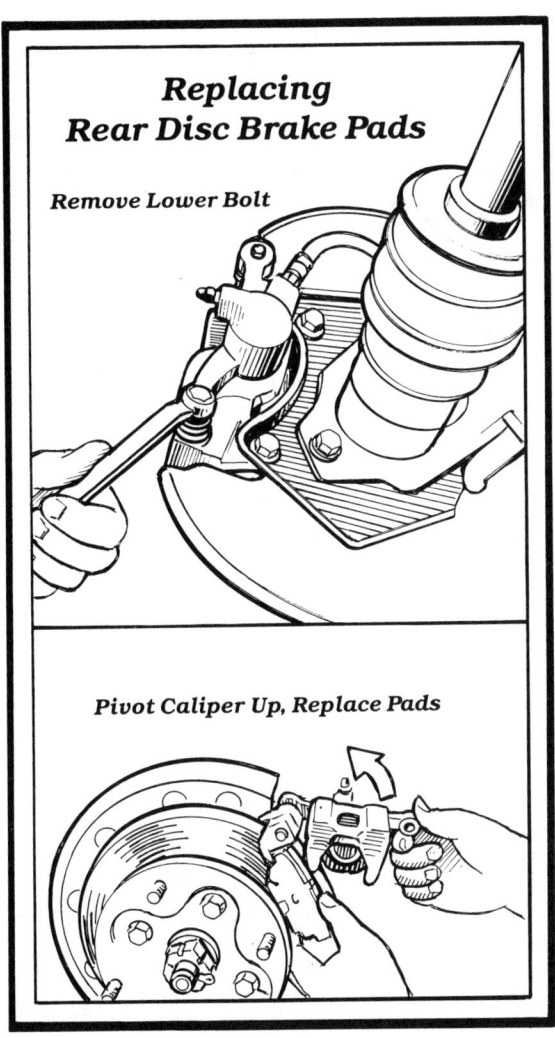

Replacing Rear Disc Brake Pads

Remove Lower Bolt

Pivot Caliper Up, Replace Pads

Step 4. Remove and Install Rear Brake Caliper.

If you are only removing the caliper so that you can remove the disc, don't disconnect the brake line. Just remove the upper caliper mounting bolt and let the caliper dangle by the string or wire (not by the brake line) while you remove the disc. If you need to remove the caliper because it's leaking, see Procedure 11, Steps 1 and 2, to disconnect the brake hose from the metal brake line. When the hose is disconnected, remove the upper bolt that attaches the caliper to the holder. The caliper is now liberated.

To install the caliper, fit it onto the holder and install the top mounting bolt. Tighten the bolt to 16-23 ft. lbs. If you didn't disconnect the brake line, go to Step 3 to install the brake pads. If you disconnected the brake line, clean the ends of the rubber brake hose and the metal brake line, then fit the metal end of the hose through the brake line bracket. Be sure the hose isn't twisted or kinked. Screw the nut on the metal brake line into the fitting on the end of the hose. Hold the hose fitting with a wrench while you tighten the nut on the brake line. Wiggle the spring clip into the slots on the sides of the brake hose fitting. Use the string or wire to hold the lower end of the caliper up while you install the pads (Step 3).

Step 5. Remove and Install Rear Brake Disc.

The caliper and brake pads have already been removed, right? Now remove the two bolts that attach the caliper holder to the axle. Lift the holder off the disc.

Non-4WD models: Follow the instructions for non-4WD models in Procedure 4, Step 1, to remove the disc. To install the disc, follow the instructions for non-4WD models in Procedure 4, Step 3.

4WD models: Follow the instructions for 4WD models in Procedure 4, Step 1, to remove the disc. To install the disc, follow the instructions for 4WD models in Procedure 4, Step 3.

EVERYONE: When the disc is on, install the caliper holder and tighten the two mounting bolts to 34-43 ft. lbs. Step 4 tells you how to install the caliper.

Step 6. Finish the Job.

Put the wheels on and snug the lug nuts. Lower the car and torque the lug nuts to 72 ft. lbs. If you disconnected any brake lines, do Procedure 2, to bleed the brake system.

4WD models: If you loosened the large axle nut, do Procedure 4, Step 4, to tighten the axle nuts.

PROCEDURE 7. REBUILD OR REPLACE WHEEL CYLINDERS (Drum Brakes Only)

Condition: Wheel cylinders of drum brakes are leaking.

Tools and Materials: Jack and jackstands, Phase 1 tool kit, new wheel cylinder(s) or wheel cylinder repair kit(s), 10mm flare nut wrench, fine steel wool and alcohol, at least a pint of DOT 3 or 4 brake fluid safety glasses.

Remarks: The wheel cylinders force the brake shoes into contact with the brake drum. If they're leaking fluid or admitting air, they won't do their job properly, and therefore you risk a dent in your fender at the very least. There are two ways to go. You can buy new wheel cylinders from Subaru or a foreign car parts store (they don't cost much), or you can rebuild the existing cylinder for about one-third the cost. Go for the new ones if you can afford it.

If you decide to rebuild the old wheel cylinders, but when you get the thing apart you find that the inside of the wheel cylinder is rusted, scored, or nicked at all, *don't* try to save money by installing a rebuild kit. The cylinder won't work properly and may contribute to your demise. Buy a new cylinder if you can't decide whether to replace or repair, take the cylinder to someone who knows. If one of the mounting bolts or the bleeder nipple breaks off the cylinder you have no choice but to replace the cylinder with a new one.

The Bendix brake people say never use a wheel cylinder hone on aluminum wheel cylinders because it removes the protective anodizing layer and brake fluid will quickly corrode the cylinder.

Step 1. Remove Wheel, Brake Drums and Shoes.

See Procedure 4, Step 1, for brake drum removal; Procedure 5, Step 3, for rear brake shoe removal.

Step 2. Remove Wheel Cylinder Components.

Remove the little rubber **dust cap** (if you have one), then use an 8mm box end wrench to loosen the **bleeding nipple** (sounds painful) on the rear of the wheel cylinder. Unscrew it one turn. Put a rag under the nipple to catch any brake fluid that might come out.

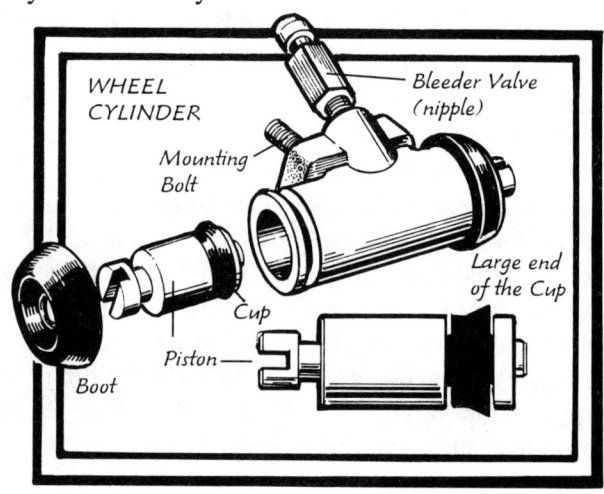

Put the **rubber boots** from each end of the wheel cylinder. As you remove the boot, out will come a **piston** with a **rubber cup** attached to the inside end. Note how the rubber cup is oriented on the end of the piston. The large flange on the cup faces toward the center of the wheel cylinder. On 1985 and newer models, a small spring will be in the cylinder, between the two pistons. Pull the spring out.

Step 3. Clean and Inspect Inside of Wheel Cylinder.

Once both pistons are out, dip a piece of steel wool in alcohol and push it into the wheel cylinder. Stick a screwdriver into the center of the steel wool and twist it around and around so the steel wool tangles with the blade—but don't let the blade touch the side of the cylinder. Put a good shine on the inside of the cylinder. Don't push the steel wool backward and forward—only 'round and 'round until the cylinder bore is nice and smooth. You can stick another screwdriver into the steel wool from the other end of the cylinder for better action.

When the inside of the cylinder is clean, inspect it for grooves and corrosion pits. If the inside of the cylinder is nice and smooth, you can rebuild the cylinder (Step 4).

Dark spots near the center of the bore are indications that the surface of the cylinder has been etched by water and crud in the brake fluid. Play dentist for a minute and gently probe the spots with a small screwdriver to see if they are indeed "cavities." If they are, that's probably the reason you're doing this procedure. If there's any doubt, replace the cylinder with a new one (Step 5). New wheel cylinders are a lot cheaper than hospital bills.

Step 4. Rebuild Wheel Cylinder.

Remove the old, tired rubber cups from the inside ends of the pistons. Pry them off with a small screwdriver, being careful to avoid scratching the piston. Clean the pistons with the steel wool and alcohol. Be sure the little holes in the end of the pistons are clean. Dry the pistons with a clean rag and blow through the holes to remove any traces of the steel wool.

Wash your hands thoroughly to remove any traces of grease. Break out your can of brake fluid and pour a little in a clean container. Dip a corner of a clean rag or your forefinger in the brake fluid and thoroughly swab out the inside of the wheel cylinder.

Take the wheel cylinder rebuild kit out of the box and put the two round cups and the clean pistons in the container with brake fluid. *Don't* soak the two large end boots. Take one of the pistons and one of the rubber cups and slip the cup into the groove of the piston. The large shoulder of the cup should be closest to the end of the piston that has the tiny holes.

Next, slide one of the rubber end boots into the groove on the other end of the piston. Push and wiggle the piston into one end of the wheel cylinder, rubber cup end first. Snap the end of the boot over the groove on the end of the wheel cylinder so the piston won't fall out. If your wheel cylinder has the little spring between the pistons, insert it now. Put the other cup and boot onto the other piston and push it into the opposite end of the wheel cylinder. Turn the pistons so the slots are vertical, as shown in the illustration. Slip the new dust cap on the bleeder valve.

Now put the brake shoes on (Procedure 5, Steps 4 and 5), then install the brake drum (Procedure 4, Steps 3 and 4). After the cylinders on both sides are rebuilt or replaced, bleed the entire brake system (Procedure 2). I mean it—it's tedious but very important.

Step 5. Replace Wheel Cylinder.

If you've done Step 4, you can ignore Step 5. It's just for people who discovered they need a new wheel cylinder. There are three easily avoided hazards to removing and replacing wheel cylinders:

1. The nut that attaches the brake line to the wheel cylinder gets rounded off because a 10mm flare-nut wrench wasn't used. If this happens, and you can't unscrew the nut, cut the metal brake line with a hacksaw and replace the line with a new one (Procedure 11). *Use a flare-nut wrench!*

2. The attaching bolts for the wheel cylinder break off when you try to unscrew the nuts, thus ruining the cylinder. This is common no matter how careful you are, or how much holy water (penetrating oil) you put on the nuts. If you're replacing the cylinder anyway, so what if they break?

3. The threads on the brake line nut get cross-threaded when they are screwed into the wheel cylinder, ruining both the cylinder and the brake line! Cross-threaded means the threads on the nut aren't aligned with the threads in the cylinder. When this happens the nut goes in at an angle, tearing up the threads and preventing the nut from going into the cylinder far enough to make a good seal. To avoid this catastrophe, move the brake line as little as possible and don't even think about using a wrench on the nut until it's screwed into the cylinder at least half way by hand.

Now, on with the show.

Use a 10mm flare-nut wrench to unscrew the **brake line nut** from the back of the wheel cylinder. Unscrew it but don't pull it away from its hole. We want to keep the brake line aligned with the hole and also avoid bending it.

Soak the two 10mm nuts on each side of the brake line connection with penetrating oil. Let it soak in for a few minutes, then unscrew the two nuts with a 10mm box-end wrench. Pull the cylinder off the backing plate being careful not to kink the brake line.

When installing a wheel cylinder, don't let any dirt, dust, or dung fall into the bleeder hole or brake line connection hole. Be sure the end of the brake line is clean and uncontaminated before you screw it in.

To install the wheel cylinder, slip the wheel cylinder bolts into their holes in the backing plate while guiding the brake line nut into its hole. Tighten the brake line nut with your fingers until you are absolutely positively sure it's not cross-threaded. It helps to wiggle the wheel cylinder a little while screwing in the brake line nut. Screw it in as far as you can with your fingers. Install the lockwashers and 10mm nuts and tighten them with the box-end wrench. Tighten the brake line nut with the 10mm flare-nut wrench.

Now put on the brake shoes and drums (Procedure 5, Steps 4-6). Install the wheels and snug the lug nuts. Lower the car and torque the lug nuts to 72 ft. lbs. After both sides are rebuilt or replaced, bleed the entire brake system (Procedure 2).

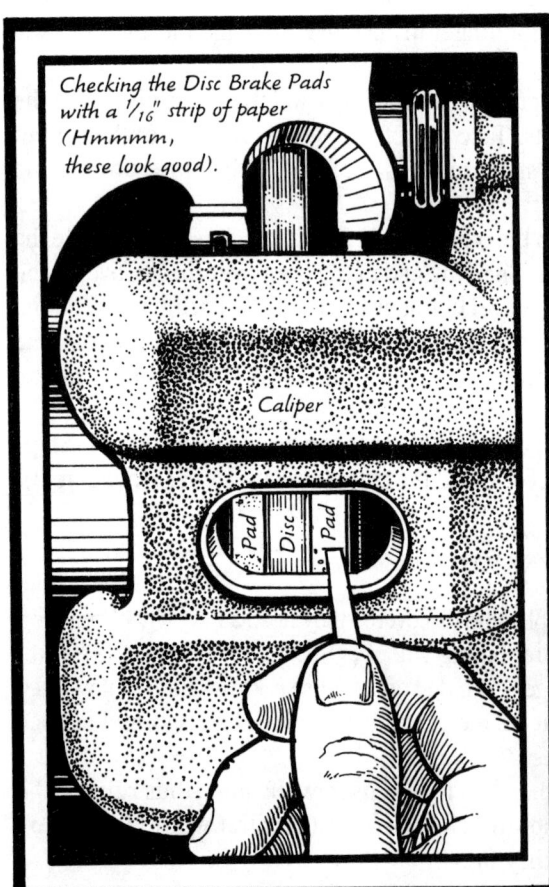

PROCEDURE 8: CHECK BRAKE PADS FOR WEAR

Condition: Regular maintenance; OR you just bought the car; OR the front brakes are squealing like a ruptured pig.

Tools and Materials: Safety glasses, dust mask, small tape measure or ruler, jack, jackstands. You may need: penetrating oil, high-temp wheel bearing grease.

CAUTION: Avoid getting grease, brake fluid, or anything but water or brake cleaner on the disc and brake pads.

Step 1. Chock, Jack, Block, and Remove Front Wheel.

Block the rear wheels, loosen the front lug nuts a little, release the handbrake, put the gearshift in NEUTRAL, and turn the ignition key to *unlock* the steering wheel. Now turn the front wheel in the *opposite* direction from the side you're going to check; in other words, turn them so you have access to the back of the wheel. Jack the car up and put it on jackstands (Chapter 3). Remove the wheel.

Step 2. Identify Disc Brake Components.

Rotate the disc by using the lug bolts to turn it. It should turn fairly easily by hand. The big flat shiny surface that rotates with the axle is the *disc* (sometimes called the rotor). The large lumpy looking hunk of metal that the disc passes through is the *caliper* and *caliper holder*.

Step 3. Measure Pad Thickness.

If you're lucky, the caliper will have an *inspection hole* in the rear for checking pad wear. Look through the hole while rotating the axle so you can see which part is the moving disc. On either side of the disc is a brake pad. Most pads have a slot in the middle that serves as a *wear indicator*. When the pads wear to the bottom of the slot it's time to change pads. If your pads don't have the wear indicator slots, cut a strip of paper 1/16" wide to measure the pad thickness. Look at the illustration to see where to measure pad thickness. *Don't* include the metal backing plate in your measurement. If the pad thickness is less than 1/16" (1.5mm), it's time for new pads (Procedure 6 for rears, Procedure 9 for fronts). Just to be safe, I change my pads when they're down to 1/8".

No inspection hole? Then the caliper must be removed to check the pads. Look at Procedure 6, Step 4, for rears or Procedure 9, Step 2A or 2B, for front caliper removal. When the caliper is off, measure the pad thickness.

Step 4. Check Disc.

Run a clean fingernail over the disc surface to check for grooves. Does your nail hang up on ridges and scoring? If so, the disc should be machined ("turned") to make it smooth again (Procedure 10).

Step 5. Check Cable Lever on Caliper (front brakes only).

Reach in the car and pull the handbrake up and release it a few times, then leave it in the OFF (down) position. Check the amount of drag on the disc by using the lug bolts to rotate the disc. Get a feel for how easy or hard it is to rotate. Now grab the little **lever** on the top of the caliper that has a cable attached to one end. Try to pull the cable end of the lever toward the rear of the car. If the disc turns easier after you pull on the lever, it means the lever isn't returning to the off position by itself and the brakes are staying on slightly. This can cause brake squeal, rapid pad wear, overheating of the brake system, engine overheating, and reduced gas mileage. Rust, collapsed springs, or a bent **spindle** in the caliper are probable culprits.

If the lever doesn't return properly, there's a chance you can fix it by lubricating the lever shaft. Locate the **rubber boot** covering the lump sticking out of the inboard side of the caliper. On some models, **another boot** covers most of the lever and the top of the boot on the side of the caliper. If you have a top boot, use pliers to pull on the end of the handbrake cable, then pull it up and out of the slot in the lever. Carefully pull the top boot off the lever.

Locate a metal clamp securing the side boot to the caliper. Spread the ends of the metal clamp with your fingers and slip it up off the boot. Be careful not to tear the boot. Pull the bottom of the boot toward the center of the car until you can lift it up over the lump on the caliper. Now move the cable lever back and forth so you can see where the shaft goes down into the caliper mechanism. Look for rusty or white-looking grease around the shaft and on the mechanism. These are indications that water has gotten into the boot. Wipe out the old grease and try squirting a little penetrating oil around the lever shaft where it goes into the top of the caliper. Work the cable lever back and forth with your hand while squirting the penetrating oil. If this doesn't loosen the lever so it returns freely, the caliper needs to be rebuilt or replaced (Procedure 10). If the penetrating oil loosened the lever, pack some high-temp wheel bearing grease around the shaft and caliper mechanism, then install the rubber boot and secure it with the clip. Replace the boot if it's torn. Install the top boot if you have one. Use pliers to connect the handbrake cable to the cable lever.

Step 6. Examine Brake Hose.

Inspect the rubber brake hoses attached to the caliper and replace them if they are hard, cracked, split, or bulging in places (Procedure 11). There are two rubber hoses between the caliper and body on cars with Bendix disc brakes; check both of them.

Step 7. Put It All Back Together.

Install the caliper if you removed it (Procedure 10, Step 9). Put the wheel back on, lower the car, torque the lug nuts to 72 ft. lbs., then install the hubcap if you removed it. Check the front brakes on the other side of the car the same way.

PROCEDURE 9: CHANGE FRONT DISC BRAKE PADS

ABOUT BRAKE PADS (Read Before You Begin!)

When buying replacement pads for disc brakes, often you can choose between *regular pads* that are quieter but wear out faster, or harder *semi-metallic pads* that tend to squeal more but last longer. The regular pads are fine for normal driving, but if you're a leadfoot or do a lot of high speed freeway cruising or mountain driving, the semi-metallic pads might be best for you. The choice is yours.

Subaru made a few subtle changes in pad and pad holder dimensions through the years that sometimes makes finding the right pads harder than installing the pads on the car. To be sure you're getting the right pads, have your chassis number, production date, and the old pads with you when you trek to the parts department. Before installing the pads, carefully compare the length, width, and dimensions of the tabs and/or notches on the ends

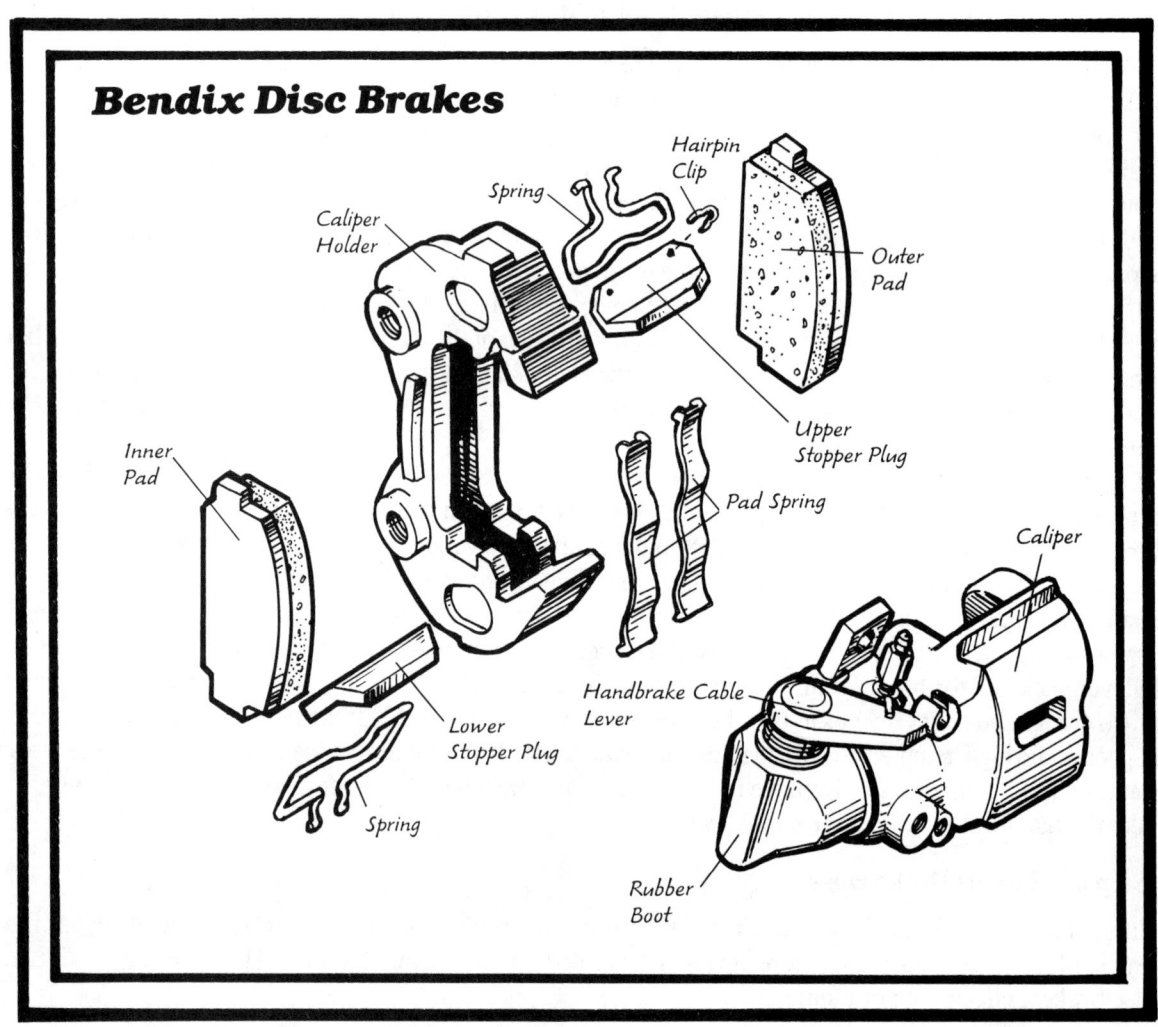

of the new pads to those on the old pads. The new pads should be free to move in the caliper holder without binding. They shouldn't be so loose they rattle either. A nice, lightly snug fit is just right. If the pads are too tight, return them for some that fit. Pads from the Subaru dealer usually fit the first time around.

For Soobs with AD systems, I urge you to always get pad kits from the Subaru dealer. The kits come complete with new pads (your choice of regular or hard linings), new spring clips, packets of silicone grease, PBC grease, and installation instructions in English and Japanese. The price of the kit is comparable to parts store prices.

When installing new pads, always replace the pads on both left and right wheels. It's the law in some states. Do one side first, so you have the other side as a reference for the proper location and placement of the pads, shims, and clips.

Condition: Brake pads are worn out; OR brake fluid or grease has gotten on the pads; OR the brakes have to come off so you can remove the disc, wheel bearing housing, or axle.

Tools and Materials: Jack and jackstands, Phase 1 tool kit, new brake pads for both front wheels, 8 new caliper hairpin clips for models with Bendix type brakes, safety glasses, dust mask, pliers and large screwdriver or brake piston wrench, small wire brush, PBC grease or antiseize compound, silicone grease for AD calipers, alcohol or spray can of brake cleaner, two pieces of wire or heavy string at least 18" long.

Remarks: When installing new brake pads, Subaru caliper pistons must be screwed into the caliper and not just pressed in like most other cars. Pressing the piston in without turning it will buckle, and thus ruin, the *handbrake spindle* inside the caliper. Some Subaru mechanics use an inexpensive garden valve wrench like the one being used in the "Brake Piston Tool in Action" illustration. Just be sure the two prongs fit squarely in the piston notches. You get these at hardware stores or nurseries. K-D Tools makes a nifty little inexpensive *brake piston wrench* (#2545, available in most auto parts stores for about ten bucks) for screwing brake pistons in. The tool is shown in the top right side of the "Brake Piston Tool in Action" illustration. You can buy brake tools that make the job easier, but they are more expensive. Subaru sells these tools for about $65. The tool I prefer is made for screwing in the rear caliper pistons on early '70s model Fords—costs about $50.

Sometimes it's possible (but usually difficult) to screw the pistons in without a piston wrench. If you don't have a brake piston wrench and get hung up trying to do it by the alternative method I describe, you can remove the calipers from the car (Procedure 10) and take them to a garage and have the pistons screwed in. If you remove the calipers you must bleed the brakes after reassembly. *Don't* try to screw the piston in by grabbing it around the edge with pliers.

CAUTION: Wear a dust mask or respirator while working on the brakes. Don't press on the brake pedal while a caliper is off the caliper holder. The piston will come flying out of the caliper like a cannonball!

REMEMBER: The kind of calipers you have depends on the year and model Subaru you have. *Bendix calipers* are on all Soobs with front disc brakes from '75-'79 and on '77-'81 Brats. *AD calipers* are on '80 and newer cars and '82-'87 Brats. There are differences in pre-1985 AD systems and 1985 and newer AD systems. The parts (pads, clips, etc) are not interchangeable, so be sure to compare your old parts to the new ones before trying to install them.

Step 1. Chock, Jack, Block and Remove Front Wheel.

Do Procedure 8, Step 1, then tie one end of a piece of wire or string to one of the coils of the strut. It's way up under the fender. Let the other end hang down for now.

Step 2A. Release Bendix Type Caliper ('72-'79 cars and '77-'81 Brats).

Use pliers to pull the end of the handbrake cable up and out of the slot in the handbrake cable lever located just above where the brake line screws into the caliper.

About 2½" from the end of the cable is a thin metal **clip** that secures the cable to a **bracket** on the caliper. Grab the bent part of the clip with pliers and lift up to remove it.

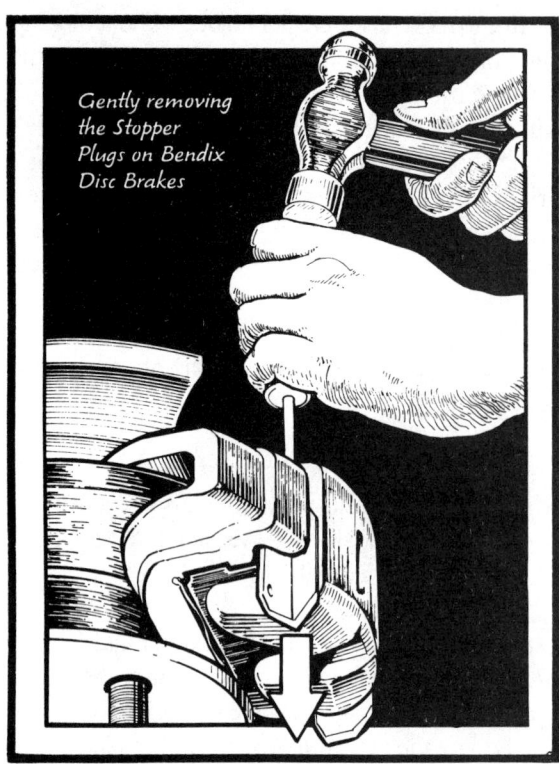

Gently removing the Stopper Plugs on Bendix Disc Brakes

Use needlenose pliers to remove the four tiny **hairpin clips** located near the outer ends of the **stopper plugs**. Place a screwdriver against the inner edge of the top stopper plug and tap lightly with a hammer. When the plug is out as far as you can get it with the screwdriver, try pulling it out with your fingers. Stuck? Put a rag on the plug to protect it, then grab it with pliers and pull it out. Remove the lower stopper plug the same way.

Push the caliper up as far as possible, then pry the bottom of the caliper out of the caliper holder. When the bottom is out, push down on the caliper and pull the top end out of the holder. The handbrake cable will slide out of the bracket as you remove the caliper. Hang the caliper up by the wire or string. Don't let it hang by the brake line!

If you encounter extreme difficulty removing the caliper from the holder, take out the two 8mm bolts that clamp the handbrake cable to the front of the disc cover.

Step 2B. Release AD Type Caliper ('80 and newer cars and '82-'87 Brats).

The end of the braided handbrake cable fits into the slotted lever on the upper inboard side of the caliper. Use pliers to grab the lump on the end of the cable, then pull rearward on the cable while you slip the cable out of the slot on the lever. Follow the cable forward to where it is fastened to a bracket. Use pliers to wiggle the thin metal spring clip off the metal fitting on the end of the brake hose.

Look at the lower inboard side of the caliper and locate a 17mm bolt. If there is a 10mm bolt near the head of the 17mm bolt, unscrew it *counterclockwise*. Unscrew the 17mm bolt *counterclockwise* until you can pull it out with your fingers. Models with solid discs have *two sets* of threads on this bolt, so be sure it's completely unscrewed before pulling it out. There's a little rubber **lock pin boot** there that you may need to hold in place with a finger while unscrewing the bolt, so it won't twist and tear.

Pull up on the bottom of the caliper and it will rotate away from the disc. Leave the top end of the caliper on the **pivot pin** (early type), or **guide pin** (later type), and tie the bottom end up out of your way with the wire or string. Don't let it dangle by the brake line.

If you are here only to measure the pads, do it now. If the pads are OK, skip down to Step 6 to install the caliper. If the pads need to be replaced, do Step 3.

Step 3. Remove and Examine Pads.

Wiggle the inner and outer pads out of the holder; just grab them with your fingers and pull straight back away from the disc. Mark them "inner" and "outer" if you're going to reuse them. As you do, notice the position of the clips that hold the pads in place, top and bottom.

Examine the pads for scoring or uneven wear. If they are worn down to the metal, I'll bet the disc is scratched and scored and needs to be resurfaced. If the pads have worn down evenly, and haven't reached the metal, the disc is probably OK. But check both sides of it for grooves, uneven wear, and dark blotchy-looking areas anyway. Remove the disc and have it machined smooth if it's rough, uneven, or has dark "hot spots" on it (Procedure 10).

Is there any brake fluid on or around the pads or any part of the brake mechanisms? Yes? Then the brake cylinder will have to be rebuilt. Even if only one side is leaking, rebuild both front calipers/cylinders at the same time (Procedure 10).

Carefully examine the rubber boot around the wheel cylinder piston. If the boot is torn, you should remove it, clean the piston with a clean rag, then install a new boot after the piston is screwed in.

All looks well? Proceed...

If you're not changing brake pads, or will have to have the wheel cylinders rebuilt, skip to Step 5.

Step 4. Screw Brake Piston Into Caliper.

Do this step only if you are installing new brake pads. Put the new pads where there is no danger of getting brake fluid on them. They must stay dry and uncontaminated.

Put one end of your clear plastic brake bleeding hose on the brake **bleeder nipple** and the other end into a jar or can. Open the **bleeder valve** at least ½ turn with your 8mm box-end wrench.

AD type: There are two ways to hold the caliper while you screw in the pistons. You can either leave the caliper attached to the caliper holder, or remove it. The best way is determined by which tool you use, how strong you are, if someone is helping, and whether you have a vast quantity of good Carma stored up. Try screwing the piston while the caliper is still on the pivot pin or guide pin. If that doesn't work, push the caliper toward the center of the car and off the pivot pin or guide pin. You might have to pry the rubber boot off its seat on the pin. Be careful so the boot isn't damaged.

After the piston is screwed in (see 4A or 4B), hang the caliper up again by the string or wire while you install the pads.

If you have a brake tool, go to Step 4A. No brake tool? Go to Step 4B.

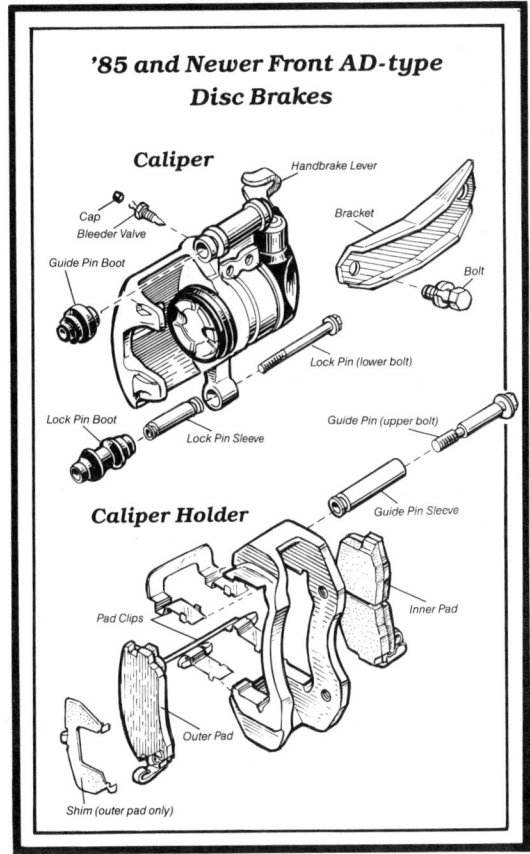

'85 and Newer Front AD-type Disc Brakes

Step 4A. Screw Piston Into Caliper (using brake tool).

Even with a brake tool, an extra pair of hands comes in handy for screwing in the brake piston. If you have K-D tool #2545, put a 17mm socket with a 3" to 6" extension and ratchet on the end of the tool. Hold the caliper firmly with one hand (or have Friend hold it) so as little pressure as possible is on the pivot bolt or pin (if the caliper is still attached to the holder). Grasp the head of the ratchet (or whatever tool you're using) and put the two round tabs on the end of the tool into the center of the brake piston *slot* (Bendix type), or in the two *notches* that angle out to the edge of the piston (AD type).

Press hard on the tool while you screw the piston *clockwise* into the caliper until the surface of the piston is even (flush) with the caliper or until it will go no further. While screwing in the piston, hold the caliper so no strain is placed on the delicate brake hose, pivot pin, or guide pin. Adjust the piston slot (Bendix) or notches (AD) so they are perpendicular to the caliper (see illustration). Just turn it a partial turn *counterclockwise* if need be. Remove the piston tool, then tighten the bleeder valve *clockwise* and remove the plastic hose.

Use a small screwdriver and fingers to carefully straighten the bellows-type **sealing rubber** that's around the edge of the piston if it turned with the piston and got twisted up. The rubber should fold neatly between the piston and cylinder bore in the caliper body.

If you can't get the piston screwed into the caliper, you will have to remove the caliper (Procedure 10, Step 4) and take it to Subaru or a garage and have them screw it in for you.

296 Chapter 13 Procedure 9, Step 4

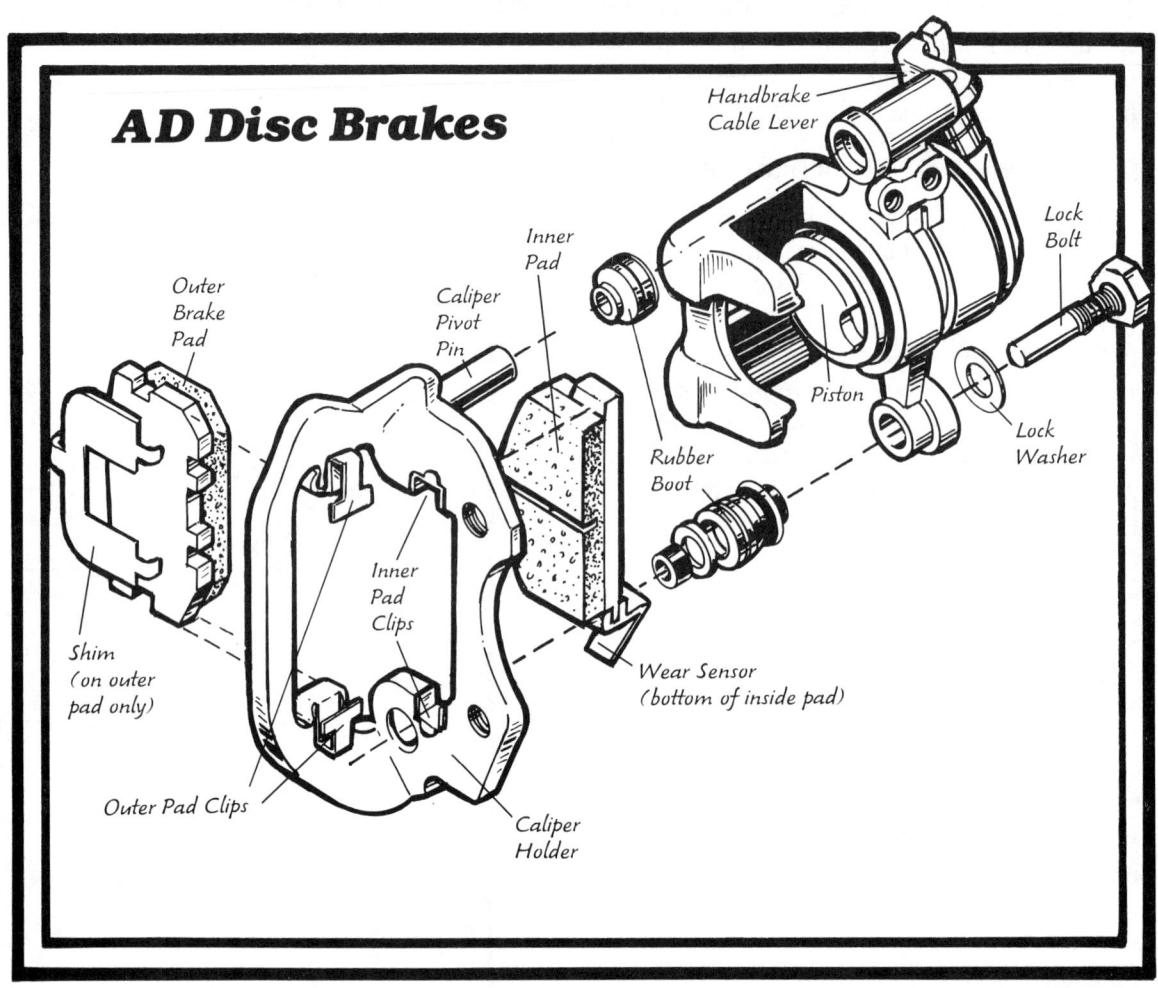

Step 4B. Screw Piston Into Caliper (no brake tool).

A Friend with helping hands is almost a necessity for accomplishing the job this way. If you have AD-type brakes, you might find it easier to leave the caliper on its pivot pin. During the operation, make sure the caliper isn't slipping back off the pivot pin.

Bendix type: Grasp the caliper firmly with one hand (or have Friend hold it) so no strain is on the brake hose. Insert the end of your largest screwdriver into the brake piston slot. Push in on the screwdriver while turning it *clockwise* until the piston is even with the cylinder bore in the caliper body, or until it will go no more. Turn the piston so the slot is perpendicular to the caliper body (see illustration). Tighten the bleeder valve and remove the plastic hose.

If the screwdriver keeps jumping out of the slot, either the screwdriver is too small or you're not getting enough pressure on the screwdriver. If the slot is getting damaged, remove the caliper (Procedure 10, Step 4) and take it to someone with a brake piston tool.

AD type: Put the ends of your largest pliers in the two notches and press hard while turning the pliers *clockwise*. I know it's hard to squeeze, push, and turn all at once. Perseverance furthers, but don't persevere if the piston notches are getting damaged. *Don't* use the pliers to grab the outer edge of the piston; scratches or burrs will cause the piston to stick in the cylinder. If you have a pair of 5" or 7" Vise Grips, snap them shut on the inner ends of the two notches. Press and turn as described above. Use a crescent wrench on the handle of the Vise Grips to turn the piston. Screw the piston in until it is flush with the end of the wheel cylinder bore in the caliper body, or until it stops. Carefully fold the bellows-type sealing rubber as described at the end of Step 3. Rotate the piston back a partial turn so the slots are perpendicular to the caliper body.

If you can't get the piston screwed in, remove the caliper (Procedure 10, Step 4) and take it to Subaru or a garage to have the piston screwed in.

Step 5. Install New Pads.

Use a clean cloth dipped in alcohol, or a spray can of brake cleaner, to clean the caliper holder and brake disc. These brake parts are your first line of safety—be *certain* you assemble them correctly.

Bendix type: Use a wire brush or emery cloth to clean the *pad springs*, both sides of the *stopper plugs*, and the surfaces on the caliper and holder that contact the stopper plugs. Smear the contact surfaces of the springs, stopper plugs, and the tabs on the ends of the pads with a little PBC grease or antiseize compound. Don't get any of the grease on the pads or disc! Clean your hands before installing the new pads.

You've labeled the old pads so you know which new pad goes where, right?

Slip the new pads into the holder while pushing forward against the pad springs until the *ears* on the pads engage in the *notches* on the holder. The new pads should touch the disc, top and bottom, front and back. Wiggle them in the holder until they do. Are they "lightly snug" as I said in the "About Brake Pads" rap?

AD type: Use a wire brush or emery cloth to clean the **pad clips** on the caliper holder. Check them for cracks and worn areas that might prevent the new pads from sliding smoothly; replace any clips that are broken, bent, or questionable. Remove the **pad shim** from the outside of the old outer pad and inspect it for damage; replace it if it's broken, bent, or rusty. If you've got new clips and shims in your brake pad set, by all means use them. Replace them one by one, so you'll be certain they're going on correctly. If you're not sure, you can look at the setup on the opposite side of your car. Your instructions from Subaru may ask you to file a small surface on the holder that the pad ends rest against; this is to assure the right "lightly snug" fit. Lubricate the pad clips, and the little *tabs* or *notches* on the ends of the brake pads with a dab of PBC grease or antiseize compound. Don't get any grease on the pads or disc. Clean your hands before installing the new pads.

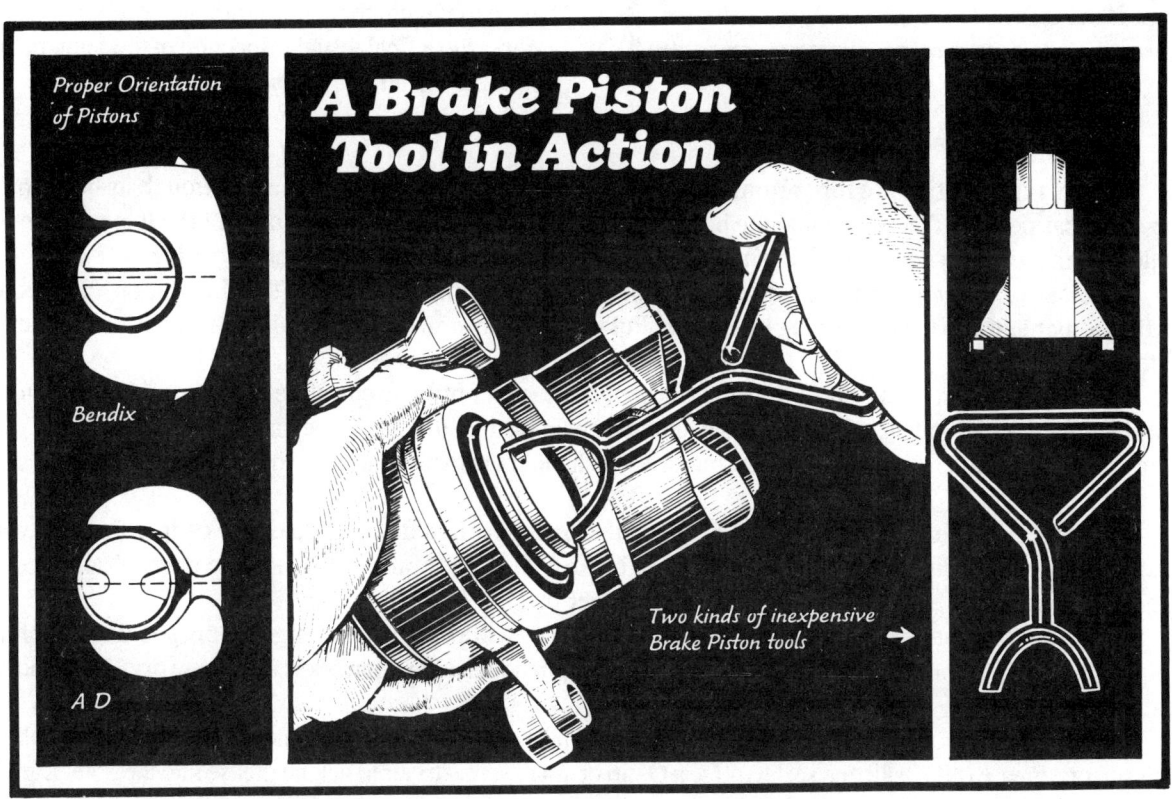

298 Chapter 13 Procedure 9, Step 6

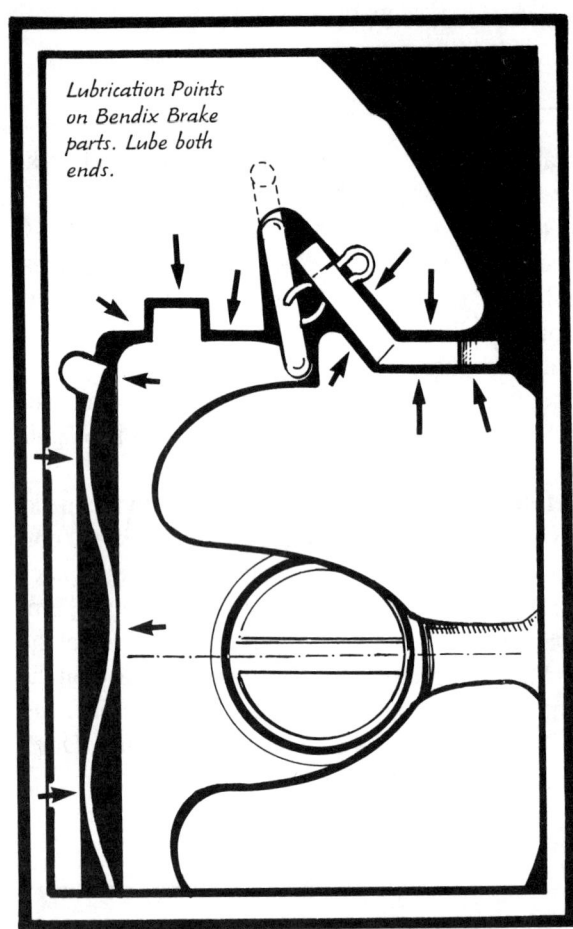

Lubrication Points on Bendix Brake parts. Lube both ends.

Outer AD pad: Smear PBC grease on the outside of the pad and inside of the pad shim (see illustration), then install the shim on the outside of the pad. If necessary, bend the little tabs slightly to make the shim snug. Install the pads so the wear indicators are at the bottom.

On early AD brakes, squeeze the springy part on the lower pad clip against the clip and fit the *notch* in the bottom of the pad over the clip. Fit the *upper notch* over the upper clip the same way.

On later AD brakes the *tabs* at the top and bottom of the pad fit into the *notches* in the clips. The wear sensors always go at the bottom of the pad.

Inner AD pad: On early AD pads, install the **wear indicator spring** that's attached to the bottom of the pad into the lower notch on the pad holder. Press down on the pad until the spring is against the pad, then slip the *tab* at the top of the pad into the *notch* in the holder.

On later AD pads, fit the *tab* and **wear indicator** at the bottom of the pad into the *notch* in the lower pad clip, then fit the *tab* at the top of the pad into the *notch* in the upper clip.

EVERYONE: Both pads should be flat against the disc and feel securely in place. Sometimes you have to wiggle them until they seat properly on the clips. Do a final visual inspection of the setup before moving ahead to the next step.

Step 6. Install Caliper.

Bendix type: Untie the caliper from the string or wire. Slide the handbrake cable through its hole on the top of the caliper. Put the caliper into the holder—top first, then the bottom. You might have to pry up on the bottom with a screwdriver to get it to slide in. Is the handbrake cable in its bracket properly?

Slide one of the *stopper plugs* between the bottom of the caliper and holder (see illustration). Pry down on the caliper and slip the upper plug into place. Put the four tiny *hairpin clips* in the four holes near the ends of the stopper plugs.

Pull the black handbrake cable housing through its bracket until you can slide the handbrake clip into its slot. Use pliers to pull on the end of the cable until the cable fits into the slot of the handbrake cable lever. Cover the cable with the little rubber boot. If you removed the handbrake cable clamp on the disc cover, bolt it on with the two 8mm bolts.

AD type: If you didn't remove the caliper from the pivot pin or guide pin, release the caliper from the wire or string and let the caliper rotate down and over the brake pads. If the brake piston slots are aligned right, they'll slip right over the little nubbins on the back of the inner pad.

If you removed the caliper from the pivot pin, be sure the caliper pivot pin or guide pin sticking out of the caliper holder is clean and shiny. Replace the rubber pivot pin boot and lockpin boots if they are dry, hard, and/or cracked.

Coat the pin (especially on the end) and the inside surface of the pivot pin hole and rubber boot on the caliper with silicone grease (NOT silicone sealer). Use a Q-tip or small screwdriver to get the grease into the hole. Lightly lubricate the pivot pin and lower lock bolt (pin) with silicone grease. Untie the caliper from the string or wire and fit it onto the pivot pin. Pull hard on the caliper toward the outside of the car and hold it there for about ten seconds. While you're holding pressure on the caliper, use a small screwdriver to gently pry up on an edge of the rubber boot that's between the caliper and caliper pivot bolt. Air trapped in the pivot pin hole, or too much silicone grease, can keep the caliper from seating properly and this causes the outer pad to drag. And that's a drag. Fit the rubber boot into the groove on the pivot pin.

Early AD type: If you have ventilated discs there will be a groove around the outer edge of the disc. If you have solid discs, the disc is one solid chunk of metal. Look at your discs to see which type you have.

Solid disc models: Clean the 17mm lockpin bolt, then smear silicone grease on the smooth end. Straighten the rubber lockpin boot between the caliper and caliper holder so the bolt can screw into the holder. If the little boot twists as you turn the bolt, hold it in place with a finger. Torque the bolt to 54 ft. lbs, then screw the 10mm bolt into the side of the lockpin housing and tighten it (not all models have this little bolt).

Ventilated disc models: Slide the *metal sleeve* out of the rubber boot that the lock bolt (lock pin) goes through. Lightly coat the outside of the sleeve and lock bolt, and the inside of the boot with silicone grease, then slide the sleeve into the boot. Stick the 17mm lock bolt through the sleeve, screw it into the caliper holder, then torque it to 17 ft. lbs. on pre-1985 models, or to 25 ft. lbs. on 1985 and newer models.

Late AD type: Follow the instructions for ventilated discs, above, to lubricate the lock pin, boot, and sleeve. Tighten the lock pin to 25 ft. lbs.

All AD types: Use pliers to grab the end of the handbrake cable and pull it rearward until you can hook it into the slot on the end of the handbrake lever. Fit the thin spring clip into its groove on the metal fitting that's on the end of the rubber brake hose.

EVERYONE: Now look at the whole assembly. Recheck the position of the shims, pads, and clips, and recheck the bolt tightness. Your life depends on these parts. Repeat Steps 1 through 6 for the opposite front brake. Unless you've jacked up just one side of the car, don't put the wheels on quite yet.

Step 7. Adjust and Bleed Front Brakes.

Check the bleeder valve on both calipers to be sure they are tight, then check the brake fluid level and add fluid if necessary. After both calipers are on, pump the brake pedal a few times to adjust the brakes. Bleed the front brakes (Procedure 2). This would be a good time to flush the brake system if it hasn't been flushed recently (Procedure 3). Check the operation of the handbrake lever; if it's not right do Procedure 15 to adjust the handbrake.

Step 8. Do This and That.

Put the wheels on and snug down the lug nuts. Remove the jack stands, lower the car to the ground, and torque the lug nuts to 72 ft. lbs. Clean up all traces of brake dust, then throw the old brake pads and the dust mask in the trash. Clean your hands before eating or smoking anything. It's a good idea to blow your nose now to remove any brake dust. This isn't intended to be funny—that stuff is dangerous. Now take your Soob for a slow and easy drive around the block to test the operation of your new brakes.

PROCEDURE 10: REMOVE AND INSTALL CALIPER AND BRAKE DISC

Condition: You weren't able to screw the brake piston into the caliper when installing new pads; OR you found a fluid leak in one or both of the brake cylinders; OR the handbrake lever on the caliper doesn't return properly; OR the pads have worn to the metal and gouged the discs so they need to be removed and turned or replaced; OR you're removing the brakes in order to remove the wheel bearing housing or axle.

Tools and Materials: Phase 1 tool kit, 3/16" chisel, PBC grease for Bendix type calipers, PBC and Silicone grease for AD type calipers, two new copper brake line gaskets for each caliper removed, two cans or jars to catch the brake fluid when the brake hose is disconnected, two pints of fresh DOT 3 or 4 brake fluid, dust mask, baggies, and rubber bands.

Remarks: Please don't try to remove the calipers when they are hot. Also, always remove the caliper and holder before trying to remove the disc.

Step 1. Loosen Axle Nuts.

Do this step ONLY if you are going to remove the disc.

'75-'78: Remove the hubcap. Locate the groove in the axle where the outer edge of the axle nut has been bent ("staked") into the groove to lock the nut in place. Tap a 3/16" chisel into the groove under the staked portion of the nut until the end of the nut is round enough to clear the threads on the axle.

'79 and newer models: Remove the hubcap. Use pliers to straighten the ends of the cotter pin that goes through the axle nut, then pull the cotter pin out.

EVERYONE: Loosen the 36mm axle nut at least one full turn counterclockwise. If it's on really tight, you can use the cheater pipe setup described in Chapter 18: *Mechanics' Tips*.

Step 2. Chock, Jack, and Block.

Chock the rear wheels, loosen the lug nuts a little, jack the car up, lower it on jack stands or blocks, then remove the wheel. (See Chapter 3 if you need details.)

Step 3. Release Calipers and Remove Pads.

See Procedure 9, Step 2A or 2B and Step 3 to release the calipers and remove the pads. If you're going to use the same pads again, mark them *left inner, left outer*, and so on. Stash them where brake fluid can't splash or drip on them. If you're replacing the pads, stash the new pads someplace clean and safe.

Step 4. Remove Calipers.

Bendix type: If you are just going to remove the disc, leave the caliper hanging by the string or wire and skip to Step 4.

If you need to remove the caliper, put a can or jar under the brake hose to catch the brake fluid. Unscrew the 14mm **"union" bolt** that attaches the end of the rubber brake hose to the caliper. Use two screwdrivers to gently pry the **union brake hose fitting** off the pin in the caliper. Hold onto the two copper union fitting gaskets until you find new ones. Reuse the old ones if you can't find new ones, but carefully check for leaks when everything is back together. Untie the caliper from the wire or string and remove it. When the fluid has drained, put a baggie and rubber band over the end of the hose to keep dust and dirt out.

Before hauling the caliper away to be rebuilt or replaced, inspect the rubber brake line hoses and replace them if they are hard, stiff, cracked, or bulging in places (Procedure 11). If you're not removing the disc, skip to Step 8 to install the caliper.

AD type: If you are just going to remove the disc and not the caliper from the car, push the caliper toward the center of the car until it slides off the *pivot pin*. Let the caliper hang by the wire or string—not by the brake hose.

To remove the caliper from the car, untie the string or wire and let it rotate down to its normal position. The *brake pads* are already out, right? Put a can or jar under the brake hose to catch the brake fluid, then unscrew the 14mm **union bolt** that attaches the **union fitting** end of the brake hose to the caliper. Use two screwdrivers to gently pry the union fitting out of the notch in the caliper body. Hold onto the two copper union fitting *gaskets* until you find new ones. Reuse the old ones if you can't find new ones, but carefully check for leaks when everything is back together.

When the hose quits dripping, put a baggie and rubber band over the end to protect it from dust and dirt. Hold a clean rag over the hole where the brake line was attached, then rotate the caliper up until it will clear the disc. Push the caliper toward the center of the car and off the pivot pin. You might have to pry the *rubber boot* out of its groove on the pivot pin.

Before hauling the calipers away to be rebuilt or replaced, inspect the rubber brake line hoses and replace them if they are worn, cracked, broken, or bulging in places (Procedure 11).

If you're not removing the disc, skip to Step 8 to replace the caliper.

Step 5. Remove Caliper Holder.

If you need to remove the disc, locate two 17mm bolts on the inboard side of the brake disc. They are slightly forward from the inside brake pad slot. Unscrew the two bolts *counterclockwise*, then pull the holder away from the disc.

Step 6. Remove Disc.

Remove the 36mm *axle nut* and *cone washer*, then try to pull the disc off the axle. If it's stuck, you may need to fetch a puller (look at the end of Procedure 4, Step 1). Subaru disc brake hubs attach to the axle just like front brake drums.

If you removed the discs because they are scratched or grooved, take them to Subaru, a machine shop, or garage and have them turned (resurfaced).

The minimum legal (and safe) thickness for the disc is:

Bendix Type:	330 in.	(8.5mm)
Early AD Type:	394 in.	(10mm) solid disc
	610 in.	(15.5mm) ventilated disc
Late AD Type:	630 in.	(16mm)

Replace the disc (Step 7) if it's worn out (less than the minimum thickness). Thin discs can't dissipate the heat properly and thus warp easily.

Step 7. Install Disc.

If the disc was worn out, unscrew the four 14mm bolts that attach it to the *hub*. Fit a new disc onto the hub, lightly oil the bolt threads, then screw them in and torque them in a crisscross (upper left, lower right, etc.) pattern to 12 ft. lbs., then around again to 22, then 32, and finally to 42 ft. lbs. It's a good idea to have the new discs turned (machined) before installing them. Even though the disc is made of heavy steel, mounting it to the hub often distorts it slightly which could cause brake squeal.

Before installing the disc on the car, peek at the **wheel bearings** and **grease seals**. The wheel bearings are the round things the axle sticks through. Look for *white* gooey-looking stuff that would indicate water has gotten inside the bearings. See any? If you do, the wheel bearings should be repacked and the grease seals replaced (Chapter 14, Procedure 9). The grease seals are the round rubber things just outside the wheel bearings. If they are hard or cracked they should be replaced (Chapter 14, Procedure 9). Everything OK? Proceed...

Clean the brake disc (even if it's new), caliper holder, mounting bolts, and caliper lock bolt with brake cleaner, or alcohol. Lightly oil the threads on the two caliper holder bolts, the splines on the axle, and the splines inside the disc hub. Wipe excess oil off with a clean rag. Clean your hands before installing the clean disc and hub.

Slide the disc and hub onto the axle, then install the *split center piece* and the *cone washer* with the raised center part facing out. Install the *axle nut* and snug it down with the 36mm socket while holding a wooden hammer handle or a piece of wood across two lug bolts to keep the hub from turning. The final tightening must be done after the wheels are on the ground.

Step 8. Install Caliper Holder and Brake Pads.

Hold the holder up to the disc so the two threaded bolt holes are between the disc and the bolt holes in the wheel bearing housing. Screw in the two 17mm mounting bolts, then torque them to 51 ft. lbs.

Install the brake pads (Procedure 9, Steps 4 and 5).

Step 9. Install Caliper.

If you had the calipers rebuilt or are replacing them, be sure the *brake piston* is screwed all the way in and the grooves (Bendix type) or notches (AD type) are positioned properly. Look at the illustration.

Bendix Type: Procedure 9, Step 6, covers Bendix caliper installation. After the caliper is installed, come back here and do Step 10 to connect the brake line.

AD Type: Do Procedure 9, Step 6, to install the caliper. After the caliper is installed, come back here and do Step 10 to connect the brake line.

Step 10. Connect Brake Line.

Inspect the rubber brake hose. Replace it if it's stiff, cracked, split, or bulging in places (Procedure 11).

Hose OK? Clean the brake line union fitting and the union bolt that attaches the fitting to the caliper. Don't put oil or anything on the threads. Blow through the end of the union bolt to be sure the little hole on the side is clean and clear. Put a new copper gasket on the union bolt, insert the bolt into the union fitting, then install another new gasket on the bolt. Install the union fitting onto the pin (Bendix) or into the slot (AD), then screw the bolt into the caliper. Torque the bolt to 15 ft. lbs.

Step 11. Finish the Job.

If the calipers were removed from the car, go back to Procedure 2 and bleed the master cylinder, then the front brakes; then follow the bleeding sequence in Procedure 2 and bleed all four wheels.

Put the wheels back on, lower the car and torque the lug nuts to 72 ft. lbs. If the axle nuts were loosened or removed, remember to torque them (Procedure 4, Step 4). Install the hubcap.

If you had the discs turned, or you installed new discs, check the handbrake adjustment (Procedure 15). The thickness of the disc affects the handbrake setting.

PROCEDURE 11: REPLACE RUBBER BRAKE HOSES

Condition: The hoses are worn, cracked, split, or bulging in places.

Tools and Materials: Phase 1 tool kit, 10mm flare nut wrench, new hoses, a couple of cans of DOT 3 or 4 brake fluid, solvent or carb cleaner, copper gaskets for the union bolt. If you are replacing hoses that connect directly to calipers, you'll need two new brake line gaskets for each caliper.

Remarks: If one brake hose is worn out, the others are probably nearing the end of the trail also. Check them carefully. When you buy a new hose, compare the length of the new against the old.

Bendix disc brake systems have two rubber hoses under *each* front fender. Be sure to check *both* of them.

To locate the rubber brake hoses for the rear wheels, follow the metal brake lines forward from the top of the brake backing plates until you come to the rubber hoses.

Step 1. Chock, Jack, and Block.

Chock the wheels, loosen the lug nuts a little, jack up the car and put it on jackstands or blocks. Remove the lug nuts then the wheel.

You don't want any dirt to get into the metal brake line or caliper when you divorce, I mean separate, the brake lines, so clean the connections on both ends of the rubber brake hose before removing it. A squirt can of carb cleaner or a stiff brush and solvent works well.

Step 2. Remove Brake Hose (all except hose ends attached to calipers).

Use a rag to catch the brake fluid that's sure to run out of the line. Keep the nut at the end of the rubber brake hose from turning with a 17mm open-end wrench while you use a 10mm flare-nut wrench to unscrew the nut on the metal brake line. When the nut is completely unscrewed, use pliers to remove the **spring clip** that attaches the rubber brake hose to the *bracket*. Pull the rubber hose away from the bracket. *Don't* pull the metal brake line away from the bracket. If it gets bent, even slightly, it will be hard to screw the nut into the new brake hose. Remove the other end of the hose the same way.

Step 3. Detach Brake Hose from Caliper.

Use a 14mm box-end wrench to unscrew the **union bolt** that attaches the brake hose to the caliper. Use two screwdrivers to gently pry the fitting off the **caliper pin** (Bendix type) or out of the groove (AD type). To remove the hose, separate the other end of the hose from the metal brake line as in Step 2.

Don't throw away the copper gaskets unless you already have new ones. The fitting will leak like a sieve without the gaskets. If you can't find new gaskets, use the old ones again, then check carefully for leaks when everything is back together.

To remove the hose on models with AD type calipers, use pliers to remove the *spring clip* that attaches the hose to the *strut bracket*. Pull the caliper end of the hose through the bracket.

Step 4. Install New Caliper Hose.

Bendix type: Clean the union bolt and union fitting. Use a new gasket on each side of the fitting. Install the fitting onto the pin, then attach the hose fitting to the caliper with the union bolt. Torque the bolt to 15 ft. lbs. Stick the other end of the hose through the bracket. Position the hose so it isn't kinked and can't rub against anything. Skip down to Step 5 to attach the remaining end.

AD type: Thread the caliper end of the hose with the union fitting through the bracket on the strut. Clean the union bolt and union fitting. Use a new gasket on each side of the fitting. Slide the union fitting into the groove in the caliper, then attach the hose fitting to the caliper with the bolt. Position the hose so it isn't kinked and can't rub against anything, then torque the bolt to 15 ft. lbs. Secure the hose to the strut bracket with the spring clip, then stick the end of the hose through the *mounting bracket* on the inside of the wheel well. Step 5 explains how to attach the rubber hose to the metal brake line.

Step 5. All Other Fittings.

You've stuck the end of the brake hose through the mounting bracket hole, right? Screw the nut on the metal brake line into the hose by hand until you're *sure* the threads have started correctly. Position the hose so there are no kinks and so the hose can't rub against anything. Secure the hose to the bracket with a spring clip. Use a 17mm wrench on the brake hose nut to keep the hose from twisting while tightening the 10mm nut with a flare nut wrench. Make it tight.

Step 6. Bleed.

After replacing the worn-out hoses, bleed the brake system (Procedure 2). When the brakes have been bled, have someone press the brake pedal a few times while you watch the hose connections for leaks. Don't forget to replace the dust caps on the bleeding nipples. That's it.

PROCEDURE 12: REMOVE AND INSTALL MASTER CYLINDER

The master cylinder sticks out from the left side of the firewall and has one large or two small semi-opaque white plastic hydraulic **fluid reservoirs** on top. If your car has a black cylindrical "master vac" brake booster, the master cylinder is mounted on the front of it. You remove the master cylinder the same way for Soobs with or without the master vac.

Condition: Master cylinder is leaking; OR no matter how much you bleed the brakes the pedal is still spongy; OR you have to bleed the brakes frequently; OR the master vac has to be removed.

Tools and Materials: Phase 1 tool kit, 10mm flare-nut wrench, three pints of fresh DOT 3 brake fluid, brake bleeding hose and jar (Procedure 2), two baggies, rags. *Optional:* Syringe or eye dropper.

Remarks: If you've determined the master cylinder isn't performing the way it should, call a few garages to see how much they'll charge to rebuild your old one. Then call Subaru and a few parts stores to see what a new or rebuilt one costs. If the prices are close, go for a new or rebuilt one. They usually come with new reservoirs and sometimes even have new reservoir caps.

Step 1. Unplug Wires, Bleed Cylinder.

Remove the spare tire if it's in the engine compartment. Place a large rag under the master cylinder to catch stray drops of brake fluid. *Brake fluid is harmful to eyes and paint, so be careful!*

If there are wires coming from the reservoir cap or caps, trace the wires to a connector located about 3" from the master cylinder. Disconnect the wires by pulling the connector apart.

Pull off the reservoir **cap(s)** and remove the little plastic **strainers** (if you have them) and put them someplace clean and safe. Use something like an eye dropper or syringe to empty the brake fluid out of the reservoir(s). Don't suck the stuff out yourself—POISON!

As an alternative, you can connect a hose to the **bleeder nipple(s)** on the side of the master cylinder, stick the other end of the hose into a can or jar, and open the bleeder valve with a 10mm wrench. Turn the nipple counterclockwise a half turn or so, and the fluid should start to flow out. Pump the brake pedal a few times to get rid of all the brake fluid. Do it to *both* master cylinder bleeder nipples. When the reservoir's empty, tighten the nipples and remove the hose. If you need to know more about bleeding, see Procedure 2.

Step 2. Remove Master Cylinder.

Remove the two brake line nuts from the bottom of the master cylinder with a 10mm flare nut wrench and pull the lines just slightly clear but don't kink the lines! Put a baggie over the end of each line to keep it clean. Remove the two 12mm nuts that connect the master cylinder to the master vac unit or firewall, one above and one below. Carefully pull the master cylinder forward and free. Pour any brake fluid remaining in the master cylinder into a suitable container. Stuff a clean rag into the hole left by the departed master cylinder. Clean the outside of the master cylinder if you're going to take it to a brake specialist for rebuilding.

Step 3. Install Master Cylinder.

Remove the rag from the hole and coat the little rod sticking out of the firewall or master vac with a fingerfull of brake fluid. Guide the rod into the rubber boot on the end of the master cylinder as you slide the master cylinder onto the two mounting studs. Don't put the nuts on yet. Now remove the plastic baggies and put the two brake lines into their respective holes in the master cylinder. Get the threads on both lines started by hand. Please make sure they're not cross-threaded. Then install and tighten the two 12mm mounting nuts and washers. Next tighten the two brake line nuts with a 10mm flare nut wrench.

Step 4. Prepare Master Cylinder for Action.

Clean each brake fluid strainer with a clean rag, then insert it into the reservoir. Replace any that are torn, broken, or greasy. Fill the reservoir(s) with fresh clean brake fluid to the MAX line. Slowly pump the brake pedal five times, then check the fluid level. Add more fluid if necessary to keep the level at the MAX line. Pump and add, pump and add until the fluid level doesn't drop.

Now bleed the master cylinder and then all four wheels (Procedure 2). After replacing the master cylinder, it will take more bleeding than usual to get the air out of the lines. Be patient and persevere. When you're finished bleeding, fill the reservoir to the MAX line. Clean each reservoir cap and round white **fluid level indicator** (if your cap has one) with a clean rag, then put the cap on the reservoir. Reconnect the electrical wires for the fluid level indicator (if you have them). Put the spare tire in its place if you removed it.

PROCEDURE 13: CHECK, REMOVE, REPLACE MASTER VAC UNIT

The master vac unit is attached via a rubber hose to the engine's intake manifold. When the engine's running, a vacuum is created in the intake manifold as the pistons suck air and fuel into the cylinders. The master vac utilizes this vacuum to reduce the amount of pressure required on the brake pedal to stop the car. A check valve in the rubber hose prevents the vacuum from flow back to the manifold.

Only coupe GSRs were equipped with master vac units until 1975, at which time all models except two-door sedans got the master vac treatment. All 1979 and newer models have master vac units (as well they should).

Condition: Everything in the brake system checks out OK, but extra force must be applied to the brake pedal before braking action occurs.

Tools and Materials: Phase 1 tool kit, 10mm flare-nut wrench, big baggie.

Remarks: If it almost takes both feet on the brake pedal to slow the car, run through the master vac check (Step 1). If the tests indicate the unit is faulty, have a Subaru dealer check the old unit with gauges before replacing it with a new one. They're expensive, so be *sure* the old one is dead before replacing it.

Step 1. Check Master Vac Operation.

Be sure the handbrake is on.

Air tightness check: Start the engine and let it run for a few minutes, then turn it off. Push on the brake pedal a few times with the same force you usually use to stop the car. If the master vac is working properly the pedal should go farther toward the floor the first time you press on it and stop farther away from the floor with each following stroke. If there is no change in the distance the pedal travels, check the **check valve** and **rubber vacuum hose** (Step 2).

Operation check: Before starting the engine, pump the brake pedal a few times using the same pressure. Make sure the pedal height doesn't vary with each pump of the pedal. Hold the pedal down and start the engine. When the engine starts the brake pedal should move toward the floor slightly. If the pedal doesn't drop a little, do Step 2.

Loaded air tightness Check: Hold the brake pedal down while the engine is running, then turn the engine off. Hold the pedal down for 30 seconds. If the pedal height stays the same, the master vac is OK. If the pedal moves up away from the floor, the master vac has a problem; do Step 2.

Step 2. Test Check Valve and Vacuum Hose.

Check the large black hose that connects the master vac to the **intake manifold** on the engine. Look for cracks, splits, and/or loose connections. Replace any hoses that are suspect.

Somewhere along the big black vacuum hose, between the master vac and the intake manifold on the engine, is a brass-colored *check valve* about the same diameter as the hose (sometimes it's almost hidden under a clamp). If it's under a clamp, remove the phillips screw, then the clamp. Use pliers to squeeze the little tabs on the spring clamps next to the check valve, then slide the clamps up the hose, away from the valve. Twist and pull the hose off each end of the check valve. The valve is now free.

Hold the valve while you blow into each end. Air should only flow through the valve in one direction—from the master vac end toward the engine end. If air passes both ways, replace the valve with a new one and test the master vac again.

Install the check valve back on the hoses so that the tapered shoulder is toward the engine. Slide the clamps into place on each end of the valve, then secure the valve in the holder and tighten the phillips screw.

Step 3. Remove Master Vac.

Remove the master cylinder (Procedure 12). Put it in a clean baggie and stash it someplace clean and safe.

Use pliers to squeeze the clamp on the end of the large black vacuum hose where it attaches to the master vac. Slide the clamp up the hose a few inches, then twist and pull the hose off the master vac.

Look at the brake pedal inside the car. About 6″ above the foot pad is a *clevis* (a U-shaped thing), with a round *clevis pin* going through it and the *brake lever*. Attached to the clevis is the *brake pushrod* that goes through the firewall and into the master vac unit. Use needlenose pliers to remove the little *cotter key* or *snap pin* on the end of the clevis pin. If there are little plastic barbs on the end of the clevis pin, squeeze them toward the pin and push the pin out of the clevis. No barbs? Just tap the clevis pin out of the clevis.

Still under the dash, remove the four 12mm nuts around the hole that the brake pushrod goes through on the firewall. Now the master vac can be removed from the car. Go back under the hood and carefully pull the unit away from the firewall without bending the master cylinder brake lines.

Step 4. Install Master Vac Unit.

Carefully slide the master vac over the brake lines, then push the four mounting bolts into the holes on the firewall. From under the dash, screw on and tighten the four 12mm mounting washers and nuts. Slide the clevis over the brake lever and install the clevis pin. Install the cotter key or snap pin in the end of the clevis pin. Bend the end of the cotter pin around the clevis pin.

Connect the black vacuum hose to the master vac unit in the engine compartment, then use pliers to slide the clamp back over the connection to secure it.

Install the master cylinder (Procedure 12). Now bleed the master cylinder and then the whole brake system (Procedure 2).

Go through Step 1 to see that the master vac is operating properly before you hit the road.

PROCEDURE 14: CHECK, REMOVE, REPLACE BRAKE LIGHT SWITCH

Condition 1: The brake lights stay on all the time. Do Steps 1 and 2.

Condition 2: Brake lights don't light up when the brake pedal is pressed. Do steps 1, 3, 4, and 5 (omit Step 2).

Remarks: If condition 2 is your problem, check the brake light *bulbs* and *fuse* (Chapter 10) before testing the brake light switch.

Tools and Materials: Step 2 requires a new rubber brake pedal stopper, Step 3 may require some penetrating oil. Steps 4 and 5 require other items.

Step 1. Locate Brake Light Switch.

Look up under the dash while pumping the brake pedal with your hand. When you release the pedal, a **rubber pad** on the brake lever pushes a plunger into a little round **switch**. See it? On some models with cruise control there will be two switches. The switch on the right is the brake light switch.

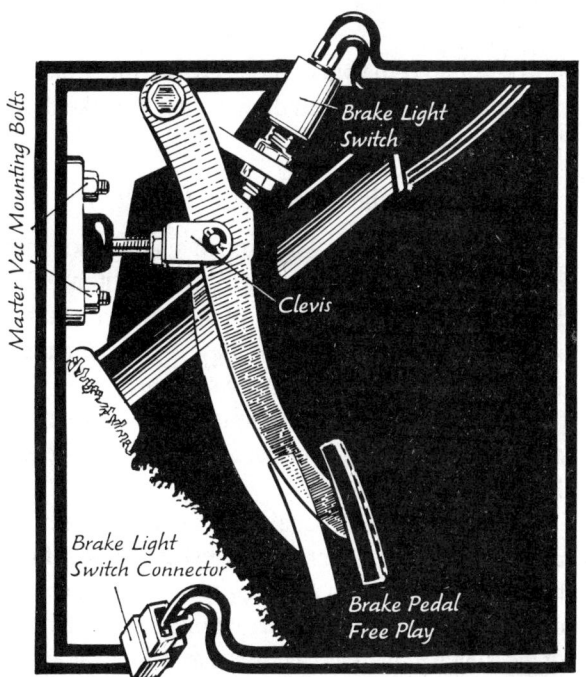

Step 2. Replace Rubber Brake Pad.

If the rubber pad is missing, the brake lights will stay on all the time. Buy a new pad from Subaru and press it into the hole. The brakes lights should go off now when the pedal is released.

Step 3. Check Plunger.

While holding the brake pedal down, push on the end of the switch with your finger to see if the plunger moves freely. If it's stuck in the switch, spray some penetrating oil on it and try to move it in and out until it slides easily. If you can't get it unstuck, you need to replace the switch (Step 5).

Step 4. Test Electrical Source.

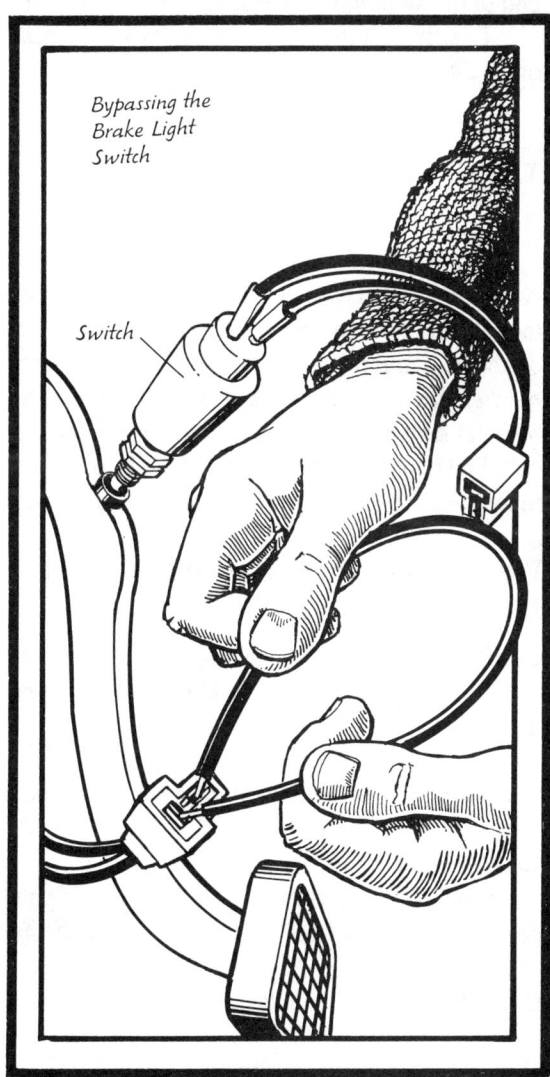

Tools and Materials: 12-volt test light, short piece of insulated wire. Follow the two wires from the switch to a plastic *connector*. Pull the connector apart. Use a 12-volt test light to check for electricity in the *two slots* of the connector that the brake light switch wires plug into. Stick one of the test light wires (or the metal probe on the test light) into one of the slots on the connector and touch the other wire to an unpainted piece of metal or screw head that's attached to the car. Try both slots. One of the slots should light the tester.

If no electricity is getting to the connector, the wire must be broken or shorted somewhere between the switch and the fuse box. You did check the fuse, didn't you? Look at Chapter 10, Procedure 5, Step 3 to track down the broken wire.

If the test light goes on, there's "juice" at the terminal. Find a short piece of spare insulated electrical wire and strip about ¼" of insulation from each end of the wire. Now stick one end of the wire into each of the terminal slots in the connector. Check the rear brake lights. If the brake lights are on, the brake light switch is bad. Replace it (Step 5). Still no lights? Either a wire is broken between the switch and brake light bulb, or the brake light system isn't grounded properly. See Chapter 10, Procedure 5.

Step 5. Replace Brake Light Switch.

Tools and Materials: 14mm open-end wrench, new switch, small ruler (either in. or cm. is OK), Friend. Disconnect the two wires coming from the switch at the plastic connector if you haven't already. Unscrew the 14mm nut that's on the opposite end of the switch from the wires. You may have to be patient here; Subaru hasn't made it particularly easy to get at because of a bend in the **mounting holder** (bracket). Slide the switch out of its holder. Remove the other nut from the switch.

Screw one of the nuts about halfway onto the new switch. Slide the switch into the holder with the plunger end pointed toward the brake lever. Hold the brake pedal down while you screw the other nut onto the switch. Don't tighten it yet.

Adjust the brake pedal height so there is .20″-.43″ (5-11mm) free play. *Free play* is the distance the pedal travels before encountering any resistance (see illustration). A little free play is important; otherwise, you could have the brake switch putting pressure on the brakes without help from your right foot. That would be a real drag. Screw the two nuts farther onto the switch to decrease the amount of free play, or farther toward the end of the switch to increase the free play. When the free play is right, tighten the 14mm nut that's closest to the plunger end of the switch, clockwise against the mounting holder. Then reconnect the wires to the plastic connector.

Finally, test the light by pressing on the brake pedal a few times while a Friend looks for the lights to turn on and off at the back of the car.

THE HANDBRAKE

The handbrake (also called *emergency* or *parking brake*) is operated by a **hand lever** (handle) between the two front seats. Two steel **cables** run from the lever to the front brakes. When the handbrake lever is pulled up, the cables tighten and push the front *brake shoes* against the brake drums or *brake pads* against the discs—depending on the year and model. The lever is held up (brake ON) by a notched locking arrangement: *pawl teeth* fall into *ratchet teeth*. To release the brake, just press the button at the end of the handbrake lever. (Aha! You remember!) The button knocks the pawl away from the ratchet teeth and lets you push the handle down.

The handbrake usually needs to be adjusted (tightened) after the discs or drums have been "turned" at a machine shop. Installing new discs or drums might necessitate loosening the handbrake cables a little.

PROCEDURE 15: ADJUST HANDBRAKE

Condition: Handbrake lever goes up nine or more notches (clicks) '75-'82; six or more notches (clicks) '83-'84; or four or more notches '85 and newer. If your handbrake won't keep your Soob from rolling on a slope, adjust it *now*.

Tools and Materials: Medium phillips screwdriver, 10mm and 12mm wrenches.

Remarks: Before adjusting the handbrake, be sure the rear brakes are adjusted (Procedure 1), and there is no air in the hydraulic system (Procedure 2). If you have disc brakes, check that the handbrake lever on the caliper at each front wheel returns fully after the handbrake is released (Procedure 8, Step 5).

CAUTION: Be sure the transmission is in 1st gear (manual) or PARK (automatics) and the wheels are blocked.

Step 1. Remove Handbrake Handle Cover.

Begin with the handle pulled up (applied). This will permit easier removal of the cover and access to the **handbrake adjusting nuts**.

'75-'79 cars and '77-'81 Brats: If there is a plastic *console* in front of the handbrake cover, remove the phillips screws located around the edges and remove the console. Lift the carpet just in front of the **handbrake cover** and remove the two phillips screws. If there are two little *containers* to the rear of the handbrake lever, remove the phillips screw in the bottom of the left container. If there is an *ashtray* in the rear of the cover, remove the ashtray, then remove the phillips screws. Push the cover toward the rear while lifting up on the front. Slide the cover over the handbrake lever.

'80 and newer cars and '82-'87 Brats: To get to the handbrake adjusting nuts, lift up on the rear edge of the plastic **panel** that's just in front of the handbrake cover. If you have 4WD, lift up on the 4WD lever, then rotate the plastic panel forward until the handbrake adjusting nuts are visible (check out the illustration).

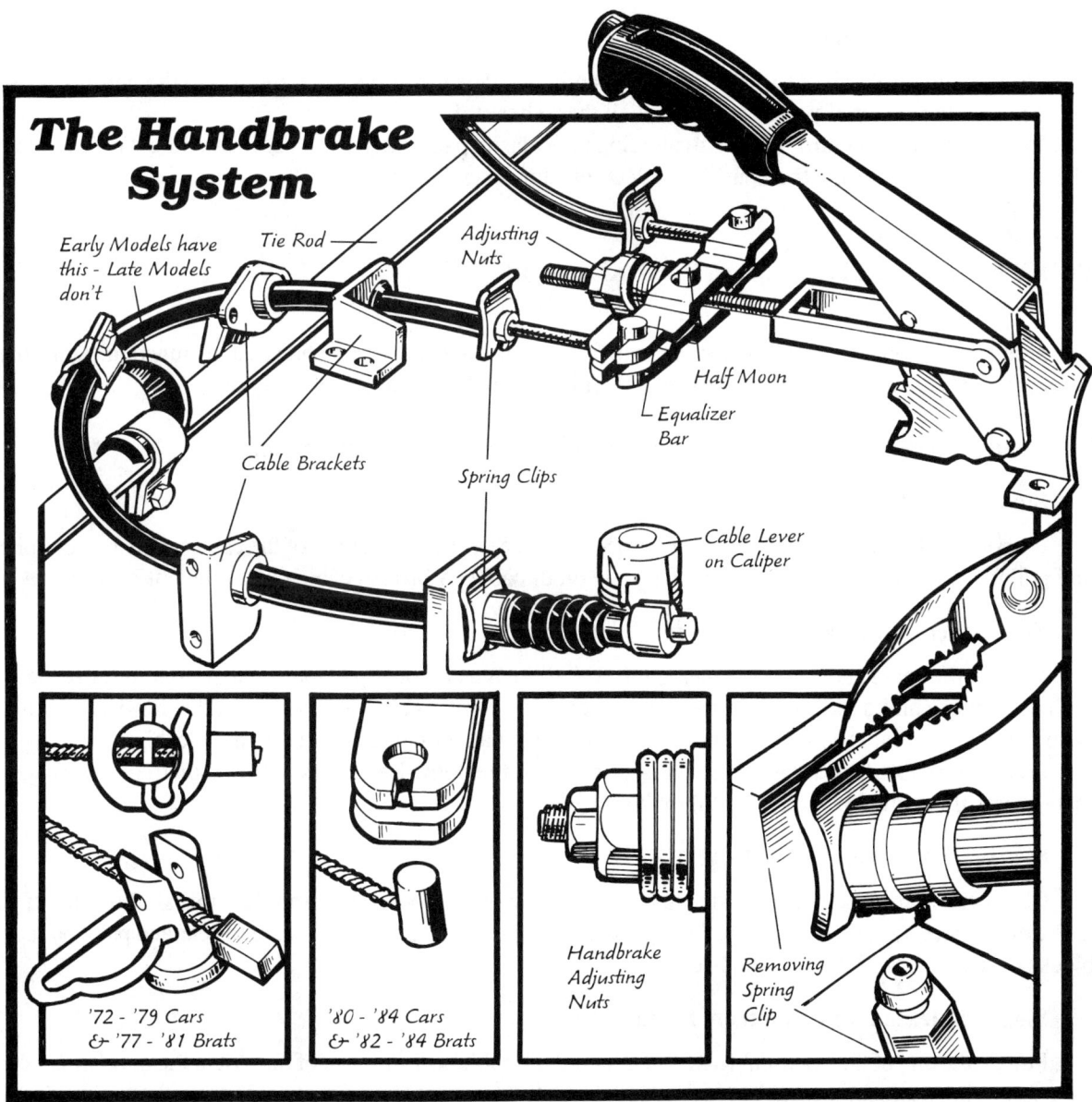

Step 2. Adjust Handbrake.

The handbrake lever pulls on a threaded **rod** that passes through an **equalizer bar**. Cables going to the front brakes are attached to each end of the bar, which is free to pivot on a half-moon shaped **pin** (actually, it's more like a ¾ moon). Thus the force applied to the lever is transmitted equally to both front brakes.

To adjust the handbrake, locate the two nuts on the front end of the threaded rod. They're right between the two cables. Hold the larger nut with a 12mm wrench while you loosen the 10mm nut just a little. Now put the handbrake handle in the OFF position (down). Turn the 12mm nut toward the equalizer bar with your fingers until you can only lift the handbrake lever 6-8 clicks (3-4 clicks '83 and newer models), using moderate force (Subaru says 55 lbs.). Put the handbrake all the way OFF again and check the pin in the center of the equalizer bar for slack. Put a finger under the pin and your thumb on top of the pin and try to move it up and down. If the pin is tight, unscrew the 12mm nut until you can wiggle the pin slightly with your fingers. If the cables are over-tightened so that the pin won't wiggle, the brakes will be on all the time. When the adjustment is correct, pull the handle up again and hold the 12mm nut with a wrench and tighten the 10mm nut against it.

Step 3. Put Cover Back On.

'75-'79 cars and '77-'81 Brats: Slide the handbrake cover over the lever and install the phillips screws. Put the console back on if you have one, and all that other stuff.

'80 and newer cars and '82-'87 Brats: Snap the plastic panel back in place. If you have 4WD, rotate the plastic panel back in place, then push the 4WD selector down.

PROCEDURE 16: REPLACE HANDBRAKE CABLE

Condition: The handbrake handle comes up with no resistance and the parking brakes don't function. Adjustment (Procedure 15) does nothing. Conclusion: One or both handbrake cables have broken.

Tools and Materials: Phase 1 tool kit, new handbrake cable, new rubber grommet.

Step 1. Find Broken Cable.

Remove the **handbrake handle cover** (Procedure 15, Step 1). Grab either of the cables with a pair of pliers and pull it toward the rear of the car. Now try the other cable. A broken cable will come out in your hands.

Step 2. Release Broken Cable.

Release the cable end from the *equalizer bar*. If there is a *clip* on top of the equalizer bar, remove the clip with needlenose pliers then push the **cable retainer** down through the hole with a small screwdriver. If there is no clip, pull the cable so it aligns with the slot in the equalizer bar, then lift up on the cable.

Follow the cable forward to where it disappears into the body. Use pliers to lift up on the *spring clip* tab that secures the **cable housing** (sheath) to the car body.

Step 3. Chock, Jack, and Block.

Chock the rear wheels. On the side that has a broken cable, loosen the front lug nuts slightly, and if you have drum brakes, loosen the axle nut a little (Procedure 6, Step 1). Jack up the front of the car and put it on secure blocks or jackstands. Remove the wheel.

Step 4. Release Cable End from Brakes.

Pull on the end of the brake cable with pliers until the cable will slide out of the slot in the *handbrake lever*. Now follow the cable toward the front of the car about three inches. Use pliers to pull up on the *spring clip* that secures the cable housing to the *bracket* on the caliper. Models with **Bendix calipers** ('72-'79 cars and '77-'81 Brats): You have a *cable clamp* on the back of the axle housing a couple of inches forward from the spring clip bracket. Remove the two 8mm bolts to remove the clamp and free the cable.

Step 5. Remove Broken Cable.

Use a 10mm wrench to release the cable housing (sheath) from the **holders** (clamps) on the tie rod (if you have one there), the **control arm** (also called the *transverse link*), and the **rear crossmember** (the black, flat piece of metal that holds up the rear of the transmission). Some automatic transmission models have an extra cable clamp on the rear crossmember. Pull the cable housing through the **cable guide** in the transmission tunnel and out of the body.

Step 6. Install New Cable.

Compare the length and hardware of the new cable with the old cable. When you're sure you have the right cable, get under the car and thread the end *without* a rubber cable protector through the cable guide that's fastened to the inside of the transmission tunnel. Push the end of the cable through the hole and inside the car.

Get in the car and install the *spring clip* that secures the cable to the body. Pull on the end of the cable and attach it to the *equalizer bar*. You might have to loosen the adjusting nuts a little. Put on the *cable retainer* and *pin* if that's your setup, or line up the cable with the slot in the equalizer bar and push the round cable end into the hole.

Get back under the car and attach the cable holders (clamps) on the *rear crossmember*, the *control arm*, and the *tie rod* (if you have one there).

Thread the cable through the bracket on the caliper, install the *spring clip* to secure the cable to the bracket, then connect the cable end to the lever arm on the caliper by slipping the cable through the slot and fitting the cable end in place. You may have to slide the little rubber boot up the cable in order to slip the cable onto the slot. If your setup has a *cable clamp* on the backing plate, install the clamp and tighten the 8mm bolts.

Put the wheel on and snug down the lug nuts. Lower the car and torque the nuts to 72 ft. lbs.

Put the hub cap on, then adjust the handbrake (Procedure 15), then do Procedure 4, Step 13, in Chapter 7.

HILL-HOLDER

Some Subarus have a unique gadget called a **hill-holder** that allows you to stop on a hill and take your foot off the brake without rolling backwards. How does this miracle work, you ask?

There's a unit called a **pressure hold valve (PHV)** in the engine compartment right below the master cylinder. Inside the PHV is a cylinder and in the cylinder is a ball that is free to roll from one end to the other. When you stop on a hill with the clutch and brake pedals depressed, the ball rolls to the rear of the cylinder and seals a hole that prevents the release of hydraulic pressure in the primary brake system when you release the brake pedal. This locks the left front and right rear brakes and prevents the car from rolling backward. When the clutch pedal is released, a cable attached to the clutch lever on the engine pulls on a lever mounted on the PHV. The lever pushes a pin against the ball and moves it away from the hole, releasing the pressure on the brakes. Nifty, eh? Works, too!

I've heard that people who live in hilly places like San Francisco and heavy-duty off-road people have developed severe love relationships with their hill-holders!

PROCEDURE 17: ADJUST HILL-HOLDER

Condition 1: When stopped on a hill, the hill-holder doesn't hold and the car slips backward. Do Steps 1 and 2.

Condition 2: The brakes stay on momentarily after the clutch pedal is released and the engine tends to stall. Do Steps 1 and 2. If the brakes are locked on so you can't drive the car at all, see Procedure 18, Step 2.

312 Chapter 13 Procedure 17, Step 1

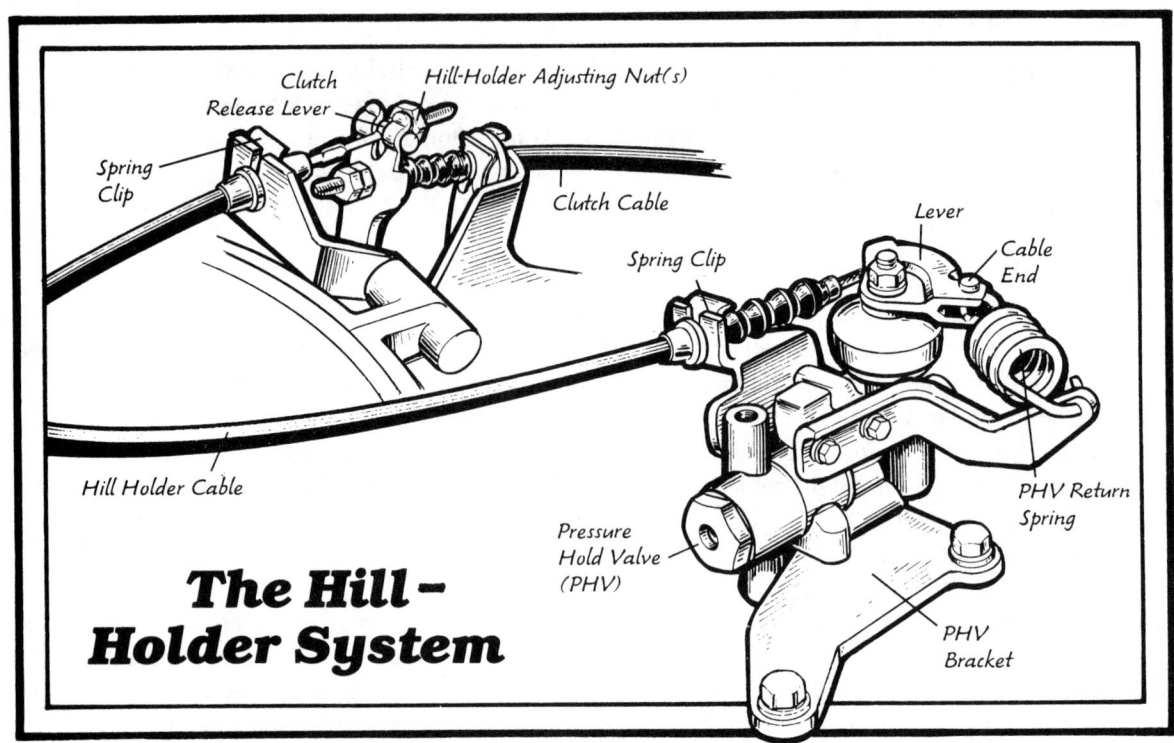

The Hill-Holder System

Condition 3: The hill-holder works fine on steep hills but not on moderate hills. Do Step 3, then Steps 1 and 2 if necessary.

Tools and Materials: For conditions 1 and 2: pliers, maybe 8mm, 10mm, and 14mm wrenches (depending on your setup), maybe a new PHV cable and/or a new PHV return spring. For condition 3, 10mm socket, ratchet, and short extension, one or two hill-holder shims (Subaru Part No. 725807000).

Remarks: The hill-holder system is designed to only work on a grade of 30 or more, so it doesn't work on extremely slight inclines.

Before adjusting the cable, try the hill-holder on a hill and apply more pressure on the brake pedal. Maybe you're just not pushing hard enough. It requires a little more than normal braking pressure on the pedal to activate the system. If pressing harder on the brake pedal before releasing it doesn't keep the car from slipping backward, do Steps 1 and 2.

Step 1. Adjust Clutch.

The clutch pedal free play has to be set correctly before adjusting the hill-holder cable. Chapter 15, Procedure 1, explains how to check and adjust the clutch.

Step 2. Adjust Hill-Holder PHV Cable.

The pressure hold valve (PHV) is located on a ledge in the engine compartment below the master cylinder. A *cable* goes from the PHV unit to the top rear of the engine and connects to the **clutch release lever** (just above where the *clutch cable* attaches to the lever). This is where you adjust the cable.

On the end of the hill-holder cable, some models have an adjusting **knob** with a *groove* on one side that fits over a small *cylinder* that sits horizontally in an indented part of the clutch release lever. (The groove/cylinder arrangement prevents the knob from turning by itself.) When adjusting the cable, the knob must be turned ½ turn at a time so the groove fits over the cylinder.

On other models, there's a 14mm **adjusting nut** locked in place with an 8mm or 10mm **locknut** (just like the nuts on the end of the clutch cable). Before adjusting the hill-holder cable, use a wrench to hold the 14mm nut while turning the 8mm or 10mm nut a couple of turns *counterclockwise* (as viewed from the end of the cable). This frees the adjusting nut so the cable can be adjusted. After the cable is adjusted, use a wrench to hold the 14mm adjusting nut while you tighten the small nut against it to lock it in place.

When adjusting the cable, always use pliers to hold the solid part of the cable on the engine side of the clutch lever while turning the **adjusting nut or knob**. In other words, don't let the cable twist while turning the adjusting nut or knob.

Condition 1: If your Soob slowly rolls backward on hills, tighten the adjusting nut or knob ½ turn *clockwise* as viewed from the end of the cable. Try the hill-holder again and tighten the nut or knob a little more if necessary. Repeat the trial-and-adjust routine until the hill-holder holds the car. If you have the double nut setup, tighten the small nut against the 14mm nut.

If you run out of threads on the cable and can't tighten the nut enough to hold the car on a hill, the cable has stretched and needs replacing (Procedure 18, Step 1). If the brakes start staying on when the clutch pedal is released, you've tightened the nut or knob too much. Loosen it a little, then try the hill-holder again.

Condition 2: If the brakes release slowly when the clutch pedal is released and the engine tends to stall, unscrew the adjustment nut or knob about ½ turn *counterclockwise* as viewed from the end of the cable. (This makes the pin in the PHV move the ball away from the hole sooner.) Try the hill-holder on a hill and loosen the nut or knob ½ turn at a time until the brakes release when you let out on the clutch pedal. If the car starts slipping backwards on the hill, you've loosened it too much. Tighten it ½ turn, then check the hill-holder operation again.

Step 3. Increase PHV Angle.

Raising the front of the PHV will activate the hill-holder system on more gradual inclines. When changing the PHV angle, insert one shim, then test the car on a hill. If you want it to activate on even lesser inclines, insert one more shim, then test it again. Never install more than two shims. If more than two shims are needed, try adjusting the cable (Step 2). If the system still doesn't work, replace the PHV unit (Procedure 19).

To raise the front of the PHV unit, loosen the two 10mm bolts that attach the **PHV bracket** to the car body. Loosen but don't remove the 10mm bolt that attaches the *brake line junction block* to the side of the PHV bracket.

Slide a U-shaped shim (Subaru Part No. 725807000) under the front end of the PHV bracket. The shim should fit around the front mounting bolt.

Tighten the two 10mm bracket bolts and the 10mm brake line junction block bolt. Test the car on a gradual slope. Insert one more shim if necessary.

PROCEDURE 18: REPLACE HILL-HOLDER CABLE AND/OR RETURN SPRING

Condition: Hill-holder cable or return spring is broken; OR you're replacing the PHV unit.

Tools and Materials: Pliers. You might need the following: 10mm and 14mm wrenches, new cable, new return spring.

Step 1. Remove Hill-Holder PHV Cable.

Unscrew the *PHV cable adjusting nut or knob* until the cable can slide up and out of the slot in the *clutch release lever* (Procedure 17, Step 2). Save the adjusting nut and the little cylinder that fits on the cable (if there is one). Use pliers to remove the *spring clip* securing the cable to the bracket located in front of the clutch lever. Pull the cable up and out of the bracket. Follow the cable from the clutch lever to the PHV unit, releasing any clips or clamps securing the cable to the engine.

There's another spring clip attaching the cable to a bracket on the PHV. Remove it with pliers. Pull the cable around the PHV lever until it lines up with the slot in the lever. Pull the round cylinder on the end of the cable up and out of the lever.

Step 2. Install Hill-Holder PHV Cable.

To install the new cable, fit the round cylinder that's on one end of the cable into the hole on the PHV lever. Align the cable with the slot and push the cylinder down into the lever. Guide the cable around the lever so the cable housing (sheath) can fit into the slot on the bracket. Install a spring clip to secure the cable to the bracket. Now thread the cable up to the clutch lever so there are no sharp bends or kinks. Fit the cable into the bracket in front of the clutch lever and secure it with a spring clip. Slide the end of the cable down into the slot on the clutch lever. If your setup has a small cylinder, install and orient it so it fits horizontally into the indented part of the lever. Screw the adjusting nut onto the end of the cable. Use the old clips to attach the new cable to the engine in the same places where the old one was attached.

Now it's trial and adjust (T and A) time. Find a nice hill with little or no traffic to test the hill-holder. Start with the adjusting nut or knob positioned near the end of the cable. Keep trying the hill-holder then turning the adjusting nut about ½ turn *clockwise* until the hill-holder holds the car (Procedure 17).

Step 3. Replace PHV Return Spring.

Emergency situation: If your problem is that the brakes are locked so the car can't move and you are stuck in rush hour traffic with a roast in the oven at home, check the **return spring** on the top rear of the PHV unit. It's a short fat dude. Spring broken? If not, do Procedure 17, Step 2, Condition 2.

If the spring is broken, pull the handbrake ON, then remove the PHV adjusting nut or knob on the clutch lever end of the cable. Pull the cable out of the slot in the clutch lever. Put the little cylinder back on the end of the cable if it came off, then screw the adjusting nut or knob back on the cable so it doesn't get lost.

Reach down to the PHV unit and rotate the lever (where the cable is attached) *clockwise* toward the broken spring. This disarms the hill-holder. Buy a new PHV spring and install it. Read the next two paragraphs to find out how.

Non-emergency situation: If the spring is broken, use another car to round up a new spring, unless you've come here from the "Emergency Situation." Use pliers to unhook the old spring from the arm sticking out on the side of the PHV, then unhook the other end from the lever on the PHV.

To install the new spring, hook one end onto the PHV lever where the old spring was attached, then use pliers to hook the other end in the hole on the arm sticking out of the PHV. If you removed the clutch end of the cable from the clutch lever, install it now (Step 2), then adjust the hill-holder (Procedure 17).

PROCEDURE 19: REMOVE AND INSTALL HILL-HOLDER (PHV Unit)

Condition: You've adjusted the hill-holder cable and checked the return spring but the pressure hold valve (PHV) still isn't working. Remember, the hill-holder wasn't designed to work on slight inclines. Test it on a fairly steep hill. Check the cable to see if it might be broken (Procedure 17) before replacing the PHV unit. They rarely wear out.

PHV units can't be rebuilt; when they die they have to be replaced with a new unit.

Tools and Materials: To remove and install the PHV unit: 10mm socket, ratchet, short extension for the ratchet, 10mm flare-nut wrench, rag. To bleed the brake system after installing the unit, look at the tools and materials list in Procedure 2.

Step 1. Remove PHV Unit.

Use the rear bleeder valve on the master cylinder to drain the brake fluid from the primary (rear) end of the master cylinder (Procedure 3, Step 1).

Loosen the adjusting nut on the clutch lever end of the hill-holder cable enough to pull the cable up and out of the slot in the lever. Use pliers to remove the spring clip that attaches the cable to the bracket on the PHV unit. Release the cable end from the lever on the PHV unit (Procedure 18, Step 1).

Lay a rag beside the PHV unit to protect the paint from brake fluid. Now use a 10mm flare-nut wrench to completely unscrew the nuts that attach the three metal brake lines to the PHV unit. One is on the top, one on the bottom, and one screws into the rear. Don't pull the pipes out of the unit yet. Don't remove the brake lines attached to the small junction box.

Remove the 10mm bolts that attach the PHV holder to the ledge on the body. Lift up on the top brake line just enough so you can raise the PHV unit enough to clear the bottom brake line. Pull forward to remove the unit. If there's a shim (a U-shaped piece of metal) between the unit and the ledge, hang on to it and install it under the front of the PHV during installation.

Step 2. Install PHV Unit.

Lift the top brake line just enough to slide the new PHV unit and bracket into position on the car. Be sure all three brake lines go into the holes on the unit. Now install the bolts that secure the bracket to the ledge on the car body but don't tighten them yet. If there was a shim under the unit, slide it between the ledge and the unit so the front mounting bolt fits into the slot of the shim. Leave the unit loose so you can wiggle it while starting the brake line nuts.

Start all three brake line nuts into the unit. Screw them in at least halfway by hand. Wiggling the unit helps. Now tighten the bolts that secure the bracket to the ledge. Tighten the brake line nuts with a 10mm flare-nut wrench.

Look at Procedure 18, Step 2, to attach one end of the cable to the lever on top of the PHV and the other end to the clutch lever. Install the spring clip that secures the cable to the bracket on the PHV unit.

Step 3. Bleed the Brake System.

Tighten the rear bleeder valve on the master cylinder, then fill the reservoir with fresh DOT 3 or 4 brake fluid. Bleed the entire brake system (Procedure 2). Don't skimp here—this is very important for your health. After the brakes are bled, you can adjust the hill-holder (Procedure 17).

316 Chapter 13

CHAPTER 14

SUSPENSION AND STEERING

You've probably followed a car on a rough road or driven beside a car on a bumpy freeway and noticed how the car's wheels were moving up and down, following the contour of the road, yet the body of the car (and the passengers) were traveling along relatively smoothly. The phenomena you were witnessing was Suspension In Action! Without a suspension system, even small bumps would just about jar your teeth out and larger bumps would cause your car to be frequently airborne, making it impossible to steer. A suspension system that's in good order makes your ride both comfortable and safe.

Steering is lumped in with suspension because they are interrelated; in fact, they share several parts in common. Together they affect how your car deals with the road. The steering "geometry" is designed so your Soob has a tendency to want to go straight ahead. Wear in the various steering parts or parts that have been knocked out of adjustment or bent by hitting curbs after late nights out on the town change the geometry of the system. These changes are evident in many ways: the car wanders mindlessly across the road, impulsively darts here and there, wears the tires in funny patterns, or makes nerve-wracking noises on rough roads. These are the symptoms; now you get to play doctor with your Soob to diagnose and cure its ills. Procedure 1 tells you how to check the various suspension and steering parts.

Before jumping into how Subaru suspension and steering work, let me first describe a couple of the interrelated parts.

WHEEL BEARING HOUSINGS

The heart of the front suspension and steering on your Soob is a heavy chunk of metal called a **wheel bear-**

ing housing (also called a **steering knuckle** or just **knuckle**). There's a wheel bearing housing near the outer end of each **front axle**, next to the brakes. Holes for the **wheel bearings** and **axles** are machined into the sides of the knuckles, the **MacPherson struts** attach to the top and the **steering ball joints** attach to the bottom. A short **steering arm** sticking out the front of the knuckle is where the steering system connects to make the wheels turn. In other words, all of the front suspension and steering components, as well as the front axles, wheel bearings, brakes, and wheels are attached directly or indirectly to the two wheel bearing housings. Pretty important chunk of metal, eh?

BALL JOINTS

A **ball joint** is not a round marijuana cigarette or a whorehouse. It's a vital part of your steering/suspension setup. It's made of two pieces: a round steel ball with an end that's threaded like a bolt (a stud) and a steel socket that surrounds the ball. The socket also has a threaded bolt or nut-like end or mounting plate attached to it. When the "bolt" (stud) on the ball is attached to one part of the car and the attaching part of the socket is secured to a different part of the car, the two car parts are securely connected yet they are free to pivot all around the radius of the ball. The flexibility offered by the ball joints allows the different parts of the suspension and steering to change relative positions even though they are securely attached to one another. It's exactly how your hip and shoulder joints work, except the material is steel instead of bone.

There are three different ball joints on each side of your Soob. Let's name them. One is at the bottom of each wheel bearing housing and allows the wheels to move up and down and turn. We'll call this one the "**steering ball joint**." A 90° ball joint is at the end of each tie rod, so let's simply call this ball joint a "**tie rod end**." The third ball joint connects the tie rod to the steering rack. We'll call this one the "**tie rod ball joint**." (The tie rods and steering rack will be described in detail along with other parts of the steering system in the steering description ahead.) As the metal parts of the ball joint gradually wear away, the balls become loose in the sockets causing excessive play (movement) in the steering and/or suspension. We'll check for play in your ball joints in Procedure 1.

SUSPENSION

Some OHC models are equipped with a **pneumatic (air) suspension** system. Dealing with this high-tech system is beyond the home mechanic's means. So if your model has air suspension, you'll have to see the dealer for repairs. Sorry. Here's how the suspension on non-pneumatic Soobs works.

The front suspension system for Subarus combines strong heavy-duty coiled springs and double action (up and down) shock absorbers into units called **MacPherson Struts** (or just **struts**). One strut is located between each front wheel and the body. The **shock absorber**, which is inside the **coil spring**, has a dual purpose—it helps the coil spring absorb the shock of irregularities in the road such as potholes, tree stumps, armadillos, etc. and also "dampens" the springs so the car doesn't continue bouncing after hitting a bump.

The top of each strut is bolted to a bracket called the **strut tower** in the engine compartment and the lower end is attached to the top of the wheel bearing housing. The wheel bearing housings are located near the wheel end of the front axles and pivot when the steering wheel is turned. The bottom ends of the struts are made so they rotate along with the wheel bearing housings, allowing the front wheels to turn.

The bottom of the wheel bearing housing is connected through the steering ball joint to a steel plate called a **control arm** (sometimes called a wishbone or transverse link). The inner end of the control arm pivots up and down on a bolt near the center of the underside of the car, just behind the engine. Without the control arm, the front wheels would be free to flop out to the side of the car or tuck under the car like retractable landing gear on an airplane.

There is one more front suspension part you need to know about. To prevent the front wheels from end-

Suspension and Steering 319

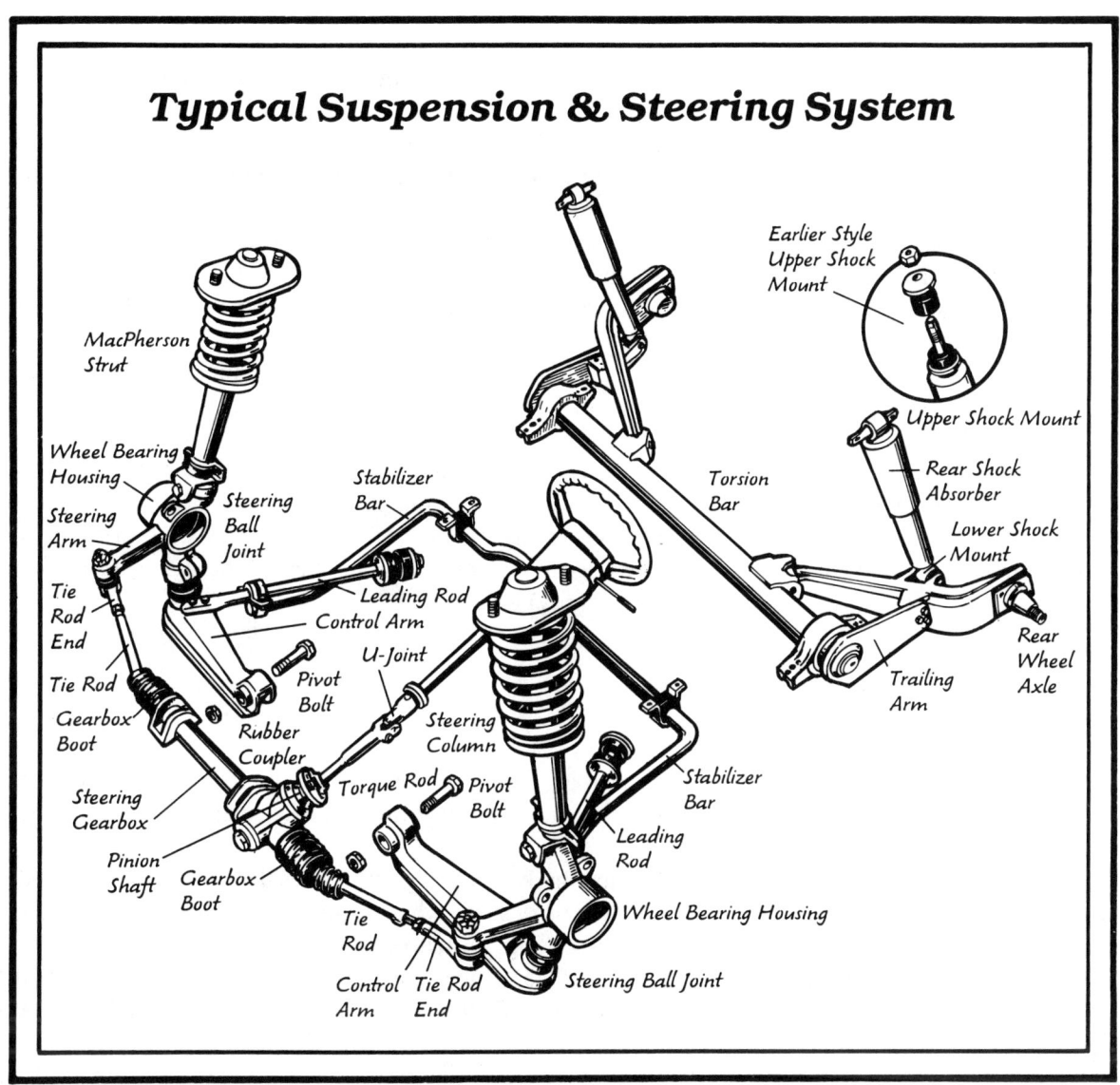

ing up under the front seats every time you hit a curb or ditch, one end of a strong steel rod called a **leading rod** is attached to the knuckle end of the control arm. The other end of the leading rod is attached securely to the car frame behind the front wheel.

The rear suspension on OHV Subarus consists of two strong steel **torsion bars**, two steel **trailing arms**, and two **shock absorbers** (shocks). The inner end of each torsion bar is bolted securely to the bottom center of the body and the outer end is mounted in a bracket about a foot and a half in front of each rear wheel. The outer end of each torsion bar is connected to the front end of a trailing arm. The trailing arm goes back to where it attaches to a rear axle and the bottom end of a shock absorber. The upper end of the shock is bolted to the body of the car.

When a rear wheel hits a bump or hole, the trailing arm twists the torsion bar. The flexing of the torsion bar absorbs the jolt. The shock absorber absorbs some of the shock, then dampens the spring action of the torsion bar so the car stops bouncing.

On OHC models, the rear suspension consists of two steel trailing arms and two shock absorbers. A strong steel coiled spring wrapped around each rear shock absorbs most of the jolt when you hit a bump. The shock absorber helps soften the shock, then dampens the coil spring so the car won't continue bouncing.

STEERING

Starting in 1981, Subaru offered power steering as an option on most models. The hydraulic system that operates the power steering is very complex and should be serviced by Subaru or a garage, not mortals like you and me. Other than the hydraulics, the system is similar to the regular steering system that I'm about to describe.

The **steering wheel** is attached to a long **steering shaft** that goes through the hollow **steering column** to a little **universal joint** (U-joint) in the engine compartment. The U-joint connects the steering shaft to one end of a shorter shaft called a **torque rod**. The torque rod connects (via a **rubber coupler**) to a **pinion shaft** that disappears into the **steering gearbox unit**. Inside the gearbox unit, a gear on the end of the pinion shaft meshes with gear teeth on a strong heavy steel bar called a **rack**. An automatic adjuster keeps the rack and pinion gears meshed properly.

As you turn the steering wheel, to the right, for example, gear teeth on the end of the pinion gear shaft engage the teeth on the rack and the rack is moved toward the right side of the car. This movement results in turned front wheels—here's how: As the rack moves it pushes on the right **tie rod** (a steel rod about as big around as your little pinky), which pushes on a short arm called a **steering arm** on the front of the right **wheel bearing housing**. This forces the front of the right wheel to move away from the car, that is, to the right. At the same time, the rack pulls on the left tie rod, which pulls inward on the steering arm on the front of the left wheel bearing housing causing the front of the left wheel to move inward (right), matching the movement of the right wheel. As you know, where the wheels go the car will surely (hopefully) follow.

WHEEL ALIGNMENT

Your front wheels have three attitudes toward the road: **caster**, **camber**, and **toe-in**. If the front end assembly is put together right, caster and camber are set for you. You can't change them without bending some of the heavy metal suspension parts.

Caster works kind of like the front wheels on supermarket shopping carts (when they work like they should, which is seldom). The wheels roll behind and below a pivot shaft, which helps the wheel decide which way it is going. In other words it makes the wheel "center-seeking"; it follows the lead of the pivot shaft.

Camber is the angle the wheels have to the road off the vertical plane. As you face the front of the car, the bottoms of the tires are slightly closer together than the tops. (Or they should be if things are right.) Subaru calls the camber angle "Zero Scrub Radius."

The toe-in, just like a pigeon-toed kid, is set so the wheels will run straight on the highway. Friction of the tires on the road tends to force them into the wall-eyed position, so you want them slightly toed-in, to counter this force. If they're wall-eyed (toed out), you will have steering and handling problems—the car will want to wander.

On Subarus the front toe-in is adjusted by changing the length of the tie rods. It's done with the Soob standing still. This is accomplished by screwing the tie rod ends farther onto or off of the tie rods. The rear wheel toe-in can be adjusted by moving the inner end of the torsion bars. Special expensive equipment is required to check the toe-in, so you have to take your Soob to Subaru or an alignment shop to have it checked and adjusted.

There's actually a fourth attitude that operates when you're turning a corner. It's called **steering axis inclination**. The wheel bearing housings are tilted so the tops of the housings are closer together than the bottoms when you look at them from the front end of the car, just the reverse of the wheel camber. This inclination is done for you by those clever Subaru engineers so that some semblance of proper wheel attitude is maintained when you zip around corners.

All this doesn't amount to diddly squat to you as long as it works OK, right? The attitudes are designed for proper road handling, safety, and minimal tire wear. They do fine until wear catches up with them; then comes the uneasy feeling that the car is doing more steering than you are, or the tires start wearing in funny patterns. Make a maintenance habit of running through Procedure 1 every 12,000 miles to locate and eliminate looseness (play) in the suspension and steering systems. You should be able to feel the play in plenty of time to do something about it.

PROCEDURE 1: CHECK SUSPENSION AND STEERING

Condition: Regular 12,000-mile maintenance; OR your Soob feels like a small boat on a stormy sea as you sail down the road; OR you hear clanks, clunks, or bangs every time you hit a bump; OR the tires are wearing in funny patterns.

Tools and Materials: Tire gauge, hard level ground, flashlight, safety glasses, Friend, large screwdriver, maybe a 12mm wrench, hammer, and a piece of chalk.

Step 1. Check Tire Pressure.

Check the tires and inflate them to the proper pressure. Chapter 7, Procedure 4, Step 2, tells you how. Read the rap on tires and tire pressure in Chapter 7 if you haven't already.

Step 2. Check Shocks and Struts.

Park the car on hard level ground and get the wheels pointing straight ahead. Bounce each corner of the car up and down a few times by pushing on the fender or end of the bumper. Pay particular attention to the first bounce. If the car bounces easier on the first push, then becomes harder, or continues to be easy to bounce, the shocks have reached the end of the trail. Healthy shocks and struts will resist your efforts equally on each push and the car will not move up and down more than twice when you stop pushing and let go.

The rear shock absorbers are long metal tubes bolted to the inside of the suspension arms just in front of where the rear wheels are attached. Be sure the car is in gear and the handbrake is on, then slide under the rear of the car. Look at the shocks where the smaller bottom part disappears into the larger top part. Any sign of wetness there means a seal inside the shock is broken and allowing the shock oil to leak out. The shock is doomed and should be replaced. Procedure 2 tells you how to do it.

To check the front shock absorber, kneel beside one of the front tires and look under the fender for the MacPherson strut. Peek through the coil spring at the shock absorber. Like the rear shocks, if you see oily wetness on the smaller part of the shock, it means the fluid is leaking and the shock should be replaced. Procedure 3 tells you how to remove the strut so you can take it to a garage to have the shock absorber replaced.

Step 3. Check for Clanks, Clunks, and Bangs.

Clanks, clunks, and bangs when you hit bumps means something is loose. Tracking down some rattles would turn even Sherlock Holmes into a babbling idiot. Usually it's the exhaust system or something rolling around in the trunk, but let's check the suspension to be sure.

If the clanks and bangs are coming from the rear of the car, put the car in 1st or Park, set the handbrake, chock the wheels, put on your safety glasses, and squeeze under the rear of the car. Don't jack it up.

Grab the bottom end of a rear shock just above the mounting bolt and shake it like you're strangling a cobra. Look for looseness in the rubber grommet at the bottom of the shock. Check both sides and tighten the shock nuts or bolts if the grommets are loose (Procedure 2, Step 4). If the grommet is gone, cracked or can't be tightened, try and round up new or used ones and install them. If you can't find any grommets the shock will have to be replaced (Procedure 2). While you're under the rear of the car, bump the exhaust pipe around a little with your hand (use a rag if the pipe is hot) to see if it's loose and hitting something. Clunks or squeaks? Turn to Chapter 12 to correct exhaust system problems.

Now crawl out and kneel beside one of the rear tires, reach over the top of the tire and grab the top of the shock. Strangle that cobra again. Try and move the shock up and down and side to side. If the shock feels loose, look at Procedure 2, Steps 1 and 4, to tighten the upper shock bolts. As with the lower grommet, if the rubber is cracked, AWOL, or can't be tightened, try and find new or used grommets to install or the shock must be replaced (Procedure 2). Check both rear shocks.

If clanks and bangs are coming from the front of the car, there's a slight possibility the MacPherson strut isn't securely bolted to the wheel bearing housing or the mounting bracket in the engine compartment. The two 14mm bolts that attach the strut to the wheel bearing housing and the two 14mm strut mounting nuts in the engine compartment should all be torqued to 29 ft. lbs.

Step 4. Vibrations or Shimmies.

Vibrations in the car, or steering wheel shimmies (steering wheel moves rapidly side to side), that increase in intensity as the car's speed increases can mean one of several things.

1. A tire is out of balance. Have the tires dynamically balanced by Subaru or an alignment shop.

2. The front wheel alignment (toe-in) is incorrect. Are the front tires wearing out faster on either the inside or outside edge? If so, have the alignment checked by Subaru, an alignment shop, or tire shop, not a department store garage.

3. A DOJ (double offset joint) or CVJ (constant velocity joint) on one of the axles is kaput. You'll feel a solid vibration in the seat of your pants rather than steering wheel shimmy. Chapter 15 tells how to check DOJs and CVJs.

4. The 4WD driveshaft is bent, out of balance, or has worn U-joints. See Chapter 15.

5. Ball joints, wheel bearings, or bushings in the front suspension are worn. We'll check all these in the next few steps.

Step 5. Check the Steering Wheel Free Play.

Open the driver's window and turn the steering wheel as you watch the left front wheel (the key has to be turned to the first click to release the steering lock). Move the steering wheel right and left a little. How much does it move before the front tire starts to move? This slack in movement is called **steering play** and should be no more than 1 inch. More than an inch? Open the hood and prop it. Have Friend rock the steering wheel back and forth while you watch the steering gearbox. Worn rubber mounting adapters will let the gearbox move instead of forcing the rack to move. If the gear box moves more than the slightest amount, see your local freindly Subaru dealer or independent garage for gearbox removal and rubber adapter replacement.

A number of other components can contribute to excessive steering play, so let's check them out. Don't forget to turn the key off.

Step 6. Check and Replace the Steering U-joint.

Open the hood and prop it. Grab the steering shaft with one hand on each side of the U-joint and twist your hands in opposite directions. Look for play in the center of the joint and where the joint attaches to the shafts. If the U-joint is loose on one of the shafts, try tightening the 12mm clamp bolt. If that doesn't remove the play, or you saw looseness in the U-joint, you need a new U-joint.

Before replacing a U-joint, make a note of which end of the U-joint has the longest clamp so you can install the new one the same as the old one. Use chalk or paint to make a line on each shaft where the slot in the clamp goes. The new U-joint slots must be in exactly the same position as they were on the old U-joint. This will keep the steering wheel centered.

Remove the two 12mm clamp bolts and nuts, then use a small hammer to tap the U-joint up the steering shaft or down the torque rod shaft until the other end can be removed. Slide the other end of the U-joint off. Try not to turn the steering wheel while the U-joint is off.

To install the new U-joint, line up the slot in the longer end of the joint with the line you made on the shaft. Slide the joint onto the shaft far enough to fit the other end of the joint onto the other shaft. Line up the slot in the other end of the U-joint with the line you made on the other shaft, then slide the joint onto the shaft. Line up the bolt holes with the flat spot or groove on the shafts, then install the 12mm pinch bolts, lockwashers, and nuts and tighten them.

Step 7. Check and Replace the Rubber Coupler.

See that round thing at the bottom of the torque rod? That's a *rubber coupler*. It has four nuts sticking out of it. Check it for play and looseness by turning the steering shaft back and forth. If the rubber is frayed, fried, or cracked in places, replace it with a new one. Here's how.

First, remove the U-joint (Step 6). Then remove the two 12mm nuts and lockwashers on the rubber coupler; they are between the two nuts on the torque rod. Wiggle the torque rod and coupler off the two bolts. You can now take the unit out of the car. Remove the two 12mm bolts, nuts, and lockwashers that attach the coupler to the torque rod. Separate the coupler from the torque rod.

Got the new coupler in hand? OK, slide the two 12mm bolts through the new coupler, then stick the bolts through the holes on the torque rod. If there's a little skirt on the coupler, it goes on the side that's away from the torque rod. Install the lockwashers and nuts and tighten them. Now put the unit back in the car. Set the coupler over the two pinion shaft bolts. Install the lockwashers and nuts and tighten them. Install the U-joint and tighten the clamp bolts (Step 6).

Recheck to make sure all the bolts are installed and snug. Your life depends on them.

Step 8. Check Tie Rod End Ball Joints.

To check the tie rod ends for play, put on your safety glasses, grab your flashlight, and slide under the front of the car (be sure the handbrake is on and the transmission is in 1st or Park). Just inside the front of each front tire is a tie rod end. It connects the steering arm of the wheel bearing housing to the tie rod, which disappears into the rubber boot under the engine.

Grab the tie rod and try to move it side to side while watching the rubber part of the tie rod end. If the rubber moves, it means the ball is loose in the socket. Now push up and pull down on the bottom of the tie rod end. Have Friend rock the steering wheel back and forth while you watch the tie rod ends. There should be NO movement in the rubber. You should be able to twist the tie rod end a little—that's normal. Tighten the castle nut to 29 ft. lb. if it appears loose (Procedure 6, Step 6).

Check the tie rod end on the other side of the car the same way. Replace the tie rod end(s) if your test tells you the ball joint is loose (Procedure 6).

Replace rubber ball joint boots that are cracked, torn, or missing (Procedure 6, Steps 1, 3, 6, and 7). You'll probably have to get the boots from Subaru.

Step 9. Check Tie Rod (Inner) Ball Joint.

Chock the rear wheels, jack up the front of the car, and block it safely. Get both wheels off the ground.

The tie rod ball joints are hiding inside the accordion-looking rubber boots where you can't see them. You can check them for wear though. Like this.

Point the front wheels straight ahead. Now get down where you can see both tie rods and lightly push out and pull in on the front of one of the tires. Watch the two tie rods. They should move at exactly the same time and move exactly the same amount. If one moves slightly before the other, one or both of the tie rod ball joints is loose. See Procedure 10. Grab the tie rod and try to move it front to back. If you hear a clunk and feel movement, the bushing in the end of the steering gearbox is worn and should be replaced (see the pros).

Check the accordion-style rubber boots on the steering gearbox for tears and holes. Procedure 10, Steps 1-8 (skip Step 6), will enlighten you about replacement.

Step 10. Check Steering Ball Joint.

The rear wheels are chocked and the front of the car is jacked up and resting on jackstands, right? The front wheels have to be off the ground for this test.

The steering ball joint connects the bottom of the wheel bearing housing to the outer end of the control arm. Here's how to test the ball joint for play. Put a large screwdriver on the control arm right next to the ball joint. Put the end of the screwdriver under the bottom of the wheel bearing housing (check the illustration). Now push down on the screwdriver handle and watch for looseness in the ball joint. If the control arm moves down under the pressure of the screwdriver more than .012" (about the thickness of the cover of this book), the ball joint is worn and should be replaced (Procedure 4).

Replace the rubber boots on the ball joints with new boots from Subaru if they are cracked, torn, or missing (Procedure 4, Steps 1, 2, 4, and 5).

Step 11. Check Control Arm Bushing.

The front of the car must be on jackstands to do this step.

To check the control arm bushing have Friend grab the bottom of the tire and try to move it in and out while you watch the inner end of the control arm. The control arm should be rigidly attached to the crossmember with no sign of play around the mounting bolt. Found some play? See Procedure 5.

Step 12. Check Wheel and Wheel Bearings.

Jack up the front of the car and put it on jackstands (if it isn't already).

If there was movement in the wheel while Friend rocked it back and forth in Step 10, but the ball joint and control arm bushing checked out OK, the wheel is loose on the hub (check the lug nuts for tightness) or the wheel bearings are shot.

Ask Friend to hold the steering wheel steady while you grasp the front wheel at the 9 and 3 o'clock positions. Rock the tire back and forth and feel for movement. Try the 12 and 6 o'clock positions. If the wheel bearing is loose, you'll feel movement in all directions and you've probably been hearing some low pitched growls and rumbling coming from the front of the car as you've been driving. See Procedure 7.

Step 13. Finish Up.

Lower the car if it's on jackstands. Now that you've diagnosed the suspension and steering, let's remedy any maladies that were observed.

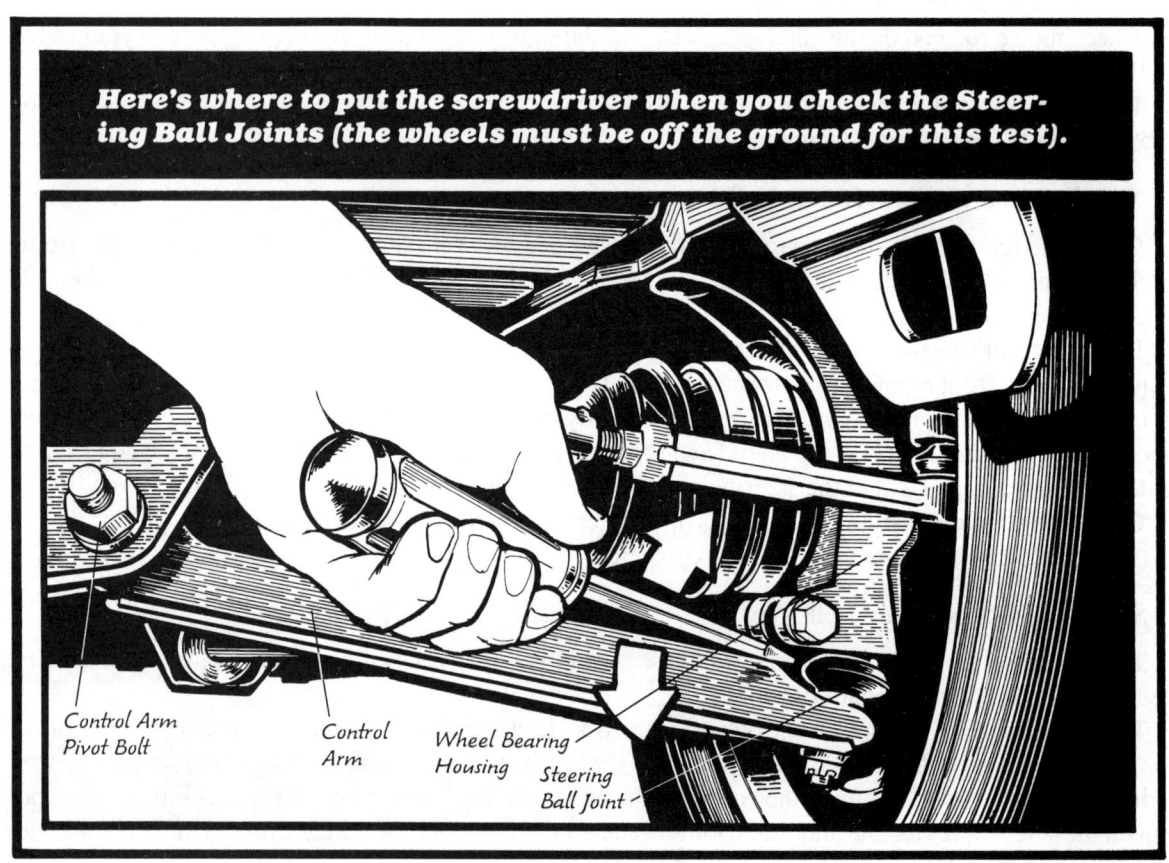

PROCEDURE 2: REPLACE REAR SHOCKS

This procedure does not cover models with pneumatic (air) suspension.

Condition: Rear shocks or shock bushings have expired.

Tools and Materials: Phase 1 tool kit, two new rear shock absorbers, penetrating oil.

Remarks: Because of the way the rear shocks are attached, all people with '75-'79 cars and '77-'81 Brats will be referred to as **NUT PEOPLE**. All people with '80 and newer cars and '82 and newer Brats are hereby named **BOLT PEOPLE**.

Always replace both rear shocks at the same time or the car's handling characteristics will change frightfully.

If the rubber grommets are worn out but the shock seems good otherwise, try to buy new ones or round up some used ones and install them.

CAUTION!: On OHC models, the rear shock absorbers are surrounded by a strong steel spring that's under a lot of tension. Once the shock absorber is removed from the car it must be taken to Subaru or a garage to have the new shock installed. DON'T remove the nuts from the top of the shock absorber!

Step 1. Locate Upper Shock Mount.

'75-'79 Cars:

Station Wagon: Fold the top of the rear seat forward and locate a plastic cap on the front edge of the wheel hump. Unscrew the phillips screws (if you have them), then pry off the plastic cap.

Sedan, Coupe, and Hardtop: There are two 10mm bolts at the bottom front edge of the rear seat, or between the seat bottom and back (push down on the rear of the seat bottom to see them). Remove the two bolts. Lift up on the seat bottom and remove the seat from the car. Remove the two 10mm bolts at the bottom of the seat back. Lift up on the cushion to unhook it, then remove it from the car. Remove the screws from the top of the cardboard panel behind the seat back. Lift up on the cardboard until it clears the hooks on the bottom, then remove it from the car. Look for two short threaded bolts sticking into the car from the round wheel hump. You might have to remove a piece of garbage bag type plastic to see them.

'77-'81 Brats: Use pliers to unscrew the two knurled nuts under the front edge (the part facing the rear) of each jump seat. Remove the seats. Unscrew the two phillips screws that secure that bulbous thing on the front edge of the round wheel well. Remove the bulbous thing.

'80 and newer cars and '82-'87 Brats: Two upper shock mounting bolts are located in the rear wheel well just inside the top of the rear tire.

Step 2. Release Upper Shock Mount.

NUT PEOPLE: Note that there are two nuts on the bolt and the end of the bolt is flattened on two sides. Squirt some penetrating oil on the mounting bolts. Use a 14mm wrench to hold the bottom nut while you remove the top nut with a 14mm wrench or socket.

Hold the square part of the mounting bolt with a crescent wrench, Vise Grips, or large pliers while you remove the bottom 14mm nut. Remove the large washer (note which side is out), then remove the rubber pad. Remove the nuts, washer, and rubber pad from the other shock.

BOLT PEOPLE: Jack up the rear of the car and put it safely on blocks. 4WD models have a lot of clearance, so you probably don't need to jack and block them. I don't, but you can if you'd rather. Use a 17mm socket and ratchet to remove the two upper shock mounting bolts. They're usually pretty tight so you might have to use a cheater bar (a 2-3' long piece of pipe) on the ratchet handle for added leverage. Use a husky ½" drive socket and ratchet if you have them.

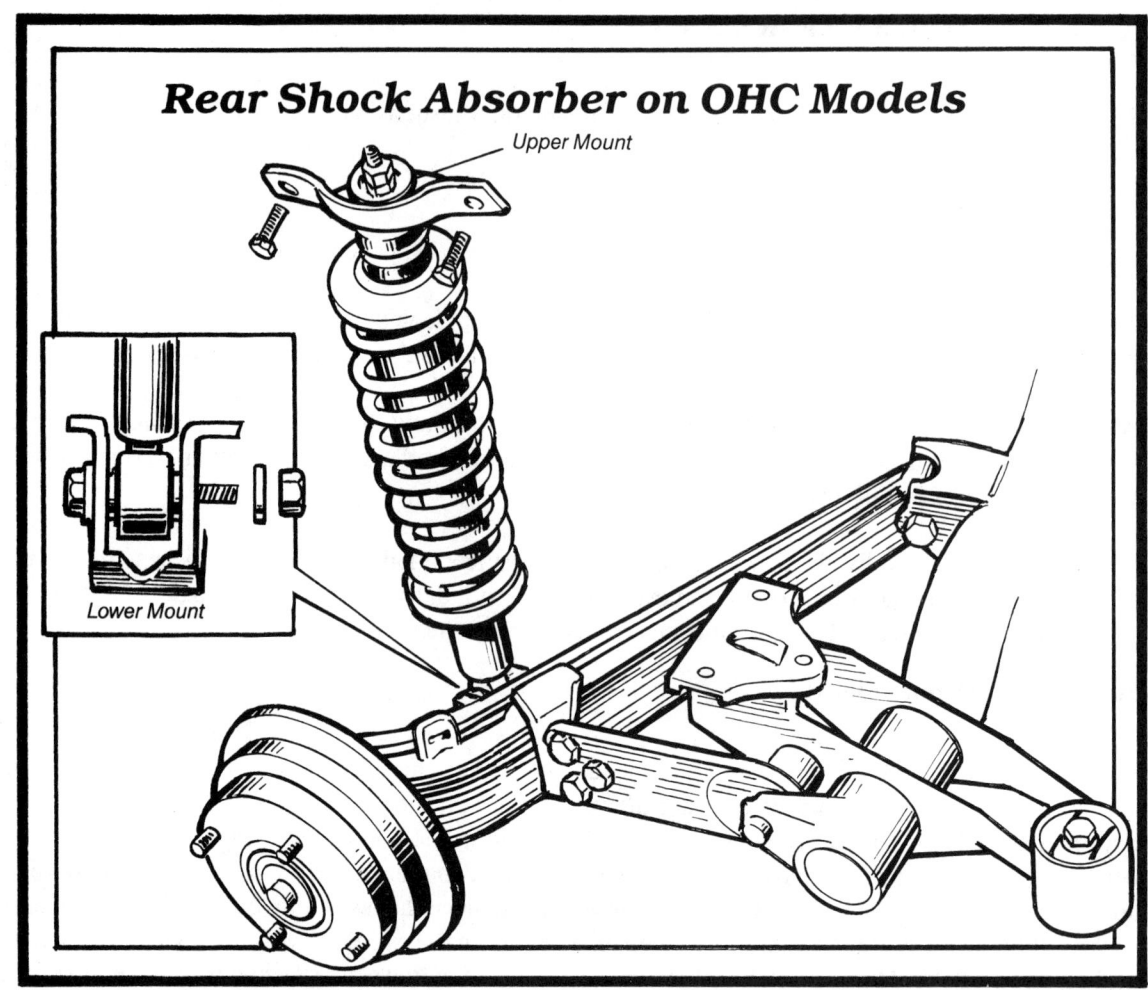

Rear Shock Absorber on OHC Models
Upper Mount
Lower Mount

Step 3. Remove Lower Shock Mounting Nut or Bolt.

NUT PEOPLE: Chock the front wheels, jack up the car, and put it safely on blocks. 4WDs have enough clearance that you probably don't need to jack them up. Choice is yours, though. Squirt some penetrating oil on the lower shock mounting nut and bolt and let it soak a few minutes. Use a 14mm wrench or socket to loosen the nut *counterclockwise* about ¼ turn. Continue to squirt penetrating oil on the nut as you loosen it to keep the threads clean. Remove the nut, lockwasher, and large washer. Slide (or pry) the shock off the mounting bolt.

BOLT PEOPLE: Squirt penetrating oil around the bolt head, between the shock and bracket, and on the nut the mounting bolt screws into. Unscrew the 17mm bolt *counterclockwise* a little at a time. We want to avoid breaking the bolt, so if it seems to tighten while you're unscrewing it, douse everything with penetrating oil, then screw the bolt back in a little; then douse everything with penetrating oil again and unscrew it a little. Repeat the in-and-out routine as many times as necessary. When the bolt is out, wrestle the shock out of its bracket.

OHC models: If you are replacing the shocks, take the old ones to Subaru or a garage to have the new shocks installed in the coil spring. Don't try to do this at home—it's very dangerous.

Step 4. Install Shock Absorber.

OHV models: Before installing a new shock, hold it upright the way it will be installed. Hold the bottom end and extend the top end as far as it will go, then push the top of the shock down until it hits bottom. Do this a few times to purge the air from the shock oil. (This isn't necessary if you're installing gas filled shocks.) Compare the resistance in the new shocks to each other and to the resistance in the old shocks. If the new shocks aren't equally hard to pump or aren't significantly harder to pump than the old shocks, you either bought some cheap dimestore shocks or the new shocks are defective. Return them and get some good ones. Don't laugh, two out of the last four "major brand" shocks I've tried to install were defective!

EVERYONE: Clean the threads of the mounting bolts and nuts with a wire brush, then give them a light coat of oil.

NUT PEOPLE: Follow the directions that came with the shocks and install a flat washer and a rubber grommet on the top installing bolt of the shock. No instructions? Install the new ones like the old ones. Hold the shock in its installed position and push the bottom rubber grommet over the lower shock mounting bolt. Install the large flat washer on the bolt with the concave side facing out toward the threads. Slide the lockwasher on the bolt, then screw the nut on the threads but don't tighten it yet. Guide the upper mounting bolt through the hole in the body.

From inside the car, install the other grommet, flat washer, and one of the mounting nuts. Follow the directions that came with the new shock and tighten the nut. No instructions? Tighten the nut until the rubber grommet bulges almost to the outer edge of the washer. Install the locknut (top nut) and tighten it while holding the bottom nut with another wrench. Go back to the lower mounting nut and tighten it to 32 ft. lbs. Now install the shock on the other side of the car.

Lower the car if it's on jackstands, install the piece of cardboard and rear seats if they were removed, or the upper shock bolt cover on station wagons and Brats. Brat people! Don't forget to install the jump seats. Now go for a nice smooth ride.

BOLT PEOPLE: Slide the bottom end of the shock into the bracket. Get the bottom bolt started into the threads, then install the top two bolts and get them started. When you're sure all the threads are straight, torque all three bolts to 85 ft. lbs.

Lower the car if it's on jackstands, then go for a ride. Quite a difference, eh?

PROCEDURE 3: REPLACE FRONT STRUTS

This procedure does not cover models with pneumatic (air) suspension.

Condition: Front shocks are worn; maybe the front coil springs are worn or broken.

Tools and Materials: Jack and jackstands, Phase 1 tool kit, rags, Friend. '80 and newer cars and '82-'87 Brats will need a can or jar to catch brake fluid, baggies and rubber bands, a pint of fresh DOT 3 OR 4 brake fluid, four new brake line to caliper gaskets, rags.

CAUTION: Once the strut assemblies are off the car, take them to a garage to have new shock absorbers installed. Special, expensive tools are required to handle the extreme tension on the coil springs. Even some experienced mechanics with proper tools have broken bones and horror stories about the time the tool slipped...

Step 1. Chock, Jack, and Block.

Loosen the front lug nuts a little, jack up the car and put it on jackstands. Remove the wheels.

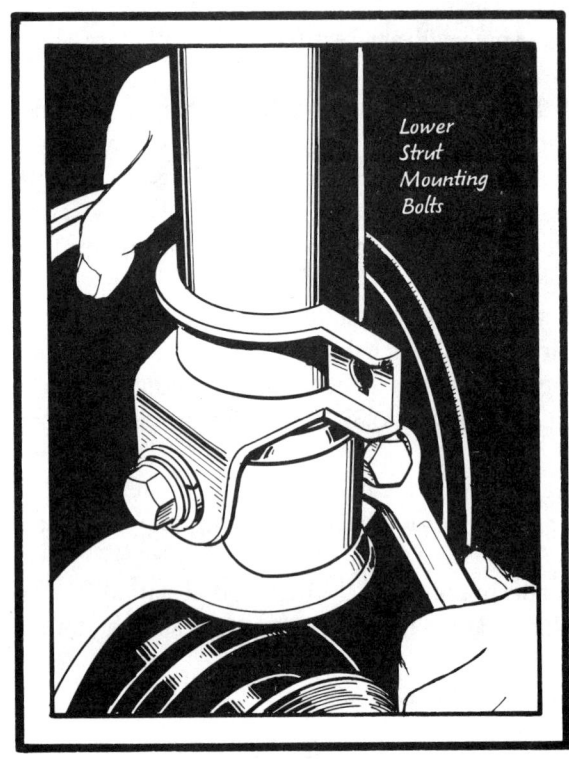

Step 2. Remove Lower Strut Mounting Bolts.

Locate two 14mm bolts near the bottom end of the strut. One bolt goes through a bracket attached to the strut and the other bolt goes through a slot on the wheel bearing housing. Remove the two bolts.

Step 3. Disconnect Tie Rod End From Bearing Housing.

See Procedure 6, Step 3, for tie rod end removal.

Step 4. Loosen Upper Strut Mounting Nuts.

Open the hood and prop it. Locate the two large strut towers in the engine compartment. They're straight above the wheels. You'll see a round black thing sticking out of each of the towers. One strut mounting nut is in front of the black thing and the other nut is to the rear of it, or on OHC models there are three nuts around the black thing. Loosen the 14mm nuts two turns. DON'T mess with the nut under the rubber cap in the center of the strut.

Step 5. Remove Brake Line.

'75 models with front drum brakes: You can't move the metal brake line out of the way. Just be very careful to not bend it while wrestling the bottom of the strut out of and into the wheel bearing housing. DON'T disconnect the brake line from the wheel cylinder.

'75-'79 models with front disc brakes and '77-'81 Brats: Push the rubber brake hose and bracket toward the engine and away from the strut. Tie them out of the way with string or wire. DON'T disconnect the brake lines!

'80 and newer cars and '82-'87 Brats: Lay some clean rags over the top of the brake caliper to protect it from brake fluid and penetrating oil.

Use pliers to remove the clip that attaches the rubber brake hose to the bracket on the side of the strut. Remove the 14mm brake line bolt (union bolt) that attaches the brake hose to the caliper. Pry the fitting out of the slot and stick the end of the hose in a can or jar to catch the fluid. Screw the union bolt back into the caliper to keep dirt out. Be careful not to let any brake fluid get on the brake pads or disc. When the fluid has drained out of the line, pull the hose toward the front of the car and through the strut bracket. Put a baggie over the end of the hose to protect it from dirt. Secure it with a rubber band.

Step 6. Separate Strut from Housing.

Tap the end of a regular-size screwdriver into the slot on the side of the wheel bearing housing until it touches the strut. Grab the strut with both hands and twist it back and forth to loosen it. If it's stuck, squirt penetrating oil into the slot and around the area where the strut fits into the housing. Let the penetrating oil do its thing for a few minutes, then try twisting the strut again. Keep at it until you can turn the strut in the housing.

Now comes the teamwork. Have Friend push down on the end of the axle while you wiggle and pull the strut toward the outside of the car and out of the housing.

If you don't have any Friends, or just want to do it yourself, you can use a long board or pipe as a pry bar to pry down on the axle. I use the removable handle from my cheap floor jack. Put one end of the pry bar under the car body at the rear of the wheel well and the middle of the bar over the axle. Push down on the end of the bar with your knee while you pull the strut out of the wheel bearing housing. Be careful! Think about where your knee will end up if the bar slips.

Step 7. Remove Strut.

To simplify installing the struts after the shock absorber is replaced, use chalk or paint to make an R (right) or L (left) on the front of the round black thing (the top of the shock) in the engine compartment so you know which side is front and which side of the car the strut is on.

Hold the strut with one hand (or have Friend hold it) while you remove the 14mm nuts and lockwashers from the upper strut bolts. Remove the strut from the car.

Now do Steps 1 through 7 for the other front strut. Remember, it's mandatory to replace left and right shocks together.

Step 8. Take Struts to Expert.

Take the struts to a garage to have the shock absorbers replaced. Tell them to be sure to check the thrust washer for cracks, and ask them to put grease on it when reassembling the strut.

Have them check the coil spring for cracks while the strut is apart.

Step 9. Orient Strut Assembly.

Install each strut on the same side it was on when you removed it. You'll know which side is which and what's front by your paint marks. If the marks disappeared (or you didn't mark them) follow the instructions below.

'75-'77 models: Look for arrows on the top of the strut near the mounting bolts. If there are arrows, follow the installation directions for '78 and newer OHV models. If there are no arrows, the top can be installed in either direction.

'78 and newer OHV models: Look at the top of the strut. If you have a two-wheel-drive Sedan, Coupe, or Hatchback and NO power steering, orient the top of the strut so the arrow near the S or Sedan is pointed toward the front of the car. If you have a Station Wagon, 4WD, or any vehicle WITH power steering, orient the strut so the arrow near the V4, 4WD, VAN, or PS is pointed toward the front.

'85 and newer OHC models: Orient the strut assemblies so the three bolts fit through the three holes in the strut towers.

Step 10. Install Strut.

Orient the strut (Step 9), then slide it up under the fender and push the two strut mounting bolts through the holes in the mounting bracket in the engine compartment. Install the flat washers, lockwashers, and nuts. Don't fully tighten the nuts yet.

Have Friend push down on the axle (or use the pry bar method) while you guide the lower end of the strut into its hole on the wheel bearing housing. Tap

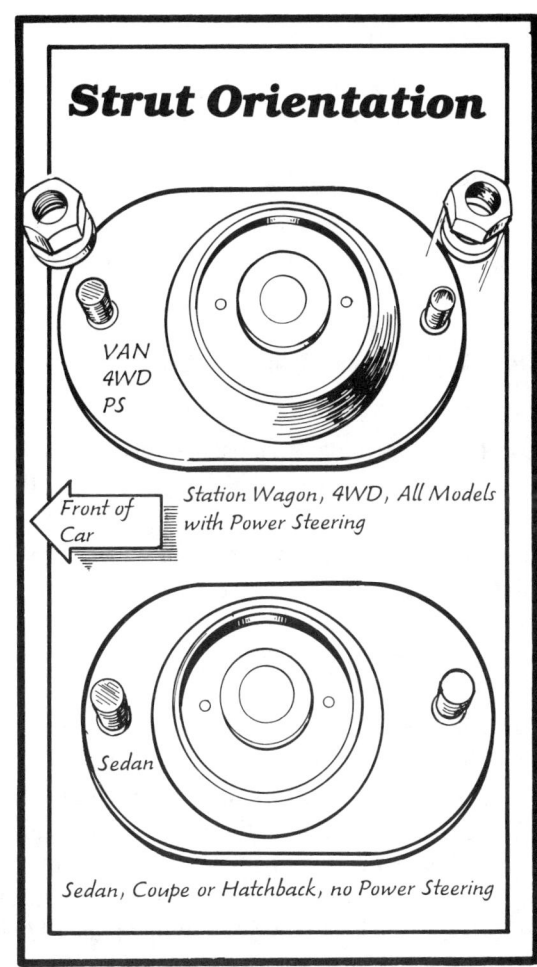

a medium screwdriver blade into the slot on the wheel bearing housing, then wiggle the housing upward until the top of the housing touches the bottom of the strut. Twist the strut so the hole in the strut bracket lines up with the hole on the housing. Wiggle the screwdriver out of the slot.

'75-'79 cars and '77-'81 Brats: Position the brake line bracket so the holes line up with the bolt holes on the housing.

EVERYONE: Install the short mounting bolt through the brake line bracket (if you have one), the strut bracket, and into the housing. Install the long mounting bolt through the brake line bracket (if you have one) and into the bolt hole that goes through the pinch bolt slot on the housing. Torque the two mounting bolts at the bottom of the strut and the mounting nuts in the engine compartment to 29 ft. lbs.

Step 11. Install Tie Rod End.

Look at Procedure 6, Step 6, to install the tie rod end. Use a new cotter pin.

Step 12. Connect Rubber Brake Hose ('80 and newer cars and '82-'87 Brats).

Check the brake line hose for cracks, and worn or bulging spots. Install a new hose if the old one is cracked, or has worn or bulging places. Chapter 13, Procedure 11, tells how to connect or replace the rubber brake line hoses. Be sure to put the hose through the inner bracket on the strut and secure it with the clip before bolting the union fitting to the caliper.

Step 13. Install Wheels.

Put the wheels on and snug down the lug nuts, lower the car, and torque the lug nuts to 72 ft. lbs. Install the hubcaps if you removed them.

Step 14. Bleed the Brakes ('80 and newer cars and '82-'87 Brats).

Fill the master cylinder with fresh brake fluid, then adjust the rear brakes (Chapter 13, Procedure 1). Bleed the master cylinder, then the front brakes, then the entire brake system (Chapter 13, Procedure 2).

PROCEDURE 4: REMOVE AND REPLACE STEERING BALL JOINT

Condition: You detected looseness in the steering ball joint when checking the suspension or steering; OR you need to remove the wheel bearing housing or the control arm.

Tools and Materials: Jack and jackstands, Phase 1 tool kit, new cotter pin for the castle nut, maybe a new ball joint, maybe a tube of Loctite Stud 'n' Bearing Mount.

'75-'79 cars and '77-'81 Brats also require three new self-locking nuts for each ball joint you remove and a ½" x ¾" spacer (see Remarks).

Remarks: It's best to replace both steering ball joints at the same time. If one joint has reached the end of the trail, the other one is probably close behind.

The ½" x ¾" spacer required to separate the ball joint from the wheel bearing housing on '75-'79 cars and '77-'81 Brats can be a ½" thick piece of metal like a chisel handle, a socket, or a nut. The spacer has to be at least ¾" wide to cover the ball joint castle nut.

If you can't find new self-locking nuts, get a tube of Loctite Stud 'n' Bearing Mount and squirt a little on the bolt threads just before screwing on the old nuts.

Step 1. Chock, Jack, and Block.

Loosen the front lug nuts a little, then jack up the front of the car and put it safely on jackstands. Remove the front wheels.

Step 2. Separate Ball Joint from Wheel Bearing Housing.

EVERYONE: Look at the illustration to see where your ball joint castle nut is located. Squirt some penetrating oil on the threads sticking out of the castle nut. Use needlenose pliers to straighten the end of the cotter pin, then pull the cotter pin out of the castle nut.

'75-'79 cars and '77-'81 Brats: Unscrew the 19mm castle nut until the top is even with the end of the stud threads. Put a ½" spacer between the castle nut and the wheel bearing housing, then continue to unscrew the castle nut. This will force the tapered ball joint stud down and out of the wheel bearing housing.

'80 and newer cars and '82-'87 Brats: Remove the 14mm bolt that attaches the top of the ball joint to the wheel bearing housing. Tap the end of a large screwdriver into the slot on the housing, then pry down on the control arm to pop the ball joint out.

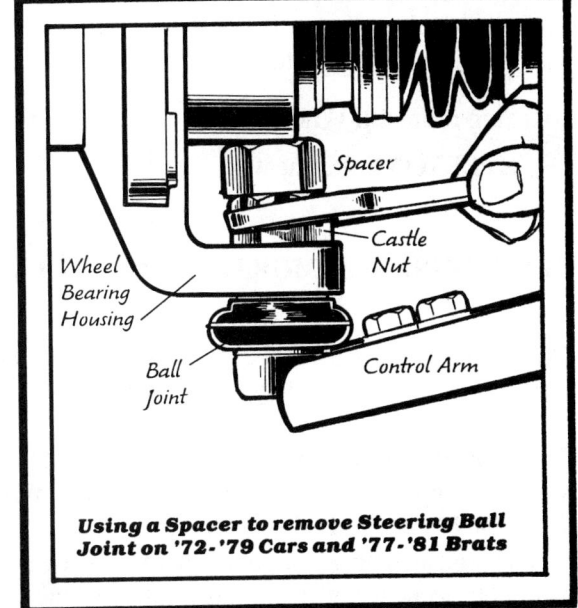

Using a Spacer to remove Steering Ball Joint on '72-'79 Cars and '77-'81 Brats

Step 3. Separate Ball Joint from Control Arm.

'75-'79 cars and '77-'81 Brats: Unscrew the three 17mm nuts that attach the bottom of the ball joint to the control arm. You'll have to hold the bolt heads with another 17mm wrench. Remove the three bolts, then push down on the control arm. If you're here to remove the ball joint, pull it out now.

'80 and newer cars and '82-'87 Brats: Unscrew the 19mm castle nut from the bottom of the control arm.

If you're removing the ball joint, put a block of wood on the end of the bolt, then tap the ball joint up and out of the control arm. Be sure there's room for it to clear the wheel bearing housing by pulling down on the control arm.

If you're here from Procedure 5 to remove the control arm, put a large screwdriver between the top of the control arm and the bottom of the wheel bearing housing. Pry down on the screwdriver the same as you do when checking the ball joint in Procedure 1, Step 10.

Step 4. Install Ball Joint.

Friction between the tapered ball joint stud and its hole in the steering arm or control arm is what prevents the bolt from turning while you tighten the castle nut—so clean the tapered surfaces of the stud and hole with a clean, dry rag before installing the ball joint.

'75-'79 cars and '77-'81 Brats: Bolt the ball joint to the bottom of the control arm with the three 17mm bolts and self-locking nuts. Be sure the rubber boot is above the end of the control arm. Torque the nuts to 90 ft. lbs. while holding the bolt heads with another wrench.

'75-'79 cars and '77-'81 Brats: Use a nail or small punch in the cotter key hole to twist the ball joint stud so the hole is going front to rear. This makes it easier to install the cotter key. Push down on the control arm far enough so you can slide the ball joint stud into its hole on the wheel bearing housing. Give the bottom of the ball joint a couple of light taps with a hammer to seat the stud in the hole. Install the castle nut and tighten it with a 19mm wrench. Tap the bottom some more if the stud turns. The torque is supposed to be 28 ft. lbs. but your torque wrench won't fit, right? So, get the bolt medium tight, then tighten it a little farther until you can slide a new cotter pin through the castle nut and bolt. Bend the ends of the cotter pin up over the top of the bolt.

'80 and newer cars and '82-'87 Brats: Slide the ball joint stud through its hole on the control arm. Use a screwdriver to spread the slot on the wheel bearing housing while you insert the upper end of the ball joint into its place. Tap up on the bottom of the control arm with a hammer (don't hit the ball joint bolt) to seat the ball joint. Install the upper mounting bolt into the housing, then screw on the castle nut. Torque them both to 29 ft. lbs. Tighten the castle nut farther if necessary to install a new cotter pin. Twist the ends of the pin over the end of the ball joint stud.

Step 5. Install Wheels.

EVERYONE: Put the wheels on and snug the lug nuts. Lower the car and torque the lug nuts to 72 ft. lbs.

PROCEDURE 5: REMOVE AND REPLACE CONTROL ARM

Condition: Control arm is bent; OR The rubber bushing on the inner end of the control arm and/or the rubber grommets on the leading rod are worn out.

Tools and Materials: EVERYONE: Jack and jackstands, Phase 1 tool kit, new cotter pins for the steering ball joint castle nuts, maybe a tube of Loctite Stud 'n' Bearing Mount (see Remarks).

'75-'79 cars and '77-'81 Brats: For each control arm you're removing; three new self-locking nuts for the ball joint attaching bolts, one self-locking leading rod nut, and one new self-locking nut for the control arm pivot bolt. Maybe new grommets for the leading rod and/or new bushings for the pivot bolt.

'80 and newer cars and '82-'87 Brats: For each control arm you're removing; two self-locking nuts for the leading rod bolts and one new self-locking nut for the inner pivot bolt. Maybe a new control arm bushing. If you're removing the leading rod to replace the grommets, you'll need new grommets and a new self-locking nut for the rear end of the rod.

Remarks: If you can't find new self-locking nuts, squirt a little Loctite Stud 'n' Bearing Mount on the bolt threads just before screwing on the old self-locking nuts.

Step 1. Chock, Jack, and Block.

Chock the rear wheels, loosen the front wheel lug nuts a little, jack up the car and put it securely on jackstands. Remove the wheels.

Step 2. Separate Control Arm from Ball Joint.

Look at Procedure 4, Step 3, to separate the control arm from the ball joint.

Step 3. Free Outer End of Control Arm.

EVERYONE: Remove the 10mm bolt and nut that attach the handbrake cable to the control arm.

'75-'79 cars and '77-'81 Brats: Locate a steel bar (about as big around as your thumb) that's welded to the top of the control arm near the ball joint. That bar is called the leading rod. Follow the leading rod a few inches rearward to a clamp that attaches the leading rod to another steel bar (the stabilizer bar). Remove the 12mm bolt from the clamp, then remove the clamp. Follow the leading rod to where it goes through a bracket on the body. Remove the 22mm nut, large washer, rubber grommet, and short piece of pipe from the end of the leading rod. Keep the parts in order so you can install them in the same place during reassembly. Install new rubber grommets if the old ones are cracked, or hard and brittle.

'80 and newer cars and '82-'87 Brats: Remove the two 17mm nuts on the bottom of the control arm right next to the ball joint castle nut. You have to look through the hole in the control arm to see them. Hold the top of the bolts with a wrench while you remove the nuts. This releases the control arm from the leading rod.

Step 4. Remove Control Arm Pivot Bolt.

Remove the 14mm nut and bolt that attaches the inner end of the control arm to the crossmember. You might have to tap the bolt out of the hole with a small screwdriver. Pull the control arm down and out of the crossmember bracket.

'75-'79 cars and '77-'81 Brats: If you're removing the control arm from the car, pull it forward until the leading rod clears it's hole in the body.

Step 5. Install Control Arm.

Inspect all the rubber grommets and replace them with new ones if they are cracked, hard and brittle, or worn thin in places.

Check the rubber bushing in the inner end of the control arm. Take it to Subaru or a machine shop and have a new one pressed in if the hole is oval shaped or the rubber is cracked.

Soak all the rubber grommets in soapy water before installing them. This helps them slide comfortably into the correct position.

'75-'79 cars and '77-'81 Brats: Be sure there's a small flat washer, then a large washer with the concave side facing the small washer, then a rubber grommet on the leading rod. Slide the small piece of pipe onto the leading rod. Stick the end of the leading rod through the bracket on the body then install a rubber grommet, a large washer with the concave side facing away from the rubber grommet and a self-locking nut. Don't tighten the nut yet.

Slide the inner end of the control arm into the bracket on the crossmember, then install the pivot bolt through the bracket and control arm bushing from the front side of the bracket. Screw the self-locking nut onto the bolt but don't tighten it yet. For now we're just using it to hold the control arm in position so it's easier to install the ball joint. We'll tighten it in Step 6.

Attach the control arm to the ball joint (Procedure 4, Step 4).

Now start tightening the nut on the end of the leading rod. Use a large screwdriver for a pry bar to move

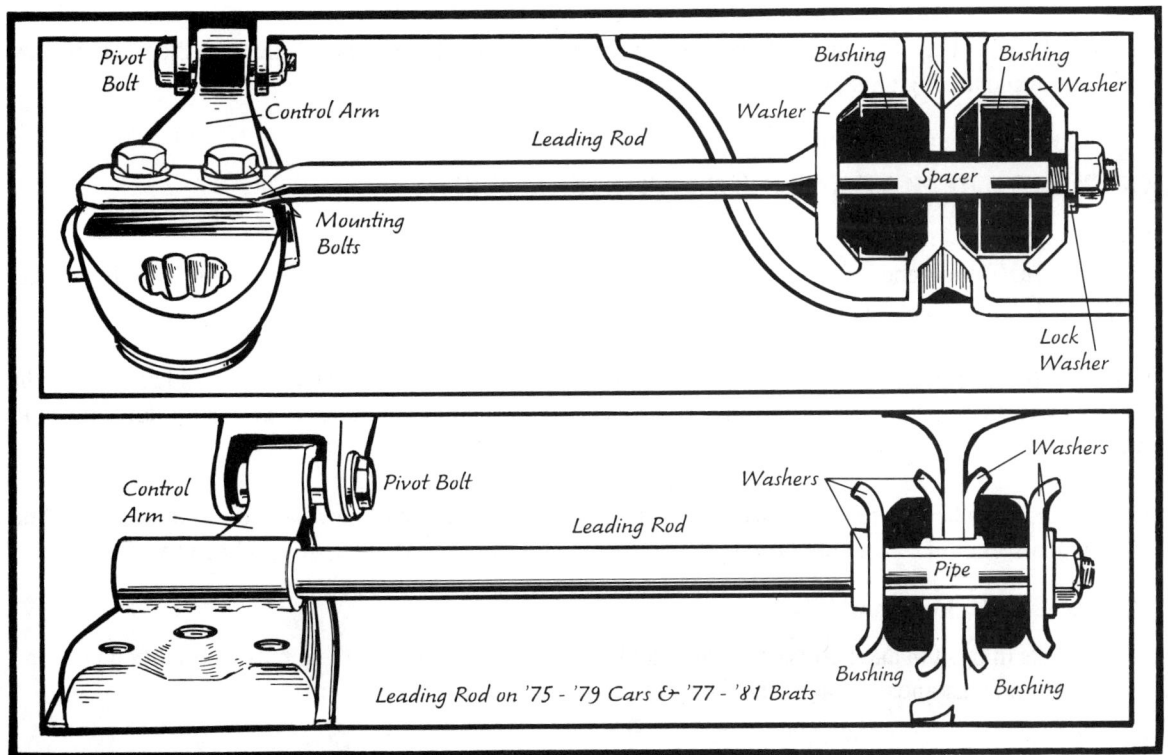

the rod around until you're sure it's centered. Torque the nut to 60 ft. lbs.

Fit the rubber grommet for the stabilizer bar clamp onto the leading rod if it was removed. Slip the tab on the bottom half of the stabilizer clamp into the slot on the top half of the clamp, then wrap the clamp around the rubber grommet. Install the 12mm bolt through the bottom clamp and screw it into the nut on the top clamp. Tighten the bolt.

Attach the handbrake cable bracket to the control arm and tighten the 10mm bolt and nut. Now you can skip down to Step 6 to tighten the nut on the pivot bolt. Be sure to do it.

'80 and newer cars and '82-'87 Brats: Slide the inner end of the control arm into the bracket on the crossmember. Stick the bolt through the bracket and control arm bushing from the front side, then start the nut but don't tighten it. Swing the outer end of the control arm up to the wheel bearing housing. Guide the ball joint stud through its hole in the control arm, then install the ball joint castle nut. Torque the nut to 29 ft. lbs., then tighten it just a little farther until the cotter pin can slide through the nut and bolt. Bend the ends of the cotter pin around the castle nut.

Install the two bolts that go through the holes in the leading rod and control arm. Now look at the nuts that go on the bolts. If they are nylon self-locking nuts (you'll see opaque nylon inside the rounded end of the nut), torque the nuts to 95 ft. lbs. No nylon? Then torque the nuts to 55 ft. lbs. You'll have to hold the bolt head with a wrench while you tighten the nuts.

Attach the handbrake cable bracket to the control arm and tighten the 10mm nut and bolt. Be sure to do Step 6.

Step 6. Install and Tighten Control Arm Pivot Bolt.

If you're here from another chapter or procedure, fit the inner end of the control arm into the bracket on the crossmember. Align the holes, then install the pivot bolt from the front side of the bracket. Wiggle it all the way in. Install a new self-locking nut on the end of the bolt. No new nut? Put some Loctite on the threads, then install the old nut. Now hold the pivot bolt head with a 14mm wrench while you torque the nut to 50 ft. lbs.

Check everything you've done to make sure it's attached, secure, and tight. Your life depends on it.

Step 7. Install Wheels.

Mount the wheels on the car, then install the lug nuts and snug them down a little with the wrench. Lower the car and torque the lug nuts to 72 ft. lbs.

PROCEDURE 6. REMOVE AND INSTALL TIE ROD ENDS

Condition: Tie rod end ball joints are worn out; OR you need to release the tie rod end for wheel bearing housing, strut, or steering box removal.

Tools and Materials: Jack and jackstands, safety glasses, a new cotter pin for each tie rod end removed, 19mm socket or box end wrench, crescent wrench, needlenose pliers, a ball joint puller or two hammers, and a block of wood.

Remarks: If a tie rod end is removed from the tie rod for the installation of new parts or whatever, you'll need to have the front end alignment checked by Subaru or an alignment shop after it's all back together.

Step 1. Chock, Jack, and Block.

Put chocks in front of and behind the rear wheels. Loosen the front wheel lug nuts a little, then jack up the car and put it on jackstands. Remove the front wheels.

Step 2. Record Location of Tie Rod End, Loosen Locknut.

This step is vital if you are separating the tie rod end from the tie rod. (Skip this step if you only need to remove the tie rod end from the wheel bearing housing and aren't removing the tie rod end from the tie rod.)

Measure the distance from the inner end of each tie rod end (not the locknut) to the shoulder on the tie rod where the rod tapers down to the threads (see illustration). Write the numbers somewhere so you can find them when you put the tie rod ends back on the tie rods.

Find two flat places on the tie rod end right next to the 19mm locknut. Use a crescent wrench on the two flat spots to hold the tie rod end while you loosen the locknut (counterclockwise, as you view the nut from the center of the car). Don't let the ball joint twist while loosening the locknut.

Step 3. Remove Tie Rod End from Wheel Bearing Housing.

Use needlenose pliers to straighten the bent end of the cotter pin that goes through the tie rod end castle nut. Pull the cotter pin out.

Use a 19mm wrench to loosen the castle nut from the ball joint and unscrew it until the top of the nut is even with the end of the ball joint stud.

I recommend that you borrow, buy, or rent a small puller to remove the tie rod end from the wheel bearing housing. Small pullers are less expensive than replacing a tie rod end that's damaged during removal. If you can't get a puller, you can try using two hammers to break the ball joint free. Put on your safety glasses, then squirt some penetrating oil around the ball joint stud where it goes through the wheel bearing housing. Wait a few minutes for the penetrating oil to seep in, then use the two hammers to simultaneously smack the sides of the steering arm through which the ball joint fits. The ball joint should drop out of the arm. Be careful not to hit the side of the castle nut or any of the brake parts. I've never had much success with this method, but all the old mechanics swear by it. Maybe I have bad ball joint Karma.

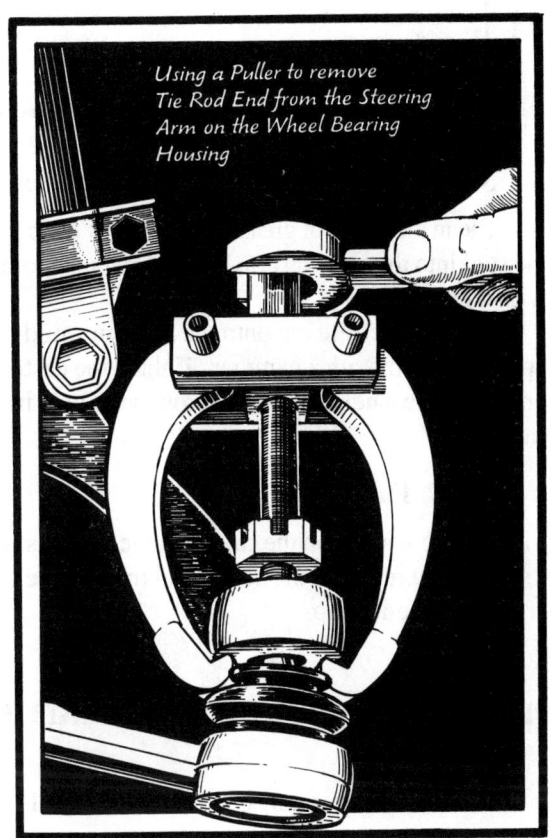

Using a Puller to remove Tie Rod End from the Steering Arm on the Wheel Bearing Housing

If all else fails, or you're getting a new tie rod end anyway, unscrew the castle nut, turn it over so the notched part is facing down and screw it onto the ball joint until the top of the nut is even with the top of the bolt. Put a block of wood on the top of the nut, then hit the block SQUARELY with the hammer and the ball joint will pop out. Remove the castle nut. If the stud turns with the nut, lightly tap the ball joint back up into the arm and hold it there while you unscrew the castle nut.

Step 4. Remove Tie Rod End from Tie Rod.

Use large pliers to keep the tie rod from turning while you unscrew the tie rod end with a crescent wrench (counterclockwise, as viewed from the outer end of the tie rod). Remove the tie rod end.

Step 5. Install Tie Rod End on Tie Rod.

Screw the locknut onto the tie rod if it was removed. Thread the tie rod end onto the tie rod to exactly the same point where it was before, using the measurements you made before removing the tie rod end. Run the locknut up against the tie rod end and tighten it with a 19mm wrench while holding the tie rod end at its flat spots with a crescent wrench.

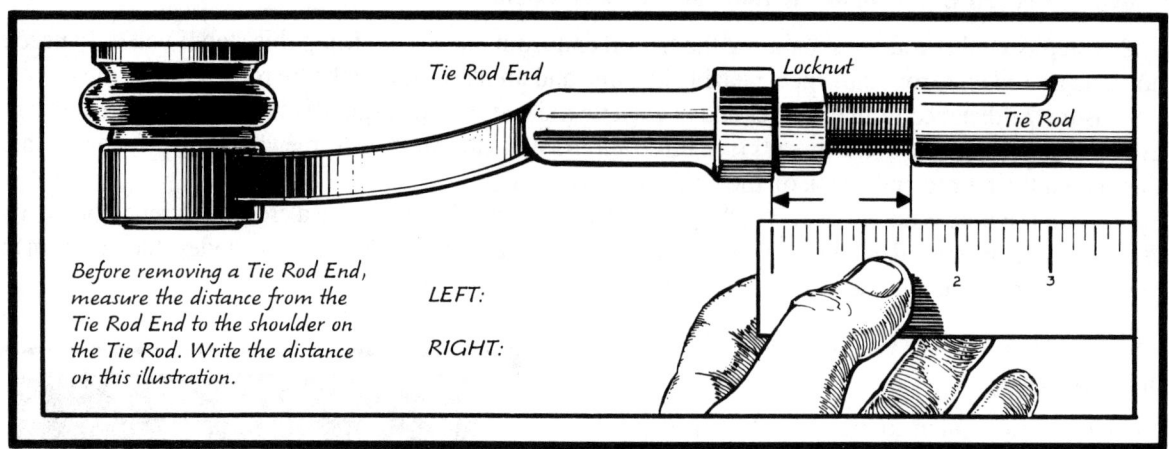

Before removing a Tie Rod End, measure the distance from the Tie Rod End to the shoulder on the Tie Rod. Write the distance on this illustration.

LEFT:

RIGHT:

Step 6. Attach Tie Rod End to Wheel Bearing Housing.

Clean all traces of grease, oil, and dirt from the tapered ball joint stud and its hole in the steering arm. Stick the stud into the steering arm hole from the bottom, then tap the bottom of the ball joint lightly a couple of times with a hammer.

Screw the castle nut onto the ball joint stud. If the stud turns with the nut, tap the bottom of the ball joint up a little more with a hammer. Tighten the castle nut to 22 ft. lbs., then tighten it a bit farther, if necessary, in order to slide a new cotter pin through the hole in the stud. When the cotter pin is in, wrap the ends around the castle nut.

Step 7. Finish Up.

Put the wheels on the car, snug the lug nuts with your wrench, lower the car and torque the lug nuts to 72 ft. lbs. If you removed the tie rod end from the tie rod you'll need to have the wheel alignment checked by Subaru or an alignment shop.

PROCEDURE 7: REMOVE AND INSTALL FRONT WHEEL BEARING HOUSING

This procedure does not cover 1975 models with front drum brakes.

Condition: Routine maintenance; OR the front wheel bearings are worn out.

Tools and Materials: Jack and jackstands, Phase 1 tool kit, two wheel-bearing grease seals for each housing that you remove, a can of high-temperature disc brake wheel-bearing grease, maybe new wheel bearings, a large two-jaw puller with at least 8″ jaws to separate the housing from the axle (you can rent these), a ½″-1″ diameter copper, brass, or aluminum rod, or hard wooden dowel at least 6 inches long (the rod or dowel used to remove and install wheel bearings is known as a "drift").

'75-'79 cars and '77-'81 Brats: You need a ½″ spacer (see the Tools and Materials section in Procedure 4).

Remarks: If you don't have access to a large puller to remove the wheel bearing housing from the axle, you can remove the double offset joint (DOJ) from the inboard end of the axle, then remove the wheel bearing housing and axle as a unit. Take the unit to Subaru or a machine shop and have the axle pressed out of the wheel bearings. Since the axle is already off the car you might as well have them press the axle back in when you're ready to assemble everything.

Step 1. Remove Front Brakes.

Do Chapter 13, Procedure 10, Steps 1-6. I'll see you back here when the brakes are off.

Step 2. Remove Disc Cover.

Locate the 12mm bolt on the disc cover. It's near the wheel bearing housing. Look behind the cover for a 12mm nut on the other end of the bolt. The nut, if you have one, is holding the bottom end of a handbrake cable bracket. Remove the nut, then remove the bolt from the outer side of the cover. Rotate the top of the cover toward the rear of the car until the brake cable bracket can clear the bolt tab on the wheel bearing housing. Pull the cover off the housing and let it hang by the handbrake cable.

Step 3. Remove Tie Rod End and Lower End of Strut from Housing.

See Procedure 3, Steps 2, 3, 4, and 6 (skip Step 5).

Step 4. Separate Steering Ball Joint from Housing.

See Procedure 4, Step 2.

Step 5. Remove Wheel Bearing Housing from Axle.

Try pulling the housing off the axle. If you're lucky it will slide right off. Not lucky? Then borrow, buy, or rent a two-jaw gear puller with a minimum of 8″ jaws, or remove the DOJ from the inboard end of the axle (Chapter 15, Procedure 4). If you have a puller, here's what to do with it: Hook the jaws over the inboard side of the housing and center the puller bolt on the end of the axle. Screw the puller bolt *clockwise* with a wrench while holding the jaws in place. The housing will begin to move out toward you. When the outer bearing comes off its seat, the housing will slide out easily for a couple of inches. Keep tightening the puller bolt and holding the jaws in position until the inner bearing clears the axle. The wheel bearing housing is now free, and you can lift it off and set it on your workbench or a clean, flat block of wood.

If the inner bearing stayed on the axle, remove it with the puller. Don't worry about damaging the seal behind the bearing because it gets replaced anyway.

If you removed the DOJ, pull the wheel bearing housing and axle away from the car. Haul it to Subaru or a machine shop to have the axle pressed out of the housing.

Step 6. Remove Bearings from Housing.

Lay the housing on the workbench or piece of wood so the inner bearing is down and the outer bearing is up. Stick your finger into the housing and push the spacer toward one side. Now you should be able to feel the inner race of the inner bearing. You can

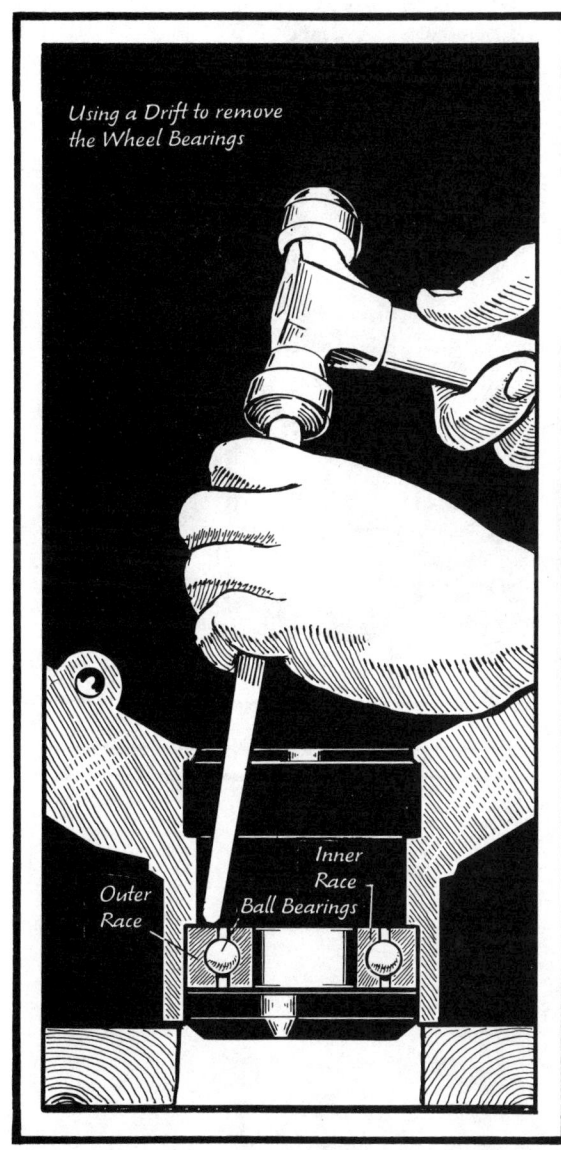

Using a Drift to remove the Wheel Bearings

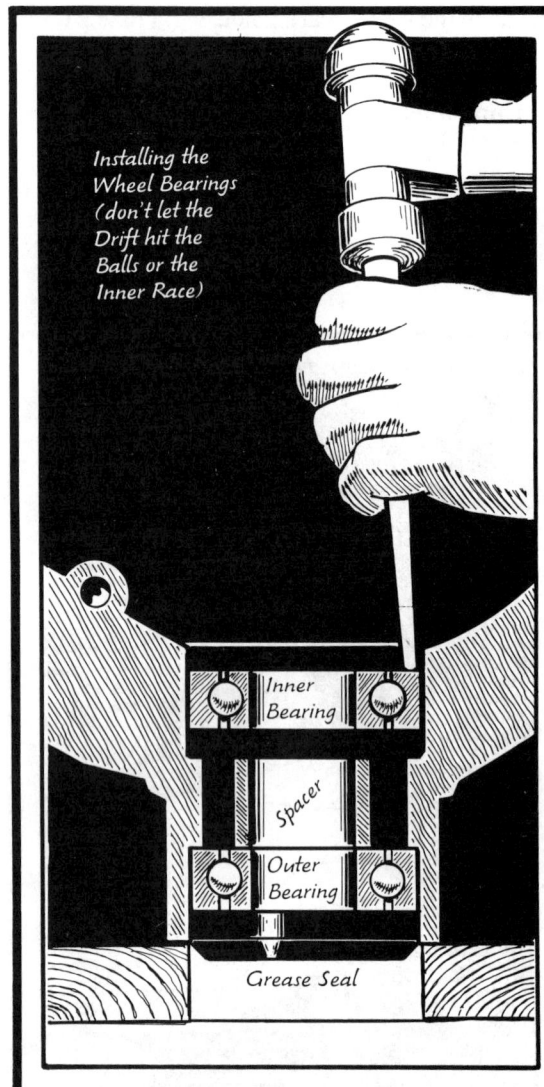

Installing the Wheel Bearings (don't let the Drift hit the Balls or the Inner Race)

feel it best where the inside of the housing is grooved. Put your "drift" in one of the grooves with the end against the race. Tap the drift lightly with a hammer (see illustration). Move the spacer around so you can tap all the way around the bearing race. Don't let the drift hit the ball bearings or inner race. Don't try to take it out in one punch, Rocky, just keep tapping round and round and soon the bearing will drop out of the housing.

If the inner bearing stayed with the axle, the above naturally won't be necessary. DON'T use a steel rod for tapping on the bearing; you run the risk of ruining it.

Now turn the housing over, remove the spacer, and tap the outer bearing out the same way you tapped the inner one out. When the bearing reaches the edge of the housing, prop the housing on its side so you can finish tapping the bearing out.

Step 7. Clean, Inspect, and Pack Wheel Bearings.

For the thrill of your life, go to Procedure 8 and clean and inspect the bearings and housing. Whether original or new, the bearings have to get packed before they're installed. When the bearings are packed with fresh grease come back here and we'll stick 'em back in the housing.

Step 8. Install Bearings in Housing.

Wasn't packing the bearings fun? OK, now lay the housing so the outer bearing hole is up. If you want, you can prop one side of the housing with a block of wood so it can't pivot on the steering and ball joint arms. (It makes installing the bearing a little easier.) Lay the bearing on the hole (either side can go in first) and LIGHTLY tap around the *outer edge* of the bearing with a hammer. DON'T tap on the smaller center part. The bearing won't go in until it's aligned perfectly with the hole. When you see the bearing start to go in all the way around, use a copper, brass, or aluminum drift and hammer to tap the bearing into the housing. Don't use a wooden dowel to install the bearing; splinters might fall into the bearing. If absolutely necessary, you can use a ratchet extension, but be sure to tap the extension against the outer race only. Tap, don't smack, the drift all around the outer bearing race until you feel and hear the bearing hit bottom. The sound of the hammer taps will change to a ringing sound. Get the same sound all the way around the bearing.

Turn the housing over and put the spacer in the hole. The gap between the spacer and housing now has to be filled with grease. Note the size of the gap, remove the spacer, then dip into the grease can again and spread enough grease around the inside of the hole to fill the gap. You won't be able to fill it completely; just get as much grease in as you can. Put the spacer in the hole again. Now install the inner bearing the same way you installed the outer bearing. Remember, tap very lightly until you're sure the bearing is going in straight. Use the drift to tap it in until you feel and hear the bearing hit bottom.

Step 9. Install Inner Grease Seal.

Before installing the new inner seal, be sure it looks just like the old one. Match 'em up. Don't install the outer grease seal until the housing is back on the car (Step 11).

Use a little wheel bearing grease to pack the grooves on the inside edge of the new seal (the part the axle goes through) and the space under the flappy lip. Lay the seal over the inner bearing hole with the flappy lip toward the outside (away from the housing). Press the outer edge of the seal straight into the housing with your thumbs. Don't push on the flappy lip. Work all the way around the edge until the seal is in as far you can go with your thumbs. Now gently use the drift-and-hammer technique around the outer edge to fully seat the seal.

Step 10. Install Wheel Bearing Housing.

If you haven't greased the constant velocity joints (CVJs) recently, this would be a convenient time to do it while the housing is out of your way (Chapter 15, Procedure 5).

Wipe off the axle shaft and the outside of the CVJ (that lumpy thing on the axle) with a clean rag. Use fine emery paper to smooth off any scratches or rust on the parts of the axle where the bearings ride. Wipe them clean again, then smear them with a light coat of grease.

Getting the housing on the axle is sometimes awkward and frustrating, but you can do it. Be patient and think about all the money you're saving by doing it yourself.

Wrap a rag around the rubber CVJ axle boot and another one around the ball joint. You wouldn't want to break anything while you're supposed to be fixing something.

Slide the housing onto the axle, being careful not to bash the grease seal with the end of the axle shaft. Line up the housing as straight as you can on the axle. Use your hammer to tap on the strut mounting arm and steering ball joint arm. You are wearing safety glasses, aren't you? Alternately tap one arm, then the other until the housing starts going onto the axle. Sometimes it slides on easily, but sometimes it's a slow, tedious process. If you don't seem to be making any progress by tapping on the strut and ball joint arms, try tapping on the *inner* race of the outer bearing. Use a copper, brass or aluminum drift and hammer. Work the drift all around the bearing race, being careful not to let the drift hit the ball bearings. Having a friend hold the housing while you tap helps a lot.

When the inner bearing gets past the outer bearing seat on the axle, the housing will slide easily for about 1½". Now you can remove the rag and fit the steering ball joint bolt into its hole on the housing. Install the ball joint nut and snug it down but don't try to tighten it yet. Push down on the housing enough that you can fit the bottom end of the strut into its hole at the top of the housing. Don't install the strut mounting bolts yet.

OK, things are looking more normal and the hard part's over. Now you can use the disc and wheel hub or brake drum to pull the axle through the housing. Here's how:

Wipe the grease seal mating surface on the inside of the disc hub or brake drum with a clean rag, then slide it onto the axle. Put the tapered split center piece on the axle, then screw the axle nut on. Use a hammer handle or wooden dowel between two lug nut studs to keep the axle from turning while you tighten the axle nut with a 36mm socket and ratchet. This draws the axle through the bearings. When you see the flappy lip on the inner grease seal make contact with the CVJ, you know the housing is on as far as it can go. Use the hammer handle to hold the hub while you unscrew the axle nut. Pull the disc or drum off the axle.

Don't worry about the outer grease seal yet. We'll get to it in the next step.

Attach the strut to the housing, then tighten the upper strut mounting nuts (Procedure 3, Step 10).

Tighten the steering ball joint nut and install a new cotter pin (Procedure 4, Step 4).

Attach the tie rod end to the housing and tighten the nut (Procedure 6, Step 6).

Step 11. Install Brakes and Outer Grease Seal.

Pack the outer seal with grease and install it in the wheel bearing housing like this: Use a rag to clean the grease off the outer edge of the seal and inside the housing where the seal fits. Orient the seal so the smooth side is out and the side with a groove is toward the housing. Press the seal into the housing with your thumbs as far as you can get it. Use a drift or ratchet extension and hammer to gently tap on the seal until it's fully seated. Use a rag to wipe off any grease that's on the outside of the seal or housing.

Pull the disc cover over the axle and fit it onto the housing. Rotate the top of the cover toward the rear of the car until you can slip the handbrake bracket on the back of the cover over the mounting tab on the housing. Rotate the cover so you can screw the 12mm bolt through the cover and into the housing. Before tightening the bolt, see if the two caliper bracket mounting bolts can slide easily through the housing and cover. Rotate the cover a little if necessary, then tighten the 12mm cover bolt. Install a lock washer and 12mm nut (if you had one) on the inner end of the bolt and tighten it.

Install the disc, the brake caliper holder, brake pads, and caliper (Chapter 13, Procedure 10, Steps 7, 8, and 9).

Step 12. Finish Up.

Install the wheels, lower the car, then torque the axle nuts (Chapter 13, Procedure 4, Step 4). Torque the lug nuts to 72 ft. lbs.

Take the Soob for a test drive. If you hear unusual noises on the side you've worked on, or the car pulls to one side, something wasn't reassembled right. This is rare, but don't drive the car until you've got it together correctly.

Have the front wheel toe-in checked by Subaru or an alignment shop.

PROCEDURE 8: CLEAN, INSPECT, AND PACK WHEEL BEARINGS WITH GREASE

You have come here from Procedure 7 or Procedure 9. Have fun!

Condition: Routine maintenance; OR wheel bearing has broken or worn out.

Tools and Materials: Can of high-temperature disc brake wheel-bearing grease, spray can of brake cleaner or carburetor cleaner, solvent, parts-cleaning pan, stiff brush, lots of clean rags and/or paper towels.

Remarks: Different brands of grease are likely to be incompatible, causing each other to deteriorate or liquify, which reduces the lubricating effect. So, clean all the old grease out of the bearings and housings before packing them with new grease.

Keep track of where the wheel bearings were installed so you can put all the pieces back in the same place during reassembly.

Step 1. Clean and Inspect Bearings.

Use a stiff parts-cleaning brush or old toothbrush and solvent to clean the bearings until they shine. Use a spray can of brake cleaner or carb cleaner to clean the places the brush can't reach.

If the balls or rollers in a bearing are dark, scratched, or chipped, the bearing should be replaced. If the balls seem too loose inside the *races* (front wheel ball bearings) or the rollers seem too loose in the *cage* (rear wheel roller bearings), take the bearings to Subaru or a garage for their opinion.

Wipe the old grease out of the wheel bearing housing or brake drum with rags or paper towels. Use brake cleaner or solvent to wash away all traces of the old grease. Dry the inside of the housing or drum with clean rags or paper towels.

On rear wheel bearings, check the outer bearing races (inside the brake drum) and the inner races (the part that fits between the axle and the bearings) for cracks, chips, and scratches. The races should be bright and shiny. A brown or blue color means the bearings have been overheated, probably due to lack of grease or dirty installation. Get a new bearing if either race is cracked, chipped, scratched, or discolored, or if the rollers are too loose inside the cage. (If the rollers fall out of the cage, you need a new bearing for sure.) Procedure 9, Step 5 tells you how to install the new races in the brake drum.

If you're checking front wheel bearings, hold the inner race with one hand while you spin the outer race with the other. (Don't use compressed air to spin the bearings—it's dangerous!) The outer race should turn easily with no signs of roughness or resistance. Get a new bearing if it feels like the balls are rolling over bumps or chips, or if there's any resistance when you spin the outer race with your hand.

When you're through cleaning the bearings, throw the greasy rags in the trash outside. Don't pile them in a corner of the garage because greasy or oily rags have a weird ability to burst into flames!

Step 2. Pack Wheel Bearings with Grease.

Wheel bearings all nice and shiny? They must be completely dry of water, solvent, and brake or carb cleaner before packing.

Here comes the fun part. Put a glob of wheel-bearing grease about the size of a golf ball in the palm of one hand. Press one side of the bearing (the larger side on rear wheel roller bearings) into the glob of grease over and over until grease oozes through the balls on front wheel bearings, or rollers on rear wheel bearings. The grease should come out the side of the bearing facing you. The idea is to pack the grease into the spaces around all the bearings. Rotate the bearing a little and keep packing until grease is oozing out all the way around the bearing. Pack the other bearing(s) the same way. Lay the packed bearings on a clean paper towel or rag. Don't you wish you could do this every day?

Now you can go to the assembly step to put the whole mess back together. Procedure 7, Step 8, covers front wheel bearing installation. For rear wheel bearing installation, do Procedure 9, Step 5, if you're installing new wheel bearings, or Procedure 9, Step 6, if you're installing the old bearings. Clean your hands before fondling the other parts or the pages of this book. Thank you.

Keep pressing the Bearing into the grease until it oozes out the opposite end. Are we having fun yet? These are Rear Wheel Bearings, but the principle is the same for the Fronts.

PROCEDURE 9: REMOVE AND INSTALL REAR WHEEL BEARINGS (Non-4WD Only)

Special tools and skills are required to remove the rear wheel bearings on 4WD Soobs. So take your four-wheeler to Subaru or a garage at least every 30,000 miles (severe conditions), or every 60,000 miles (normal conditions) to have the rear wheel bearings inspected and, if necessary, packed with fresh grease.

Condition: 30,000 severe miles or 60,000 normal miles maintenance; OR a rear wheel bearing has broken or worn out.

Tools and Materials: Phase 1 tool kit, safety glasses and dust mask, wheel-bearing grease (get high-temperature disc brake wheel-bearing grease even though you don't have disc brakes on the rear), several rags or paper towels, spray can of brake cleaner or solvent, stiff brush, wash pan, maybe new wheel bearings, two new lock plates for the axle nuts, two new grease seals.

'80 and newer models: You also need two new rear axle O-rings. (The old ones can be reused in a pinch if they aren't broken.)

To install new rear wheel bearings, you need a ½" to 1" diameter copper, brass, or aluminum rod (called a "drift") at least six inches long. You can use a hard wooden dowel if you clean the splinters and dirt out of the inside of the drum before packing it with grease.

CAUTION! While repacking or replacing the wheel bearings, don't get any grease on the brake shoes, drums, pads, or discs. If you accidentally do, use brake cleaner to remove it, or replace the shoes or pads with new ones.

Step 1. Chock, Jack, Block, and Remove Brake Drum.

Flip to Chapter 13, Procedure 4, Step 1, to get the car on jackstands with the wheels and rear brake drums removed, or if you have rear disc brakes, see Chapter 13, Procedure 6, to remove the rotors. Please read the **CAUTION! WARNING!** in the remarks at the beginning of Chapter 13.

Step 2. Remove Inner Wheel Bearing.

Sometimes the inner wheel bearing comes off the axle with the brake drum or disc. If this is the case, skip to Step 3.

Bearing is still on the axle? OK, use your two largest screwdrivers to gently pry the bearing off the axle. Gently, I said. Hook the ends of the screwdrivers behind the bearing cage on opposite sides, then lightly push the handles toward the car. The screwdrivers will pivot on the brake shoes and pry out on the bearing. If you have drum brakes and the bearing refuses to budge, remove the brake shoes (Chapter 13, Procedure 5, Step 3) and try again. You can get a better angle with the brake shoes out of the way. If the bearing still refuses to budge, you'll need to buy, rent, or borrow a gear puller, or put everything back together and take it to Subaru or a garage to have the bearings packed or replaced. It's cheaper to find a puller.

Replace the bearing with a new one if the puller bends the bearing cage (the thing that holds the rollers in) while removing the bearing.

Step 3. Remove Grease Seal, Spacer, and O-Ring.

Use a large screwdriver to pry the rubber grease seal out of the bearing hole on the inside of the brake drum. If the inner wheel bearing is still in the drum, pull it out now.

Remove the spacer from the axle. It's that shiny round thing around the axle right next to the backing plate. '80 and newer models have a rubber O-ring behind the spacer. Remove it.

Step 4. Clean, Inspect, and Pack Bearings with Grease.

For a cheap thrill, do Procedure 8 to clean, inspect, and pack the wheel bearings, then come back here for reassembly. If you found that the wheel bearings were all good, skip step 5. It's only for people who need to install new bearings.

Step 5. Install New Wheel Bearings.

If you bought new bearings to install in the drums, you've made sure you bought the right ones, eh? You should have new bearings with exactly the same numbers stamped on them as the old bearings—or a darn good explanation from the parts man about why the numbers are different.

The bearing that fits into the brake drum from the brake side is the inner bearing, and the one you install from the axle nut side of the drum is the outer bearing. The inner bearing is always larger than the outer one.

Each bearing has two races, an inner and outer. The outer race is pressed tightly into the drum and stays there until you knock it out with a drift (punch, dull chisel, copper, brass, aluminum, or wooden rod). The inner bearing race is the part that fits between the axle and the rollers in the bearing cage. You can usually slide the inner race (and bearing) off the axle with your fingers, or pry it off with screwdrivers.

OK, to install new bearings you have to knock the old outer races out of the drum, then put new ones in. Yes, it's tempting to leave the old outer races in the drum and just slide in a new bearing, but don't. The life of the new bearing will be shortened drastically.

To remove the old outer races, put on your safety glasses, then stick a finger into the drum and locate the inner edge of the bearing race. It sticks up a little higher than the inside of the drum. Got it? Now lay the drum so the lug studs are sticking up. Put a drift (preferably a copper, brass, or aluminum rod) inside the drum and against the lip on the bottom race. (In a pinch a screwdriver, dull chisel, or flat-nosed punch will work.) Tap all around the inside circumference of the race until it begins to move out of the brake drum. Keep tapping around the race until it falls out. Have a look at the illustration. Now turn the drum over and tap the other race out the same way.

Before installing the new bearing races, use brake cleaner or solvent to remove all traces of old grease from inside the drum (Procedure 8, Step 1, paragraph 2). Lay the new outer race in its hole so the thicker, heavy side of the race goes in first. LIGHTLY tap all around the edge with a hammer until the race starts going into the drum. Remove it if it gets crooked and start again. Once the edge of the race is flush with the drum, put the drift on the edge of the race and continue tapping all around the circumference until it's fully seated in the drum. Don't let the drift slip and scratch the bearing surface. The sound the hammer makes will change from a ding to a dong when the race hits bottom. Or is it a dong to a ding? Anyway, install the other outer race the same way.

Now pack the new bearings with grease if you haven't already (Procedure 8, Step 2).

Step 6. Put It All Back Together.

What an exhilarating experience packing wheel bearings is. I wish I could have been there to watch. Is the mess all cleaned up? Now let's put it all back together.

Clean all the old grease off the axle without getting any on the brake shoes.

'80 and newer models: Install a new rubber O-ring onto the inner end of the axle.

EVERYONE: Clean the spacer and install it on the axle with the concave (dished) side, facing away from you. Slide the freshly packed inner (larger) wheel bearing on the axle. The larger edge goes on first. Slide it up against the spacer. Use a screwdriver and hammer to lightly tap around the inner race of the bearing if you can't slide it all the way on with your fingers (don't hit the rollers).

Drum brake models: Clean your hands and install the brake shoes if they were removed (Chapter 13, Procedure 5, Step 5). Don't get any grease on the shoes. If your model has manual adjusting brake shoes, turn the brake adjuster bolt a couple of turns counterclockwise (Chapter 13, Procedure 1, Step 2).

EVERYONE: The inside of the brake drum or disc has been spotlessly cleaned, right? Pack grease inside the drum or disc until it's level with the edge of the wheel bearing races. If you accidentally get grease on the part of the drum or disc where the brake shoes or pads rub, clean it off with solvent or brake cleaner. Now pack grease on the axle until it's even with the inner race on the inside bearing.

Press a new grease seal into the inner hole of the brake drum or disc with your thumbs. The "open" side of the seal with a groove in it goes toward the inside and the smooth side with the "lips" faces the outside. Use a drift or ratchet extension and hammer to gently tap all the way around the outer edge of the seal to seat it completely. Put grease in the lips of the seal, then wipe away the excess grease around the seal with a clean rag.

Stand the drum or disc on its edge and insert the outer (smaller) bearing into its hole. Keep greasy fingers away from the friction surface on the drum or disc.

Grab the drum or disc so your fingers won't get pinched between the drum and brake shoes or backing plate,. Hold the outer bearing in with your thumbs, line up the hole in the drum with the axle and slide the drum straight onto the axle. Wiggle it all the way on. Do Chapter 13, Procedure 4, Steps 3 and 4, to install the washers, lockplates, cotter pin, etc. and to tighten the axle nuts. If you have rear disc brakes, skip to Step 7.

Drum brake people: If you don't have self-adjusting brakes, adjust the brakes (Chapter 13, Procedure 1,

Step 2). Don't forget to adjust both rear brakes.

Step 7. Install Wheels.

Put the wheels on and snug the lug nuts. Lower the car and torque the lug nuts to 72 ft. lbs. Install the hubcaps (if you have them). Take the Soob for a spin, listening for any unusual squeals or grinding noises from your freshly done wheel bearings. All smooth and quiet? You've done the job well.

PROCEDURE 10: REMOVE AND INSTALL STEERING GEARBOX BOOTS, TIE RODS, AND TIE ROD BALL JOINTS

Condition: Rubber steering gearbox boots are torn or missing; OR tie rod is bent; OR tie rod ball joint is worn out.

Tools and Materials: Phase 1 tool kit, tie rod end ball-joint puller, new rubber gearbox boots and/or new tie rod and tie rod ball joint, new ball joint lock plate if the ball joint is removed.

Remarks: The gearbox boots and tie rod ball joints can be replaced without removing the steering gearbox.

Step 1. Chock, Jack, Block, and Remove Front Wheels.

Chock the rear wheels, loosen the front wheel lug nuts a little, jack up the front of the car and put it securely on jackstands. Remove the front wheels.

Step 2. Release Tie Rod End from Wheel Bearing Housing.

Do Procedure 3, Step 3, to free the tie rod end.

Step 3. Remove Tie Rod End.

Be sure to measure and write down the position of the tie rod end before removing it (Procedure 6, Steps 2 and 3).

If you're only replacing the tie rod end, Procedure 6, Step 5 tells you how to install the new one. Once the new tie rod is on, go ahead and do Procedure 6, Steps 6 and 7, to put everything back together. No need to come back here.

If you're removing the tie rod and/or the gearbox boot, come back here after removing the tie rod end.

Step 4. Remove Exhaust Shields.

If there are thin metal shields (a little larger than your hand) between the rubber tie rod boots and the exhaust pipe, remove them (newer models only have one on the left side). The front of the shields is attached to the bottom of the motor mount with a 14mm nut. The rear of the shields is attached with either 10mm nuts on the top rear of the crossmember or a 10mm bolt on the side of the crossmember. The crossmember is that big black contoured steel plate the steering box is bolted to.

Step 5. Remove and Install Gearbox Boot.

'75-'79 cars and '77-'81 Brats: Remove the bolt and nut securing the handbrake cable strap to the tie rod. Spread the clamp enough to pull it off the tie rod. Install the nut and bolt on the clamp so they don't get lost. Replace the rubber strap if it's broken or funky.

Clean the outside of the boot you're going to remove with a rag to prevent dirt from falling into the gearbox.

There's a small plastic vent tube that connects the right and left gearbox boots on all '75-'79 models and '81 and newer OHV models with power steering. It runs along the front side of the steering gearbox. Twist the tube out of its connection on the boot you're replacing.

'75-'79 models: The boot clamp around the large end of the boot looks like a thick square rubber band. There isn't a clamp on the small end of the boot.

'80 and newer models: A large spring clamp is hiding under the flappy thing on the large end of the boot and there's a smaller spring clamp on the small end of the boot. Some models have another spring clamp about two grooves away from the small end of the boot that clamps the boot to the tie rod ball joint.

EVERYONE: Remove the rubber bands or springs, then slide the boot off the gearbox and tie rod.

If you're here to remove the tie rod and ball joint, skip to Step 6 now. Come back here to install the boot after the new ball joint is installed.

Before installing the gearbox boot, use a rag to clean dirt and grease off the tie rod and the groove in the gearbox where the boot fits. To install the boot, slide it over the tie rod and ball joint and onto the gearbox so the large end fits into the groove. Due to limited space on some models, you might have to use a couple of long screwdrivers to push the end of the boot onto the gearbox. Be careful—don't tear or puncture the boot.

'75-'79 and OHV models with Power Steering: Turn the boot so the vent tube connection is toward the front of the car.

EVERYONE: Pull the boot over the ball joint until the indentation in the boot (about two rings away from the small end of the boot) fits into the groove in the ball joint. Fit the small end of the boot into the groove on the tie rod. Install the rubber or spring clamps. If you have a vent tube, be sure the end is clean, then insert it into the small opening in the boot. Skip to Step 7 to put everything back together.

Step 6. Remove and Install Tie Rods and Tie Rod Ball Joints.

The rubber boot is off the tie rod (Step 5), right? The tie rod ball joint is that squarish thing the tie rod is attached to. They are inseparable and have to be replaced as a unit.

Locate the lock plate that's bent over the flat sides of the ball joint. Use a screwdriver and hammer to gently bend the lock plate away from the ball joint so you can fit a crescent wrench on the flat sides. Put a 19mm open-end wrench on the flat places on the steering rack right next to the ball joint. Unscrew the ball joint *counterclockwise* as viewed from the tie rod (not the rack). Be sure you're holding the rack firmly with the 19mm wrench. If the rack turns too much it might damage the gear teeth on the rack or pinion shafts. Remove the ball joint, then the lock plate.

To install the tie rod and ball joint, first slide a new lock plate onto the rack so the little tab fits into the notch on the rack. Screw the ball joint onto the rack, then use the crescent and 19mm wrenches to tighten it. The torque is supposed to be 58 ft. lbs., but you can't get a torque wrench on it, right? So get it as tight as you can with the two wrenches, then use a hammer to bend the lock plate over the flat sides of the ball joint. Install the rubber boot (Step 5).

Step 7. Do This and That.

Install the exhaust shield(s), backtracking the way you took them off in Step 4. Torque the engine mounting nut to 22 ft. lbs. ('75-'79 models), or 25 ft. lbs. ('80 and newer models).

'75-'79 cars and '77-'81 Brats: Attach the handbrake cable to the tie rod. Install the clamp on the gearbox side of the little bump on the tie rod. No bump? Then install it on the flat places on the tie rod.

EVERYONE: Do Procedure 6, Steps 5 and 6 to install the tie rod end on the tie rod and to attach the tie rod end to the wheel bearing housing.

Step 8. Finish Up.

Install the wheels, snug the lug nuts, lower the car, torque the lug nuts to 72 ft. lbs. Put the hubcaps on if you have them. Have the toe-in checked by Subaru or an alignment shop.

PROCEDURE 11: CHECK AND ADJUST GROUND CLEARANCE (4WD Only)

This Procedure only applies to '79 and newer OHV 4WD cars and Brats.

Condition: Your Soob seems to be sagging; OR there are deep ruts in your driveway and you need just a little more ground clearance.

Tools and Materials: Only a tire gauge and tape measure are required to check the ground clearance. To adjust the front height, a 21mm open-end or crescent wrench and chalk or paint are needed. To adjust the rear height, a 19mm socket and ratchet is all you need.

Remarks: If the ground clearance is adjusted higher than its maximum range, you'll hear weird noises (clunks and squawks) when driving, due to the decrease in the rebound stroke in the suspension system. Make a low rider or high rider out of your Chevy or Ford, but keep the ground clearance on your Soob within the specified ranges.

If you change the front or rear ground clearance, have the front wheel toe-in checked by Subaru or an alignment shop. Changing the ground clearance also affects the aim of the headlights. Have them adjusted by Subaru.

Step 1. Check Tire Pressure and Unload Car.

Inflate all four tires to the proper pressure (Chapter 7, Procedure 4, Step 2). Check the air pressure in the spare tire while you're at it. Park on a solid, level surface, turn off the engine, put the transmission in gear or PARK, and set the handbrake.

The car must be unloaded before checking the ground clearance, so remove heavy stuff like tool boxes, sacks of cement, dead bodies, etc. from the car before taking measurements.

Step 2. Measure and Adjust Front Ground Clearance.

Grab your tape measure and crawl under the front end. Check the front ground clearance by measuring from the ground to the center of each control arm pivot bolt. Be sure to hold the tape measure straight up and down.

If one side of the car is higher than the other, or you want to raise or lower the car slightly, here's how to adjust it: Look over the top of the front tire and locate two 21mm nuts just below the coil spring on the strut. Use chalk or paint to mark one of the flat sides of each nut so you can keep track of how far you've turned it. To increase the ground clearance, turn the nuts so the outside edge (the side facing you) moves to your right.

Soobs usually come from the factory with the front suspension in the lowest position. In the lowest position, the bottom of the adjusting nuts will be resting against the steel plate below the coil spring holder. From this position you can only raise the car a maximum of 0.98" (25mm). If someone has raised it already, you can turn the nuts to the left to lower it. Be sure to turn both nuts on each side the same direction and exactly the same amount. Keep measuring the ground clearance and adjusting the nuts until the ground clearance is where you want it. Be sure both sides of the car are the same height.

Have the headlights adjusted and the toe-in checked by Subaru or an alignment shop after changing the front ground clearance. If you hear clunks and/or squawks when you hit bumps, you've raised the car above its maximum range. Lower the car a little at a time until the noises go away.

Step 3. Check and Adjust Rear Ground Clearance.

This step only applies to '80 and newer OHV 4WD cars and '82-'87 Brats.

Find the torsion bar tube that goes across the bottom of the car. It's just in front of the rear wheels. Hold the tape measure straight up and down and check the distance from the ground to the bracket on the end of the tube. Be sure to measure in the same place on both sides of the car.

To change the ground clearance, find a rubber plug under the rear seat. On Brats it will be between the two jump seats. Remove the rubber plug from the top, then use a 19mm socket and ratchet to turn the bolt that's in the hole. Turn the bolt *clockwise* to increase the ground clearance or *counterclockwise* to reduce ground clearance. Soobs usually come from the factory with the rear adjustment set between the minimum and maximum adjustment so you can go up or down about 1-1/8" (30mm). Turn the bolt a little, then check your measurement again. When the height is where you want it, install the rubber plug in the hole and install the rear seat. If you hear clunks (while driving) after raising the car, you've probably gone beyond the maximum adjustment. Lower the rear of the car a little bit at a time until the noise goes away.

348   Chapter 14

CHAPTER 15
CLUTCH, TRANSMISSION AND DRIVESHAFTS

If your Starship Subaru has a manual transmission (also called a *standard transmission* or *stick shift*), it has a **clutch assembly** that links the engine to the transmission. Without the clutch, the engine would be mechanically connected to the front wheels all the time, making it impossible to stop the car without turning the engine off, and making it next to impossible to shift the gears.

The parts of the clutch assembly are: the engine **flywheel**, which is bolted to the rear end of the engine crankshaft; a spring-loaded **pressure plate** (also called a *clutch cover*), which is bolted to the outer edge of the rear surface of the flywheel; a **clutch disc** with a friction surface on both sides that's sandwiched between the flywheel and pressure plate; and a **throwout bearing**, which pushes on the pressure plate when the clutch pedal is pressed down. The clutch disc is attached to the transmission via the splined **transmission mainshaft**. A small **pilot bearing** in the crankshaft (on early models) or in the flywheel (on late models) supports the front end of the transmission shaft.

As long as the clutch pedal inside the car is up, the engine is connected to the transmission; the clutch disc (and transmission shaft) will turn with the flywheel because it's squeezed tightly against the flywheel by the pressure plate. When you push down on the clutch pedal, the **clutch cable** attached to the top of the pedal pulls rearward on the upper end of a **clutch release lever** on the front of the transmission. The lever pivots (on a ball inside the transmission *bell housing*) and the lower end of the lever presses the throwout bearing against the center of the clutch pressure plate compressing its springs. When the springs in the pressure plate are compressed, the pressure of the plate against the clutch disc is released. This allows the engine to run without turning the clutch disc and transmission shaft.

AUTOMATICS

Soobs with automatic transmissions have a fluid-filled **torque converter** linking the engine to the transmission. The fluid, rather than mechanical, connection is the key to the torque converter's magical ability to let the engine idle while the transmission is in gear. The torque converter is like a large donut filled with transmission fluid. Inside, a "shell" with vanes like a windmill turns around, forcing the fluid to operate another shell with vanes. (Blow against a child's pinwheel with an electric fan, and you'll get the idea.) The outer shell of the torque converter is attached to the engine crankshaft via a **torque plate** (the *flywheel* on manual trans models), and the inner part of the torque converter is connected to a splined transmission shaft. When the engine speed increases, the fluid around the vanes of the outer shell of the torque converter moves causing the inner part to turn the transmission gears.

THE TRANSMISSION AND BEYOND

I'm not going to go into the complexities of transmissions in this book. Suffice it to say, you've got a number of movable gears of different sizes in there. When you move the shift lever, you engage gears of different sizes. You convert the revolutions of the engine into different ratios of speed (five in a five-speed, plus reverse), depending on the power and speed needs of the car.

Both manual and automatic shift Subarus have a combined transmission and differential called a **transaxle**. Short shafts sticking out from each side of the transaxle are attached to **double offset joints** (DOJs) which in turn are attached to solid steel **axleshafts**. The outer ends of the axleshafts connect to **constant velocity joints**

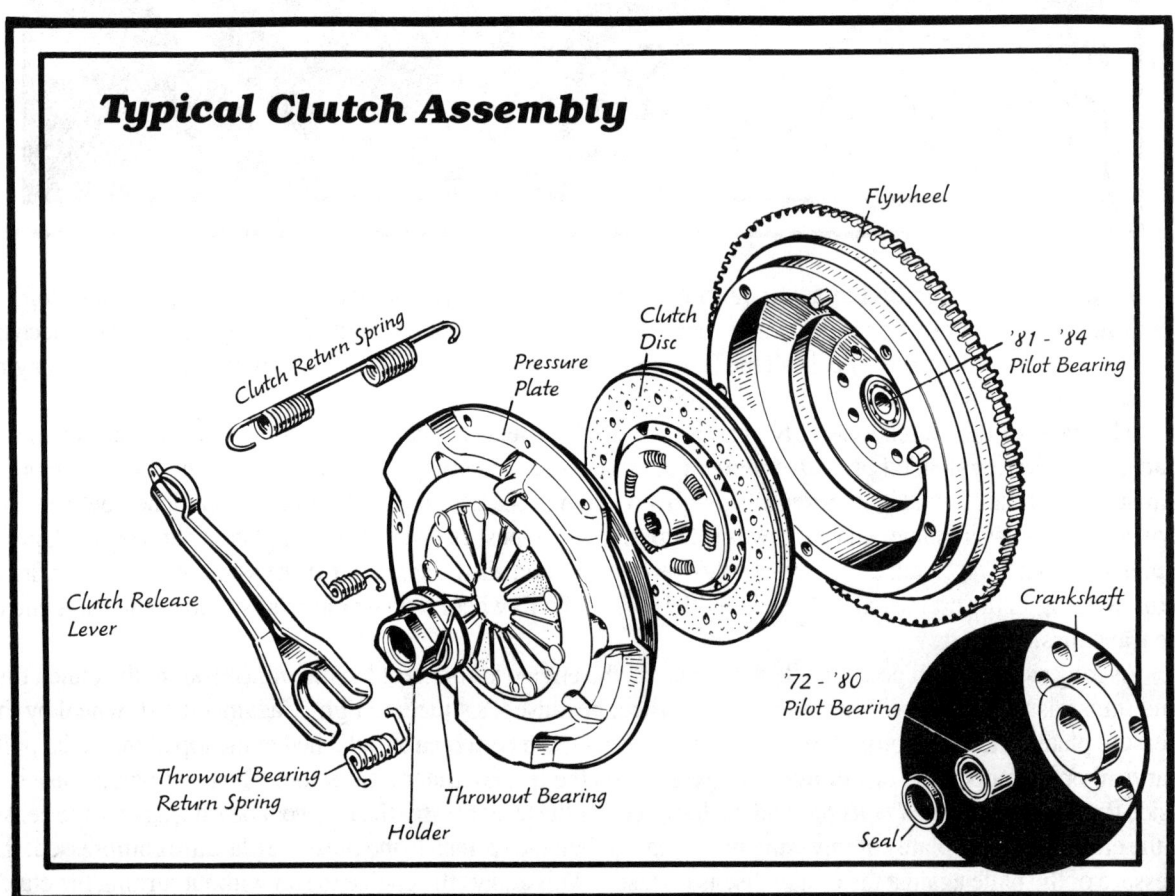

(CVJs) just inside the front **wheel bearing housings**. Another steel shaft goes from the outer end of the CVJs through the wheel bearings in the wheel bearing housings, then attaches to the brake drums or discs (depending on the year and model). The wheels are attached to the brake drums or discs. When the clutch is engaged (pedal up) and the transmission is in gear, the gears inside the transmission mechanically link the engine to the axleshafts and thence through the CVJ's, etc., to the front wheels.

On Starships with 4WD, a long hollow steel **driveshaft** with **universal joints** (U-joints) on each end connects the rear end of the transmission to the **rear differential**. OHC models have two driveshafts, end to end, connected in the middle with a U-joint. A center (carrier) bearing next to the middle U-joint is mounted in a bracket that's attached to the car body.

Short axles with U-joints or double offset joints (DOJs) on each end connect the rear differential to the rear wheels.

The DOJs, CVJs, and U-joints provide flexibility in the axles and driveshaft so all four wheels can move up and down while being turned by the axles. They allow the front wheels to turn right and left as well.

GETTING AT THESE PARTS

To replace the clutch disc, pressure plate, flywheel, throwout bearing, and pilot bearing, the engine has to be removed. The procedures for removing the engine and replacing the worn-out parts are in Chapter 17. Clutch cable adjustment and replacement can be done without removing the engine, and in fact are fairly simple.

Since the transmission and differential are combined into a transaxle, it's a very heavy, unwieldy unit. Removing it is nearly impossible without a hoist to lift the car five feet off the ground. Even if you could remove it easily, specialized tools are required (hydraulic press, transmission jigs, special wrenches, etc.) to repair the inner workings, so it's really beyond our means. When transmission or differential problems develop, I suggest taking the car to Subaru or a transmission shop for repair. Buying a used transaxle from a salvage yard might save you some money. Whether you have your transaxle rebuilt or buy a used one, be sure it comes with a written guarantee that not only covers the transaxle but also the labor charges for removing and installing it again if it's defective.

Replacing the DOJs and CVJs or their rubber boots on the front axles is dirty and greasy, but not too difficult. On 4WD models, removing the 4WD driveshaft and rear axleshafts for U-joint or DOJ replacement is easy.

Something else we home mechanics can do to keep our manual transmission Subaru Starships up to Federation standards is replace the bushings in the gearshift lever so it doesn't buzz at us like a pissed-off rattlesnake.

Here's a guide that will direct you to the appropriate procedure to remedy clutch, transmission, axleshaft, and driveshaft problems:

1. Clutch pedal goes down more than ½" before any resistance is felt.

   Clutch cable out of adjustment (Procedure 1)

2. Clutch "slips" on hills or during acceleration (engine speed increases but the car speed doesn't). A smell like burning underwear wafts into the car.

   Clutch disc, pressure plate, or flywheel worn (Procedure 12)

3. A squeal is heard when the clutch pedal is pressed (engine running).

   Worn throwout bearing (Procedure 12)

352 Chapter 15

4. Difficulty shifting gears.

   Clutch cable out of adjustment (Procedure 1); worn pressure plate (Procedure 12); dry or worn pilot bearing (Procedure 12); transmission innards worn (take it to a garage).

5. No resistance at clutch pedal or pedal is flat on the floor.

   Clutch cable broken (Procedure 2)

6. Car jerks forward even when clutch is released slowly (clutch "grabbing").

   Clutch cable improperly routed (Procedure 2); clutch disc worn (Procedure 12)

7. Oil drips between engine and transmission.

   Rear main seal leaking (Procedure 12)

8. Knocking noise when the car is turned sharply.

   DOJ and/or CVJ worn (Procedure 3)

9. You hear a clunk when you let the clutch pedal up (engage the clutch).

   DOJ, CVJ, or U-joint worn (Procedure 3)

10. Loud knocking when starter is engaged.

    Faulty starter, teeth missing from starter drive gear, or edge of flywheel (Chapter 10, Procedure 10)

11. Howl, squeal, or whine while driving.

    Transmission and/or differential low on oil (Chapter 7, Procedure 2, Steps 2 and 3, and Procedure 3, Step 7); worn bearings or gears in transmission or differential (take it to a garage)

12. Car shivers and shakes when clutch pedal is released (clutch chatter).

    Improperly routed clutch cable (Procedure 2); worn or warped pressure plate, flywheel, or clutch disc, oil on clutch disc (Procedure 12); improper adjustment of pitching stopper (Chapter 17)

13. Cars equipped with a hill-holder: engine tends to stumble and die when the clutch pedal is released.

    Check clutch adjustment (Procedure 1), then check hill-holder adjustment (Chapter 13, Procedure 17)

14. Gearshift rattles or buzzes.

    Worn bushings or rubber O-rings in the gearshift lever (Procedure 11)

PROCEDURE 1: CHECK AND ADJUST CLUTCH CABLE

Condition: Routine maintenance; OR you were directed here by the clutch troubleshooting guide.

Tools and Materials: Ruler or tape measure, 10mm and 14mm wrenches, pliers or Vise Grips, maybe a Friend.

Step 1. Check Clutch "Free Play" Adjustment.

Set your ruler or tape measure perpendicular to the clutch pedal pad so you can measure how far the clutch pedal moves toward the floorboard before resistance is felt. This distance is called "free play." Push on the pedal with your hand, and eyeball the ruler. The pedal should move at least ½" (13mm) but not more than ¾" (20mm). If it moves shorter or farther before resistance, do Step 2 to adjust the free play.

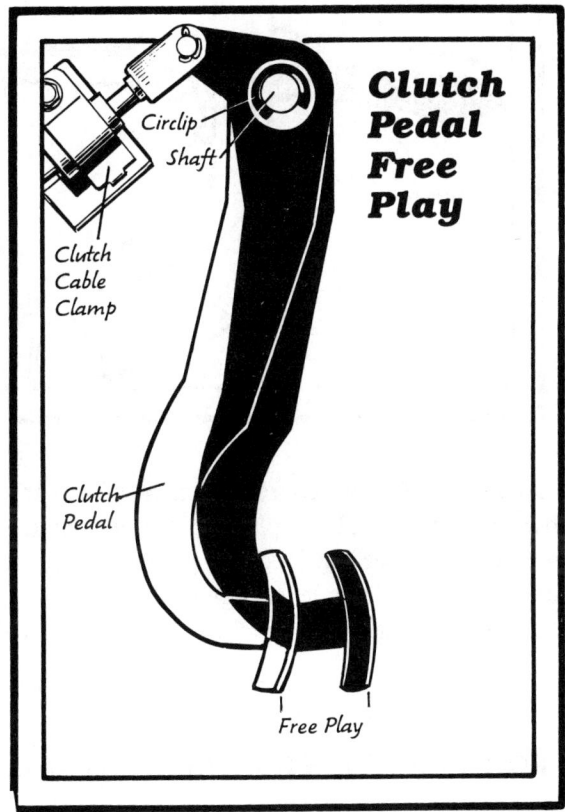

Step 2. Adjust Clutch Pedal Free Play.

If you're not sure where the clutch end of the clutch cable is, have Friend press and release the clutch while you watch for movement in the engine compartment. Remove the spare tire if it's in your way. You'll see a cable pulling on a short **lever** on the top or left (driver's) side of the transmission bell housing. There will be a 10mm and a 14mm nut right next to it on the end of the cable. A **spring** with hooked ends is attached between the lever and the engine. If you have a hill-holder, there will be two cables attached to the lever. The clutch cable is the one that sticks through the lever from the rear, and the hill-holder cable sticks through the lever from the front. You'll need to check the hill-holder adjustment after adjusting the clutch.

To adjust the clutch pedal free play, hold the 14mm nut on the clutch cable with a wrench while you loosen the 10mm nut a few turns (*counterclockwise* as viewed from the front of the car). The 10mm nut is a locknut to hold the other one in position. The 14mm nut is the one that adjusts the free play. To avoid twisting the cable, use your pliers or Vise Grips to hold the solid metal part of the cable (between the threaded part and the braided cable part) while you turn the 14mm nut. If you have less than ½" free play, turn the 14mm nut *counterclockwise* (as viewed from the front of the car) to increase the free play. If you have more than ¾" free play, turn the

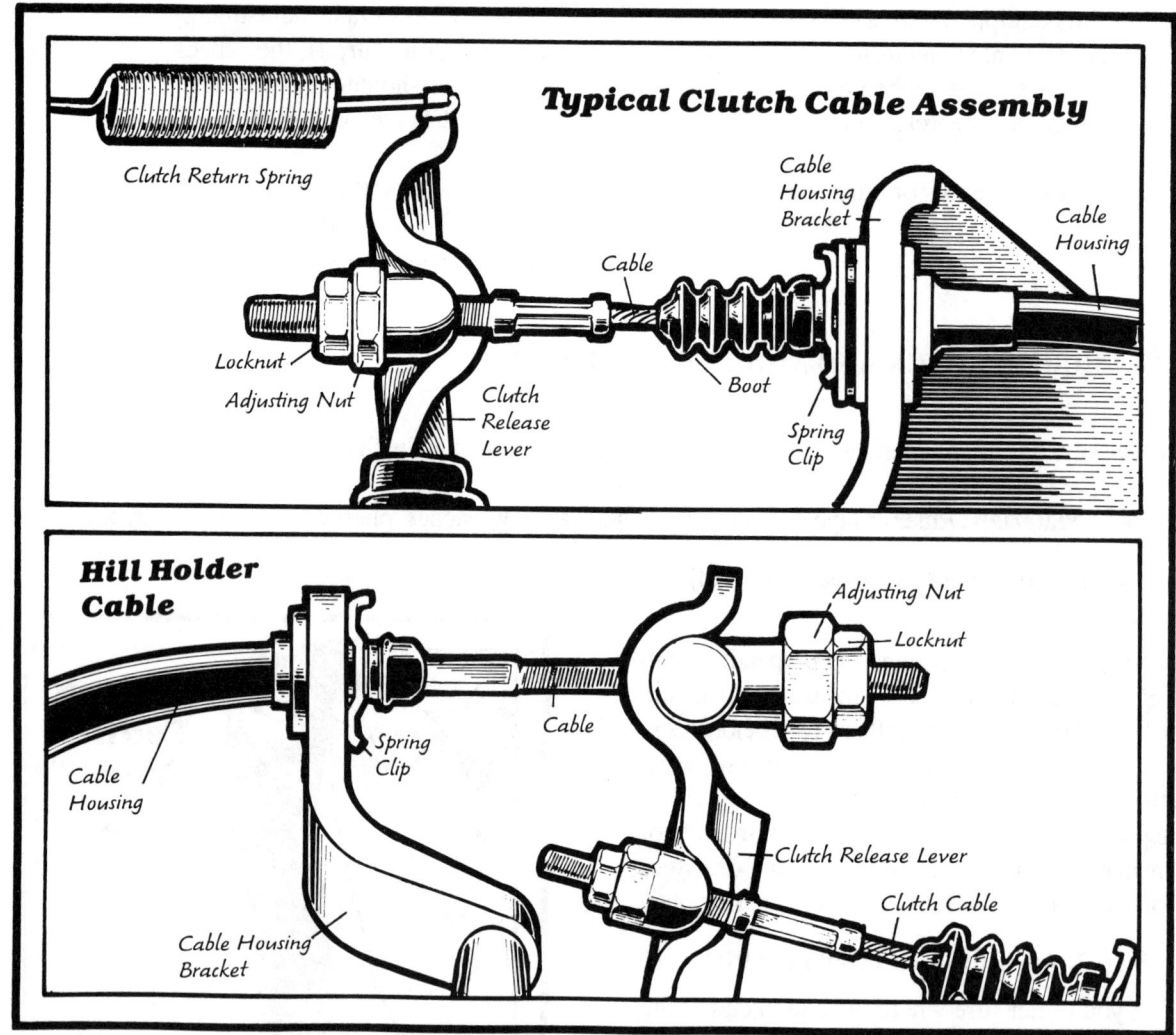

nut *clockwise* (as viewed from the front of the car) to decrease the free play. Turn the 14mm nut a turn or two, then check the pedal free play again. Keep turning the nut and checking until you have the proper free play.

When the free play is correct, screw the 10mm nut clockwise until it touches the 14mm nut. Hold the 14mm nut with a wrench while you tighten the 10mm nut against it. This locks the nuts so they can't move. That's all there is to adjusting the clutch. If you have a hill-holder, check the adjustment (Chapter 13, Procedure 17, Step 2).

PROCEDURE 2: REPLACE CLUTCH CABLE

The clutch cable consists of a braided wire cable which slides back and forth inside a semi-rigid **cable housing**. One end of the braided cable is attached to the top of the clutch pedal and the other end to the clutch release lever. The pedal end of the cable housing is attached to the **clutch pedal bracket** inside the car with a clamp. The engine end of the housing is attached to a bracket with a spring clip a few inches behind the clutch release lever.

The braided wire cable rarely breaks near the ends, where you would expect it to break. Usually it breaks inside the housing. Sometimes you can tell if the cable is becoming frayed inside the housing and about to break because it becomes harder and harder to push the pedal down. If you notice the clutch pedal becoming stiffer, save yourself from the hassle of a roadside breakdown by removing the cable and checking it for smooth operation.

Replace it with a new one if the braided wire doesn't slide easily and smoothly inside the cable housing.

Often the end of the cable housing breaks where it's attached to the clutch pedal bracket inside the car. This happens suddenly and without warning, and you're left without a working clutch. (A good reason to carry a spare clutch cable along with spare drive belts! The top of the spare tire is a convenient place to stash spare parts.)

Condition: Clutch pedal offers no resistance or is lying against the floorboard; OR the clutch pedal is getting harder and harder to push down.

Tools and Materials: New clutch cable, 10mm and 14mm wrenches, 10mm socket and ratchet, small screwdriver, pliers, flashlight, a couple of dabs of grease, safety glasses, patience.

Remarks: This procedure does not cover OHC Turbo models.

Step 1. Remove Old Clutch Cable.

See Procedure 1, Step 2, if you're not sure where the engine end of the clutch cable is located.

Unhook the **clutch return spring** from the end of the clutch return lever. Note where the other end of the spring is attached so you can hook it there during reassembly. If you have a hill-holder, don't mess with the two adjusting nuts on the end of the hill-holder cable (the upper cable).

Use a wrench to hold the 14mm nut on the end of the clutch cable while you loosen the 10mm nut. Now use pliers to hold the solid metal part of the cable (just behind the threaded part) while you remove both nuts from the cable. You'll use the nuts on the new cable, so stash them someplace safe.

Use pliers to slide the spring clip off the **cable housing bracket** located a few inches behind the clutch return lever. Pull the rubber boot, large flat washer, and rubber grommet toward the engine. Now pull the cable housing to the rear until the thin braided wire can slide out of the slot in the bracket.

'75-'79 models: The cable housing goes through a **rubber sling** located a few inches behind the clutch cable bracket. The sling is pulled toward the center of the car by a spring. Unhook the spring from the car body, then slide the sling off the housing.

'80 and newer models: Remove the 4-6 phillips screws securing the plastic **trim panel** to the bottom of the dash in front of the driver's seat. Remove the trim panel and lay it aside.

EVERYONE: Now the fun begins. Grab your flashlight or drop light and look under the dash at the top of the clutch pedal. The clutch cable housing is bolted to the **clutch pedal bracket** with one or two 10mm bolts. It's on the right side of the pedal on '75-'79 models and on the left side on '80 and newer models. Use a 10mm socket and ratchet to remove the bolt(s). Wiggle the **clamp** off the cable housing

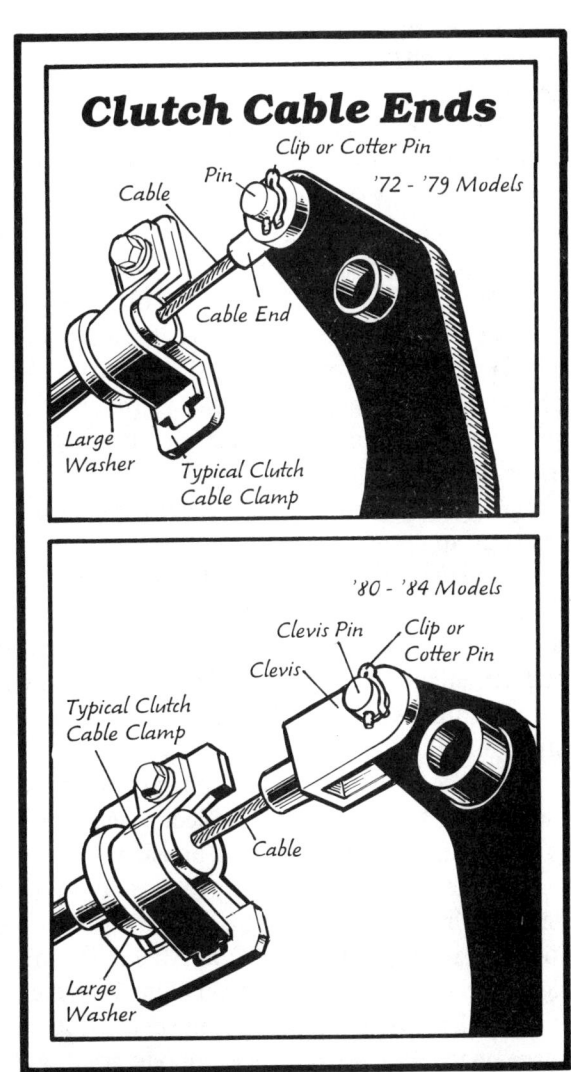

and stash the bolt and clamp where they won't get lost. Note how the large washers and rubber grommet on the end of the cable housing fit into a groove on the pedal bracket.

Now look at the left end of the horizontal shaft that the clutch and brake pedals pivot on. There's a horseshoe-shaped circlip around the very end of the shaft (see the clutch pedal free play illustration). Place the end of a small screwdriver in one of the spaces in the clip and push it off the shaft. Don't pry it off the end or it'll get bent and ruined. If there's a washer on the end of the shaft, remove it. Now slowly pull the clutch pedal off the pivot shaft. Watch for a thin washer that fits between the clutch pedal and brake pedal. Leave the washer on the shaft. Whew, now things are a little handier!

'75-'79 models: The round cable end is held onto the pin on the clutch pedal with a cotter pin or hairpin-type clip. Use pliers to remove the pin or clip. Slide the cable end off the pin.

'80 and newer models: The end of the cable is attached to the clutch pedal with a U-shaped clevis and pin. Use pliers to remove the cotter pin in the end of the clevis pin, then push the clevis pin out of the clutch pedal.

EVERYONE: Crawl out from under the dash. While you're giving your back a rest, carefully note how the clutch cable is routed in the engine compartment. Does it go over or under the heater hoses, the steering shaft, etc.? You'll need to thread the new cable through the engine compartment exactly the same way.

From inside the car, pry the rubber grommet out of the firewall where the clutch cable passes through. Remove the old cable by pulling it through the firewall into the passenger compartment. Throw it away.

Step 2. Install Clutch Cable.

Now creep back under the dash and push the threaded end of the cable through the hole in the firewall. Get out and thread the cable through the engine compartment exactly like the old cable. Crawl back under the dash and get ready to connect the cable end to the clutch pedal.

'75-'79 models: Fit the round cable end onto the pin on the clutch pedal. Install the hairpin clip or cotter pin into the top of the clutch pedal pin. If you have a cotter pin, bend the ends around the pin.

'80 and newer models: Fit the U-shaped clevis over the end of the clutch pedal, align the holes, then slip the clevis pin through the holes. Fit a cotter pin into the hole on the clevis pin, then bend the ends of the cotter pin around the clevis pin.

EVERYONE: Smear a light coat of grease on the clutch pedal shaft. Be sure there's a fiber bushing in each side of the clutch pedal where it fits onto the pivot shaft. Slide the clutch pedal onto the pivot shaft. If there was a washer on the end of the shaft, slip it onto the shaft. Safety glasses on? Fit the open end of the circlip into the groove on the end of the shaft, then use a screwdriver to push the clip into place. Put a finger on the end of the shaft while installing the clip just in case it tries to fly away. Check the clip all around to make sure it's securely in the groove.

Wiggle the grommet into place in the firewall hole so the edge of the hole fits into the groove on the big end of the grommet.

Now fit the large washers and rubber spacer on the cable housing into the groove on the clutch pedal bracket. Fit the tab on the clamp into the slot on the bracket, then fold it over the cable housing. You might have to squeeze the washers together to make them fit into the groove. When the clamp is in place, hold it there while you install and tighten the 10mm bolt. You're now through with the clutch pedal end of the process.

Be sure the cable is routed properly in the engine compartment. (Don't forget to put it through the rubber sling on '75-'79 models.)

Pull the rubber boot away from the braided wire inside the cable so you can slip its end into the slot on the clutch cable bracket. Pull the cable housing forward through the bracket so you can insert the spring clip in the groove near the end of the cable housing.

Fit the threaded end of the cable into the hole on the clutch release lever, then install the 14mm nut on the cable so the rounded part is toward the lever. Adjust the clutch (Procedure 1). Now install the 10mm nut and lock it against the 14mm nut. You'll hold the 14mm nut with another wrench so it doesn't turn when you snug down the 10mm nut. Don't forget to hook up the clutch lever return spring.

Hook the rubber sling up to the body by its spring ('75-'79 models). Screw the plastic trim panel back in place on the dash ('80 and newer models).

PROCEDURE 3: CHECK DOJs, CVJs, and U-JOINTS

Condition: Routine maintenance; OR you feel a solid vibration that increases with speed; OR you hear a knocking sound when making sharp turns; OR you hear a clunk when you let the clutch pedal up.

Tools and Materials: Jack and jackstands, safety glasses, rags.

Remarks: Drive train vibrations caused by worn DOJs, CVJs, U-joints, bent driveshaft or axles are harsh, solid vibrations felt in the seat of your pants. The vibration intensity increases with car speed. (Vibrations caused by improper wheel balance or wheel alignment are softer and you feel them more on the steering wheel.) It's difficult to check DOJs and CVJs because they normally have *a little* looseness (play) in them. It's a good idea to check them while they're in good condition to get a feel for the proper amount of play. Then you'll be able to detect wear when it occurs. The CVJ and axleshaft are inseparable and must be replaced as a unit. Expensive (and built to stay that way).

Step 1. Quick CVJ Check.

Find a large deserted parking lot where you can drive in circles. Turn the steering wheel either direction as far as it will go, then make a few slow circles while listening for clanks and clunks. Turn the steering wheel the other direction and try again. No sounds? The CVJs are probably good.

If you hear clunks while turning but the clunk goes away when the wheels are straightened out, or you're here from the 12,000-mile tune-up procedure, do Step 2.

Step 2. Check DOJs, CVJs, U-joints.

Chock the rear wheels, then jack up the front of the car and put it on jackstands. Put the transmission in Neutral, then release the handbrake.

To locate the front DOJs, CVJs, and axleshafts, crawl under the front of the car. Look at the inboard side of each front wheel for a black, wavy rubber boot. That's the **CVJ boot**. The **axleshaft** is a steel rod a little larger than your thumb coming out of the CVJ boot. The shaft disappears into the rubber **DOJ boot** on the transmission end of the shaft.

Check CVJs: Try to push and pull the axleshaft into and out of the CVJ while watching for play (movement) where the shaft disappears into the CVJ boot. You should be able to move the shaft in and out very slightly. Now twist the axleshaft as if you're screwing and unscrewing it. At most the amount of play should be a very slight.

Evaluation: If the axleshaft moves in and out more than 1/16", can be twisted more than a barely perceptible amount, and/or makes dry sounding clunks when you move it, the joint is worn and/or needs to be cleaned and repacked with grease (Procedure 5). It's worthwhile to try cleaning and greasing the joint before replacing it because they're very expensive. If fresh grease doesn't quiet the joint, it should be replaced (Procedure 7).

Check DOJs: DOJs are normally a little wobbly on the axleshaft. The only check you can do is the "twist test," like you did with the CVJs. Hold the round DOJ with one hand while twisting the axleshaft with the other. If there's more than a slight movement and/or you hear a dry clunk or click when twisting the shaft, the DOJ should be cleaned and greased (Procedure 4).

Lower the car when you're through checking, cleaning, and greasing, or replacing the front DOJs or CVJs.

Step 3. Check 4WD Driveshaft and Axleshafts.

All 4WD models have a long, black **driveshaft tube** connecting the rear end of the transmission to the rear differential. A U-joint on each end allows the driveshaft to rotate smoothly even though the transmission and differential aren't perfectly aligned. OHC 4WD models have two driveshafts, connected in the middle with a U-joint. Axleshafts between the rear differential and rear wheels carry the power to the rear wheels.

'75-'78 4WD station wagons: There are U-joints on each end of the rear axleshafts. Check them the same way you check the U-joints on the driveshaft (see the Check U-joints section later in this step).

'79 and newer cars and all Brats: There's a DOJ on each end of the rear axleshafts. Check them the same way you check the DOJs on the front axleshafts (Step 2).

Check U-joints (4WD only): A U-joint consists of an X-shaped piece of steel called a **cross** that has four grease filled cups on the ends containing needle bearings. U-shaped pieces of steel called **yokes** are attached on opposite sides of the cross. The U-joint cups fit into holes in the ends of the yokes, and are secured by C-shaped clips. As the needle bearings and bearing surfaces on the ends of the cross wear away, slack develops and the U-joint should be replaced with a new one. Fortunately, Subaru U-joints are very durable and rarely need to be replaced. If you find a worn U-joint, remove the driveshaft (Procedure 8), or the axleshaft(s) on '75-'79 station wagons (Procedure 9), then take the shaft to Subaru or a machine shop and have them install the new U-joint(s). U-joints should be checked regularly, and here's how you do it:

Hold the yoke on one side of the U-joint with one hand while twisting the yoke on the other side. Look for movement where the cross disappears into the cups in the yokes. Check all the U-joints this way. Don't forget the center U-joint on OHC models. If you see *any* movement, the U-joint is worn and should be replaced. If there's enough movement so you hear a click when twisting the yokes, install a new U-joint before driving the car! New U-joints are relatively inexpensive, but if one breaks while cruising down the road, the driveshaft will flail about under the car, damaging the yokes and other delicate things like brake lines. If the rear driveshaft U-joint breaks, the driveshaft can fall off the car, causing frantic havoc on a busy freeway.

PROCEDURE 4: REMOVE AND INSTALL DOJ AND DOJ BOOT

Condition: Routine maintenance; OR a DOJ is worn out; OR a DOJ boot is torn; OR the DOJ is being removed so you can install a new CVJ boot or CVJ.

Tools and Materials: Safety glasses, Friend, maybe new DOJ(s) or DOJ boots and clamps, DOJ/CVJ grease (see Remarks), 5/32" or 3/16" (5mm or 6mm) punch (see Remarks), hammer, external snap ring (circlip) pliers (preferably with 90° jaws), 14mm wrench, 14mm socket and ratchet, very small screwdriver, medium screwdriver, pliers, torque wrench, flashlight or droplight, maybe a new roll pin, LOTS of rags and/or paper towels, jack and jackstands.

Remarks: The DOJ must be removed from the axleshaft to be cleaned and greased or to replace the DOJ boot. You have to get under the car to remove the left (driver's side) DOJ because the steering shaft, heater hoses, etc. are in the way. You can remove the right (passenger's side) DOJ from above (through the engine compartment) except on Turbo models. Turbo owners should have Subaru or a garage replace the right front DOJ and/or boot when they wear out.

Subaru sells DOJ/CVJ grease in little tubes that make it easy to pack the joints. If you can't get the Subaru grease, use molybdenum wheel bearing grease.

The perfect punch for removing Subaru DOJs is a 3/16" Sears Craftsman #42885 WF. It's just the right length to tap in until the tapered part of the tool hits the DOJ. The roll pin will clear the transaxleshaft but will stay in the DOJ housing so it doesn't fly out and get lost. If any roll pin taps out easily, replace it with a new one (they're cheap).

CAUTION: Wear safety glasses while working under the car.

Step 1. Separate DOJ from Transaxle, Rear Differential, or Rear Stub Axle.

Front DOJs: Chock the rear wheels, then jack up the front of the car and put it on jackstands. Release the handbrake. If you're removing the right DOJ, remove the spare tire if it's in the engine compartment.

Remove the **inner control arm pivot bolt** for the side you're working on (Chapter 14, Procedure 5, Step 4).

Rear DOJs (4WD): Chock the front wheels, then jack up the rear of the car and put it on jackstands.

Look at Chapter 14, Procedure 2. If you're a "Nut" person, remove the **lower shock absorber mounting nut** on the side you're working on, then pull the shock off the mounting bolt. If you're a "Bolt" person, remove the two **upper shock absorber mounting bolts** on that side.

EVERYONE: To remove the left front DOJ or rear DOJ (4WD only), crawl under the car with a 5/32" or 3/16" (5mm or 6mm) punch, hammer, and flashlight or drop light. Rotate the DOJ you're removing until you see a small hole with a roll pin in it. It's in the small part of the DOJ on the opposite end from the rubber boot. Use the punch and hammer to drive the pin far enough out of the DOJ so the DOJ can slide away from the transaxle. If you're working on a rear DOJ, drive the pins out of both DOJs on the axle (it's easier to remove the whole axleshaft so you can put it on a table to work on it).

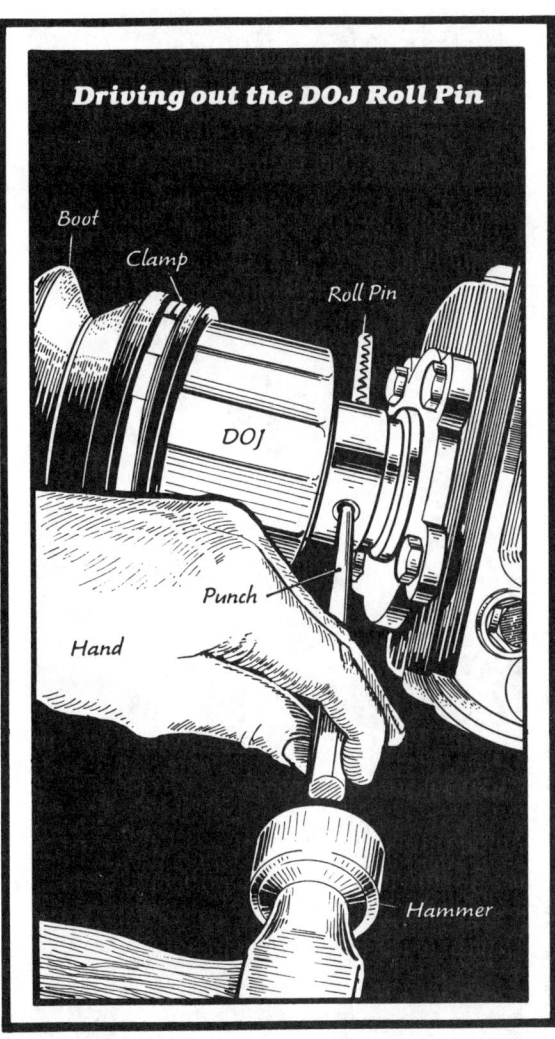

To remove the right front DOJ, open the hood and remove the spare tire if you haven't already. Rotate the right wheel until you see the roll pin in the small part of the DOJ. Use a 5/32" or 3/16" (5mm or 6mm) punch and hammer to tap the roll pin out far enough so the DOJ can slide toward the front wheel.

To remove the DOJ from the transaxle (front), have Friend pull out gently on the bottom of the front tire while you pull the DOJ off the transaxle. To remove the DOJ from the rear differential, have Friend push down gently on the rear tire while you pull the DOJ off the differential. If you're working on the rear, you can pull the DOJ off the wheel "stub" axle now.

Step 2. Remove DOJ and/or CVJ Boot Clamps.

On some Soobs, a large rubber band covers the clamp that secures the boot to the DOJ or CVJ. If your large clamp is covered, slide the rubber band off the clamp.

Two kinds of clamps are used on different year models. One kind wraps tightly around the boot twice before being pinched in a small band that fits around the clamp. The other type has a split-band around the clamp that holds a thicker, lever-like part of the clamp. The split-band lever-type clamp can be reused if it isn't bent or funky. Replace the large double-wrap-type clamps with new ones, and use the old large clamps on the small end of the boot. If someone has replaced the boot before, they may have replaced the original type clamps with

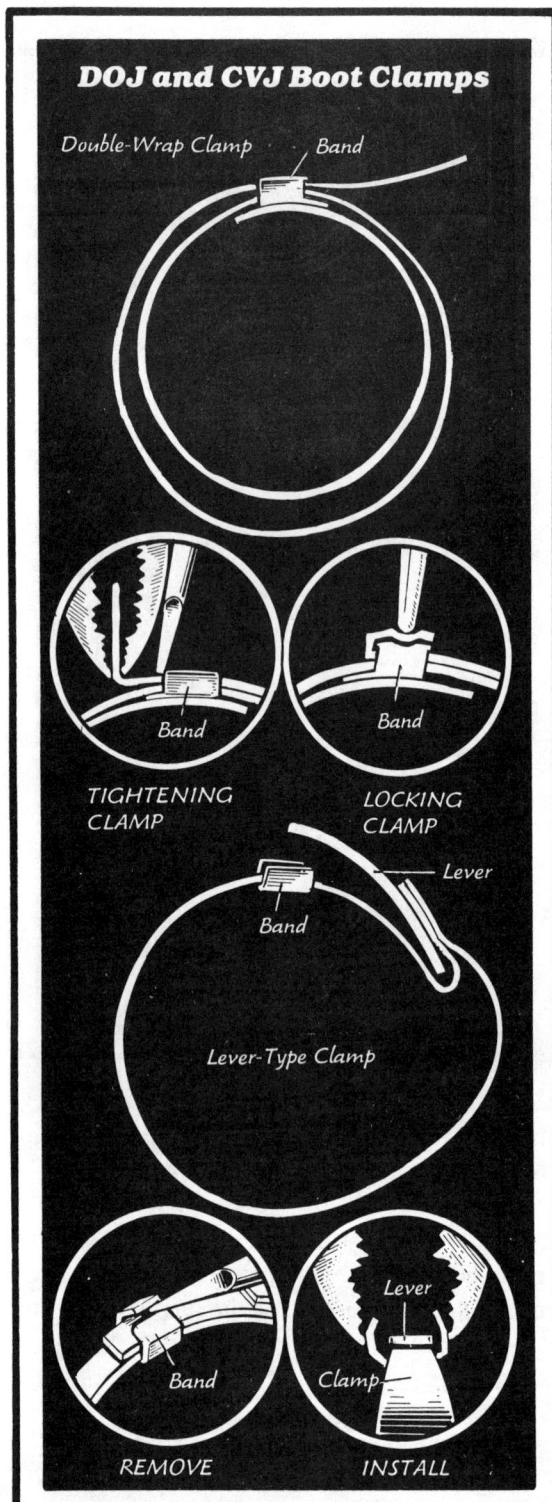

large hose clamps. You can use hose clamps in place of the boot clamps everywhere except for the large clamp on the left front DOJ, where there isn't enough clearance for the clamp screw to rotate between the DOJ and the steering gear. If you use hose clamps, use the ones with the smallest clamp screw you can find.

Look for a split in the center part of the band. If you find a split, pry the band open with a small screwdriver or knife, then lift up on the lever that was held by the band. Lift the lever far enough to wiggle the clamp off the boot. No split in the band? The end of the clamp is probably folded over the band. Bend the clamp end off the band, then wiggle a small screwdriver under the band and pry up and down to loosen it. Now you can pull the thin clamp through the band. Loosen the clamp enough to slide it off the boot. Remove both clamps on the boot, then twist and slide the boot away from the DOJ or CVJ.

Step 3. Remove DOJ.

Now that the boot is out of the way, you can see the greasy innards of the DOJ. Wipe some of the grease away from the inside edge of the **DOJ housing**. While you're wiping away the grease, you'll notice grooves for the ball bearings on the inside of the housing. There's a thin wire clip in a slot just inside the opening of the housing. Slide the end of a small screwdriver into one of the ball bearing grooves so it's under the wire, then gently pry the wire out of the housing. Find the ends of the wire, then remove it from the axleshaft. Now you can slide the DOJ housing off the axle. What's left is the **ball cage** and **ball bearings**. Wipe the grease off the end of the axle so you can see the ends of a circlip. Use the tire to rotate the axle so you can get to the circlip with circlip pliers. If you're working underneath the car on the left DOJ, you can pull the control arm down slightly, then pull the axle toward the rear of the car a few inches for better access. Hold a finger on the end of the axleshaft while you use external snap ring pliers to remove the circlip from the end of the axleshaft. Your finger will keep the circlip from flying off. When the circlip is off, pull the ball cage off the axleshaft.

If there's a thick snap ring left on the axle when the ball cage is removed, you can remove it and throw it away. Subaru decided it wasn't needed, like an appendix. It just makes removing and installing the DOJ and CVJ boots more difficult. (You need hefty external snap ring pliers to get it off.)

If you're replacing the DOJ or CVJ boot, slide the DOJ boot off the axle now. Otherwise, leave it on the axleshaft.

Step 4. Clean, Inspect, and Grease DOJ.

Use rags or paper towels to wipe as much grease as possible from the ball cage and from inside the DOJ housing and boot. Use solvent to wash the ball cage, DOJ housing, circlip, wire ring, and boot clamps until they're spotlessly clean and shiny. Let them dry.

If the balls fall out of the cage easily, or if the balls are bluish-colored instead of clear and bright (you should be able to see your reflection in them), the DOJ should be replaced with a new one. Feel all the grooves inside the housing where the balls fit for worn or rough places. If you can feel a slight ridge where the balls have worn into the housing, replace the DOJ with a new one. Use a new circlip and wire ring if the old ones are bent and funky. The plug in the small end of the DOJ housing should be securely fastened to the housing. If it isn't, try peening the housing with a punch and hammer to tighten it, or replace the DOJ. Everything look good?

If you have a tube of grease, press the nozzle end of the tube against the grooves on the end of the bearing cage where you can see the ball bearings. Squeeze the tube so grease oozes out around the balls. Squeeze grease into each groove on both sides of the bearing cage. Now smear grease on the outside of the ball cage and ball bearings.

If the grease you're using isn't in a tube, pack about two inches of grease into the bottom of the DOJ housing and smear some in each of the ball bearing grooves. Smear grease all over the ball bearings. When you install the housing on the ball bearings, push it on as far as possible so the grease will be forced through the bearing cage and around the bearings.

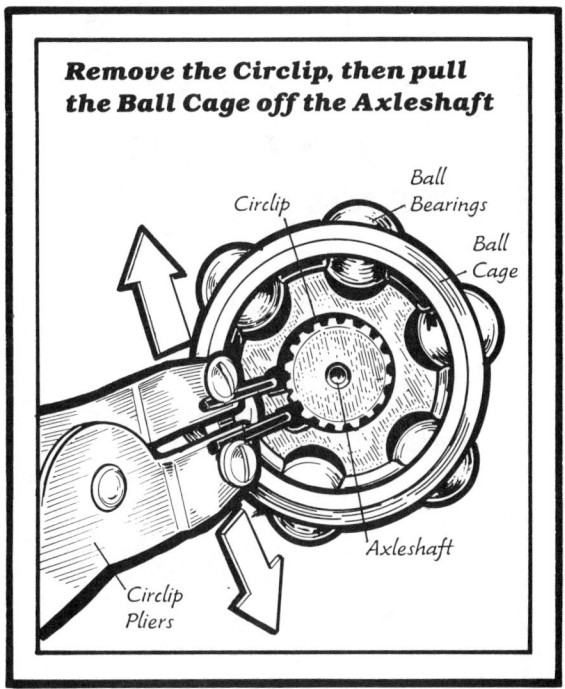

Remove the Circlip, then pull the Ball Cage off the Axleshaft

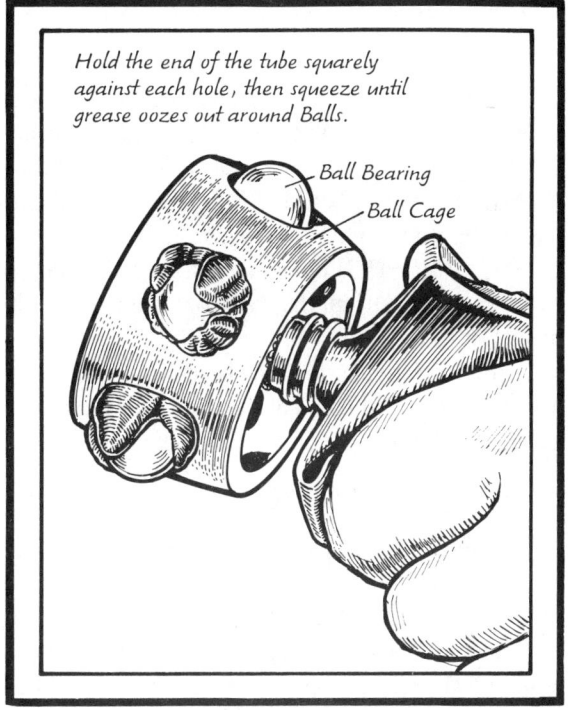

Hold the end of the tube squarely against each hole, then squeeze until grease oozes out around Balls.

Step 5. Install DOJ Boot and DOJ on Axleshaft.

Put a thin coating of grease in the grooves of the boot where the clamps fit. It makes the clamps easier to tighten. Slide a clamp for the small end of the boot onto the axle (if you removed the old one), then slide the small

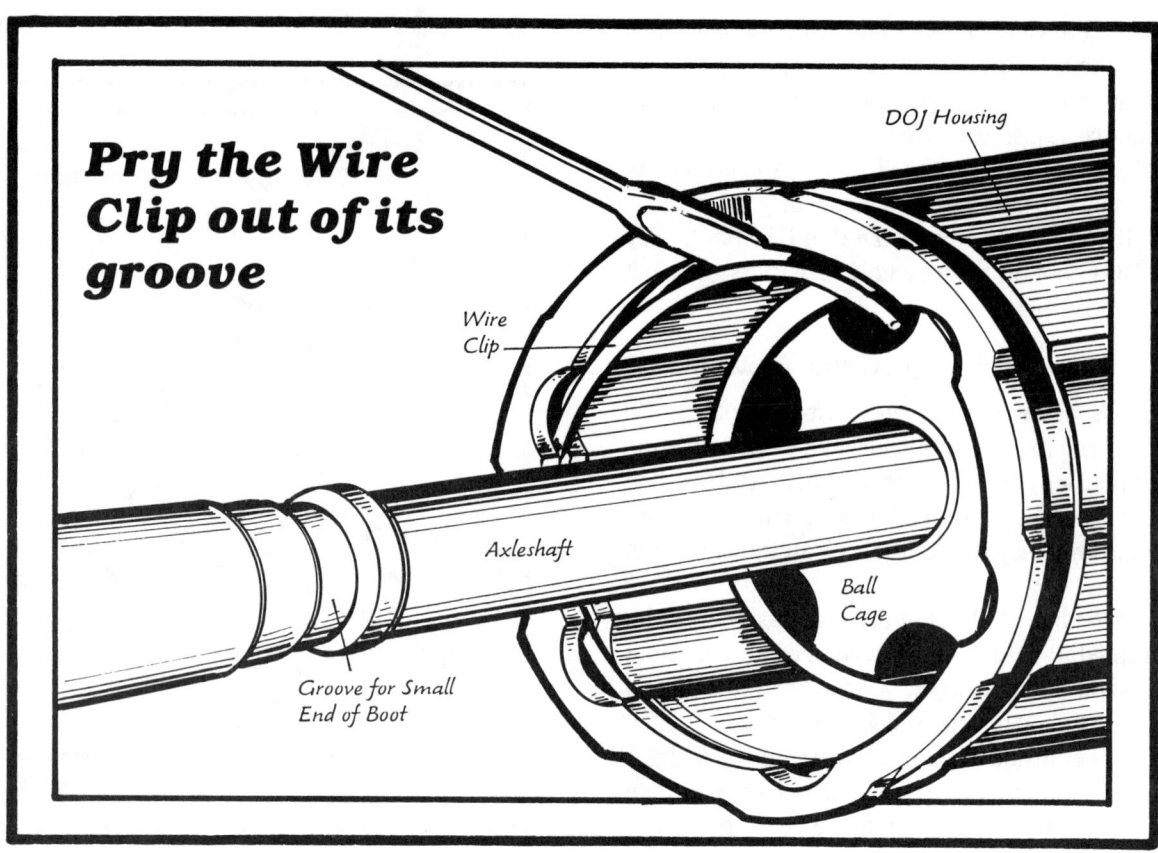

Pry the Wire Clip out of its groove

end of the boot on (if you removed the boot). Align the splines on the shaft with the splines on the ball cage, then fit the ball cage onto the axle with the recessed side toward the end of the axleshaft. Use snap-ring pliers to install the circlip into the groove. To be sure the circlip is seated properly, tap a screwdriver against the clip all the way around. You should be able to rotate the circlip around the shaft fairly easily by hooking one end of the circlip pliers in one of the circlip holes.

Wiggle the DOJ housing onto the ball cage, then install the wire ring into the groove just inside the edge of the housing. Orient the wire so the ends aren't in a ball groove. Feel all the way around to be sure it's seated properly.

Slide the small end of the boot into the groove on the axleshaft. Wipe the grease off the outside of the DOJ housing, then fit the end of the boot over the edge of the DOJ housing so the ridge inside the boot fits into the groove on the outside of the housing.

Step 6. Install Boot Clamps.

Fit the boot clamps into the grooves on the boot. It's best to tighten the large clamp first so the grease doesn't get out of the boot and dirt doesn't get in. Be sure the boot is properly seated in the groove on the housing or axle before you tighten the clamp. Here's how to tighten the clamps:

Lever-type clamps: Press the lever down into the band and hold it there while you use a screwdriver to bend the sides of the band over the lever. Use pliers to squeeze the sides of the band together gently until the two sides touch. Give the band a tap or two with the hammer to be sure it's tight.

Double-wrap-type clamp: Wrap the clamp around the boot twice, threading it through the band each time. Place a screwdriver against the band to hold it while you pull on the loose end of the clamp. Be sure the clamp is in the groove on the boot. Keep the screwdriver against the band while you grab the clamp with pliers as close as possible to the screwdriver. Use the pliers as a lever against the screwdriver to pull the clamp through the band. When the clamp is as tight as you can get it, keep pulling on the pliers while you bend the clamp end over the band. Try to rotate the boot on the DOJ housing or axle. If the boot slips off the housing or rotates easily, you need to get the clamp tighter—try again.

When you're satisfied the boot clamp is tight enough, lift the end so it's 90° to the clamp. Put a medium screwdriver blade, punch, or pointed center punch on the center of the band and tap it with a hammer to crimp the band. Leaving enough clamp to cover the band, use the pliers to bend the excess clamp back and forth until it breaks. Now use the hammer to flatten the clamp against the band.

Hose clamps: Fit the clamp into the groove on the boot, then use a screwdriver to tighten the clamp. Be sure the clamp is in the groove all the way around. If the clamp is too wide to fit in the groove, it might slip off the boot—get a narrower clamp. Don't use a hose clamp on the large end of the left, front DOJ.

People without tubes of grease: If you didn't have a tube of grease to pack the bearings, but packed the grease in the bottom of the housing instead, press the housing onto the axle. You'll hear and feel the grease being forced through the ball cage.

Front DOJ people: Wait until the DOJ is attached to the transaxle before tightening the clamp on the small end of the boot. Now you can install the DOJ on the transaxle (Step 7).

Rear (4WD) DOJ people: Gently push the DOJ onto the axle until it stops, then pull it toward the end until it stops. Now that you know how far it moves, position it approximately centered on the shaft. Now install the clamp on the small end of the boot.

Step 7. Attach DOJ to Transaxle, Rear Differential, or Stub Axle.

Have Friend ready to pull out on the bottom of the front wheel or push down on the rear wheel when you have the roll pin holes aligned.

The hole in the DOJ must align perfectly with the hole in the shaft or the roll pin won't fit. There's an easy way to tell which way the DOJ goes. Look in the splined end of the DOJ for the roll pin holes. One hole will be centered on one of the splines and the other hole will be centered on a groove. The holes in the splined shaft on the transaxle, rear differential, and stub axle are the same; one side is centered on a spline, the other side is centered on a groove. When fitting the DOJ onto the shaft, you have to match opposites. In other words, align the centered spline in the DOJ with the centered groove on the shaft or vice versa. When the DOJ is on and you're sure the holes are aligned, tap the roll pin in with a hammer. Use the punch and hammer to tap it in flush with the DOJ. If the pin taps in too easily, replace it with a new one (they're cheap).

Install front DOJ: Have Friend pull out on the bottom of the wheel while you slip the DOJ onto the shaft. When you're sure the holes are aligned perfectly, tap the roll pin in with a hammer. Use the punch and hammer to tap it flush.

Install rear (4WD) DOJs: The two DOJs on the rear axleshaft are slightly different. Measure the distance across the metal dust shields next to the roll pin holes. The shield for the inner DOJ that attaches to the differential will be just over 2½" (64.5mm) across. The shield for the outer stub axle DOJ will be just over 2¾" (70.5mm).

Align the roll pin holes for the outer DOJ and stub axle, then install the DOJ and roll pin. Align the holes for the inner DOJ and differential shaft. Have Friend push down on the rear wheel while you slip the DOJ onto the shaft. Install the roll pin.

Step 8. Finish Up.

Front DOJ people: Slide the smaller end of the boot into the groove on the axle. If the boot is distorted and part of it won't pop out, there's a vacuum inside that must be relieved. Slide a very small screwdriver under the edge of the small end of the boot, then lift the edge so air can enter the boot. Be careful not to tear the boot. Pull out on the boot if necessary.

When the boot is straight, be sure the ridge on the inside of the boot is in the groove on the axle. Slide the small clamp into its slot on the boot and tighten it the same way you tightened the large clamp (Step 5). Wipe the boot with a clean rag to remove excess grease.

Install the control arm pivot bolt and nut, and torque it to 54 ft. lbs (Chapter 14, Procedure 5, Step 6).

Rear DOJ people: Attach the end of the shock absorber (Chapter 14, Procedure 2, Step 4).

EVERYONE: Use clean rags to wipe the grease off the DOJ housing and boot and the axleshaft. Lower the car, clean your tools, throw the greasy rags in the outside trash can, then clean your hands, and you're finished. Now that you've been through the ordeal once and know what you're doing, the next time you replace a DOJ or boot it will be a lot easier.

PROCEDURE 5: REPACK CVJ WITH FRESH GREASE

Condition: Routine maintenance; OR you're installing a new CVJ boot; OR you hear clunks, clanks, or clicks when making sharp turns.

Tools and Materials: Same as Procedure 4, maybe new CVJ boot(s).

Remarks: Clean the suspension, wheel bearing housing, and other parts around the CVJ first to prevent dirt from getting into the CVJs while repacking them and/or replacing the boots. Use your garden hose or cruise down to the carwash.

Step 1. Chock, Jack, and Block.

Chock the rear wheels. Jack up the front of the car and put it on jackstands. Release the handbrake and put the gearshift in Neutral.

Step 2. Remove CVJ Boot, Clean and Grease CVJ.

Clean the outside of the boot with a rag so dirt can't fall into the CVJ.

See Procedure 4, Step 5, to release the boot clamps. Twist and slide the boot toward the center of the car until it clears the CVJ.

Use rags or paper towels to wipe the old grease off the CVJ and out of the boot.

If you have a tube of grease, press the nozzle end of the tube against the ball bearing grooves right next to the axle. Squirt fresh grease into the grooves until you see it forcing the old grease out around the balls (the old grease will be black and the fresh grease will be dark grey). Use the tire to rotate the joint so you can get to all the grooves. Wipe the old grease off the joint, then squirt more fresh grease into the grooves. Smear some fresh grease around the outside of the joint and inside the boot. It should take about half the tube to pack the bearings and grease the inside of the boot.

If you don't have a tube of grease, use your fingers to pack fresh grease into the grooves on the inner end of the joint. Rotate the tire so you can get to all the grooves. Take your time and try to get as much fresh grease as possible into the joint. Use a rag to wipe off the old grease as it oozes out around the balls. When the joint is packed, smear fresh grease over as much of the joint as possible, then put a couple of two-finger scoops of grease inside the boot. Spread it around just inside the edge.

Step 3. Install CVJ Boot.

Slide the CVJ boot into position so the small end fits in the groove on the axleshaft and the large end fits in the groove on the joint. Position the clamps, then tighten them. Procedure 4, Step 6, tells you how.

Step 4. Finish Up.

When the clamps are secure, crawl out from under the car and clean your hands. Pretty yucky, eh? Be sure the rear wheels are blocked, then lower the car to the ground.

PROCEDURE 6: REPLACE CVJ BOOT

Condition: CVJ boot is torn.

Tools and Materials: Same as Procedures 4 and 5 plus a new CVJ boot.

Remarks: The DOJ must be removed before you install a CVJ boot. I've seen ads for "split" CVJ boots you can install without having to remove the DOJ. You just cut the old boot off, then wrap a new split boot around the CVJ and glue the edges together. I haven't tried them, because replacing a CVJ boot is an opportune time to clean and grease the DOJ. A split boot might be a good thing to add to the spare parts stash for emergencies.

Step 1. Remove DOJ.

Chock the rear wheels, then jack the car up and put it on jackstands.
Do Steps 1-4 of Procedure 4 to remove the DOJ on the side with the torn CVJ boot.

Step 2. Remove CVJ Boot.

Remove the clamps on the torn CVJ boot (Procedure 4, Step 2). Pull the old boot off the DOJ end of the axleshaft. Clean the axleshaft with rags so dirt won't get in the new boot when you install it.

Step 3. Clean and Grease CVJ.

See Procedure 5, Step 2, to pack the CVJ with fresh grease.

Step 4. Install New CVJ Boot.

Clean your hands, then fit the large end of the new boot over the axleshaft and slide it onto the CVJ. Install the clamps on the CVJ (Procedure 4, Step 3).

Step 5. Install DOJ and Finish Up.

When the new CVJ boot is installed and the clamps are secure, do Procedure 4, Steps 5-8, to install the DOJ. Install and tighten the control arm pivot bolt (Chapter 14, Procedure 5, Step 6). Clean your hands and tools, then lower the car.

PROCEDURE 7: REPLACE CVJ AND FRONT AXLE SHAFT

The CVJ and axleshafts are inseparable, so unfortunately they must be installed as a complete unit. You have to take a lot of things apart to remove the front axle, so it's an opportune time to inspect the brake shoes or pads, drum or disc, wheel bearings, grease seals, and MacPherson struts. If you can afford it, replace any parts that are nearing the end of the trail while it's handy and save yourself the hassle of replacing them later.

It takes a a special tool to install the new axle in the wheel bearing housing, so you'll have to remove the housing and axle and take them to Subaru, a garage, or a machine shop to have the old axle pressed out of the wheel bearing housing and the new axle pressed in. It shouldn't cost much.

Condition: CVJ is worn out; OR axleshaft is bent; OR the threads on the end of the axleshaft are damaged beyond repair.

Tools and Materials: Same as Procedure 4, plus those listed in Chapter 13, Procedure 6 if you have drum brakes, or Chapter 13, Procedure 10 if you have disc brakes; and Chapter 14, Procedure 7.

Remarks: This procedure does not cover 1975 models with front drum brakes.

Step 1. Chock, Jack, and Block.

Chock the rear wheels, then slightly loosen the lug nuts on the side you're removing. Look at Chapter 13, Procedure 4, Step 1, to see how to loosen the large axle nut. When the lug nuts and axle nuts are loose, jack up the front of the car and put it on jackstands. Release the handbrake (down). Gently push on the car to be sure it's securely on the jackstands.

Step 2. Remove DOJ.

See Procedure 4, Steps 1-3, in this chapter to remove the DOJ from the axleshaft.

Step 3. Remove Brakes.

Do Chapter 13, Procedure 10, Steps 1-6, to remove the caliper and disc. When the disc is removed, do Chapter 14, Procedure 7, Step 2, to remove the disc cover. Stash the brake pads and disc where they won't get dirty or greasy. While the brake pads are handy, check them for wear and buy new ones if they're getting thin. Check the caliper for signs of leaking brake fluid and if you find a leak, have them rebuilt or replace them with new ones.

Step 4. Remove Wheel Bearing Housing.

See Chapter 14, Procedure 7, Steps 3 and 4, to remove the wheel bearing housing. You're removing the axle and the housing as a unit so you won't need a puller. Note where the axle goes through the body, then pull the whole thing off the car and take it to Subaru, a garage, or machine shop. Have them press the old axle out of the housing and press the new one in. While the axle is out would be an opportune time to repack the wheel bearings with grease and replace the wheel-bearing grease seals (Chapter 14, Procedure 7, Steps 6-9). When the new axle is in the housing, you're ready to put it all back together.

Step 5. Install Front Axleshaft and Wheel Bearing Housing.

Slip the inner (DOJ) end of the axle through the slot on the body, then install the wheel bearing housing (Chapter 14, Procedure 7, Step 10). You won't have to hammer the housing onto the axle because it's already installed.

Step 6. Install DOJ.

Do Procedure 4, Steps 4-7, in this chapter to clean and grease the DOJ, then assemble and install it. When the DOJ is attached to the transaxle, install and tighten the control arm pivot bolt (Chapter 14, Procedure 5, Step 6).

Step 7. Install Brakes and Outer Grease Seal.

OK, things are looking a little more normal now. The only parts left to install are the brakes and wheels. Do Chapter 14, Procedure 7, Step 11, to install the disc cover, the brakes, and the outer grease seal.

Step 8. Finish Up.

The brakes are all back together on the car, right? If any brake lines were disconnected, be sure and bleed the brake system (Chapter 13, Procedure 2).

Install the wheels and snug the lug nuts with a wrench. Snug the axle nut with the 36mm socket if you haven't already.

Now do Chapter 14, Procedure 7, Step 12 to finish the job. You deserve a gold star (or a purple heart?) for your efforts!

PROCEDURE 8: REMOVE AND INSTALL DRIVESHAFT (4WD Models Only)

Condition: Vibration from worn out U-joint(s); OR the driveshaft tube is dented or bent; OR you're removing the rear differential.

Tools and Materials: Jack, jackstands, two 12mm wrenches, oil drain pan, rags.

Remarks: You can't drive the car with the driveshaft removed because all the gear oil in the transaxle will leak out.

If the U-joints are worn out, remove the driveshaft, take it to Subaru or a machine shop and have them install the new U-joints. If the driveshaft is bent, a machine shop can replace the tube for you, or you might find a good used driveshaft at a salvage yard. New ones are expensive.

Step 1. Chock, Jack, and Block.

Set the handbrake, chock the front wheels, then jack up the rear of the car and put it on jackstands. Put the gearshift in Neutral.

Crawl under the rear of the car with two 12mm wrenches and your oil drain pan or several rags. Place the oil pan or some rags beneath the rear end of the transaxle to catch gear oil that might dribble out when the driveshaft is removed.

The rear end of the driveshaft is bolted to a round flange on the front of the rear differential. Hold the bolt heads with a wrench while you remove the nuts. When the nuts are all removed, support the weight of the driveshaft while you remove the bolts.

OHC models: If you only need to remove the rear driveshaft, mark the two yokes where the driveshafts connect so you can bolt them together in exactly the same position. Remove the four bolts and nuts the same way you did at the rear end of the shaft. If you need to remove both driveshafts, remove the two bolts that attach the center bearing assembly to the body. It's near the middle of the drive shaft.

EVERYONE: Now support the entire driveshaft and gently pull it out of the rear of the transaxle, or away from the front driveshaft if you're only removing the rear shaft on an OHC model. Don't let it crash to the floor. Haul the driveshaft away for repairs.

OHC models: If you didn't remove the two driveshafts separately to make it easier to transport, you can separate the two halves of the driveshaft the same way you disconnected the rear shaft from the differential. Use paint or a punch to mark the two flanges so you can bolt them back together in exactly the same position, then remove the four bolts and nuts.

Step 2. Install Driveshaft.

OHC models: If you separated the two driveshafts, align the matchmarks you made, then bolt the two flanges together. Tighten the bolts.

EVERYONE: Clean the part of the driveshaft that fits into the rear of the transaxle. Align the splines on the driveshaft end with the splines on the shaft in the transaxle and carefully slip the driveshaft into the transaxle.

OHC models: Fit the center bearing into position against the bottom of the car body, then install and tighten the two mounting bolts.

EVERYONE: Reattach the rear end of the driveshaft to the rear differential with the four bolts and nuts. Hold the bolt heads with one wrench while you tighten the nuts with the other wrench. That's all there is to it. Lower the car to the ground.

PROCEDURE 9: REMOVE AND INSTALL REAR AXLE SHAFTS ON '75-'78 4WD MODELS (Except Brats)

Condition: U-joints or slip joints in the rear axleshaft are worn out.

Tools and Materials: Jack, jackstands, two 12mm wrenches.

Remarks: Once you've removed the axleshaft, take it to Subaru or a machine shop to have the new U-joints installed. Have them check the slip joint in the middle of the shaft before installing the U-joints. If the slip joint is worn out, ask how much it will cost to rebuild it, then compare that figure to the price for a good used axleshaft from a salvage yard. New axleshafts are expensive. If you find a good used one, carefully check the U-joints and have new ones installed if necessary.

CAUTION: Be careful not to damage the rubber boot on the axleshaft during removal or installation.

Step 1. Chock, Jack, and Block.

Set the handbrake, chock the front wheels, then jack up the rear of the car and put it on jackstands. Put the gearshift in Neutral.

Step 2. Remove Rear Axle Shaft.

Crawl under the rear of the car with two 12mm wrenches. The outer end of the axleshaft is attached to a **flange yoke** on the inside of the wheel with four 12mm bolts and nuts. Remove the four nuts, then support the shaft while you remove the bolts. Hold the axleshaft so you can fit a wrench into the space on the differential side of the inner U-joint. Pull out on the axleshaft as you unscrew the bolt. When the bolt is out, pull the end of the axleshaft out of the differential.

If you removed the axleshaft because the U-joints are worn out, take it to Subaru or a machine shop and have them install new U-joints (see Remarks).

Step 3. Install Rear Axleshaft.

Clean the end of the shaft that fits into the differential, then install the attaching bolt into the yoke if you removed it. Align the splines and gently slip the end of the axleshaft into the differential. Hold the shaft in a position so you can screw the bolt into the differential and tighten it. Attach the outer end of the shaft to the flange on the inside of the wheel with the four bolts and nuts. Hold each bolt with one wrench while you tighten the nut with another wrench. Lower the car and you're finished.

PROCEDURE 10: REMOVE AND INSTALL REAR DIFFERENTIAL (4WD Only)

Condition: Rear differential is howling like a wolf: OR differential case is cracked; OR you're replacing one of the differential mounts.

Tools and Materials: Jack, jackstands, drain pan, 17mm socket and ratchet, ¾" drive ratchet (to drain the differential oil).

Step 1. Drain Rear Differential Oil.

Chapter 7, Procedure 15, Step 6, tells you how.

Step 2. Chock, Jack, and Block.

Chock the front wheels, set the handbrake, then jack up the rear end of the car and put it on jackstands.

Step 3. Remove Rear Axle Shafts.

'75-'78 models (except Brats): Remove both rear axleshafts (Procedure 9, Step 2).
'79 and newer cars and all Brats: Remove the rear axleshafts (Procedure 4, Step 1).

Step 4. Remove Driveshaft.

Remove the driveshaft (Procedure 8, Step 2).

Step 5. Remove Rear Differential.

Place your jack under the differential to support it while you remove the mounting bolts and nuts.

Remove the two 17mm nuts that attach the top rear of the differential to a black piece of steel going across the top rear of the differential (the rear differential mount).

The front of the differential is held in place by two bolts and lockwashers (pre-'80 models) or four nuts and lockwashers ('80 and newer models). The 17mm bolts or nuts are on the bottom front of the differential. Hold the differential steady while you remove them. Lower the jack and drag the differential out from under the car. Haul it away to be rebuilt, or round up a guaranteed used one to install. When shopping for a used one, remove the drain plug and check it for chunks of metal stuck to the magnetic plug to determine the condition of the bearings and gears inside. Reject it if there are any large chunks or flakes of metal stuck to the magnet.

Step 6. Install Rear Differential.

Put the differential on your jack and raise it into position. Hold it steady while you install the bolts or nuts on the bottom front and the two nuts on the top rear. Torque all the bolts or nuts to 50 ft. lbs.

Install the rear axleshafts: Procedure 9, Step 3, for '75-'78 cars, or Procedure 4, Step 7, for '79 and newer cars and all Brats.

Reattach the shock absorbers if you removed one end (Chapter 14, Procedure 2, Step 4).

Lower the car to the ground, then fill the differential with fresh gear oil (Chapter 7, Procedure 15, Step 6).

PROCEDURE 11: REPLACE GEARSHIFT LEVER BUSHINGS (Manual Transmission OHV Models Only)

Is that gearshift buzz driving you nuts and you're tired of holding it with your hand or using bungy cord, pillows, blankets, or coats to muffle the sound. Then this procedure is for you. Replacing worn-out gearshift lever bushings is probably the easiest way to make your Soob seem 50,000 miles younger!

Condition: The gearshift buzz is driving you nuts.

Tools and Materials: Phillips screwdriver, contact cement, crescent wrench, 10mm and 12mm wrenches, punch, gloves, rags, solvent, paper clip or wire pliers, grease (wheel bearing, silicone, or white lithium), maybe a new dust boot for the bottom of the gearshift lever(s). Here are the parts you'll need for the various years and models. You'll have to get them from the Subaru dealer (they're all pretty cheap).

'75 and newer non-4WD models: Non-hardening adhesive for the rubber boots (see Remarks), two new fiber bushings and two new rubber bushings for the transmission rod that attaches to the gearshift lever bracket, maybe a new fiber bushing and rubber cushion for the bottom of the lever.

'75-'79 4WD cars and '77-'81 Brats: The gearshift lever and 4WD selector lever require the same bushings. If you need to replace the bushings in the 4WD lever, follow the directions for replacing the gearshift bushings. For each lever you'll need two new fiber bushings for the sides and a new rubber bushing for the bottom. You'll need some non-hardening adhesive for the rubber boots (see Remarks).

'80 and newer 4WD cars and '82-'87 Brats: For the gearshift lever, you'll need a new rubber bushing for the bottom of the lever and two new fiber bushings and two new rubber bushings for the sides. For the 4WD selector you'll need two fiber and two rubber bushings for the lever and two smaller fiber bushings for the rod. You'll also need two 17mm wrenches (if you don't have two, you can substitute a crescent wrench for one of them).

Remarks: On some models the rubber boots are glued to the body to hold them in place and make them watertight. Use a non-hardening glue like silicone sealer, rubber cement, or butyl rubber bathtub caulk to glue the boots down when you're finished.

This procedure does not cover OHC models.

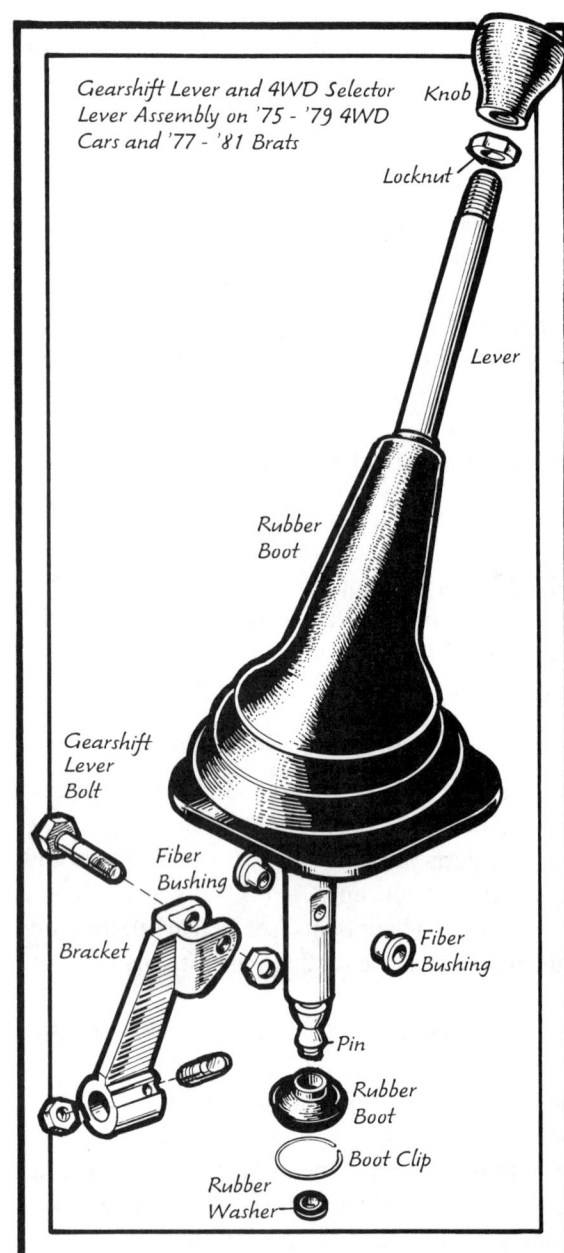

Gearshift Lever and 4WD Selector Lever Assembly on '75 - '79 4WD Cars and '77 - '81 Brats

Knob
Locknut
Lever
Rubber Boot
Gearshift Lever Bolt
Fiber Bushing
Bracket
Fiber Bushing
Pin
Rubber Boot
Boot Clip
Rubber Washer

Step 1. Remove Gearshift Knob.

You may or may not have to take off the **gearshift knob** to remove the **rubber boot** or **console**. (Or you might just want to replace the old knob with a fancy new one.) Hold the knob while using a crescent wrench to turn the lock nut at the bottom of the knob slightly *clockwise* (as viewed from the top). Now unscrew the knob (*counterclockwise* as viewed from the top) to remove it.

Step 2. Remove Console.

'75-'79 cars and '77-'81 Brats: If there's a plastic console around the bottom of the gearshift lever, remove the phillips screws on the sides and along the rear edge, then remove the console.

'80 and newer cars and '82-'87 Brats: The console consists of three panels: one around the gearshift lever, one around the handbrake lever, and a small panel between the two larger ones. If you have 4WD, the 4WD selector lever sticks through the center panel. Here's how you remove all three panels.

Pry out on the sides of the flat middle panel located between the gearshift console and the hand brake console. It pops right off. If you have 4WD, slide the panel off the 4WD selector lever. Next remove the two phillips screws on the front sides of the gearshift console, the two screws at the rear of the console, and the screw in the bottom center of the little storage tray in the handbrake console. Wiggle the rear console off the handbrake lever and set it aside. Now you can remove the front console.

Step 3. Remove Rubber Gearshift Boot.

'75-'79 cars and '77-'81 Brats: The edge of the boot is glued to the body. Gently press the edge of the boot toward the lever all the way around to release it. Slide it up the lever out of your way.

'80 and newer cars and '82-'87 Brats: Remove the phillips screws and metal plate that secure the boot to the body. Non-4WD models can now slide the boot up the gearshift lever out of the way. 4WD models will have to wait until the 4WD rod is disconnected.

Step 4. Remove 4WD Selector Lever and Rod ('80 and newer cars and '82-'87 Brats only).

Use two 17mm wrenches or crescent wrenches, or one of each, to remove the 17mm nut on the rear end of the horizontal shaft just to the right of the bottom of the gearshift lever. There are flat places on the shaft so you can hold it with a wrench while unscrewing the nut. Don't let the shaft twist, or a hard-to-get-to bushing might get damaged. Remove the nut and lock washer.

"Dual Range" (High and Low 4WD) models have a small black switch (the 4WD dashlight switch) sticking through a bracket at the rear of the selector lever. The switch has to be removed. Be sure the ignition switch is OFF, then push on the small tab on the rear side of the bracket to release the switch. Push the switch through the bracket and lay it on the floor. If you're here to replace the switch, follow the wires a couple of inches to connectors. Note the colors of the wires on both sides of the connector before you pull them apart. (One wire is probably black-to-black. The other wire might be red-to-green. Why? I don't know.)

Lift the 4WD lever as high as possible. Now remove the two 12mm nuts and flat washers from the right side of the lever. Slide the lever off the two studs. There should be a rubber bushing and a fiber bushing on each side of the top hole, and a smaller fiber bushing on each side of the bottom hole. If they stayed on the stud, remove them.

Now you can wiggle the front end of the rod off the horizontal shaft and remove it. Pull the rubber gearshift boot rearward over the shaft, then slide the boot up the gearshift lever.

Step 5. Remove Gearshift Lever Bolt and Bushings.

4WD models: A bolt goes through a U-shaped bracket from the transmission and through the gearshift lever. The bushings you're going to replace are in the sides and on the bottom of the gearshift lever.

Non-4WD models: A bracket on the front of the gearshift lever attaches the lever to a rod from the transmission. The bushings you're going to replace are in the end of the rod and at the bottom of the gearshift lever.

EVERYONE: Use a 10mm or 12mm wrench, to remove the nut from the bolt sticking through the side of the gearshift lever or bracket. You'll have to hold the bolt head with a 12mm wrench. Remove the nut and bolt, then pull the lever rearward. Remove the bushings from the sides of the gearshift lever or rod depending on your setup. If there's a metal spacer in the bushings, remove it also.

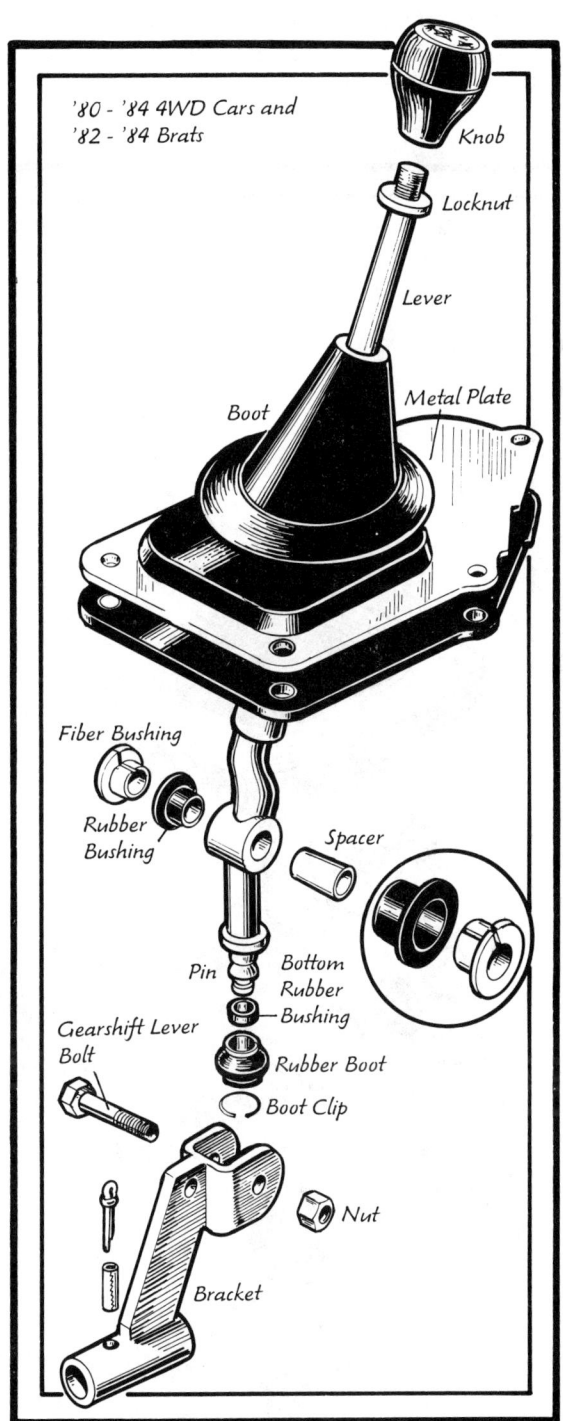

Step 6. Remove Gearshift Lever.

4WD models: Pull straight up on the lever to remove it. It will pop out of the rubber boot at the bottom. Look for a small rubber bushing on the bottom end of the lever. No rubber? Then you'll probably have to fish it out of the lever socket after the dust boot is removed (a piece of wire like a paper clip with a hook on the end will probably get it).

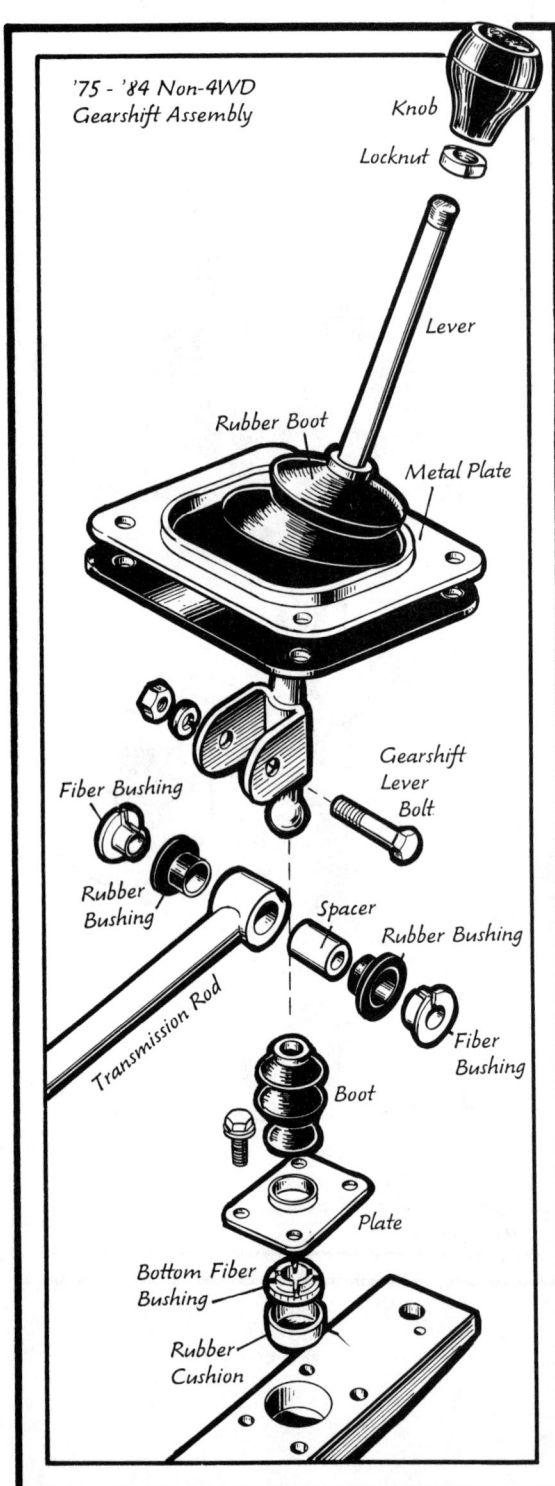

'75 - '84 Non-4WD Gearshift Assembly

Non-4WD models: Worn bushings in the rod from the transmission are the usual cause of the gearshift buzz. The bottom bushing tends to outlive the car. Here's how to check the bottom bushing, though, just in case. Try to pull up and push down on the gearshift lever. Now rotate the lever around in the bottom socket. If you don't feel any looseness and the lever moves smoothly, the bottom bushing is good and doesn't need replacement. If you only need to replace the bushings in the rod, skip down to Step 8.

If the bottom bushing felt worn and you want to replace it, remove the four screws or bolts from the plate around the bottom of the lever. Pull up on the gearshift lever to remove it.

Step 7. Replace Bushing on the Bottom of the Gearshift Lever.

4WD models: The bottom of the gearshift lever fits into a socket covered by a rubber dust boot. To clean and grease the socket, remove the wire ring or spring from the bottom edge of the rubber dust boot, then peel the boot off the socket. Replace the rubber boot if it's torn or funky. Use rags or paper towels and solvent (or spray cans of carb cleaner or brake cleaner) to clean the bottom end of the lever and inside the socket. Dig the crud out of the socket with a small screwdriver.

Smear grease around the tapered top edge of the socket but DON'T pack grease down into the hole (if you do, you won't be able to install the lever!). Install the rubber dust boot on the socket and secure it with the wire ring or spring.

Install a new rubber bushing onto the pin on the bottom of the lever. The groove in the bushing goes toward the bottom end of the lever. Now smear grease on the bottom of the lever and on the rubber bushing. Orient the gearshift lever (front and rear), then stick it through the hole in the rubber boot. Push the lever down into the socket far enough so the pivot bolt holes in the lever and the bracket are aligned. If the lever won't go down far enough, there's too much grease in the socket. Remove the boot and scrape out some of the grease, then try again. When the holes are aligned, skip down to Step 8 to install the bushings.

Non-4WD models: The rubber boot is attached to the metal plate by a piece of wire twisted on the end. Find the end of the wire (usually on the left side of the boot), then use pliers to untwist it. Remove the plate and boot from the gearshift lever.

'75-'79 Non-4WD models: A ball on the end of the lever fits tightly into the fiber bushing. Support the bushing on the jaws of a vise or between two blocks of wood while you tap a bolt or punch through the bottom end to force the ball out of the old bushing. Use rags and solvent to clean the end of the lever, then smear grease on the ball.

To install the new bushing, warm up your oven until it's between 140°F and 158°F (60°C-79°C), then set the new bushing in the oven for about ten minutes. Use gloves or a rag to retrieve the bushing from the oven and set it on a table with the top side up. Press the ball on the gearshift lever down into the bushing while it's still warm.

'80 and newer non-4WD models: Pry the fiber bushing off the end of the gearshift lever. Clean the ball on the end of the lever, then smear fresh grease on the ball and inside the new bushing. Press the new bushing onto the ball, then smear grease on the outside of the bushing.

Non-4WD models: Check the rubber cushion the bushing sits in, and if it's torn, hard, or worn thin in places, replace it. Clean the bottom of the metal plate and the surface where the metal plate attaches to the car. Put the small end of the rubber boot onto the lever so it fits in the groove. Fit the large end of the boot over the lip on the metal plate. If one side of the plate is wider than the other, the wide side goes toward the left (driver's) side of the car. Wrap a thin piece of wire around the bottom of the boot, then use pliers to twist the ends until the boot is on tight.

Make a bead of sealant (silicone or butyl rubber) around the top edge of the hole where the rubber cushion and bushing go. Attach the metal plate to the car with the four screws or bolts. Remember, if the plate is wider on one side, the wide part goes on the driver's side.

Step 8. Install New Gearshift Lever Bushings or Transmission Rod Bushings.

You've replaced the rubber bushing on the bottom of the lever and installed it in the socket, right? If so, continue.

Smear fresh grease on all the new bushings, inside and out. If your setup has a metal spacer, clean the spacer, then coat it with grease.

'75-'79 4WD cars and '77-'81 Brats: Install a new fiber bushing into each side of the gearshift lever, then position the lever in the U-shaped bracket. Install and tighten the bolt and nut.

'80 and newer 4WD cars and '82-'87 Brats: Install new rubber bushings, then new fiber bushings, on each side of the gearshift lever. Slide the spacer into the bushings, then install and tighten the bolt and nut.

Non-4WD models: Insert a new rubber bushing, then a new fiber bushing into each side of the transmission rod. Slide the metal spacer into the bushings. Fit the U-shaped part of the gearshift lever over the end of the transmission rod, then install and tighten the gearshift lever bolt and nut.

Step 9. Install Large Rubber Gearshift Lever Boot.

Fit the rubber boot over the gearshift lever if you removed it.

'80 and newer 4WD cars and '82-'87 Brats: Fit the horizontal shaft near the right rear side of the gearshift through its hole in the boot.

'80 and newer cars and '82-'87 Brats: Fit the metal plate onto the rubber boot so the holes in the plate and boot align with the holes in the body. You might have to wiggle the boot around while installing the screws. Install and tighten all the screws.

'75-'79 cars and '77-'81 Brats: There's a groove around the large end of the boot. Fit the boot in the hole so the flap on the bottom side of the groove is below the hole and the flap on top of the groove is above the hole. To keep the boot in place, use contact cement or silicone sealer to glue the bottom of the top flap to the body.

Step 10. Assemble 4WD Selector Lever and Rod ('80 and newer 4WD cars and '82-'87 Brats only).

Fit the connector rod onto the horizontal shaft sticking out of the left rear corner of the boot. Wiggle it into position so the stud on the rear end of the rod is on the right side. Be sure the wavy washer is still on the stud.

Smear grease on the rubber and fiber bushings, then install them in the top hole on the 4WD shift lever the same way you installed the bushings in the gearshift lever. Grease, then install, two smaller fiber bushings in the bottom hole on the lever. Install the 4WD shift lever so the bottom hole fits over the stud on the rod and the upper hole fits over the stud on the bracket. Install a flat washer on each stud, then install and tighten the two 12mm nuts.

Install the lockwasher and nut on the horizontal shaft. Be sure the tabs on the ends of the shaft and rod are meshed properly, then hold the shaft with a wrench while you tighten the nut. Get it tight.

Dual Range Models: Pull the black switch back through its hole and wiggle it around until the tab locks it into place.

Step 11. Finish Up.

If you removed the gearshift knob, be sure a lock nut is on the gearshift lever, then screw on the knob (*clockwise*) as far as it will go. Next turn it *counterclockwise* until the shift pattern or emblem is oriented the way you want it. Hold the knob in that position while you tighten the lock nut against the bottom of the knob (*counterclockwise* as viewed from the top).

'75-'79 cars and '77-'81 Brats: Fit the carpet back into place if you removed it. Secure the top front edge of the carpet with the clips.

'80 and newer cars and '82-'87 Brats: Install the front console over the gearshift lever and wiggle it into place. Now install the rear console over the handbrake lever and wiggle it into place. Install and tighten the two screws on the front sides of the front console and the two screws on the top rear of the front console. Install and tighten the screw that fits in the bottom of the little storage compartment on the rear console. If you have 4WD, fit the center console section over the 4WD lever, then snap it into place. Non-4WD models can just snap the center console into place.

PROCEDURE 12: REPLACE CLUTCH, THROWOUT BEARING, PILOT BEARING (OHV Models Only)

Condition: Some or all of the clutch components are worn out.

Tools and Materials: All the tools to remove the engine and clutch are listed in Chapter 17, Procedures 1 and 3. For insurance, it's a good idea to replace the clutch disc, pressure plate, pilot bearing, throwout bearing, and rear crankshaft seal while the engine is out so you won't have to remove it again for a long time (hopefully).

Remarks: Before removing the engine, do a compression check (Chapter 7, Procedure 11). If one or more cylinders has a low compression reading, it would be an opportune time to do a ring and valve job while the engine is removed.

Also, while the engine is out, check the entire engine for oil leaks. If the seal behind the crankshaft pulley on the front of the engine, the oil pump, or the oil pan is leaking, replace the seal or gaskets while the engine is out. It's a lot easier.

Step 1. Remove Engine.

Do Chapter 17, Procedure 1, to remove the engine.

Step 2. Remove Clutch Disc and Pressure Plate.

Do Chapter 17, Procedure 3, Steps 1 and 2, to remove the pressure plate and clutch disc. Also do Step 3 if you're replacing the front crankshaft seal.

Step 3. Remove Flywheel.

Do Chapter 17, Procedure 3, Step 4, to remove the flywheel. Once it's off, take it to a machine shop and have it resurfaced. This will smooth the wrinkles out so the new clutch disc will work better and last longer.

Step 4. Remove Pilot Bearing.

'75-'80 models: To remove the old pilot bearing from the rear end of the crankshaft, you'll either have to haul the engine to a machine shop or garage and have them remove it for you, or rent a very small bearing puller and do it yourself (see Chapter 18, Procedure 8). When the old pilot bearing is out, put grease inside the new bearing, then use a hammer to gently tap the new bearing into the hole in the crankshaft. Be sure it's going in straight. Use an extension and socket with a slightly smaller outside diameter than the bearing to tap the bearing in until it's recessed in the crank about ¼". If there was a small grease seal in the end of the crank, tap a new one in with the same socket you used to install the pilot bearing. The seal should end up recessed in the crank about 1/8".

'81 and newer models: The pilot bearing is in the center of the flywheel. Use a hammer and punch or a socket with a slightly smaller diameter than the bearing to tap it out toward the clutch side of the flywheel.

Pilot bearings for 1600cc engines are brown and slightly larger than the black ones used in 1800cc flywheels. Be sure you have the right one. Coat the outer edge of the new pilot bearing with oil, then from the clutch side of the flywheel, use a hammer to gently tap the new pilot bearing into the flywheel until it's flush. Don't tap it in too far.

Step 5. Replace Crankshaft Seal(s).

This step is for people with leaking front and/or rear crankshaft seals.

Once the flywheel and/or crank pulley have been removed, slide a small screwdriver between the seal and crankshaft, being careful not to scratch the crank. To remove the rear seal, use the end of the crank and the screwdriver to lever the old seal out the rear of the flywheel housing. To remove the front seal, lever the screwdriver against crankcase to pop the seal out.

See Chapter 17, Procedure 15, to install the new rear crank seal. Chapter 17, Procedure 20, tells how to install a new front crank seal.

Step 6. Replace Throwout Bearing.

The throwout bearing is that round thing that fits around the splined shaft sticking out of front end of the transmission. It's attached to the clutch release lever with two springs.

To remove the throwout bearing, use a small screwdriver or needlenose pliers to unhook the springs from the little ears on the sides of the throwout bearing holder. Slide the bearing and holder off the transmission shaft.

If you don't have a vise or two blocks of wood handy, take the throwout bearing and holder to the machine shop and have the old bearing removed and the new bearing pressed on.

If you have a vise or a couple of wood blocks, support the sides of the throwout bearing so the bearing holder is hanging down. Use a punch or screwdriver to tap the holder out of the inside of the bearing. It isn't tight and usually taps out easily.

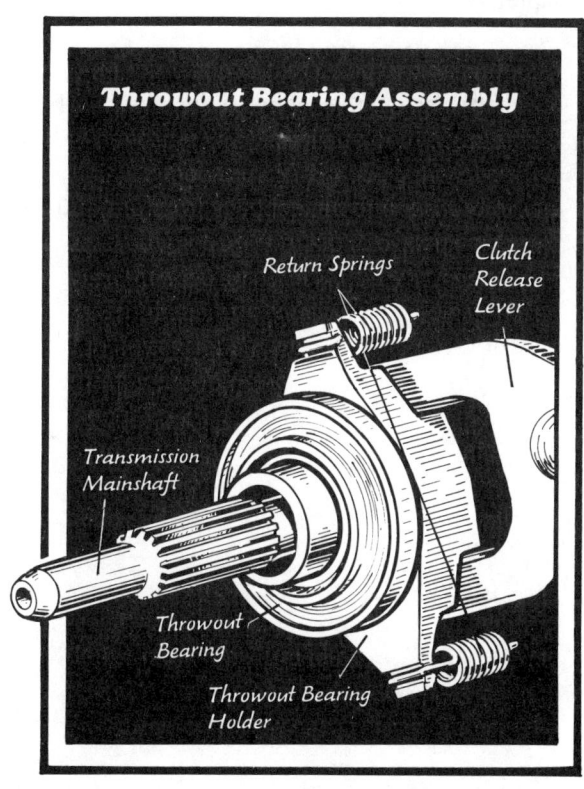

Throwout Bearing Assembly

Check the old bearing to see which side was out, then use a punch or screwdriver and hammer to tap the new bearing onto the holder the same way. Only tap on the thick inner race of the bearing, not on the rounded part. Tap it on all the way.

Use a rag to clean the shaft on the transmission where the throwout bearing fits. Now spread a very thin coat of grease on the shaft. Dab grease on the two dimples on the backside of the bearing holder, then slide the bearing holder on the shaft so the bearing is toward the front. Use needlenose pliers to hook the two small springs over the ears on the sides of the bearing holder.

Be sure the springs return the throwout bearing to the rear of the shaft. If it doesn't return, the throwout bearing will wear out quickly. Here's how to check it:

Push rearward on the end of the clutch release lever to force the bearing toward the front end of the shaft. When you let go of the lever, the throwout bearing should return to the rear of the shaft. Push on the bearing to be sure it returned all the way. If it didn't, or you feel resistance as the bearing slides back and forth on the shaft, remove the springs and slide the throwout bearing and its holder off the shaft. Check the inner surface of the holder where you tapped while removing the holder from the bearing. The tapping may have created burrs along the edge. If necessary, use a file to remove the burrs, then reinstall the bearing and holder.

Step 7. Install Flywheel, Clutch Disc, and Pressure Plate.

Do Chapter 17, Procedure 17, to install the flywheel. Chapter 17, Procedure 18, tells you how to install the clutch disc and pressure plate.

Step 8. Other Things.

There will never be a more convenient time than now to fix any oil leaks the engine may have. If the engine is cool, it's also a good time to adjust the valves while they're so handy.

Step 9. Install Engine.

Yep, the instructions are in Chapter 17, Procedures 32-34. Hopefully you won't need Procedure 35 in Chapter 17.

Step 10. Adjust Clutch.

Before starting the engine, adjust the clutch (Procedure 1 in this chapter).

Step 11. One More Thing.

Whew! Now do Chapter 7, Procedure 4, Steps 12 and 13. You'll be glad you did.

CHAPTER 16
COOLING SYSTEM

"Since the engine of the **Starship** *Subaru* runs by burning a fuel/air mixture, it's logical, Capt. Quirk, that heat is generated."

"Explain, Mr. Schpock."

"Each of the four combustion chambers of the *Starship Subaru* reaches temperatures of over 4,000°F (2222°C) when the engine is running at normal operating temperature. Some of the heat is carried away by the exhaust system, some by the lubricating oil, and some is radiated directly into the surrounding air, but mainly the engine temperature is controlled by the *cooling system*."

"How, Mr. Schpock?"

"Narrow passages called **water jackets** surround the cylinders in the crankcase and the combustion chambers in the cylinder heads. A mixture of water and antifreeze (called **coolant**) is pumped through the water jackets by a **water pump**. The pump is turned by a **drive belt** which is driven by a pulley on the end of the engine **crankshaft**. Most of the heat generated in the combustion chambers is absorbed by the coolant as it flows through the water jackets. The heated coolant is pumped from the engine through the **upper radiator hose** to a vertical tank built into the right side of the **radiator**. The coolant radiates the absorbed heat to the outside air as it is pumped across the radiator through small, finned tubes to a vertical tank on the left side of the radiator. Since the radiator is in the front of the vehicle it receives a constant flow of onrushing air to carry the heat away. The cooled coolant then flows through the **lower radiator hose** to the water pump where it is pumped through the water jackets again to absorb more heat."

"Exceptions, Mr. Schpock?"

"There is an exception, Capt. Quirk. When the engine is cold, a **thermostat** closes the passageway between the engine and upper radiator hose, thus restricting the coolant from flowing to the radiator. Once the coolant temperature in the engine reaches 185°F (85°C) the thermostat opens and the coolant flows normally. The reason for the thermostat is that a lot of engine wear occurs while the engine is cold, so it's best for the engine to warm up to operating temperature quickly."

"Is that all, Mr. Schpock?"

"Almost, Capt. Quirk. When we get stuck in rush hour traffic jams like those around the Los Angeles galaxy and there's no air flowing through the radiator, a **thermoswitch** on the right side of the radiator automatically turns on an electric **cooling fan** when the coolant temperature reaches 208°F (98°C). The fan draws air through the radiator to dissipate the heat. The thermoswitch turns the fan off when the coolant temperature drops to 195°F (91°C). Some Starships made in the '70s also have an **engine driven fan** mounted on the front of the engine. The same drive belt that turns the water pump turns the fan on the engine.

"One more thing, Captain. Located under the dashboard behind the radio is another small radiator and fan. This is the **heater** that heats the cabin and crew. When the heater control knob or lever on the dashboard is set to the *HOT* position, hot coolant from the engine flows through **heater hoses** to the small radiator. Turning the fan switch to *ON* blows hot air into the passenger compartment, like a campaigning politician from the Washington, D.C. Nebula."

"Elaborate on the coolant, Mr. Schpock."

"Plain water freezes at 32°F (0°C), boils at 212°F (100°C), and allows rust and corrosion to form inside the cooling system. A 50/50 solution of antifreeze and water freezes at about -32°F (-35°C), boils at about 220°F (105°C), and inhibits the formation of rust and corrosion. So it's logical that straight water should not be used in a cooling system. Straight antifreeze shouldn't be used either because water dissipates heat better than antifreeze. Antifreeze wears out with use so it should be replaced at least every two years (yearly in severe weather). The use of distilled or bottled water in the cooling system is preferred (but not always available) in order to prevent mineral deposits from building up inside the system.

"Like you, Capt. Quirk, the cooling system is more efficient when under pressure. For instance, the boiling temperature of coolant at sea level is around 220°F (105°C). Add 15 pounds of pressure and the boiling point rises to about 265°F (130°C). Since the normal operating temperature is near 200°F (94°C), it is essential that the cooling system be pressurized in order for the *Subaru* to keep its cool under strain when more heat is generated, such as cruising at higher warp speeds.

"The amount of pressure in the cooling system is regulated by the **radiator cap**. That's why you should never remove the radiator cap when the engine is hot—the coolant may be hotter than its normal boiling temperature, but doesn't boil because it's under pressure. When the radiator cap is removed quickly, the pressure drops, and the boiling point suddenly falls well below the temperature of the coolant. The result: a dangerous geyser of super-hot liquid."

"What are the procedures for maintaining the cooling system, Mr. Schpock?"

"Following is a list of diagnostic, maintenance, and repair procedures that will keep the *Starship Subaru* cool even when operating at speeds above the legal speed of Warp 55. If they are performed at appropriate Star Date intervals, we will never be caught with the hood up, the radiator bellowing clouds of steam, and our thumbs out trying to hitch a ride to the next galaxy."

"Anything else, Mr. Schpock?"

"That is all, Capt. Quirk."

"Beam us up, Snotty."

As Mr. Schpock says, regular maintenance of the cooling system is the best way to avoid getting stranded due to an overheated engine. To keep a cool engine (and temper), go through Procedures 1-3 when you do the 12,000 mile or 12-month tune-up and massage.

Cooling System 379

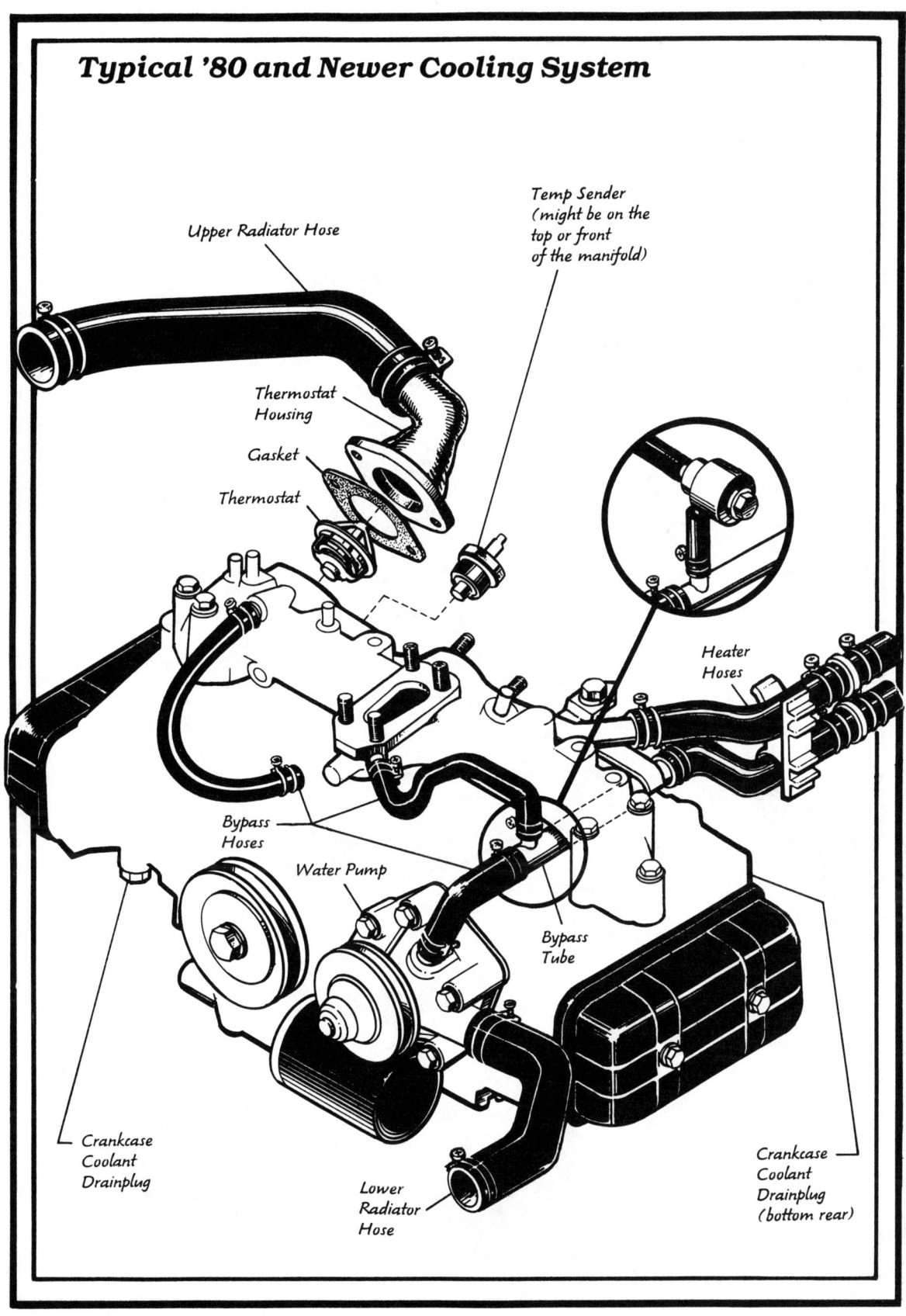

380 Chapter 16

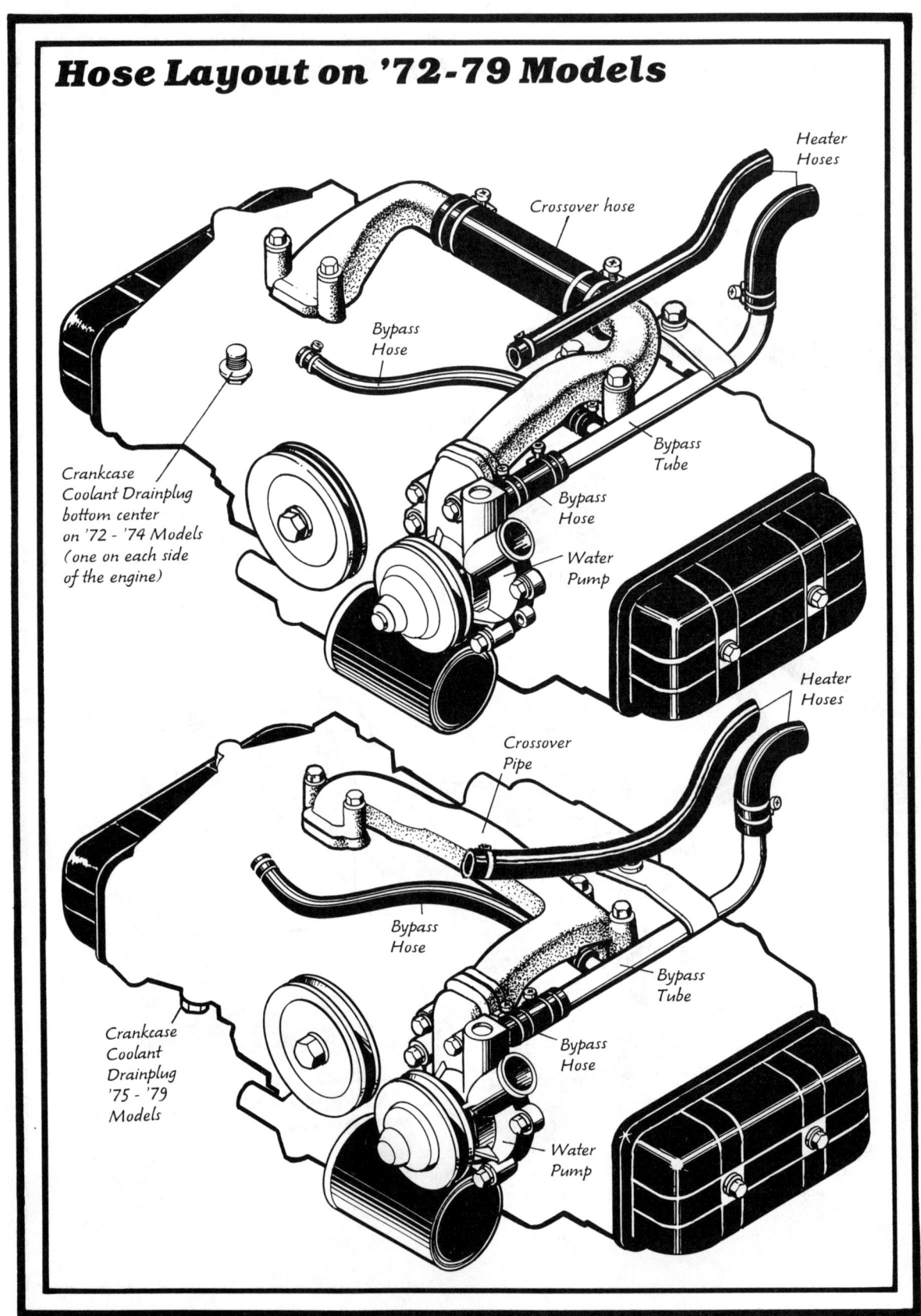

PROCEDURE 1: CHECK COOLANT LEVEL

Conditions: Regular maintenance; OR engine overheating; OR replacing coolant.

Tools and Materials: You might need some coolant (50/50 antifreeze/distilled water mix), rag. Distilled or bottled water is preferred but not essential.

Remark: CAUTION! The best time to check the radiator level is when the engine is cold. If the engine is hot, wait for five minutes before removing the radiator cap. You don't have to remove the radiator cap to check the coolant level on OHC models.

Step 1. Check Coolant Level.

See Chapter 7, Procedure 2, Step 8, to check the coolant level.

PROCEDURE 2: CHECK AND REPLACE HOSES AND CLAMPS

Conditions: Regular maintenance; OR you have to add coolant to the radiator frequently; OR a hose or clamp is broken; OR the engine is overheating.

Tools and Materials: To check hoses—safety glasses, at least one good eyeball, one hand with a few good fingers and a thumb. To replace hoses—new hose(s), regular and/or phillips screwdriver, knife, wire brush and/or emery cloth, maybe new hose clamps.

Remarks: First, a word about **hose clamps**. Subaru hose clamps consist of a piece of wire twisted so it goes around the hose twice, a screw, a tiny washer that fits on the end of the screw, and a flat piece of metal (screw plate) with three holes in it for the screw and the two hooked ends of the wire. The clamps won't work without the little washer on the end of the screw because the screw is small enough to slide through the wire ear.

A hose clamp is worn out if the wire is broken, the screw is rusted to the screw plate, or the head of the screw touches the screw plate without clamping the hose sufficiently. You can replace the Subaru wire-style clamps with band-type hose clamps that are available in parts stores. Be sure the new clamp is the same size as the old one.

Now, how tight is tight? Overtightened clamps will cut into the rubber and can cause the hose to leak. A correctly tightened clamp will indent the rubber slightly without cutting it. If there's crud between the hose and its fitting, the hose will leak no matter how much you tighten the clamp.

Step 1. Check Radiator Hoses.

Locate the large hoses coming out of the top right and lower left corners of the radiator. Put your safety glasses on. Squeeze the hoses and look for cracks, pinholes, soft mushy spots, bulging spots (especially near the hose clamps), and hard, stiff areas that feel brittle. Replace the hose if any of these abnormalities are found (Steps 2 and 3).

White crud at the end of a hose or around the clamp means the hose has been leaking. If the hose seems good otherwise, try tightening the screw in the clamp (clockwise) a little to stop the leak. You might have to remove the hose and clean the inside of the hose and its fitting. Replace the clamp if it's broken or already tightened as far as it can go.

Step 2. Remove Radiator Hoses.

Replacing the two radiator hoses is easy. If you're going to replace the lower hose, first drain the radiator into a clean catch pan (Procedure 3, Step 1). Replacing the top hose will cause a little coolant to be lost, but not enough to warrant the hassle of draining the radiator. If any of the clamps are rusty or deformed, buy new ones.

Completely loosen the hose clamps on each end of the hose and slide them up the hose away from the ends. Hold the hose tightly near one of its ends and give it a few good twists to break it loose from the fitting. Pull and wiggle the hose off. If you're replacing the hose and it won't come off easily, cut the hose off with a sharp knife. Don't use a screwdriver to lever a hose off, especially if it's stuck hard onto the radiator. You may damage the radiator (it's made of soft stuff). Next pull and twist the other end free. Save the clamps if they're good.

Step 3. Install Radiator Hoses.

When the old hose is off, clean the fittings with a wire brush or emery cloth until they're smooth. Slip the hose clamps onto the center of the new hose. Put them on so you can get to the screw with a screwdriver when they're in the installed position. Moisten the inside of the hose with water or antifreeze and slide the hose onto its fittings. Push the clamps into place about ½" from the end of the hose and tighten them with your regular or phillips screwdriver.

If you drained the radiator, tighten the **radiator drain valve** and install the coolant (Procedure 3, Step 3). Run the engine for a few minutes, then check for leaks. Look for coolant oozing out around the ends of the hose. Check the coolant level after driving a few miles.

Step 4. Check Heater Hoses.

Remove the spare tire if it's in the engine compartment. Locate two thumb-size heater hoses coming out near the center of the firewall just to the right (passenger's) side of the master cylinder, and a little lower. The two hoses go to the rear of the engine. If you have air conditioning, don't confuse the two heater hoses with one or two air conditioning hoses that go from the firewall to the air conditioning compressor on the left front of the engine.

Start at the firewall and work toward the engine squeezing each hose every inch or so. The hoses should be flexible and not feel like they're cracking as you squeeze them. If they feel harder and more brittle as you get closer to the engine, they need a fix.

Step 5. Repair or Replace Heater Hoses.

A little coolant will be lost when you replace heater hoses, but not enough to warrant draining the radiator. You'll need to use a different car or have someone take you to the parts store to get new hoses. You can't drive your Soob with the heater hoses off. If you're stuck out in the boonies, see Procedure 10, Step 6, A.4 for a quick fix that will get you back on the road without any new parts.

'75-'79 models: To repair these hoses, determine where along the hose it starts becoming hard and brittle. If the hoses are hard and brittle from the engine right up to the firewall, take the car to Subaru or a garage and have them replace the hoses. Believe me, it's not worth the under-the-dash hassle to do it yourself.

Luckily, however, the hoses are usually only brittle for a few inches on the engine end. If you have at least three inches of good hose coming out of the firewall, you can repair the hose easily. How? First, make a note where each hose connects to the engine so you won't get them mixed up, then get out your Boy Scout knife and cut the hoses at least three inches away from the firewall. Loosen the clamps that secure the other ends of the hoses to the engine, then twist and pull the hoses off. Take the hoses to a parts store and get replacements that are the same inside diameter and length as the ones you cut off. Also, get a proper diameter **heater hose splicer** and two more hose clamps for each hose you're replacing.

Splicers are short metal or plastic tubes that connect the new hose to the old hose stubs you left sticking out of the firewall. Just push the splicer halfway into the hose sticking out of the firewall, then slip one end of the new hose onto the remaining half of the splicer. Use water or antifreeze as a lubricant if necessary. Put a new hose clamp on each side of the splice and tighten it.

Use a wire brush or emery cloth to clean the fitting on the engine where the old hose was connected. Slide a hose clamp onto the new hose, then slip the end of the new hose onto the fitting. Slide the clamp to the end of the hose and tighten it. Run the engine for a few minutes, then check for leaks. Add coolant to the radiator if necessary.

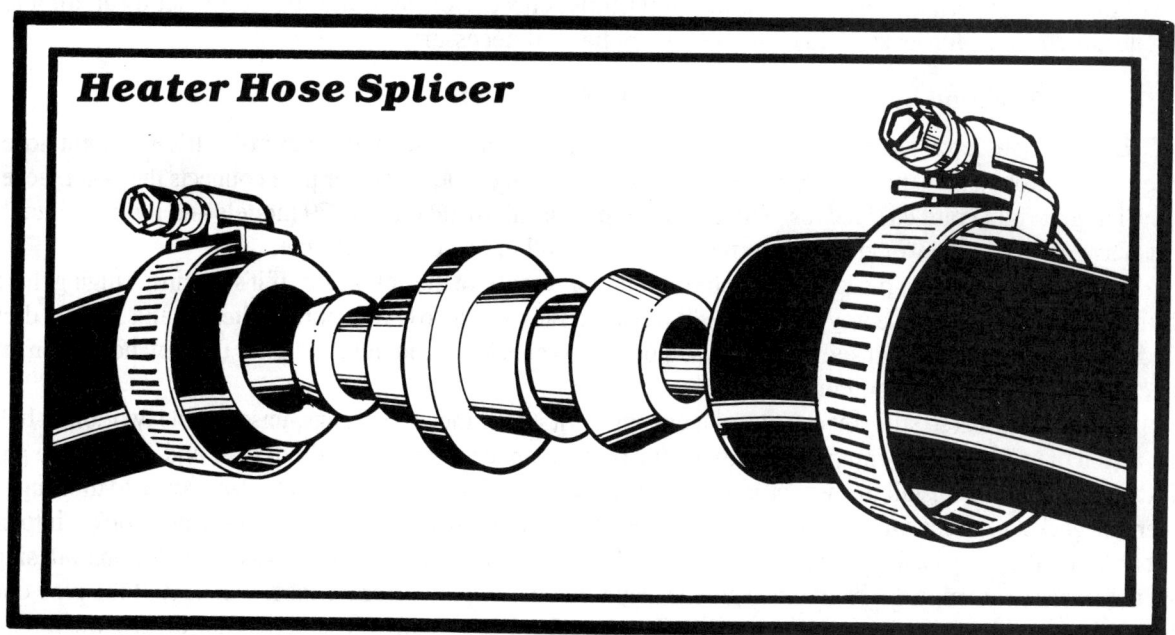
Heater Hose Splicer

'80 and newer models: There are four heater hoses on these models. Two short ones on the engine connect to two longer ones that go from the engine to connections on the firewall. To replace these hoses, loosen the clamps at each end, then wiggle or cut the hose off the connection. If possible, get new hoses from Subaru because they're curved in just the right places so they won't rub against anything in the engine compartment. If a Subaru dealer isn't handy, take the hoses to a parts store and get replacement hoses of the same inside diameter and length as the old ones. Use a wire brush or emery cloth to clean the metal tubes (fittings) where the hoses connect. Slip the clamps onto the new hose, push the hose onto the fittings (use water or antifreeze to make them slide on easier), then position and tighten the hose clamps. Start the engine and let it run for a few minutes while you check for leaks. Top up the coolant level in the radiator if need be.

Step 6. Check and Replace Bypass Hoses.

When the engine is cold and the thermostat is closed, small **bypass hoses** allow the coolant to circulate through water jackets in the crankcase and intake manifold, so the engine warms up quicker.

The largest bypass hose connects the water pump to a metal **bypass tube** mounted on the top left side of the engine. The other end of the bypass tube connects to one of the heater hoses.

'75 and newer non-Turbo models have a small bypass hose connected to the intake manifold just below the front of the carburetor.

'80 and newer OHV Soobs also have a small bypass hose on the right front side of the intake manifold that connects either to the top right side of the crankcase or the bottom front of the intake manifold.

'83-'84 Turbos and '85 and newer OHC models: There are two thumb-size bypass hoses attached to the back of the thermostat housing.

EVERYONE: Look at the bypass hose chart for your engine and year. Check the hoses the same way you checked the radiator and heater hoses. Some of the small ones are difficult to get at but check them anyway and replace them NOW if they are cracked, bulging in spots, or appear to have one foot in the grave. It's a lot easier to do it now than at the side of the road with trucks splashing mud in your face. If possible, get the hoses from Subaru; they're curved in the right places so they won't rub against hot engine parts.

Need to replace them? OK, loosen the hose clamps, then twist and pull the hose off the fittings. Round up new hose clamps if yours are funky, and a new hose the same length and inside diameter as the old one. Clean the metal fittings with a wire brush or emery paper, then lubricate the inside of the hose with water or antifreeze. Slide the hose clamps onto the new hose, slide the end of the new hose onto the fitting, move the clamp to the end of the hose, then tighten it with a regular or phillips screwdriver. Start the engine and let it run for a few minutes, then check for leaks. Add coolant to the radiator if necessary.

Step 7. Check and Replace Crossover Hose ('75-'77 only).

'75-'77 Soobs have a rubber hose in the **crossover pipe** behind the intake manifold. It's a straight hose a little smaller around than the radiator hoses and about 7 ½" long. The crossover pipe connects the water jackets in the left and right crankcase halves. The crossover pipe is all-metal on '78-'79 models and it's built into the crankcase on '80 and newer engines. Some '77s have the all-metal crossover pipe.

To find the crossover pipe, look behind the carburetor just above the crankcase. If it's leaking, bulging, hard, or brittle, replace it the same way as you would replace a radiator hose (Procedure 2, Steps 2 and 3). You don't need to drain the radiator, but some coolant will be lost so check the coolant level after the new hose is on and the engine has run for a few minutes.

If the new hose is so stiff you can't bend it enough to fit it over the pipe fittings, unscrew the two 10mm bolts that attach the right crossover pipe fitting to the top of the crankcase between cylinders #1 and #2. Pry the pipe off the crankcase and install the new crossover hose but don't tighten the clamps yet. Use a knife to thoroughly clean the gasket surfaces on the pipe and crankcase. Twist a rag or paper towel into a point and stick it into the bolt holes on the crankcase to remove any water in the holes. Smear a light coat of gasket sealer on both sides of a new **crossover-pipe-to-crankcase gasket**, lay it in position on the crankcase, then install the pipe onto the crankcase and tighten the two 10mm bolts. Careful! Those are small bolts and it's easy to strip the threads or break the bolts. Now tighten the hose clamps.

Start the engine and let it run for a few minutes. Check for leaks, then check the coolant level in the radiator.

PROCEDURE 3: DRAIN RADIATOR, CHANGE COOLANT, FLUSH COOLING SYSTEM

Conditions: Regular maintenance; OR you just bought the car; OR the engine is overheating.

Tools and Materials: Catch pan, funnel, one gallon of ethylene glycol antifreeze (make sure it's phosphorous-free), one gallon of distilled water, screw-top plastic containers for disposal of the old antifreeze.

If you are going to flush the cooling system, park the car so you can reach the filler neck on the radiator with a garden hose.

If you are going to drain the crankcase, you'll need a 10mm and 14mm socket and ratchet, and one long (about 12") or several short ratchet extensions.

Optional: On some models there's a little tube on the bottom of the radiator drain valve. If you put a two-foot-long piece of 3/16" or ¼" inside-diameter hose on the tube, you can drain the coolant into the catch pan without making a mess. Some models already have a short hose on the tube.

Remarks: If you use distilled water and change the antifreeze every year, the cooling system can go two years before needing a flush job. If you just bought the car, or can't remember how many years ago you last changed the antifreeze, the cooling system should be flushed (like a toilet) to rid it of accumulated rust, sludge, and doo doo.

CAUTION!: Sweet-tasting ethylene glycol is lethal to cats, dogs, kids, and other crawling things. Don't let it stand in the open; cap the old coolant and discard it.

Don't drain the crankcase while the engine is hot; you could damage the engine as well as yourself.

Step 1. Drain Radiator.

Pull the handbrake on, set the heater control to **HOT**, block the rear wheels, then remove the radiator cap (Procedure 1, Step 1).

Locate the radiator **drain valve bolt**. It's a flat little plastic gizmo that sticks out of the radiator toward the engine. On '75-'76 manual transmission non-California cars, it's on the lower left corner (driver's side) of the radiator and easy to reach. For '75-'76 automatic transmission and California cars, and all Soobs '77 and newer, it's on the lower right corner of the radiator and not so handy. On most models it helps to release that large **preheater tube** from the bottom of the air cleaner horn and move it out of the way. Just squeeze the tabs on the clamp and slide it down the hose, then grab the end of the hose and twist and pull it off the air cleaner.

If there is a short tube pointing down between the drain valve and radiator, attach one end of a 3/16″ or ¼″ inside-diameter hose to the tube and stick the other end in the drain pan—less mess this way. Some models already have the hose. If you don't have the right size hose or there's no tube on your drain valve, remove the flat piece of sheet metal below the drain valve (four 10mm bolts), then slide the catch pan under the valve and catch as much coolant as possible when you open the valve.

Unscrew the drain valve *counterclockwise*. If you can't move it with your fingers, use pliers, but don't force it. The drain valve is a plastic bolt with a slot in it. The more you unscrew it the faster the coolant will drain. You can loosen it a few turns to get a steady flow, then set the bolt so the stream is aimed at the drain pan. If you're not trying to catch or save the coolant, you can remove the bolt completely. Be careful not to lose the rubber washer that fits between the bolt and radiator. Peel it off the radiator if it's stuck there. After the radiator has drained, pour the old coolant into screw-top plastic containers and put them in the trash. Don't pour it down the drain. If you are going to drain the crankcase, do Step 2. If you are just draining the radiator for a repair job, do Step 3 to refill the radiator.

Step 2. Drain Crankcase and Flush Cooling System.

Remarks: If you're here from the carburetor removal procedure in Chapter 11, you only need to remove one of the crankcase drain plugs. You don't need to drain the radiator.

Remove the 14mm plug in front of the exhaust pipe on the passenger's side, and behind the exhaust pipe on the driver's side. (Unscrewing the three or four 10mm bolts and removing those flat pieces of sheet metal that are in your way makes the job a little easier.) These plugs drain the engine water jackets. Use a 14mm socket (and swivel joint if necessary) on the end of a long ratchet extension to unscrew the two plugs (*counterclockwise* as viewed from the bottom of the engine). If nothing comes out of the cylinder heads when the drain plugs are removed, stick a screwdriver into the holes to break up the sediment that's blocking the drain. Drain the coolant into the catch pan.

If you are changing to fresh new antifreeze, you should flush as much crud out of the system as possible. Here's how:

When the old coolant has drained, remove the drain valve bolt and rubber washer from the radiator so large chunks of crud can float out with the water. Now stick the garden hose into the radiator and turn the water on enough to keep the radiator full while washing the crud out of the engine. Water should be coming out the bottom of both cylinder heads and the radiator drain valve. Be sure the garden hose is keeping the radiator full. Use a screwdriver or piece of wire to open the drain holes if they get plugged with crud that's on the way out.

When the water coming out of the radiator and crankcase is clear, turn the hose off. As soon as the flow stops, install and tighten the two drain plugs in the bottom of the cylinder heads. Be sure each plug has an aluminum washer. Install the sheet metal pieces to the bottom of the car, if you removed them.

Step 3. Install Coolant.

Install and tighten the radiator drain plug bolt and rubber washer. On carb models, fit the big black preheater tube to the bottom of the air cleaner if you removed it.

Drain plug tight? If you drained the radiator for a hose repair or engine work and are going to use the same coolant again, it's a good idea to filter it through a fine screen as you pour it into the radiator. At least fish out the big chunks of grease, sticks, leaves, $100 bills, etc.

Put a clean funnel in the radiator filler neck. If you're changing to new antifreeze, pour ¾-gallon of fresh antifreeze into the radiator, then fill the radiator with distilled water. If you are using the old coolant, pour the old coolant in and add fresh coolant until the radiator is full (OHC models), or until the fluid level reaches the little horizontal plate in the radiator (OHV models). Install and tighten the radiator cap. On OHC models, be sure the coolant level in the reservoir is between the FULL and LOW lines. Start the engine and let it warm up to operating temperature. When the thermostat opens, the coolant level in the radiator will drop.

OHC models: Coolant will be sucked out of the reservoir to fill the radiator. Check the fluid level in the reservoir after driving a few miles and add more coolant if need be. If the reservoir is empty, wait until the engine cools off, then remove the radiator cap and check the fluid level in the radiator.

OHV models: You'll need to wait until the engine cools off, then add more coolant until it reaches the horizontal plate in the radiator. Put the radiator cap on tight. Check the coolant level and add some if necessary after driving a few miles (Procedure 1).

Record the antifreeze change in the maintenance log at the end of Chapter 7.

WATER PUMP

Symptoms of a worn-out water pump are: (1) squeals up front when you first start the car in the morning; (2) the pulley on the water pump can be wiggled up and down or side to side by hand; (3) coolant leaking from the water pump. To be sure it's the pump leaking and not the little **bypass** hose above the pump, use a small mirror to peek behind the bottom of the pulley. There's a little hole in the water pump housing where coolant will leak if the seals in the water pump are worn out. You'll see drips or other signs of water residue at the hole. If the bypass hose is the problem, see Procedure 2.

PROCEDURE 4: REPLACE WATER PUMP

Conditions: Water pump leaks; OR the pulley on the water pump feels loose indicating worn-out bearings; OR the pump squeaks and squeals at you when you first start the engine in the morning, then gets quieter after a few moments. As time goes by, the squeak will last longer, and longer, and longer.

Tools and Materials: 10mm socket and ratchet, a short extension for the ratchet, regular and/or phillips screwdriver, a new or rebuilt water pump, a water-pump-to-engine mounting gasket, silicone gasket sealer. **'75-'79 models** also need a 12mm socket. **OHC models** also need a new rubber O-ring for the water pump pipe.

While the water pump is off, carefully inspect the water pump bypass hose (Procedure 2). If the hose shows signs of wear, replace it now while it's handy.

Remarks: People used to rebuild their own water pumps, but in this disposable age we just replace them with new or factory rebuilt ones.

Step 1. Drain Radiator and Crankcase. (Procedure 3, Steps 1 and 2).

Step 2. Remove A/C Fan (some models) and Drive Belt(s).

'83-'84 Turbo models and OHC models with air conditioning (A/C): A fan is mounted to the front of the water pump with four bolts.

'83-'84 Turbo models: First remove the fan guard that's attached to the radiator just above the fan. Now remove the four bolts in the center of the fan and pull the fan out. Stash it someplace safe.

OHC models with A/C: The round, finned chunk of aluminum between the fan and water pump is the fan clutch. The clutch is attached to the end of the water pump with four bolts and nuts. Remove the nuts, then carefully pull the fan forward, off the bolts, and wiggle it out of the engine compartment. Don't bang the fan against the radiator. Remove the four bolts in the end of the water pump pulley, then remove the pulley.

EVERYONE: See Chapter 10, Procedure 3, to remove the drive belt(s) on your model. Remove only the belt(s) that turn the water pump or that are in the way.

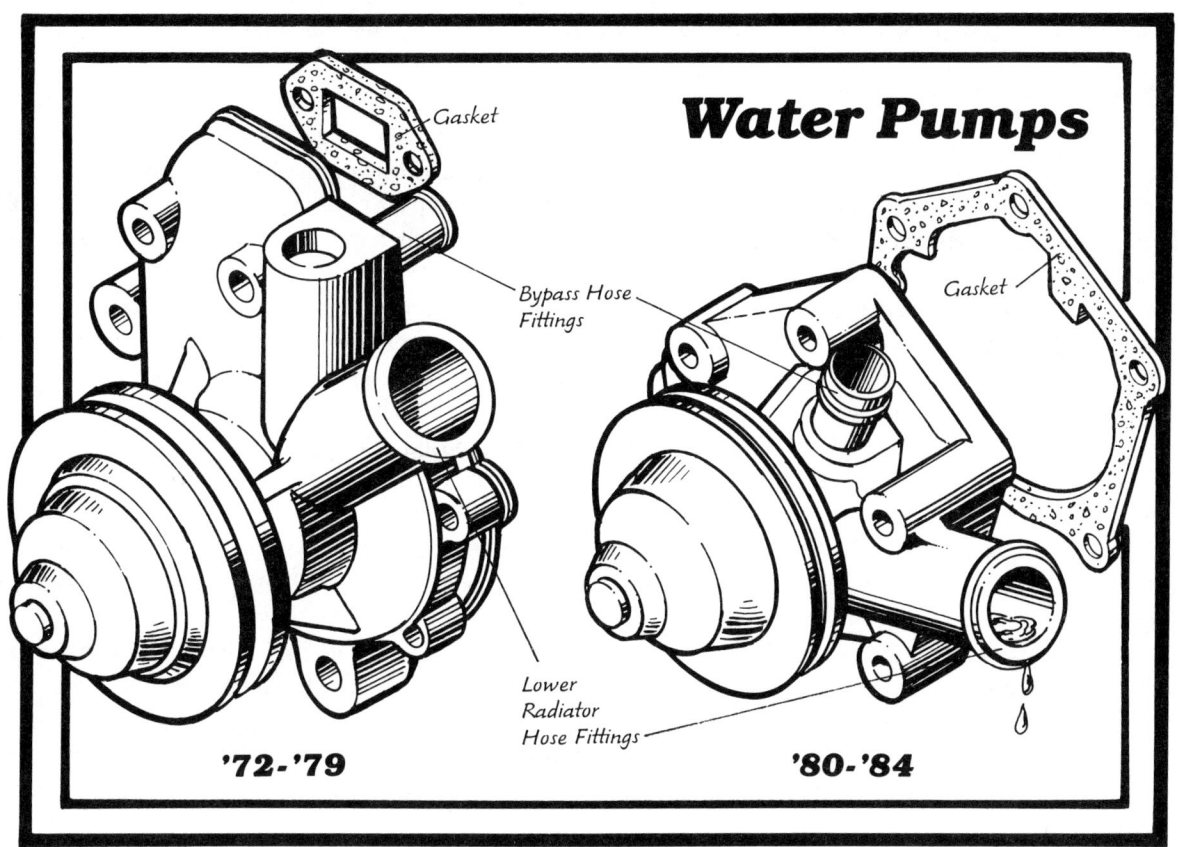

Water Pumps — '72–'79, '80–'84

Step 3. Unbolt Water Pump.

If you're replacing the water pump **bypass hose**, and you have air conditioning (A/C), you might have to remove the A/C **compressor** and **bracket** in order to get to the rear bypass hose clamp.

OHC models: See Chapter 7, Procedure 8, Step 2, to remove the front cam belt covers. Cover the cam belt near the water pump with a plastic bag so no coolant, oil, or dirt can get on the belt when the pump is removed. This is important, so tape the plastic on securely.

EVERYONE: Use a regular or phillips screwdriver to loosen the clamps that attach the small bypass hose and the large radiator hose to the water pump. Pull the radiator hose off and tuck it out of the way. On OHC models the radiator hose is attached to the end of a long pipe sticking out of the left side of the water pump. Remove the bolts that attach the long water-pump pipe to the top of the left cylinder head. Wiggle the pipe out of the water pump.

'83-'84 Turbo models: The **timing plate** is attached to the water pump with two of the bolts. Note its location and be sure it's correctly positioned when installing the new water pump.

OHC models: There is a small piece of packing between the right side of the water pump and the crankcase. This prevents dirt and stuff from getting inside the cam belt covers. Save the packing when you remove the water pump and be sure you install it when you put the water pump on.

Unscrew the five bolts around the edge of the water pump. If the water pump doesn't fall off in your hand when the bolts are removed, put a large screwdriver between the large hose connection and the engine and carefully pry the water pump off. Pull the bypass hose off the fitting as you remove the pump. Be careful not to bang the pump against the delicate radiator.

Use a wire brush, putty knife, emery paper, dull knife blade, or whatever works, to clean the **gasket surface** on the engine where the water passages connect. On '75-'79 models it will be a small square affair on the front end of the crossover pipe on the top of the engine right next to the bypass hose. On '80 and newer models it's the size and shape of the water pump and on the front of the engine. Be sure the gasket surface is absolutely clean and smooth. Clean the threads on the mounting bolts with a wire brush, then give them a light coat of oil.

Step 4. Install Water Pump.

If you haven't replaced the water-pump bypass hose recently and it's showing signs of wear, replace it now while the pump's off (Procedure 2, Step 6). Be sure to clean the hose fitting on the **bypass pipe**.

If you're replacing the bypass hose, install the new hose on the bypass pipe on the engine. Push the new hose onto the pipe to where the old hose was installed, then slide a clamp to the end of the hose and tighten it. Slide the other clamp onto the hose.

OHC models: Remove the old O-ring, then clean the ends of the long water-pump pipe with a wire brush or emery cloth. Install a new rubber O-ring on the end of the pipe. Put a very light coat of silicone gasket sealer on the O-ring, then press the pipe into the water pump in the same position it was on the old pump.

EVERYONE: Put a thin, even coating of silicone gasket sealer on the mating (gasket) surface of the water pump. Lay the new gasket in position on the pump, then coat the exposed side of the gasket with gasket sealer.

'75-'79 models: Slip the two 10mm bolts through the two holes on the top of the pump to hold the gasket in place. Fit the bypass hose onto the bypass fitting as you position the pump on the engine. Get the two 10mm bolts started into the threads with your fingers, then install and get the other three bolts started into the threads. Tighten the top two 10mm bolts first, then tighten the three 12mm bolts. Position, then tighten the bypass hose clamp.

'80 and newer OHV models: Put the longest mounting bolt through the hole between the two hose fittings on the pump and another bolt through one of the other holes. The bolts you just slipped in are to hold the gasket in place while you install the pump. Position the pump on the engine, get the two bolts started into the threads, then install the other three bolts and get them started. Turbo people, don't forget to install the *timing plate*. Use your socket to tighten the five bolts evenly. Fit the end of the bypass hose onto the fitting, then position and tighten the hose clamp.

OHC models: Fit the water pump onto the engine, then install and tighten the mounting bolts. Be sure that little piece of packing is between the right side of the water pump and the crankcase. Install and tighten the bolts that attach the long pipe to the left cylinder head. Remove the plastic wrapping from the cam belts and check to see that no coolant is on them. If you find any, wipe it off completely with a clean dry rag.

EVERYONE: Connect the bypass hose to the top of the water pump, then slide the clamp into place and tighten it.

Step 5. Reconnect Everything Else.

'83-'84 Turbo models: Screw one of the mounting bolts for the fan a couple of turns into one of the holes on the water pump. Fit the fan on so the bolt slips into one of the slots on the round fan-mounting surface. Now install the other three bolts. Tighten all four bolts. Install the fan guard on the radiator and tighten the bolts.

OHC models: Install the front cam belt covers (Chapter 7, Procedure 8, Step 4). Install the pulley on the end of the water pump and gently tighten the mounting bolts.

EVERYONE: Install the radiator hose on the water pump fitting, then position and tighten the hose clamp. Install the A/C bracket and compressor if you removed them. Inspect the drive belt(s) for cracks and frayed edges, then install and adjust it/them (Chapter 10, Procedure 3).

OHC models with A/C: Fit the fan and clutch assembly onto the water pump pulley, then install and tighten the four mounting nuts.

EVERYONE: See Procedure 3 to close the radiator drain valve, install the crankcase drain plugs, then fill the radiator with fresh coolant. In a pinch you can use the old coolant if it looks clean. Replace it with fresh coolant if it's rusty brown, or has chunks of dirt, grease, or a nuclear submarine floating in it.

Start the engine and check for leaks. After the engine has warmed up, add more coolant if needed.

PROCEDURE 5: REPLACE THERMOSWITCH

The **thermoswitch** is located on the rear right (passenger's) side of the radiator, below the radiator hose. To test the thermoswitch, look at Procedure 9, Step 6, B.1.

Condition: Thermoswitch doesn't activate the electric fan.

Tools and Materials: 19mm open-end wrench, a 10mm or 12mm wrench depending on the size of the nut on your battery terminal, new thermoswitch and gasket. Maybe a battery terminal puller.

Remarks: Have the new thermoswitch ready to screw in when you pull the old one out so only a little coolant will be lost.

Step 1. Disconnect Negative (-) Battery Terminal.

See Chapter 10, Procedure 1, Step 3, to disconnect the negative battery cable. On some models you might need to remove the battery to get to the thermoswitch (Chapter 10, Procedure 1, Step 7).

Step 2. Disconnect Thermoswitch Wire.

On some models the connection is at the switch—just pull the connecter off. On other models the wire is built into the switch, so follow the wire to a male-female connector a few inches from the thermoswitch. Pull on the each side of the connection to disconnect the wires. Don't pull on the wires.

Step 3. Remove Old Thermoswitch, Install New One.

The thermoswitch location varies up and down the right side of the radiator on different models and years. On some it's easy to get to, and on others it's difficult without removing the upper radiator hose (Procedure 2, Step 2) or loosening the battery hold-down bracket and sliding the battery out of the way (Chapter 10, Procedure 1). Look the situation over carefully, then do whatever you need to do to get a 19mm wrench on the nut behind the switch.

Get the new switch and gasket ready and close at hand. Unscrew the old switch with a 19mm open-end wrench and quickly screw the new one in. Tighten the switch with the wrench (don't overtighten it or it might break). Connect the wire to the switch, then reconnect the radiator hose, battery bracket, and/or whatever you had to move to get to the switch. Add coolant to the radiator if the level is low.

Step 4. Connect Battery.

Install the battery if you removed it (Chapter 10, Procedure 1, Step 7). Install safety glasses on your face, then clean the battery terminal post and inside the battery cable clamp with a wire brush. Fit the clamp over the post, wiggle it down as far as you can, then tighten the nut on the pinch bolt (usually a 10mm or 12mm nut).

PROCEDURE 6: REMOVE, CHECK, AND INSTALL THERMOSTAT

Condition 1: Engine overheats. The thermostat is sticking or stuck in the closed position.

Condition 2: Engine underheats. It takes a long time for the engine to warm up to normal operating temperature and the interior heater output is poor. The thermostat is AWOL or stuck in the open position.

Tools and Materials: 12mm socket, ratchet, an extension for the ratchet at least 4" long, new thermostat-housing gasket, silicone gasket sealer, wire brush, rags or paper towels, knife, emery cloth, maybe a new thermostat. To test the thermostat you'll need a cooking pot and the kitchen stove.

Remarks: Some coolant will be lost when you remove the thermostat housing but not enough to warrant draining the radiator. On '80 and newer models you might want to disconnect and move some of the hoses around the thermostat housing so it's more accessible. To avoid confusion during reassembly, use masking tape and a marker to label each hose and whatever it's connected to before disconnecting it.

Step 1. Remove Thermostat Housing.

Carb models: Remove the *spare tire* if it's in the engine compartment and the *air cleaner* if it's in your way (Chapter 7, Procedure 5, Step 4). If you remove the air cleaner, cover the carburetor with a clean rag.

EVERYONE: Follow the upper radiator hose from the top right side of the radiator to where it connects to the *intake manifold* on the engine. The aluminum thing at the end of the hose is the **thermostat housing**. If the thermostat housing is round and bulbous, and there is nothing attached to the top, skip the rest of this paragraph. If there is a plastic gizmo with wires sprouting from its top mounted to the top of the thermostat cover, be sure the ignition switch is OFF. Don't turn it on until the thermostat housing is back on the engine and the wires you're about to disconnect are reconnected (it could damage electrical things). OK, disconnect the wire harness from the gizmo mounted to the top of the thermostat housing. There are also two thumb-size hoses connected to the back of the housing. Squeeze the ears on the clamps and pull the hoses off their fittings.

Loosen the hose clamp that attaches the radiator hose to the thermostat housing, then pull the hose off the fitting (Procedure 2). Prop the end of the hose so it's pointing up to prevent coolant from running out of the radiator. Locate the two 12mm bolts that secure the thermostat housing to the intake manifold. Make a note if other things are held in place by the bolts, then unscrew the bolts *counterclockwise*. Remove the housing and gasket. Just pull out on the brass **thermostat** to remove it.

No thermostat? Some jerk left it out thinking the engine would run cooler. That's why you've been stuck with slow warmups and a weak heater. Buy a new thermostat and skip to Step 3 to install it.

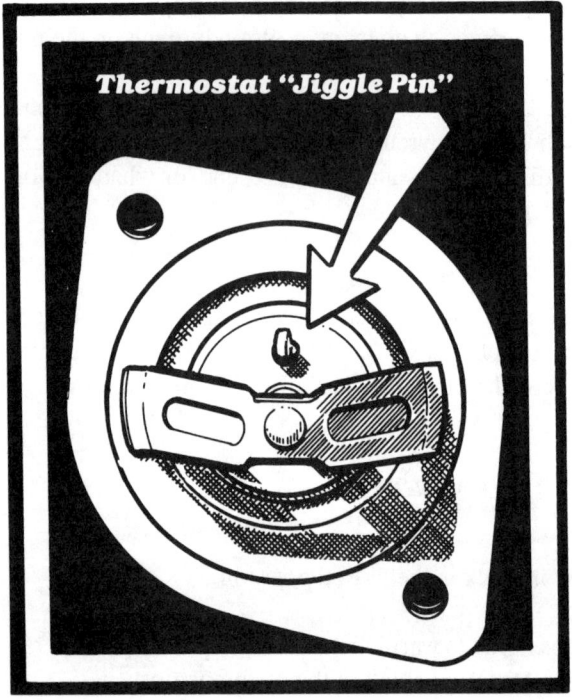

Step 2. Check Thermostat.

If your condition was Condition 1 (engine overheats), the thermostat may not be opening. Here's how to check it:

Put the thermostat in a cooking pot of water, put it on the stove, and turn on the heat. Watch the thermostat as the water heats up. The round center part of the thermostat should move toward the spring end just before the water starts to boil. This allows water to flow through the center of the thermostat (see illustration). If the center part doesn't open before the water boils, or is rusted or locked to the outer part, buy a new thermostat and install it (Step 3). Fish the thermostat out of the cooking pot, then wash the cooking pot thoroughly with soap and water before anyone has a chance to cook in it. Antifreeze is an additive you definitely don't want in your food.

Dealing with Condition 2 (engine underheats): If the engine takes a long time to warm up and the interior heater doesn't warm your toes the way it should, see if the thermostat is stuck in the open position. If the round center part doesn't seat against the large round part (see illustration) when the thermostat is cool, the thermostat is broken. Buy a new thermostat and install it (Step 3).

If you live in Eskimo-type country or where the temperature stays below zero frequently, you might have to cover the grille with something like cardboard, plastic, or blankets to block the flow of frigid air through the radiator. If you do this, check the temperature gauge frequently to be sure the engine isn't overheating. It's easy to overcompensate.

Step 3. Install Thermostat.

Clean the gasket mating surfaces on the intake manifold and thermostat housing with a knife and emery cloth. Clean the bolt threads with a wire brush and give them a light coat of oil. Use a knife and emery cloth to clean the hose fitting on the thermostat housing. Clean up any dirt and gasket material that might have fallen into the intake manifold. Twist the end of a rag or paper towel to a point and clean the bolt holes in the manifold. Be sure there's no antifreeze or water in the bolt holes or you won't be able to screw the bolts in all the way.

Install the thermostat in the intake manifold so the spring end is inside the manifold. Rotate the thermostat so the loose little "*jiggle pin*" near one edge is at the top. Or, if there's an arrow stamped on the thermostat, point the arrow UP. No jiggle pin or arrow? Look for a small notch on the outer edge of the thermostat or on the round center part. Orient the thermostat so the notch is at the top. If the thermostat mounts horizontally, point the arrow or locate the jiggle pin or notch toward the rear of the car.

Coat both sides of the new gasket with silicone gasket sealer. Be sure the gasket surface on the manifold is dry before installing the new gasket. Put the gasket on the manifold, then install the housing. Slip in the two 12mm bolts (be sure any other things held by the bolts are in place) and tighten the bolts. Install the radiator hose and tighten its clamp. Reconnect any other hoses or wires you disconnected.

If your model has a plastic gizmo on top of the thermostat housing, connect the two thumb-size hoses to the fittings on the rear of the housing and secure them with the hose clamps. Reconnect the wiring harness to the plastic gizmo on top of the housing.

Install the spare tire, and the air cleaner, if you removed it (Chapter 7, Procedure 5, Step 5).

Use a can, jar, or glass of water to clean the top of the engine where coolant spilled when the hoses were disconnected. Don't get water on the distributor or electrical connections in the engine compart-

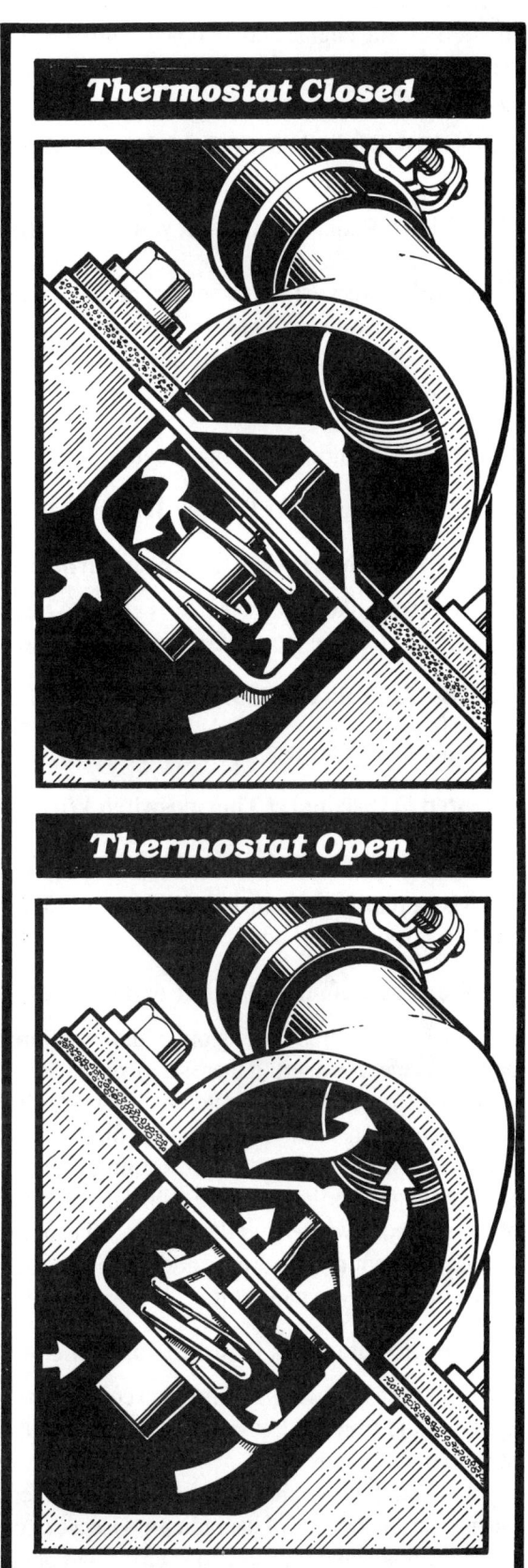

ment. Start the engine and let it warm up, then check for leaks. Add coolant to the radiator if the level is low (Chapter 7, Procedure 2, Step 8).

PROCEDURE 7: REMOVE AND INSTALL RADIATOR

Conditions: Radiator leaks; OR you suspect the radiator is clogged; OR you're removing the engine.

Tools and Materials: 12mm socket, ratchet, small ratchet extension, regular and/or phillips screwdriver, catch pan. If you have an automatic transmission, you'll need a couple of baggies and rubber bands, and a can or jar. If it's time to replace the coolant, you'll need one gallon of fresh ethylene glycol antifreeze and one gallon of distilled water.

Remarks: Radiators are delicate dudes, so avoid close encounters with sharp objects.

Step 1. Disconnect Battery Terminals. (Procedure 5, Step 1.)

Step 2. Remove Air Cleaner on Carb Models.

If it looks like the air cleaner is going to be in your way (on some models it is), see Chapter 7, Procedure 5, Step 3, to remove the air cleaner. Be sure and cover the top of the carburetor with a clean rag.

Step 3. Drain the Radiator. (Procedure 3, Step 1.)

Step 4. Disconnect Upper and Lower Radiator Hoses. (Procedure 2, Step 2.)

Step 5. Disconnect Thermoswitch Wire. (Procedure 5, Step 2.)

Step 6. Disconnect Radiator Ground Wire.

Use a phillips screwdriver to disconnect the radiator end of the small **ground wire** connecting the top of the radiator to the car body.

Step 7. Disconnect Electric Fan Motor.

Follow the wires coming out of the **fan motor** to connectors. Label the wires for which goes where, then pull the connectors apart. If there's a *wiring harness* (a bundle of wires wrapped in tape) attached to the fan bracket, unwrap the rubber tab(s) to release the harness from the bracket. Late OHV models with air conditioning also have a fan mounted on the left side of the radiator. Disconnect it just like the other fan motor.

OHC models with air conditioning: Remove the three or four bolts that attach the shroud to the left side of the radiator. It's the one around the fan that's bolted to the water pump. Two bolts are near the top outer edge of the shroud, two are near the bottom. One of the bottom bolts is inside the shroud. You'll probably have to remove the bottom bolts from underneath the car. When the bolts are out, hang the shroud over the fan as close to the engine as you can get it.

Step 8. Automatic Transmission Vehicles Only.

Two hoses from the transmission connect to the left side of the radiator. These hoses carry automatic transmission fluid from the transmission to a tank built into the radiator. The fluid is cooled in the tank, then pumped back to the transmission.

Loosen the two small hose clamps on the left side of the radiator. One is on the upper half and the other one is near the bottom of the radiator. Use a can or jar to catch the automatic transmission fluid that will come out of the hoses and radiator. To keep dirt out of the hoses, put baggies over the hose ends and secure them with rubber bands.

Step 9. Haul Out the Radiator.

Two 12mm bolts along the top of the radiator attach it to the car. On some models you have to look through holes in the body to see them. Hold the top of the radiator so it can't fall against the engine while you remove the bolts *counterclockwise*. Carefully lift straight up on the radiator to remove it. It ain't heavy, brother. Don't bump it on anything.

Air conditioned cars have another radiator in front of the engine radiator. Tie the top of it to the body with wire or string so it can't fall against the engine.

On some models the bottom of the radiator sits on two **rubber pads** that fit over two pins sticking up from the body. If the pads came off with the radiator, remove them from the radiator and put them back on the pins. On other models the pins are built into the bottom of the radiator and covered with rubber pads that fit into holes in the body. Remove the pads before hauling the radiator away for repair.

Stash the radiator somewhere safe if you're not hauling it away to be repaired. A flattened cardboard box will protect the delicate fins and tubes during storage or transit.

Before taking the radiator to a shop for cleaning or repair, remove the fan shroud or bracket, whichever you have (Procedure 8, Step 2).

Step 10. Install Radiator.

Be sure the rubber pads (cushions) are on the pins that secure the bottom of the radiator.

Mount the **fan shroud** or bracket onto the radiator if it was removed (Procedure 8, Step 5).

Remove the string or wire holding the air conditioner radiator if you tied it up.

Carefully lower the radiator into position so the rubber cushions fit into the holes.

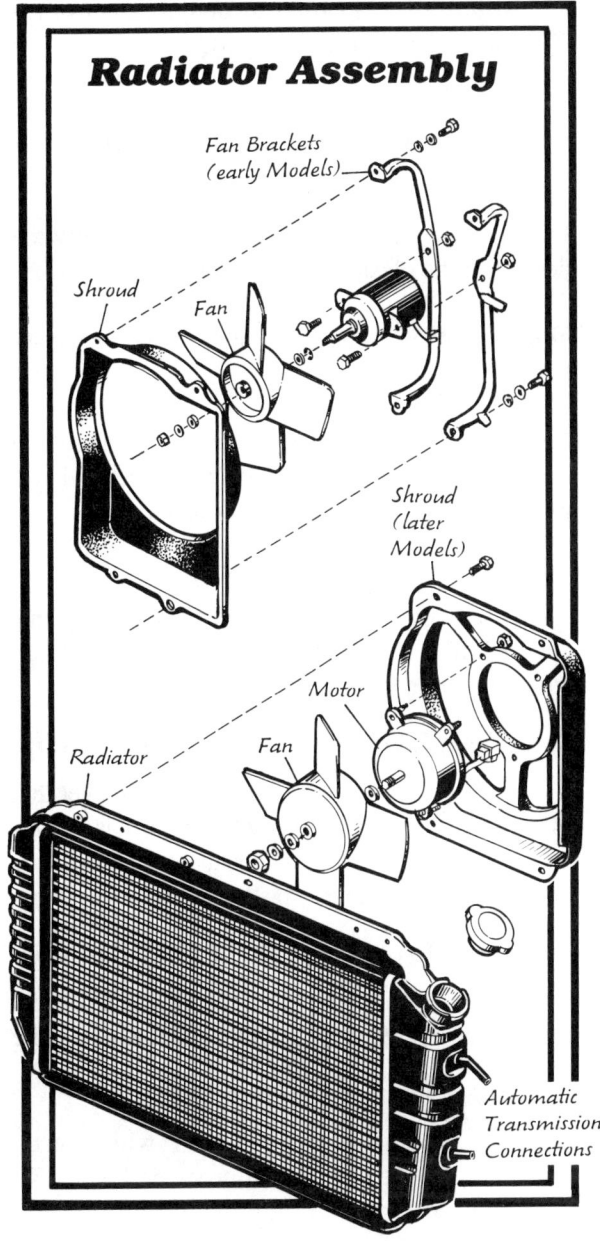

Install the two 12mm bolts to secure the top of the radiator and tighten them. Be sure the bolts are going through the mounting holes in the air conditioner radiator if you have one.

Clean, then connect the wire terminals to the thermoswitch and electric fan(s). Attach the wiring harness to the fan bracket with the rubber tab(s). Clean the contact surface on the little ground wire that attaches to the top of the radiator, then install the screw and tighten it. Install the radiator hoses (Procedure 2).

OHC models with A/C: Fit the left shroud onto the radiator, then install and tighten the mounting bolts.
Clean the battery posts and cable clamps, then connect the cables to the battery (Procedure 5, Step 4).
Automatic transmission people: Connect the two hoses to the left side of the radiator. Tighten the clamps.
Carb people: Install the air cleaner (Chapter 7, Procedure 5, Step 5), if you removed it.
EVERYONE: Tighten the drain plug, then fill the radiator (Procedure 3, Step 3). Start the engine and let it warm up to operating temperature while you check for leaks. Check the coolant level after the engine has warmed up then cooled off. Add coolant if necessary, then tighten the radiator cap. Check the level again after driving a few miles.

Automatic transmission people: Check the automatic transmission fluid level after driving a few miles (Chapter 7, Procedure 1, Step 3).

PROCEDURE 8: REMOVE AND REPLACE ELECTRIC COOLING FAN MOTOR

Condition: You checked the fan and thermoswitch (Procedure 9, Step 6, B.1) and determined the fan motor is dead; OR the plastic fan is broken.

Tools and Materials: 8mm, 10mm, and 12mm sockets, ratchet, short ratchet extension, maybe a new plastic fan or new fan motor.

Remarks: You can remove the fan motor without removing the radiator. It's a hassle on later models due to limited space, but it can be done. If you're also removing the radiator for repair (Procedure 7, Steps 1-7), it's easier to remove the fan after the radiator is out.

Step 1. Unplug the Electrics.

Disconnect the negative (-) battery cable clamp (Procedure 5, Step 1). Now disconnect the fan motor wires (Procedure 7, Step 7). If a *wiring harness* is attached to the fan bracket, release the harness from the bracket by unwrapping the rubber tab(s).

Step 2. Remove Fan Assembly from Radiator.

The fan is mounted in a *shroud* or bracket that's bolted to the radiator. It all comes off as a unit. On carb models, if it looks like the air cleaner horn is in the way, remove the air cleaner (Chapter 7, Procedure 5, Step 4).

Locate the four 10mm bolts that attach the corners of the shroud or bracket to the radiator. Remove the bolts and lift the unit straight up. Be careful not to bang it against old mister radiator.

Step 3. Remove Fan Motor from Shroud or Bracket.

On '75-'79 models the fan motor is attached to the shroud or bracket by two 12mm nuts. Some '80 and newer models have three nuts. Lucky devils. Remove the mounting nuts and lockwashers to free the fan.

Step 4. Remove Fan from Motor.

Hold the fan blades from turning while you unscrew the nut from the end of the fan shaft. Note the order of washers on the outside and inside of the fan. They have to go back in the same places during reassembly.

If the motor is dead, call a few electric motor shops and ask how much they charge to rebuild a motor like yours. Compare their prices with the price of a guaranteed motor from a junkyard. Then call Subaru to ask the price of a new one. I'm just trying to save you some hard-earned dollars here.

Step 5. Assemble Fan, Motor, and Shroud or Bracket.

Slide the plastic fan blade and washers onto the motor shaft in the same order as you removed them. Screw the nut on the end of the shaft and tighten it while holding the fan to keep it from turning.

Slide the two or three mounting bolts on the motor through the holes in the shroud or bracket. Put on the lockwashers and nuts and tighten them.

Step 6. Install Fan Assembly.

Gently lower the fan assembly into its position on the radiator. Install the four 10mm mounting bolts and tighten them.

Install the radiator if you removed it (Procedure 7, Step 10) and fill it with coolant (Procedure 3, Step 3). Install the air cleaner if you removed it (Chapter 7, Procedure 5, Step 5).

Connect the fan motor wires to the wiring harness, then attach the wiring harness to the fan bracket with the rubber tab(s). Clean and connect the negative battery clamp and post (Procedure 5, Step 4).

Start the engine and let it warm up. The fan should come on when the needle on the temperature gauge goes a little past the halfway mark. Check the coolant level and add some if necessary.

PROCEDURE 9: REMOVE AND REPAIR ENGINE DRIVEN FAN

'75-'78 4WDs and '75-'79 models with air conditioning have a fan mounted to the top front of the engine. The fan is turned by the alternator/water pump drive belt.

To check the engine driven fan bearings, turn the engine off if it's running. Grab two fan blades opposite each other and try moving the fan up and down, then side to side. Looseness or clunking sounds mean the bearings are worn out. Another way to check is to start the engine, then place the metal end of a long (at least 12″) screwdriver on the round **shaft holder** behind the fan. Keep the screwdriver away from the fan and drive belt. Keep the screwdriver solidly on the shaft and lean over and put the end of the screwdriver handle on the bone just in front of your ear. Keep long hair, ties, jewelry, etc. away from the fan blades and drive belt. You can actually listen to the inside of the bearings this way. Good bearings will make a light, smooth, even sound. Worn bearings make an irregular rumbling sound and/or a tortured screech.

Some people eliminate the engine-driven fan by removing the fan and pulley, then replacing the drive belt with a drive belt for a non-4WD model. This seems to work OK in mild climates if the car is driven normally, but heavy off-road driving in a hot climate might cause the engine to overheat without the extra fan.

Condition: Rumbling sounds are coming from the engine-driven fan; OR the plastic fan is broken.

Tools and Materials: 10mm and 12mm sockets and ratchet, internal and external snap-ring pliers, maybe a new fan blade or new bearings.

Step 1. Remove Drive Belt.

Loosen the drive belt adjusting-bolts on the alternator, then push down on the alternator until the drive belt can be removed (Chapter 10, Procedure 3, Step 2).

Step 2. Remove Fan, Pulley, and Bearings.

Bend the lock tabs away from the four 10mm bolts on the front of the fan, then remove the bolts and pull the fan off. Look in the rear (engine) side of the pulley for a **snap-ring**. Remove the snap-ring with *internal* snap-ring pliers, then pull or tap the pulley off. Use *external* snap-ring pliers to remove the small snap-ring on the front end of the shaft. Now you can pull the **outer bearing**, **spacer** and **inner bearing** off the shaft. If they're stuck, put on your safety glasses and use a puller or a screwdriver or chisel and hammer to tap them off the shaft.

Step 3. Install Bearings, Pulley, and Fan.

Use sandpaper or emery cloth to clean the inside of the pulley and the shaft where the bearings fit. Lightly oil the shaft, then slide one of the new bearings on. If it's tight, use a screwdriver and hammer to gently tap on the inner race of the bearing (the part that fits around the shaft). Tap the bearing all the way on, then install the spacer, then the other bearing. Tap it on far enough to install the external snap-ring into the groove on the end of the shaft.

Fit the pulley over the bearings, tap it on if necessary, then install the internal snap-ring in the rear end of the pulley. Be sure the snap-ring is in the groove all the way around.

Install the fan on the pulley with the lock plates and four 10mm bolts. Tighten the bolts, then use pliers to bend the lock plates against the sides of the bolt heads.

Step 4. Install and Adjust Drive Belt.

Look at Chapter 10, Procedure 3, to install and adjust the drive belt.

PROCEDURE 10: CHECK CAUSES OF OVERHEATING

Condition: Engine is overheating.

Tools and Materials: Depending on how far your checks take you, you may need: test light, jumper wire (a piece of insulated wire with alligator clips on the ends), phillips screwdriver, etc.

Remarks: Most overheating is caused by owners not taking the time to do periodic tune-up, lubrication, and maintenance of their cars. If your engine starts running a little hotter than normal, run through this procedure BEFORE you get stuck in rush hour traffic with your hood up and your radiator and temper bellowing clouds of steam.

Step 1. Check Coolant (Procedure 1.)

Step 2. Check and Adjust Drive Belt. (Chapter 10, Procedure 3.)

Step 3. Check Hoses and Clamps. (Procedure 2.)

Step 4. Check Water Pump. (Procedure 3.)

Step 5. Check Front of Radiator for Trash and Debris. (Chapter 7, Procedure 4, Step 7.)

Step 6. Pressure Test Cooling System and Cap.

Report to the Bridge: Have the radiator cap and cooling system pressure-tested by Subaru, a garage, or radiator shop. If the cap won't hold at least 13 lbs. of pressure, replace it with a new one.

If you have cooling system pressure leaks or coolant leaks, check the items under A; if you don't have pressure or coolant leaks, skip ahead to B.

A. Pressure Leaks: If the cooling system fails the Captain Quirk pressure test, do the following:

1. Check the seams around the edges of the radiator and where the **cooling fins** connect to the **tanks** on the sides of the radiator. A slow leak will eventually dissolve the black paint and expose the brass radiator and/or form a greenish deposit. If the radiator is leaking, remove it and have it repaired at a reputable radiator repair shop. (Procedure 7).

2. Check the thermostat housing (that bulbous thing on the engine where the upper radiator hose connects). If it leaks, remove it and replace the gasket (Procedure 6).

3. Check the water-pump-hose connections and use a mirror to look at the bottom of the water pump behind the pulley. There's a little hole back there where coolant will come out if a **seal** inside the water pump has died. If the water pump leaks, replace it (Procedure 4).

4. Check all of the radiator, bypass, and heater hoses in the engine compartment. Tighten any loose clamps and replace any leaking hoses (Procedure 2). See if the heater or heater hoses under the dash are leaking (is the carpet wet and smelly?). If there's a leak inside the car have Subaru or a garage determine whether the heater hoses or the heater radiator is leaking. Let them fix it.

If you're stuck on the side of the road and it's a heater hose leaking, you can bypass the heater and drive on home or to a garage. All you need is a knife and a phillips screwdriver. Here's how: Determine which hose is leaking and where. If the leak is *more* than a foot from the engine, cut the hose right next to the leak on the engine side. Disconnect the good hose from its fitting on the engine. Slide the hose clamp off the good hose and put it on the end of the short hose still connected to the engine. Connect the end of the short hose to that fitting where the good hose was connected and tighten the clamp.

If the leak is *less* than a foot from the engine, cut the leaking hose 3" from the firewall ('75-'79 models) or disconnect the hose from the fitting on the firewall ('80 and newer models). Cut at least one foot off the firewall end of the hose. Disconnect both heater hoses from the engine. Slide the hose clamps off the engine end of the hoses and install them on the ends of the short hose. Install the ends of the short hose onto the fittings on the engine and tighten the clamps.

If you can tell which hose is leaking but can't tell where, just cut a 12" chunk out of the good hose and install it between the fittings on the engine. You'll have to replace both heater hoses this way, but at least you're mobile and both hoses should probably be replaced anyway.

Whichever way you do it, you'll end up with a short hose going from the *bypass tube* to a fitting on the *intake manifold*. Add coolant to the radiator if need be. Your toes will probably get cold if it's winter, but at least you are on the road again. Replace the heater hose(s) right away (Procedure 2).

5. Check the **crankcase drain plugs** on the bottom of the cylinder heads. If tightening the plugs doesn't keep them from leaking, remove the plugs and install new aluminum washers. Procedure 3, Step 5 tells you where the plugs are located and how to remove them.

6. Check where the *intake manifold* bolts to the top of the cylinder heads. Manifold leaking? Tighten the three mounting bolts on each end of the manifold to 16 ft. lbs. If that doesn't stop the leak, you need to replace the intake manifold gaskets. It's a nasty, difficult job on later models with Power Steering and/or Air Conditioning. Here's a generic description of how to do it, but keep in mind you might have to move or remove other things on later models with accessories. DON'T try this if your engine is fuel-injected. Take it to Subaru and have them fix it.

Carb models only: Drain the radiator (Procedure 3, Step 1), then remove the drain plugs in the bottom of the cylinder heads and drain the engine crankcase (Procedure 3, Step 2). Remove the *air cleaner* (Chapter 7, Procedure 5, Step 4), and if your engine has an EGR pipe that connects the intake manifold to the right cylinder head, remove it (Chapter 17). Now remove the the three bolts from each end of the manifold. Pry the manifold up just enough to remove the old gaskets. Plug the holes in the cylinder head with clean rags so no crud can fall into the engine, then clean the gasket surfaces on the head and manifold with a knife and emery cloth. When the gasket surfaces are clean, remove the rags and slip in new gaskets (one on each end of the manifold). Use a wire brush to clean the threads on the bolts, then install the bolts and torque them to 16 ft. lbs.

Install the EGR tube if you removed it (Chapter 17), and the air cleaner (Chapter 7, Procedure 5, Step 5). Install the drain plugs and aluminum washers in the bottom of the cylinder heads, fill the radiator with coolant (Procedure 3, Step 2), then start the engine and let it warm up to operating temperature. After the engine has warmed up and cooled off, retorque the intake manifold bolts to 16 ft. lbs. Check the coolant level, add some if necessary, then install the radiator cap. Check the coolant level after driving a few miles.

B. No pressure leaks: If the cooling system passed the Captain Quirk pressure test (and there are no signs of coolant leaks) but the engine still overheats, do this:

1. Check the *electric fan* and *thermoswitch*. Start the engine and let it warm up. When the temperature gauge needle goes slightly past the midway point, the electric fan on the right side of the radiator should kick on and stay on until the needle drops to around the midway point. No fan? Feel the upper radiator hose; it should be hot if the thermostat opened. If the hose is cool or just warm, check the thermostat (Procedure 6). If the radiator hose is hot but the fan doesn't go on, read on, Brother.

Check the *fuse* for the fan in the *fuse box* (Chapter 10, Procedure 2, Step 1). Even if the fuse looks good, take it out and clean the ends of the fuse and the copper clips in the fuse box with fine emery paper. Put the fuse back into its slot, then start the engine to see if the fan goes on when the temperature gauge crosses the halfway mark. Sometimes fuses look perfectly good but won't carry the electric current. If the fan still doesn't come on, install a new or different fuse and try again.

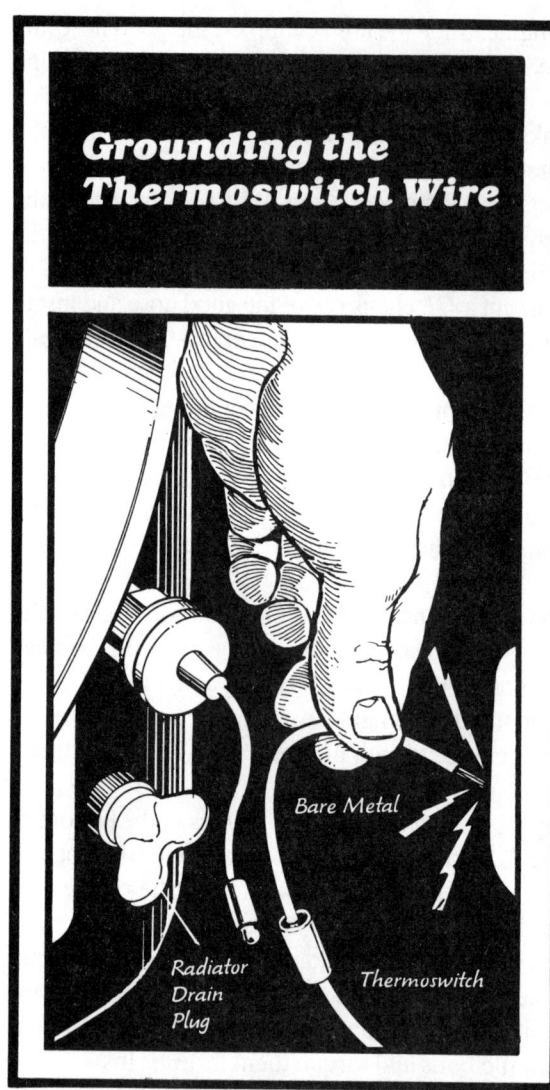

Grounding the Thermoswitch Wire

Bare Metal
Radiator Drain Plug
Thermoswitch

Still no fan? Remove the two phillips head screws that attach a short piece of wire to the top right side of the radiator and to the body in front of the radiator. Clean the ends of the wire and the area around the screw holes with emery paper until the metal is clean and bright. Put the wire and screws back in place and tighten them. Start the engine again to see if the fan goes on when the temperature gauge crosses the halfway mark.

Still no fan? Locate the brass *thermoswitch* on the right side of the radiator below the upper hose connection. Disconnect the thermoswitch wire (Procedure 5, Step 2). Turn the ignition switch to **ON** but don't start the engine. Clip one end of your jumper wire (or stick one end of an extra piece of wire) into the female end of the connector where the thermoswitch was plugged in. Ground (touch) the other end of the wire to bare unpainted metal or the negative (-) terminal of the battery. The electric fan on the radiator should burst into life. If it does, the fan is good but the thermoswitch is kaput.

If you're stuck at the side of the road, attach the end of the wire to a screw or bolt on the engine or body so it stays grounded. (Don't attach it to an electrical connection like the ones on the coil.) With the wire grounded the fan will be on whenever the key is on. On '80 models the fan will stay on all the time so you'll have to disconnect the wire when you turn the key off. Replace the thermoswitch as soon as possible (Procedure 5).

If the fan still shows no sign of life, leave the thermoswitch wire grounded (have Friend ground it if necessary), turn the ignition switch to **ON** but don't start the engine. Check the wires at the fan motor with your test light to see if they are getting juice (electric current). Here's how: Disconnect the fan wires and touch the pointed end of your test light to the end of one of the wires coming out of the wiring harness (not the wires coming out of the fan) and touch the other end of the test light to bare metal. Test both wires. One of the wires should light the test light. No juice? The wires to the fan motor are broken or disconnected somewhere. Chapter 10 tells how to trace broken wires.

If the wires are OK and the fan has juice but refuses to whir for you, replace the fan motor (Procedure 8).

2. Check the *thermostat*. Let the engine cool a little if it's hot, then remove and check the thermostat (Procedure 6).

3. Check the engine **temperature sending unit** (temp sender) and the **temperature gauge** in the dashboard. A broken temperature sending unit or gauge might lie and tell you the engine is running hot when it's not. Faulty gauges usually show one temperature constantly or the needle moves erratically while the engine is running. The needle should point to the COLD end of the gauge when the ignition key is **OFF**. Replace the temperature sending unit if the needle wanders around on the gauge. If the gauge always indicates an overheating condition, borrow or buy an *engine thermometer* and take your engine's temperature through the radiator filler neck. When the engine is warmed up, the coolant should be between 195° and 208°. Probably closer to 195° since you're checking it after it's passed through the radiator. If the gauge is showing hot but the thermometer is within the

normal range, replace the temperature sending unit.

On all '75-'81 models and '82-'84 models with Hitachi carburetors, the temperature sending unit is located on the right rear side of the intake manifold near the thermostat housing. On '82 and newer models with Carter-Weber carburetors, the temp sender is on the right front side of the intake manifold opposite the thermostat housing. The temp sender on fuel-injected models is on the right side of the intake manifold near the thermostat housing. It might be on the front or rear of the manifold. The temp sending units have one wire connection on '75-'81 models and two wires in a plastic connector on '82 and newer models.

To remove the temp sending unit, disconnect the wires, then unscrew it with a 17mm deep socket or box-end wrench. Have the new sending unit ready to screw in so only a little coolant will be lost. Screw in the new unit and tighten it. Connect the wire(s), start the engine and look for coolant leaks at the sending unit. Does the gauge work now? If not, you'll have to have Subaru or a garage replace the gauge in the dashboard.

4. Check brakes. Put the car in *Neutral* on level ground, handbrake *OFF*, and push. The car should move. If it doesn't, the brakes are stuck, so go to Chapter 13 and read the introduction to brake problems.

5. Check for slipping clutch. Chapter 15.

6. Do the 12,000-mile tune-up in Chapter 7. Pay particular attention to ignition timing, valve clearance, engine compression, and carburetor adjustment (you'll have to have Subaru or a garage check the *duty ratio* on '80 and newer models).

7. Other things. If you've gone through all the tests and the car still overheats, here are a few possibilities to try before slashing your wrists:

Change the engine and transmission oil. Maybe they're too thick.

Have the cooling system "back flushed" by a radiator shop. They can also do a flow test to see if the inside of the radiator is clogged and needs to be removed and reconditioned. If necessary, you can remove it and install it yourself (Procedure 7).

Check the exhaust system for dents that could restrict the flow of exhaust gases (Chapter 12).

Take the engine apart (Chapter 17) and check for seizing pistons and bearings. (This is your next-to-last resort.)

Move to a cooler climate or only drive the car in the wintertime. (This is your last resort.)

PROCEDURE 11: EMERGENCY OVERHEATING!

Condition: You're cruising along and suddenly notice the needle on the temperature gauge is indicating *HOT*. What should you do? What would Capt. Quirk do?

If the alternator charge light is on, the drive belt is probably broken and not turning the water pump. Check the drive belt(s) (Chapter 10, Procedure 3).

If you're driving up a steep grade on a hot day with a heavy load, do Step 1. There's probably nothing wrong with the car; it's just being overworked. When the temperature gauge drops to normal, start the car and drive on—with one eye on the temperature gauge. If you have a tachometer, use a gear that allows the engine to turn between 2,500 and 3,000 rpm. If the engine quickly overheats again, pull over and go through Steps 1-3.

Step 1. Don't Panic—Just Act!

Turn the air conditioner *OFF* if it's on. Set the heater control to *HOT* and the fan switch to *ON*. As soon as it's safe, pull off the road and turn the engine off. Turn the ignition switch to *ON* but don't start the engine. If you have air conditioning, set the control knob to *ON*. These moves will release excess engine heat into the air.

Step 2. Evaluation.

Open and prop the hood. DON'T try to remove the radiator cap now. Let the engine cool for ten minutes (or at least until the fan turns itself off) before trying to remove the cap. Due to the aluminum crankcase, Subaru engines cool off quicker than most cars. Check the following things while the engine cools. Be careful—everything under the hood will be **HOT**. Keep fingers away from the fan(s) even if they're off because they could kick on any time.

The *electric fan motor* should be whirring like mad trying to cool things off. The fan isn't on? See Procedure 10, Step 6, B-1.

Check the *drive belt(s)*. Too loose or broken? See Chapter 10, Procedure 3. Wait until the engine has cooled a little before trying to adjust or replace the drive belt. You do have a spare drive belt stashed on the spare tire, don't you?

Look for *coolant leaks* on the engine and radiator (Procedure 10, Step 6, A. 1-6). That will tell you everywhere the cooling system could be leaking (and a quick remedy for heater hose leaks).

Check the engine *oil level* (Chapter 7, Procedure 2, Step 1).

Use the end of a hammer, screwdriver, or the lug wrench to tap (not bang) on the *thermostat housing*. It's on the engine end of the large black radiator hose that's attached to the top right (passenger's) side of the radiator. If your model has a plastic gizmo mounted to the top of the thermostat housing, tap on the side of the metal housing, not on the plastic gizmo on top of the housing. If the thermostat is stuck closed, the tapping might jar it loose.

See if a newspaper or something is blocking the *flow of air* through the front of the radiator. If necessary, remove the phillips screws around the edge of the grille, pull the grille off the car, remove the offending obstacle, then install the grille.

Step 3. Check Coolant Level.

See Chapter 7, Procedure 2, Step 8, to check the coolant level.

If the coolant level is low, ideally you should add an antifreeze/water mixture, but if you're out on the road, find some clean water. Don't use dirty, funky water from the roadside ditch; it'll clog the cooling system.

Pour coolant (or water) into the radiator until it's full (OHC models), or up to the little metal plate inside the filler neck (OHV models). If you noticed a coolant leak on the radiator or hoses, install the radiator cap but don't tighten it. This way the system won't pressurize and force the coolant out. If you didn't see any leaks, install the cap and tighten it. Lower the hood, then drive slowly for awhile (air conditioner OFF). Keep an eye on the temperature gauge. If the engine overheats again, go through Procedure 10, Steps 1-6 if you have your tools handy. No tools? Have Snotty beam you up, or call someone to tow you home.

Everything seems OK? If you added water only to the radiator, remember to add antifreeze when you get home and the engine is cold. If the coolant level is low again, check the hoses and clamps (Procedure 2), and the water pump (Procedure 4).

CHAPTER 17
ENGINE REMOVAL AND REPAIR

Removing and rebuilding OHC models is not specifically covered in this chapter. If you want to do the job yourself, you'll have to buy the factory manual for your year and model. This chapter is for those of you with an abundance of perseverance, the ability to keep things reasonably well organized, and a willingness to get really greasy. The more experienced you are (mechanically speaking), the easier this chapter will be for you. An experienced Friend to help would be a definite asset.

Even though all OHV Subaru engines are basically the same, the emission control devices attached to these engines have changed drastically over the years. I've made the engine removal and repair procedures as detailed as possible given the multitude of changes, but some parts on your model may differ slightly from those described in the text. If they do, take notes during the disassembly so you'll know how to put it back together. I'll warn you about procedures that require professional assistance.

The single most important factor for the successful removal and installation of your engine is also one of the easiest. I'm talking about the use of masking tape and an indelible pen (like a Sharpie) to label hoses, wires, cables, and engine parts as you disconnect or remove them from the engine. This is something you can and must do! If you label *everything* you disconnect while removing the engine, the labels will attract your attention (like little flags) when you install the engine. Remove the labels as you reconnect things and you'll be assured everything is reconnected when all the "flags" are gone.

If you have to disconnect a hose or wire that isn't mentioned in the text and you don't know what it's called, make up a name for it (*Gizmo 1*, for example) and label *both ends* before disconnecting it. During reassembly you'll know that *Gizmo 1* attaches to *Gizmo 1*, *Gizmo 2* attaches to *Gizmo 2*, and so on. Do the same with any engine parts not mentioned in the text.

As you remove parts from the engine, put the nuts, bolts, and washers in plastic sandwich baggies and/or plastic bread bags, then label the baggies and tape them to the part. This will make reassembly a breeze.

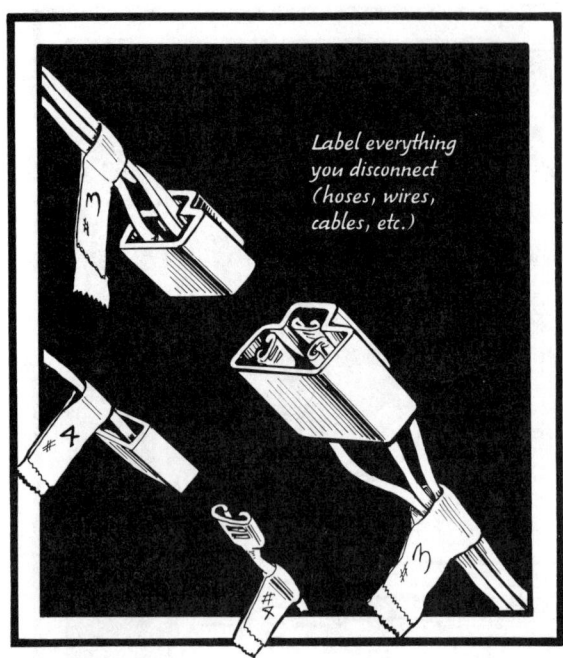

Label everything you disconnect (hoses, wires, cables, etc.)

Once again, here's something you can (and should) do to help you remember where everything for your particular Subaru attaches. Round up a camera and take pictures of the engine compartment from several angles before disconnecting anything. (It was too much to ask Joe to illustrate all the variations.) If you're doing a ring and valve job or a rebuild, take pictures of the engine from several angles before and during the dismantling procedures. Have the pictures developed as soon as the engine is as far apart as you're going to disassemble it. The pics will come in handy when you start putting it all back together. If you're only replacing the clutch components or oil seals, you probably won't need to take disassembly pictures.

In other words, the more thoroughly you label things during engine removal and disassembly, the more fun you'll have putting the puzzle back together after the repair work is done.

Before yanking the engine out by its roots and reducing it to several piles of parts, let's be sure engine removal is really necessary. This chapter does not cover the removal, repair, and installation of fuel-injected Turbo engines.

REASONS FOR ENGINE REMOVAL

Following is a list of problems that require removal of the engine for repair.

Worn-out clutch components: You've gone through the clutch troubleshooting guide in Chapter 15 and determined the clutch and/or throwout bearing are worn out.

Rear crankshaft oil seal leaks: See the Oil Leaks section of Chapter 9 to determine if it's really the crank seal that's leaking.

Leaking head gasket: If the tests in Chapter 9: *Troubleshooting*, indicate the head gaskets are leaking.

Engine makes a knocking sound: See the Noises section in Chapter 9 to diagnose engine knocks. A LOUD knocking from the engine means something's definitely amiss—so get ready to rebuild the engine. DON'T start the engine, you may do more damage.

Worn-out piston rings: You can tell the engine is burning a lot of oil by the blue cloud following your Soob, and you have to add oil to the engine frequently. If the numbers on the compression test in Chapter 7 were higher after you squirted oil in the cylinders, the rings aren't holding compression like they should. You can try doctoring your engine with one of the "mechanic in a can" remedies that claim to clean and loosen gummed-up piston rings. If that doesn't work or the engine has around 100,000 miles on it, a ring and valve job is probably needed.

Burned valve(s): The compression check in Chapter 7 showed that one or more cylinders had significantly less compression than the others and squirting oil into the cylinders didn't raise the compression. Drive the car for a few days and do another compression check. Maybe a carbon flake was preventing the valves from seating properly in the head. If there's no improvement after checking the compression two or three times, you need to remove the heads for a valve job.

Worn out camshaft and/or lifters: You'll know the cam and lifters are wearing out if the gap between one or more of the valves and the adjuster is extremely loose at every valve adjustment. Eventually you'll run out of adjustment threads on the bolt and the valve will still be loose. If it's the lobe on the camshaft wearing out, the valves opposite each other on the engine will both be loose. If it's just a lifter wearing out, only the valve operated by that lifter will be loose. Either way, you have to remove and disassemble the engine to repair it.

Or: Chief engineer Snotty has informed the bridge that the dilithium crystal supply for the thrusters is dangerously low.

WHAT IF?

If you've come to the inescapable conclusion that the engine needs to be removed and repaired, the cheapest way is to do it yourself. If you're unsure about diving into the innards of your engine, you might still save some money by removing the engine, stripping the accessories, then taking it to a garage to have them do the internal repair. Compare the cost of having the garage remove and strip the engine to the cost of renting an engine hoist twice to remove and install the engine yourself.

If the engine has a lot of miles on it and needs a complete rebuild, you have four choices: buy a new or rebuilt engine, find a used engine, rebuild your engine, or have Subaru or a garage rebuild it. Let's consider these one at a time.

New engine or rebuilt engine: Call Subaru and garages that specialize in Subarus for the price of a new or rebuilt engine for your year and model. Better be seated when you make this call—the price might send you into cardiac arrest. Ask how much you would save by removing your old engine and installing the new one yourself and if they'll give you anything for your old engine. What kind of warranty does the new engine have?

A company called ATK North America imports high quality rebuilt engines from Japan which they can ship directly to you. In California call them at (800) 631-5446. If you live outside California, the number is (800) 421-3746. Be sure to ask them about the warranty and shipping costs.

Used engine: It may be possible to find a low-mileage Soob that has just been wrecked and towed to a junkyard. If you locate one, check the number of miles on the odometer and, if the engine still runs, do a compression check. See if they'll give you a warranty with the engine. Maybe you can trade in your old engine to save some money.

Several companies are importing guaranteed low-mileage used Subaru engines from Japan. The engines usually come with the engine's compression readings stamped on a tag and are often complete with alternator, carburetor, clutch, and other major parts. The prices seem pretty reasonable. Check the classified ads and local garages to find these engines.

Not all Subaru engines are interchangeable, so be sure the used engine will work in your particular year and model. If you decide to go the used engine route, you can easily have your old engine out and the new, used one installed in a couple of days (one, if you really hustle and don't run into any problems). It would be a good idea to install new front and rear crankshaft seals, new clutch disc, and a new oil pump before installing the engine.

Rebuild your engine: It's impossible to tell what it's going to cost to rebuild your engine until it's apart and checked by a machine shop, and comparative prices have been gathered from the Subaru dealer and parts stores. You can eliminate profit and labor costs by doing it yourself, so it will probably cost less than buying a new or rebuilt engine. If some of the major parts on your engine must be replaced (cylinder heads, pistons, crankshaft, crankcase), buying a rebuilt engine might be cheaper. Counting machine shop time and rounding up the parts, it will probably take at least one, and maybe two, weeks to completely rebuild the engine yourself.

Have someone else rebuild your engine: If you're not up for doing the rebuild yourself, you can still save money. Remove the engine, strip the accessories and hardware, and take it to a machine shop or garage to have it rebuilt. When the engine is rebuilt, drag it home and reinstall it yourself. Call around for "ballpark" figures for the parts and labor. They won't be able to tell you exactly what it's going to cost until they know which parts are reusable and which parts must be replaced. Don't forget to include the cost of renting an engine hoist twice to remove and install the engine.

MACHINE SHOPS

Before you take your engine or engine parts to a machine shop, call the local hotrod places and car dealers and ask the service managers to recommend the best machine shop. There's usually one machine shop in town that has the reputation of being "The Best." That's the one for you.

GARAGES

If you're going to have a garage rebuild or repair your engine, be sure they're knowledgeable about Subarus. The job requires special tools and techniques that most garages and gas station mechanics aren't aware of. They might screw things up. An experienced mechanic with this book should be able to do a good job.

WAYS TO REMOVE THE ENGINE

Using a Cherry Picker: Garages use a hoist called a "cherry picker" to lift the engine out of the car once everything is disconnected. You can rent a cherry picker, or maybe borrow one from a friendly garage, making engine removal and installation relatively easy. You'll need Friend to operate the hoist while you guide the engine in or out of the car. After doing it a few times, one person can slowly and carefully do it alone.

Using a Neighbor: Subaru engines weigh between 180 and 250 lbs. When removing an engine at home, I use a 4' to 6' piece of chain or a cable-type bicycle lock wrapped around a strong 4x4 board, and a strong neighbor (Peter Porinsh) to remove and install the engine. The first time or two, it helped to have Billy Trucker around to guide the engine while Peter and I hoisted it out or in. Peter and I have done it alone, but it's easier with an extra person to help guide it in. This method takes a lot of muscle, so don't try it if you have a weak back and/or don't have a former football player for a neighbor. A longer board with two people on each end and someone to guide the engine out and back in would make it easier.

When using this technique, attach the board as close to the engine as possible so you don't have to lift any higher than necessary for the engine to clear the front of the car. Measure the distance between the engine and the board when removing the engine so you'll know where to attach it when you're ready to put the engine back in. It's a real bummer to lift the engine into the car and find the board hits the fenders before the engine is low enough to install. Guess how I found this out.

Bear in mind that a tumbling engine can be lethal. I strongly advise you to use a cherry picker if at all possible, or at least have put in some time with other procedures in this book before you tackle engine removal yourself. You'll then have a fair idea of the heft and feel of Subaru components.

ENGINE STAND

Since Subaru oil pans are rounded on the bottom, you'll need something to hold the engine once it's removed. If you're only replacing the clutch and/or the rear crank seal, an old tire and/or several blocks of wood will work OK. But for a complete rebuild, replacing the head gaskets, or doing a ring and valve job, you'll have to roll the engine onto its front and rear ends several times; an engine stand makes the job a lot easier. Also, if the oil pan is removed, you have to protect the oil pickup tube that hangs down from the crankcase. I've designed a simple stand you can make out of wood that works very well. There's a sketch of the stand somewhere nearby.

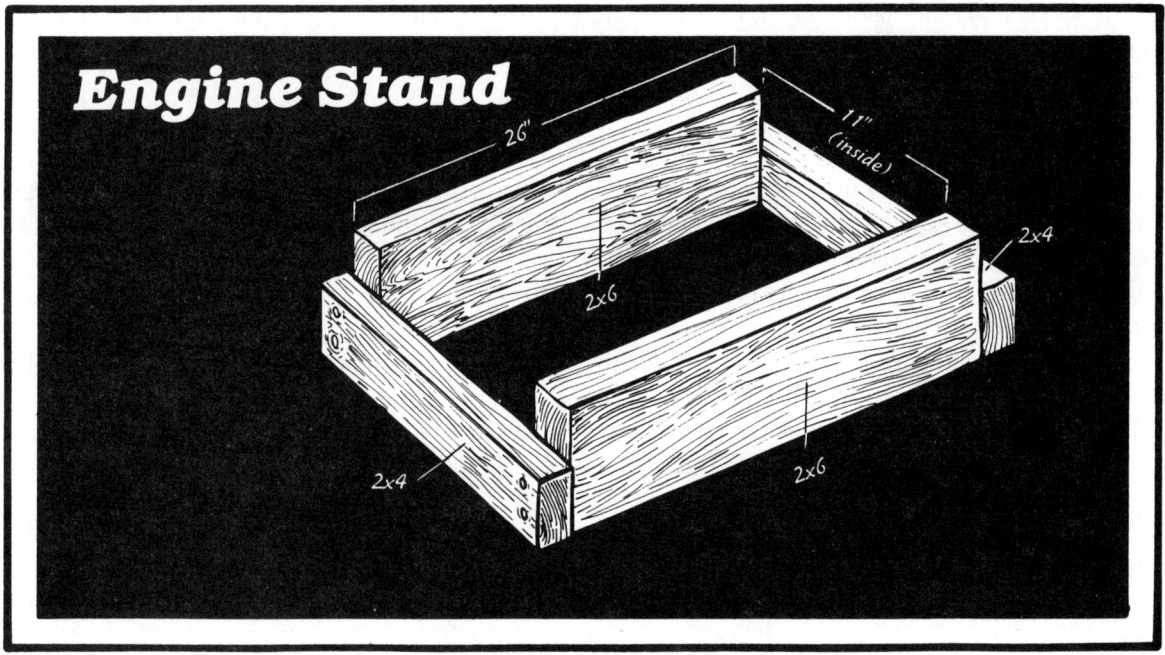

NOW WHAT?

If you've decided to remove the engine and repair it yourself, read through the procedures that apply to your engine's problem(s) so you'll know which tools and materials are necessary to successfully complete the job. I strongly urge you to read Chapter 2: *Orientation*, Chapter 3: *Safety*, and Chapter 4: *How A Subaru Works* before removing the engine. You'll find the illustrations in Chapter 2 and Chapter 4 very helpful during engine removal and repair.

As you remove and disassemble the engine, go slow, baggie and label EVERYTHING as you disconnect or remove it, and take lots of pictures. Having Friend around to read the instructions and help you wrestle with the engine will make the job easier and more fun. Have a pencil and paper handy to jot down notes. Also, as you take things apart, make a shopping list of parts and supplies you'll need during reassembly. The shopping list will save several extra trips to the parts store.

If you rebuild your engine using this book, please let me know. I'm very curious about how many home mechanics are rebuilding their own engines these days.

PROCEDURE 1: REMOVE ENGINE

Condition: You've determined the engine must be removed for repair or replacement; OR you want to impress Jodie Foster.

Tools and Materials: Phase 1 tool kit, catch pan(s) for oil and coolant, plastic jugs to dispose of the oil and coolant, masking tape, indelible marker, plastic baggies, an old three-pound coffee can, a cherry picker engine hoist, or two or more strong Friends and the materials mentioned above under Ways to Remove the Engine.

Remarks: On models with air conditioning (A/C), if the A/C compressor is mounted between the alternator and carburetor, have Subaru or a garage discharge the gas in the system before disconnecting anything from the engine. You'll have to have the system recharged when the engine is back in the car. If the A/C compressor is mounted between the alternator and left fender, you might be able to move the compressor out of the way far enough to remove the engine without discharging the system and disconnecting the A/C hoses. Check it carefully and have the system discharged if there's any doubt.

Step 1. Get Ready.

If at all possible, drive or drag the car to a carwash and wash the top and bottom of the engine and transmission thoroughly (Chapter 7, Procedure 5, Step 2). You'll be glad you did. (If you have 4WD, remove the **skid plate** before going to the carwash.)

Park the car on level ground where the engine is going to be removed. Set the handbrake, put the gearshift in Neutral, and block the rear wheels.

Open the hood and prop it in the "Way Up" position (Chapter 2: *Orientation*). Remove the spare tire if it's in the engine compartment.

4WD models: Remove the skid plate beneath the engine. It's held on with four or five 12mm bolts or 5.5mm allen head bolts. Baggie the bolts as "Skid Plate" and stash the plate out of the way.

Step 2. Drain Engine Oil.

If you're here only for a clutch or rear seal repair and the engine isn't due for an oil change, skip to Step 3.

Drain the engine oil (Chapter 7, Procedure 3, Step 1). While the oil drains, you can disconnect things on the engine.

Step 3. Disconnect Battery Cables.

Disconnect both **battery cable clamps** from the battery (Chapter 10, Procedure 1, Step 3).

Follow the **negative (-) battery cable** to where it connects to the engine. Unscrew the bolt and pull the cable out of the way. If other wires from the body are attached to the engine with this bolt, label them "Negative Battery Cable Bolt," then disconnect them. Screw the bolt back into its hole.

Follow the **positive (+) battery cable** toward the starter and remove the 12mm bolt that attaches a **cable bracket** to the cylinder head (not all models have this). Remove the bracket, then screw the bolt back into its hole.

Step 4. Remove Air Cleaner and Hot Air Intake Hose.

Look at Chapter 7, Procedure 5, Step 4, to remove the **air cleaner**. Remove the **hot air intake hose** (Chapter 12, Procedure 3, Step 1).

Step 5. Remove Power Steering Pump and Bracket (models with power steering only).

Skip this step if you don't have power steering.

CAUTION: Don't remove the hoses from the rear of the power steering reservoir. It's unnecessary and would make a big mess.

Remove and label the **power steering (P/S) drive belt** (Chapter 10, Procedure 3, Step 4).

Now remove the nut on the rear center of the **power steering reservoir tank** and the two bolts on the lower right side of the **P/S unit**. They're between the reservoir and the drive belt pulley. Lift the P/S unit away from the engine and lay it on the firewall shelf where the spare tire sits. Be careful not to kink or damage the hoses. Prop the tank upright so the fluid won't run out and make a mess. Remove the three bolts that attach the P/S bracket to the front of the engine. Label and baggie all the P/S bolts, washers, and nuts.

Step 6. Remove Air Conditioner Compressor from Engine.

Skip this step if you don't have air conditioning.

CAUTION! See Remark. Unless the A/C system has been discharged, don't disconnect any hoses from the air conditioner. The high-pressure gas inside can damage you severely. If you determined the hoses must be removed in order to remove the engine and you've had the system discharged, label the hoses and their fittings. Use a crescent wrench to disconnect the hoses from the compressor. There might also be an electrical wire attached to the compressor to label and disconnect.

Since there are several different compressor mountings, I can't tell you exactly how your compressor is attached, but here's a generic description. Remove the **air conditioner drive belt** (Chapter 10, Procedure 3, Step 3), label the belt "A/C," then remove the bolts that attach the **compressor** to a heavy metal plate or to brackets mounted on the engine. Baggie the bolts as "A/C." If you disconnected the hoses from the compressor, remove the compressor from the engine and set it upright so the fluid won't run out. Tuck the hoses out of the way. If the compressor is mounted between the alternator and fender and you didn't disconnect the compressor hoses, pull the compressor toward the fender and use wire, rope, twine, or an old necktie to tie it to the bracket that holds the jack. If you don't have a floor jack, remove the Subaru jack before tying the compressor to the bracket; you'll need the jack later for engine removal.

Step 7. Disconnect Hoses Relating to the Fuel System.

'75-'79 cars and '77-'80 Brats: Put a rag below the fitting on the left rear side of the carburetor where the **fuel line** attaches. Label the hose, release the clamp, then pull the hose off the carb. Plug the end of the hose with a punch or phillips screwdriver, then prop the hose toward the rear of the engine compartment so gas won't drain out of it.

'77-'79 models: See if a couple of hoses from the left side of the **intake manifold** cross behind the engine and connect to metal pipes near the engine oil dipstick. The pipes connect to the round black **canister** in the corner of the engine compartment. If you have these hoses, label them ("Fuel 1," "Fuel 2," etc.), then disconnect them.

'81 Brats: You'll have four **hoses** connected to metal **pipes** near the right rear corner of the engine, just behind the engine oil dipstick. Label the hoses and pipes ("Hose 1," "Hose 2," etc.) then disconnect them.

'80 and newer cars and '82-'87 Brats: You'll have two or three hoses attached to the top left side of the carb. Two of the hoses go to the left rear corner of the engine compartment, and one hose goes to a metal pipe near the left strut tower. These hoses might go through a clamp that's mounted to the strut tower. If so, remove the clamp. Follow the hoses from the carb to where they connect to metal pipes or the fuel pump. Label the hoses "Fuel 1," "Fuel 2," and "Fuel 3" (if you have it), then disconnect them.

You've probably been nervously avoiding the thought of disconnecting that bundle of hoses located between the **oil filler tube** and **left strut tower**. Right? Don't worry, it's a piece of cake. Get your tape and marking pen and label one of the hoses and the pipe it's connected to, "Hose 1." Label another hose and pipe "Hose 2," and so on until they're all labeled and disconnected. Easy, eh?

Step 8. Disconnect Brake Booster Vacuum Hose.

Follow the thumb-size hose from the round black **master vac** (right behind the master cylinder) to where it connects to a **check valve** mounted in a bracket. If the bracket is mounted to the side of the oil filler tube (early models), disconnect the hose from the *rear* of the check valve. If the bracket is mounted to the left strut tower, disconnect the hose from the *front* of the check valve. If there's no check valve, follow the hose to where it connects to the intake manifold and disconnect it there. Label the hose, then cover the open end with tape to keep dirt out. Tuck the hose out of the way.

Step 9. Electrical Disconnections.

Alternator: Disconnect the white plastic electrical connector on the rear of the alternator or a few inches from it. Label, then disconnect the smaller wires attached to the rear of the alternator (a push-on connector, screw, or 8mm nut). Use the letter stamped on the rear of the alternator next to the terminals for the label. Put the nut or screw back onto the alternator. Tuck the wires out of the way, away from the engine.

Electric fan wires: Follow the wires from the **fan motor** on the right side of the radiator to plastic connectors. Wipe the wires off with a rag if they're oily, then label them "Fan." If the two wires don't join in a common connector, put a label on each side of the connector. Label the wires "Fan 1" and "Fan 2." Do the same with the **air conditioner fan** on the left side of the radiator if you have one.

Thermoswitch wire: Find the round brass **thermoswitch** on the right rear side of the radiator. Some thermoswitch wires disconnect right at the thermoswitch and some disconnect a few inches away. Label the wire "Thermoswitch," then disconnect it.

Coil wire: Pull the large high-tension wire out of the center of the distributor cap. Pry the wire out of the plastic holder on the engine, then tuck the wire out of the way.

Automatic choke: Follow the wire coming out of the round automatic choke housing on the side of the carburetor to a connector. Label the wire on each side of the connector "Choke," then disconnect the wires.

'75-'76 models: Label, then disconnect the following wires:

Anti-diesel valve: If there's a hexagonal thing about the size of your thumb on the left front side of the carburetor with a wire coming out of it, follow the wire to a connector, label the wires "Anti-diesel Valve," then disconnect them.

Temperature sending switch: On the right side of the intake manifold near the carburetor there's a wire connected to what looks like a large bolt. Label the wire "Temp Sending Switch," then disconnect it.

Oil pressure switch: The oil pressure switch (OPS) is located on the bottom front of the engine, to the right of the oil pump. Label the wire "OPS," then disconnect it.

Distributor wire: There's a push-on connector on the side of the distributor. Label the wire "Dist.," then disconnect it from the distributor and pull it away from the engine, out of the way.

'77 and newer models: Starting in 1977, Soobs have a large plastic harness connector that disconnects most of the wires from the engine to the body. Some models also have a distributor wire harness connector. Follow the bundle(s) of wires from the engine to where they connect to another bundle of wires with a plastic connector. To disconnect the connectors, squeeze the tab(s) on the side, then separate the two halves. The location of the harness connectors wandered around in the engine compartment over the years, so here are directions to find them.

'77-'79 models: The connectors are located near the left rear corner of the engine.

'80-'81 models: The connectors are located near the ignition coil on the right side of the engine compartment. No distributor connector? See below.

'82 and newer models: The large connectors are located near the right strut tower, just above the windshield washer fluid reservoir. There also might be a single wire connector to disconnect.

'80 and newer models: If your distributor wires connect directly to the coil, look on the coil for a "+" near one of the small screw terminals and a "-" near the other screw terminal. Label the wires "Coil +" and "Coil-" (or "Front" and "Rear"), then use an 8mm wrench to release the wires from the coil. Screw the nuts back onto the coil.

EVERYONE: Once the connectors are divorced (I mean separated), coil the bundle(s) of wires and stash them on the engine so they aren't dangling around and in the way.

Step 10. Vacuum Hoses Disconnections.

Automatic transmission models: Near the rear of the engine, between the differential and engine dipsticks, you'll see a metal tube coming from under the car that connects to a rubber **vacuum hose** that's connected to the engine. Label the hose and tube "Trans," then pull the hose off the tube. Put tape over the ends of the tube and hose.

'80 California models: You'll have three vacuum hoses connected between the engine and a small boxlike **altitude compensator** located near the right strut tower. Label the hoses and their fittings 1, 2, and 3 (or whatever), then disconnect them from the altitude compensator.

'81 and newer models with Hitachi carburetor: A rubber vacuum hose or two goes from the right side of the **intake manifold** to the right rear corner of the engine compartment. There it connects to two **vacuum switches**. Label the engine end of the hose(s) and the fitting(s) "Vacuum Switch 1," and if you have two hoses, "Vacuum Switch 2," then disconnect it/them.

Right next to the vacuum switches is a large electrical **wiring harness** that connects the engine to the computer located inside the car. Label the two halves of the connector "ECU" (electronic control unit), then separate the connector.

Cruise control: If you have cruise control, find a vacuum line going from the engine to a reservoir on the firewall. Label the engine end of the hose and where it connects to the engine "CC," then disconnect the hose and tuck it out of the way.

OK, that should take care of the electrical, vacuum, and fuel disconnections. Look around for others that need to be labeled and disconnected.

Step 11. Install Oil Drain Plug, Drain Oil Filter.

If you didn't drain the oil, skip this step.

Put the **oil plug** back in the oil pan, then remove the **oil filter** and drain it into the catch pan. When most of the oil is out of the filter, toss it in the trash. Empty the catch pan in a suitable container for disposal. Clean the catch pan.

Step 12. Drain Radiator.

Remove and baggie the four 10mm bolts that attach a flat piece of sheet metal to the body just below the right exhaust pipe. This will make it easier to get to the radiator drain valve.

Look at Chapter 16, Procedure 3, Steps 1 and 2, to drain the radiator and crankcase. If the antifreeze has been replaced recently and you want to use it again, be sure the catch pan is very clean before draining the radiator and crankcase into it.

Step 13. Mechanical Disconnections.

Accelerator cable: Do Chapter 11, Procedure 3, Steps 2 and 3, to disconnect the accelerator cable from the carburetor, and the cable housing from the bracket behind the carburetor. Put the screw and clamp back on the bracket. Tuck the cable out of the way.

Clutch return spring (manual transmission only): Disconnect and remove the clutch return spring between the clutch release lever and the intake manifold or bracket on the rear of the engine (Chapter 15, Procedure 2, Step 1). Put the spring in the coffee can.

Hill-holder cable: If your model has a hill-holder, see Chapter 13, Procedure 18, Step 1, to release the hill-holder cable from the clutch return lever and bracket. Release any plastic clips that attach the cable to the engine, then tuck the cable away from the engine.

Pitching stopper: The pitching stopper is that small rod from the top rear of the engine to the firewall. Remove the nut, large flat washer, and rubber grommet from the front end of the rod where it sticks through the bracket on the engine. Don't mess with the nut on the rear side of the engine bracket. Remove the nut that attaches the rod to the firewall. Wiggle the rod off the bolt on the firewall, then out of the engine bracket. Put the rubber grommet, washer, and nut back on the rod. Put the washer and nut back on the bolt on the firewall. Put the rod in the coffee can. If the pitching stopper is connected to the transmission with a cable, leave the cable attached but tuck the rod away from the engine.

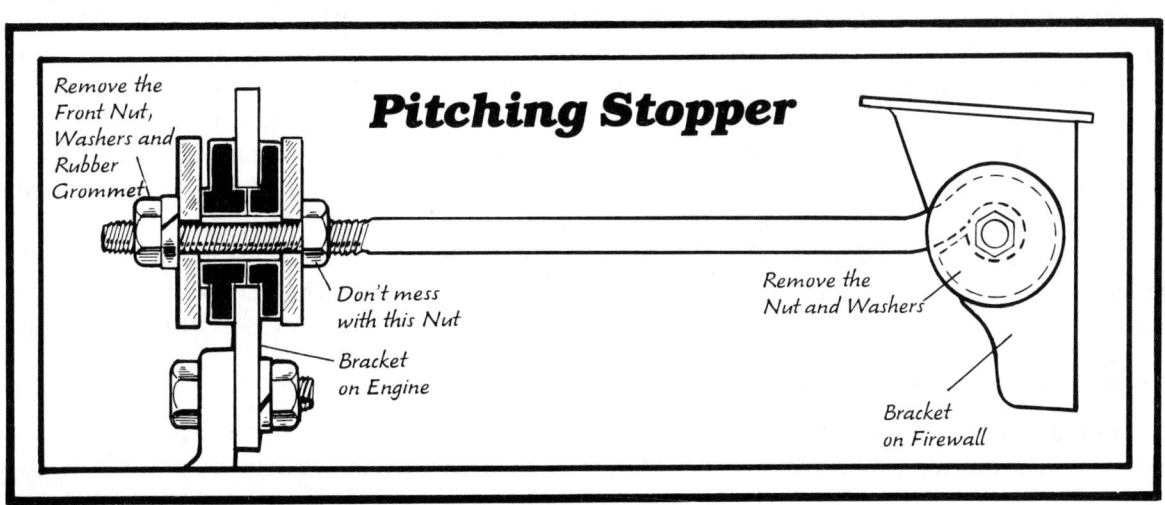

Automatic transmission models: The **torque converter** on the transmission is bolted to a **torque plate** (drive plate) on the engine with four bolts. To disconnect them, remove the **rubber plug** from the timing hole on the **flywheel housing.** Use a socket on the crankshaft pulley bolt to rotate the engine until you can see a bolt head through the timing hole. Use a socket and ratchet to remove the bolt. Be careful—don't let the bolt fall down into the flywheel housing! Keep rotating the engine and removing bolts until all four bolts are out. Baggie them as "Torque Plate." Note the position of the bolt hole on the torque converter relative to the timing hole on the flywheel housing. You'll want the torque converter in this position when you install the engine.

Step 14. Disconnect Heater Hoses.

The heater hoses are those two thumb-size hoses coming out of the firewall just to the right of the master cylinder.

Before disconnecting the heater hoses, label them so you'll know where they go during reassembly.

'75-'79 models: Disconnect the heater hoses from the intake manifold and bypass pipe on the left side of the engine. If you're not sure where the heater hoses connect, look at the illustration in Chapter 16.

'80 and newer models: Disconnect the heater hoses from the hose splicers located near the rear of the engine.

Step 15. Remove Radiator.

The coolant has been drained from the radiator and engine. Right? Tighten the radiator drain plug and install the plugs in the cylinder heads. If you're going to reuse the antifreeze, stash it someplace clean and safe so kids and pets can't get to it. It's poison! If you plan to refill the radiator with new antifreeze, put the old antifreeze in plastic jugs and toss it in the trash.

Look at Chapter 16, Procedure 7, to remove the radiator. It's very delicate, so stash it someplace safe where the kids can't use it for a dart board.

Step 16. Chock, Jack, and Block.

See Chapter 3, Procedure 1, to raise the front of the car and put it on jackstands. You don't need to remove the front wheels.

Now use a floor jack or the car jack and a short block of wood to jack up the bottom front of the transmission until the engine is raised about 1 inch. If the exhaust system is in the way, guide the jack between the pipes.

Step 17. Mechanical Disconnections Under the Car.

Look at the right exhaust pipe where it connects to the bottom of the cylinder head. If the mounting bolts for the exhaust pipe are covered by a sheet metal **air stove** wrapped around the exhaust pipe, remove the two 10mm bolts from the air stove. Spread the two sheet metal pieces until they can be separated and removed from the exhaust pipe. Put the two pieces back together and screw the bolts into the holes. Toss the stove in the can.

Remove and baggie the four 14mm nuts and washers securing the exhaust pipes to the bottom of the cylinder heads. Pull the exhaust pipes down just far enough to clear the studs on the heads. If you can't lower the exhaust pipe assembly far enough to clear the studs on the cylinder heads, remove the bolt that attaches the rear of the exhaust pipe assembly to a bracket on the body. Careful, don't let the assembly fall on you.

'75-'79 cars and '77-'81 Brats: Slide under the car and locate two 14mm bolts on each side of the oil pan on the bottom of the engine. The bolts attach the engine to steel brackets. Remove the four bolts and baggie them as "Engine Mounts."

'80 and newer cars and '82-'87 Brats: From the engine compartment, locate the 14mm bolts that attach the engine to the steel **engine mounts** near the bottom rear corner of the engine. The bolt heads are pointed downward toward the outside of the car at about 45 degrees. Baggie the bolts and washers as "Engine Mounts."

Step 18. Unbolt Engine From Transaxle.

Bottom two nuts: Locate the two 14mm or 17mm nuts at the bottom rear corners of the engine screwed onto studs that point toward the rear of the car. On some models, it's possible to remove the nuts from above, but other models (especially some '80 and newer models) have too much stuff in the way, so you'll have to crawl under the car and reach the nuts with a socket on the end of a long extension. The lower nut on the left side is the most difficult to remove because of the steering shaft (a 12-point box-end wrench is helpful). Reminding you of perseverance and the Thrill of a Challenge is the only way I can help. It might take a while, but eventually you'll get them off. Remove and baggie the nuts and washers. Lower the car if you jacked it up.

Top two bolts and nuts: Remove the two 14mm or 17mm bolts, nuts and washers securing the top of the flywheel housing to the transmission. They go through the top corners of the flywheel housing and the transaxle housing. On some models, one of the bolts also attaches the top of the starter to the transaxle. You'll have to use a wrench to hold one end while you unscrew the other end. Baggie the bolts, nuts, and washers with the bottom two nuts and washers.

Step 19. Finally, Remove the Engine.

Make one last check for hoses and wires that connect the engine to the body. Label any you find, then disconnect them.

'75-'79 cars and '77-'81 Brats: Attach one end of a steel cable or chain to the hole on the top rear center of the engine where the pitching stopper was attached.

'80 and newer cars and '82-'87 Brats: Attach one end of a steel cable or chain to the short horizontal steel bracket that's bolted to the front center of the flywheel housing.

EVERYONE: Pull the cable or chain over the top of the engine so it clears the top of the carburetor.

If you're using a board to remove the engine, wrap the chain or cable around the board to take up excess length (so the board is as close to the fenders as possible), then hook the other end of the chain or cable to the hook on the top front corner of the engine.

If you're using a cherry picker, slide it into position so the end of the hoist is a foot or so above the carburetor. Put the chain through the large hook on the end of the cherry picker, then attach the other end of the chain to the hook on the top front corner of the engine.

Use the engine hoist, or a board and two or more strong Friends, to lift the engine slightly, then pull the engine forward until it clears the shaft sticking out of the transmission. Lift the engine over the front of the car and set it gently on the floor or in an old tire. Block the sides with wood so it can't fall over. Remove the cable, chain, board, engine hoist or whatever you used to get the engine out.

If you're just replacing the clutch and pressure plate, the work can easily be done on the floor. If you're going to rebuild the engine or do a ring and valve job, you've probably made an engine stand already. Have Friends help you set the engine into the center of the engine stand. If you're setting it on a table, be sure the table is sturdy enough hold the weight.

Congratulations! Removing the engine wasn't so bad, was it?

ENGINE DISASSEMBLY

Engine rebuilders: Do the following steps in order. Some parts must be removed in a certain sequence, so don't skip around.

Clutch and/or rear crankshaft seal replacers: Start with Procedure 3. You'll be directed where to go next at the end of each step.

Valve job and/or piston ring people: If you *aren't* replacing the clutch or rear crankshaft seal, start with Procedure 4. You'll be directed where to go at the end of each step.

PROCEDURE 2: REMOVE DISTRIBUTOR

Condition: Engine rebuild; OR you were sent here from another chapter.

Tools and Materials: 12mm wrench, small file or hammer and punch or something sharp, masking tape, indelible marker, maybe a new rubber 0-ring for the distributor housing.

Remarks: Before removing the **distributor**, set the engine to top dead center firing position for cylinder #1 and carefully mark where the distributor is set so you'll know which way it goes during reassembly. If you're here from another chapter, don't rotate the crank after the distributor is removed or you'll have to reset it before installing the distributor.

Step 1. Mark Distributor.

Set the engine to top dead center (TDC) firing position for cylinder #1 (Chapter 7, Procedure 5, Step 6). Once you're sure the rotor is pointed to the #1 spark plug wire, use masking tape and a marker to number all four **spark plug wires** so you'll know which cylinders they're for.
   Distributor removers: If you're here from another chapter only to remove the distributor, disconnect the spark plug wires from cylinders #1 and #3, then pry those wires out of the plastic clips (looms) and prop the distributor cap out of the way.
   Rebuilders: Disconnect the spark plug wires from all four spark plugs, then pry the wires out of the wire looms located between the spark plugs and distributor. Remove the distributor cap with the wires still attached. Stash the cap someplace where it won't get damaged.
   EVERYONE: With the engine set at TDC for cylinder #1, use a small file, a hammer and punch, or a sharp object to make a small mark on the top edge of the distributor exactly where the rotor is pointing. Also make a mark where the distributor hold-down bolt is located in the slot at the bottom of the distributor. If you're here only to replace the distributor, Procedure 21 tells you how to install the distributor.

Step 2. Remove Distributor.

Remove the 12mm bolt(s) at the bottom of the distributor that attach the distributor plate to the crankcase. OHV models: don't mess with the adjustment bolt on the front of the distributor. Grab the distributor with both hands and twist side-to-side as you pull the distributor up and out of the crankcase. Stash it someplace safe if you're not hauling it away for repairs.

PROCEDURE 3: REMOVE CLUTCH COMPONENTS (Manual), TORQUE PLATE (Automatics), FRONT AND REAR CRANKSHAFT SEALS

Condition: Engine rebuild; OR piston ring replacement; OR clutch parts are worn out; OR front or rear crank seal is leaking.

Tools and Materials: Phase 1 tool set, maybe new front and rear crank seals. People with manual transmissions will need a dust mask or respirator, clutch alignment tool, and maybe new clutch disc, pressure plate, throwout bearing, pilot bearing, front and rear crank seals.

Remarks: When replacing the **clutch disc**, it's best to have the **flywheel** resurfaced by a machine shop so the new disc will wear evenly. If you're really short on money or time, carefully inspect the clutch surface on the flywheel. If there are no grooves, cracks, or dark blotchy-looking "hot spot" areas, you can get by without resurfacing (the new clutch disc might not last as long, though).
   While the engine is out, it's a good idea to replace the **front** and **rear crank seals** (everyone), and the **throwout bearing** and **pilot bearing** (manual transmission). This is insurance that you won't have to remove the engine again soon just to install a small inexpensive part. If you aren't sure what the clutch parts look like, see the illustration at the start of Chapter 15.

CAUTION: Wear a dust mask or respirator to protect you from the black clutch dust. It's harmful to your health,

Step 1. Lock the Engine.

Remove the **rubber plug** from the timing hole of the flywheel housing and toss it in the coffee can. Look through the timing hole while you use a socket and ratchet on the **crank pulley** to rotate the engine until you see a small hole drilled in the flywheel (or torque plate on automatics). Stick a strong punch, phillips or regular screwdriver through the timing hole and into the small hole. This keeps the crankshaft from turning while you loosen the bolts on the pressure plate, flywheel, torque plate, and/or front pulley.

Step 2. Remove Clutch Pressure Plate and Clutch Disc (manual trans only).

Loosen the six 10mm or 12mm bolts around the outer edge of the **pressure plate** one turn at a time until they're all loose, then remove and baggie them as "Pressure Plate."

Clean the oil and grease off your hands, then use a screwdriver to pry the pressure plate gently off the alignment pins on the flywheel. Remove the pressure plate and clutch disc and put them someplace where there's no chance of getting oil or grease on them.

Inspect the flywheel for grooves, scratches, cracks, and dark blotchy-looking "hot spots." If you find any of these, remove the flywheel and have it resurfaced (Step 4) after you do Step 3. If you're only replacing the clutch and you aren't going to resurface the flywheel or replace the front or rear crankshaft seal, skip to Procedure 18.

Step 3. Loosen Front Crankshaft Pulley Nut, Remove Front Crankshaft Seal.

Skip this step if you're only replacing the clutch and aren't replacing the front seal. Engine rebuilders and front seal replacers, do this step.

See Chapter 10, Procedure 3, to remove the **drive belt(s)**. If the drive belts are looking a bit shabby, put them on your shopping list.

Lock the engine (Step 1), then use a socket and ratchet to loosen the **crankshaft pulley nut** enough to turn by hand (counterclockwise as viewed from the front of the engine).

Rebuilders: Loosen the bolt but leave the pulley on the engine. You'll use the pulley to turn the crankshaft during disassembly. Go on to Step 4.

Seal replacers: Remove the bolt, then the pulley. You may have to use two screwdrivers to pry the pulley off the crank. Carefully pry the old seal out of the crankcase with a screwdriver. Be careful not to scratch the crankcase. Go to Procedure 20 to install a new seal.

Step 4. Remove Flywheel (manual trans) or Torque Plate (auto trans).

Do this step only if you're rebuilding the engine, having the flywheel resurfaced, or replacing the rear crank seal.

Lock the engine (Step 1). Remove the eight 14mm bolts near the center of the flywheel or torque plate. Baggie the bolts as "Flywheel," then wiggle the flywheel or torque plate off the crankshaft. Careful—don't drop the flywheel on your toes. It's heavy! On '80 and newer automatics there's a small, round **back plate** on the rear of the torque plate. Stash it with the torque plate. If you *aren't* rebuilding the engine or replacing the rear crank seal, go to Procedure 17 to install the flywheel or torque plate. Rebuilders and rear seal replacers, do Step 5.

Step 5. Remove Rear Crankshaft Seal.

This step is only for engine rebuilders and rear seal replacers.

Slide a small screwdriver between the outer edge of the crank and the inner edge of the rubber seal. Carefully pry the seal out of the crankcase and save it to compare to the new seal. Don't scratch the case with the screwdriver. If you're only here to replace the rear crank seal, go to Procedure 15 to install a new seal.

PROCEDURE 4: REMOVE INTAKE MANIFOLD AND CYLINDER HEADS

Condition: Engine rebuild, valve job, piston ring replacement.

Tools and Materials: Phase 1 tool set, special head-nut-removing socket (Subaru part no. 499987006), and a short, thin-walled 17mm socket, baggies, marker. If you're replacing the piston rings you'll need a piston ring compressor and piston pin (wrist pin) puller.

Remarks: If you have a good torque wrench and the two special sockets, you should have no trouble removing and installing the cylinder heads on 1600cc and 1800cc engines. If you're replacing the piston rings, I recommend that you have Subaru or a garage that specializes in Subarus remove and install the **pistons** for you (unless you're an experienced mechanic or you have Friend helping you who is).

Step 1. Remove Air Suction Valve(s).

'75-'81 models: Skip this step.

'82 and newer models: Depending on your model, you may or may not have an **air suction valve (ASV)** mounted on the top rear corner of one or both cylinder heads. Air suction valves look similar to the EGR valve (there's an illustration of an EGR valve in Chapter 12). Each ASV is attached to a bracket which is attached to the cylinder head. A pipe connects the valve to the exhaust port on the bottom of the cylinder head. If you don't have air suction valve(s), skip this step.

If you have an air suction valve, label and disconnect the small rubber vacuum hose(s) and/or the electrical connection from the valve. If necessary, remove the large rubber hoses so you can loosen the nuts that attach the pipe to the suction valve and to the exhaust port. Remove the pipe. Put any of the large hoses you removed back on the valve so you'll know where they go during reassembly. Now remove the two bolts that attach the bracket to the cylinder head. You don't need to remove the valve from the bracket. Remove the ASV from the other cylinder head if you have one. Baggie the bolts as "ASV" and stash the valve(s) someplace where they won't get stepped on.

Step 2. Remove Exhaust Gas Recirculation (EGR) Tube.

'75-'76 California cars and all '77 and newer models: Find the metal **EGR tube** that connects the right cylinder head to the right center rear of the intake manifold. The tube attaches to the cylinder head at the lower rear corner on '74-'80 models and to the top rear corner on '81 and newer models. If there's a thin metal shield covering the manifold end of the tube, loosen the two 10mm bolts on the shield, then slide the shield far enough away from the manifold so you can get a wrench on the nut. Before unscrewing the 17mm nuts, squirt lots of penetrating oil around each end of the pipe where it goes through the nuts. To prevent bending the pipe, unscrew both nuts completely before pulling the pipe off. If the pipe starts bending when the nuts are turned, tighten the nut, and douse the pipe with more penetrating oil and let it soak for awhile. Screw the nut in and out, gradually unscrewing it farther each time. Remove the pipe.

Step 3. Disconnect Water Bypass Hoses.

Loosen the clamp on the small **water bypass hose** attached to the bottom front of the intake manifold, then label and disconnect the hose. '80 and newer models might also have a small hose between the right front side of the manifold and the top right side of the crankcase. Label, then disconnect the crankcase end of the hose and leave the other end connected to the intake manifold.

Step 4. Remove Air Pump (1975 models only).

Unless you're here for a rebuild, skip this step.

If you have 4WD, label and remove the drive belt for the belt-driven fan if you haven't already (Chapter 10, Procedure 3, Step 6). Remove and baggie the two bolts on the belt adjustment idler pulley bracket and remove the bracket. Now remove the fan and pulley (Chapter 16, Procedure 9, Step 2). See Chapter 12, Procedure 3, Step 2, to remove the air pump. Baggie the air pump bolts.

Step 5. Remove Alternator.

See Chapter 10, Procedure 7, Step 2, to remove the alternator. Also remove the 12mm bolt that attaches the slotted bracket to the cylinder head. If you're here for a rebuild, remove the 12mm bolts that attach the alternator bracket(s) to the crankcase. Baggie the bolts as "ALT." If you're only here for a valve job, leave the bracket(s) on the crankcase but remove any bolts that attach the bracket(s) to the left cylinder head.

Step 6. Remove Intake Manifold.

'77 and newer models: Disconnect and label the wire from the **oil pressure switch** located on the lower front side of the engine.

Disconnect the black hose from the top of the left valve cover if it wasn't removed with the air cleaner. There might be a clamp attaching the upper end of the hose to the oil filler pipe. If there is, release the clamp.

EVERYONE: If the hose for the master vac unit is attached to the oil filler tube, remove the phillips screw and pull the hose out of the clamp. Put the screw back in its hole so it won't get lost.

Remove the three 12mm bolts that attach each end of the manifold to the cylinder heads. Baggie the bolts and any brackets held on by the bolts as "Intake Manifold," then lift the manifold gently while looking for wires or hoses that need to be disconnected. If you find any, first label them, then disconnect them from the engine. Make a note to connect them during assembly. Lift the manifold off the engine and set it out of the way. Keep the top of the carburetor covered so nothing can fall into it.

Step 7. Remove Air Injection System ('75-'80 models only).

The **air injection system** (AIS) is that spider-like thing connected to the top front and rear of each cylinder head. Squirt lots of penetrating oil on the threads of the attaching nuts and on the pipes where they go into the nuts. Use a 14mm flare-nut wrench (if you have one), or a 14mm open-end wrench to unscrew the fittings from the heads. If they're stuck or hard to turn, douse them with more "holy water," then wait a while. Don't bend the pipe as you remove the nuts. Remove the 10mm bolt and clamp that attaches the AIS to the oil filler tube. Lift the entire air injection system off the engine as a unit. Install the bolt and clamp back into the oil filler tube.

Step 8. Remove Cylinder Heads.

If there's a bracket between the left cylinder head and oil filler tube, remove the bolts, then the bracket. Baggie the bolts and bracket as "Oil Filler Bracket Bolts."

Remove the two 12mm bolts from each valve cover. Pry the valve covers off and lay them under the cylinder heads to catch oil that might drip out of the engine.

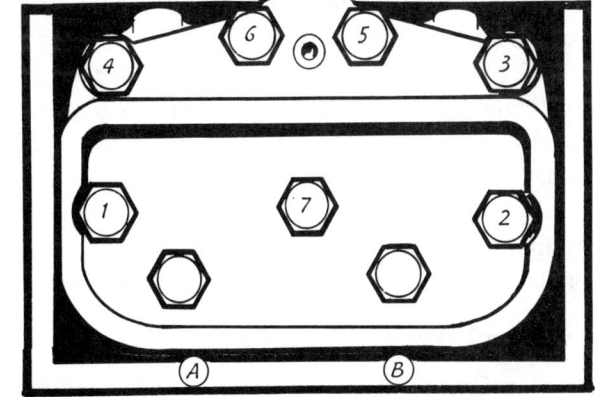

Use a thin-walled 17mm socket (or the special Subaru tool) and a ratchet to remove the two nuts or bolts holding each rocker arm assembly on the heads. Remove the rocker assemblies and lay them in the valve covers. Pull the four push rods out of the bottom of each head and lay them in the valve covers.

'80 and newer models: If the bottom of your cylinder heads have two 10mm bolts, labeled "A" and "B" in the illustration, remove them.

EVERYONE: Follow the cylinder head nut-loosening sequence to remove the other seven nuts and flat washers from each head. Put the nuts, bolts and washers, in a baggie labeled "Head Nuts."

Use a block of wood or wooden hammer handle to tap the heads off the studs. Tap on the square surface on the front and rear corners of the heads, not on the exhaust pipe studs. If the heads are stuck, squirt penetrating oil around the studs where they stick out of the cylinder head and let it soak for awhile. NEVER put anything between the cylinder head and crankcase to pry the head off. The heads sometimes get hung up on crud that's on the studs. If this happens to you, keep squirting penetrating oil on the studs and pushing the head in and out. Wipe the crud off the studs as you go and eventually the heads will come off.

If you're only doing a valve job or replacing the head gaskets and *not* replacing the piston rings or rebuilding the engine, skip to Procedure 10.

PROCEDURE 5: REMOVE PISTONS

Condition: Engine rebuild; OR piston ring replacement.

Tools and Materials: Long, thin needlenose pliers, 14mm allen head wrench, piston pin removal tool, small center punch or nail, hammer, safety glasses, baggies, marker.

Remarks: To remove the pistons, you must first remove the water pump, flywheel housing, and two hex-head crankcase plugs on the front of the engine so you can get to the piston pin circlips.

Removing the pistons requires a special tool that only a garage specializing in Subarus will have. Getting the pistons out and in is a rather tricky operation, so read through the procedure first to find out what's involved, then decide whether you think it's something you can do. If you're not up for it, you can easily remove the water pump and flywheel housing, then haul the engine to a garage and let the professionals remove the crankcase plugs and pistons, deglaze the cylinders, install new piston rings, and put the pistons back in the crankcase. You can install the flywheel housing and water pump at home.

For those of you who are intrepid enough to want to remove and install the pistons yourselves, first you must beg, borrow, or buy a Subaru piston pin puller and a 14mm (or 9/16″) allen head wrench, then ignore my advice later in this procedure that suggests taking the engine to a garage for piston removal and installation.

Step 1. Remove Flywheel Housing.

The clutch and flywheel (or torque plate on automatics) have been removed already, right?

Gently roll the engine forward so the rear end is up and you can get to the oil pan bolts. Remove the five 10mm bolts and washers on the rear edge of the **oil pan**. These bolts attach the oil pan to the flywheel housing. Baggie them as "Oil Pan."

On manual transmission cars, remove the two 10mm bolts that attach a small piece of sheet metal to the bottom of the flywheel housing. Put the bolts in the "Oil Pan" baggie.

Roll the engine so it's upright with the oil pan down. Remove the 12mm bolts inside the rear of the flywheel housing and the two bolts at the bottom rear corners. Baggie the bolts as "Flywheel Housing."

Tap on the front sides of the flywheel housing with a block of wood or wooden hammer handle until it comes off the alignment dowels. DON'T use a screwdriver between the housing and crankcase to pry it off. You might damage the sealing surface and create an oil leak.

Step 2. Remove Water Pump.

See Chapter 16, Procedure 4, Step 3, to remove the water pump. Baggie the bolts as "Water Pump."

Step 3. Remove Crankcase Plugs.

The allen head (hex-head) **crankcase plugs** are on the front of the crankcase. One is on the left side where the water pump was mounted, and the other one is in the same position on the right side. '80 and newer models have two plugs on the right side of the engine. The plug you're after is the smaller one closer to the center of the crankcase. Put on your safety glasses, then smack the plugs a few times square on the head with the hammer. This should loosen them enough to unscrew with the allen wrench. If they're still tight, you may have to use a cheater bar on the end of the allen wrench. Unscrew the two plugs and toss them in the can.

Step 4. Remove Pistons.

Now's the time to take the engine to Subaru or a garage that specializes in Subarus to have the pistons removed and installed. If the engine has over 80,000 miles, I suggest having the rod bearings replaced while the pistons are out. Maybe they'll show you how to use the tools and let you do the work so you can save some money. Maybe someday a tool maker will start offering inexpensive piston pin pullers so you can do the job at home. If you're only doing a ring and valve job, when you get the engine back with new rings (and maybe new rod bearings) installed, see Procedure 7 to replace any leaking gaskets on the engine and Procedure 10 to clean all the parts before putting the engine back together. Then go to Procedure 14 to install the flywheel housing.

If you're removing the pistons yourself, finish this step. If someone else is removing the pistons for you, and you're doing the rest of the rebuild, skip down to Procedure 6.

If you're determined to remove the pistons on a 1600cc or 1800cc engine yourself, here's how.

Slide the crank pulley back on the end of the crankshaft if you removed it, then use the pulley to rotate the engine so the #1 piston is flush with the outside edge of the crankcase.

During assembly, each piston must be oriented the same way (top and bottom) and go back in the same cylinder. To keep the pistons in order, use a knife blade, razor blade, or putty knife to scrape the carbon off the top half of the piston, then use a hammer and small center punch or nail to make a small dot in the top half of the #1 piston. Don't make the dot close to the edge of the piston. Scrape the carbon on piston #2, then make two dots on the top half. Rotate the engine so pistons #3 and #4 are flush with the crankcase. Clean and mark pistons #3 and #4 with three and four dots. Don't get carried away with the hammer and punch; just make the dots deep enough so you can barely see or feel them. If you don't have a punch or nail, just make small scratches in the top of the pistons with a knife or the edge of a small screwdriver to number the pistons.

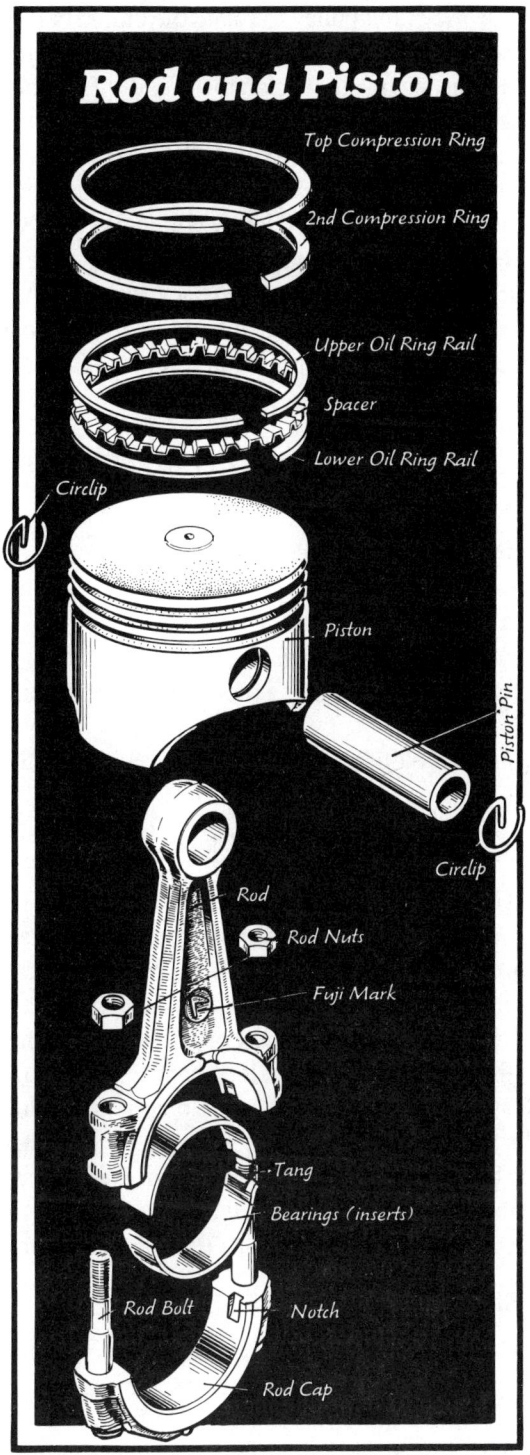

When all the pistons are marked, use the crankshaft pulley to rotate the engine so you can see the #1 and #2 piston pin **circlips** through the crankcase plug holes on the front side of the engine. Use long, thin needlenose pliers to remove the circlips. Baggie them as "Circlips." Insert the piston pin puller into one of the **piston pins**, then tighten the adjusting nut on the tool. Use the slide hammer part of the tool to tap the pin out of the piston. Now remove the other piston pin the same way. Keep track of the piston pins so you'll know which piston they go with.

Use the crank pulley to rotate the crankshaft; the **connecting rods** will push the pistons toward the ends of the cylinders. Rotate the crank farther until you can see the ends of the rods through the holes in the crankcase. Fit the piston pins back into the ends of the rods, then rotate the crankshaft again. The piston pins will push against the bottom of the pistons forcing them part way out of the crankcase. If there's much of a ridge in the cylinders, you'll have to turn pretty hard on the crank. Pull the pistons out of the cylinders, then rotate the crankshaft again so you can remove the piston pins through the crankcase holes. Slip the piston pins into the pistons you just removed so you'll know which pin goes with which piston.

Remove pistons #3 and #4 the same way. The holes for removing the piston pins are in the rear of the case. Be sure to insert each piston pin back into its piston and baggie the circlips with the others.

If you're going to replace the **rod bearings**, do the next procedure. If you're only replacing the **piston rings**, skip to Procedure 9, Step 2, to inspect the pistons and cylinders and remove the old rings.

PROCEDURE 6: LOOSEN CONNECTING ROD NUTS OR BOLTS AND REMOVE RODS

Condition: Engine rebuild; OR you've removed the pistons and want to install new rod bearings without splitting the case.

Tools and Materials: 14mm socket, ½" drive ratchet, long extension for the ratchet (at least 6"), 3/8" to ½" adapter, 2x4 board or strong broom handle approximately 3 feet long, center punch, hammer, four rags, Friend.

Remarks: Do this step only if you're rebuilding the engine or replacing the rod bearings without splitting the case.

Step 1. Loosen Rod Bolts or Nuts.

The rods are attached to the crankshaft with 14mm nuts. They're tight, so have Friend hold the crankcase and/or use a long piece of wood or broom handle stuck through the head studs to keep the engine from rolling over when you loosen the rods. Wrap the end of each rod with a rag to protect the cylinder from getting scratched. Be careful not to scratch the cylinder with the socket, extension, or ratchet.

Put the appropriate socket on a long extension, then use a 3/8" to ½" adapter and ½" drive ratchet. You'll need the extra leverage of the long handle. Rotate the engine so the end of the rod you're going to loosen is nearest the outside of the engine. Angle a board or broom handle through the head studs so it diagonally crosses the center of the cylinder you're working on. Arrange the ratchet so it's about 90° (perpendicular) to the top of the board as viewed from the ends of the head studs. Get the socket on the rod nut or bolt, let the extension rest on the board, then pull on the ratchet handle while pushing on the top of the board. Pop! The nut will come loose. Loosen all eight rod nuts (or bolts) the same way.

Step 2. Remove and Number Rods.

CAUTION! While removing the rods, and once they're off the crank, be very careful not to scratch, nick, or ding the shiny bearing surfaces of the crank.

Remarks: If you're splitting the case for a rebuild, skip to Procedure 7 now. I'll tell you when to come back and do this step.

If you've returned here after splitting the case, remove the rods from the crank one at a time and mark them as described below. The rod closest to the front end of the crankshaft (the pulley end) is #1, the next one is #2, then #3, and the last one (closest to the flywheel end) is #4.

If you didn't split the case, rotate the crankshaft so the end of the #1 rod is close to the outside of the cylinder. Reach into the cylinder and unscrew the rod bolts or nuts, then pull the rod out of the cylinder. If the rod cap remained on the crank, rotate the cap so you can pull it off. If the rod cap, bolts, or nuts fell down into the engine, fish them out with your fingers or a magnet. If the rod is tight on the crank, use a broom handle and hammer to reach in and tap on the bolts until the rod can be removed. Be sure the rod end doesn't scratch the cylinder.

When the #1 rod and rod cap are off, fit any bearing shells (inserts) that fell out back into their original position in the rod or cap. Use a rag to wipe the oil off the sides of the rod and cap, and you'll see engraved numbers or lines (markings) on one side of the rod and cap. Assemble the rod with the bolts or nuts so the markings are on the same side of the rod. Notice how the numbers or lines go from the rod to the rod caps. The marking on each rod will be different so you can tell which rod and rod cap go together during reassembly.

The rods must go back on the crank in the same position, so you need to mark them. Turn the rod so the engraved marking is down. The other side of the rod should be blank (unless the engine has been disassembled before and the rods are already marked). Use a pointed punch and hammer to put one dot on the flat part of the rod right next to the rod cap and one dot on the flat part of the rod cap. Tap very lightly with the hammer when numbering the rods. You only need to make tiny dots. Now remove the rod and cap for cylinder #2 and mark it with two dots on the rod and two dots on the rod cap. Rotate the crank so the ends of the other two rods are close to the outer end of the cylinder. Remove and mark the #3 rod and cap with three dots and the #4 rod and cap with four dots.

If you're going all the way (rebuild) and came back here to remove the rods from the crankshaft, you can go to Procedure 9 now.

If you aren't doing a rebuild but want to replace leaking gaskets on the engine, check out procedure 7. If the crank and connecting rods appear to be in good condition, you can install new rod bearings without splitting the case. If so, skip to Procedure 9 after doing Procedure 7.

PROCEDURE 7: REMOVE THIS AND THAT

Condition: You're doing a complete rebuild; OR you want to install new gaskets on things like the oil filler tube, oil pan, water crossover pipe ('75-'79 models), or oil pump; OR a head gasket leaked water into the engine and you want to clean the inside of the engine thoroughly (good idea!); OR you were sent here from another chapter.

Tools and Materials: Phase 1 tool set.

Remarks: At the end of each step, I'll indicate which procedure and step tells you how to install each part. If you aren't splitting the case, go to that procedure to install the part. If you're doing a rebuild, take the parts off and continue.

Step 1. Remove Oil Filler Tube and Engine Dipstick.

Remove the two 12mm bolts at the base of the oil filler tube. The bracket for the water bypass pipe (and on 4WD models an L-shaped bracket) is attached with one of the bolts. Baggie the bolts and bracket as "Oil Filler." Remove the oil filler tube. You can now remove the water bypass pipe and hoses attached to it as a unit. See Procedure 25 to install the tube.

Pull the engine oil dipstick out of its hole and stash it in the coffee can.

Step 2. Remove Water Crossover Pipe ('75-'79 only).

Remove, and baggie as "Crossover Pipe," the four 10mm bolts and washers that hold the tube across the top of the engine. Remove the tube. See Procedure 24 to install the crossover pipe.

Step 3. Remove Oil Pan.

Remove the oil pan only if you're splitting the case, replacing the oil pan gasket, or a broken head gasket leaked water into the engine.

CAUTION! Once the oil pan is off the crankcase, the **oil pickup tube** on the bottom of the engine is vulnerable to damage. Don't let the weight of the engine rest on the tube and don't use the tube for a handle or lever point. Don't remove the tube from the case unless it gets bent. If the pickup tube or the screen in the bottom of the round end of the tube is damaged, have Subaru or a garage install a new one for you. To remove the oil pan, put a pile of rags beneath the engine to catch oil that's still in the engine. Roll the engine so the rear end is on the bottom, then remove the 10mm bolts around the edge of the oil pan and put them in the "Oil Pan" baggie. Be sure to remove all the washers with the bolts. Some models have a flat washer and a lock washer, while other models only have lock washers. Use a screwdriver to gently pry the oil pan off the crankcase.

If you're going to split the case, remove and baggie the 12mm bolt, nut, and washers that attach the oil pickup tube to the bottom center of the case. Label the baggie "Oil Pickup Tube." If you aren't splitting the case, don't mess with the bolt.

If you're doing a rebuild and the engine has **hydraulic valve lifters** ('83 and newer models with automatic transmissions), they can be removed at this point. Look at Procedure 8, Step 4, to make a holder so you can keep them in order. Tilt the engine to one side until the lifters start sliding out of their holes, then set the engine up straight. Don't let the lifters fall out and get mixed up. Put the lifters in the holder in order, then tilt the engine the other way to remove the lifters from the other side. Procedure 16 covers installing the oil pan.

Step 4. Remove Oil Pump.

Leave the engine with the rear end facing down. Remove the four 10mm bolts and washers located on the corners of the **oil pump**. Baggie the bolts as "Oil Pump." Try to wiggle the pump out of the crankcase.

If the pump is stuck, use a block of wood and hammer to gently tap it out of the crankcase. Tap up alternately on the large steel nut sticking out of the right side of the pump and on the edge of the oil filter mount. If you're splitting the case and the oil pump is difficult to remove, wait until the case is split and the pump will fall out. If you aren't splitting the case, you'll have to keep trying until the pump comes out.

Procedure 19, Step 1, covers oil pump installation.

Step 5. Remove Oil Pressure Switch (OPS).

On models with an oil pressure *gauge*, the OPS is screwed into the bottom of the oil pump. Label, then disconnect the wire from the OPS. Use a 14mm open-end wrench to unscrew the switch from the oil pump.

On models with an oil pressure *warning light*, the OPS is screwed into the crankcase just to the left of where the oil pump mounts. Use large pliers to unscrew the OPS counterclockwise as viewed from the wire terminal end. Stash it with the oil pump bolts.

PROCEDURE 8: SPLIT THE CRANKCASE.

Condition: Engine rebuild.

Tools and Materials: Phase 1 tool set, 2' to 3' long strong broom handle or 2 x 4 piece of wood, two 24" pieces of wire or strong string, four 4" to 6" pieces of small rubber hose to hold the followers in the case (vacuum line hose works well), maybe a magnet. No hose? You can tie the followers together with wire or string, but using hose is quicker.

Step 1. Remove Camshaft Thrustplate Bolts.

Do this step only if you're going to split the case.

Rotate the crankshaft until you can see two 10mm bolts through the holes in the **cam gear** (the larger of the two gears on the rear surface of the engine). Use a small screwdriver and hammer to bend the lock tabs away from the bolt heads, then remove the two bolts and lock plates. Baggie the bolts and lock plates as "Cam Bolts."

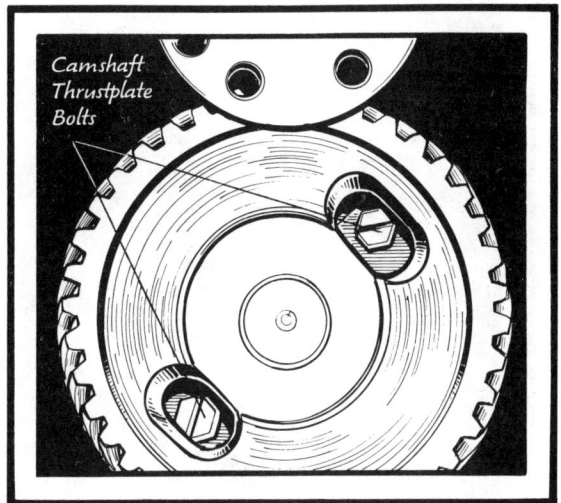

Step 2. Secure Cam Followers.

If you're going to use a new **camshaft** and **cam followers**, skip this step. If you're planning to reuse the old cam and followers, the followers must go back in the same positions in the case during reassembly. Unless they're held in place when the case is split, they'll all fall out and get mixed up. Here's how to keep them in order.

Tilt the case onto the rear surface. Use your fingers or a magnet, if necessary, to pull the cam followers toward the outside of the case as far as possible. Fold a short piece of small rubber hose into a U-shape, then wedge it between a pair of the cam followers. Do this to all four pairs. If you don't have the right size rubber hoses, tie pieces of wire or string tightly around the pairs of followers so they can't fall out when the case is split.

Two Ways to Hold the Cam Followers — With a piece of Rubber Hose / Or with Wire

Step 3. Remove Case Bolts and Nuts.

Tilt the engine right side up, then tie a piece of wire or string around each end of the crankshaft. Pull the wires tight and wrap them around two of the head studs for the #2 and #4 cylinders to keep the crank from falling out when the case is split. Now tilt the engine back onto its rear surface.

While removing the case bolts, use the board or broom handle through the head studs to keep the case from turning, the same way you did when loosening the rod nuts or bolts. A Friend to hold the case makes loosening the bolts a lot easier.

Remove the 12mm bolt, nut, and washers securing the oil pickup tube to the bottom center of the crankcase. Baggie them as "Oil Pickup Tube."

Remove the 12mm and 14mm bolts or nuts along the top of the crankcase. The front one is probably attaching the **front engine hanger** (hook). Baggie the bolts, nuts, washers and hanger as "Top Case Bolts."

Remove the two 10mm case bolts located above and below the front end of the crankshaft. Baggie them as "Front Case Bolts."

Remove the two 14mm bolts behind cylinder #3 and compare their length as you remove them. If one is longer than the other baggie them separately as "Upper Rear Case Bolt" and as "Lower Rear Case Bolt." If they're both the same length, baggie them together as "Rear Case Bolts." On 4WD models there will be a steel bracket attached with the upper case bolt. Baggie the bracket with the case bolt(s).

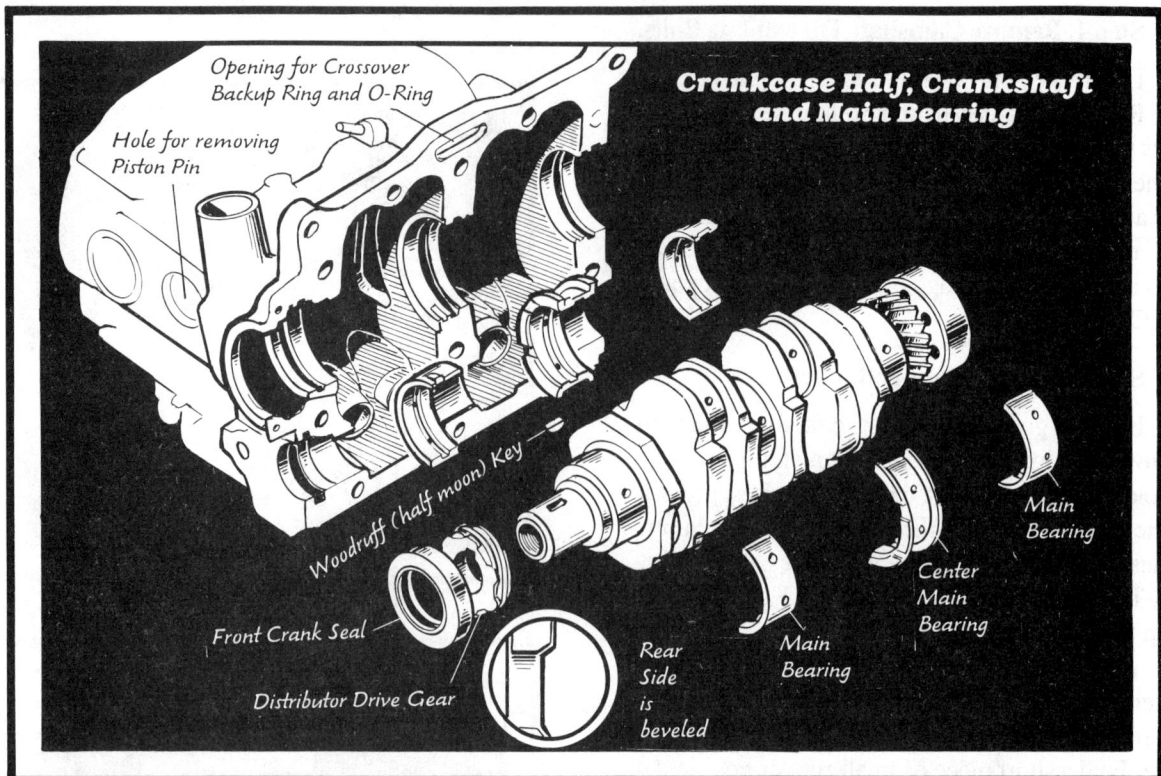

Crankcase Half, Crankshaft and Main Bearing

Remove the two bolts in front of cylinder #2. If they're different lengths, baggie them as "Upper Front Case Bolts" or "Lower Front Case Bolts."

Now look for a 14mm bolt between and slightly below cylinders #1 and #3. It's recessed in the case. See it? Remove and baggie the bolt as "Center Case Bolt."

Now comes the big moment! Use a block of wood and a hammer to alternately tap outward against the case where the distributor fits and where the oil filler tube mounts. Don't hit the case with the hammer. Keep tapping on the block of wood until the case halves separate slightly. If the case is stuck together, it's probably stuck on an alignment bushing at the top front corner. Tap more around the distributor housing. If possible, have Friend hold the left side of the case while you tap on the right side.

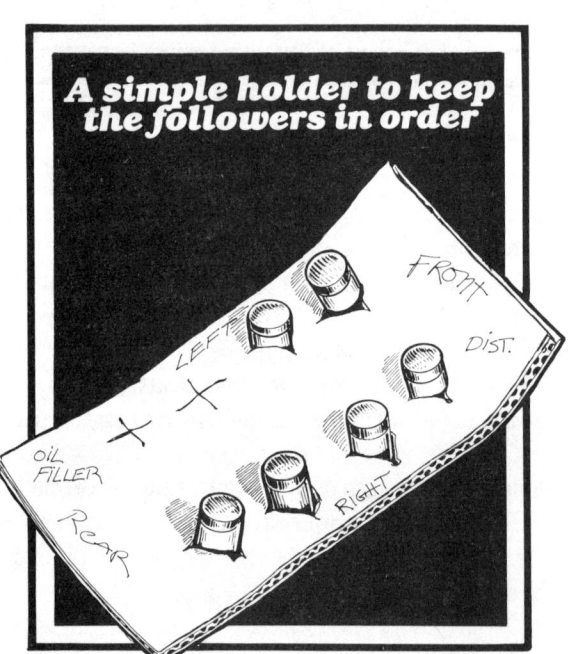

A simple holder to keep the followers in order

When the case has separated slightly all the way around, slowly pull the right half of the case (#1 and #3) away from the left half. Hold the side containing the crankshaft with one hand while you gently lay the other half to the side. Don't set it on the oil pickup tube. Pull the camshaft out of the case and set the camshaft aside also. Hold the crankshaft in the case while you untie the wires holding the crankshaft to the head studs. Lift the crankshaft out of the case and lay it on a rag.

Step 4. Remove Cam Followers.

When the engine is reassembled the cam followers must go back in the same positions. Here's how I keep my followers in order.

Round up a piece of heavy cardboard (like a cardboard box) about the size of this book and mark the top center of the cardboard "Front" and the bottom center "Rear." Just below and to the right of "Front" write "Distributor" and just above and to the left of "Rear" write "Oil Filler." Mark the right and left edges "Right and Left." Now use a knife to cut four pairs of 1″ Xs vertically between the words "Front" and "Rear." Set the crankcase right side up (lean the right half on the head studs because of the oil pick up tube), then hold the cardboard next to the inside of the *left* case half so the word "Front" is next to the front of the engine. Remove the front cam follower and stick it into the front left X (the side with oil filler marked on it). Remove the other three followers on the left side and stick them in the cardboard in order. Now remove the four followers from the right side of the case and put them in the cardboard in order. If the followers fall out of the cardboard, cut smaller Xs next to the original Xs and use them. Stash the cardboard someplace safe so the followers won't get knocked out.

Step 5. Remove Distributor Drive Gear from Crank.

Pull the **distributor drive gear** off the front end of the crankshaft. See how the rear side of the gear is beveled and the other side is flat? You'll need to remember this when you reassemble the crank. Put the gear in the coffee can.

OK, that's as far apart as we can take the engine. Take a few minutes to clean your tools and put them away, mop up puddles of oil and grease, and clean up your work area. Now it's time to see which parts in the various piles scattered about you need to be replaced or reconditioned.

PROCEDURE 9: INSPECT PARTS AND A FIELD TRIP TO THE MACHINE SHOP AND PARTS STORES

Condition: The parts of your engine are scattered or piled around you. You need to know which parts can be used again and which parts should be given a military funeral.

Tools and Materials: To inspect the parts; clean rags or paper towels, feeler gauge, a good pair of eyes, baggies, and marker. At the machine shop and parts stores you need; the parts you want the machinist to inspect and recondition, your parts list, paper and pen, maybe a calculator.

Remarks: If you didn't split the case, inspect only those parts which are applicable to you.

If you're only doing a valve job, take only the applicable parts to the machinist. If you're replacing the piston rings, have the machinist measure the cylinders, then deglaze them if the size is OK. If you removed the rods without splitting the case and the bearings were suspect, take the connecting rods and bearings along for the machinist's opinion.

Have the serial numbers for your engine and chassis, the engine type, and the production date for your car with you when trekking to the machine shop and parts stores (Chapter 2: *Orientation*).

Step 1. Inspect Rod and Main Bearings.

Rebuilders: If you haven't removed the rods from the crankshaft and marked them, do it now (Procedure 6, Step 2). Be sure to keep the rod caps with the same rod, and number them as they are removed. I'll see you here when the rods are off.

EVERYONE: The thin metal shells in the rods and rod caps are the **rod bearings** (sometimes called inserts). The larger shells in the case that fit around the crank are the **main bearings**. If you haven't split the case, you can't check the main bearings.

Use a clean rag to wipe the inside of each rod, rod cap, and the six main bearings in the case where the crank fits so you can inspect the bearing shells. Are they all uniformly gray and smooth? If so, the crank and rods are probably in good condition. If any of the bearings are burned black or have scratches, grooves, galled or etched areas, or missing chunks of bearing material, the crank will probably need to be ground (machined) and the rod(s) with bad bearings checked by the machine shop. Leave the bad (or questionable) bearings in the rod until the machine shop checks them. If the crank needs to be ground, the case will have to be split if you haven't done so already (Procedures 7 and 8).

Wiggle all the bearing shells out of the rods, rod caps, and case (if the case was split). If you're short of money and might have to use the same bearings, baggie and label the rod and main bearings so you can put them back in the same location during reassembly. I strongly suggest replacing the bearings while the engine is apart. If necessary, wire mommy for the money.

Step 2. Inspect Cylinders and Pistons.

Wipe the inside of cylinders with a clean rag, then look for cracks or deep scratches in the walls of each cylinder. Put your finger into each of the cylinders and feel for a ridge near the outer edge. This ridge is the original size of the cylinder before the piston rings wore the cylinder walls away slightly. Subaru cylinders wear out very slowly, so unless you have over 100,000 miles on the engine (or ran the engine with a funky air filter), you shouldn't find much ridge. The machine shop can tell you the exact amount of wear by measuring it with a micrometer.

Checking the pistons is easy. The two piston rings near the flat top of the piston are the **compression rings** and they should be free to rotate around the piston. The third ring (closest to the piston pin) is the **oil control ring** (oil ring). On '79 and newer models, there are stopper pins in the oil ring grooves of the pistons so the oil rings aren't free to rotate as the top two rings do. Here's how to check the piston ring grooves for wear. Get your feeler gauges and try to fit a .004" blade between the *compression rings* and grooves all the way around the pistons. If the blade fits easily between the piston ring and groove, the groove, and thus the piston, is worn out. If the blade won't fit, check the sides and tops of the pistons for deep scratches, galled areas, or cracks—signs the pistons are ready to be made into ashtrays. Pistons all look good? Pry the ends of the rings apart with your thumbs and slip them off the pistons. You can buy piston ring spreaders and save wear and tear on the thumbs, but if you're short of money, well. . . . Be careful not to scratch the pistons with the ends of the rings as you remove them. When the old rings are off, stash the pistons someplace where they won't get dropped or stepped on.

If the cylinders are only very slightly ridged, and have no deep scratches or score marks in them, they can be deglazed and reused. If the pistons had no deep scratches, cracks, or worn out ring grooves, they can be cleaned and fitted with new piston rings.

Replace any of the pistons that failed the inspection with new ones that have the same letter stamped on the flat top of the piston.

Step 3. Inspect Camshaft, Cam Followers, and Push Rods.

Clean the camshaft with a rag, then carefully inspect the lobes (bumps) and each side of the lobes where the followers ride for signs of pitting or scratches. The high point of each lobe should be flat with no sign of roundness in the direction parallel with the shaft. Your camshaft can be reground if it is pitted, scratched, or rounded.

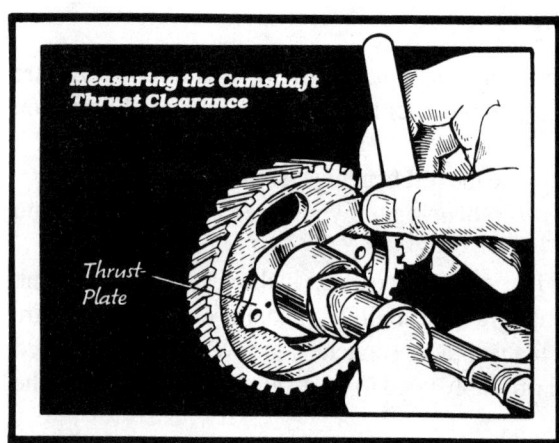

Inspect the teeth on the cam gear for chips, cracks, and wear. The machinist can help you with this. If the gear is worn out or damaged but the camshaft is still good, you can have the machinist install a new cam gear.

Whip out your feeler gauges and measure the distance between the camshaft and the thrust plate. The thrust plate is between the cam and the cam gear and has two holes in it. It's free to rotate around the cam. The clearance should be between .0008" and .035" (.020mm-.090mm). Subaru says the maximum allowable clearance is .008" (.2mm), but if the clearance is more than .004" (.1mm), have the machinist press the gear on farther so it's within the normal specifications or it might "knock" at low engine rpm.

Wipe the smooth top of each cam follower with a rag. Lay something straight, like the side of a straight screwdriver, across the top of each follower. Is there space between the screwdriver and the top of the follower? Are the tops pitted? Good followers will be flat or slightly domed on top and have no pits or scratches. A circular pattern on the top is normal. If the cam or followers are suspect, take them to the machine shop for an opinion.

Wipe the oil off the **push rods**, then roll them one at a time across a smooth table top. A bent push rod will appear to flop as it rolls across the table. Replace any bent ones with new ones from the Subaru dealer.

Step 4. Inspect Oil Pump.

If the engine has over 80,000 miles on it, or you determined in Chapter 9 that the oil pump isn't pumping like it should, I recommend that you buy a new oil pump. Like your heart, the oil pump supplies the vital juice to all the critical areas of the engine, so it's best not to gamble with it. Oil pumps aren't very expensive, and it's worth the investment. You can have the old pump checked by Subaru but that might cost as much as buying a new one.

Step 5. Inspect Crankcase.

Wiggle each of the studs sticking out of the case. If any studs came out while removing the head nuts, screw them back into the case. If any studs are loose, try tightening them with large pliers (not on the threads). If any studs can't be tightened, have the machine shop install helicoils in the case.

Check the case for cracks, especially where it bolts to the flywheel housing. Are there large, deeply pitted areas on the inside of the case (indicating that the engine had water in the oil for a long period of time)? Check for deep scratches or pitted areas in the main bearing and cam bearing saddles and the sealing surface where the two case halves join together. Ask the machinist if you're not sure what you're looking for or if you notice something questionable.

Step 6. To the Machine Shop.

Gather the following parts to take to the machine shop.

Cylinder heads for a valve job: Ask the machinist if he has new valves for your heads in case any are needed, or if you should supply them. If new valves are required, be sure the new valves match the old valves, or come with new valve keepers. Newer-type valves won't work with old style valve keepers.

Ask the machinist to check the spark plug threads, remove any broken bolts (intake manifold, exhaust, etc.) and install helicoils if necessary. It's advisable to have both heads resurfaced and new core plugs installed.

Crankshaft: The machinist can tell you if the crank needs to be turned (ground) and what size rod and main bearings you'll need. If the crank doesn't need turning, have it cleaned and polished. On '75-'80 models with manual transmissions, have a new pilot bearing and pilot bearing seal installed (you'll probably have to get the bearing and seal from Subaru). If you want to install the new pilot bearing yourself, see Chapter 15, Procedure 12, Step 4.

Crankcase: Have the cylinders checked for wear. If the wear on the worst cylinder is less than .004", the cylinders are good. If the wear is between .004" and .006", the cylinders are marginal. Over .006" wear, forget it. Even new piston rings won't hold compression in worn out cylinders. You'll have to round up another case or find a machine shop that can bore the cylinders so oversize pistons can be installed.

If the cylinder sizes are good and there are no deep scratches in the bores, have the case cleaned, the cylinders deglazed (lightly honed so the new piston rings will "seat" to the cylinders), and the ridges in the cylinders removed (if there are any). Have broken bolts removed and helicoils installed wherever threads in the case are damaged or missing. It's a good idea to have helicoils installed in the case where the four rocker arm bolts screw into it.

Connecting rods: Have the piston pin holes checked for wear. Some Subaru rods have replaceable piston pin bushings. Replace the rods or the bushings if the piston pin hole is worn out.

If the rod bearings in any of the rods were black, deeply scratched, or had spun inside the rod, have the rod checked for size and straightness and reconditioned if necessary.

Pistons: If the pistons passed the inspection in Step 2, have them cleaned. Have the machinist install new rings if you're unsure about installing them yourself. (If you break one during installation, you'll probably have to buy a whole new set since rings aren't sold individually.)

Camshaft and cam followers: Have the machinist look at them. If they're worn out, see how much it costs to have them reground. Check that price against new ones from Subaru and parts stores.

Flywheel: To be resurfaced. On '81 and newer models with manual transmissions, have a new pilot bearing installed. If you want to install it yourself, see Chapter 15, Procedure 12, Step 4.

And now: Ask the machinist for an estimate of what the machining and cleaning will cost. If he sells parts, get his price for the parts listed in Step 7. Maybe you should sit down before you hear the total!

If the amount is nearing or beyond your budget, have the machinist wait to start working on your parts while you gather the prices for the rest of the parts and supplies needed to get the engine back together. Determine the total cost to rebuild your engine, then compare that figure to a rebuilt or used engine.

Step 7. On to the Parts Stores.

Here's a list of things you'll need in addition to the machine shop work. Get prices from a couple of parts stores and from the Subaru dealer. Prices vary radically for the same part, so you can save a lot of money by comparison shopping. Some parts are a lot cheaper from parts stores and some are cheaper from Subaru.

See Chapter 5 for the brands of some parts and supplies that I've found to work well.

PARTS:

Main bearings if you split the case.

Rod bearings if you removed the rods.

Piston rings if you removed the pistons.

Pistons if yours were worn out or damaged.

Pin bushings for the rods if your engine has them and they were worn out.

Complete **gasket set** if you're rebuilding the engine or doing a ring and valve job. Otherwise, get only the gaskets and seals needed for the parts you removed. New front and rear crankshaft seals should be in the gasket set. If not, buy them.

Camshaft and **lifters** if yours were shot.

Oil pump if the engine is nearing or past 80,000 miles.

Oil pressure switch.

Pilot bearing for manual transmission models (and **seal** on pre-'81 models).

Push rods. Replace only those that are bent or worn on the ends. Get them from the Subaru dealer.

Clutch disc and pressure plate. Replacing these parts now is insurance against having to remove the engine again soon. If you're short on money, have the machinist, the Subaru dealer, or a garage check the old ones for you.

Any washers, nuts, bolts, engine studs, screws, push-ons for wires—all that little stuff you've been writing down on a list.

'82 and newer models require a new **O-ring** for the rear end of the crankshaft.

SUPPLIES YOU'LL NEED:

A small can or tube of antiseize compound. Before screwing any bolts into the crankcase or cylinder heads, coat the threads with antiseize compound. I prefer the Jet-Lube brand.

At least one gallon of **solvent, fiber parts brush,** and **wash pan** for cleaning parts.

A tube of **silicone gasket sealer.** I like the blue kind better than the clear because it's easier to see where you've spread sealer.

A tube of **Permatex #2A gasket sealer.**

Oil squirt gun full of the kind of oil you're going to use in the engine.

A sheet of **fine emery cloth.**

For a rebuild you'll need a tube of **Lubriplate Engine Assembly Grease** OR a tube of **Molybdium Disulfide Engine Assembly Lube.**

Twelve quarts of the **oil** you plan to use.

Three **oil filters.**
Hand cleaner.
Clean rags and **paper towels.**
Spray can of **carburetor cleaner.**
Wheel bearing grease or Bosch grease.
Maybe the 12,000-mile **tune-up parts** if it's almost time to replace them (Chapter 7, Procedure 5).

If you removed the clutch, a **clutch alignment tool** makes clutch installation easier. If you can't buy or borrow one, you can use the "eyeball method" to center the clutch plate.

'75-'79 models: Pull the new head gaskets out of the gasket set. If they are wrapped in plastic bags, peel the plastic away from one gasket slightly and feel the surface. If the gasket surface feels tacky and sticky, you won't need head gasket sealer. If the gaskets are dry and not sticky, get the head gasket sealer recommended below for '80 and newer models.

'80 and newer models: If you removed the cylinder heads, Subaru recommends using only genuine Subaru **head gasket sealer** when installing new head gaskets (Subaru part #004403008 or Dow Corning #92-024). In reality, the stuff is hard to get. If you can't find it, use General Motors gasket sealer (GM part #1050026). The GM can has a handy brush built into the cap for applying the stuff.

PROCEDURE 10: CLEAN, CLEAN, CLEAN

Condition: The engine has been at least partially disassembled and dirty engine parts are scattered everywhere.

Tools and Materials: A large catch pan or old dishpan (approximately two gallon capacity), a stiff fiber parts-cleaning brush, a small wire brush, spray can of carb cleaner.

Step 1. Clean Everything.

While the machine shop does its thing, you can clean all the engine parts lying around the garage, things like nuts, bolts, hoses, brackets, and oil pan. Use a catch pan full of solvent and a parts cleaning brush to remove all traces of dirt and grease. Use a wire brush to clean the threads of all the bolts.

If you're reusing the cam followers, wash them one at a time so they don't get mixed up. Squirt carb cleaner through the hole in the end until it shoots out the side.

Don't dunk the carburetor, distributor, alternator, or water pump in the solvent; just clean the outside. Clean the rocker arm assemblies, but don't take them apart. Lay the parts on clean rags or paper towels. Just before installing the parts, give them a shot of carb cleaner to remove dirt or dust that might have accumulated since their solvent bath. When it comes to engine assembly, cleanliness really is next to godliness (whatever that is).

Now is an opportune time to turn to Chapter 12 and clean the following parts if your engine has them: the EGR valve and pipe (Procedure 1, Step 2); the PCV valve (Procedure 2, Step 2); and the air injection system reed valves (Procedure 3, Step 3).

You can paint the valve covers, air cleaner, oil filler tube, and water bypass pipe any color you want; but don't paint aluminum parts (like the crankcase or cylinder heads) because they won't dissipate heat as well. A picture painted on the top of the air cleaner will probably give you a chuckle every time you check the oil.

PROCEDURE 11: ASSEMBLE CRANKSHAFT AND CRANKCASE

Condition: The engine parts are back from the machine shop, there's a stack of new parts and assembly supplies lying around somewhere, all the rest of the engine parts have been spotlessly cleaned and some may have even been repainted. Your little heart is throbbing in anticipation of putting everything back together.

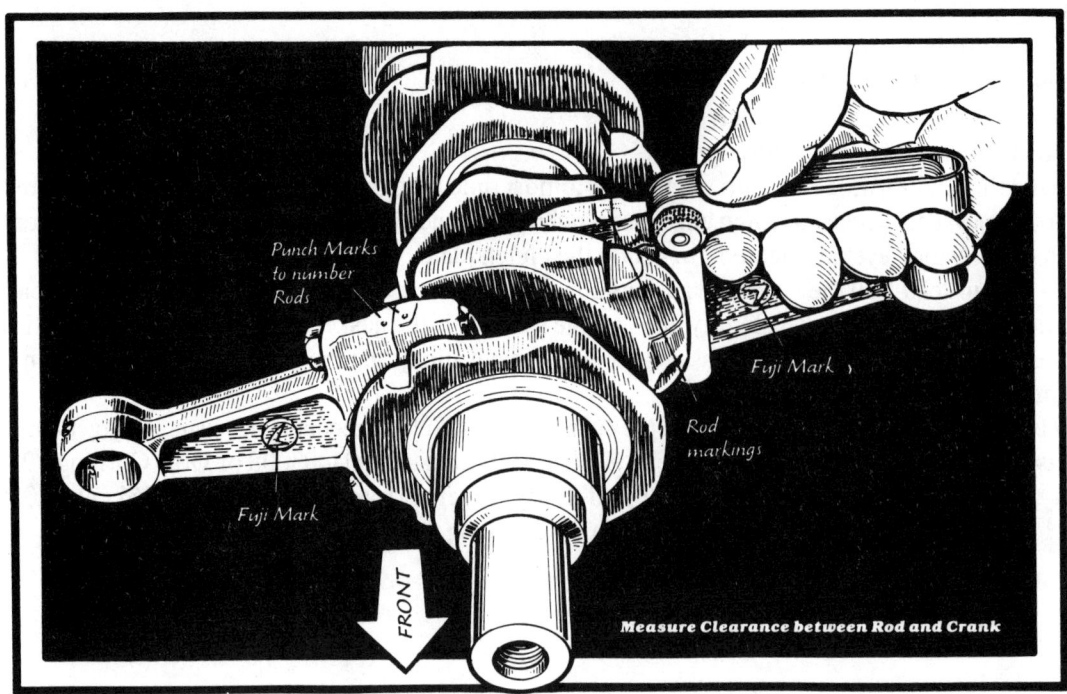

Measure Clearance between Rod and Crank

Tools and Materials: Phase 1 tool kit including a good torque wrench, a large sturdy bucket (five gallon plastic paint buckets work well). If you're going to install the pistons on a 1600cc or 1800cc engine, you'll need a piston ring compressor. If you didn't have the pistons cleaned and the rings installed at the machine shop, you'll need a ring groove cleaner or a piece of one of the old rings, and maybe a piston ring spreader (if your thumbs are tender). Parts and assembly supplies required are listed in the shopping list in Procedure 9.
Remarks: If you removed the connecting rods from the crankshaft *without* splitting the case, you'll only need to do Steps 1 and 3 of this procedure.

Step 1. Pep Talk.

OK folks, so far so good. You've done all the dirty cleanup work and legwork running around gathering parts and supplies. Now it's time for the fun part! Take your time and enjoy the assembly. Please read each step all the way through before doing it, then take a moment to check your work at the end of each step. Take a break if you get tired to avoid burn out. Remember, you're going to be very proud of yourself in just a few hours!

Step 2. Prepare Crankcase for Assembly.

Clean all the head bolt studs on both case halves with a wire brush and emery cloth. Check the threads on the studs by screwing one of the head nuts all the way onto each stud. You should be able to screw them on by hand if the threads are clean. Use emery paper to clean the smooth, unthreaded part of the head studs.

Use a light wire brush, a pocket knife, and emery cloth to thoroughly clean the case surfaces around the cylinders where the heads fit. Don't scratch the aluminum, but be sure ALL the old gasket material, carbon, and rust are off the surface. Pay particular attention to the areas around the head studs. Use carb cleaner and a rag for a final clean and check of the surface. This is very important to prevent head gasket leaks.

Check the following sealing surfaces on the crankcase: where the case halves fit together, where the oil pan bolts on, where the oil pump goes and where the flywheel housing attaches. Use fine emery paper to smooth off burrs, gasket sealer, or pieces of old gaskets.

Rinse the case halves again with fresh solvent or carb cleaner. Squirt or pour the cleaner into the oil passages (holes) in each main bearing saddle and through the oil pickup tube. Put the case halves someplace clean to dry.

Step 3. Assemble Crankshaft.

The method for installing the rods on the crank depends on whether or not the case has been split and the crankshaft removed. Therefore, in this step, those of you who removed the rods *without* splitting the case will be referred to as "Bearing Replacers." If you split the case, follow the instructions for "Rebuilders." Of course, everyone does the EVERYONE sections.

EVERYONE: Clean your hands, then squirt carb cleaner through the holes in each rod and main bearing journal on the crank, and give each connecting rod a shot of carb cleaner. Now squirt fresh oil on each journal. Arrange the rods and rod caps so they are numbered 1-4, left to right. If your engine has rod nuts, install the bolts in the rod caps and lay the nuts next to the rods. If you only have rod bolts, lay them next to the rods.

Rebuilders: Spread a clean towel or paper towels on the workbench. Lay the clean crank on the towel so the pulley end is to your left. If the woodruff (half-moon) key was removed from the pulley end of the crankshaft, gently tap it into the groove. Line up the groove in the distributor drive gear with the woodruff key on the crank, then slide the gear all the way on. The beveled side of the gear goes toward the rear of the crank.

EVERYONE: Break out the new rod bearings. Avoid touching the inside (concave) part of the bearing shells with your fingers; handle them only by the outside surfaces or edges. There should be eight identical half shells. Smear a little oil on the concave sides of two of the bearings, then fit them around one of the connecting rod journals and see if they fit. Be careful not to scratch the shiny parts of the crankshaft. The inside diameter of the shells should be exactly the same size as the outside diameter of the rod journals on the crank. If they're too small, there will be a slight gap between the ends of the shells when you put the two halves together. If they're too big, you will have too much clearance between the crankshaft and the bearing halves. If you feel the bearing size is incorrect, take the bearings and crank to the machinist for his opinion.

Rebuilders: Check the main bearing shells on the crank the same way you checked the rod bearings. Again, if something doesn't seem exactly right, haul it to the machine shop for a dose of sage advice.

EVERYONE: Notice that each bearing shell has a little tang on the outside of one end. The tangs fit into notches on the rods and caps (rod bearings) or notches in the crankcase (main bearings) to keep the bearings from spinning with the crankshaft. Install one of the rod bearing shells in each rod and rod cap so the little tang on the bearing fits into the notch. The ends of the bearings should end up flush with the ends of the rods and caps. Coat the bearings with engine assembly lube, then squirt oil on the threads of the rod bolts. Put oil on the rod nuts if your engine has nuts. Coat the four rod throws and three main bearing journals on the crankshaft with assembly lube.

When you install the rods on the crank, the Fuji symbol mark on the shaft part of the rod always faces the pulley end of the crank. Got that? Be sure the number of punch marks you made during disassembly are the same for the rod and cap, and that they're on the same side of the rod. The rods must be installed in their original position on the crank.

On 1600cc and 1800cc engines, the rod bolts must fit into the rod caps a certain way. Look at the rod cap to be sure the flat side of the bolt head is aligned with the flat spot on the rod cap. If it isn't, remove the bolt and insert it into the rod cap so the flat parts match.

Bearing replacers: The engine should be sitting in the stand top side up. Here's the tricky part of replacing rod bearings without splitting the case. Go slowly, think, and be sure the rods and caps go back on the crank in the correct order and that they are oriented correctly. Friend to help would make it easier.

To install the rods on the crank, you'll have to hold the rod cap on the crank from the opposite side of the crankcase while you install the rod. Here's how. Separate the rod and rod cap, then hold them in their installed position in front of the appropriate cylinder (remember, the Fuji mark goes toward the pulley end of the crank). Note whether the engraved markings or the punch marks you made on the cap are on the top surface. Lay the rod aside. To get the cap on the crank, rotate the cap a half turn from its installed position so the bearing side is facing the crankshaft. The markings or punch mark(s) that were on top will now be on the bottom. Carefully fit the cap onto the crank, then rotate the cap to its installed position. Use a long screwdriver through the cylinder on the opposite side of the case to push on the rod cap and hold it in place on the crank while you gently install the rod, then the bolts or nuts. If the rod pushes the rod bolts out of the cap, you'll have to start all over. Tighten the bolts or nuts finger tight for now. We'll torque them later. Is the Fuji mark facing the front of the engine and are the markings or punch marks on the same side of the rod? Check it carefully and try again if something's not right. Install the other three rods on the crank the same way.

Rebuilders: Install the #1 rod and cap on the offset rod throw closest to the pulley end of the crank. Be careful not to scratch the crank with the rod bolts. The punch marks you made during disassembly must be on the same side of the rod and the Fuji mark on the rod must be facing the pulley end of the crank. Install the 14mm rod nuts and snug them down finger tight. Now install the #2 rod and cap the same way on the second crank throw from the pulley end. Install the #3 rod and cap on the third offset journal, then the #4 rod and cap. Don't confuse the main bearing journals with the rod journals.

EVERYONE: Now use a socket and extension on the torque wrench to torque all the rod bolts or nuts to 10 ft. lbs., then grab each rod by the small end and wiggle it back and forth toward the front and rear of the crank. This helps seat the bearings in the rod and cap. Next torque bolts or nuts to 20 ft. lbs., wiggle them back and forth a little, then torque them all to 30 ft. lbs. Rebuilders will have to hold one end of the crank down (or have Friend hold it) while you torque the bolts or nuts.

Rebuilders: When all the rods are torqued, lift the crank by the ends and rotate it *slowly*. If any rods are tight enough to rotate with the crank, lay the crank on the table and tap lightly on the sides of the sticking rod where the rod and cap join. Try the rotating test again. If any rods are still tight and sticking, remove the bolts or nuts on the tight rod(s) and inspect the bearings to see if the tangs are engaged in the notches correctly. Are there scratches in the bearing that would indicate dirt or a burr on the crank? If all looks well, put more assembly lube on the bearings and crank, then install the rod again. Try moving it at each torque setting. If the crank is scratching the bearing or the rod tightens on the crank as you torque it, take the crank and rod to the machine shop for guidance.

Bearing replacers: Lay rags or paper towels between the rod ends and cylinders to prevent scratches. Now use the crank pulley to rotate the crankshaft *slowly* while you watch the rods. The rod ends should stay on the rags or paper towels. Remove any rods that turn with the crankshaft so they hit the top side of the cylinder. Check the bearings, then install the rod again. If it's still tight, take the rod, bearings, and engine to the machinist for salvation. All's well? Continue.

EVERYONE: When the crank is assembled so all the rods move smoothly, whip out your feeler gauges and measure the clearance between the rods and crankshaft. Here's how: Slide a .003" (.070mm) gauge between the crank and rod. If the blade slips in easily, you have enough clearance. Now try a .012" (.30mm) blade. If the blade won't fit or fits snugly, there isn't too much clearance. You're in good shape. If the .003" blade won't fit, there isn't enough clearance. Or, if the .012" blade fits loosely, there's too much clearance. Have the machine shop check it for you.

Bearing replacers: You can go to Procedure 12 now.

Step 4. Install Main Bearings and Valve Lifters.

Set the #2 and #4 (left) case half in the bucket so the head studs are down and the main bearing saddles are up. Be sure the bucket is sturdy enough to hold the weight of the engine. Set the other case half right side up and tilted onto the head studs.

Install the two large main bearing shells in the center main bearing saddles and the other four bearings in the outer bearing saddles. Don't touch the inside of the bearings with your fingers. Be sure the tangs on the shells fit into the notches in the case. The ends of the bearings should end up flush with the case surface. If the tangs on the two large center bearings don't match the notches in the case, you have the wrong bearings. Subaru changed the tang orientation starting with engine #76650, so the partsperson will need your engine number to give you the correct bearings.

Coat the main bearings and the camshaft saddles in the crankcase with assembly lube.

'83 and newer models with hydraulic lifters (cam followers): You can wait until the case is together to install the lifters. Skip down to Step 5.

EVERYONE (except people with hydraulic lifters): Smear assembly lube in each cam follower hole in the case halves and all over each of the cam followers. Install the followers in their original holes if you're reusing the old followers. New or refaced followers can go in any of the holes. The flat end of the followers goes toward the camshaft.

Use the wires or rubber hoses you used during disassembly to secure the lifters in the #1 and #3 (right) case half.

Step 5. Install Crankshaft and Camshaft.

Main bearings all loobed up? Good. Smear assembly lube on the crankshaft main bearing journals, then arrange the rods on the crankshaft so the #1 and #3 rods are on one side of the crank and the #2 and #4 rods are on the other. Rotate the crank so the #4 rod is extended from the center of the crank and the #2 rod is kind of tucked up into the crank. Now grab the ends of the #1 and #3 rods and pick up the whole assembly. Gently lower it into the case half that's in the bucket so the main bearing journals on the crank fit into the main bearings in the case. Be sure the pulley end of the crank is toward the front of the crankcase. The crank has to be aligned almost perfectly before it can slip into the bearings. See that the #2 and #4 rods are hanging down into the cylinders. Once the crank is in, let the #1 and #3 rods rest against the top of the case.

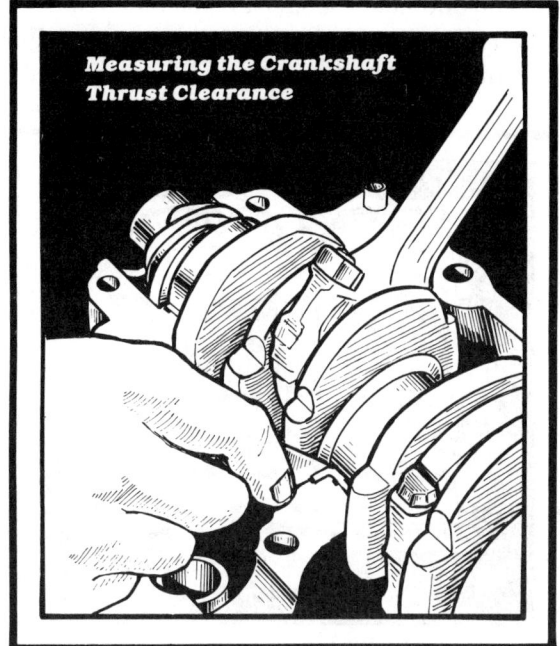

Whip out the feeler gauges again and measure the clearance between the side of the center main bearing journal on the crankshaft and the shoulder on the center main bearing. This is the thrust clearance and should be between .002" and .005" (.047-.137mm). It's imperative that you have at least .002" clearance or the engine will seize the first time it warms up. Subaru says it's allowable for the clearance to be as much as .011" (.30mm), but the more clearance above .005" you have, the more likely it is that the engine will have a disconcerting knock when it's all put back together. See your friendly machinist if the clearance is less or more than it should be.

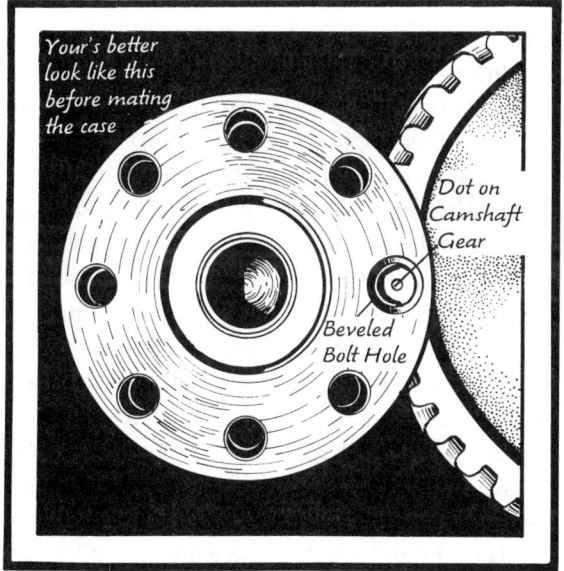

Now look at the flywheel end of the crank. One of the flywheel bolt holes has a chamfered (beveled) edge around it and thus looks a little different than the other bolt holes. Rotate the crank until the chamfered hole is toward the camshaft side of the crank.

Find the camshaft and put assembly lube on all the lobes (bumps) and on the smooth surfaces that ride in the case bores. Cams don't ride in bearings. Look on the side of the cam gear opposite the camshaft. There's a punch mark on one of the gear teeth. The gear tooth with the dot goes between the two gear teeth on the crank gear that you can see if you look through the chamfered hole. Hold the cam parallel to the crank just above the cam bores in the case. Fit the tooth with the dot into the crank gear so you can see it through the chamfered hole. Keep the gears meshed while you lower the cam into the case bores. You should be able to rotate the crank so you can see the dot through the hole. Look at the illustration.

Step 6. Mate the Case Halves.

Round up the baggies with the crankcase bolts, nuts, and washers. Arrange them on the table in order so you'll know where they all go, then put antiseize compound or oil on all the threads.

As you install the various bolts and nuts that hold the crankcase together, install them in the order I give you, then *gently* snug them down with a socket and ratchet. Don't tighten them yet; they get torqued in a certain pattern later.

'80 and newer models: If you removed the crossover backup ring from the top center of the crankcase, install it into the case half that's in the bucket. Find the new crossover O-ring, give it a light coat of oil, then fit it around the backup ring.

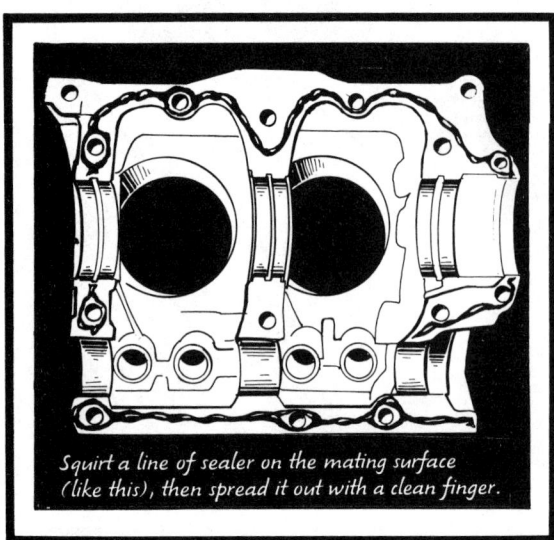
Squirt a line of sealer on the mating surface (like this), then spread it out with a clean finger.

EVERYONE: Squeeze a bead of silicone gasket sealer on one of the case halves (as shown in the illustration), then use a clean finger to spread it into a thin layer that covers the entire mating surface. Don't get any sealer on the crankshaft.

'80 and newer models: Spread sealer around the crossover O-ring at the top center of the crankcase.

EVERYONE: Balance the #1 and #3 rods on the crank so they are sticking straight up. If they won't stay erect, have Friend hold them up while you mate the case halves. (Right, Dr. Ruth?)

Grab the #1 and #3 case half by the head studs and carefully lower it onto the case half in the bucket. Be sure the long bolt sticking out of the case (on some models) is going into its hole and that the main bearings are aligned.

Gently wiggle the case half down until the mating surfaces meet. You might have to squeeze the corners of the case a little with your hands to seat the alignment dowels.

Insert the long 14mm case bolt, with a washer, into the hole between the #1 and #3 cylinders and snug it down.

Install a 14mm washer and nut on the stud in the top center of the case. Snug the bolt and nut.

Install the appropriate 14mm bolts and washers behind the #3 cylinder and snug them down. If you have an L-shaped steel bracket (4WD case stiffener), install it when you install the top rear bolt.

Pick the case up and set it in the engine stand so the flywheel end is down and the pulley end is up. Install the appropriate bolts and washers in the holes in front of cylinder #2. Lightly snug the bolts.

Install two 12mm bolts and washers in the holes on the top of the case. Install the 12mm bolt, washer, and nut that attach the oil pickup tube to the bottom of the case. Install the two 10mm bolts and washers on the front of the case, above and below the front end of the crank.

Have Friend hold the case while you follow the torque pattern and torque the six 14mm bolts and the 12mm nuts (two on the top of the case and one on the bottom) to 10 ft. lbs. The torque on the two 10mm bolts on the front of the case is only 4 ft. lbs., so just lightly snug them down with a ratchet. Next, follow

Crankcase Bolt tightening sequence

the torque pattern and torque the 12mm and 14mm bolts and nuts to 20 ft. lbs. Also torque the 12mm pickup tube bolt on the bottom to 20 ft. lbs. Finally, follow the pattern and torque only the 14mm nuts or bolts to 35 ft. lbs. Do the final pattern at least twice.

Roll the engine so the top is up. Put a rag or paper towel between the rods and cylinders so the cylinders won't get scratched. Slide the crank pulley on the end of the crank and turn it slowly to see that the crank rotates freely. If it binds in places or is hard to turn, loosen the 14mm bolts and torque them one at a time to see which one is causing the problem. If the crank is still hard to turn, split the case again and see that the main bearings are installed properly. All's well? Continue.

Rotate the crank so you can check the timing mark on the cam gear through the chamfered hole on the crankshaft. You might have to rotate the crank twice. If you can't see the dot through the chamfered hole, split the case and install the cam correctly. If the cam is installed right, install the two 10mm camshaft thrust plate bolts using two new lock plates from the gasket set. Be sure the small tabs on the lock plates fit into the small holes on the thrust plate. Tighten the two bolts with a large screwdriver. Careful, the bolts are small so don't overtighten them. Use needlenose pliers to bend the lock tabs against the bolt heads.

The case is mated!

PROCEDURE 12: INSTALL PISTONS (1600cc and 1800cc Engines Only)

Set the engine so the flywheel end is down and the pulley end is up. This will enable you to align the ends of the rods with the holes in the case as you install the piston pins. If you have difficulty looking down through the crankcase holes when the engine is in this position, get a box to stand on.

When installing the pistons, remember that "Top" is toward the top of the crankcase when the engine is in its normal position.

Condition: Engine rebuild; OR you're doing a ring and valve job.

Tools and Materials: Fresh engine oil, piston ring compressor, needlenose pliers, hammer with a wooden handle.

Remarks: If you're not up for installing the pistons, have Subaru or a garage install them for you.

Step 1. Clean Pistons, Install Rings.

If the machine shop didn't clean the pistons for you, spread one of the *old* compression rings until it breaks. Notice how far it spreads before breaking, then keep this in mind when installing the compression rings. Use the square, unbroken end of the ring you just broke to scrape all the carbon, dirt, and grease out of the ring grooves. Take your time and get the grooves spotless. Be careful to not damage the sides of the grooves while cleaning. Use a putty knife to scrape the carbon off the tops of the pistons, then wash the pistons in solvent. Use solvent and fine emery cloth to remove the two brown rings around the piston pins. The brown rings are varnishlike stuff formed from heat and oil vapors inside the crankcase. They make removing and installing the piston pins difficult.

Open the box of new rings and read the instructions. See which side of the ring goes toward the top of the piston. There might be a dot or letter on the top side of the ring, or nothing if it doesn't matter. One edge of the inside or outside of the ring might have a notch or chamfered edge. Be sure to put the rings on the pistons according to the manufacturer's instructions. Install the rings in the following order.

The third ring is the oil ring and fits in the bottom groove next to the piston pin. Install the spacer (that funny wiggly-looking ring) into the bottom ring groove. On '79 and newer models, install the oil ring spacer so the ends of the spacer (the gap) is on the opposite side of the piston from the stopper pin. Hook one end of a thin oil ring rail into the gap between the top of the spacer and the ring groove, then gently wrap the rest of the ring around the piston until it fits into the groove. Hook one end of the other oil ring rail into the gap between the bottom of the spacer and the ring groove. Wind the rail around the piston and it will slide into place. Be sure the rails are evenly securing the spacer all the way around.

Use a ring spreader or your thumbs to carefully install the second ring in the middle groove. Follow the manufacturer's instructions for top and bottom.

Install the top ring in the top ring groove according to the instructions.

Check the top two rings to be sure they are free to move in the grooves all the way around the piston.

Install the rings on the other three pistons the same way.

Step 2. Lubricate.

Squirt some oil in each of the cylinders and smear it around so there's a light coat of oil on the entire cylinder. Smear some oil in the piston pin holes on the ends of the rods.

Remove the piston pins from the pistons and give the pin and the holes in the pistons a light coat of oil. Slide the pin in and out of the piston to see that it moves freely. You should be able to push the pin in and out with your fingers. Use fine emery paper to remove any burrs in the pin holes. Keep each piston pin with its piston so they don't get mixed up.

Squirt oil on the pistons and rings and smear the oil all around the sides of the pistons. Don't worry about the top. Move the rings so oil can get down into all the grooves.

Step 3. Gap the Rings.

Rotate the rings in the ring grooves so the gaps are arranged to match the illustration for your year. This is important so take your time and get it right.

Step 4. Install Pistons.

Slip the crank pulley onto the crankshaft and rotate the engine so the end of the #1 rod is aligned with the piston pin hole on the front side of the crankcase. Remove the rags in cylinders #1 and #2. Find the #1 piston and hold it up to the cylinder in its installed position. The punch mark you made during disassembly should be toward the top of the case. If both circlips were removed, use needlenose pliers to install a circlip on the side of the piston that will be closest to cylinder #3. Here's how you install circlips. Grab a circlip and look at it. See how the little tang in the center of the circlip is bent so it sticks out slightly on one side of the clip? When you install the circlip, the tang should point toward the outside of the piston (away from the piston pin). Grab the tang with needlenose pliers, then hook the end of the circlip in the groove in the piston. Twist and push the clip into place. Check it carefully to be sure it's fully seated all the way around.

To install the pistons, clean the ring compressor and fit it around the #1 piston so it covers all three rings. Orient the tightening mechanism on the compressor toward the top of the piston so it will fit between the two head studs. Be careful not to rotate the ring compressor when it's on the piston so the ring gaps won't be moved. Tighten the compressor, then fit the piston into the #1 cylinder (punch marks toward the top of the crankcase) until the ring compressor hits the case. Tap around the edge of the ring compressor with the end of a wooden hammer handle until it's square with the crankcase and touching it all the way around.

Hold the ring compressor with one hand while you tap the piston into the cylinder with the end of a wooden hammer handle. The piston should slide in easily. If the piston stops before it's in all the way, don't keep smacking it with the hammer handle. Remove the piston, take the ring compressor off and check the rings. If all looks well, install the compressor again being sure the rings are fully compressed and the compressor is square with the case before installing the piston again. When all the rings slide into the cylinder, the ring compressor will fall off in your hand.

Continue tapping the piston into the cylinder until you can see the piston pin hole through the hole on the front of the case. Reach in with your finger and rotate the piston if it doesn't line up with the hole exactly. Look through the piston pin hole to be sure you installed the circlip on the other side of the piston.

Step 5. Install Piston Pin.

The end of the rod should be visible through the crankcase hole and piston pin hole. Use a long, thin, clean screwdriver to reach through the piston pin hole and align the hole in the rod with the center of the piston pin hole. Rotate the crank, tap the piston in further, or do whatever is necessary to align the hole in the piston exactly with the hole in the rod. Give the pin a light coat of oil, then wiggle it into the hole in the piston. It will slide in until it hits the end of the rod. Gently wiggle the pin until it slides through the rod end. (You might need to rock the crank pulley back and forth a little.) Push the pin in far enough to install the outer circlip in its groove. If the pin is tight, use a small socket on the end of an extension to *gently* tap the pin in far enough to install the circlip.

Fit a circlip in piston #2 on the side closest to cylinder #4 (if the clip was removed). Install the piston for cylinder #2 the same way you installed #1. Be sure to install the circlip.

Use the crank pulley to rotate the crank back and forth a little while watching the pistons. They should move in and out within the cylinder. If they only move outward, away from the crank, you've missed the piston pin hole in the rod. Remove the pin and start over. If you don't have a piston pin puller you can push the piston out of the cylinder by rotating the crank. Remove the circlip, then pull the pin out of the piston. Do Steps 2, 3, and 4 to reinstall the piston, piston pin, and circlip.

Pistons #1 and #2 installed correctly? Good. Use the pulley to rotate the crank so the tops of the two pistons are flush with the outer surface of the crankcase. Due to the new rings, you might have to use a socket and ratchet on the pulley nut to rotate the crank now.

Roll the engine so the front is down and the flywheel end is up. Be sure circlips are installed in the #3 and #4 pistons on the side closest to cylinders #1 and #2. Install piston #3, then piston #4. Don't forget to install the circlips after the piston pins are installed. If you need to rotate the crank a little to align the hole in the rod and piston, screw a couple of flywheel bolts into the end of the crank, then use a hammer handle or large screwdriver between the bolts to move the crank.

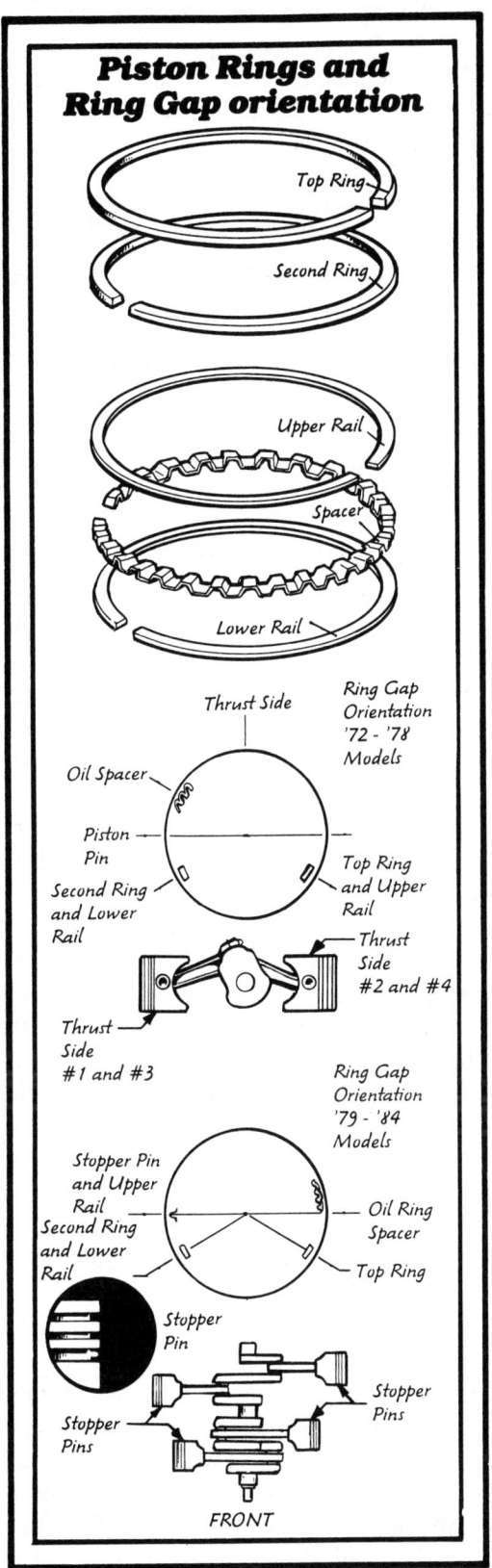

When all four pistons are installed, set the crankcase so the top side is up. Use a socket and ratchet on the crank pulley nut to rotate the crank a couple of turns. Make one final check to be sure all the piston pin circlips are installed. If any pistons pop out of the cylinders, the piston pin didn't go through the hole in the rod. Try again.

Now that the pistons are correctly installed, round up the two crankcase plugs and clean the threads with a wire brush. In the gasket set, find two new aluminum washers that will fit on the plugs. Coat the threads of the plugs with Permatex #2 gasket sealer, then screw them into the crankcase. Use the hex tool and torque wrench to tighten the plugs to 50 ft. lbs.

PROCEDURE 13: INSTALL CYLINDER HEADS, PUSH RODS, AND ROCKER ARMS

Condition: Cylinder heads have been removed.

Tools and Materials: New cylinder head gaskets, special head torquing socket (Subaru part #499987006), thin wall 17mm socket, torque wrench, maybe head gasket sealer (see the rap at the end of the parts section in Procedure 9, Step 3).

Step 1. Prep for Cylinder Head Installation.

Use a long thin screwdriver, rags, and solvent or carb cleaner to clean inside the holes in the cylinder heads where the mounting studs fit. Machine shops often miss crud that accumulates in the holes when they clean the heads.

Screw a spark plug into each of the spark plug holes to be sure the threads are in good condition. If any are stripped or funky, have the machine shop install helicoils.

'75-'76 California cars and all '77 and newer models: Find the cylinder head with the threaded hole for the EGR tube. This head must be installed on the right side of the engine (cylinders #1 and #3). Mark it or lay it on that side of the engine now so you won't forget.

EVERYONE: Round up the rocker arm assemblies and pushrods. Clean them if you haven't already. Find the rocker assembly with an "**R**" stamped on the shaft between the two center rocker arms. This is the rocker arm assembly for the right (#1 and #3) cylinder head.

Rotate the crank so all four pistons are away from the cylinder head surface of the crankcase. Use a clean rag or paper towel to wipe the oil out of the cylinders so it won't dribble out on the head mounting surface. Squirt carb cleaner on a rag or paper towel and clean the head gasket surfaces on the crankcase and cylinder heads to remove all traces of oil.

Lightly oil the threads on the head studs, then remove the excess oil with a rag or paper towel. The cylinder head mounting nuts, bolts, and washers have been spotlessly cleaned, right? If not, do it now. Spread out the nuts, bolts, and washers on a clean rag and squirt oil on the nut and bolt threads, and on both sides of the washers.

Look in the gasket set for the head gaskets. They are large and black. If they're wrapped with thin cellophane that's stuck to the gasket, don't remove the cellophane until just before you install the gasket on the crankcase.

Step 2. Install Cylinder Heads.

OK, now that everything is cleaned and oiled, we can install the cylinder heads. Install one cylinder head at a time and be sure to follow the pattern for your particular year to torque the heads. The torque pattern illustrations are in Chapter 7, Procedure 15, Step 3. Look it up now and put a marker in the book so you can find it again easily.

If your head gaskets are wrapped in cellophane, peel the cellophane off one gasket now. If your head gaskets aren't sticky feeling, follow the directions for '80 and newer models and use gasket sealer on the gaskets.

'80 and newer models: Use a small brush to spread a light coat of head gasket sealer on both sides of one head gasket. Quickly install the gasket on the crankcase. Be sure all the holes are aligned properly.

EVERYONE: Install a head gasket on one side of the engine. The outline of the gasket should match the outline of the crankcase.

Now fit a cylinder head onto the studs and push it against the head gasket. Be sure the head with the EGR hole goes on the right side. Fit a washer over the center mounting stud so the rounded side of the washer is toward the outside and the flat side is against the head. Install a nut on the stud and lightly snug it down with a 17mm socket and ratchet. Install washers (rounded side out) and nuts on the rest of the head studs but don't tighten them yet.

Install the rocker arm assembly on the cylinder head with two nuts or bolts, depending on your setup. Don't use washers for the rocker assembly mounting bolts or nuts. Don't install the pushrods yet; we'll install them after the heads are torqued.

Step 3. Torque Cylinder Heads.

The cylinder heads get torqued in three stages. Go through the pattern with your torque wrench at least twice at each stage. Here's how:

First stage: Follow the torque pattern and torque the head to 14 ft. lbs. ('75-'78 models) or 22 ft. lbs. ('79 and newer models).

Second stage: Follow the torque pattern and torque the head to 28 ft. lbs. ('75-'78 models) or 43 ft. lbs. ('79 and newer models).

The Rocker Assembly with a R goes on the right side.

Third stage: Follow the pattern and torque the head to 43 ft. lbs. ('75-'78 models) or 47 ft. lbs ('79 and newer models).

If your head has two 10mm bolts that fit in holes in the bottom, install the two bolts and snug them down. Repeat Steps 2 and 3 to install the other cylinder head.

Step 4. Install Push Rods and Rocker Arm Assemblies.

'83 and newer models with automatic transmissions: Roll the engine onto the flywheel end and install the hydraulic lifters. Roll the engine upright again.

EVERYONE: Remove the nuts or bolts securing the rocker arm assemblies, then remove the assemblies. Squirt oil into the hole in one end of each push rod until it runs out the other end. Insert a push rod into each of the holes at the bottom of the cylinder heads. Push and wiggle each push rod a little to make it seat in the cam follower.

Install the rocker arm assemblies on the cylinder heads again as you did in Step 2. Remember, the one stamped "**R**" goes on the right side. The rocker assembly mounting nuts or bolts don't get washers under them. Be sure the ends of the push rods are all fitting into their sockets on the bottoms of the rocker arms before tightening the bolts or nuts. Tighten the bolts or nuts a couple of turns at a time until they're snug. Now tighten them to the same torque setting you used in Stage 3 (Step 3).

PROCEDURE 14: INSTALL FLYWHEEL HOUSING

Condition: Flywheel housing was removed.

Tools and Materials: 12mm and maybe a 14mm socket, ratchet, extension, torque wrench, wire brush, silicone gasket sealer, spray can of carb cleaner, oil, antiseize compound.

Step 1. Do It.

Use a wire brush to clean the flywheel housing bolts, then give them a light coat of antiseize compound. (Use oil if you don't have antiseize.)

Use carb cleaner and a clean rag to clean the seal surface on the end of the crankshaft, the hole in the flywheel housing where the seal fits, and the mating surfaces of the crankcase and flywheel housing. Squirt some oil on the crank and cam gears.

Be sure the two dowel pins are on the crankcase or flywheel housing. One might be on each and that's OK, just so they're both there.

Apply a thin layer of silicone gasket sealer to the mating surface of the flywheel housing. Align the dowel pins with their holes, then install the housing on the case. You might have to tap the housing with a hammer handle to get it on the pins. If you have two 14mm flywheel housing bolts, they go in the lower corners of the housing. Install all the bolts, snug them down evenly, then torque them in a crisscross pattern to 19 ft. lbs.

PROCEDURE 15: INSTALL REAR CRANKSHAFT SEAL

Condition: Engine rebuild; OR seal was leaking.

Tools and Materials: New rear crank seal, Permatex #2 gasket sealer, wire brush, grease (white lithium or wheel bearing), maybe a hammer.

Step 1. Do It.

The seal surface on the crankshaft and in the flywheel housing have been cleaned with carb cleaner, right?

Rough up the outer surface of the new seal with a wire brush. This will make the seal stick better. Be careful not to damage the tiny spring inside the seal or the two lips on the inner edge of the seal.

Pack grease into the groove between the two seal lips that fit against the crankshaft. Now coat the outer edge of the seal with Permatex #2 gasket sealer.

Hold the seal up to the end of the crank so the smooth side is toward you. The side with a groove should face the engine. Carefully wiggle the seal over the end of the crank. Put your thumbs on opposite sides of the seal and press it into the flywheel housing. Press all around the edge until the seal is flush with the flywheel housing. Don't press it in any farther. That's all there is to it.

If you didn't remove the oil pan, skip to Procedure 17.

PROCEDURE 16: INSTALL OIL PAN

Condition: Oil pan has been removed.

Tools and Materials: 10mm socket and ratchet, new oil pan gasket, wire brush, antiseize compound or engine oil, white lithium or wheel bearing grease.

Step 1. Do It.

Roll the engine so the flywheel end is up. The inside of the oil pan is so clean you could eat soup out of it. Right? Use a wire brush, then carb cleaner and a clean rag to clean the gasket surfaces thoroughly on the oil pan and crankcase. Clean all the oil pan bolts and washers, then lightly coat the threads with antiseize compound. Use oil if you don't have antiseize.

Find the new oil pan gasket in the gasket set and lay it on the oil pan so all the holes are aligned. Look carefully; it will only fit one way. One end has six holes and the other end has five. Lightly coat one side of the new gasket with white lithium grease or wheel bearing grease, then flip the gasket over and coat the other side.

Put a lockwasher on each of the oil pan bolts, then a flat washer if your engine has them. Next put a couple of the bolts through the oil pan and gasket to hold the gasket in place and install the oil pan on the engine. Get all the bolts started in their holes before tightening any of them. Once they're all started, snug them down.

They only torque to 4 ft. lbs., so be careful not to overtighten them. If you tighten them too much it will break the gasket or bolt!

Manual transmission people: Install the small sheet metal plate across the bottom of the flywheel housing.

PROCEDURE 17: INSTALL FLYWHEEL (Manual Trans), OR TORQUE PLATE (Automatic Trans)

Condition: Flywheel or torque plate has been removed.

Tools and Materials: Permatex #2 gasket sealer, 14mm socket, extension, torque wrench, punch or phillips screwdriver to lock the flywheel.

Step 1. Do It.

Use a wire brush to clean the threads of the flywheel or torque plate bolts. Use carb cleaner and a rag to clean the flywheel, torque plate, small back plate for the torque plate (if you have one), and the end of the crankshaft.

Put a thin coat of Permatex #2 gasket sealer on the end of the crank and on the threads of the bolts.

'82 and newer models: Install a new O-ring on the end of the crankshaft.

EVERYONE: The flywheel or torque plate (and back plate if you have one) will only fit on the crank in one position, so hold whichever you have up to the crank and rotate it until all the holes are aligned with the holes in the crank. If you have a back plate, align the small notch on the outer edge with the small hole in the torque plate. Fit the flywheel or torque plate (and back plate if you have it) on the end of the crank, then install the mounting bolts. Turn the flywheel until you can lock the engine (Procedure 3, Step 1), then snug the bolts down in a crisscross pattern. Torque the bolts in a diagonal, crisscross pattern to 33 ft. lbs. Now check them by going around in a circle.

PROCEDURE 18: INSTALL CLUTCH (Manual Transmission Models Only)

Condition: Clutch has been removed.

Tools and Materials: 10mm or 12mm socket, torque wrench, clutch alignment tool, new clutch disc and/or pressure plate if the old ones were worn out or oily.

Step 1. Do It.

'75-'80 models: Put a dab of grease on your pinky and smear it in the pilot bearing that's in the end of the crankshaft. Wipe off any grease that gets on the outside of the crank.

EVERYONE: Clean the smooth flat surface on the pressure plate with carb cleaner. Clean your hands before handling the clutch disc. If you're installing a new clutch disc and/or pressure plate, carefully compare the new parts to the old. If you notice anything different, take both parts back to the parts store for an explanation. It would be a bummer to get the engine installed, then find you'd installed the wrong part.

Fit the clutch alignment tool through the outside of the pressure plate, then install the clutch disc onto the tool so the side with springs is toward the pressure plate (away from the flywheel). Support the weight of the pressure plate with one hand while you stick the end of the alignment tool into the pilot bearing.

There may be an "0" stamped near the edge of the pressure plate and one somewhere on the flywheel. If there is, orient the pressure plate so the "0" is 120° or more away from the "0" on the flywheel. (Not all pressure plates have the 0, so don't worry if you don't have it.) Slip the pressure plate onto the dowels in the flywheel. Be sure the bolt holes line up, then install the six pressure-plate bolts. Screw the bolts in until the lockwashers barely touch the pressure plate. Use a socket and ratchet to tighten the bolts one turn at a time in a diagonal, criss-cross pattern until they're *lightly* snug.

If you don't have a clutch alignment tool, install the disc and pressure plate and tighten the bolts evenly until the clutch disc can barely be moved with your fingers. Using a flashlight or drop light, look through the splined hole in the disc and move the disc around until it's perfectly aligned with the pilot bearing. The closer it's aligned, the easier it will be to install the engine.

If the pressure plate bolt heads are 10mm, the torque is only 7 ft. lbs. Put your hand on the head of the ratchet and snug them all down evenly. If the bolt heads are 12mm, torque the bolts to 12 ft. lbs. Remove the clutch alignment tool.

PROCEDURE 19: INSTALL OIL PUMP AND OIL PRESSURE SWITCH

Condition: Oil pump and/or oil pressure switch have been removed.

Tools and Materials: Oil pump, oil pressure switch, new rubber O-ring(s) for the pump, 10mm socket and ratchet, phillips screwdriver, large pliers or 14mm open-end wrench depending on your oil pressure switch.

Step 1. Install Oil Pump.

If you've taken the old oil pump apart, inspected it (Procedure 9, Step 4), and decided to use it again, you'll need two new O-rings to install between the two pump body pieces. They should match the old O-rings exactly. Install the round center piece in the pump housing, then the squarish gear, then a large O-ring into the groove on the pump body. Install the small ball and spring (wide end toward the outside), then an O-ring in the recessed area around the spring. Install the pump cover and tighten the two phillips screws.

Whether you're installing a new oil pump or the old pump, check the two phillips screws on the rear of the pump for tightness.

Hold the pump up to the case in its installed position. See the hole on the round part of the pump that matches a hole in the lower right side of the pump hole in the case? Squirt engine assembly lube into both holes. Also squirt the lube into the two holes on the pump where the oil filter mounts. The assembly lube will prime the pump.

Put a dab of assembly lube or grease around the edge of the recessed hole on the back of the oil pump, then insert a new O-ring in the hole. The grease will hold the O-ring while the pump is installed. The O-ring should fit into the recessed area of the pump exactly. If it's too large or small you've got the wrong O-ring. Check this carefully—it's very important.

Insert a couple of the short oil pump mounting bolts in their holes in the pump, then install a new oil pump gasket on the rear of the pump. Don't use gasket sealer. Be sure the large hole in the gasket is around the O-ring and all four small mounting bolt holes align with the holes in the pump.

Smear oil inside the crankcase where the pump fits, and put a dab of oil on the O-ring. Rotate the crankshaft so the slot in the oil pump hole of the crankcase (the camshaft end) is vertical. Turn the oil pump shaft blade so it's vertical like the slot in the end of the camshaft, then wiggle the oil pump into the crankcase. If it's a tight fit, gently tap it in with the end of a wooden hammer handle. If it refuses to go in all the way, the shaft isn't aligned with the slot. Remove the pump and try again.

When the pump is all the way in the case, install and tighten the four 10mm bolts. The long bolt goes on the bottom of the pump, next to the oil filter bracket. The bolts are small, so just get them good and snug.

Install a new oil filter on the pump (Chapter 7, Procedure 3, Step 3).

Step 2. Install Oil Pressure Switch (OPS).

It's a good idea to install a new OPS when you do a ring and/or valve job, or rebuild the engine. They're inexpensive.

Clean the threads on the oil pressure switch, then give them a light coat of Permatex #2. Don't get any gasket sealer in the small hole in the end of the switch. Screw the OPS into the crankcase next the oil pump, or into the bottom of the oil pump depending on your setup.

If yours screws into the case, use large pliers to get the switch snug. The threads are tapered so don't overtighten it. Don't squeeze hard on the switch with the pliers or you might distort the diaphragm inside.

If your OPS screws into the bottom of the oil pump, use a 14mm open-end wrench to snug it down. The threads are tapered so don't crank on it too hard.

PROCEDURE 20: INSTALL FRONT CRANKSHAFT SEAL AND CRANKSHAFT PULLEY

Condition: Engine rebuild; OR the old seal was leaking.

Tools and Materials: Phase 1 tool set, new front crankshaft seal, wire brush, Permatex #2 gasket sealer, grease.

Step 1. Install Front Crank Seal.

Rebuilders: Be sure the crankshaft key is in the slot on the front end of the crankshaft and the distributor drive gear is on the crank. The flat side of the drive gear should be toward the pulley end of the crank. If you see a beveled area where the gear fits on the crank, pull the gear out and turn it around.

EVERYONE: Crank key and distributor drive gear installed correctly? OK, use carb cleaner to clean the seal surface in the crankcase. Use a wire brush to rough up the outer edge of the seal so it will hold better. Pack white lithium or wheel bearing grease between the two lips on the inner edge of the seal where it rides against the crank. Smear Permatex #2 gasket sealer around the outer edge of the seal, then install it in the crankcase so the flat side faces out and the grooved side is toward the engine. Press the seal in evenly with your thumbs until it's flush with the case. Go slow so you don't push it in too far.

If you accidentally push the seal in too far, gently pry it out with a screwdriver, inspect the lips for damage and see that the small spring is still in its groove on the inner side of the seal. Replace the seal if the lips or spring are torn or damaged. Try installing the seal again, a little slower this time.

Step 2. Install Crankshaft Pulley.

Smear oil on the smooth shiny seal surface of the crank pulley. Align the groove inside the pulley with the woodruff key, then slide the pulley onto the crank. Install the pulley bolt and washer and snug them down. Use the socket and ratchet to rotate the crank so you can lock it in position with a punch or phillips screwdriver (Procedure 3, Step 1). Torque the pulley nut to 40 ft. lb., then remove the punch or phillips screwdriver from the timing hole.

PROCEDURE 21: INSTALL DISTRIBUTOR

Condition: The distributor has been removed.

Tools and Materials: 10mm socket, ratchet, and extension. Maybe a new distributor 0-ring. If the crankshaft has been rotated since the distributor was removed (engine rebuild, etc.) you'll need a socket and ratchet for the crank pulley nut so you can rotate the crank.

Step 1. Set Cylinder #1 to TDC Firing Position.

If you set the engine to TDC firing position for cylinder #1 and marked the distributor before removing it, and you haven't rotated the crank at all since, skip to Step 2. If the crank has been rotated or you're not sure where it's set now, do this step before installing the distributor.

To set the engine to TDC firing position for cylinder #1, remove the valve cover for cylinders #1 and #3 (if it's on). Use a socket and ratchet on the crank pulley nut to rotate the crank *clockwise* as viewed from the front of the engine. Watch the rocker arm for the *intake* valve of *cylinder#1*. (If you're not sure which one to watch, see the illustration in Chapter 7, Procedure 16, Step 4.) As you rotate the crank, the rocker arm will push the end of the intake valve toward the cylinder head (opening the valve). Rotate the engine farther and the top end

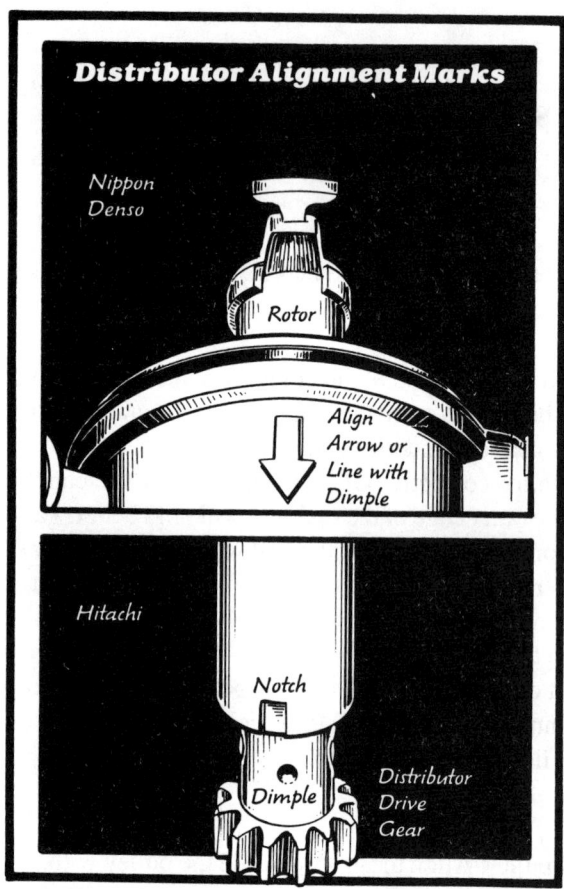

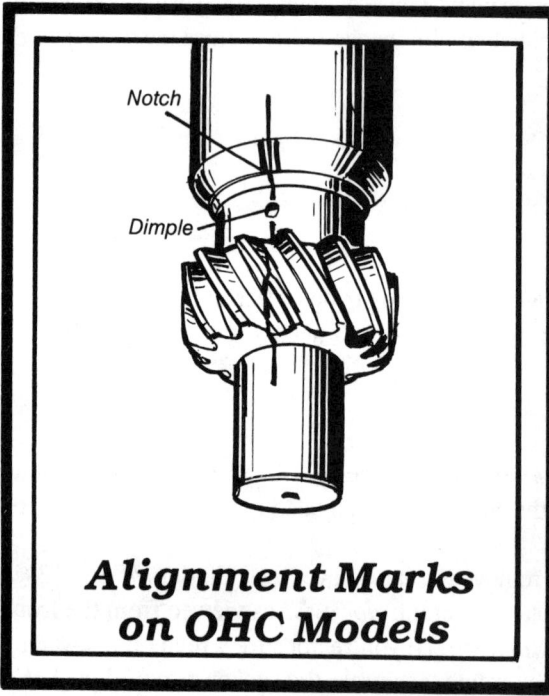

Alignment Marks on OHC Models

of the rocker arm will move away from the cylinder head (valve closes). As the valve starts closing, look in the timing hole on the flywheel housing. You'll see the single line on the flywheel go by. Keep rotating the engine and you'll see the timing marks appear on the flywheel. Set the engine so the "0" on the flywheel is aligned with the pointer on the flywheel housing. The engine is now set at TDC firing position for cylinder #1.

Step 2. Install Distributor.

Rebuilders: Remove the rubber 0-ring from its groove on the long shaft housing part of the distributor body. Find a new 0-ring in the gasket set that matches the old one. Put oil on the new ring and on the distributor shaft housing, then wiggle the new 0-ring onto the shaft housing and into its groove. Be careful not to tear the new O-ring on the gear teeth. Install the distributor hold-down plate on the distributor if you removed it.

EVERYONE: Fit the rotor onto the distributor shaft and point it to the mark you made on the top edge of the distributor housing before removing the distributor. No mark? Look at the illustration and align the dimple at the bottom of the distributor shaft (just above the distributor drive gear) with the notch in the end of the shaft housing (Hitachi distributor), or align the dimple with the arrow (or line) on the side of the distributor body (Nippon Denso distributor). Don't confuse the dimple with the spring pin that holds the gear on the shaft. When the dimple and arrow or notch are aligned, the distributor is set at firing position for #1 cylinder. Use a pen, chalk, or paint to make a mark on the top edge of the distributor housing where the rotor is pointing.

Squirt oil on the distributor drive gear and the rubber O-ring, then lower the distributor into the case. When the 0-ring reaches the case, turn the distributor housing so the mounting bracket aligns with the distributor hold-down bolt hole in the crankcase. Align the rotor with your mark on the housing, then push the distributor all the way into the case. You may have to turn the rotor slightly so the teeth will mesh with the drive gear on the crank. Turn the distributor body until the mark you made on the mounting bracket is aligned with the hold-down bolt.

If you are installing a new distributor, or you didn't mark the old one, center the slot on the distributor on the bolt hole. Is the rotor still pointing at (or very close to) your mark on the distributor? If not, you'll need to pull the distributor back out until you can turn the rotor slightly so a different tooth on the distributor gear engages with the gear on the crankshaft. Keep trying and you'll get it so the bolt hole in the case aligns with your mark on the hold-down bracket and the rotor points to the mark on the distributor housing. Install and tighten the 10mm hold-down bolt(s) and washer(s). Check the ignition timing as soon as you start the engine.

PROCEDURE 22: ADJUST VALVES, INSTALL VALVE COVERS

Condition: Cylinder heads were removed or retorqued.

Tools and Materials: The tools for adjusting the valves are listed in Chapter 7, Procedure 7.

Step 1. Adjust Valves (except models with hydraulic lifter).

Turn to Chapter 7, Procedure 7, to adjust the valves and install the valve covers. Come back here when you're finished.

Step 2. Adjust Valves on Models with Hydraulic Lifters.

You'll have to fit the distributor cap on the distributor for this step so you can tell which spark plug wire the rotor is pointing toward. If you're not sure which of the valves are intake and which are exhaust, see the illustration in Chapter 7, Procedure 7.

Adjusting hydraulic valve lifters is done in two stages. I'll tell you how to adjust the valves right after I tell you how to set the engine for the two stages.

Stage 1: Set the engine to Top Dead Center (TDC) firing position for cylinder #1. (See Chapter 7, Procedure 5, Step 6, if you're not sure how this is done.) The rotor should be pointing toward the #1 spark plug wire in the distributor cap and the pointer on the flywheel housing should be pointing to the 0 on the torque plate.

While the engine is in the Stage 1 position you can adjust the intake and exhaust valves for cylinder #1, the exhaust valve for cylinder #3, and the intake valve for cylinder #4.

Skip down to the *Adjust Valves* section to adjust these valves now. When you're finished, come back and do Stage 2.

Stage 2: Use the socket and ratchet on the pulley bolt to rotate the crank *clockwise* (as viewed from the front of the engine) one complete turn (360°). The rotor should now be pointing to the spark plug wire on the distributor cap for cylinder #2. The pointer should be pointing at the 0 on the torque plate.

While the engine is set in the Stage 2 position, adjust the intake and exhaust valves for cylinder #2, the intake valve for cylinder #3, and the exhaust valve for cylinder #4.

Adjust valves: Go slowly and pay attention to which valves you're adjusting. Adjust only the valves for whichever stage the engine is set for.

Use a thin screwdriver to bend the lock tabs away from the valve-adjusting nuts at the bottom of the rocker arms. Use a 12mm box-end wrench to loosen the locknuts a couple of turns *counterclockwise*. Hold the locknuts with the wrench while you use a small crescent wrench or 6mm open-end wrench to screw the valve adjustment bolts *clockwise* (as viewed from the end of the bolt) four complete turns. Do this on all the valves you're adjusting.

Let the engine rest like this for 15 minutes to relieve the pressure in the valve lifters.

After 15 minutes, use the small wrench to slowly turn the adjusting bolt *counterclockwise*. While turning the bolt, grab the end of the pushrod with your other hand and gently try to rotate it. Also watch the upper end of the rocker arm to see when it stops moving. You're looking for the point where the rocker arm just barely touches the pushrod. You should be able to rotate the pushrod, and the rocker arm should stop moving at the same time. Subaru calls this the "Zero Point." When you reach the zero point, unscrew the bolt *counterclockwise* 1½ (1.5) more turns. The valve is now adjusted. Hold the adjusting bolt with the small wrench while you tighten the locknut against the rocker arm. Use pliers to bend the lockplate against the locknut. Adjust the other valves in the stage the same way.

When the appropriate valves have been adjusted for Stage 1, set the engine for Stage 2 and adjust those valves. When you're finished with Stage 2, install the valve covers (Chapter 7, Procedure 7, Step 6).

PROCEDURE 23: INSTALL ALL THAT LITTLE STUFF ON THE ENGINE

OK, the big stuff has been assembled. This procedure covers installing the following parts on the engine: crossover pipe ('75-'79 models), water pump, air injection system (AIS), alternator, intake manifold, spark plugs, distributor cap, and spark plug wires. Install these parts in the order of the steps.

Condition: Engine rebuild; OR you've removed some of the various parts on the engine.

Tools and Materials: Phase 1 tool set, new gaskets for some of the parts you'll be installing, silicone gasket sealer, antiseize compound, fine emery cloth.

Step 1. Install Crossover Pipe.

On 1980-1984 models, the crossover pipe is built into the case so you can skip this step.

Use fine emery cloth to clean the mating surfaces of the crankcase and crossover pipe fittings. Now is an opportune time to replace the hose between the fittings on early models (Chapter 16, Procedure 2, Step 6). At least inspect the old one thoroughly for cracks and soft spots.

Be sure there's no water, dirt, or crud in the crossover fitting bolt holes on top of the crankcase. Clean the threads on the bolts, then give them a light coat of antiseize compound or engine oil.

Look in the gasket set for two gaskets that match the shape of the crossover pipe fittings. Coat both sides of the gaskets with silicone gasket sealer, then place them in position on the crankcase. Set the bypass pipe or hose and fittings on the crankcase and install the bolts and washers. Snug the bolts down with a 10mm socket and ratchet. Be careful not to overtighten them (they might break or strip the threads in the case).

Step 2. Install Oil Filler Tube and Small Bypass Pipe.

Clean the threads on the oil filler tube bolts with a wire brush, then give the threads a light coat of antiseize compound or engine oil. Use emery paper to clean the mating surfaces on the crankcase and the bottom of the oil filler tube. Find the new gasket that matches the shape of the bottom of the oil filler tube (it usually has lots of little holes in it). Smear silicone gasket sealer on both sides of the gasket, then lay it on the crankcase in its installed position. Set the oil filler tube on the gasket so it points toward the left side of the engine. Stick a bolt through the bracket on the small bypass pipe, then install it on the oil filler tube. On 4WD models, there will be an L-shaped steel bracket that attaches to one of the oil filler bolts. Orient the bracket so the hole in one end is aligned with the engine mounting bolt hole and the other end is on the oil filler mount. Tighten both 12mm bolts. If your engine has a bracket between the oil filler tube and the top of the cylinder head, install the bracket and tighten the bolts.

Step 3. Install Water Pump.

See Chapter 16, Procedure 4, Step 4, to install the water pump. This is a good time to replace the short bypass hose that connects the water pump and bypass pipe. At least inspect it carefully.

Step 4. Install Air Injection System (if you have one).

The air injection system found on some '75-'80 models is a spiderlike set of pipes that attaches to the top corners of the cylinder heads. If you don't have an AIS, skip this step.

You've cleaned the reed valves already. Right? Oh, well. Use a wire brush to clean the threads on the flare nuts, then lightly coat the threads with antiseize compound or engine oil. Set the AIS system on the engine so the flare nuts fit into the holes on the top corners of the cylinder heads. Screw the nuts into the heads a few turns by hand to be sure none are cross-threaded, then use an open-end wrench to evenly tighten the nuts.

If your AIS system attaches to the oil filler tube, fit the pipe under the clamp, then tighten the 10mm bolt. Tighten the four 10mm bolts on the square reed valve cover.

Step 5. Install Alternator.

If you have air conditioning, install the compressor bracket(s) as you install the alternator brackets.

Install the larger alternator bracket that mounts near the center of the crankcase. Screw the 12mm mounting bolts into the case finger tight. If your setup has a smaller bracket attached to the left side of the large bracket, attach it loosely to the cylinder head with a 12mm bolt. Now torque the bracket bolts to 14 ft. lbs.

If the slotted adjustment bracket is still attached to the alternator, remove the adjusting bolt from the alternator. Install the slotted adjustment bracket on the top front of the left cylinder head and tighten the bolt with your fingers.

Depending on your setup, install the alternator on the large bracket with the two 12mm bolts and nuts or with the long 12mm bolt and nut. A spark plug wire loom might be on one or more of the attaching nuts. Just get the nuts finger tight. Now screw the adjusting bolt through the adjustment slot on the bracket and into the ear on the alternator. When everything is lined up, torque the bolt at the bottom of the slotted bracket to 14 ft. lbs.

Install the alternator drive belt and adjust the belt tension (Chapter 10, Procedure 3).

Step 6. Install Intake Manifold.

You've cleaned the EGR valve and tube, the EGR passage in the manifold, the mating surfaces on the intake manifold and cylinder heads, right? Use a wire brush to clean the manifold mounting bolts, then coat the threads with antiseize compound or engine oil.

Set new intake manifold gaskets in place on top of the cylinder heads. Don't use gasket sealer. Set the manifold in position and install the mounting bolts, washers, and any brackets that were attached with the bolts. It's obvious where the long bolts go. Torque the bolts to 15 ft. lbs.

Connect the small water bypass hose from the bypass pipe to the bottom front of the manifold or carburetor. If you have a bypass hose from the right side of the intake manifold to the crankcase, connect it now. Tighten the hose clamps.

Install the EGR tube between the manifold and cylinder head. Put antiseize compound on the threads, then screw in both nuts with your fingers until you're sure they aren't cross-threaded. Tighten the nuts with a wrench. If your EGR pipe has a heat shield, slide it into position near the top of the pipe, then tighten the two 10mm bolts.

Reconnect the vacuum hose(s) from the intake manifold to other parts of the engine (vacuum advance/retard unit on the distributor, for example). Look for other vacuum hoses or electrical wires on the intake manifold that can be connected to the engine now.

Step 7. Install Spark Plugs, Distributor Cap, and Spark Plug Wires

Check and adjust the spark plug gaps (Chapter 7, Procedure 11, Step 3). Smear a light coat of antiseize compound on the threads.

Rebuilders: Install the spark plugs in the cylinder heads, but don't tighten them with the spark plug socket yet.

EVERYONE (except rebuilders): Install the spark plugs and tighten them with the spark plug socket and ratchet (Chapter 7, Procedure 11, Steps 3 and 6).

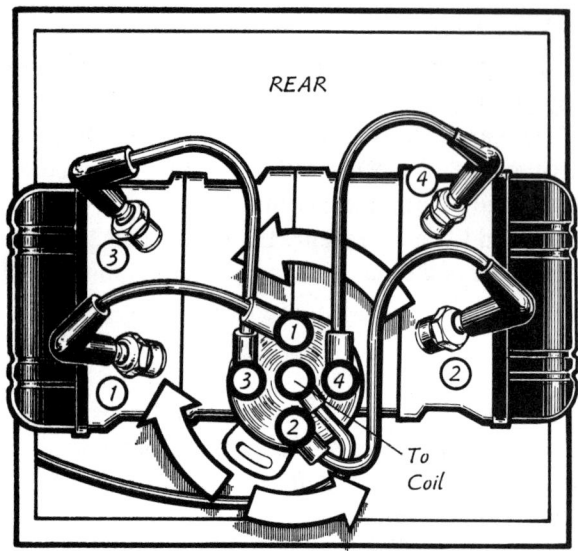

EVERYONE: Inspect the distributor cap and rotor (Chapter 7, Procedure 9, Steps 2 and 3). Replace them with new ones if they're getting funky. Use a Volt/Ohm meter to check the resistance of the spark plug wires (Chapter 10, Procedure 13). Replace them if the resistance values are higher than normal.

Install the distributor dust shield (if you have one), then the rotor. Set the engine to firing position for cylinder #1. Note where the rotor is pointing.

Fit the distributor cap on the distributor so the tabs fit into the notches. Secure the cap with the spring clips. Thread the wire from the #1 distributor post (remember where the rotor is pointing?) to the #1 spark plug. Push the end of the spark plug wire onto the plug until you feel it snap into place. If you didn't mark the spark plug wires, go *counterclockwise* around the distributor cap from the #1 spark plug wire. The wires connect to cylinder #3, then #2, then #4. Install the spark plug wires in the plastic wire looms.

Step 8. Do This and That.

If you removed the drain plugs from the bottom of the cylinder heads, round up the plugs and clean the threads with a wire brush. Coat the threads with antiseize compound or Permatex #2. Find new aluminum washers in the gasket set that fit the plugs. If you didn't get new washers, you can use the old ones if they aren't broken or bent. Screw the plugs into the bottom of the heads and tighten them with a 14mm socket and ratchet.

If you're installing a new throwout bearing, see Chapter 15, Procedure 12, Step 6.

Find a tiny new rubber O-ring for the dipstick tube. Remove the old O-ring, then put some oil on the thicker part of the stick where the O-ring fits. Slide the new O-ring into the slot. Stick the dipstick into the dipstick tube on the crankcase.

'75 models: See Chapter 12, Procedure 3, Step 2, to install the air pump.

'82 and newer models: Install the air suction valves (ASVs) if you have them.

Power Steering models: Install the power steering bracket on the front of the engine. Torque the three bolts to 25 ft. lbs.

PROCEDURE 24: INSTALL THE ENGINE

OK. The repair work has been done. Look around for unfinished business that should be taken care of before the engine is installed. Take a few minutes and clean your tools and work area so you won't be tripping over things while wrestling the engine into the car. Be careful while installing the engine; it's heavy. Have someone available to help guide the engine into place on the transaxle.

Condition: Engine has been removed for repair.

Tools and Materials: Phase 1 tool set, cherry picker engine hoist or strong Friend(s). If you rebuilt the engine or removed the cylinder heads for a valve job or gasket replacement, you'll need the tune-up tools and special sockets for retorquing the cylinder heads.

Remarks: Once the engine is in, remove the labels as you reconnect the hoses and wires so you'll know which ones still need to be connected.

Procedure 24, Step 1   Engine Removal and Repair   447

Some Grease Pit Lore: When I was rebuilding engines at the old Grease Pit Garage, one of my cohorts would occasionally sneak a piston pin circlip onto my workbench just before I was ready to install a freshly rebuilt engine. Upon seeing the circlip I would panic (Freak Out, as we said in those days) at the thought of having to take the engine apart again to install the circlip I'd forgotten. After an hour or so of my ranting and raving, the culprit would confess and we would all have a good laugh.

This kind of joke ended suddenly when the person who put the circlip on the workbench forgot about it and left the garage for the day before I found it. No one else knew he had left the clip so no one could confess. There was no way I could be sure whether it was a joke or whether I had actually forgotten to install the clip without taking the engine apart—which I did. Needless to say, I was pissed off when I found all the circlips in place. The next day the scoundrel apologized profusely, and bought me a case of German beer. We're still good friends.

Step 1. Stick It In.

Cover the carburetor with a clean rag, then attach the cherry picker or board to the engine. If you're using a board, do you remember how much space to leave above the board? If not, you'll have to guess. Use a floor jack or the Subaru jack to raise the transaxle about 1".

Automatic transmission people: Turn the crank so one of the mounting holes on the torque plate is in the center of the timing hole. If you've moved the torque converter on the transaxle, rotate it so a mounting hole will align with the timing hole on the engine.

EVERYONE: Raise the engine high enough to clear the front of the car, then lower it into the engine compartment.

Manual transmission people: Tilt the rear of the engine down slightly so it matches the angle of the shaft sticking out of the transmission. Align the transmission shaft with the hole in the pressure plate.

EVERYONE: Align the two bottom engine mounting studs with the holes in the transaxle housing. Gently push the engine toward the transaxle. If everything is aligned, the engine will slide right in. On manual transmission models, you might have to wiggle the engine or turn the crank pulley a little so the splines on the transmission shaft can slide into the clutch disc.

Once the engine slides in so the flywheel housing touches the transmission housing all the way around, you can remove the hoist. Install the two upper mounting nuts, bolts, and washers, then install the two nuts and washers on the lower engine mounting studs. Tighten all four mounting nuts.

'75-'79 models: Install all four 14mm bolts that attach the bottom of the engine to the two motor mount arms. Turn the bolts several turns with your fingers to be sure they aren't cross-threaded or hitting the arms. While installing the bolts you can wiggle the engine and/or the arms, or raise or lower the jack to align the holes. When the bolts are all in and tight, lower and remove the jack under the transmission.

'80 and newer models: Guide the two motor-mount bolts through the holes in the motor-mount brackets. Lower the jack under the transmission a little at a time until you can screw the bolts into the crankcase a few turns with your fingers. Tighten the bolts, then lower the jack all the way.

Automatic transmission people: Use a socket on the crank pulley to rotate the engine until one of the driveplate bolt holes is in the center of the timing hole on the flywheel housing. Use a screwdriver to rotate the torque converter until a bolt hole aligns with the hole in the torque plate. If you can't move the torque converter with a screwdriver, jack up the front of the car until both wheels are off the ground. Rotate the front wheels the same direction until a bolt hole on the torque converter is aligned with the hole on the drive plate. Install one of the bolts until it's finger tight, then lower the car. Use a socket on the crank pulley bolt to turn the engine so you can install the other three bolts finger tight. Now torque all four bolts to 20 ft. lbs.

Install new exhaust pipe gaskets on the studs on the bottom of the cylinder heads. If there are bumps on one side of the gaskets, install the bumpy side toward the exhaust pipe assembly (away from the cylinder head). Don't use gasket sealer on the gaskets. Push the exhaust pipe assembly over the mounting studs, then install and tighten the lockwashers and nuts. If you have an air stove, install it on the right exhaust pipe with the 10mm nuts. Install and tighten the exhaust pipe assembly bolt at the rear of the transmission if you removed it.

EVERYONE: THE ENGINE IS IN! Now let's see how well you labeled the wires and hoses as you disconnected them.

Step 2. Electrical Connections.

If your model has large wiring-harness connectors, align the tabs, grooves, or the shape of the connectors (they'll only fit one way), then connect them. Be sure they lock into place.

Connect the following wires to their respective gizmos. Even if you have harness connectors, go through this list to be sure everthing's properly hooked up.

Oil pressure switch wire: To the oil pressure switch on the front of the engine.

Automatic choke wire: To the wire attached to the round automatic choke unit on the top right side of the carb. It's on the top left side if you have a Carter/Weber carb.

Anti-diesel valve wire: To the thumb-size gizmo sticking out of the left front corner of the carb.

Temperature sending switch wire: To the temperature sending switch on the right side of the intake manifold.

Distributor wire: It attaches either to the two poles on the coil, to a plastic wire connector, or to a push-on connector on the side of the distributor.

Large high-tension coil wire: To the center of the distributor cap. Fit the wire into the plastic spark plug wire loom.

Alternator wires: To the rear of the alternator. You did label the small wires, didn't you?

Step 3. Mechanical Connections.

Pitching stopper: Install the front end of the pitching stopper rod and bushing through the bracket on the rear of the engine, then slip the rear end onto its mount on the firewall. You may have to wiggle it to get it on the stud. Install and tighten the nuts and washers on both ends of the pitching stopper.

Clutch return spring: Connect one end of the spring to the clutch release lever and the other end to the left side of the intake manifold or to a bracket on the engine, depending on your setup.

Hill-holder cable: If you have a hill-holder, see Chapter 13, Procedure 18, Step 1, to connect the cable to the clutch release lever and mounting bracket. You'll have to wait until you can drive the car to adjust the cable (Chapter 13, Procedure 17).

Fuel line(s): Connect the fuel line to the carburetor or fuel pump. Now reconnect the fuel return hose and the vent hose (if you have them).

Heater hoses: Reconnect the heater hoses to the intake manifold and the bypass pipe or to the two splicers on the rear of the engine. Tighten the clamps.

Accelerator cable: See Chapter 11, Procedure 3, Steps 6 and 7, to attach the accelerator cable to the bracket and carburetor.

Adjust clutch (manual transmissions): Check the clutch free play and adjust it if necessary (Chapter 15, Procedure 1).

Hoses: Check the entire engine for disconnected hoses. Aren't you glad you carefully labeled each hose as you disconnected it. If your model has a master vac unit, be sure to connect the large vacuum hose to the check valve or intake manifold. Don't forget to connect the vacuum line to the automatic transmission, if you have one.

Air conditioner compressor: If your model has air conditioning, wrestle the compressor back onto its bracket, then install the mounting bolts. If the mounting bolts are also the drive belt adjustment bolts, don't tighten them until the drive belt is installed. If the mounting bolts are not involved with the belt adjustment, tighten them. If you had to remove the hoses from the compressor, slide them onto the fittings and tighten the clamps.

Power steering pump: If you have power steering, install the power steering pump on its bracket and tighten the two bolts and the nut on the rear to 35 ft. lbs.

Drive belts: See Chapter 10, Procedure 3, to inspect, install, and adjust the alternator drive belt. Install the air conditioner belt, then the power steering belt, if you have them. Why not install all new belts while it's convenient?

'75 4WD models with a belt driven fan: See Chapter 10, Procedure 3, Step 6, to install and adjust the drive belt.

Radiator and hoses: See Chapter 16, Procedure 7, Step 8, to install the radiator. Connect the radiator hoses to the engine (Chapter 16, Procedure 2, Step 3). Connect the thermoswitch wire, the electric fan motor wires, and the radiator ground wire. They should all be labeled.

If you have an automatic transmission, don't forget to connect the transmission oil cooler hoses to the side of the radiator.

Cruise control: If you disconnected any vacuum hoses, cables, or little chains during engine removal, reconnect them now.

Final check: Take a few minutes to check the engine carefully for unfinished business. Check your notebook for things you might have written about wires and hoses on your model that weren't mentioned in the text.

Step 4. Do This and That.

Engine oil: See that the drain plug is installed and tight in the oil pan, and that the oil filter is installed. Add fresh oil to the engine until it reaches the top line on the engine dipstick (Chapter 7, Procedure 3, Step 5).

Coolant: Be sure the radiator drain plug and cylinder head drain plugs are installed and tight, then add fresh coolant to the radiator (Chapter 16, Procedure 3, Step 3). Check for hose clamps that are loose.

Battery connections: Clean, then attach the engine end of the negative battery cable to the engine. Clean the battery posts and cable clamps, then attach the cables to the battery (Chapter 10, Procedure 1, Step 3). If you removed it, attach the positive battery cable bracket to the right cylinder head.

Now take a minute to clear the tools, rags, and beer cans away from the engine compartment. Look for wires and hoses that haven't been reconnected. Clean your hands, then put something on the car seat to protect it from your greasy body, and get ready to start the engine.

PROCEDURE 25: PRE-STARTING PROCEDURE

Before starting the engine, we need to be sure the oil pump is working so all those new parts receive a good supply of the slippery stuff. Here's how:

Step 1. Check Oil Pressure.

Remove the spark plugs, then remove the coil wire from the center of the distributor cap and ground it with your jumper wire (Chapter 7, Procedure 11, Step 4). Get in the car and crank the engine for about 15 seconds while watching the oil pressure warning light or oil pressure gauge, depending on your setup. After 15 seconds, let the starter cool for two or three minutes, then crank the engine for another 15 seconds. Do this until the oil pressure light goes out or the oil pressure gauge starts moving. Don't worry if it takes several tries; the oil filter and oil galleys in the engine have to fill up with oil before any pressure can develop in the system. If you crank the engine a dozen times or more and still have no oil pressure, see Procedure 27, *DON'T PANIC*.

Step 2. Install Spark Plugs, Connect Gauges, Final Check.

OK, you have oil pressure, right? Install and tighten the spark plugs (Chapter 7, Procedure 11, Step 6). Fit the spark plug wires on the appropriate spark plugs and push them into place. Remove the jumper wire and reconnect the coil wire to the distributor. Before starting the engine, give it one more quick check, top and bottom, for oil, gas, and coolant leaks. If you find any, remedy the problem.

Use small phillips screwdrivers, punches, or tape to plug the small vacuum hoses or pipes that are normally connected to the air cleaner (Chapter 7, Procedure 5, Step 4).

Hook up the tack/dwell gauge (if you have one) so you can adjust the engine idle speed.

If the distributor was removed (or just moved), or you messed with the point gap or air gap, hook up the timing light so you can time the engine as soon as it starts (Chapter 7, Procedure 13).

Have a screwdriver handy so you can adjust the idle speed (Chapter 7, Procedure 12, Step 6).

Check the engine compartment for loose rags, tools, and wires that might get caught in the drive belts.

PROCEDURE 26: START YOUR ENGINE!

The big moment has arrived! All the neighbors are hanging around to watch the big event, the kids are laughing at the nervous look on your face, your hands are sweaty and shaking. Right? It still happens to me everytime I start an engine I've rebuilt.

More Grease Pit Lore: Before starting a freshly rebuilt engine at the Grease Pit, we would play Tschaikovsky's *Capriccio Italien* very loud while taking turns blowing a certain kind of smoke down the carburetor to give the engine good *Car*ma. It seemed to work!

Step 1. Start the Engine.

OK, start the engine and listen to it purr. If it won't start, skip down to the ***DON'T PANIC*** section (Procedure 27). Let the engine warm up enough to idle, then check the points dwell if you have breaker points (Chapter 7, Procedure 10, Step 3), and the ignition timing (Chapter 7, Procedure 13, Step 3). Now adjust the idle speed to about 1200 rpm and let the engine warm up until the electric cooling fan turns on. Lower the idle speed to the normal setting, then turn the engine off. While the engine is warming up, check the temperature gauge frequently and turn the engine off if the gauge goes over ¾ of the way toward the HOT end of the scale. If the engine overheats, check the thermoswitch wire and electric fan motor wires (Chapter 16, Procedure 10, Step 6, B.1).

Step 2. A Very Important Step.

If you didn't remove the cylinder heads, skip this step.

Whew, aren't you proud of yourself? Now let the engine cool for at least four hours. I know you want to hop in and go for a ride, but don't. You're not quite ready to boldly go where no Soob has gone before.

When the engine has cooled down, retorque the heads (Chapter 7, Procedure 6). This is very important! You'll see how much the head bolts have loosened when you retorque them. If you skip the retorqueing, the head gaskets will start leaking within a few hundred miles. After the heads are torqued, do Chapter 7, Procedure 7, to adjust the valves. If you have hydraulic valve lifters, do Procedure 22, Step 2, in this chapter to adjust the valves, then you can forget about adjusting them until you remove the rocker arm assemblies again (or until the lifters start making clicking noises).

While the engine is cooling (or before you drive the car), install the flat piece of sheet metal below the right exhaust pipe and tighten the 10mm bolts. Install the air cleaner (Chapter 7, Procedure 5, Step 5). Be sure all the hoses are connected.

Step 3. What Else But—

Go for a ride. If you installed new piston rings, find a deserted street or highway, put the transmission in 3rd gear (DRIVE on automatics), and accelerate quickly up to about 55 mph, then let up on the gas pedal until you're down to about 20 mph. Do this about a dozen times to "seat" the rings. You might need to adjust the carburetor after driving a few miles (Chapter 7, Procedure 12).

If you have a hill-holder, find a hill and adjust the hill-holder cable (Chapter 13, Procedure 17).

Step 4. Don't Skip This!

If you've done a ring and valve job or rebuilt the engine, change the **engine oil** and **oil filter** after driving about 300 miles. Also at 300 miles, **retorque the heads** (*everyone*) and **adjust the valves** (*except cars with hydraulic lifters*). Do the same things (oil and filter change, retorque heads, and adjust valves) again after driving another 1000 miles. The reason: the new parts are "breaking in" and the oil gets contaminated with fine metal particles that can cause premature wear on the engine parts. After the 1,300-mile oil and filter change, head retorque and valve adjustment, get on the maintenance schedule in Chapter 7. You'll be glad you did.

PROCEDURE 27: DON'T PANIC!

This little section is to prevent suicide, ulcers, and/or divorce, in case the engine doesn't have oil pressure or won't start right away.

No oil pressure: You're sure you put oil in the engine? Check it. Is the correct wire connected to the oil pressure switch? Check it. If everything seems OK, the most likely reason you're not getting oil pressure is that the oil pump is not primed so it can't suck oil out of the oil pan. Try this: remove the oil pressure switch and crank the engine for a couple of seconds. If oil squirts out the OPS hole, install the oil pressure switch and crank the engine some more. If the gauge still shows no oil pressure, replace the oil pressure switch.

If oil doesn't squirt out of the OPS hole when the switch is removed, remove the oil pump and squirt more engine assembly lube into the pump holes until the pump is packed, and into the oil pickup hole in the crankcase (Procedure 19, Step 1). Install the pump and try cranking the engine again.

Still no pressure? This is a bit risky if you run the engine too long, but by now you're probably ready to try anything. Install the spark plugs and coil wire, then start the engine while watching the oil pressure light or gauge. Once the engine starts, if the light doesn't go off or the gauge doesn't move within 10 to 15 seconds, turn the engine off. If you run the engine without oil pressure for more than a few seconds, the bearings will be damaged and you'll have to take the whole thing apart and start over again. If the oil warning light goes off or the gauge starts showing pressure now, everything is OK; the oil pump just wasn't primed. If you still don't have oil pressure after running the engine for a few seconds, it's time to seek professional advice.

Engine won't start: You have oil pressure, but the engine won't start. Here's what to check for.

Electrical checks: Be sure the distributor wires are connected to the coil and that the rotor and distributor are installed properly. Do Chapter 9, Procedure 1B, to see if the coil and spark plugs are getting a good supply of electricity (juice).

If you removed the distributor, try rotating it a bit one way, then try to start the engine. If it doesn't start, rotate the distributor the other direction and try again. If the engine starts, set the ignition timing and tighten the distributor bolt (Chapter 7, Procedure 13). If the engine still won't start, set the engine to TDC firing position for cylinder #1 and see if the rotor is pointing directly at the #1 spark plug post (Chapter 7, Procedure 4). If it isn't, remove the distributor bolt, lift the distributor slightly, and turn the rotor so it points to #1. Rotate it just a bit further, then push the distributor back down into the crankcase. Install the hold-down bolt, then try to start the engine. Time it as soon as it starts (Chapter 7, Procedure 13). If the spark plugs are getting spark but the engine won't start, do the fuel check below.

Fuel check: If you have a Hitachi carburetor, look at the round sight glass on the left side of the carb. If you don't see a line across the glass indicating the carb is getting gas, see Chapter 11, Procedure 4, to check the fuel supply.

If the engine still refuses to start, it's time to seek professional assistance.

Chapter 17

CHAPTER 18
MECHANIC'S TIPS, SECRETS, ODDS 'N ENDS

This chapter is a grab bag of things to help get you past unexpected and unwelcome circumstances—like broken bolts, stripped threads, and having to use a brake drum or gear puller. The *condition* under which you need the procedure is stated in the procedure's name and, since the procedures are all short, the *tools and materials* required for the procedures will be found within the procedure or steps. Don't forget your goggles when dealing with things like stuck or stubborn bolts, wheel pullers, or where you'll be using a hammer or hacksaw.

PROCEDURE 1: HOW TO CURE HICCUPS

Pour a glass of fresh water and put a *drinking straw* in it. (There's probably a leftover straw from the local fast food cesspool in the glove box or under the seats.) Set the glass on a table, stick a finger firmly into each ear, then drink the water through the straw. Like magic, the hiccups are gone. I've never seen this method fail! What other automotive repair manual gives you practical, down-to-earth information like this?

PROCEDURE 2: HIGH-PERFORMANCE PARTS RAP (Making It Go!)

I confess. I was a teenage hot rodder in the late fifties when Detroit was cranking out cars with big muscles (not just big cars). I cut my teeth (so to speak) at the age of 14 by replacing the four-cylinder engine in my

Model A Ford with a big V8 engine. Then it was on to a hopped-up '57 Chevy and finally to a very fast '62 Corvette, before my primary interests (and expenses) changed to the fairer sex. Even though I don't hang out at drag strips anymore, I still enjoy driving cars that respond to my occasionally impulsive right foot. Through the years, however, I've come to the conclusion that every engine modification done to a car in the name of "performance" shortens the life of the car. The main reason is that if the car will go faster, you'll at least occasionally drive it harder and faster than you would if the car was "stock" (everything factory original). So keep in mind that you sacrifice longevity (and sometimes reliability and economy) when you make engine modifications. Certain suspension modifications, however, might make your car a little safer to drive and more economical than a stock model as well as more fun to drive.

As of this writing (1989), finding high-performance engine and suspension parts for Subarus is not easy. In fact, the only bolt-on engine modification available that I'm aware of is the installation of a *Weber carburetor*. I put a Weber on my '78 Brat and was thrilled with the increase in power, smoother operation, and unchanged gas mileage. I love my Weber!

However, there are a couple of problems with converting to a Weber: (1) they're illegal in some states except for racing and off-road use, and (2) they come with no installation instructions. Unless you have a good understanding of how to bypass some of the emission control systems (or know someone who does), you could possibly create some expensive problems. Installing a Weber on an '80 or newer model would be especially difficult because the original electronic carburetor is integrated into the fuel and ignition systems. Ah, for the simple days of yore when you could just bolt on a different carburetor and drive away.

The good people at Redline, Inc. (the Weber importers), will probably develop a "Street Lethal" kit for Subarus someday (like they have for some other cars). These are legal and come with all the necessary fittings and instructions. If you're interested in a Weber, shop around at the parts stores for the best price, or if no one in your area sells Webers, call Redline, Inc., at (800) 262-1565 if you live in California or (800) 932-3787 if you live outside California. They'll be able to direct you to the nearest dealer.

ADDCO Co., in Florida, sells suspension modification parts in the form of a *heavy-duty stabilizer bar* for the front and an *anti-sway bar* for the rear. These bars reduce the amount your Soob tilts when going around corners and curves and thus keeps the weight more evenly distributed to all four wheels so you have better balance, stability, and therefore traction. The installation of the bars is a relatively simple bolt-on operation. Their catalog includes a good rap called "Handling: What It Is—And How to Get It." Call ADDCO Co. at (305) 844-2531.

The addition of a plastic or rubber "*air dam*" mounted below the front bumper will help keep your Soob's nose down at high speed and thus increase traction and aerodynamics. An air dam will probably improve your gas mileage slightly and also make your Soob look meaner. Kamei U.S.A., Inc., 5213 W. Broadway, Minneapolis, MN 55429, and Flex Dam (you'll have to get these through a parts store) are two companies that make air dams. Rear spoilers or "whales tails" are only effective at speeds in excess of 100 mph, so they are a waste of money on a Subaru.

If your local parts stores can't get the high-performance suspension parts or air dams, call Mike at Mahneke Motors in Goleta, California, (805) 964-4068.

PROCEDURE 3: TOUGH OR BROKEN NUTS, SCREWS, AND BOLTS

First, be absolutely certain you're turning the nut, bolt, or screw the right direction to remove it. Bolts and screws turn *counterclockwise* as viewed from the head. Nuts turn *counterclockwise* as viewed from the threaded end of the bolt, stud, or screw.

Step 1. Dealing with Tight Nuts.

If you have a nut that refuses to budge, sprinkle it repeatedly with *penetrating oil* (holy water) and let it soak for a few minutes. (WD-40 isn't technically penetrating oil, but it's often thin enough to do the job; Marvel Mystery oil also works well.) If possible, use a *6-point box-end wrench* or *6-point socket* to get a better grip on the nut and to avoid rounding off its corners. (Open-end wrenches and 12-point sockets are more likely to slip, damaging the nut.) Find a *cheater bar* (a piece of pipe large enough to slide over the wrench) and slip it onto the wrench handle for added leverage. Pull counterclockwise on the end of the cheater bar. **CAUTION:** Cheater bars and the wrench handles they hold tend to slip; make sure the socket or wrench is securely on the nut or bolt head, and the cheater pipe is well over the shaft of the wrench handle.

If the points on a nut or bolt head get rounded off, try *Vise Grip* or *Channel Lock* pliers first (see Chapter 5: *Tools*). If they don't work, take the next smaller size socket out of the box, file down the sides of the nut a little and jam the socket down on the nut with a hammer. Sprinkle a little more holy water while mumbling whatever incantations one mumbles while sprinkling holy water, then put the ratchet on the socket and turn the nut off.

When all else fails, use a hacksaw or chisel to cut off one side of the nut. Make the cut parallel to the stud, then use the Vise Grips to unscrew what's left of the nut.

Step 2. Dealing with Stubborn Bolts and Screws.

Repeatedly sprinkle the bolt or screw with penetrating oil and let it soak. Give the head of the bolt or screw a few solid whacks straight on the head with a hammer. The straighter the blows, the more effective they will be. If you can't get to a screw with the hammer, fit the screwdriver blade into the slot, then rap on the other end of the screwdriver. You hope the hammering will jar the threads loose so the bolt or screw can be removed. If a tight bolt still won't move, use a *cheater bar* on the wrench as described in Step 1.

Sawing the Nut

If the corners of a bolt get rounded off so the wrench slips, try using Vise Grips or Channel Lock pliers. If that fails, file down the sides of bolt head, then jam the next smaller socket on with a hammer and try the ratchet again. (You may have to use the hammer and a screwdriver or chisel to get the bolt out of the socket once you've unscrewed it.)

If the slot in a screwhead gets widened and tapered so the screwdriver slips out easily when you try to turn it, try straightening the sides of the slot with a hacksaw or small file, then use a larger screwdriver. If you can grab the screwhead with Vise Grips, clamp them on, then use the Vise Grips and screwdriver together to turn the screw.

When the slots on phillips head screws disappear, use a hacksaw to cut a slot in the head, then use a regular screwdriver. If you can grab the head with Vise Grips, clamp them on and use the Vise Grips and screwdriver together. Another technique is to clamp the Vise Grips onto the shaft of the screwdriver as a turning handle. This allows you to use maximum force to hold the screwdriver in the slots. Remember, *counterclockwise* to unscrew it.

Step 3. Broken Bolts or Screws.

If a bolt or screwhead breaks off and there's still a stub of it left sticking out, soak it with penetrating oil, then smack the stub squarely on the head with a hammer a few times. Use Vise Grips or Channel Locks to grab the stub and turn it out. If you have access to a *propane torch* and the stub is in a place where there's absolutely no danger of starting a fire, heat up the area around the stub (not the stub itself), then try removing it with Vise Grips or Channel Locks.

If the bolt or screw is broken off flush with whatever it's screwed into, you'll need to round up an *electric drill, drill bits, center punch*, and a gizmo called an *"easy out"* of the right size for your broken bolt or screw.

Your friendly parts store counterperson should be able to tell you which size to use. Tap the center punch exactly in the center of the broken part, then drill a small hole straight through the center of the bolt. If you drill a crooked hole, the easy out probably won't work and you also run the risk of damaging the hole threads. Have Friend help you align the drill bit so it's straight while you drill the hole.

Next, drill the hole to the proper size for the easy out. The proper drill bit size should be stamped on the side of the easy out, or ask the parts person what size to use. Use the hammer to tap the easy out into the hole, then use a crescent wrench to gently unscrew the broken bolt. Be very careful not to break the easy out. You'd be in real trouble then because easy outs are made of super-hard material and can't be drilled out. If you're not up for all this, take the car or the part with the broken bolt to a garage or machine shop and have them remove the broken bolt or screw.

PROCEDURE 4: DEALING WITH BROKEN OR STRIPPED STUDS

A stud is a headless bolt with threads on both ends—what a way to go through life! Studs you might have to deal with are on the cylinder head where the exhaust manifold attaches, and the cylinder heads are attached to the crankcase with long studs. If the nut is rusted to the stud so the stud comes out when you unscrew the nut, buy and install a new stud and nut. Put *Loctight* (a compound you find at the parts store) on the threads before screwing it in so it won't come out the next time.

Step 1. Removing and Installing Studs.

Studs are removed and installed by using two nuts locked together on the exposed stud threads or by *very careful* use of Vise Grips or pliers on the nonthreaded (middle) portion of the stud.

To use the two-nut method, screw two nuts onto the stud far enough so the end of the stud sticks through the outside nut. Lock the nuts by tightening them toward each other with two wrenches. Now remove the stud by turning the inside nut *counterclockwise* with your wrench. Install the stud by turning the outside nut *clockwise*.

If you're removing a stud with stripped threads, just grab it with Vise Grips or Channel Locks and unscrew it. You'll be putting in a new stud anyway.

When using Vise Grips or pliers to install good or new studs, be careful to not damage the threads on either end. Grab it only at the unthreaded place in the middle. Be sure the threads you're screwing the stud into are clean and in good condition. Grab the stud as close to the center as possible and don't squeeze any tighter than necessary.

Step 2. Removing Broken Studs.

Follow the instructions in Procedure 2, Step 3, for removing broken bolts and screws.

Step 3. Other Troubles with Studs.

When you're tightening a nut on a stud and the nut keeps turning without tightening, you have a stripped nut, a stripped stud, or a stud that's pulling out. First remove the nut from the stud, either pulling or prying it off as you turn it, then examine both the nut and the stud for stripping—flat and mashed places on the threads. Perhaps the stud is unhurt and all you need is a new nut. If the stud is stripped, you have to remove the stud and replace it with a new one from the Subaru dealer (Step 1).

If the stud itself pulls out as you tighten the nut, the threads that hold the stud are usually stripped. You'll need to have Subaru, a garage, or a machine shop drill and tap (thread) the hole for a larger stud. Better yet, have them install a *Helicoil* into the stripped hole so you can use the original stud. I prefer Helicoils because they're made of tough steel and are less likely to strip out again later.

PROCEDURE 5: STARTING A NUT

Here are a few tricks to getting a nut started on a bolt or stud, especially if you can't see the place where you are working and have to feel. Use your index finger to hold the nut on the end of the stud and twist the nut around with your thumb and second finger. Twist it *counterclockwise* a little until you feel the threads slip into place, then *clockwise* to screw it on.

If the threads are so bunged up on a stud that the nut won't start, tap it a little with a small hammer as you turn it with a box-end wrench until it's down one thread; then it should go on with the wrench.

If the space around a nut is too confining to let you turn the nut with your fingers, hold the nut onto the end of the stud with your forefinger and turn it on with the point of a screwdriver. Use a wrench to tighten it.

If the bolt you are putting a nut on tends to turn, you can often wedge the bolt with a small screwdriver or knife blade to hold it still while you start the nut.

PROCEDURE 6: TIGHTENING THINGS HELD ON BY MORE THAN ONE BOLT OR NUT

Anywhere a part is held on with more than one bolt or nut, never tighten first one nut or bolt all the way, then the next one. Always tighten them gradually in sequence: first tighten one a little, then the one opposite the first one a little, then one next to the first one a little, and so on until they are all fairly tight. This puts equal stress on the part or parts. Do the final tightening the same way until they are all tightened or torqued. This will save you broken assemblies and distorted plates, such as the cylinder heads and clutch pressure plate.

PROCEDURE 7: HOW TO USE A TORQUE WRENCH

Torque is measured in foot pounds (ft. lbs.), inch pounds (in. lbs.), or meter kilograms (Mkg). I assume you have a ft. lbs. torque wrench. Inch pounds can be converted to ft. lbs. by dividing by 12. The U.S. ft. lb. represents the number of pounds applied to the end of a wrench one foot long (more technically, the leverage one foot away from the center of the nut or bolt you are turning).

Torque wrenches come in three basic types: one slips or clicks when the preset torque is reached, another has a dial you read as you turn, and the third (cheapest and most common) type has a skinny rod coming up from the head of the wrench with a point on the end of it that points to numbers (the torque you've reached) on a calibrated arc scale on the handle. Here's how to use all these kinds of torque wrenches.

First, be sure the bolt and/or nut threads are clean and lightly oiled. Find the correct *torque value*; these are given right in the procedure you're dealing with. Attach the correct socket, then hold the torque wrench and socket firmly on the nut or bolt with one hand on the head (socket end) of the wrench. Stay clear of the pointer rod if your wrench has one. Get yourself in position where you can see the reading clearly on the arc scale or dial. Now pull on the handle of the torque wrench with a steady, slow pull until the pointer or dial needle points to the correct number, or until you hear a click (depending on type). Don't add extra torque "just to be sure." Trust your torque wrench! If you're doing a set of bolts (such as on the head or clutch housing) first run all the bolts in the series up to about half the final torque, then up to ¾ of the final torque, then up to the final torque all around. Go around again to be sure none were missed.

PROCEDURE 8: MECHANICS' QUICK DWELL TEST

For those of you with breaker-type distributors, this is a quick way to set the points dwell without having to put everything back together and starting the engine between checks.

You'll need a Friend for this one. Hook up the *dwell gauge*, then pull the *coil wire* out of the center of the distributor cap and ground it with your *jumper wire* (clip the other end to a piece of bare metal on the car). Remove the distributor cap and rotor, then slightly loosen the *points holding screws*. Insert the tip of a medium screwdriver between the *nipples and slot*, or in the *point gap adjusting screw*, depending on your setup.

Be sure the transmission is in Neutral or PARK and the handbrake is ON, then have Friend crank the engine. Adjust the point gap with the screwdriver while watching the dwell meter. When the dwell is correct for your car's specifications, tell Friend to stop cranking the engine. Tighten the points' holding screws, then have Friend crank the engine again and check the dwell reading again. When the dwell is right on, have Friend turn the ignition OFF. Install the rotor and distributor cap. Unclip the jumper wire and plug the coil wire back into the distributor cap. Disconnect the dwell gauge and you're finished.

PROCEDURE 9: HOW TO USE A PULLER (Wheel, Gear, Drum, Etc.)

A puller is a device that grabs onto something and pulls it off or out. There are several types of pullers and many "special application" pullers. They usually have a large bolt in the middle that does the pulling and various types of arms and legs that grab onto what they were built to pull.

A **drum puller** is one built to pull brake drums or discs; they usually have a round *plate* or three *arms* that attach to three lug studs with lug nuts. A "tower" that holds the large bolt through its center is positioned against the end of the axle. Turning the bolt with a wrench forces the arms to pull the drum off the axle.

A word of caution about wheel and drum pullers. When you tighten the center bolt on the puller and the drum or disc doesn't seem to budge, there is a lot of pent-up energy in the puller. The puller could conceivably come flying off. So be sure to wear safety glasses and stand to one side while tightening the large bolt.

A **gear** or **bearing puller** has two or three arms with hooks (jaws) on the ends. They hook over the back of the gear or bearing so when the large screw is turned, the gear or bearing is pulled off the shaft it's mounted on. The same rules apply as for the wheel and drum pullers.

You might need a three-arm (jaw) puller to remove stubborn brake drums or brake discs, and a two-arm (jaw) puller to remove the front wheel bearing housing, tie rod ball joints, and rear wheel bearings on non-4WD models. You can usually find a variety of pullers at your local equipment rental place; if you take one home and find you can't make it fit, take it back. These people are usually understanding and will often help you with further advice on selecting and using pullers. Just ask.

PROCEDURE 10: HOW TO SPLICE ELECTRICAL WIRE AND REPLACE WIRE CONNECTORS

Step 1. Simple Splice.

If you're making a wire longer by adding a piece of wire to it, be sure the wire you're adding is the same gauge or thicker than the wire you're adding it to. (If it's a narrower gauge, it may overheat at that point.)

Strip about ½" of the plastic insulation away from the ends of both wires. Use a *wire stripping tool* if you have one. If not, a knife or in an emergency, your teeth will do. Make *certain* all the juice is off to any wire still attached to the car, and be extra careful not to nick or cut the wire still inside. Twist the bare wire strands on the exposed ends a couple of times so they're wrapped up tight with no loose strands sticking out. Arrange the two wires so they form an X and touch at the points where the insulation ends and the bare wire begins. Hold that point tight with a thumb and forefinger while you twist the two wires together into a spiral shape. Fold the spiral onto the insulation of one of the wires, then give the wires a little tug to test the strength of the splice. Wrap *insulating tape* (electrician's black tape) around one of the wires starting about an inch back from the bare wires. Keep wrapping the tape round and round toward the bare wires until they're covered, then continue wrapping the tape about an inch past the splice. If the tape doesn't seem to stick too well, cut another piece that's a little longer, and spiral wrap again, going the opposite direction.

Step 2. Install Wire Connector.

Wire connectors are available individually or in plastic packets at your local auto supply store. If one comes detached from its wire, it's easy to put on a new one.

If you're splicing two wires together and have a new insulated in-line wire connector handy or you're replacing a connector on the end of a wire, first strip the insulation from the end(s) of the wire(s) as described in Step 1. Stick the twisted bare wire into the wire hole end of the connector, then squeeze that end of the connector with wire stripping pliers or regular pliers. Squeeze the end of the connector as tight as you can. If you're splicing two wires together, install the other wire in the other end of the connector, same as you did with the first, and squeeze with the pliers. Test with a slight tug to make sure the wires are securely attached.

PROCEDURE 11: REPLACE SPEEDOMETER CABLE (OHV Models Only)

First be sure the cable is broken before replacing it.

This procedure does not cover OHC models.

'80 and newer OHV cars and '82-'87 Brats: Remove the plastic panel on the lower left side of the dash. It's held on with phillips screws.

EVERYONE: With flashlight in hand, crawl under and look at the backside of the dashboard for a black, pencil-size cable screwed into the back of the speedometer. The other end of the cable goes through the firewall into the engine compartment. The cable connects to the back of the speedometer by a threaded *plastic ring* which loosens *counterclockwise* by hand to let you pull the end of the cable out of the speedometer. Use pliers if the ring is real tight. (Careful of all those wires under there!) When the ring is loose, just pull the cable free from the back of the speedometer.

Inside this cable is a smaller wire cable with a square end. Gently twirl the square end of the cable with your fingers. If it twists slightly, then stops, the cable is probably good and it's the speedometer that isn't working. Have Subaru or a garage fix or replace it for you. If the cable twists freely with your fingers, give it a little tug to see if it pulls out of the housing. If the inner cable comes completely out, the cable is broken and needs to be replaced. Here's how.

Remove the spare tire if it's in the engine compartment. Now follow the speedometer cable through the firewall into the engine compartment. The other end of the cable attaches to the *transmission*, usually on the top right side. It's attached with a *plastic ring* similar to the one on the speedometer end that you unscrewed with your fingers. Unscrew the ring, using pliers if necessary, then release any *plastic clips* that secure the cable to the car body or engine parts. Pull the old cable through the firewall into the engine compartment.

Now push the speedometer end of the new cable through the hole from the engine side. Get under the dash again and thread the cable through the wires and stuff so you can attach it easily to the rear of the speedometer. Screw the plastic ring onto the threaded stub on the speedometer with your fingers. Fit the rubber grommet around the cable so water and air can't come in through the hole in the firewall. Attach the other end of the cable to the transmission; turn the ring down snugly with your fingers. Reattach the cable to body and/or engine with the plastic clips. Drive the car and see if the speedometer works now. It should.

PROCEDURE 12: REMOVE AND INSTALL INSIDE DOOR PANELS (to Get at Locks, Latch Mechanisms, Window Cranks, Etc.)

Inside your doors are the works for the window crank, lock, door handle mechanisms, and maybe a radio speaker. The door panel is made of fiberboard covered with vinyl and/or fabric and is held on with clips and the door hardware (handles, armrest). It's easy to remove so that you can get at what's inside, for repair or replacement. Use Step 1 alone if you need to replace a broken window crank. Step 2 tells you how to remove and install the armrests and Step 3 tells you how to remove and install the panel.

Step 1. Remove and Install Window Crank.

The window crank is attached to the window operating mechanism inside the door with a U-shaped clip. You'll need a tiny hook (which you can make out of a strong paper clip) to reach between the window crank and the plastic trim ring to remove the clip. I use a Mac tool #SW50 to remove the clips. Here's how: Turn the crank so the handle part is pointing straight up. Push the plastic trim ring away from the handle while you insert your hook through the small opening at the base of the handle. Hook the end of the clip and pull up to remove it. Once the clip is off, the window crank will slide right off. You can remove the trim ring now.

To install the window crank, fit the plastic trim ring into its hole in the door panel. The clip usually gets stretched a little during removal, so squeeze the clip and bend it so the sides are almost touching. Now fit the clip into the slots on the sides of the window crank so the closed end of the clip is toward the handle. Fit the crank onto the shaft, then wiggle the crank while you push it toward the door. When the clip snaps into its groove on the shaft, the crank is installed. If the crank comes off easily, bend the clip so the sides are closer together before installing it on the crank, then push the crank onto the shaft again.

Step 2. Remove and Install Armrests.

The armrest is held on by two or more phillips screws. On some models you may have to pry off a little rubber or plastic plug with a regular screwdriver in order to get at the screw heads. The screws go up through the armrest at about a 45° angle. Unscrew the screws and the armrest should come right off.

To install the armrest, hold it in position while you install the two screws. It's a little tricky to get the screws started, but perseverance will further.

Step 3. Remove and Install the Door Panel.

Before removing the door panel you must first remove the window crank (Step 1), the armrest (Step 2), and the plastic trim around the door handle. Here's how to remove the door handle trim. Pull the door handle toward the inside of the car as far as possible while you remove the phillips screw located in the center of the plastic trim. Remove the screw and wiggle the trim over the handle.

The panel is attached to the door with little clips around the edges. To remove it, slide a large screwdriver between the panel and the door, then twist the screwdriver side-to-side. One of the clips should pop out of its hole in the door. Slip your fingers behind the panel and pull toward you while you get the screwdriver as close as possible to the next clip. Pop that clip with the screwdriver. Now go around the bottom and sides of the panel placing your fingers or the screwdriver as close as possible to the clips to avoid breaking the panel. The top of the panel is either secured with clips like the sides and bottom or it hooks over the top edge of the door. If you have them, remove the clips along the top edge. When all the clips have been released, gently lift the panel away from the door. On some models you'll have to lift up slightly on the panel to unhook the top edge. If you've removed the panel to install speakers, do it now. Just be sure the speakers won't get crunched when you roll the windows down.

Now you can get to the inside door handle, the window operating mechanism, the door lock, and the nuts that attach the outside door handle. If you're here because the inside door handle isn't working, or because you can't lock the door from the inside but you can from the outside, see if one of the long thin rods that go from the inside door handle to the rear of the door is broken. If the other door is working properly, remove its panel and compare the two mechanisms.

To install the door panel, fit it into position over the window operating shaft and inside door handle. If yours is the type that hooks over the top edge of the door, be sure the panel is securely hooked all along the top edge. Align the clips with the holes in the door, then push them in one at a time. Tap around the outer edge of the panel with your fist to seat them fully. Install the arm rest, window crank, and door handle trim and you're finished.

PROCEDURE 13: SOME TIPS FROM *POOR RICHARD'S RABBIT BOOK*

Remarks: The following jewels of wisdom were stolen from Richard Sealey's masterpiece *How to Keep Your*

Volkswagen Rabbit Alive. Although they were written for Rabbits, they are equally applicable to Subarus.

Need a Drop of Oil?

Should you be out in the proverbial boonies and stuck for a spot of oil, remove the dipstick and use the oil adhering to the tip. Clever, huh?

The world record for transferring a pint of oil from the engine to a container using the "one-drop-at-a-time" method is 4 hours, 26 minutes, 12 seconds. (Richard Sealey holds the record.)

Drive Belt Broken?

If one of the drive belts ("fan belts") on the front of the engine breaks and you don't have a spare, you can substitute the leg of a nylon stocking or pair of tights for a belt. That is, if you're wearing nylon stockings or tights. Remove the tights and cut one of the legs off close to the crotch. Pull the liberated leg into a long, thin "belt" and slip it around the pulleys just as you would a real drive belt. Now tie a square knot to attach the ends of the stocking leg. Snug it down as tight as possible. Cut off any excess nylon. Should work fine until you get to civilization.

Buy a new belt at the next parts store you pass. If you don't have a nylon stocking, woven nylon string such as used with camping gear will sometimes work, if you can tie it tight enough. A friend carries a stocking or leg from a panty hose in his on-board emergency tool kit. He's too cheap to carry a spare drive belt and says he likes to help damsels in distress. The nylon stocking emergency drive belt fits any car.

Gas Tank Leak?

During one of my travels, I bounced off a sand dune into a pile of rocks, one that put four tiny holes into the Rabbit's gas tank. Since welding equipment is hard to find in the middle of the Mojave, I whipped out a bar of Dial and had at the tank. If this disaster should happen to you, rub bar soap into the offending split or pinhole. Of course, if you've trashed out your gas tank on a rock and there's a huge gash in it, this method won't work. However, it works beautifully for small holes. Continue rubbing the soap into the holes until the gas no longer flows. Repair the gas tank as soon as you have tools. The temporary repair on the Rabbit has lasted three years. You might say it's part of a continuing experiment.

Shelter

Let me dispel one myth. It isn't a good idea to keep a car in a heated garage. It's lovely to have heat when working on a car but storing a car in one is not so good. If the car underbody is coated with salt from winter roads, the warmth of the surrounding atmosphere will accelerate the rusting process. Rinse off salt and dirt from beneath the car before putting it into any garage, warm or freezing. (You'd think that after 100 years, and the scheming of thousands of engineers, they'd have come up with truly rust-proof production cars. Even fiberglass Corvettes can develop frame rot.)

And Yet Another Gem from Richard Sealey!

Many years ago a certain well-known dairy company started a nationwide competition to find a catchy jingle to promote their canned milk. A cowboy from the Midwest sent in the following prize-winning entry:

> No tits to pull,
> no hay to pitch,
> Just punch a hole
> in the son of a bitch!

(Un)fortunately this jingle was never used. If you know of other time-saving and/or labor-saving tips, please let me know. ASA NISI MASA!

MAIL BAG

Thanks to those who sent me letters with compliments, complaints, and suggestions about the first edition of this book. And to a couple of people who wanted more things covered in the manual, my apologies. To keep the size and price of the manual reasonable, I have to draw the line somewhere; and I've tried to include the procedures most people are likely to need.

Here are a few suggestions sent in by readers. If your catalytic converter blows out, you might be able to find one in a mail order catalog, like J. C. Whitney, or at your local muffler shop for about half of what it would cost from the dealer.

Carburetor cleaner is great for removing DOJ/CVJ grease from the upholstery.

Split DOJ/CVJ boots are available at a major auto parts chain run by three guys called Manny, Moe, and Jack.

Be sure the plug in the end of the DOJ housing is securely in place before installing the DOJ. It makes a terrible mess and you have to take everything apart again if the plug is loose or missing.

At 3,000 miles, check the front DOJ and CVJ boots for cracks, the water pump and oil pressure gauge for leakage, and the distributor for a grinding sound indicating the distributor bearings are worn out.

One fellow wrote saying the Subaru dealer's parts books didn't show the head torquing tool (#499987006). I suggested that he have the dealer send in an order with that part number, even though it wasn't in the book. Sure enough, they sent him the tool. Perseverance furthers!

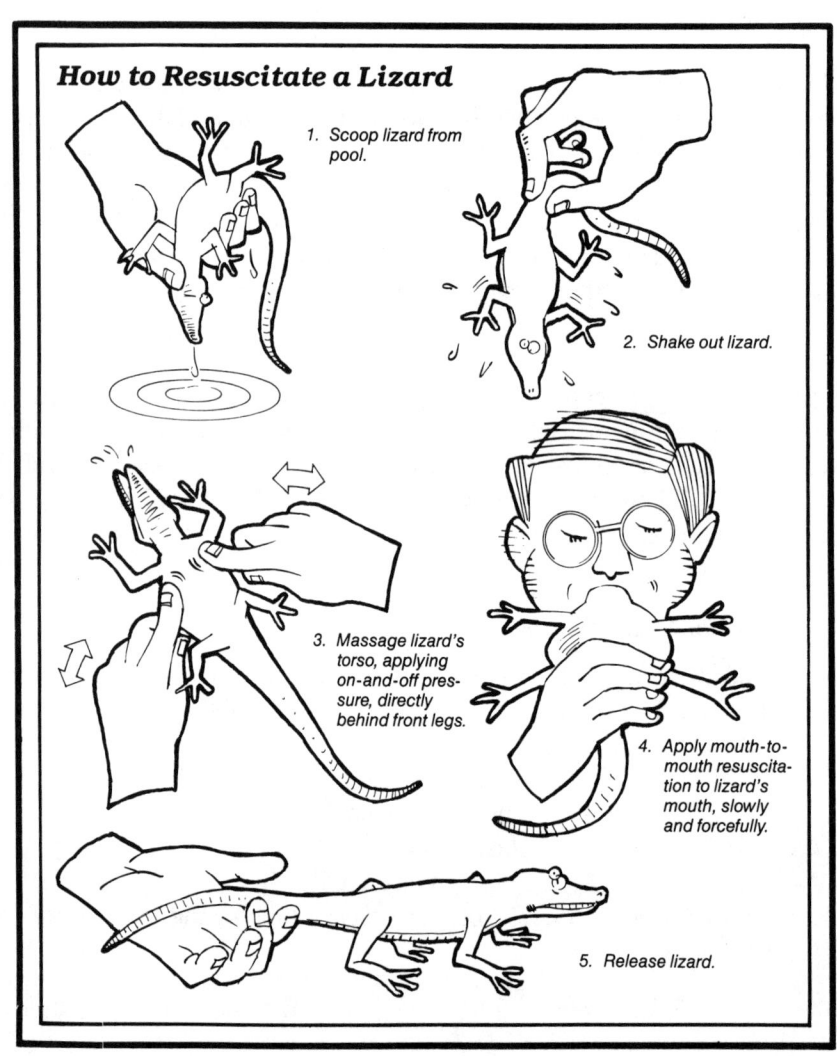

INDEX

A

Accessory System (see Electrical System)
Accelerator Cable
  check and replace 212
Air Conditioning, about 36
  caution about 22, 405
  discharge 405
  drive belt 178
  hoses 405, 406
    install 448
    remove 406
Air Cleaner
  air filter element
    check and replace 86, 87
  install 95
  lid, remove 87
  remove 93
  secondary ('80 models)
    check, replace 254
Alternator (see Charging System)
Amperage Output (see Charging System)
Antifreeze (see Cooling System)
Automatic Choke (see Choke)
Automatic Transmission, about 41, 350
  (see also Transmission, Transaxle)
  change fluid 138
  check fluid level 78
  fluid types 70
  hoses 392
  recommended brands 71
  towing limit 29
Axleshafts, about 43, 318
  (see also Constant Velocity Joints,
    Double Offset Joints)
  front, remove and install 365
  rear, '75-'78 remove and install 367
    '79-'84 remove and install 358

B

Backfire 155
Backup Lights (see Electrical System,
  rear lights)
Ball Joints, about 318
  check 323
  remove and install
    steering ball joint 330
    tie rod ball joints 344
    tie rod ends 334
Battery, about 38, 89
  caution with 89, 169
  charge 171
  checking, with charging system
    problems 171
  cleaning 169
  fluid level maintenance 89
  jump starting 172
  life span 169
  remove and install 172
  remove clamps and cables 169
Bearings (see Clutch, throwout bearing;
  Connecting Rods, bearings; Crankshaft,
    main bearings; Wheel Bearing Housing;
    Wheel Bearings)
Block (see Crankcase)
Bolts (see Nuts)
Brain (see Emission Control)
Brakes, about 267
  adjust (rear) 272
  bleed 273
  booster (see Master Vac)
  cautions about 274, 277
  disc brakes, about 268
    caliper and disc
      check 291, 294
        remove and install 300
    noise 161, 292
    pads, about 268, 292
      inspect 290
      replace (front brakes) 292
      replace (rear brakes) 280
      special tool 293, 295
    rear discs,
      check and replace 280
    rotor (same as disc)
  drum brakes, about 268
    inspect 277
    puller 279
    shoes, check 277
      replace, rear 281
    wheel cylinders, check 279
      rebuild or replace 288

fluid
   caution about 274
   check level 79, 274
   leaks, check for 271
   replace 276
handbrake, about 271, 308
   adjust 308
   replace cables 310
Hill Holder, about 311
   adjust 311
   replace cable 313
   replace PHV unit 314
hoses, check 279, 291
   remove and replace 302
linings (see drum brakes)
master cylinder, about 267
   remove and install 267
master vac, about 267
   check and replace 305
pedal height, adjust 308
problems 160, 271
self-adjusting 270, 284
shoes (see drum brakes)
wheel cylinders (see drum brakes)
Brake Lights (see Electrical System, rear lights)
Breaker Bar (see Tools, about)
Bulbs (see Electrical System)

C

Cable (see Accelerator; Brakes; handbrake, Hill Holder; Cable)
Caliper (see Brakes, disc brakes)
Camshaft, about 34
   cam followers, about 34
      inspect 424
      install 430
      remove 422
   hydraulic valve lifters
      about and adjust 443
   inspect 424
   install 431
   remove 422
Carburetor, about 36-37, 124, 205
   (see also Choke)
   accelerator pump, about 148
      check 156
   anti-diesel valve
      check and replace 155, 241

Carter/Weber, remove and install 238
   checks 156, 215
   choke 148
   clean 124
   electronic control, about 245
   fondle 228
   Hitachi, about 206
      Emergency! 237
      install 235
      quicky clean/rebuild 237
      rebuild 222-235
      remove 219
   idle speed, adjust 124
   mixture, adjust 124
   orientation 206
   power system, about 148
   problems 209
   spray cleaner 124
Catalytic Converter (see Emission Control)
Charging System, about 167
   alternator
      belt, check tension 176
         adjust, replace 176
      remove and install 193
   diagnosis 192
   voltage regulator, about 168
      replace 194
Cherry Picker (for engine removal) 404
Chevy Corvair 13, 32
Chock, Jack and Block
   (see Jacking Up Your Subaru)
Choke 148, 210 (see also Carburetor)
   adjustment check 154, 240
Clutch, about 349
   adjust 353
   alignment tool 439
   cable, replace 354
   disc, about 350
      install 439
      remove 412
   free play
      check and adjust 353
   pilot bearing, about 349
      remove 375
      replace 374
   pressure plate, about 349
      install 439
      remove 412
   release lever, about 349, 351
      replace 374

throwout bearing, about 349
    replace 374
  troubleshooting guide 351
Coil, about 38
  check 152, 200
  replace 200
Compression, about 42, 125
  gauge, using it 127
  test and evaluation 127
  testing for bad rings 128
Condenser (see Distributor)
Connecting Rods, about 33
  bearings, about 35
  caps, about 33
  install 429
  remove 418
Constant Velocity (CV) Joint, about 43, 350
  boot, replace 365
    clamp
      install 362
      remove 359
    grease 364
    replace 365
Coolant (see Cooling System)
Cooling System, about 377
  check coolant level 80, 381
  coolant, about 377
    antifreeze 71, 377
    caution, about 384
    change 384
    flush 384
  drain crankcase 385
  fan, about 35, 377, 394, 397
    electric motor
      check 397
      replace 394
    engine driven fan
      remove and repair 395
  hoses
    check and replace 381
  overheating 396
    emergency 399
  radiator, about 377
    cap 378
    drain 384
    remove and install 393
  thermoswitch, about 377
    check 397
    replace 389
  temperature gauge, check 399

  thermostat, about 377
    check and replace 389
  underheating 339
  water pump, about 36, 377, 386
    belt (see Drive Belt)
    replace 386
Crank (see Crankshaft)
Crankcase, about 33
  assemble 427
  checking 425
  cylinder bores, checking 424, 425
  mate 432
  split 420
Cranking System, about 168
  (also see Starter Motor)
  diagnosis 195-197
Crankshaft, about 33
  assemble 427
  front seal, replace 412, 441
  inspect 425
  install 431
  main bearings, about 35
    inspect 423
    install 430
    remove 423
  pulley, about 35, 96
    install 441
    mark 95
    remove 413
  rear seal, replace 412
    install 438
  woodruff key 429
CV joint (see Constant Velocity Joint)
Cylinder Head, about 33
  gasket, check for leaks 160
  install 436
  remove 413
  torquing it 98
Cylinder, about 32
  (see also Crankcase and Pistons)
  checking 424

D

Differential, about 43
  (also see Transaxle)
  change oil 138
  check oil level 77

rear 4WD differential, about 32, 351
   change oil 138, 141
   check oil level 136
   remove and install 368
Disc Brakes (see Brakes, disc)
Distributor, about 17, 38, 115
  air gap, check and adjust 116
  breakerless, about 40, 116
   check and adjust 116
  cap
   check 115
   install 119
   replace 120
  condenser, about 40, 123
   replace 123
  install 441
  lubricate 125
  mechanical advance, check 118, 135
  points, about 39
   adjust 122
   fiber block 121
   gap, check 121, 122
   inspect 121
   replace 123
  remove 411
  rotor 38, 116
   remove and inspect 116
   install 119
  set timing 132
  shaft, check 116
  vacuum unit
   check 118, 135
   replace 119
Don't Panic! 451
Door Hardware, about 459
   remove and install 459
Double Offset Joint, about 43, 350, 357
  check 81, 357
  clamps
   install 362
   remove 359
  grease 361
  inspect 361
  remove and install 358
Drivebelts, about 36
  adjust or replace, 179-182
  inspect 79, 177
Driveshaft (4WD), about 351
  check 357
  remove and install 366

Dr. McJoy 14, 21
Drum Brakes (see Brakes, drum)
Dwell
  adjust 122
  meter connections 122
  quick test 457

E

Easy Out 455
EGR (see Emissions Control)
Electrical System, about 165
  (see also Battery, Charging System,
   Cranking System, Ignition System)
  accessory system 168
  bulbs, how to replace 185-189
  circuits, about 166, 167
  dash lights, replace 187
  emergency flashers 26, 189
  fuses and fusible links, about 166
   check and replace 173
  headlight, replace 183
  horn, check, replace 202
   stuck 202
  lights, check 88
  oil pressure light, test and replace 157
  parking light, replace 185, 186
  problems, how to diagnose 189-192
  rear lights
   brake light, problems 306
   replace 185
  side marker lamp and lens, replace 185
  turn signal light, replace 189
  flasher unit, replace 189
  voltage, checking 192
  wires and switches, checking 189
   splice 458
Emergency Brake (see Brakes, handbrake)
Emissions Control, about 243-248
  air injection system 246, 248
   check, replace 252
  altitude compensator
   check, replace 261
  anti-afterburning valve 245, 247
   check, replace 259
  brain 208, 247
  canister 248
   check, replace 254
  catalyst 247, 262, 265
  catalytic converter (see catalyst)

coasting bypass system 245
  check, adjust 258
dashpot 246
  check, replace 261
EGR valve 245, 249
  check, replace 248
evaporative control system 208, 248
  check 248
hot air control system 246
  check, repair 255
PCV valve 244
  check, replace 251
specification sticker 20
vacuum advance/retard unit 245, 247
  check, replace 119
Engine
  about and how it works 31
  crankcase (see Crankcase)
  diagnosing problems 152, 402
  disassembly 411
  drive plate
    install 439
    remove 412
  hoist 404
  install 446
  layout 31
  noises 161
  orientation 14-18
  parts of, 33
  parts 53
  removal 404
    reasons for 402
  smells 162
  stand 404
  wash 92
Exhaust System, about 262
  replace 263

F

Fan (see Cooling System)
Fan Belt (see Drivebelt)
Feeler Gauge
  how to use 101
Firing Order 42
Fluid Level Checks 75
Flywheel, about 43, 349
  install 439
  remove and inspect 412
Foster, Jody 405

Four Strokes 42
Front End (see Ball Joints; MacPherson Strut; Steering; Suspension)
Front Crossmember 24
Fuel Injection, about 11, 205
  orientation 11
Fuel Supply System
  about 11, 36, 205
  carburetor (see Carburetor)
  cautions, about 209
  filters, about 205
    replace 209
  pump, about 36, 205
    check power to 217
    replace 216
  tests 153, 215
  vapor separator 205
    replace 209
Fuses (see Electrical System, fuses)
Fusible Links (see Electrical System fuses)

G

Garage Materials 52
Gas Stop Fluid Level Checks 75
Gas Mileage 147
Gasoline (see Fuel Supply System)
Gearshift (also see Transmission)
  replace bushings 369
Grille, remove and install 183
Ground Clearance, check and adjust 346

H

Handbrake (see Brakes, handbrake)
Heads (see Cylinder Head)
Headlights (see Electrical System, headlights)
Hiccups, cure 453
High Performance Parts 453
Hitler, Adolph 13
History 32
Horn (see Electrical System, horn)
Hoses (see Air Conditioning; Cooling System; Automatic Transmission)
Hydraulics (see Brakes)
How to Use this Book 9
  procedure layout 10
  year and model variations 10
Hydraulic Valve Lifters (see Camshaft)

Index

I

Idle, adjust (see Carburetor)
Ignition System, about 38-40, 168
  (see also Coil, Distributor, Spark Plugs)
Ignition Switch (see also Electrical System)
  check 195
Ignition Timing
  check and adjust 132
Intake Manifold
  install 446
  remove 415

J

Jack Location 27
Jacking Up Your Subaru 23-29
  block 28
  chock 24, 27
  floorjack 24
  jack points 24, 28
Jackstands 23
  positions 25

L

Lens (see Electrical System)
Lights (see Electrical System)
Lizard, revive 460
Lubrication 67
Lug Nuts
  torque pattern 26

M

Machine Shop
  at the, 423, 425
Madame Noogies' Massage Parlor 73
Main Bearings (see Crankshaft)
Maintenance Schedules 73-74
MacPherson Struts, about 318
  check 321
  remove and install 327
Manual Transmission (see Transaxle,
  Transmission, Clutch)
Massage
  body 90
  major 136
  minor 85
Muffler (see Exhaust System)

N

Numbers 19
Nuts, Bolts, Screws and Studs
  remove stuck or damaged ones 454-456
  starting and tightening 457

O

Oil, about 67-70
  additives 68
  change 81
  check level 75-78
  filter, about 36, 69
    replace 82
    wrench 83
  leaks 158
  other oils 68
  pan, about 33
    install 438
    remove 420
  pressure
    check 157
    lack of 156, 451
    oil pressure switch
      check 157
      install 440
      remove 420
  pump, about 36
    inspect 425
    install 440
    remove 420
  quality 67
  transmission oil, 70
  used oil 85
  viscosity 69
  weight 69
Orientation
  engine compartment 14
  which way is up 14
  year and model variations 10

P

Parking Lights (see Electrical System)
Parts, about 53
  store, at the 426
Penetrating Oil, about 53
Pistons, about 33
  inspect 424

Index

install 433
remove 416
rings, about 33
  compressor 433
  install 433
  remove 424
  test for bad rings 128
Pleiades 14
Points (see Distributor)
Porinsh, Peter 404
Porsche 13, 32
  Ferdinand 13
Power Steering
  check fluid level 78
  remove pump 406
Poor Richard's Rabbit Book 461
Production Date 20
Puller 458
Push Rods, about 34
  check 424

Q

Quirk, Captain 14, 377, 399

R

Radiator (see Cooling System)
Rear Lights (see Electrical System)
Reward Yourself 91
Rings (see Pistons)
Rocker Arms (see Valves, rocker arms)
Rods (see Connecting Rods)
Rotor (see Distributor)

S

Safety 21-23
Schpock, Mr. 14, 377
Seven Sisters 14
Shimmies 322
Shock Absorbers 318
  (see also MacPherson Struts)
  check 321
  replace rear, 325
Side Marker Lamp (see Electrical System)
Solenoid (see Starter Motor)
Snotty 14, 20, 29, 378, 400
Spare Parts 53
Spare Tire, about 26, 28

install 28
location 27
Spark Plugs, about 38, 125
  remove and inspect 125
  clean and gap 126
  gapper 126
  install 128
  test 153
Spark Plug Wires, about 38
  check and replace 201
Speedometer Cable, check and replace 459
SPFI, about 37, 207
  also see Fuel Injection, Fuel System
Starship Subaru 14, 208, 349, 377
Starter Motor, about 168
  checking 195-197
  remove and install 197
Steering, about 317-321
  ball joint (see Ball Joints)
  check 321
  gearbox, 320
    boots, replace 344
Struts (see MacPherson Struts)
Suspension, about 317-321
  check 321

T

Taillights (see Electrical System)
Tape Deck Maintenance 90
Temperature, about 377
  sending unit 398
Thermostat (see Cooling System)
Throwout Bearing (see Clutch)
Tie Rod End (see Ball Joint)
Timing
  doing it 132
  light 133
  marks 95, 134
  pointer 87, 134
Tires, about 71-73
  buying 72
  change 26
  check pressure 85
  pressure gauge 85
  spare, about 26
Tools, about 45-46
  (also see Torque Wrench)
  don't leave town without 52
  optional and special 50

phase I 47
phase II 50
phase III 52
safety with 54
tune-up 49
Torsion Bars 43, 319
Torque Converter, about 43
    attach 448
    detach 410
Torque Plate (see Engine, drive plate)
Torque Wrench, about 45
    how to use 457
Towing 29
Transaxle, about 32, 349
    filler tube 77, 140
    check level 77
    gearshift lever bushings
        replace 369
    layout 32
Transmission
    (see Automatic Transmission; Transaxle)
Troubleshooting
    clutch, transmission, driveshafts 351
    cooling system 396
    engine, etc. 151
Trucker, Billy 388
Turbo, about 16, 37, 207
Turn Signals (see Electrical System)
Tune-up, about 65-75
    tools 49

U

Universal Joints, about 43, 351
    check 357

V

V-belt (see Drivebelt)
Vacuum Unit (see Distributor)
Valves, about 33, 34
    adjusting bolt 102
    check and adjust 99-105
        hydraulic 443
    cover
        install 104
        gasket 104
        remove 98
    rocker arm, about 34, 101, 436
        install 436
        remove 415
    timing mark, alignment 95, 100
    valve lifters
        mechanical (see Camshaft, cam followers)
        hydraulic (see Camshaft, hydraulic lifters)
Vehicle Identification Number (VIN) 20
Voltage checks 192
Voltage Regulator (see Charging System)
Volt/Ohm Meter (VOM)
    how to use 198
VW 13, 32

W

Water Pump (see Cooling System)
Wash Engine 92
Wheel alignment 320
Wheel Bearing Housing, about 317
    remove and install 336
Wheel Bearings
    clean and grease 340
    front, check 324
        remove and install 336
    rear, check 280
        remove and install 341
Wheel Chock 24, 27
Wheel Rotors (see Brakes, disc)
Windshield Washer Fluid
    check fluid level 79
Wiper Blades
    check and replace 88
Woodruff key (see Crankshaft)
Wrenches (see Tools)

Other Books from John Muir Publications

Travel Books by Rick Steves
Asia Through the Back Door, 4th ed., 400 pp. $16.95
Europe 101: History, Art, and Culture for the Traveler, 4th ed., 372 pp. $15.95
Mona Winks: Self-Guided Tours of Europe's Top Museums, 2nd ed., 456 pp. $16.95
Rick Steves' Best of the Baltics and Russia, 1995 ed. 144 pp. $9.95
Rick Steves' Best of Europe, 1995 ed., 544 pp. $16.95
Rick Steves' Best of France, Belgium, and the Netherlands, 1995 ed., 240 pp. $12.95
Rick Steves' Best of Germany, Austria, and Switzerland, 1995 ed., 240 pp. $12.95
Rick Steves' Best of Great Britain, 1995 ed., 192 pp. $11.95
Rick Steves' Best of Italy, 1995 ed., 208 pp. $11.95
Rick Steves' Best of Scandinavia, 1995 ed., 192 pp. $11.95
Rick Steves' Best of Spain and Portugal, 1995 ed., 192 pp. $11.95
Rick Steves' Europe Through the Back Door, 13th ed., 480 pp. $17.95
Rick Steves' French Phrase Book, 2nd ed., 112 pp. $4.95
Rick Steves' German Phrase Book, 2nd ed., 112 pp. $4.95
Rick Steves' Italian Phrase Book, 2nd ed., 112 pp. $4.95
Rick Steves' Spanish and Portuguese Phrase Book, 2nd ed., 288 pp. $5.95
Rick Steves' French/German/Italian Phrase Book, 288 pp. $6.95

A Natural Destination Series
Belize: A Natural Destination, 2nd ed., 304 pp. $16.95
Costa Rica: A Natural Destination, 3rd ed., 400 pp. $17.95
Guatemala: A Natural Destination, 336 pp. $16.95

Undiscovered Islands Series
Undiscovered Islands of the Caribbean, 3rd ed., 264 pp. $14.95
Undiscovered Islands of the Mediterranean, 2nd ed., 256 pp. $13.95
Undiscovered Islands of the U.S. and Canadian West Coast, 288 pp. $12.95

For Birding Enthusiasts
The Birder's Guide to Bed and Breakfasts: U.S. and Canada, 288 pp. $15.95
The Visitor's Guide to the Birds of the Central National Parks: U.S. and Canada, 400 pp. $15.95
The Visitor's Guide to the Birds of the Eastern National Parks: U.S. and Canada, 400 pp. $15.95
The Visitor's Guide to the Birds of the Rocky Mountain National Parks: U.S. and Canada, 432 pp. $15.95

Unique Travel Series
Each is 112 pages and $10.95 paperback.
Unique Arizona
Unique California
Unique Colorado
Unique Florida
Unique New England
Unique New Mexico
Unique Texas
Unique Washington

2 to 22 Days Itinerary Planners
2 to 22 Days in the American Southwest, 1995 ed., 192 pp. $11.95
2 to 22 Days in Asia, 192 pp. $10.95
2 to 22 Days in Australia, 192 pp. $10.95
2 to 22 Days in California, 1995 ed., 192 pp. $11.95
2 to 22 Days in Eastern Canada, 1995 ed., 240 pp $12.95
2 to 22 Days in Florida, 1995 ed., 192 pp. $11.95
2 to 22 Days Around the Great Lakes, 1995 ed., 192 pp. $11.95
2 to 22 Days in Hawaii, 1995 ed., 192 pp. $11.95
2 to 22 Days in New England, 1995 ed., 192 pp. $11.95
2 to 22 Days in New Zealand, 192 pp. $10.95
2 to 22 Days in the Pacific Northwest, 1995 ed., 192 pp. $11.95
2 to 22 Days in the Rockies, 1995 ed., 192 pp. $11.95
2 to 22 Days in Texas, 1995 ed., 192 pp. $11.95
2 to 22 Days in Thailand, 192 pp. $10.95
22 Days Around the World, 264 pp. $13.95

Other Terrific Travel Titles
The 100 Best Small Art Towns in America, 224 pp. $12.95
Elderhostels: The Students' Choice, 2nd ed., 304 pp. $15.95
Environmental Vacations: Volunteer Projects to Save the Planet, 2nd ed., 248 pp. $16.95
A Foreign Visitor's Guide to America, 224 pp. $12.95
Great Cities of Eastern Europe, 256 pp. $16.95
Indian America: A Traveler's Companion, 3rd ed., 432 pp. $18.95
Interior Furnishings Southwest, 256 pp. $19.95
Opera! The Guide to Western Europe's Great Houses, 296 pp. $18.95
Paintbrushes and Pistols: How the Taos Artists Sold the West, 288 pp. $17.95
The People's Guide to Mexico, 10th ed., 608 pp. $19.95
Ranch Vacations: The Complete Guide to Guest and Resort, Fly-Fishing, and Cross-Country Skiing Ranches, 3rd ed., 512 pp. $19.95
The Shopper's Guide to Art and Crafts in the Hawaiian Islands, 272 pp. $13.95
The Shopper's Guide to Mexico, 224 pp. $9.95
Understanding Europeans, 272 pp. $14.95
A Viewer's Guide to Art: A Glossary of Gods, People, and Creatures, 144 pp. $10.95
Watch It Made in the U.S.A.: A Visitor's Guide to the Companies that Make Your Favorite Products, 272 pp. $16.95

Parenting Titles
Being a Father: Family, Work, and Self, 176 pp. $12.95
Preconception: A Woman's Guide to Preparing for Pregnancy and Parenthood, 232 pp. $14.95
Schooling at Home: Parents, Kids, and Learning, 264 pp. $14.95
Teens: A Fresh Look, 240 pp. $14.95

Automotive Titles
The Greaseless Guide to Car Care Confidence, 224 pp. $14.95
How to Keep Your Datsun/Nissan Alive, 544 pp. $21.95
How to Keep Your Subaru Alive, 480 pp. $21.95
How to Keep Your Toyota Pickup Alive, 392 pp. $21.95
How to Keep Your VW Alive, 25th Anniversary ed., 464 pp. spiral bound $25

TITLES FOR YOUNG READERS AGES 8 AND UP

American Origins Series
Each is 48 pages and $12.95 hardcover.
Tracing Our English Roots
Tracing Our French Roots (available 7/95)
Tracing Our German Roots
Tracing Our Irish Roots
Tracing Our Italian Roots
Tracing Our Japanese Roots
Tracing Our Jewish Roots
Tracing Our Polish Roots

Bizarre & Beautiful Series
Each is 48 pages and $14.95 hardcover, $9.95 paperback.
Bizarre & Beautiful Ears
Bizarre & Beautiful Eyes
Bizarre & Beautiful Feelers
Bizarre & Beautiful Noses
Bizarre & Beautiful Tongues

Environmental Titles
Habitats: Where the Wild Things Live, 48 pp. $9.95
The Indian Way: Learning to Communicate with Mother Earth, 114 pp. $9.95
Rads, Ergs, and Cheeseburgers: The Kids' Guide to Energy and the Environment, 108 pp. $12.95
The Kids' Environment Book: What's Awry and Why, 192 pp. $13.95

Extremely Weird Series
Each is 48 pages and $9.95 paperback, $14.95 hardcover.
Extremely Weird Bats
Extremely Weird Birds
Extremely Weird Endangered Species
Extremely Weird Fishes
Extremely Weird Frogs
Extremely Weird Insects
Extremely Weird Mammals
Extremely Weird Micro Monsters
Extremely Weird Primates
Extremely Weird Reptiles
Extremely Weird Sea Creatures
Extremely Weird Snakes
Extremely Weird Spiders

Kidding Around Travel Series
All are 64 pages and $9.95 paperback, except for Kidding Around Spain and Kidding Around the National Parks of the Southwest, which are 108 pages and $12.95 paperback.
Kidding Around Atlanta
Kidding Around Boston, 2nd ed.
Kidding Around Chicago, 2nd ed.
Kidding Around the Hawaiian Islands
Kidding Around London
Kidding Around Los Angeles
Kidding Around the National Parks of the Southwest
Kidding Around New York City, 2nd ed.
Kidding Around Paris
Kidding Around Philadelphia
Kidding Around San Diego
Kidding Around San Francisco
Kidding Around Santa Fe
Kidding Around Seattle
Kidding Around Spain
Kidding Around Washington, D.C.

Kids Explore Series
Written by kids for kids, all are $9.95 paperback.
Kids Explore America's African American Heritage, 128 pp.
Kids Explore the Gifts of Children with Special Needs, 128 pp.
Kids Explore America's Hispanic Heritage, 112 pp.
Kids Explore America's Japanese American Heritage, 144 pp.

Masters of Motion Series
Each is 48 pages and $9.95 paperback.
How to Drive an Indy Race Car
How to Fly a 747
How to Fly the Space Shuttle

Rainbow Warrior Artists Series
Each is 48 pages and $14.95 hardcover. ($9.95 paperback editions available 4/95.)
Native Artists of Africa
Native Artists of Europe
Native Artists of North America

Rough and Ready Series
Each is 48 pages and $12.95 hardcover. ($9.95 paperback editions available 4/95.)
Rough and Ready Cowboys
Rough and Ready Homesteaders
Rough and Ready Loggers
Rough and Ready Outlaws and Lawmen
Rough and Ready Prospectors
Rough and Ready Railroaders

X-ray Vision Series
Each is 48 pages and $9.95 paperback.
Looking Inside the Brain
Looking Inside Cartoon Animation
Looking Inside Caves and Caverns
Looking Inside Sports Aerodynamics
Looking Inside Sunken Treasures
Looking Inside Telescopes and the Night Sky

Ordering Information
Please check your local bookstore for our books, or call **1-800-888-7504** to order direct. All orders are shipped via UPS; see chart below to calculate your shipping charge for U.S. destinations. **No post office boxes please; we must have a street address to ensure delivery.** If the book you request is not available, we will hold your check until we can ship it. Foreign orders will be shipped surface rate unless otherwise requested; please enclose $3 for the first item and $1 for each additional item.

For U.S. Orders Totaling	Add
Up to $15.00	$4.25
$15.01 to $45.00	$5.25
$45.01 to $75.00	$6.25
$75.01 or more	$7.25

Methods of Payment
Check, money order, American Express, MasterCard, or Visa. We cannot be responsible for cash sent through the mail. For credit card orders, include your card number, expiration date, and your signature, or call **1-800-888-7504**. American Express card orders can only be shipped to billing address of cardholder. Sorry, no C.O.D.'s. Residents of sunny New Mexico, add 6.25% tax to total.

Address all orders and inquiries to:
John Muir Publications
P.O. Box 613
Santa Fe, NM 87504
(505) 982-4078
(800) 888-7504